The Moody Atlas of the Bible

Barry J. Beitzel

Cartographer: Nick Rowland F. R. G. S.

Unless otherwise indicated, the Scripture translation used in this book is the author's own.

Scripture quotations marked KJV are taken from the King James Version.

Scripture quotations marked ASV are taken from the *American Standard Version*.

ISBN: 978-0-8024-0441-1

Worldwide co-edition organized and produced by Lion Hudson plc
Wilkinson House
Jordan Hill Road
Oxford OX2 8DR
England

Tel: +44 (0) 1865 302750
Fax: +44 (0) 1865 302757
email: coed@lionhudson.com
www.lionhudson.com

Moody Publishers
820 N. LaSalle Boulevard
Chicago, IL 60610

1 3 5 7 9 10 8 6 4 2

Printed in China

To Carol, my closest and dearest friend,
my sure companion on the journey of faith
and on the journey to the sites.

CONTENTS

TABLE OF ABBREVIATIONS

1QapGen	*Genesis Apocryphon* from Qumran cave 1
1QM	*War of the Children of Light against the Children of Darkness* from Qumran cave 1
3Q15	Copper Scroll from Qumran cave 3
4QEn[d]	*Enoch* fragment from Qumran cave 4
4QSam	*Samuel* from Qumran cave 4
Akk.	Akkadian
Ar.	Arabic
Aram.	Aramaic
ARMT	Archives royales de Mari: transcriptions et traductions.
Br.	Brook
ca.	*circa* [approximately]
ch.	chapter(s)
DN	divine name [male or female]
EA	siglum for the Tell el-Amarna tablets
Eg.	Egyptian
ELS	D. Baldi, ed., *Enchiridion Locorum Sanctorum. Documenta S. Evangelii Loca Respicientia.* Jerusalem: Franciscan Printing Press, 1982.
EN	ethnic name
Gk.	Greek
Heb.	Hebrew; or, in the context of a scriptural citation: *Hebrews*
J.	Jebel [Arabic word for mountain]
Kh.	Khirbet [Arabic word for ruins]
L.	Lake
Lat.	Latin
LXX	A. Rahlfs, ed., *Septuaginta*. Stuttgart: Württembergische Bibelanstalt, 1962.
LXX[A]	Codex Alexandrinus
LXX[B]	Codex Vaticanus
LXX[S]	Codex Sinaiticus
MT	Mas(s)oretic Text [the Hebrew text of the Old Testament]
Mt./Mts.	Mountain, Mountains
N./n.	Nahr [Hebrew word for river or stream]; or, when used with Africa: North
PN	personal name [male or female; ancient, classical, medieval or modern]
R./r.	River
RN	royal name [male or female; a non-Israelite/Judahite monarch]
RNn	royal name [a king of Israel (the northern kingdom) during the divided monarchy]
RNs	royal name [a king of Judah (the southern kingdom) during the divided monarchy]
SP	Samaritan Pentateuch
ss	superscription [heading found at the beginning of many Psalms]
Sum.	Sumerian
T.	Tel/Tell [Hebrew/Arabic word for artificial earthen occupational mound]
Ug.	Ugaritic
Vulg.	Vulgate
W./w.	Wadi [Arabic word for intermittent water channel]

MAPS AND FIGURES

PREFACE

"Geography is a flavor." Thus Starbucks proclaims as a banner on its sales displays around the world or on the side of a one pound bag of its coffee. The market strategy of the international conglomerate continues by affirming: You can tell a lot about a coffee if you know where it's from, because every bean has a distinctive flavor particular to its land of origin. Coffees from Arabia are legendary for their berrylike flavors and winelike qualities. Those from Africa are remarkable for their floral aromas and citrusy tastes. Coffees from Latin America are celebrated for their great balance, medium body, tangy brightness, and consistent quality. And those from Asia-Pacific are popular for smooth, earthy, and exotic flavors, with low acidity and full body.

A similar claim can be made with respect to the biblical storyline: it exudes a distinctive flavor that is particular to the Land where it originated. Much of the biblical storyline's character and aromatic quality reflect the specific geographic realities at the place of its birth and enactment. Thus for example, the Land of God's covenantal promises might have been created with the aroma of an environment without blemish; it might have been permeated with the flavor of ecological or climatological perfection. It might have been endowed with the taste of a tropical rain forest through which coursed an effusion of crystal-clear waters; it might have been brought into existence with the texture and brightness of a thickly carpeted grassy meadow or the scent of an elegant garden suffused with the pungent fragrance of blossoms, mosses, and flowers. It might have been—but it was not. As I will attempt to demonstrate, this Land of promise that God prepared as the stage on which his storyline would be enacted is a locale that embodied the direst of geographic and environmental hardship. Innately possessing meager physical and economic resources, and positioned where it was caught inescapably in a maelstrom of relentless political upheaval, this Land has yielded up to its residents a simple, tenuous, mystifying, and precarious existence throughout the biblical epoch, even under the best of circumstances. It is an important and helpful insight to recognize that God prepared a *certain kind of land*, situated at *a particular location*, fashioned to elicit *a specific and appropriate response*. This is not to say that I believe the Bible was designed to teach the subject of geography, or any other of the sciences. It is merely to observe that the Bible often characteristically transmits its storyline through the geographic medium. To the degree one appreciates the flavor and parameters of the medium, so also one should be able to understand more fully the revelatory import and texture of a given biblical text.

The essence of geography has imbued the biblical storyline with a distinctive flavor. It is not the flavor of most of North America, Europe, or much of the rest of the world, but it is nonetheless a robust and full-bodied flavor, one that is a function of a peculiar geography. Capturing *this* flavor will depend to a large extent on one's ability to recover and assess the Bible's particular geographical horizon. St. Jerome, who lived in this Land for many years, wrote concerning geography's role in the enterprise of biblical interpretation: "Just as those who have seen Athens understand Greek history better, and just as those who have sailed from Troy . . . to Sicily, and from there to Ostia Tiberias [Rome's port on the Tyrrhenian Sea, fully developed in the 2nd century A.D. by the emperor Hadrian; **see map 26**] understand better the 3rd Book of (the poet) Virgil, so one who has seen the land of Judah with his own eyes or has become personally acquainted with the historical references to the ancient towns . . . will surely comprehend the Holy Scriptures with a much clearer understanding."[1] Geography *does* play a critical role and *does* make a decisive difference, whether one has in mind the particular scent of a coffee bean or the distinctive flavor of a biblical storyline!

Geography is understood in the *Atlas* to define three separate, if somewhat overlapping concepts: physical geography (a description of those topographic and environmental features that characterize and embody the land), regional geography (a description of those political and territorial subdivisions that comprise the land), and historical geography (a diachronic unfolding of those events that have transpired in the land, which are conducive to a geographical explanation). Chapter one of the *Atlas* addresses aspects of physical geography, as well as setting forth many of the major parameters of regional geography; chapter two seeks to present an overview of historical geography. It is not my purpose in chapter two to supply a full and running commentary on the whole of the biblical narratives discussed, which would require separate volumes in themselves, but only to provide a geographic sketch sufficient to elucidate a given map. To a certain degree, chapter two adheres to the aphorism of Thomas Fuller: " . . . the eye will learn more in an hour from a Mappe, than the eare can learn in a day from discourse."[2]

Anyone today who wishes to write on the biblical world faces the vexed question of nomenclature, but this issue is perhaps most acute and protracted for the geographer. Given the climate of contemporary Middle Eastern politics, it becomes almost impossible for the Bible geographer to employ certain words—*e.g.*, Israel/Palestine, Jordan/Transjordan, West

Bank/Samaria-Judea, Gulf of Aqaba/Gulf of Elat, Persian Gulf/Arabian Gulf, or even Armenia or Syria, *etc.*—without creating the impression that a certain political statement is being made or a particular nationalist or religious ideology is being endorsed.[3] With this reality in mind, I wish at the outset to state as candidly and clearly as I know how to my readers—be they Christian, Jewish, or Muslim—that my agenda is purely historical and that when I use these or other such terms, even in a post-biblical or a modern context, their use should not be construed as espousing any particular contemporary political or ecclesial conviction.

Another problem faced by any author of an Atlas is the tension between the area covered by a map and the scale at which it can be covered. If the area to be covered is large, then the scale must be small, or else the map will not fit on the size of a printed page. But this can make for an extremely vague and imprecise map. Alternatively, if the map were to be composed at a large scale, then the area covered must be small, or again the map will be larger than page size. Now the map can be extraordinarily detailed but may lack the larger perspective or be without fixed geographic points. My effort here has been to keep the scale as large as possible and yet to avoid cropping off an important section of a map or placing an arrow that points off the map toward a designated spot. On a few occasions, however, to have an arrow pointing seemingly to the margin of a page was unavoidable, though admittedly this can be an irritating practice. Of similar practices, Plutarch once complained: "Geographers . . . crowd onto the edges of their maps parts of the world which elude their knowledge, adding notes in the margin to the effect that beyond this lies nothing but sandy deserts without water and full of wild beasts, unapproachable bogs, or frozen sea."[4] I trust that my readers will be more understanding. But my approach to this problem of area covered versus scale has sometimes necessitated that a map legend be positioned adjacent to, but not on, the map itself.

Complexities of phonetics between several writing systems used in the biblical world are profound, and a certain amount of inconsistency in the spelling of proper names is unavoidable. Nevertheless, a measure of systemization has been attempted. Names that have a well-known English form have been retained in the *Atlas* (*e.g.,* Jerusalem, Babylon, Greece); names that are generally transliterated into English in a certain form retain that customary form here (*e.g.,* Akkad, Tyre, Aleppo, Carchemish), even though the transliteration may be slightly imprecise; names not occurring in English are rendered phonetically in English script (*e.g.,* Negeb, Wadi Far`ah, Kafr Bir'im), normally without vowel length marks or diacritical indicators (note that both length marks and diacritical signs *are* used where feasible when transcribing words that are not proper names). Arabic names may be spelled with or without the definite article (*el-* or *al-*, but often assimilated into the sound of the following consonant) (*e.g.,* Tell el-Amarna, not Tell Amarna, or Jebel Magharah, not Jebel el-Magharah). Finally, frequently cited bodies of water that serve as important geographical points of reference on a map have been assigned a static spelling throughout the volume (*e.g.,* Mediterranean Sea, not also Upper Sea, Great Sea, Western Sea, Great Syrian Sea, Great Green Sea, Mare Internum, Mare Nostrum, Sea of the Maiden, Sea of Isis, or *tâmtu elītu*; Dead Sea, not also Salt Sea, Sea of the Arabah, Mare Maledictum, *al-bahaire el-maita*, Devil's Sea, Stinking Sea), even though such spellings will admittedly be anachronistic on some maps. In a similar vein, historical periodization indicated by terms such as "(Late) Bronze Age" or "(Early) Iron Age" reflects a classification of architectural forms and/or decorative styles of ancient pottery. It has nothing to do with metalworking or any other form of metallurgic technology.

Beyond those common abbreviations found in the Table of Abbreviations, individual maps show abbreviations, symbols, and explanatory boxes in the legend and sometimes on the body of the map itself. Use of the question mark, traditionally employed on Bible maps to denote cities of uncertain location, has been avoided in the *Atlas* because of irritation or even possible confusion to the reader. By this, however, I do not wish to imply certainty where the identity of a site remains in doubt. Instead of a question mark, I have uniformly used the symbol [o] for a city whose location is judged to be uncertain; it was thought that this symbol is both less conspicuous on a map and less susceptible to misinterpretation.

Among the back matter, the reader will encounter three Indexes (Map Citation Index, Scripture Citation Index, General Index). The Map Citation Index is organized according to map number, not page number (for a complete list of maps arranged according to page number, refer to the Table of Maps and Figures found among the front matter). It should be stressed that the Map Citation Index is not a Gazetteer (a comprehensive index of all geographic names referenced in the Bible, sometimes including information concerning the pronunciation of each entry, together with a description of its present location and name); inasmuch as Gazetteers already exist in a variety of readily accessible versions and formats, there seemed to be no need to reinvent the wheel. The Scripture Citation Index is arranged according to page number in the *Atlas*; it is also keyed to English versification, which is sometimes at variance with the versification of the MT. The General Index intends to include many proper names and major subjects addressed in the text, with some limitations. Thus for example, frequently-cited biblical characters (*e.g.,* Abraham, David, Jesus) are not included in the Index, since there are whole blocks of maps/text dedicated to these individuals (in such cases, refer to the Table of Maps and Figures found among the front matter). Likewise, frequently referenced classical writers (*e.g.,* Josephus, Pliny) are not included in the Index, as the relevant source data are documented in the Notes. Also, I have deliberately limited the number of geographical names in the General Index, hoping to minimize overlap with corresponding information contained comprehensively in the Map Citation Index. Names of most foreign monarchs have been subsumed in the General Index under their national identity (*e.g.,* Assyrian monarchs, Persian monarchs, Roman emperors), but all other data have been arranged alphabetically.

Finally, this *Atlas* could never have become a reality without the diligent labor of a host of individuals, and my thanks to them here is more than a mere accommodation to tradition. These include Greg Thornton, Vice President at Moody Publishers; Dave DeWit, project co-ordinator at Moody Publishers; Tim Dowley, London, Project Editor; Nick Rowland, Cambridge, England, cartographer; and Nick Jones, co-edition coordinator, at Lion Hudson, Oxford, England. All maps are new and digitized. The text has been completely rewritten and greatly expanded, with ample supporting documentation provided.

I wish to communicate thankfulness to the Board of Regents of Trinity Evangelical Divinity School, whose mission-minded sabbatical program has substantially helped to undergird and sustain a project of this breadth and scope. I also express profound indebtedness to my Teaching Assistant, Mr. A. D. Riddle, who has invested countless hours and concentrated energies in checking my work and in preparing the Indexes. And to Professors Davis Young, Walter Kaiser, James Hoffmeier, and Douglas Moo, who read parts of the manuscript and offered helpful insight and counsel, I express sincere appreciation. Naturally, any remaining errors are my responsibility alone. Finally, I shall never be able to estimate fairly, much less to repay, the debt of gratitude that I owe my wife and family. Without their joyful sacrifices of time, and their steadfast patience and encouragement since its inception, this project could never have been brought to consummation.

For myself, the study of geography culminates in doxology. I confess to resonating with the prophetic declaration: "That which fills the whole earth is his glory" (Isa. 6:3b), or with the analogous refrain found on the lips of the psalmist:

"Let us come into his presence with thanksgiving;
    let us make a joyful noise to him with songs of praise!
For the Lord is a great God
    and a great King above all gods.
The depths of the earth are in his hand;
    the mountain peaks also belong to him.
The sea is his, for he made it;
    and his hands formed the dry land.
Come, let us worship and bow down,
    let us kneel before the Lord, our Maker!
For he is our God,
    and we are the people of his pasture,
    the sheep under his care" (Ps. 95:2–7a).

Baalbek, Lebanon
May, 2009

ENDNOTES

1 St. Jerome, "Praefatio Hieronymi in librum Paralipomenon juxta LXX Interpretes," in J.-P. Migne, ed., *Patrologiae cursus completus: omnium SS. patrum, doctorum scriptorumque ecclesiasticorum*, Patrologiae Latinae 29, (Turnhout, Belgium: Brepols, 1880), 423a, author's translation.

2 Thomas Fuller, *A Pisgah-sight of Palestine and The Confines thereof, with the Historie of the old and new Testament acted thereon*, (London: J. Williams, 1650), 3.

3 *e.g.*, the *National Geographic Atlas of the World* [8th edition] was widely accused of displaying political bias by using the name "Persian Gulf," with the words "Arabian Gulf" appearing in brackets beneath. A delicate geographical issue not limited to the Middle East, *Rand McNally's World Atlas* [7th edition] experienced significant fallout from its primary use of "Peking" [and not "Beijing"].

4 Plutarch, *Lives: Theseus*

CHAPTER 1

The Physical Geography of the Land

ROLE OF GEOGRAPHY IN UNDERSTANDING HISTORY

Western civilization has commonly embraced the logic of Greek philosophical categories and has endeavored to describe cosmic realities in terms of "time and space." Individuals, ideas, movements, and even the courses of nations are often interpreted precisely in accordance with these canons. Hence, designations are invariably employed in analyzing civilizations past and present: pre-/post-, Early/Late, B.C./A.D., East/West, Oriental/Occidental, Near East/Far East/Middle East.[1] (Note the first word in this paragraph!)

Christian theology itself has not escaped such an encompassing mode of thinking: God may be described in terms that are corollary to time (*infinity, eternality*) or space (*omnipresence*). And Christianity asserts that those attributes of deity were willingly relinquished by Christ through the drama of incarnation, when he became "locked in time and space." Accordingly, even upon superficial reflection, one can begin to comprehend something of the far-reaching significance of the temporal and spatial disciplines: history and geography respectively.

Moreover, history is in many respects inseparably bound by and subject to geographic limitations. Geography is an impelling force that both initiates and limits the nature and extent of political history, what we might call geopolitics. Geologic formation and rock type have a decisive effect on altitude, manner and extent of erosion, location and quantity of water supply, and physical topography. These, in turn, have a profound bearing on certain aspects of climate, raw materials, soil formation, and land use—factors that may alternatively repel or attract human settlement and certainly influence the location, density, and socioeconomic makeup of a settlement. Where settlements are founded, roadways are eventually opened and used by migrants, traders, or armies, and culture ultimately arrives at a particular location. Stated more succinctly, "With every step back in time, history becomes more and more geographical until, in the beginning, it is all geography."[2]

In short, factors of geography often dictate where and how geopolitics will occur. Surely it is geographically significant that ancient civilizations emerged on the banks of rivers. Ancient Egypt owed its existence to the Nile; Mesopotamia drew its life sustenance from the Tigris and Euphrates; the Indus Valley civilization was situated along the river by the same name; the Hittite Empire rested astride the Halys; Old Indian culture sprang to life in the Brahmaputra and Ganges river valleys; ancient China had its Yellow River and the Yangtze; and European culture emerged on the banks of the Tiber, Thames, Danube, Rhine, and Seine. Nor is it inconsequential that the Roman Empire was able to expand as far as the Danube and Rhine rivers, a boundary which for part of the 20th century also corresponded to the Iron Curtain. Even in 21st-century America, virtually every major commercial and industrial city has an outlet to river, ocean, or the Great Lakes network. Those few exceptions are located at the hub of important interstate highways or airline routes.

Other factors of geography, such as earthquake activity and volcanic eruption, have likewise played their part in fashioning history.[3] It is axiomatic that the face of much of western Asia and eastern Africa has been formed through seismic activity. A huge fissure in the earth's surface has been the single dominant factor in shaping the landscape of western Syria, Lebanon, Israel, Jordan, Ethiopia, Uganda, Tanzania, Mozambique, and the island of Madagascar. [**See map 13.**]

In western Asia, earthquake activity has always meant that certain areas were inhospitable to human occupation, causing arterial travel to be funneled into an essentially north-south grid. The seismic forces that produced the mighty Himalayan chain, on the other hand, created what in antiquity was an impenetrable longitudinal barrier that caused culture to expand and traffic to flow on an essentially east-west axis. Vast badlands of congealed lava confront a potential settler in a dreary terrain broken only occasionally by basaltic plugs or cinder cones, gaunt reminders of bygone volcanic activity. More important is the harsh reality that this volcanic activity often rendered the soil totally unsuitable for human productivity. In antiquity it always presented a cruelly hostile environment that was intolerably painful to the limbs of pack animals, and thus precluded any sort of arterial traffic.

Volcanic eruptions can bring a segment of history to an abrupt termination. The image of Vesuvius's eruption upon Pompeii in A.D. 79 often comes to mind. The 1815 eruption of Tambora on Indonesia created a casualty count of approximately 92,000 and produced an ash cloud in the upper atmosphere that reflected sunlight back into space and produced a year without summer. The 1883 eruption of Krakatoa was audible across one-third of the earth's surface, caused a tsunami that was perceptible in all oceans of the world, adversely modified climate on a global scale for several years, and killed more than 36,000 people. Yet in vivid contrast to all these events stands the eruption of the Greek island of Santorini (Thera), located in the south Aegean Sea approximately midway between mainland Greece and Crete. [**See maps 111 and 112 for location.**]

Santorini's explosivity index at ground zero is calculated to have been more than 15 times greater than the force of the atomic explosion over Hiroshima. In the wake of the colossal eruption that occurred on Santorini around 1525 B.C. (±100 years, whether dated archaeologically or radiometrically), some 32 square miles of earth collapsed into a caldera of approximately 2,250 feet in depth. When the Aegean waters rushed into this newly created and superheated chasm (estimated to have been in excess of 2550° F.), a gigantic tsunami was formed that is estimated to have been as high as 800 feet at its apex. Within 20 minutes, this massive tidal wave—also propelling an enormous volume of searing, toxic gases—catastrophically struck Crete at an estimated speed of 200 miles per hour and at a height of 200 to 300 feet.[4] Pumice laminated the vestige of Santorini with a volcanic deposit ranging in depth from between 65 and 195 feet. A cloud of pumice, ash, and lava estimated at between 8.5 and 11.25 cubic miles in volume was thrust some 50 miles into the sky where a predominantly northwesterly wind blew it toward Crete. The thick blanket of falling ash would have created an atmosphere of lethal air, producing polluted water, rancid food, and diverse diseases. What is more, basaltic cores the size of a person's head were hurled like missiles directly from Santorini to Crete. Waterborne pumice fragments manifesting a Santorini origin have been found across the entire stretch of the eastern Mediterranean basin, even at inland places as far away as Israel and Egypt.[5] It is not difficult to comprehend how the entire Minoan culture on Santorini was brought to a disastrous, abrupt end, nor how a number of Minoan palaces on Crete were severely damaged and may even have been destroyed at that time.

Mountains, deserts, and oceans have all influenced the location or nature of geopolitics. Today's newspapers often contain lead stories having to do with the continental effects of El Niño, salination, widespread famine and food shortages, or global warming. Some of those same geographic factors played a profound role in ancient Near Eastern geopolitics. Famines were often described in ancient literature, and scholars have amply demonstrated how climate fluctuations in antiquity had an adverse effect on ancient culture.[6]

A "Mediterranean theater" of history existed from the demise of the Persian navy at the Battle of Salamis (480 B.C.) until the defeat of the Spanish Armada (A.D. 1588). Northern and southern shores regularly vied for political and cultural superiority. But after the oceanic voyages of Christopher Columbus, Vasco da Gama, and Ferdinand Magellan, the geopolitical sovereignty of the Mediterranean was challenged as the Renaissance and some of its important cities began to fade and "history" moved westward.

Natural resources represent yet another geographic factor that has influenced the location and nature of geopolitics. A wide array of ancient documentation explicitly addressed the need to maintain control over the tin of Afghanistan, the cedar of Lebanon, the silver of Assyria, the copper of Cyprus, the gold of Spain, and the ivory of the African interior. And who can doubt that the whole complexion of modern geopolitics has been dramatically altered by the OPEC cartel? Indeed, geography represents the stage on which the pageant of history is presented, without which history itself would wander about aimlessly as a vagrant.[7] To paraphrase the aphorism commonly but probably erroneously ascribed to Will Durant, civilization exists by geographic consent, subject to change without notice.[8]

Geography's effect upon history extends also to the theoretical domain. Like the effect of environment on culture, geography actually establishes the boundaries within which history must operate. Students of the effect of geography on history have made a most helpful distinction between its *determining* effect and its *limiting* effect. Where a frigid winter climate necessitates the wearing of heavy clothing, there is nothing in the temperature itself that decrees whether people shall wear sealskins or Shetland wool, *but they must procure and wear winter clothing.* When a region unsuitable for agriculture somehow becomes populated, very little in the environment predetermines which domestic animals shall be grazed or whether food shall be secured with hooks, nets, traps, or spears, *but a non-agrarian society will surely emerge.*

It is geographically pertinent that places in the Near East manifesting the most ancient human habitation—Mt. Carmel, Shanidar, Çatal Hüyük, Jarmo, Hacilar [**map 23**]—are situated precisely in areas that receive an average annual rainfall capable of sustaining the spontaneous generation of wild grains that can support human existence. It is also geographically pertinent that certain plants and animals are peculiar to only one hemisphere, or that writing arose where, when, and in the form that it did. These all represent expressions of geopolitical history that have been and continue to be subject to the limitations and indirect controls of geography.

Many of the same limitations are discernible even in our modern technological world, where deserts can be extensively irrigated or the effects of oppressive heat can be mitigated by air-conditioning; where Landsat photography equipped with infrared capability can discover vast reservoirs of fresh water buried deep in the cavities of the earth's interior, or cloud-seeding and widespread irrigation can lessen the gravity of an arid environment; where rampaging rivers can be restrained by huge dams and even harnessed for hydroelectric purposes; where formidable mountain barriers can be leveled, penetrated, or easily surmounted; and where air travel can put faraway places within quick and convenient reach. One might imagine how much more defined and deeply etched such geographical limitations would have been in a world that existed before such technological sophistication—one like the biblical world.

ROLE OF GEOGRAPHY IN UNDERSTANDING THE BIBLE[9]

Matters of "time and space" remain among the difficulties that vex a 21st-century student of the Bible. The proclamations of Scripture were occasioned and penned from distinctive settings, yet modern students of the Bible live in a different millennium and adhere to a different worldview. Most live on a different continent. So in our desire to properly interpret and apply the Bible, we must ensure as much as possible that our enterprise is built knowledgeably upon the grid of the Bible's own environment. At the outset, it is imperative for one to view geography (space) as something more than a superfluity that can be arbitrarily divorced from biblical interpretation. To the contrary, the biblical portrait of both Israel and the Church is painted on several levels, including the territorial level.[10]

In point of fact, biblical narratives are often driven by the notion of "space." An incident may be said to have occurred on a certain hill, in a particular valley, on a discreet plain, at a given town. At times the name of the place itself becomes an important part of the revelation, frequently including a wordplay or pun on the name in order to reinforce the location of the event in public consciousness. Occasionally an aspect of geography becomes a theological axis around which an entire biblical book revolves, or a large portion of a book is particularly rich in geographical metaphor: for example, fertility and the book of Deuteronomy, forestation and the book of Isaiah, hydrology and the book of Psalms, or agriculture and the book of Joel. Often it is precisely a geographical reference or allusion that enables scholars to assign a book to a place of origin (such as Amos in Israel's northern kingdom, or James in the eastern Mediterranean basin).

Perhaps even more profoundly, Jewish faith in the Old Testament was inextricably tied to space, and "land" became the prism of this faith. Land/space was an arena in which God acted mightily on behalf of his people. (Consider the call and covenant with Abraham and his descendants, the Exodus/Sinai motif, the conquest/settlement of the land, the captivity away from the land, the return to the land, the New Israel.) Many of God's promises related directly to the original possession (or later restoration) of a particular parcel of real estate. It is not an overstatement to declare that, during its years of recorded biblical history, Israel's rootage in this "land" provided its faithful their foundational identity, security, and even prosperity.

When they were not in possession of their land, Israelites were often described in terms that reflected the precarious connotations of landlessness, aimlessness, and estrangement:

- "Sojourning" (Gen. 12:10; 15:13; 47:4; Ex. 6:4; Deut. 10:19b; 26:5b; cf. Heb. 11:13)—A *sojourner* was a resident-alien who did not belong and could not settle down to enjoy the privileges afforded the citizen.
- "Wandering" (Num. 32:13; Hos. 9:17; Deut. 26:5b)—A *wanderer* was someone en route to nowhere. He was not just between stops, but actually had no specified destination or home.
- "Going into exile" (2 Kings 18:11; Isa. 5:13; 49:21; Ezek. 39:23; Ezra 1:11)—An *exile* was someone who had been forcibly uprooted or disenfranchised from his own land and obliged to live in another "place."

Whether removed to Egypt, Babylon, or elsewhere, landlessness was tantamount to hopelessness. Israel's covenantal faith was very much based on and grounded in events that transpired at certain places *in this world*. There was an acute consciousness of a national home, a definable geographic domain in which even the soil was divinely consecrated, what one may call "the holy land."[11] One can rightly characterize Israel's faith by its "here and now" essence—one where the ascetic principle of 1 John 2:15–17 was largely absent.

Similarly, in the New Testament gospels, much of the teaching of Jesus may be related to where he was situated at the time. Jesus talked about "living water" while at Jacob's well (John 4:10); He called himself the "bread of life" while at Capernaum, where basaltic grain mills were manufactured (John 6:48); he declared Peter to be the "rock" against which "the gates of Hades will not prevail" while in Caesarea Philippi, a site otherwise known in the classical world for the Eleusian Oracles and the daughter of Demeter being carried off by Hades, god of the underworld (Matt. 16:18); and he spoke about faith that can move a mountain while on the road to Bethphage, from which his disciples could easily have looked southward and seen evidence of a mountain that had been physically "moved" by Herod the Great in order to construct his palace/fortress site of Herodium (Matt. 21:21–22).

In a few instances Jesus appeared to go out of his way in order to teach a lesson at a particular location. On one such occasion he told a parable about a certain nobleman who journeyed to a distant country in order to obtain royal power. However, his appointment was opposed by a delegation of local citizens, who had sent an embassy to state their objections to his reign. So, when he returned with his newfound authority, this nobleman ruthlessly attacked those who had opposed him and had been disloyal to him (Luke 19:11–27). This "parable" is eerily reminiscent of real-life events surrounding the eldest son of Herod the Great—Archelaus. After Herod's death in 4 B.C., Archelaus traveled from Judea to Rome to obtain an "ethnarchy"—an official sanction to rule over a province. The Jewish historian Josephus tells us Archelaus was awarded the title over the protest of more than 8,000 Jews in Rome, including a delegation that had also traveled from Judea.[12] After returning to Judea with his new power, Archelaus wasted no time in ruthlessly extracting vengeance on his detractors. Josephus also wrote that Archelaus focused much time and attention on the New Testament city of Jericho and its immediate environs: he rebuilt the Herodian palace at Jericho in splendid fashion, he built a town near Jericho that he named for himself, and he diverted irrigation waters to his date-palm plantations located only two miles from Jericho.[13]

It is of interest to note that Jesus told his parable as he was departing Jericho en route to Jerusalem, which means that his listeners would have been on the Roman road bordering the recently reconstructed Herodian palace and adjacent to the irrigation channels that carried water out of the Judean hill country to Jericho and its environs. Indeed, many of Jesus' teachings are arguably related to his distinctive geographical surroundings. He talked about various kinds of soil, the east wind, the flowers of the field, and branches abiding in vines. One later observes a geographical correlation between the uniquely centrifugal form of Jesus' Great Commission in Acts 1:8 ("[from] Jerusalem, [then] in all Judea and Samaria, and [finally] to the ends of the earth") and that book's presentation of the expansion of the early apostolic movement.

And for Christian faith as well—not only for Jewish faith—many crucially important aspects of biblical history have transpired in *very precise places on earth*—not just in empty space nor in heaven (e.g., the location of the birth, crucifixion, resurrection, and ascension of Christ; the flow of the early apostolic missionary journeys; etc.). If the Christian gospel were simply a matter of otherworldliness or concerned only with spiritual or moral values, gaining an appreciation of the spatial dimension of the Bible would hardly matter, and seminal events in the New Testament would hardly have been geographically located in the text by the biblical writers. But it is neither of these! Central to the kerygma of the New Testament is the foundational claim that God became human at a definite moment in time and at a precise point in space. To be unaware of or to neglect the geographical DNA of the Bible or the biblical world will therefore often mean that one may run afoul of the biblical argument or that reality may dissolve into sentimentalism.

Armed with a geographical knowledge of the Bible, one is better able to understand references such as "the former and latter rains," "the strong east wind," or "a land flowing with milk and honey." Similarly, one can better appreciate the scorching effect of Israel's hot sun; the implications of "no rainfall" and the importance of dew for crop survival; the prevalence of fertility (Baal) worship; the nature of Egyptian, Canaanite, and Mesopotamian deities; the migrations of Abraham, Moses, and Nehemiah; the terrain Joshua's forces could conquer but over which the Philistines could not run their chariots; the astounding success of David in eluding Saul's manhunt; the social psychology of the ministry of John the Baptist; the motivation(s) behind Jesus' astute move from Nazareth to Capernaum; and the staggering distances traveled by the apostle Paul. In addition, the pronouncements of the prophets make more sense as they predicted a stunning day to come when valleys will be lifted, mountains will be lowered, uneven and rough ground will be made level and smooth, and even when the water of the Dead Sea will become crystal clear and nourish abundant sea life.

Cultivating a spatial awareness is a necessary and valuable component in any serious study of the Bible. Like the Bible itself, faith is formulated from within the spatial and temporal context of which it was a part. Hence, the geographical discipline should become both the object and the vehicle of some of the most rewarding and enlightening Bible study; it is clearly worthy of a detailed investigation.

Old Testament Jericho sits adjacent to the most prolific spring in eastern Canaan (above site in picture). The scars of archaeological excavation are apparent on the tell.

A GEOGRAPHICAL INTRODUCTION TO THE WORLD OF PALESTINE

AS A COMPONENT OF THE FERTILE CRESCENT[14]

Wrapped like a mantle around the Mediterranean, Black, and Caspian seas is a vast geologic formation of elevated and rugged mountains, known as the Alpine-Himalayan chain. [**See map 1.**] This rocky and convoluted landscape stretches eastward from the Pyrenees Mountains of northern Spain in a nearly unbroken 7,000-mile line to the towering Himalayan chain of India and Nepal and the Tsinling Shan range of inland China. Near the center of this sprawling alpine uplift stand the lofty Taurus, Pontus, Urartu, and Kurdistan Mountains of Turkey (rising at places to an elevation of nearly 17,000 feet, with peaks snow-clad year round) and the Zagros and Elburz ranges of Iran (a few peaks of which ascend over 18,000 feet, the highest in all the Near East). Whether Akkadian, Egyptian, Assyrian, Babylonian, Phoenician, Persian, or Greek, ancient civilization was never fully able to transcend or penetrate such formidable terrain for imperialistic purposes. Indeed, all Near Eastern empires prior to the time of Julius Caesar were largely restrained by this northern barrier. Moreover, there always lurked in those dim and mountainous recesses fierce peoples who periodically threatened Semitic domination of the northern frontier.

Farther south, extending eastward from the Atlantic shores of North Africa, is an enormous expanse of almost waterless terrain. Known across that continent as the Sahara Desert, this barren and desolate environment stretches beyond the Red Sea and spans the entire Arabian Peninsula as the Arabian Desert. The arid zone crosses the mountains of Iran to the north side and continues through the Salt Desert (Dasht-e Kavir), Tarim Basin, and into the Gobi Desert of southern Mongolia. Broadening at places to more than 1,000 miles in width, and stretching nearly 5,000 miles across two continents, this band of savage, foreboding sand was yet another impassable barrier to imperialism and civilization in antiquity.

Hemmed in by these two natural barriers of mountain and desert lies a thin, semicircular strip of comparatively arable land that arches northward from the southeastern corner of the Mediterranean Sea near Gaza (Acts 8:26) [**map 2**], through Israel, Lebanon, and western Syria. Near the northeastern corner of the Mediterranean, this strip bends eastward and then curves southeastward, essentially following the flood plains of the Tigris and Euphrates river valleys as far as the head of the Persian Gulf. Since the days of the Egyptologist James Breasted,[15] this strip of land has been known as the "Fertile Crescent." In this Crescent, humankind invented the plow, the wheel, the lever and screw, and the arch. Here they learned how to domesticate animals, to cultivate grains and become a food producer, to cluster buildings and build cities, to work metals, and to write (first pictographically and later alphabetically). It was in this crescent of civilization that humanity developed art, music, literature, law, mathematics, philosophy, medicine, astronomy, cartography, chemistry, and the calendar.

At the risk of oversimplification, the Fertile Crescent may be divided into two topographic spheres, known respectively as "Mesopotamia" and "Levant." The word "Mesopotamia" (a Greek term meaning "[the land] between the rivers"), was applied to the eastern sphere as early as the writings of Polybius, Strabo, and Josephus (200 B.C. to A.D. 100).[16] Earlier still, the translators of the Septuagint (*LXX*) employed the word to designate the district from which the patriarch Abraham had emigrated (Gen. 24:10), rendered by Hebrew scribes as Aram-naharaim ("Aram of the two rivers"). It is likely that this Hebrew expression should be understood to demarcate only the land between the Euphrates and the Balih rivers, known also as Paddan-aram ("the field of Aram" [e.g., Gen. 28:2f; 33:18; 35:9]), and not the entire terrain between the Tigris and Euphrates. [**See maps 2 and 30.**] Nevertheless, contemporary references to "Mesopotamia" conventionally denote the "island" of land bounded on the west and south by the Euphrates, on the east by the Tigris, and on the north by the outliers of the Taurus and Kurdistan mountains. The low-lying plain of Mesopotamia lies at an altitude of about 1,625 feet in some northern sectors and slopes gently toward the Persian Gulf. [**See map 2.**]

Variations in precipitation differentiate Mesopotamia into a wet and dry steppe. The wet steppe receives more than twelve inches of rainfall annually. It is characterized by red-brown sediment, perennial grasses, herbs, and bushes, especially as one moves from west to east. This area between the Euphrates and the Balih rivers is most closely associated with the biblical patriarchs and consists of low, stony hills that are bare of vegetation except when watered in the spring. Between the Balih and the Habur rivers, the steppe is less arid and even relatively fertile in the springtime and early summer. The area is quite suitable for pasturage, yet survival in this part of the steppe depended on the numerous wells scattered throughout the terrain (Gen. 24:11; 29:2). The area does not seem to have been heavily occupied or cultivated in antiquity.

The upper Habur River appears on the map in the shape of an inverted triangle where the land flattens considerably. Adequate rainfall and good soil has allowed agriculture to flourish here since high antiquity, producing an abundance of the best grain in all of Mesopotamia. Flanking either side of the southern point of this triangle, mountainous outcroppings retain the soil and mineral deposits washed down from the north. Accordingly, this region tends to remain grassy throughout even the summer and autumn months, so it provided lush grazing grounds for Mesopotamian shepherds who would migrate during the spring and summer from their native areas south of the Euphrates. The mountains also sustain essentially all the native timber available in Mesopotamia—pine, oak, terebinth, and pistachio trees. In modern times poplar trees have been planted throughout much of Mesopotamia, both as windbreaks and for architectural usage.

Most of the dry steppe, by way of contrast, is characterized by gray gypsum desert soils, shallow-rooted seasonal grasses, scattered shrubs, and—where the soil is deep enough—marginal dry-farming of winter crops. Below the eight-inch precipitation line, only limited-scale irrigation farming is practiced. The flood plain of the middle Euphrates, particularly in the area of Deir ez-Zor and south, is as deep as 300 feet and up to eight miles wide. The humus soil deposited there by the Euphrates and Habur is ideal for agriculture, and an entire network of settlements is known to have existed in this region throughout the biblical period. On a much more limited scale, the same conditions exist along a short section of the middle Tigris, in the area around Samarra, where the deposition of the Tigris and the Lower Zab has created a bed of rich alluvial sediments. The soil of south Mesopotamia is uniformly hard and nearly impenetrable. The landscape exhibits windblown formations and dunes, a result of sand blowing off the Arabian Desert. At the same time, southern Mesopotamia has always had to contend with the problem of a higher water table brought on by over-irrigation, thus producing an ever-increasing soil salination. Some authorities, in fact, suggest that the decline of the Sumerian civilization there, and the subsequent shift northward of the cultural centers, can be attributed to the creeping salination of the soil.[17] This is far from certain, though we do know that the Sumerian economy depended heavily on locally grown grain yields, far beyond what could be produced later in antiquity or any time since.[18]

The region between the confluence of the Tigris and Euphrates and the Persian Gulf is known as the Shatt el-Arab waterway. Twice daily the water level in this vicinity rises and falls by about six feet, a cause of periodic boundary disputes between Iraq and Iran. Geographically speaking, the fluctuation permits salt water from the Gulf to penetrate inland, thereby creating a marshy area that severely restricts human settlement.

This general overview enables one to realize that the phrase "Fertile Crescent" is quite open to misinterpretation. More accurately, most of Mesopotamia can be called "fertile" only by way of contrast with its arid, desert neighbor, and only along

Both the city of Diyarbekir (on the horizon) and local sheep (right of river) draw their sustenance from the waters of the upper Tigris river.

Geographical Barriers and the Ancient World

A
B
C
1
2
3
4
NORTH SEA
BALTIC SEA
ATLANTIC OCEAN
Thames R.
Vistula R.
E U R O P E
Rhine R.
Danube R.
Dniester R.
Dnieper R.
Volga R.
Loire R.
A L P S
Don R.
Rhone R.
Po R.
Danube R.
CASP
BLACK SEA
CAUCASUS MTS.
PYRENEES
DINARIC ALPS
Maritsa R.
Douro R.
Ebro R.
PONTUS MTS.
URARTU MTS.
Tagus R.
ELBURZ
TAURUS MTS.
KURDISTAN MTS.
M E D I T E R R A N E A N S E A
FERTILE CRESCENT
Tigris R.
ZAGROS MTS.
ATLAS MTS.
SYRIAN DESERT
Euphrates R.
Area of ancient Canaan
S A H A R A
D E S E R T
Nile R.
RED SEA
ARAB
DES
Lake Chad
Blue Nile R.
A F R I C A
White Nile R.
Lake Victoria
Alpine-Himalayan Mountain Belt
Afro-Arabian Rift Valley
0 500 1000 Miles
0 500 1000 1500 Kilometers

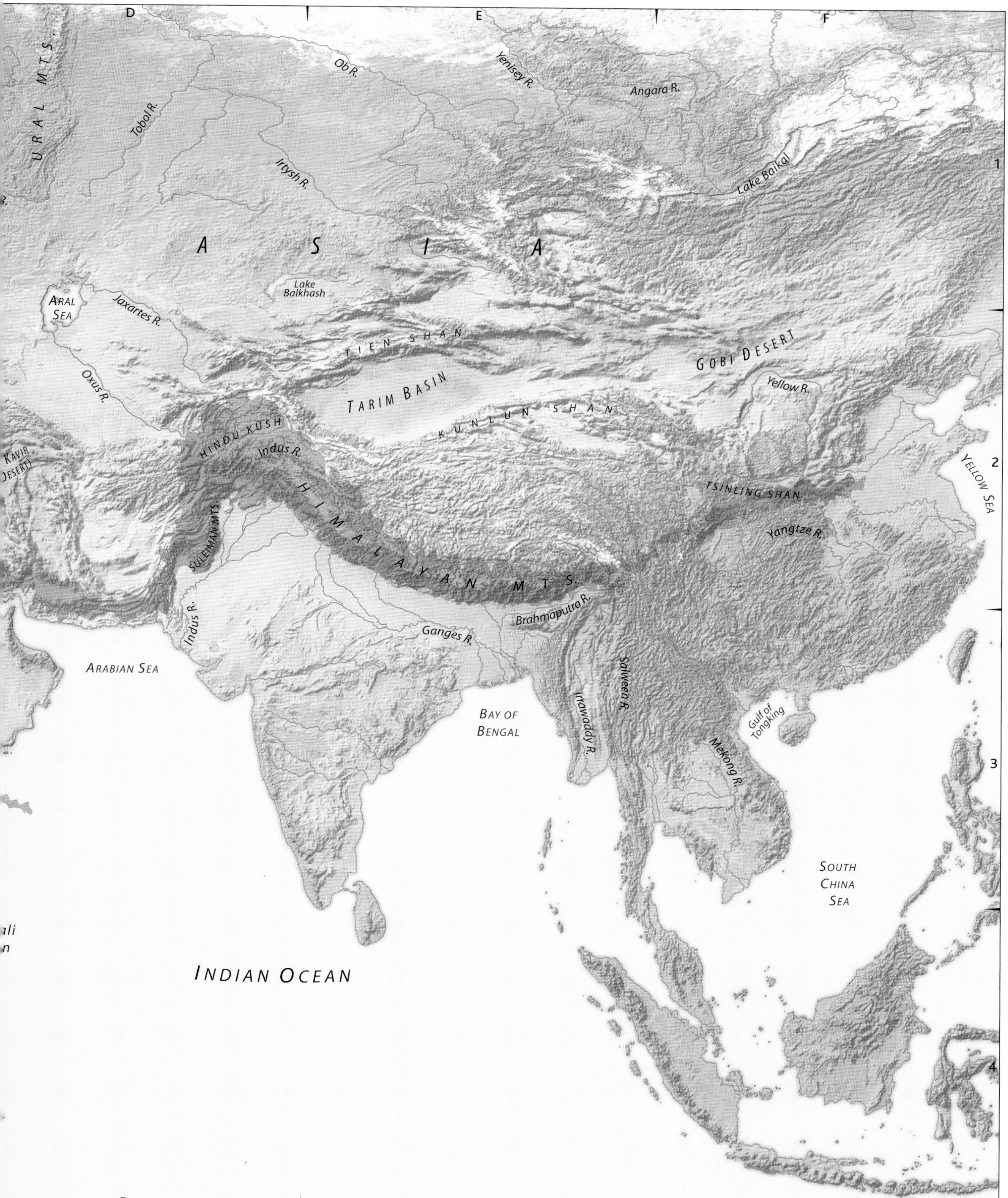
D
E
F
URAL MTS.
Ob R.
Yenisey R.
Angara R.
Tobol R.
Irtysh R.
Lake Baikal
1
A S I A
Lake Balkhash
ARAL SEA
Jaxartes R.
TIEN SHAN
GOBI DESERT
Oxus R.
Yellow R.
TARIM BASIN
KUNLUN SHAN
HINDU KUSH
Indus R.
KAVIR DESERT
2
YELLOW SEA
HIMALAYAN MTS.
TSINLING SHAN
SULEIMAN MTS.
Yangtze R.
Indus R.
Brahmaputra R.
Ganges R.
ARABIAN SEA
Salween R.
Irrawaddy R.
BAY OF BENGAL
Gulf of Tongking
Mekong R.
3
SOUTH CHINA SEA
INDIAN OCEAN
4
D
E
F

Mesopotamia

map 2

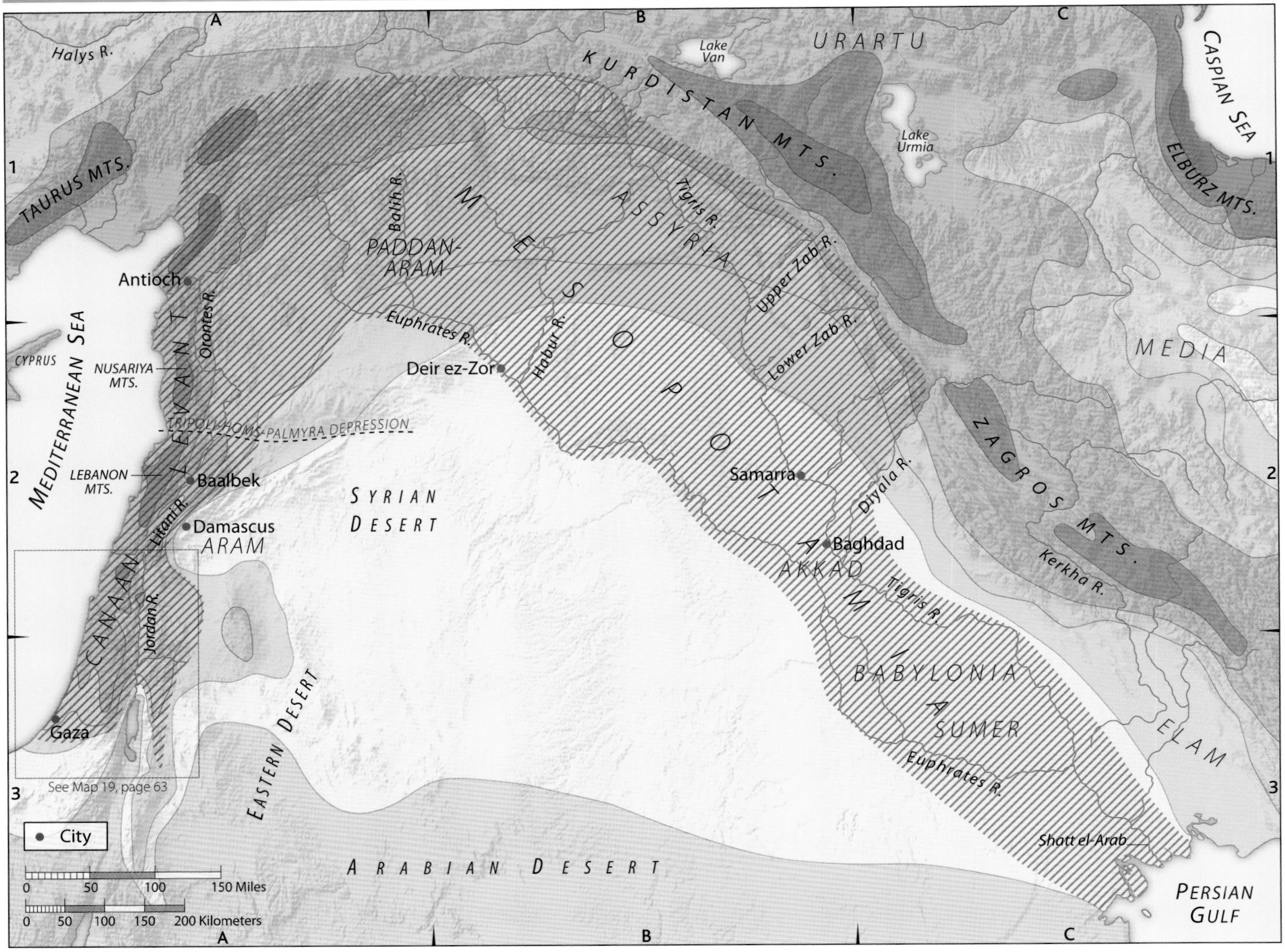

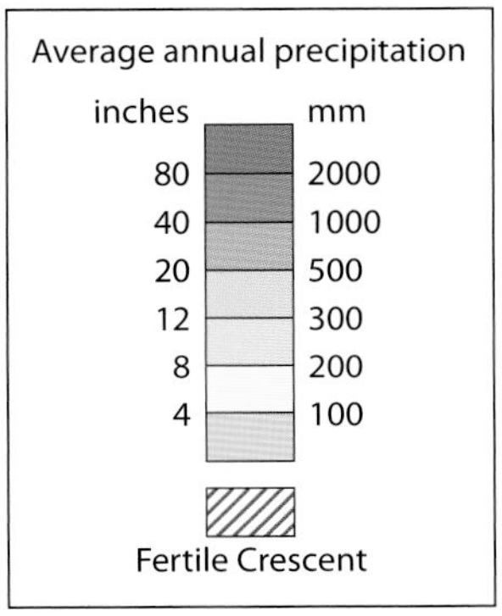

the sinuous ribbons of greenery in the flood plains of the Tigris and Euphrates rivers, their tributaries, and interlocking canal systems.

The western sphere of the Fertile Crescent is called the Levant, a French word meaning "rising" that refers to either the rising of the sun or the heights/rising of mountains as viewed from a ship on the Mediterranean headed in that direction. This geographic area consists of a double alignment of mountain belts enclosing the northern portion of the Afro-Arabian fault line. [**See maps 1 and 13.**] Longitudinally segmented by three "depressions," these belts comprise a series of four sets of parallel ranges [**See map 3**]:

1. Beginning in the north, near Antioch and the Amuq Plain, is the Nusariya mountain chain, which technically includes Mt. Cassius. [**See map 109.**] This chain dominates the western horizon, while the Zawiya chain and its northern outliers rise in the east. It stretches as far south as the so-called Tripoli-Homs-Palmyra depression—a valley through which courses the el-Kabir (Eleutherus) River that demarcates the modern border between Syria and Lebanon.
2. In the territory south of this lateral gap stand the mighty Lebanon Mountains in the western field of view. Opposite them on the east, the Anti-Lebanon chain is found, which achieves its greatest height in the southern extremity at Mt. Hermon. The Lebanons range as far as the deep gorge created by the Litani River (immediately north of Tyre), extending east past the site of Dan and on to the flat steppe that separates the hills of Damascus and the basaltic plateau of Jebel Druze.
3. Proceeding south, spanning the area between the so-called Litani-Dan-Steppeland depression and the Beersheba-Zered depression, stand the highlands of Galilee, Samaria, and Judah on the western front. Prominent in the east are the Golan Heights, the Gilead Plateau, and the Moabite Highlands.

Virtually encircled by modern roads, Tel Dan sits adjacent to the river Dan (N. Qadi) in steppeland just south of Mt. Hermon.

4. South of the Beersheba-Zered depression as far as the Red Sea, the western vista features the wild and forbidding slopes of the Wilderness of Zin and the modern Negeb. The eastern horizon is dominated by the towering sandstone highlands of Edom and the spectacular granite mountains of Midian. (Whether or not this fourth area is technically to be included in the Levant remains an open question. Primarily because this is a geographic discussion, the section is mentioned here in the text, but will be excluded from the map and from subsequent discussion in this section.)

Separating these parallel mountain ranges is the Great Rift Valley (the northernmost portion of the Afro-Arabian Rift Valley). In the north, the Nusariya and Zawiya mountains fall precipitously—more than 3,000 feet—into this chasm, known there as the Ghab ("thicket" or "depression"), which is drained by the meandering Orontes River. South of that, the Lebanon and Anti-Lebanon Mountains, which rise to heights in excess of 10,000 feet, fall off abruptly into the trough, known in that region as the Beqa` ("a place of stagnant water"), drained primarily by the Litani and Abana rivers. Continuing south, the highlands of Galilee, Samaria, and northern Judah, and the heights of Golan and Gilead, drop off into the narrow chasm referred to as the Arabah ("wasteland, desert-plain"). This depression north of the Dead Sea may also be identified as the Jordan Rift Valley, named for the river that drains it.

It is instructive to analyze the Levant using a longitudinal cross section. From such a perspective, the Levant itself bears the shape of a mountain, highest in the center, with certain topographic and physiographic features mirrored on the two sloping sides. The key to the geography of the Levant is its towering apex. The lofty elevation of the Lebanon and Anti-Lebanon Mountains far exceeds that of the ranges to the north or the south. In addition, they exhibit an unusual feature of geological structure not present in adjoining regions: a substantial substratum of impermeable, nonporous rocks within their uplift. Because of this layer, water is forced to the surface in vast quantities, producing hundreds of large and prolific springs at the unusually high altitude of 4,000 to 5,000 feet above sea level. Some of these torrents have a flow of several thousand cubic feet per second and emerge from the sides of the mountains as small rivers or cascading rivulets. They form the headwaters of at least four major rivers: the Litani, the Abana, the Orontes, and the Jordan.

In a number of fundamental ways, a certain symmetry can also be observed in the two outlying river valleys (especially prior to the 20th century, when dams were erected on each river). Both the Orontes and Jordan rivers had steep gradients, particularly near their headwaters in the elevated heights of Lebanon, and were so fast-moving that they were erosive instead of depository in nature. Neither river has been navigable to any degree throughout history. In their descents, both rivers had to cut through a basaltic dam in antiquity, thereby creating an intermediate lake (Lake of Homs on the Orontes; Lake Hula on the Jordan). Both rivers have seasonal flows that are unfavorable to the agricultural cycle, so were of little value for irrigational purposes. The soils around the

Orontes and Jordan are of similar types: alluvial soils along the banks, saline at certain places (especially along the Jordan).

The sets of mountains flanking the Lebanon and Anti-Lebanon ranges on the north and south sides are themselves symmetrical in certain respects. Both are comprised mostly of limestone and manifest an internal transverse valley (Ugarit Valley in the north; Jezreel [Esdraelon] Valley in the south). Both ranges have an approximate longitudinal shape and comparative elevation of 2,500 to 3,500 feet, with peaks approaching 4,500 to 5,000 feet. They each receive similar rainfall amounts (20 to 40 inches annually) in similar seasonal patterns. In both cases, precipitation amounts increase toward the north and on their western flanks, precisely on terrain where farming is least productive and irrigation has negligible value. The soils of both ranges produce similar growth: Mediterranean scrubs, tamarisk, and brushwood cover many slopes; seasonal grasses suitable only for grazing survive on plateaus; reed grass grows in swamps; and anemones, poppies, and wildflowers abound. Food crops include grains (wheat, barley, maize), and a wide range of vegetables can be grown on the coastal plains. Citrus trees as well as many fig, carob, olive, and date trees can be found; the few hardwood forests that were not pillaged in earlier history are exceedingly small. Stratification in both of these lands provides comparatively meager mineral resources, mainly asphalt deposits and mineral springs. Both mountainous areas are flanked on the west by a fairly narrow, flat coastline, consisting mainly of sand and sand dunes.

AS A LAND PREPARED BY GOD

Theological borders

Even though Israel's borders are discussed in more than one biblical text, significant questions of location remain with respect to three of the four borders. Perhaps a proper starting point for a discussion of these borders is the acknowledgement that they were frequently set at natural topographic locations: the Dead Sea, the Sea of Galilee, the Mediterranean, major mountains and rivers, etc. This provides warrant for suggesting that many of the lesser-known segments of the border descriptions may also have been situated at natural geographical points. The following treatment will include a delineation of fixed points, an analysis of lesser known but nevertheless important points of reference, and some discussion of the issues involved. Each segment will culminate with a summary of where the evidence seems to point.

Western border

(Num. 34:6; Josh. 15:4; 16:3, 8; 17:9; 19:29; cf. Ezek. 47:20; 48:1)
The western border happily presents no problem in identification. It extends to the Great Sea, the Mediterranean, from the northern extremity of the tribe of Asher (Josh. 19:29) to the southern extremity of the tribe of Judah (Josh. 15:4).

Northern border

(Num. 34:7–9; cf. Ezek. 47:15–17; 48:1–7)
Taken as a whole, the biblical texts indicate that the northern border extended eastward from the Mediterranean on a line that ran to Zedad, passing Mt. Hor and Lebo-hamath. From Zedad, the line continued via Ziphron to Hazar-enan, where it turned toward the border of Hauran. Of these places, only two can be identified positively, and both are situated on the edge of the Syrian/Eastern Desert. Zedad should be situated at modern Sadad, about 40 miles east of the Orontes and 65 miles northeast of Damascus, just east of the present-day Damascus-Homs highway. [**See map 4.**]

Hauran doubtless refers to the plateau that extends east of the Sea of Galilee and is dominated by Jebel Druze. (Mt. Hauran was classical Auranitis.) The name Hauran for this region is frequently attested in neo-Assyrian texts as early as Shalmaneser III,[19] and in fact, Hauran became the name of an Assyrian province[20] near the territory of Damascus, as is also seen in the wording of the Ezekiel texts. [**See map 78.**] Owing to these two identifications, it is reasonable to seek the intermediate sites of Ziphron and Hazar-enan along the perimeter of the same desert wasteland. The site of Hazar-enan is often equated with the lush and historically significant oasis of Qaryatein,[21] based on the meaning of the Hebrew name ("village of a spring"). Beyond this, the exact course of the northern border becomes a matter of uncertainty.

There are a number of indications, however, which combine to suggest that this border might have corresponded to a clearly established boundary in antiquity. First, the site of Lebo-hamath[22] should be associated with modern Lebweh, a town located in the forest region of the watershed that divides the Orontes and Litani rivers, some 15 miles northeast of Baalbek, along the Riblah-Baalbek highway. [**See map 25.**] The site was attested in Egyptian, Assyrian, and classical literatures[23] as a city of some prominence. Located between Kadesh on the Orontes and Baalbek, Lebo-hamath was situated in a territory commonly recognized in antiquity as a major boundary in the Beqa` Valley (1 Kings 8:65; 1 Chron. 13:5; 2 Chron. 7:8).

Second, in the place of Lebo-hamath, Ezekiel (47:16) references the site of Berothai, a town otherwise located in the central Beqa` Valley (2 Sam. 8:8) and generally thought to be reflected in the modern town of Brital, situated just south of Baalbek. However, Ezekiel goes on to specify that Berothai lay "on the *border* between Damascus and Hamath." (In 2 Kings 23:33 and 25:21, the site of Riblah [Rablah] is said to have been "in the land of Hamath.") It seems reasonable, then, that Ezekiel was describing this sector of Israel's northern border in a way that closely corresponded to an internationally recognized buffer zone in his day.

The book of Numbers marks the northern border between Lebo-hamath and the Mediterranean at Mt. Hor, a site which

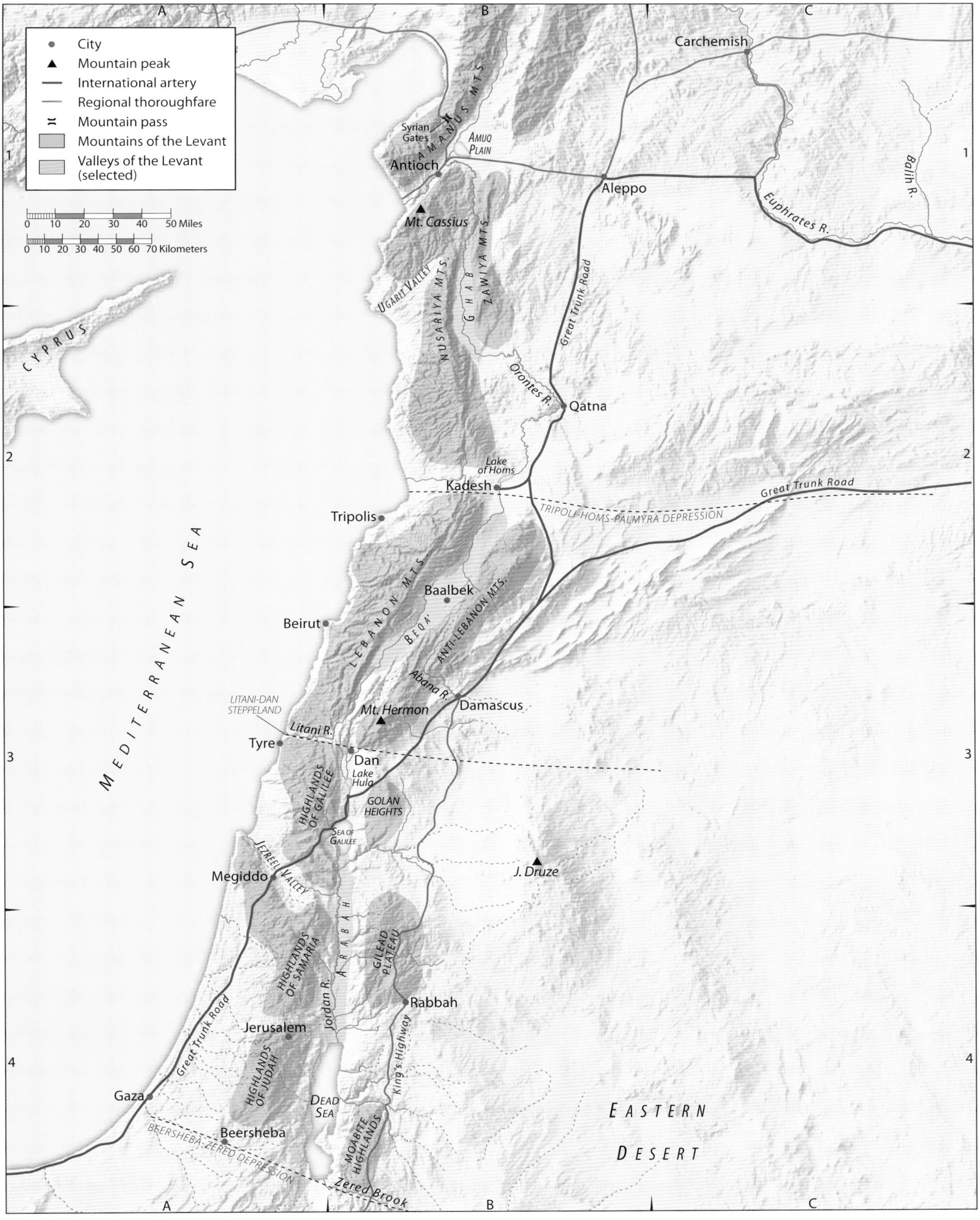
City
Mountain peak
International artery
Regional thoroughfare
Mountain pass
Mountains of the Levant
Valleys of the Levant (selected)
0 10 20 30 40 50 Miles
0 10 20 30 40 50 60 70 Kilometers
Carchemish
Syrian Gates
AMANUS MTS.
AMUQ PLAIN
Antioch
Aleppo
Balih R.
Euphrates R.
Mt. Cassius
ZAWIYA MTS.
GHAB
NUSARIYA MTS.
UGARIT VALLEY
CYPRUS
Great Trunk Road
Orontes R.
Qatna
Lake of Homs
Kadesh
Great Trunk Road
TRIPOLI-HOMS-PALMYRA DEPRESSION
Tripolis
MEDITERRANEAN SEA
LEBANON MTS.
Baalbek
ANTI-LEBANON MTS.
BEQA'
Beirut
Abana R.
Damascus
Mt. Hermon
LITANI-DAN STEPPELAND
Litani R.
Tyre
Dan
Lake Hula
HIGHLANDS OF GALILEE
GOLAN HEIGHTS
SEA OF GALILEE
JEZREEL VALLEY
Megiddo
J. Druze
ARABAH
GILEAD PLATEAU
HIGHLANDS OF SAMARIA
Jordan R.
Rabbah
Jerusalem
Great Trunk Road
King's Highway
HIGHLANDS OF JUDAH
Gaza
DEAD SEA
MOABITE HIGHLANDS
Beersheba
BEERSHEBA-ZERED DEPRESSION
Zered Brook
EASTERN DESERT

cannot be definitively located but which must refer to one of the summits within the northern Lebanon range between Lebweh and the Sea. A number of prominent peaks, both inland (Akkar, Makmel, Mneitri, Sannin) and along the coast (Ras Shakkah), have been identified with biblical Mt. Hor.

Although any proposal is ultimately speculative, a fairly strong case can be developed for identifying Mt. Hor with modern Mt. Akkar. First, as already mentioned, the northern border at other points appears to have followed the line of a natural, ancient boundary. The western portion of that same boundary extended westward from Homs through what is known as the Tripolis-Homs-Palmyra depression. [**See map 3.**] Also running through much of this depression was the el-Kabir River, which empties into the Mediterranean just south of modern Sumra/Simyra. This depression now forms the boundary between the modern countries of Syria and Lebanon after sitting approximate to an established boundary during several periods of antiquity.[24] Juxtaposed to this valley at the northernmost extremity of the Lebanon range stands the lofty Mt. Akkar. Unlike other candidates for Mt. Hor, Mt. Akkar rises contiguous to this ancient and longstanding boundary.

Moreover, it is of interest that, instead of listing Mt. Hor between the Mediterranean and Lebo-hamath in the northern border, Ezekiel (47:15; 48:1) made reference to "the way of Hethlon," an unknown site but one which may be reflected in the name of the modern town Heitela, located some 23 miles northeast of Tripolis and only about two miles from the el-Kabir River.[25]

Given the location of the fixed sites and the repeated suggestion that other places may be associated with what was an established boundary in antiquity, it seems feasible that Israel's northern border stretched along the northern edges of the Lebanon and Anti-Lebanon Mountains, following the course of the el-Kabir River as far as the vicinity of the Lake of Homs, then running south in the Beqa` as far as the outer flanks of the Anti-Lebanon Mountain (the area of Lebo-hamath). It then skirted that mountain in an eastward direction as far as the Eastern Desert (the vicinity of Sadad), where it essentially followed the fringes of the desert to the area of Mt. Hauran.

Other biblical texts at first blush seem to indicate that Israel's border extended to "the great river, the river Euphrates" (e.g., Gen. 15:18; Josh. 1:4; cf. Deut. 11:24). One problem in deciphering this expression is related to its exact application: it may be employed to describe Israel's *northern* frontier (e.g., Gen. 15:18; cf. Ex. 23:31) or Israel's *eastern* frontier (e.g., Deut. 11:24). This ambiguity has led some writers to interpret the terminology in these texts not as a delineated border, but rather as idealized territorial terminal points, anticipating the grandeur of David's or Solomon's kingdom when Israelite control extended as far afield as the Euphrates (1 Kings 4:21; 1 Chron. 18:3; 2 Chron. 9:26).

Support for this view may be found in the more expansive corollary reference to the "river of Egypt" (the easternmost arm of the Nile Delta) in the Genesis 15 text, whereas the territorial border text of Numbers 34:5 and the tribal border text of Joshua 15:4 (cf. Ezek. 47:19; 48:28) more narrowly restrict that southern frontier to the "brook/wadi of Egypt" (W. el-Arish). Other authorities regard the more enlarged description of Genesis 15 to be geographically related to the Persian (Assyrian?) provincial name "Beyond the River," indicating the territory of Palestine and Syria (cf. Ezra 4:10–11, 16–17, 20; 5:3; 6:6, 8, 13; 8:36; Neh. 2:7, 9; 3:7),[26] whereas the Numbers 34 and Joshua 15 texts have in view only the geography of the land of Canaan. Still other scholars regard the words "the great river" as a reference to the aforementioned el-Kabir River, to which an interpolation ("the river Euphrates") was added later.[27] After all, the modern Arabic name of this river (Nahr el-Kabir) means "the great river"—a well-deserved name, as the el-Kabir drains the greatest extent of Lebanon's coastal ranges. In this final scenario, amid the political realities of the United Monarchy, "the great river" might have come to assume a double meaning, referring both to Israel's actual northern border at the el-Kabir, as well as to its idealized frontier at the Euphrates. In any event, the Euphrates terminology is excluded from texts delineating the specific borders of biblical Israel.

Eastern border

(Num. 34:10–12; Josh. 13:8–23; cf. Ezek. 47:18)
A determination of the eastern border will depend upon two related issues: (1) the course one charts for the northern border; and (2) the relevance one assigns the battles against Sihon and Og (Num. 21:21–35). Placement of all sites mentioned in conjunction with the eastern border is a matter of conjecture, except the Sea of Galilee and the Jordan River. But it is precisely involving the Jordan that a major issue surfaces: Were the territories east of the Jordan and eventually occupied by the tribes of Reuben, Gad, and East Manasseh *beyond* or *within* the territory given Israel? Stated otherwise, did Israel's occupation of its land commence at the crossing of the Jordan River (Josh. 3) or did it commence at the crossing of the Arnon River (Num. 21:13; cf. Deut. 2:16–37; Judg. 11:13–26)?

Many recent studies have adopted the former option, with the result that the eastern border of Israel has been drawn at the Jordan River, between the Sea of Galilee and the Dead Sea. However, such a view may be greatly influenced by Christian hymnology[28] and must inherently embrace the premise that the eastern border of biblical Israel corresponds to the eastern border of the entity known as Canaan. Such a view is at variance with the verdict of Joshua 22 (esp. vv. 9–11, 13, 32), where the three Transjordanian tribes are clearly portrayed as being part of Israel and part of its 12 tribes, yet they were allotted territories beyond the eastern border of Canaan

Theological Borders of the Holy Land

map 4

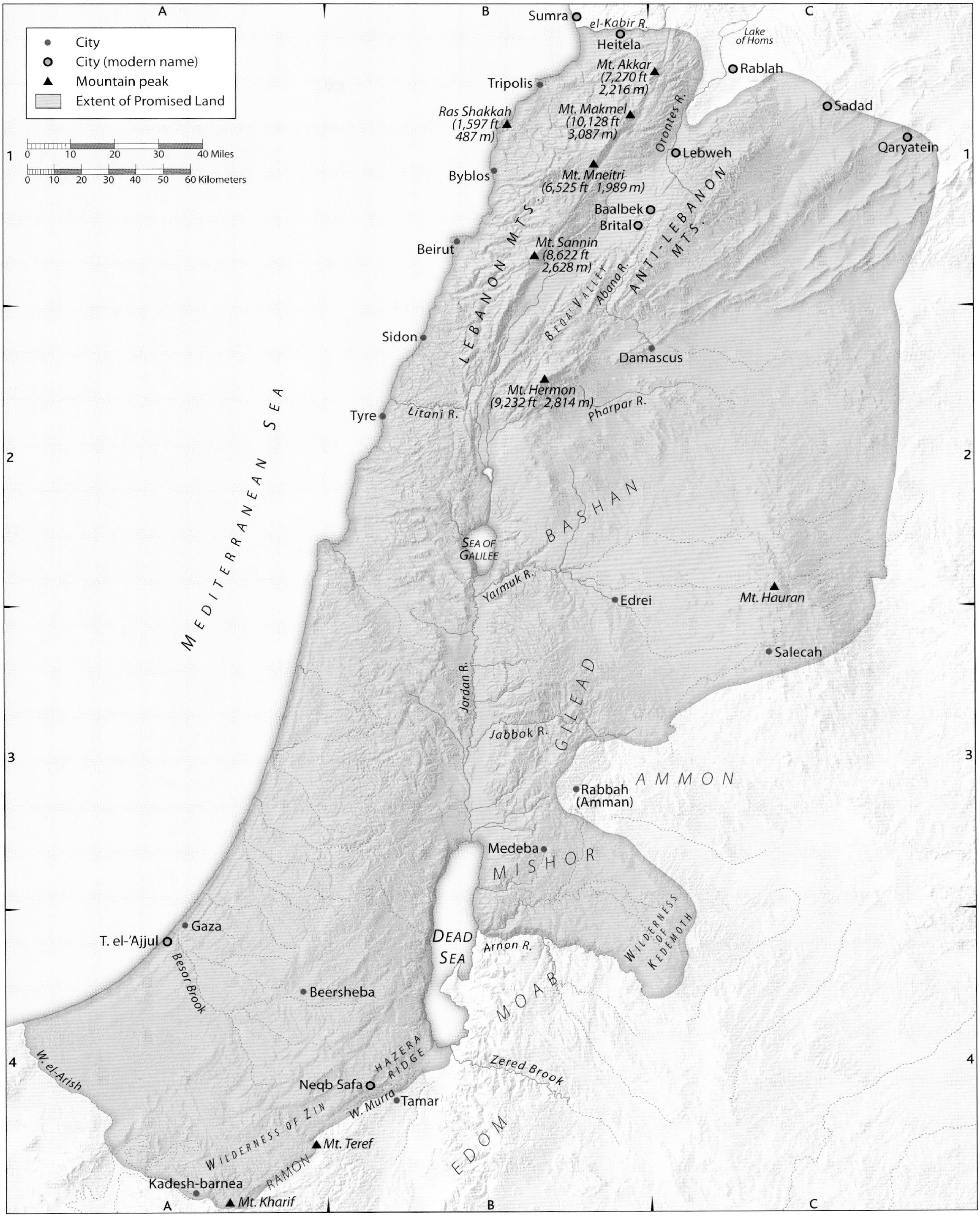
City
City (modern name)
Mountain peak
Extent of Promised Land
0 10 20 30 40 Miles
0 10 20 30 40 50 60 Kilometers
Sumra
el-Kabir R.
Heitela
Lake of Homs
Mt. Akkar (7,270 ft 2,216 m)
Rablah
Tripolis
Mt. Makmel (10,128 ft 3,087 m)
Ras Shakkah (1,597 ft 487 m)
Orontes R.
Sadad
Qaryatein
Lebweh
Byblos
Mt. Mneitri (6,525 ft 1,989 m)
Baalbek
Brital
LEBANON MTS.
ANTI-LEBANON MTS.
Beirut
Mt. Sannin (8,622 ft 2,628 m)
BEQA' VALLEY
Abana R.
Sidon
Damascus
Mt. Hermon (9,232 ft 2,814 m)
Pharpar R.
Tyre
Litani R.
MEDITERRANEAN SEA
BASHAN
SEA OF GALILEE
Yarmuk R.
Edrei
Mt. Hauran
Salecah
Jordan R.
GILEAD
Jabbok R.
AMMON
Rabbah (Amman)
Medeba
MISHOR
Gaza
T. el-'Ajjul
DEAD SEA
Arnon R.
WILDERNESS OF KEDEMOTH
Besor Brook
Beersheba
MOAB
W. el-Arish
HAZERA RIDGE
Zered Brook
Neqb Safa
W. Murra
Tamar
WILDERNESS OF ZIN
Mt. Teref
EDOM
RAMON
Kadesh-barnea
Mt. Kharif

(which does end at the Jordan River). Those tribes were given land in Bashan (Josh. 13:11–12; 17:1; 20:7; 22:7), in Gilead (Josh. 13:31; 17:1), and in the Mishor (Josh. 13:9, 20:8), in contradistinction to the "land of Canaan" (Josh. 22:9, 10, 32).[29]

The weight of certain biblical data can suggest an alternate hypothesis that the border of Israel's allotted land should be extended east as far as the fringes of the Eastern Desert, roughly approximating a line that could be drawn from the region of Mt. Hauran (the end of the northern border) to the wilderness of Kedemoth (near the Arnon), the place from which Moses had dispatched spies to Sihon, king of Heshbon (Deut. 2:24–26), and which was later allotted to the tribe of Reuben (Josh. 13:18). This hypothesis is supported by three lines of reasoning.

1. Deuteronomy 2—3 reviews the victories gained over Sihon and Og and the territorial allocation of their land to the two and a half tribes of Israel. This allotment included terrain from the Arnon to Mt. Hermon, taking in the lands of the Mishor, Gilead, and Bashan as far as Salecah and Edrei (Deut. 3:8; cf. 4:48; Josh. 13:8–12). At the same time, Deuteronomy 2:12 declares that just as the Edomites had destroyed the Horites in order to gain for themselves a possession of land, so Israel dispossessed other peoples to gain its inheritance. The wording here is unequivocal and logically requires that the passage be interpreted in one of two ways: either it is a historical description of those victories gained over the two Amorite kings—Sihon and Og—or it is a much later insertion in the text added in historical retrospect to describe what eventually took place in the biblical conquest under Joshua.

   Now, the question in Deuteronomy 2:12 is not whether post-Mosaic expressions exist in the biblical text, but whether this verse represents one such specimen. It seems that the whole of this chapter presents a rather sustained argument that pivots on a sharp distinction between those territories excluded from Israel's inheritance (Edom, Moab, Ammon) and those included in its inheritance (Bashan, Gilead, Mishor). In this regard, verse 12 seems to assert that both Edom and Israel received their respective territories by sovereign prerogative, not military skill. Because of that, there is established a clear theological reason Israel must not conquer land beyond its own perimeter (cf. Judg. 11:13–28; 2 Chron. 20:10; see also Deut. 2:20–22—an Ammonite and Edomite exodus?). If this is the case, verse 12 would then form part of the fabric of the entire narrative and could not easily be dismissed editorially. But even if verse 12 were taken as a later insertion, one is still left with a similar, transparent assertion in verses 24 and 31, which normally have not been regarded as later insertions.[30] If the theme developed in these verses is best understood to refer to the historical events surrounding the defeat of kings Sihon and Og as an integral part of the narrative as a whole, verse 12 is then a completely lucid and unambiguous statement regarding the eastern boundary of Israel (Josh. 12:6).

2. At the command of God, due consideration was given the territory east of the Jordan River in the apportionment of cities of refuge (Num. 35:9–34; Deut. 4:41–43; 19:1–10; Josh. 20:1–9) and levitical cities (Lev. 25:32–33; Num. 35:1–8; Josh. 21:8–42; 1 Chron. 6:54–81); in the latter instance, ten of the 48 levitical cities were located in Transjordanian territory. [**See map 41.**] Whereas the territory of the tribe of Manasseh was divided as a result of that tribe's own request, Levi's territorial inheritance was split as a result of divine prescription, a thought that seems illogical and even preposterous if the territories east of the Jordan are to be excluded from the inheritance of Israel.
3. The attitudes displayed by Moses (Num. 32) and Joshua (Josh. 22) cohere with this thesis. Though Moses first objected when confronted with the request for Transjordanian inheritance, it is crucial to understand the nature of his response. It had been a *national* effort that brought about Israelite control of eastern territories, he stressed; any lesser effort could weaken the resolve of the remaining tribes and lead ultimately to divine judgment. As a result, Moses laid down a precondition before the two and a half tribes could receive Transjordanian inheritance: their armed men must join in the fight for Canaan! Moses' concern was one of justice and potential faintheartedness, not one of irreconcilability with the plan and purposes of God. And later, after the two and a half tribes had fulfilled their vow and the land of Canaan had been secured, Joshua—by divine directive—dispatched those tribes to their rightful inheritance with the blessing and instruction of the Lord.

One may object that this hypothesis is not in harmony with Numbers 34:10–12, where the Jordan River is clearly demarcated as the eastern border. Perhaps this objection can be addressed both geopolitically and contextually. On the one hand, a case can be made that Numbers 34 is delineating the frontiers of the land of Canaan (which on the east extended as far as the Jordan), not the whole of the land given to biblical Israel (vv. 2, 29). On the other, the context of Numbers 34 seems to refer to the land that at the time remained unconquered but eventually would be occupied by the remaining nine and a half tribes (vv. 2, 13–15; cf. Deut. 1:7–8). An unrealized territorial objective in the narrative, that perimeter stood in marked contrast to the already vanquished territories previously controlled by Sihon and Og (Num. 21) but now theoretically given to the tribes of Reuben, Gad, and East Manasseh (Num. 32). Numbers 34, therefore, seems to be describing a territory *that was yet to be conquered* (Canaan), in contrast to the entire territory divinely apportioned and destined for biblical Israel's inheritance. In light of these considerations, then, it seems that no necessary discrepancy exists between this narrative, other biblical texts related to the placement of the eastern border, and a hypothesis that traces the eastern border along the frontier of the great Eastern Desert.

Southern border

(Num. 34:3–5; Josh. 15:1–4; cf. Ezek. 47:19; 48:28)
The crucial issue to be decided in relation to Israel's southern border has to do with where this border met the Mediterranean Sea. Did this occur at the "river" of Egypt (the easternmost segment of the Nile Delta) or at the "brook/wadi" of Egypt (the W. el-Arish)? All four biblical texts that delineate the southern border of Israel employ the lexeme *naḥal* ("brook/wadi"), not *nāhār* ("river").[31] The expression "the wadi of [the land of] Egypt" occurs in cuneiform texts as early as Tiglath-pileser III and Sargon II, describing military actions south of Gaza, but not inside Egypt.[32]

The book of Judith (1:7–11), describing how Nebuchadnezzar attempted to conscript an army in order to wage war against the Medes, provides a detailed listing of places: Cilicia, Damascus, the mountains of Lebanon, Carmel, Gilead, Upper Galilee, Esdraelon, Samaria, Jerusalem . . . Kadesh, the wadi of Egypt, Tahpanhes, Ra`amses, Goshen, Memphis, and Ethiopia. The geographical sequence of this text is clearly proceeding in a southerly direction, thereby placing the wadi of Egypt between Kadesh (either Kadesh-barnea or Kadesh of Judah) and Tahpanhes (T. Defana, an outpost on the main road between Palestine and the Nile Delta). [**See map 33.**] One should also note the *LXX* rendition of Isaiah 27:12, where *naḥal miṣrayim* ("brook/wadi of Egypt") is rendered *Rhinocorura*, the Greek word for the classical settlement occupied today by the townlet El-Arish.[33] [**See map 118.**]

The vast W. el-Arish system is the most prominent geographical feature south of the populated areas of Palestine. It courses for almost 150 miles before it is emptied into the Mediterranean Sea about 50 miles south of Gaza, draining most of northern Sinai, the western portions of the modern Negeb, and part of southern Philistia. [**See map 34.**] Modern geographers sometimes describe W. el-Arish as being situated on a natural geological border between the Negeb plateau and Sinai.[34] All of this evidence favors identifying the biblical "brook/wadi of Egypt" with the modern W. el-Arish.[35]

Related to this data is the placement of the site of Kadesh-barnea. Along the western edge of the modern Negeb plateau are three important springs that have been associated with its location: Ain Qadeis, Ain Qudeirat (about six miles to the northwest), and Ain Quseima (another four miles to the northwest). All three springs are situated along the W. el-Arish geological boundary, none is clearly eliminated on the basis of ceramic remains, and each offers a distinctive consideration when attempting to locate Kadesh-barnea. The candidacy of Ain Qadeis rests on three considerations: (1) in both biblical border descriptions (Num. 34:4; Josh. 15:3–4) that provide an east-west sequence, Kadesh-barnea is listed *before* Hazar-addar and Azmon; (2) this site retains the namesake of the biblical city; and (3) the site is situated on the edge of a large open plain capable of accommodating a large encampment. Ain Qudeirat offers the advantage of a copious water supply, by far the largest in the area. And Ain Quseima is located very near an important intersection of two roads that link the Negeb with Sinai and Egypt. [**See map 27.**] Not surprisingly, therefore, each of these three sites has been identified as Kadesh-barnea at one time or another.

One infers from the biblical texts that Israel encamped at Kadesh-barnea for the greater part of 40 years (Deut. 1:46; 2:14). Geographically speaking, this entire area offers a generally hostile and bleak environment for human occupation, so it may be that all three of these sites, as well as all of the intermediate territory, was required to accommodate Israel's encampment. Nevertheless, for the sake of map facilitation, Kadesh-barnea has been located at Ain Qadeis, Hazar-addar at Ain Qudeirat, and Azmon at Ain Quseima, though these placements are quite tentative. [**See map 22 (B15–16).**]

As with the other borders, the southern border of Israel was most likely set primarily in accordance with natural geographic features. Following a semicircular arc, this border probably extended in a southwesterly direction from the Dead Sea, via the Rift Valley and Tamar, to the environs of the Wadi Murra. Here it passed by the Hazera ridge and came to the Ascent of Akrabbim ("ascent of the scorpions"), which is commonly affiliated with Neqb Safa.[36] There an early Israeli road from Beersheba, which crosses Jebel Hathira, plunges abruptly into Wadi Murra. From that point, it is reasonable to infer that the border continued to follow the contour of the wadi in a southwesterly course until eventually it arrived in the vicinity of a slender, diagonal corridor of Turonian limestone, which extends about 30 miles from Mt. Teref to Mt. Kharif and separates the Rimmon summit from the Eocene acreage to its north. After traversing that corridor to its opposite end, one is only about five miles from the upper courses of the W. Kadesh (a tributary of the el-Arish drainage system). Following the tributary past Ain Qadeis (Kadesh-barnea), then past Ain Qudeirat and Ain Quseima, the southern border seems to have followed the course of this "brook/wadi of Egypt" the entire distance to the Mediterranean.

Historical terminology

Unfortunately, the southern Levant had neither a geographically nor a chronologically inclusive name in antiquity. Instead, the land of biblical Israel is designated by an array of biblical and/or secular terms, none of which can be understood to be completely coextensive with Israel's theological borders (or one another), and none of which can be applied across the entire span of biblical history without creating some anachronism.

In many cases in antiquity, names that previously had been employed to denote a god or a major population group were simply borrowed and reapplied to designate a geopolitical entity that was home to that group. For example, the name "Canaan" derived from the Canaanites; "Palestine" owed its existence to the Philistines; and "[the land of] Hatti" originally designated a series of neo-Hittite city-states located approximately between Carchemish and Damascus [**map 3**] whose residents seem to be descendants of Heth (e.g., Gen. 10:15; 1 Chron. 1:13) and/or devotees of the god Hatti.[37] Both the Canaanites and the Hittites were said to be among the "occupants of the land" at the time of Israel's settlement (Deut. 7:1; Josh. 3:10; 12:8; cf. Gen. 15:18–21; Ex. 3:8, 17), and the Philistines are known to have emigrated to that land around 1200 B.C.

Canaan

The term Canaan/Canaanite(s) is well attested throughout much of second-millennium B.C. literature.[38] To judge from this usage, Canaan appears to have been the conventional term to designate Egypt's southern holdings in Asia, in contrast to Amurru (Amorite land north of the el-Kabir River). Canaan extended from the southern towns of Gaza and Raphia [**map 44**] as far north as the el-Kabir River valley and the site of Sumra/Simyra.[39] The general picture that emerges, therefore, is that Near Eastern and biblical citations bear a remarkable similarity in their delineation of Canaan. (See the earlier discussion of Israel's theological borders.) Such an assertion may bear consequences regarding the antiquity and essential historicity of those narratives containing Israel's borders.

Prior to archaeological discoveries at Nuzi [**map 23**], the word "Canaan" was generally thought to be derived from a Semitic verb meaning "to bend/bow down/be low," because Canaanites occupied the lowland near the sea, in contrast to the hill country of the Amorites (Num. 13:29; Josh. 5:1; cf. Isa. 23:11). A related theory was that Canaan was the place the sun "bends down" (sets), so a Canaanite was by definition a "westerner.[40] But at Nuzi the word *kinaḫḫu*[41] was found to refer to a red-purple substance extracted from murex seashells and used in the dyeing of fabric, especially wool.

Ancient literature is replete with references to the great esteem given someone who was clothed in purple. Murex dye, being natural and not manufactured, was highly prized because it never faded. The lucrative murex industry was concentrated north of Caesarea, on the Mediterranean, where an abundant supply of murex shells regularly washed ashore. At Tyre, a large number of the shells have been found on the site of an ancient dye factory,[42] and clear evidence of the dyeing process has also been found at Dor.[43] Further indication that murex dyeing was an economically pivotal industry in that region may be found in certain Canaanite place-names in the vicinity. For example, Zarephath comes from a verb meaning "to dye," and Zobah derives from a verb denoting the dyeing of cloth. The word "Canaanite" itself is sometimes rendered "trader/merchant."[44] As a result, it appears preferable to understand Canaan as "the purple land," and Canaanites as "the people of the purple land" (from which the concept of trading generally could easily derive).

We learn from Greek literature that the cultural heirs of this dye industry in the first millennium were called Phoenicians, which derives from the Greek word *phoinix* ("purple"). Even as late as the New Testament, it seems that references to Canaanites and Phoenicians were still being used somewhat interchangeably. (Matthew 15:22 refers to a Canaanite woman; Mark's version of the same story calls her a Syro-Phoenician woman [Mark 7:26].) It appears then that "Canaan" differs from "Phoenicia" only in two fundamental ways: (1) the former is a Semitic word whereas the latter is of Greek extraction; and (2) the former is employed in the second millennium B.C. whereas the latter becomes a normative term in the first millennium B.C. If we follow the logic of all this evidence, it appears that the same word first connoted the process of dyeing, in time was extended to the people involved in the process, and eventually evolved to include the territory/province where those people were a dominant population group.

Palestine

For reasons as yet unclear to us, much of the biblical world experienced a major political upheaval around 1200 B.C., stemming largely from companies of invaders referred to in Egyptian sources as "Sea Peoples." Scholars have long pondered what occasioned this southeastward movement of approximately 14 people groups: Denyen, Lukka, Shardanu, Masha, Arinna, Karkisha, Pitassa, Kashka, Akawasha, Tursha, Sheklesh, Peleset (Philistines), Tjekker, and Weshesh. (These are approximate spellings.) Although two or three of these groups also appear in earlier literature from the Levant or Egypt, there seems to have been a rather widespread migration around this time. Was their displacement a function of climate change that may have produced famine, a consequence of the political turbulence that surrounded the Battle of Troy or the Dorian invasion of Greece, or some other factor? Whatever the case, before striking at the heart of Egypt, various contingents of the Sea Peoples were probably responsible for the demise of the Hittite Empire centered in Asia Minor, the capture of the island of Cyprus, and the ravaging and/or reoccupation of many cities across the Levant: Ugarit, Alalakh, Carchemish, T. Sukas, Tyre, Sidon, Hazor, Acco, Dor, and a host of sites in the Philistine plain. The Egyptians withstood the Sea Peoples, however, and their literature indicates that the Philistines were repelled from Egyptian soil toward the northeast,[45] where they later inhabited southwestern Canaan, which became known as the Philistine plain.

The place from which the Philistines emigrated also continues to be a debated issue.[46] The biblical tradition that they hailed from Caphtor (Crete) is not decisive because that text declares the Philistines were brought from Caphtor in the same way the Israelites were brought from Egypt (Amos 9:7; cf. Gen. 10:14; 1 Chron. 1:12; Jer. 47:4; Ezek. 25:16; Zeph. 2:5). That is to say, the Bible may not be stipulating the aboriginal home of either people. Some scholars argue that Philistines migrated from Greece, basing their opinion on certain aspects of their material culture (stylized coffins, characteristic pottery, etc.) or on biblical words found in Philistine narratives (*champion, lord, helmet, chest*). Others have asserted that the Philistines originated along the seacoasts of modern southwestern Turkey, predicated on Greek epics and the *LXX* rendering of Caphtor ("Cappadocia") in Deuteronomy 2:23 and Amos 9:7. But this all remains highly speculative, in part because of a paucity of explicitly Philistine texts and in part because the Philistines began to undergo the process of cultural assimilation soon after their arrival in Canaan. The only sure conclusion one can reach is that the word *Palestine* as a discreet geographical entity obviously derives from the Philistines.

It is sometimes asserted today that the term "Palestine" did not come into existence as a designation for the land of Israel until the mid-second century A.D. when, as political punishment for the Bar-Kochba revolt, the Emperor Hadrian deliberately co-opted the name of Israel's ancient enemies—the Philistines—and simply Latinized it to create obvious pejorative connotations.[47] According to this viewpoint, the earliest use of "Palestine" represented early Roman propaganda, with intense anti-Jewish political implications. If so, then any present-day use of the word *Palestine* in reference to history before the time of Hadrian is at best dangerously anachronistic and historically erroneous, and, at worst, anti-biblical[48] or even anti-Jewish.

Yet there is evidence to indicate otherwise. To begin with, the name *Palestine* appears thirteen times in neo-Assyrian texts from as early as Adad-nirari III (810–782 B.C.), Tiglath-pileser III (744–727 B.C.), and Sargon II (721–705 B.C.).[49] It is unlikely that any of those citations envisioned the land of Israel as a whole (as opposed to the region of Philistia). In fact, in one text Palestine is used in contrast to both Israel (literally, "the land of Omri") and Edom.[50] However, in eleven instances, the word *Palestine* is prefaced by the semantic indicator for "land/country," which gives unmistakable indication that the reference is to a discreet geographical entity. Similarly, an inscribed Egyptian statuette,[51] dating presumably from the 27th dynasty (945–715 B.C.),[52] makes reference to a "commissioner of Canaan and Palestine" (written *Plst*). In this case, the term *Palestine* is used in contradistinction to the territory of Canaan. One can again observe that the term is definitely found in a geographical/provincial (not political) context.

Part of the extensive archaeological remains from the New Palace period (c. 1700–1400 B.C.) at Zakros, on the southeast coast of Crete. Some authorities believe the Philistines may have hailed from Crete.

More germane to this contention, however, are the results of a computer search available through the *Thesaurus Linguae Graecae* (University of California at Irvine). A search for "Palestine" as a proper name in texts written before the end of the first Christian century revealed 196 complete citations in Greek or Latin literature (excluding possible partial attestations of the word or citations found in small fragments of Greek papyri). Many of the citations do not apply to this argument for one reason or another.[53] However, the *TLG* search uncovered almost two dozen references to Palestine, dating between the fifth century B.C. and the first century A.D. (before Hadrian [A.D. 117–138]), where the term is used in an unambiguous context that cannot refer to, or be restricted to, Philistia and/or the Philistines.[54] Admittedly, the geographical details of classical writers may sometimes become confused, but surely it strains credulity to imagine that such a number of unequivocal citations could be summarily dismissed on such grounds.

Additional evidence for the use of "Palestine" before the time of Hadrian comes from an early Jewish source tentatively dated to the last half of the first century B.C.[55] Moreover, the Babylonian Talmud—composed before, during, and immediately after Hadrian's reign—contains a few references to Palestine as a distinct, identifiable geographical entity.[56] The references are not political in nature and are manifestly not pejorative in tone. It is difficult to conceive that an emperor's whim would influence such an orthodox and authoritative body of Jewish literature—especially from as far away as Babylon. [**Note the eastern extent of the Roman Empire on map 98.**] At stake was the very core of its identity.

Accordingly, based on this unambiguous empirical data from a host of primary sources—widely differentiated linguistically, conceptually, geographically, and chronologically—no factual basis exists for objecting to the use of "Palestine" in reference to biblical or historical matters prior to the time of Hadrian.[57]

Israel

The name Israel ultimately derives from the patriarch Jacob, whose name was changed to Israel (Gen. 32:28). The expression "children of Israel" began to be employed rather commonly of the patriarchal descendants when they became enslaved in Egypt (Ex. 1:9–12; 2:23, 25; 3:9–11; etc.). Later, the name Israel came to be applied to the northern kingdom of Ephraim, in contrast to the southern kingdom of Judah (1 Kings 12:18–20; 1 Chron. 5:17; etc.). Still later, after the collapse of the northern kingdom, "Israel" was occasionally used to denote the southern kingdom of Judah (Jer. 10:1).

Still, it is difficult to identify a biblical passage in which the word *Israel* is utilized explicitly to denote a specific stretch of geography. Admittedly, the expression "land of Israel" occurs (1 Sam. 13:19; 1 Chron. 22:2; 2 Chron. 2:17; Ezek. 40:2; 47:18), but it is always linked to the terrain occupied or to be occupied by some or all of the people of Israel, and its extent fluctuates accordingly.

Outside of the Bible, "Israel" (i.e., the Israel of the Bible) occurs in three early texts. The oldest of these is a granite stela from the fifth year of Merneptah (1209 B.C.). [**See text at maps 42 and 43 for translation.**] The carved slab mentions Israel, but does so in a way that seems to point to an ethnic entity, and therefore the citation offers little assistance in defining the geographical boundaries of Israel. However, the Merneptah Stela represents the only extra-biblical witness to Israel before the ninth century B.C., when the name appears on two separate inscriptions.

The Black Obelisk is written in cuneiform and dates to the sixth year of Assyrian king Shalmaneser III (853 B.C.) when Ahab supplied 2,000 chariots and 10,000 soldiers to a coalition that fought against Shalmaneser's forces. [**See text at map 70.**] The inscription makes reference to Ahab as "the king of Israel."[58] A few years later (c. 835 B.C.), king Mesha of Moab had a basalt stela inscribed with a dedication to Chemosh, his god, in which he boasted that he took back territory that earlier had been conquered by Omri, "king of Israel."[59] According to the Bible, Mesha of Moab was a subject of Israel during the days of Omri and Ahab who rebelled at the death of Ahab (2 Kings 3:4–5). However, an ensuing battle recorded in the Bible ended in a Moabite defeat (2 Kings 3:9–27). Attempting to harmonize this biblical verdict with the claim of victory on the Mesha Stela, some scholars argue that Mesha's conquest over Israel dates a little later, during the reign of Jehoahaz.[60] Neither of these ninth-century B.C. inscriptions supplies geographic information of the sort that enables one to draw specific borders for Israel. Yet both are quite helpful in that each explicitly identifies by name a particular individual also known in the Bible as a "king of Israel." The Mesha Inscription is also very useful in that it is rich in biblical terminology.[61]

Geopolitical districts

Before engaging in a more extended discussion of the natural topographical features of Palestine, it is necessary to define and briefly delineate certain terms used in Scripture to signify the various geographical and/or geopolitical subdivisions of the land. In order to do this, however, it will be helpful to first introduce two modern geographical words that are sometimes employed to designate this land: *Cisjordan* ("this side [the west side] of the Jordan River") and *Transjordan* ("across [the east side] the Jordan River"). We have already seen how the Jordan River has served as both a geographical and a political boundary at various times. And before proceeding, it is essential to understand the provisional nature of these subdivisions. The frontiers of a particular district may have fluctuated over the centuries, and they cannot be precisely fixed for every period. This problem is especially aggravated when one attempts to fix

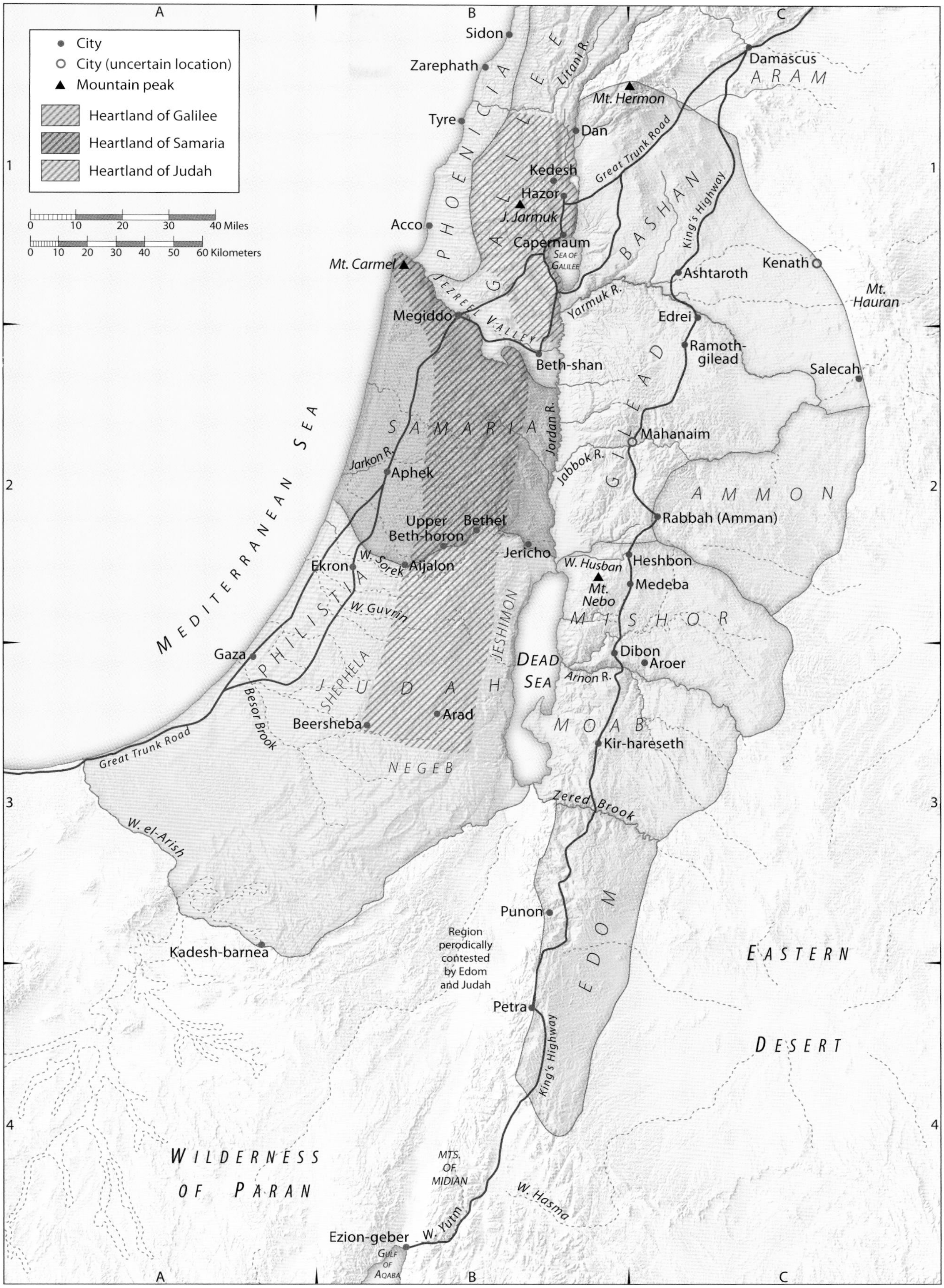
City
City (uncertain location)
Mountain peak
Heartland of Galilee
Heartland of Samaria
Heartland of Judah
0 10 20 30 40 Miles
0 10 20 30 40 50 60 Kilometers
A
B
C
1
2
3
4
Sidon
Zarephath
Tyre
Acco
Mt. Carmel
PHOENICIA
GALILEE
Litani R.
Mt. Hermon
Dan
Kedesh
Hazor
J. Jarmuk
Capernaum
Sea of Galilee
Damascus
ARAM
Great Trunk Road
BASHAN
King's Highway
Ashtaroth
Kenath
Mt. Hauran
Yarmuk R.
Edrei
Ramoth-gilead
Salecah
Jezreel Valley
Megiddo
Beth-shan
SAMARIA
Jordan R.
GILEAD
Mahanaim
Jabbok R.
AMMON
Rabbah (Amman)
MEDITERRANEAN SEA
Jarkon R.
Aphek
Upper Beth-horon
Bethel
Jericho
W. Husban
Heshbon
Mt. Nebo
Medeba
Ekron
W. Sorek
Aijalon
PHILISTIA
W. Guvrin
JESHIMON
MISHOR
Gaza
SHEPHELA
JUDAH
DEAD SEA
Dibon
Aroer
Arnon R.
Besor Brook
Beersheba
Arad
MOAB
Kir-hareseth
Great Trunk Road
NEGEB
Zered Brook
W. el-Arish
EDOM
Punon
Region perodically contested by Edom and Judah
Kadesh-barnea
EASTERN DESERT
Petra
King's Highway
WILDERNESS OF PARAN
MTS. OF MIDIAN
W. Hasma
W. Yutm
Ezion-geber
Gulf of Aqaba

frontiers of a district that existed throughout a large segment of biblical history, perhaps remaining in existence for more than a millennium. Moreover, it is necessary to bear in mind that one and the same stretch of geography frequently bore dissimilar names during different periods.

Cisjordan

From a geopolitical perspective, Cisjordan can be said to be divided into four districts during most of biblical history. From north to south those four sections were Phoenicia, Galilee, Samaria, and Judah/Judea. [**See maps 5 and 6.**]

Phoenicia

Phoenicia in the Old Testament is usually defined as a slender tract of coastland that stretched some 125 miles from the el-Kabir River to Mt. Carmel and was flanked on its east by the mountains of Lebanon and Galilee. By New Testament times, Mt. Carmel had fallen into the hands of monarchs from Tyre,[62] so Phoenicia extended as far south as the plain of Dor. Phoenicia was the scene of two biblical miracles: at Zarephath, Elisha revived a widow's son who had stopped breathing (1 Kings 17:8–24), and in the region of Tyre and Sidon, Jesus healed a Syro-Phoenician woman's daughter (Mark 7:24–30). Phoenicia also played host to a number of early apostolic travels.

Galilee

Just inland from the southern sector of Phoenicia lay the Galilean district, the northernmost territory actually occupied by ancient Israel. The heartland of Galilee, stretching from the Litani River and the site of Dan in the north as far south as the Jezreel valley, measured about 50 miles north-south and some 25 miles east-west. The district was at all times divided by a slender lateral valley that followed a fault line extending east from Acco/Ptolemais and ran to modern Rosh Pinna (just about ten miles due north of the Sea of Galilee). This Beth Kerem valley divides Galilee into two subdivisions: Upper Galilee and Lower Galilee.[63] The distinction is geographic and not administrative. Upper Galilee's rugged, virtually impassable terrain exceeds 3,300 feet, with part of its center boasting the highest altitude in all of Cisjordan. (J. Jarmuk is nearly 4,000 feet above sea level.) [**See map 18.**] The peaks of Lower Galilee remain below 2,000 feet high. Most biblical references to Galilee, including all New Testament references, are to Lower Galilee.

Because of its northerly location, Galilee was perhaps more vulnerable to cultural and military absorption (Isa. 9:1; Matt. 4:15–16; 2 Kings 15:29). Though inhabited during the settlement period by the tribes of Naphtali, Issachar, Zebulun, and perhaps part of Asher, from the Babylonian captivity onward (1 Kings 9:10–14), the Gentile population in Galilee remained dominant. [**See map 40.**] Therefore, the district was suspect both ideologically (John 1:46; cf. 7:41, 52) and linguistically (Matt. 26:73b).

Notwithstanding, Galilee became very important to Jew and Christian alike. For Jews, the city of Tiberias gradually became the center for Talmudic scholarship after the destruction of Jerusalem in A.D. 70; here the Sanhedrin last sat, here the Mishna was edited, here were centered the families of Ben Asher and Ben Naphtali of Masoretic tradition, here the revered Aleppo Codex (the oldest and most complete Hebrew Bible in existence) was created, and here one finds the tombs of the Jewish sages Maimonides, Rabbi Akiba, and Johanan ben Zekkai. For Christians, Galilee was a center of Jesus' activities. He spent his boyhood in the sleepy village of Nazareth, headquartered his ministry in the important center of Capernaum, and, perhaps most interestingly, performed most of his public miracles here.

Samaria

To the south of Galilee stands the third subdivision—Samaria. It was known earlier as the hill country of Ephraim (Josh. 17:15; 19:50; Judg. 3:27; 4:5; 1 Sam. 1:1; 9:4; 1 Kings 4:8; 2 Kings 5:22)—not to be confused with the hill country of Judah. (See below.) The district of Samaria eventually drew its name from the third and final capital city of the northern kingdom (1 Kings 16:24). The heartland of Samaria stretched from the edge of the Jezreel valley as far south as the vicinity of a natural topographic line that extended west from Jericho, via the W. Makkuk, as far as Ophrah. [**See maps 18 and 37 for W. Makkuk.**] From there the border proceeded past Bethel and Upper Beth-horon, where it began its descent to Aijalon (cf. Josh. 10:11–12) and broke into the Coastal Plain opposite Gezer. Samaria, therefore, encompassed an area approximately 40 miles north-south and some 30 miles east-west. (From Josephus's description, one infers that New Testament Samaria was slightly reduced in its southern precinct.)[64]

The natural geographic center of Samaria was at the city of Shechem, located in the vale between Mt. Ebal and Mt. Gerizim [**map 11**], adjacent to the modern city of Nablus. [**See map 118.**] Here the principal road coming north from Jerusalem (Central Ridge Road) linked with a secondary roadway (Ephraim lateral road) that connected Samaria with both the Mediterranean and the Jordan River. Not unexpectedly, therefore, Shechem witnessed periods of protracted occupation dating back as far as 4000 B.C. During much of the second millennium B.C., Shechem vied with Jerusalem for supremacy of central Palestine. The site was where Abraham first erected an altar and worshiped the Lord in Canaan (Gen. 12:6), where the bones of Joseph finally came to rest (Josh. 24:32; cf. Gen. 50:25–26; Ex. 13:19), where Israel's first attempt at monarchy was launched (Judg. 9), where the division of Israel's united monarchy occurred (1 Kings 12:1–16), where the first capital of the northern kingdom of Israel was situated (1 Kings 12:25), and where Jesus confronted a woman at the well (John 4:5).

Although eclipsed by the city of Samaria during most of the period of the divided monarchy, Shechem's ascendancy was reasserted after the Assyrians brought an end to the northern kingdom in 722 B.C. Captives from abroad were settled in Samarian cities (2 Kings 17:24–34). [**See also maps 76 and 77.**] Some of the refugees embraced a number of articles within Judaism and in time came to regard themselves as Jews (e.g., Ezra 4:2). Their bid for membership was largely repudiated by the post-exilic Jewish community, however, which set into motion a religious animosity that persisted throughout the remainder of the biblical period (Luke 9:52–53; John 4:9; 8:48). Nevertheless, Samaritanism has survived the centuries. One medieval report located some 400 Samaritans in Damascus.[65] Contemporary estimates of the Samaritan population in Israel range between 550 and 800 people who continue to celebrate the Passover annually atop Mt. Gerizim, their holy mountain (John 4:20).

Judah

The fourth major geopolitical subdivision of Cisjordan was Judah, referred to in earlier history as the hill country of Judah (Josh. 11:21; 15:48; 20:7; 21:11; cf. 2 Chron. 21:11; 27:4; Luke 1:65). According to 2 Kings 23:8, Judah extended from Geba, a strategic town located about five miles north of Jerusalem [**map 22**], as far south as Beersheba (Zech. 14:10). Thus, when understood also in the context of Israel's northern frontier at the city of Dan, this conforms to the recurring formula found in the Old Testament ("from Dan to Beersheba"), which denotes the practical boundaries of Israel's heartland (Judg. 20:1; 1 Sam. 3:20; 2 Sam. 3:10; 17:11; 24:2, 15; 1 Kings 4:25). The heartland of Judah may also be specifically delineated on its lateral axis, extending east as far as the precipitous descent into the Judean wilderness (Jeshimon [Num. 21:20; cf. 1 Sam. 26:1—Hachilah overlooks Jeshimon]) and as far west as the steep and rocky descent into a slender moat that divides it from the Shephela. (See below.) The heartland of Judah took in no more than 50 miles north-south and only about 20 miles east-west. Judah was only rarely attractive to empire builders as a very small territory that was largely comprised of large tracts of uncultivable soil, was rather isolated from international traffic, and never experienced independent material prosperity. One authority[66] described it as a secluded land that promoted a pastoral lifestyle and was a locale for fortresses, shrines, and villages.

Idumea

In addition to the four *major* geopolitical entities of Cisjordan, the province of Idumea played a secondary role in post-exilic and New Testament politics. Idumea is the Greek name for Edom applied specifically to Edomite refugees who fled northwest in order to avoid the growing pressure from their Nabatean neighbors. [**See map 6.**] Though constantly fluctuating, being alternately detached from and reannexed to Judea, Idumean territory eventually stretched from the area of Beth-zur, near Hebron, as far south as Beersheba, and from the Dead Sea to the edge of the Philistine plain. [**See map 85.**] Maccabean rulers eventually subjugated Idumea. [**See map 92.**] One of them (Alexander Janneus) appointed a local Idumean chieftain, Antipater, over the region. Ironically, it was from the loins of Antipater that Herod the Great would be born in due course. As "king of the Jews" (Matt. 2:1), Herod was not so disposed to decentralize authority.

Transjordan

Old Testament Transjordan is composed of five geopolitical entities. From north to south they include Bashan, Gilead, Mishor, Moab, and Edom [**see map 5**]. The term "Transjordan" defines specifically the stretch of geography between Mt. Hermon and the Gulf of Aqaba (some 250 miles), and from the Jordan valley to fringes of the Eastern Desert (between 30 and 80 miles). The geopolitical character of this region is actually much more complicated than that of its Cisjordanian neighbor, and to attempt to address both Old Testament and New Testament Transjordania in a single discussion is only partially possible and certainly open to the possibility of imprecision. But again, the primary purpose here is to supply approximate location of geopolitical terms used in Scripture.

Bashan

Bashan means "a fruitful/smooth land" (Josh. 9:10; 1 Kings 4:13; 2 Kings 10:33) and is the name of the territory that Israel's forces wrested from Og's control (Num. 21:33–35). It included 60 walled cities (Deut. 3:4–5) and was assigned to East Manasseh (Deut. 3:13). Bashan stretched for some 35 miles from Mt. Hermon (Josh. 12:4–5) down to the Yarmuk River[67] and extended as far east as Kenath (Num. 32:42) and Salecah (Deut. 3:10), towns situated on Mt. Hauran. During New Testament times, the region north of the Yarmuk essentially consisted of the provinces that made up the tetrarchy of Herod Philip, son of Herod the Great.[68] [**See maps 6 and 100.**]

Gilead

Transjordan's second basic entity is Gilead. Though the Bible occasionally appears to utilize this word generically to refer to all of occupied Transjordan (Deut. 34:1–4; Josh. 22:9), the geopolitical entity of Gilead specifies the high, mountainous, oval-shaped dome that is, topographically speaking, an eastern extension of the Samarian elevation (Judg. 10:4; 1 Sam. 13:7; 2 Sam. 2:9; 2 Kings 10:33). This dome rises just a few miles south of the Yarmuk and extends south more or less as far as the W. Husban that flows into the Jordan opposite Jericho. [**See also map 18.**] Longitudinally, the Gilead dome was divided by the deep gorge cut by the Jabbok River, which divided Gilead into halves (cf. Josh. 12:5; 13:31, the northern half; Deut. 3:12; Josh. 12:2, the southern half). On its eastern frontier, Gilead can only be defined negatively: it did not include the land of Ammon (Num. 21:23–24; Judg. 11:13; cf. 1 Sam. 11:1–4), so consequently it did not extend as far as the Eastern Desert in its southeastern quadrant.

The probable meaning of the name itself ("rugged land"), in contrast to its neighbors to the north (Bashan means "smooth land") and south (Mishor means "tableland/plateau"), may help clarify Gilead's borders. Thus delineated, the hill country of Gilead (Gen. 31:21, 23, 25; Deut. 3:12) encompassed some 35 miles north-south and not more than about 30 miles east-west. Most of northern Gilead became part of the inheritance of East Manasseh, whereas southern Gilead was allotted to the tribe of Gad. [**See map 40.**] The whole of the dome was effectively colonized by Israel, probably because its raised elevation permitted sufficient rainfall to support some forestation, agriculture, and animal husbandry (2 Sam. 18:6; Num. 32:1–4, 16, 26; Josh. 22:8). [**See map 19.**] The medicinal "balm of Gilead,"[69] whatever its exact character, was highly prized in antiquity (Jer. 8:22; 46:11; cf. Gen. 37:25).

Many Greek cities that had been established during the Alexandrian era formed a Transjordanian nucleus of (largely unsuccessful) opposition to the Jewish independence forged by the Hasmoneans. [**See maps 90 and 92.**] But when Pompey's legions brought an end to Hasmonean dominance, many of those cities were restored to their Hellenistic compatriots. In some cases individual cities found it necessary to band together into mutual leagues of protection from their non-Greek neighbors, just as they were also bound together economically and socially. One such confederation, known as the Decapolis ("ten cities"), was comprised of sites primarily situated along the trade arteries of central and northern Transjordan. This group is mentioned both in the Bible (Matt. 4:25; Mark 5:20; 7:31) and in classical sources.[70] In the New Testament era, the cities probably included, from north to south: Damascus, Raphana, Canatha, Hippos, Gadara, Scythopolis, Pella, Dion, Gerasa, and Philadelphia. [**See map 6.**][71] While the purpose of such a loose Hellenistic confederation is at variance with any attempt to define clear geographical frontiers, one can conclude that the heartland of the Decapolis stretched across the Gilead highlands.

Mishor

South of Old Testament Gilead lay the Mishor ("tableland," e.g., Deut. 3:10; 4:43; Josh. 20:8), which stretched in the north from Heshbon (Josh. 13:10) and Medeba (Josh. 13:16) about 25 miles south to the cities of Aroer (Josh. 13:9) and Dibon (Jer. 48:22), situated just north of the Arnon canyon and near the King's Highway. Other towns included in the Mishor were Nebo (Jer. 48:22); Shittim (where the Israelites entered into illicit sexual relations with Moabite women [Num. 25:1f]); Beth-peor (near where Moses was buried [Josh. 13:20; Deut. 34:6] and where Balaam uttered his untoward blessings [Num. 22:41; 23:13–14]); and Bezer, one of Israel's cities of refuge (Deut. 4:43).

The Mishor became the inheritance of the tribe of Reuben. [**See map 40.**] Yet because the Mishor was geographically intermediate to the core holdings of both Israel and Moab, the struggle to control it began as early as the period of the Judges (Judg. 3:12–30, implicit), continuing into the time of the united monarchy (1 Sam. 14:47; 2 Sam. 8:2, 12), and into the days of Ahab and Moabite king Mesha. But in the thinking of the prophets, Israel's control of the Mishor area had been relinquished to the Moabites (Isa. 15:1–9; 16:8–9; Jer. 48:1–5, 21–25, 34–36, 45–47; Ezek. 25:8–11). It is probable that this political ebb and flow may help explain why Reubenites seem to have been unable to play a considerable role in Israel's later history, despite being the descendants of Jacob's firstborn (Gen. 29:32; 49:3–4).

Moab/Perea

The higher plateau extending south from the Arnon as far as the Zered brook represented the nucleus of Moabite territory, with its capital city at Kir-hareseth (2 Kings 3:25; Isa. 16:7; cf. Num. 22:36; Isa. 15:1 [Kir of Moab means "town of Moab"]). During the New Testament era, the district of Perea[72] occupied the western portion of what had been the Mishor and Moab.

The historian Josephus wrote that the district of Perea extended north as far as the city of Pella and south as far as Machaerus (a fortress city overlooking the Dead Sea, where Herod Antipas is reported to have beheaded John the Baptist). Moreover, Josephus reports, Perea extended from the Jordan River as far east as Philadelphia. Finally, he stated that the capital city of Perea was at Gadara (T. Gadur, not to be confused with the Decapolis Gadara [Umm Qeis]).[73] Josephus's northern and eastern boundaries are puzzling, inasmuch as both Pella and Philadelphia were part of the Decapolis region. Perhaps his description should be construed to mean that the frontiers of the Pellan and Philadelphian city-states bordered on Perea. In any event, biblical geographers reasonably follow natural topographic and archaeological criteria, setting the eastern border essentially at a north-south line that runs from the upper Arnon as far north as the vicinity of J. Munif. From there it appears the northern border followed the downstream contours of the W. Yabis, which empties into the Jordan opposite the site of Aenon.

Edom

The final Transjordanian district to be enumerated is Edom, sometimes known as Seir (Gen. 32:3; Num. 24:18; Judg. 5:4; Isa. 21:11) or Mt. Seir (Gen. 14:6; Deut. 1:2; 2:5). Edom designates the land and kingdom perched atop the long, slender ridge of lofty mountains that extend southward from the Zered brook most of the way to the Gulf of Aqaba. Edom's

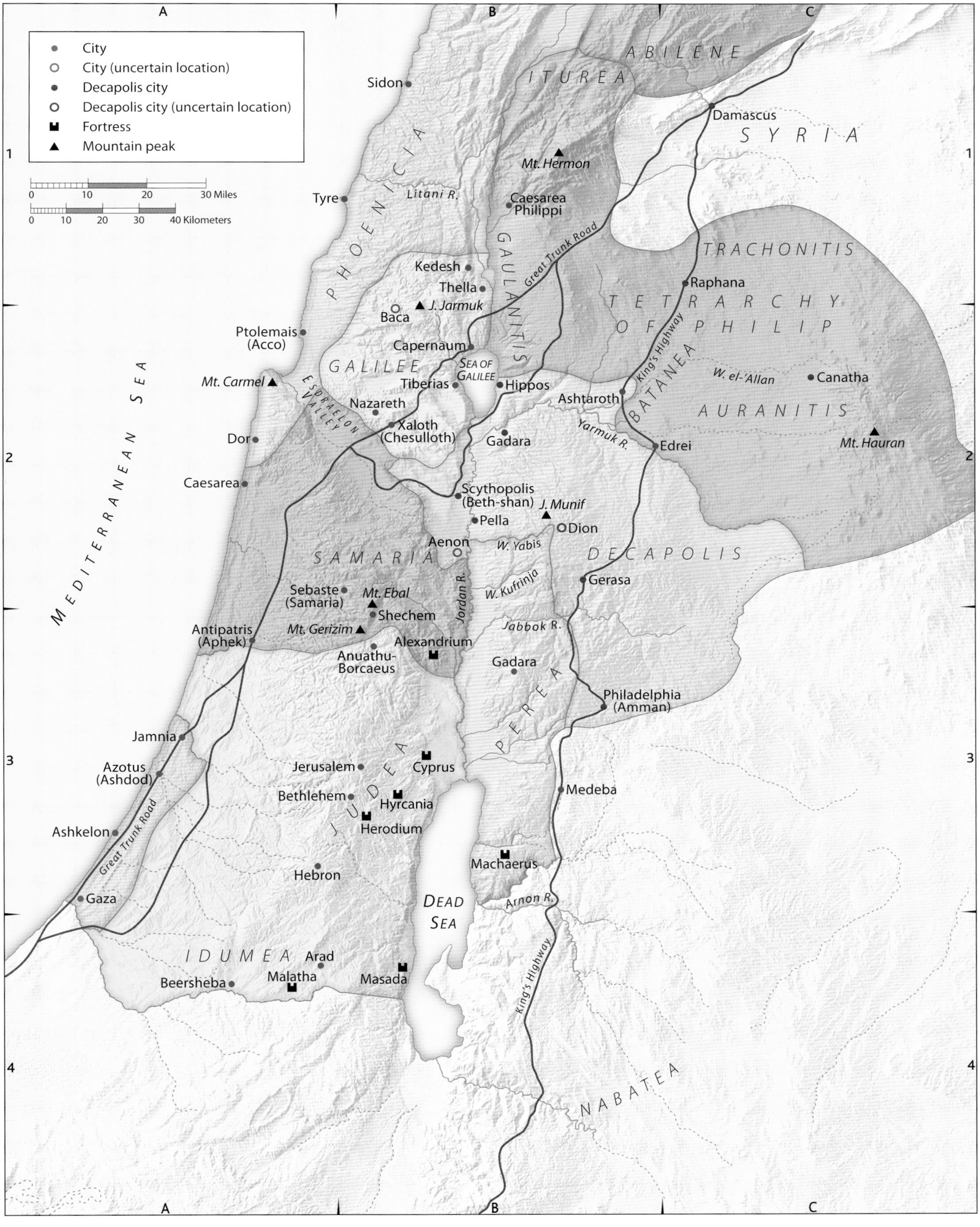
City
City (uncertain location)
Decapolis city
Decapolis city (uncertain location)
Fortress
Mountain peak
0 10 20 30 Miles
0 10 20 30 40 Kilometers
A
B
C
1
2
3
4
ABILENE
ITUREA
Sidon
Damascus
SYRIA
Mt. Hermon
PHOENICIA
Tyre
Litani R.
Caesarea Philippi
GAULANITIS
Great Trunk Road
TRACHONITIS
Kedesh
Thella
Raphana
TETRARCHY OF PHILIP
Baca
J. Jarmuk
Ptolemais (Acco)
Capernaum
King's Highway
BATANEA
GALILEE
Sea of Galilee
Mt. Carmel
Tiberias
Hippos
W. el-'Allan
Canatha
ESDRAELON VALLEY
Ashtaroth
Nazareth
AURANITIS
MEDITERRANEAN SEA
Xaloth (Chesulloth)
Gadara
Yarmuk R.
Mt. Hauran
Dor
Edrei
Caesarea
Scythopolis (Beth-shan)
J. Munif
Pella
Dion
Aenon
W. Yabis
SAMARIA
DECAPOLIS
Jordan R.
W. Kufrinja
Gerasa
Sebaste (Samaria)
Mt. Ebal
Shechem
Mt. Gerizim
Jabbok R.
Antipatris (Aphek)
Alexandrium
Anuathu-Borcaeus
Gadara
PEREA
Philadelphia (Amman)
Jamnia
Azotus (Ashdod)
Jerusalem
Cyprus
JUDEA
Medeba
Bethlehem
Hyrcania
Ashkelon
Herodium
Great Trunk Road
Machaerus
Hebron
Gaza
DEAD SEA
Arnon R.
IDUMEA
Arad
Malatha
Masada
Beersheba
King's Highway
NABATEA

heartland, however, stretched southward from the Zered about 70 miles to a plateau that overlooks the W. Hasma, part of a massive sand-covered dissection in the earth that extended in a southeastward direction and represented the gateway to southern Arabia. [**See maps 25 and 63.**] Most of the heights of Edom rise in excess of 4,000 feet above sea level, and for more than half its distance longitudinally the elevated terrain sustains a height above 5,000 feet. What is more, this forbidding landscape was plainly circumscribed on the west by the Arabah and on the east by the lowlands of the Eastern Desert. The result is that Edom itself was only 10 to 15 miles on an east-west axis, riding the elevated ridge with a series of fortresses and towns that basically aligned the King's Highway.

The combination of natural and man-made fortification rendered Edom an impenetrable barrier to lateral traffic. About 25 miles south of the Zered, a fault line has created a canyon that fans eastward from the Arabah some eight or nine miles. At the foot of this remarkable wadi lies the site of ancient Punon, an important center for copper mining and where, according to the Bible (Num. 33:42), the Israelites encamped en route from Kadesh-barnea to the plains of Moab. Moses requested that the king of Edom permit Israel passage through Edomite territory to the King's Highway (Num. 20:14–21). But the king refused, thereby requiring the Israelite entourage to journey about 100 additional miles over arid terrain and through torrid heat, just to skirt Edom (Deut. 2:1–8). This psychological defeat was surely related to the "fiery serpent" incident (Num. 21:4–9; 33:42–49), in which Moses was obliged to lift up a copper serpent in this wilderness. One can appreciate from the geographical context why the Edomite king's refusal would have gone unchallenged, even though the Edomites are unlikely to have outnumbered the Israelites.

The gigantic cliffs and steep gorges of Edom, even from the more gentle slopes of Punon's pass, represented an inaccessible objective that, at Edomite whim, would continue to exist in splendid isolation (Obad. 3).

Situated adjacent to the western Edomite mountains about 20 miles south of Punon is a cavity-like canyon containing the impressive remains of Petra, the fabulous capital of the Nabatean kingdom, later occupied by the Romans.[74] Though obscurity surrounds their ancestral roots, the Nabateans came to occupy Edom in the third century B.C., and by the first century B.C. their influence was felt from Damascus to Gaza, and into the interior of Arabia. Much of their power was due to the control they exerted over part of a lucrative trade network extending at that time from the Saudi Arabian interior to the western Mediterranean. The site of Petra was approached through a slender one-mile corridor, flanked on either side by high perpendicular cliffs that almost touch at a few places. The basin housing the actual city was surrounded by colorful sandstone cliffs that held carved structures and tombs of what in antiquity was a city laden with great wealth.

Continuing south from Edom's heartland for about 40 miles, from the W. Hasma down to the W. Yutm, near the Gulf of Aqaba, lies an extremely narrow wedge of impassable granite mountains. These mountains of Midian rise to heights approaching 5,800 feet above the sea. In this region, archaeological remains reveal a culture completely distinct from its Palestinian counterpart and is sometimes described as Midianite. It is in this "Midianite culture" that some scholars believe Moses may have found asylum when he fled from the pharaoh and there served his father-in-law, a priest of Midian (Ex. 2:15–17; 3:1).

Façade of el-Khazneh ("the Treasury"), a magnificent 1st-century A.D. tomb carved into the rose-red sandstone of Petra, measures some 130 feet high and 95 feet wide. Corinthian columns in the lower level each stand 50 feet high.

GEOGRAPHICAL OVERVIEW OF THE LAND OF BIBLICAL ISRAEL'S TERRITORIAL INHERITANCE

THE LAND'S PHYSICAL TOPOGRAPHY

It is a small land

Perhaps one of the first discoveries made in the study of the land is the recognition of its small size. As defined above, the nucleus of biblical Israel's Cisjordanian inheritance covers about 6,800 square miles, and its Transjordanian inheritance incorporates another 3,900 square miles, for a total area of approximately 10,700 square miles. Accordingly, the land's overall size is roughly the same as the state of Massachusetts, the countries of Belgium or Rwanda, or Lake Erie.

Modern readers of the Bible tend to think in "Rand McNally" terms, and they are often quite surprised to realize, for example, that there are less than 30 air miles between the Sea of Galilee and the Mediterranean shoreline. A mere 80 to 100 miles separate the western fringes of the Eastern Desert (in eastern Jordan) from the Mediterranean. Only about 65 miles separate the Sea of Galilee and Jerusalem.

As was stated previously, the traditional northern and southern perimeters of Israel's heartland are frequently described in the Bible as "from Dan to Beersheba." In actuality, those two perimeter points are separated by something on the order of only 150 air miles. In American terms, the equivalent would be "from Chicago to Peoria" or "from Los Angeles to San Diego." In Europe, the approximate distance would be "from London to Manchester" or "from Milan to Venice." The territory involved is astonishingly small in size.

It is a strategically located land

Despite its diminutive size, this land is strategically located in both an intercontinental and an interoceanic context. [**See map 1.**] As an intercontinental land bridge, it was in antiquity the single option for any land travel between Africa and either Asia or Europe. As an interoceanic land bridge, it sits adjacent to the only landmass separating the world of the Indian Ocean and the world of the Atlantic Ocean. In this latter respect, widespread trade and communication since high antiquity have brought commodities from faraway worlds to the Fertile Crescent (cloves from Thailand; cinnamon from Malaysia; cassia, silk, calamus, spikenard, indigo, millet, and sesame from India; lapis lazuli and tin from Afghanistan; silver from Spain).

Because this land formed the fulcrum point for both land and sea interaction in antiquity, it also became an international cultural bridge. Its strategic location makes it the place where East met West and where North met South. Since high antiquity, mighty powers with international political and economic aspirations have been poised at its borders. Historically speaking, what happened in this land was almost always a function of what was occurring or had recently occurred in the domain of one of its neighbors. Rare indeed have been those moments in time when citizens of this land were masters of their own destiny.

During the biblical period, the fate of this tiny but strategic land was largely determined by outsiders, be they Egyptians, Assyrians, Babylonians, Persians, Parthians, Greeks, Seleucids, Ptolemies, or Romans. In this regard, the Philistines, and even the Israelites themselves, must be regarded as territorial foreigners who migrated there. The same trend has continued in post-biblical history with the Muslim caliphs, the Christian Crusaders, the Egyptian Mamlukes, the Ottoman Turks, and the British Mandatories. Across this "bridge" have marched the armies of Thutmosis III, Amenhotep II, Seti I, Ramesses II, Merneptah, Shishak I, Necho II, Shalmaneser III, Tiglath-pileser III, Shalmaneser V, Sargon II, Sennacherib, Esarhaddon, Ashurbanipal, Nebuchadnezzar II, Cambyses II, Xerxes I, Artaxerxes III, Alexander III (the Great), Ptolemy I, Antiochus III, Antiochus IV, Herod the Great, Pompey, Vespasian, Titus, Saladin, Richard the Lionhearted, Napoleon, and Edmund Allenby, together with a host of lesser-known generals. [**See maps 7, 44, 76, 77, and 80.**] This land remains one of the most volatile and strategic areas of the world today.

It is a variable land

In spite of its small size, the land reflects an amazing, almost mosaic-like variability. Viewed through a sociological lens, variety is evident in the Old Testament's delineation of the various "ites" in the land: Girgashites, Canaanites, Hivites, Hittites, Amorites, Perizzites, Jebusites, Kenizzites, Kadmonites, Kenites, Rephaim, etc. (Gen. 10:16–18; 15:19–21; Ex. 3:8; 13:5; Num. 13:29; Deut. 7:1; 20:17; Josh. 3:10; 12:8; 24:11; Judg. 3:5; 1 Kings 9:20; cf. Acts 13:19). From a perspective of historical colonialism, the land has been variously known as Canaan, Palestine, Hatti, Djahy, Hurru, Retenu, etc. But the following view of variability has to do with the land's variegated and multiform topography. The land on its lateral axis is broken into at least four distinct physiographical zones. [**See map 8.**]

Coastal Plain

In scope, the Coastal Plain defines that longitudinal maritime strip that extends from the southern end of the Philistine

The Strategic Location of Palestine

map 7

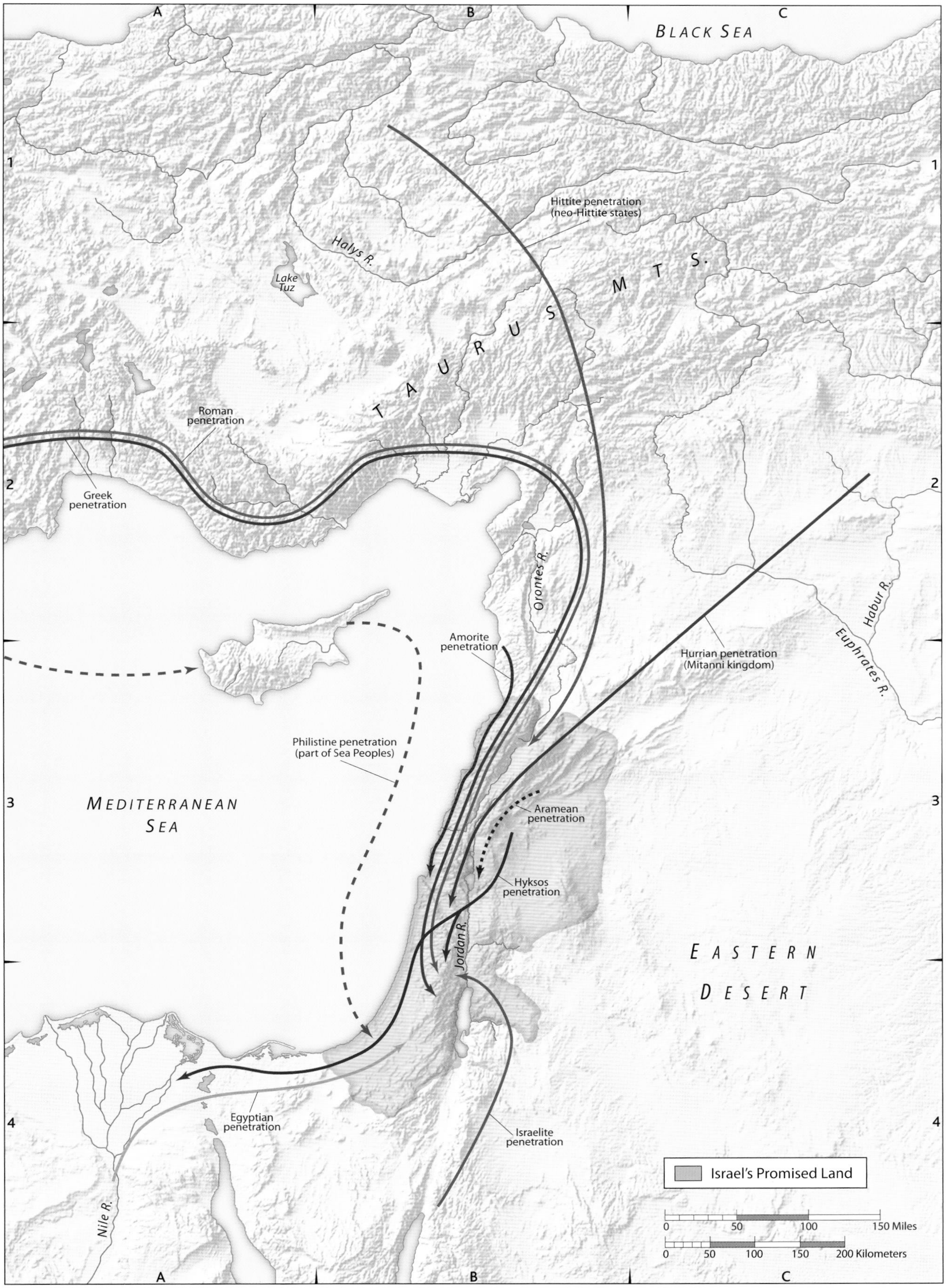
A
B
C
BLACK SEA
1
Hittite penetration (neo-Hittite states)
Halys R.
Lake Tuz
TAURUS MTS.
Roman penetration
2
Greek penetration
Orontes R.
Habur R.
Euphrates R.
Amorite penetration
Hurrian penetration (Mitanni kingdom)
Philistine penetration (part of Sea Peoples)
3
MEDITERRANEAN SEA
Aramean penetration
Hyksos penetration
Jordan R.
EASTERN DESERT
Egyptian penetration
4
Israelite penetration
Israel's Promised Land
0
50
100
150 Miles
0
50
100
150
200 Kilometers
Nile R.

Plain (at W. el-Arish) as far as the northern end of the Asher Plain (near modern Rosh HaNiqra, which corresponds to the end of the "Green Line," the boundary between modern Israel and Lebanon). This plain is internally segmented by three natural barriers—Mt. Carmel, the Crocodile River, and the Jarkon River—creating four distinct plains. Moreover, for geographical reasons to be explained below, it is desirable to further divide the northernmost of these plains. Therefore, the Coastal Plain is comprised of five parts, from north to south known as (1) the Asher Plain (from Rosh HaNiqra to the vicinity of Acco; cf. Josh. 17:10–11; 19:24–26); (2) the Acco Plain (the crescent-shaped bay stretching around to Mt. Carmel; cf. Judg. 4:13–16; 5:21); (3) the Dor Plain (a very narrow slice of land situated between Mt. Carmel and the Crocodile River; cf. Josh. 17:15–18); (4) the Sharon Plain (the lowlands between the swamps of the Crocodile River as far south as the Jarkon; cf. 1 Kings 4:10; 1 Chron. 5:16; 27:29; Isa. 33:9; 35:2; 65:10; Song of Songs 2:1); and (5) the Philistine Plain (the area to the south of the Jarkon).

The Coastal Plain can be characterized by three words: "low" (a reference to its comparative elevation), "open" (a reference to its flat topography), and "fertile" (a reference to the plain's agricultural productivity in modern times). Aside from a few inland slopes on the extreme eastern flank of Philistia that rise to a level approaching 650 feet above the sea, most of the Coastal Plain remains below 350 feet in altitude and much of it is lower than 150 feet above sea level.[75] An examination of **map 22** reveals that biblical towns in this plain tended to be situated not in its center, but rather at the coastline (Acco, Caesarea, Joppa, Ashkelon, Gaza) or toward its eastern edges (Socoh, Aphek, Gezer, Ekron, Gath, Ziklag). Likewise, **map 27** shows that the artery of international transportation (Great Trunk Road) ran along the eastern skirt of this plain, and not through its center. Most likely the plain's lowness and relative flatness, combined with the kurkar ridges that aligned much of the Mediterranean shoreline [**see map 16**] and impeded natural drainage, created a fair amount of swampiness in the plain throughout antiquity. Such a geographic impediment is probably why the Coastal Plain played a negligible, almost nonexistent role in biblical history. Aside from two brief reports about Gerar (Gen. 20; 26), this plain is not referenced in any of the patriarchal narratives. [**See maps 31 and 32.**] None of the battles of the Israelite settlement took place there [**maps 38 and 39**], none of the plain was occupied by Israel in its initial settlement [**maps 42 and 43**], none of the cities of refuge and almost none of the levitical cities were situated there [**map 41**], none of the judges [**map 45**] or prophets in Israel [**map 73**] hailed from there, and none of the recorded ministry of Jesus occurred there [**maps 102 and 103**].

In addition to being low, the plain is also open. Unlike the Central Mountain Spine of Galilee, Samaria, and Judah, which tended to remain more geographically closed and isolated as a result of its elevated and contorted topography, the Coastal Plain offered an inviting, virtually unobstructed landscape for the flow of traffic. Although the land as a whole was previously described as an intercontinental land bridge, it was the Coastal Plain south of Mt. Carmel that especially formed such a bridge. Its openness also connoted mobility. Military conflict during the early biblical period included the dimension of chariot warfare (e.g., Ex. 14:6; Deut. 20:1; Josh. 11:4; Judg. 1:19; 4:3; 2 Sam. 1:6; note also the prohibition of Deut. 17:16). In contrast to its neighboring mountains, this plain offered a terrain that was conducive to the use of chariots, including lightning-fast strikes that would have been unhampered by large

A signature city erected by Herod the Great, Caesarea sits adjacent to the Mediterranean Sea. Its remains include a Roman theater (foreground of picture, reconstructed) and a Roman aqueduct (background of picture) dilapidated today as a result of the further inlet of the sea.

The Geographical Regions of Palestine

map 8

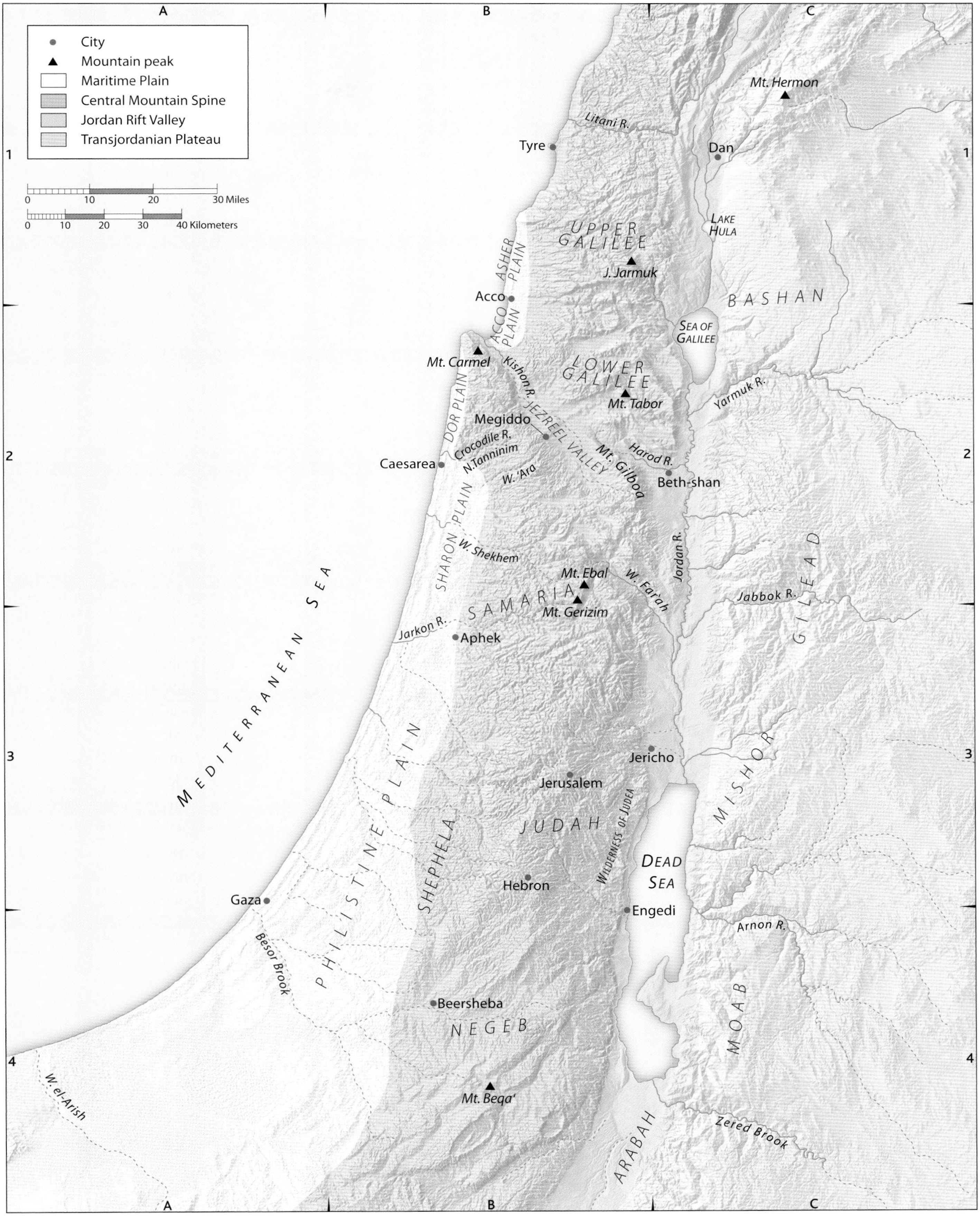

City
Mountain peak
Maritime Plain
Central Mountain Spine
Jordan Rift Valley
Transjordanian Plateau
0 10 20 30 Miles
0 10 20 30 40 Kilometers
A
B
C
1
2
3
4
Mt. Hermon
Litani R.
Tyre
Dan
Lake Hula
Upper Galilee
Asher Plain
J. Jarmuk
Acco
Bashan
Acco Plain
Sea of Galilee
Mt. Carmel
Kishon R.
Lower Galilee
Mt. Tabor
Dor Plain
Yarmuk R.
Megiddo
Jezreel Valley
Crocodile R.
N.Tanninim
Harod R.
Caesarea
Mt. Gilboa
W. 'Ara
Beth-shan
Sharon Plain
W. Shekhem
Jordan R.
Gilead
Mt. Ebal
W. Far'ah
Mediterranean Sea
Samaria
Jabbok R.
Mt. Gerizim
Jarkon R.
Aphek
Jericho
Jerusalem
Mishor
Judah
Wilderness of Judea
Shephela
Dead Sea
Hebron
Gaza
Engedi
Philistine Plain
Arnon R.
Besor Brook
Beersheba
Moab
Negeb
W. el-Arish
Mt. Beqa'
Arabah
Zered Brook

boulders and hilly landscape. In fact, there exists a striking correspondence between the extent of terrain over which the Canaanites could run their chariots and terrain Israel did not capture in the settlement (Josh. 17:16–18). [**See maps 42 and 43.**] Alternatively, openness may help explain why the Philistines were unable to survive as an indigenous political entity beyond the biblical period, whereas the more secluded Israelites succeeded in perpetuating an enduring sense of national identity.

Finally, this plain is fertile; at least, it has become fertile in modern times. A glance at a modern map of Israel [**map 118**] shows that most of the western terrain allotted Israel by the United Nations Partition Accords of 1947 is situated on the Coastal Plain, which at that time was extremely marshy and even malaria infested. But after the area became properly drained in the 1950s, an agricultural bonanza was revealed as deep layers of exceedingly rich topsoil eroded from the flanking mountains were uncovered, and as a major agricultural effort was successfully undertaken.

Central Mountain Spine

Consisting of the highlands of Galilee, Samaria, Judah, and the Negeb, the Central Mountain Spine is exactly the opposite of the Coastal Plain in character and topography. The plain is "low, open, and fertile"; the spine is "high, closed, and sterile."

While the plain ascends to only some 650 feet at its highest points, the central spine is about 1,500 feet above sea level at its lowest point, with many segments rising in excess of 3,000 feet above the sea. Where the two zones meet, this contrast in altitude can be quite pronounced. One might travel inland from the Mediterranean a distance of only three to four miles while simultaneously ascending in elevation about a half mile.

Moreover, the spine is closed. Actually a series of convoluted, interlocking mountain ranges, the spine stands as a natural obstruction to lateral traffic, except where it is broken by the Jezreel/Esdraelon Valley. At some places along its difficult undulation, it would be necessary for one to cross over as many as four or five distinct ridges, each separated by deeply etched wadi beds to get from one side to the other. Because of its elevated and jumbled terrain, the spine has been more isolated and less susceptible to international adventurism or foreign assault. Only rarely has this zone proved to be attractive to empire builders.

Finally, the spine is sterile and unproductive. Composed of hard limestones that lack precious minerals or other natural resources, and eroded to bare bedrock in substantial tracts, it seems unlikely that this sterile stone mountain, ranging only 10 to 30 miles in width, should ever have been viewed as a political asset.

Yet it is precisely on this mountain that much of the biblical story line unfolds. Here is where the patriarchs lived, built altars [**map 32**], and communed with their God. Here is where the battles of the conquest took place [**maps 37, 38, and 39**], where Israel occupied its land [**maps 42 and 43**], and where many of its national institutions were founded [**maps 41, 45, and 73**]. Here is where in due course the capital cities of the northern kingdom (Shechem, then Tirzah, and finally Samaria) and the southern kingdom (Jerusalem) were situated. Here is where post-exilic Judaism took root [**map 85**], and here is where much of the recorded ministry of Christ transpired [**maps 102 and 103**].

Galilee. Though an offshoot of the loftier mountains of Lebanon, the heights of Upper Galilee nevertheless offer a very complex topography. Jebel Jarmuk (Mt. Meron) boasts the highest point in all of Cisjordan [**map 18**], but it is surrounded by other crests that ascend above 3,000 feet. Its elevated terrain and fragmented topography have rendered Upper Galilee less suited for intensive settlement, despite its heavier annual rainfall. The region has never possessed what can be called a large city. Lower Galilee on the east side continues the rugged contours of its northern neighbor. One discovers there a large elevated limestone outcropping [**map 16**] that drops off precipitously on its eastern flank into the Sea of Galilee. Included in this region are the heights of Mt. Tabor, the cliffs of Arbel, and the volcanic Horns of Hattin. By way of contrast, the central and western portions of Lower Galilee offer the most level terrain in the entire mountain spine. The area is composed of several parallel ridges running more or less on an east-west axis, between which are relatively open basins that become almost contiguous on the west side. [**See map 10.**]

Jezreel/Esdraelon Valley. Between the heights of Lower Galilee and Samaria extends a valley that ultimately links the Jordan valley with the Coastal Plain at Acco. [**See map 10.**] Shaped like an arrow that points toward the Mediterranean, this valley is known in the Hebrew Old Testament as the Jezreel valley ("God has sown" or "May God sow," e.g., Josh. 17:16; Judg. 6:33; Hos. 1:5; 2:22) and in the New Testament era by its Greek reflex, Esdraelon.[76] A slender shaft of the arrow, at points not more than two miles wide, stretches from Beth-shan to the town of Jezreel, hemmed in by Mt. Moreh in the north and Mt. Gilboa in the south, and drained by the Harod River. Near this territory was the scene of Gideon's triumphant victory over the Midianites (Judg. 7) and of Saul's humiliating defeat at the hands of the Philistines (1 Sam. 29—31). The base of the arrow's head spans some 18 miles, from the vicinity of Jenin north to Mt. Tabor, and from those two points it extends about 20 miles to its apex, just west of Jokneam and near the Kishon River, where Sisera's chariot became lodged in its quagmire (Judg. 5:21; cf. Ps. 83:9). [**See map 50.**] The head of this arrow, sometimes referred to as the plain of Megiddo (2 Chron. 35:22; Zech. 12:11), is low and flat. The plain is covered with an extremely thick blanket of black topsoil, more than 300 feet deep in places, which has been formed by the decomposition and erosion of Galilean basalts.

The Elevation of Palestine

map 9

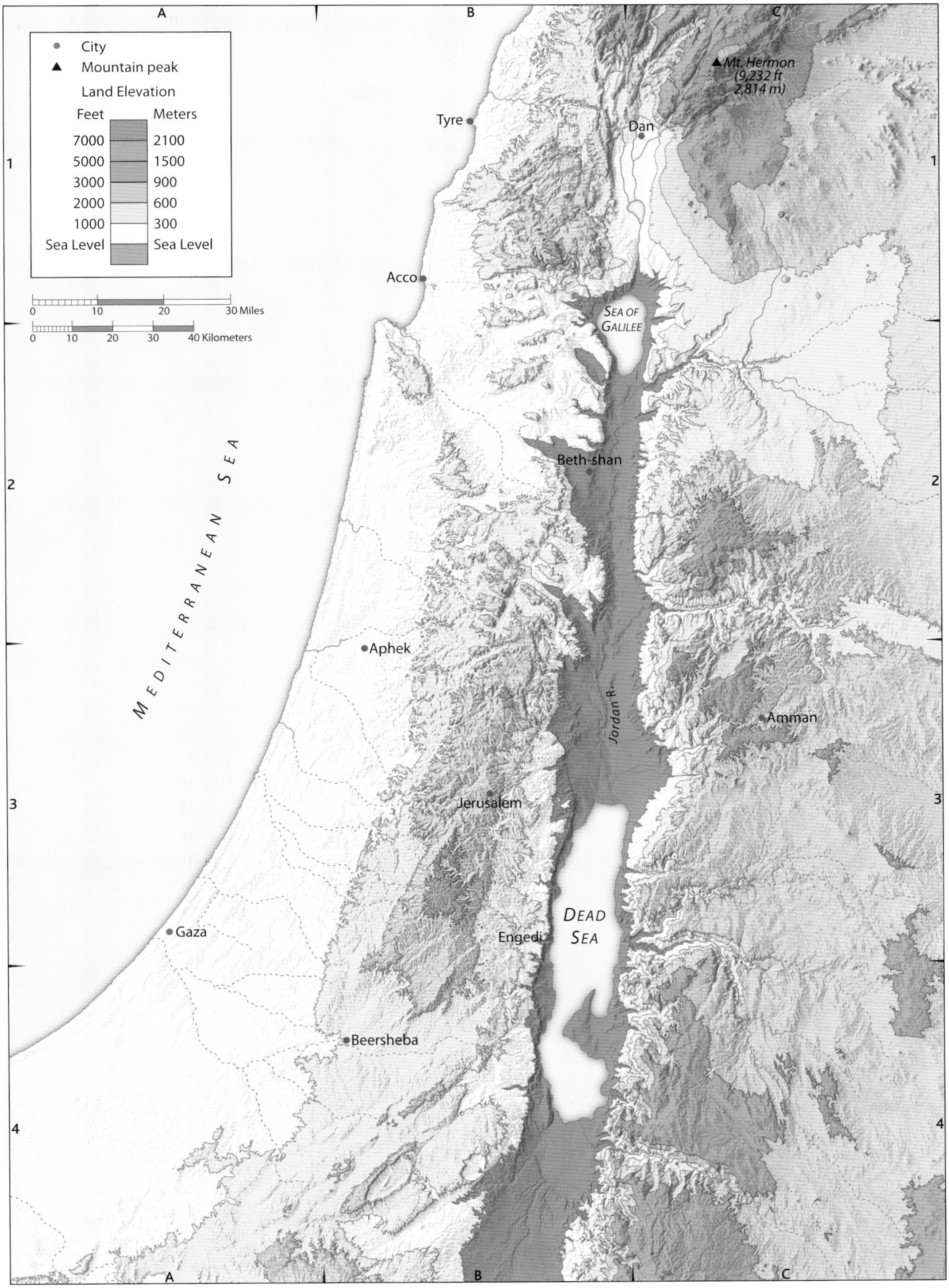
A
B
C
City
Mountain peak
Land Elevation
Feet
Meters
7000
2100
5000
1500
3000
900
2000
600
1000
300
Sea Level
Sea Level
0
10
20
30 Miles
0
10
20
30
40 Kilometers
1
2
3
4
Mt. Hermon (9,232 ft 2,814 m)
Tyre
Dan
Acco
Sea of Galilee
Beth-shan
Mediterranean Sea
Aphek
Jordan R.
Amman
Jerusalem
Dead Sea
Engedi
Gaza
Beersheba

The Jezreel Valley

map 10

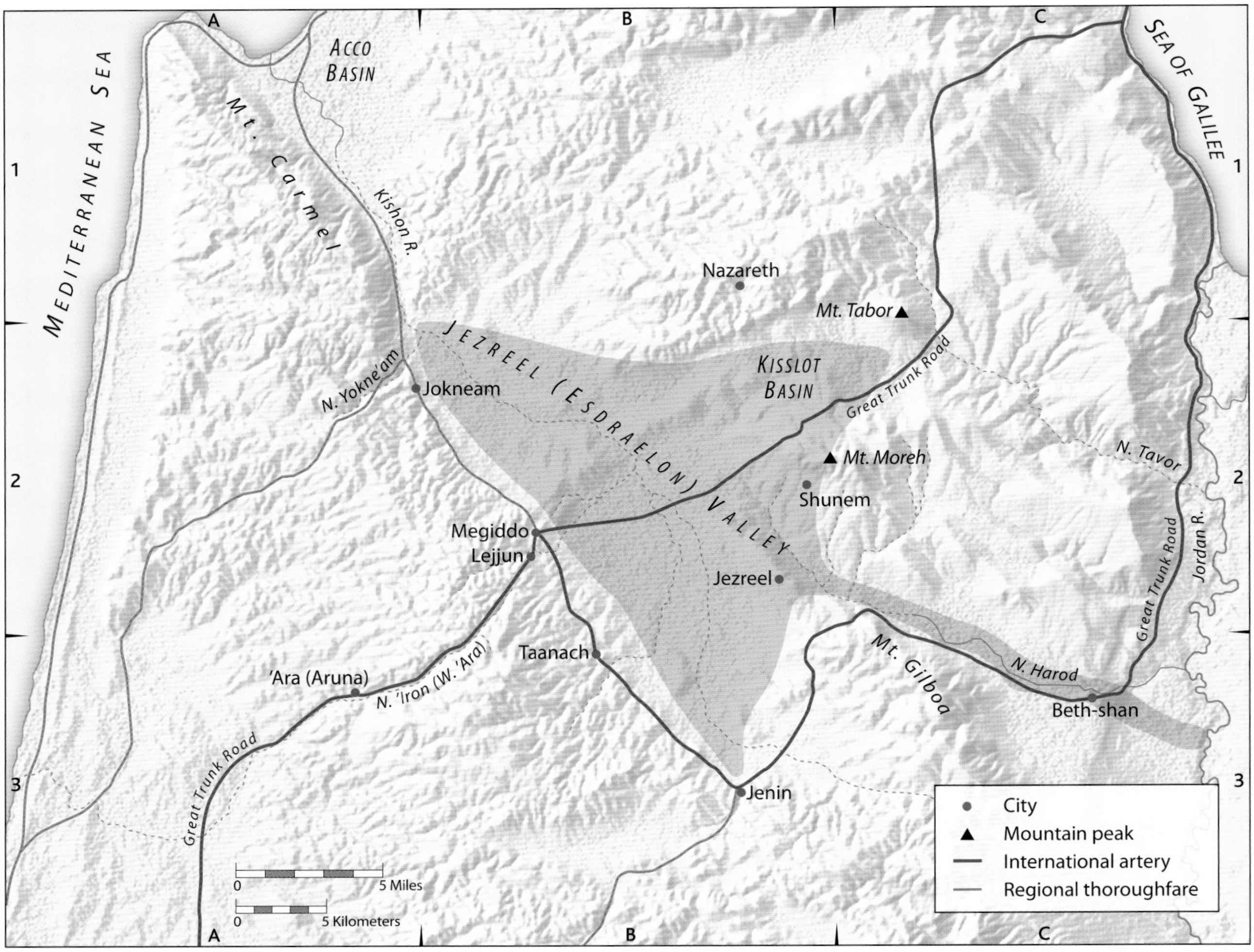

While the plain of Jezreel had multiple passage gates, the major transportation artery known as the Great Trunk Road [**maps 10 and 27**] went through the gate at Megiddo. This city's 20 archaeological strata reflect an almost continuous occupation through the early Roman period. Actually, the installation city of Megiddo was of major importance during every historical period without exception; it is no exaggeration to assert that it was one of the most militarily strategic points in all of the southwestern Fertile Crescent. From the late fourth millennium B.C. until even the 20th century, Megiddo[77] has been the scene of repeated military confrontations.[78]

Samaria. South of the Jezreel lay the mountainous district of Samaria—an intermediate and transitional area between Galilee and Judah in terms of altitude, vegetation, and climate. Mt. Carmel ("vineyard/garden of God"), in the extreme northwest, was proverbial in the Bible for its beauty (Song of Songs 7:5) and fertility (Isa. 35:2; Jer. 50:19). The mountain is amply attested in ancient literature as the place of a shrine.[79] Perhaps it was in this context that Mt. Carmel served as the scene of Elijah's religious contest with the prophets of Baal (1 Kings 18:17–40) and elsewhere as a place of spiritual retreat for Elisha (2 Kings 2:25; 4:25). In the extreme northeast, the heights of Samaria are otherwise known as the limestone mountains of Gilboa. Other Samarian mountains, Mt. Ebal and Mt. Gerizim, enclose the valley within which lies the principal town of Shechem. [**See map 11.**] Mountainous throughout, the peaks of J. el-Qurein, J. `Ayrukabba, J. `en-`Ena, and J. el-`Aṣur (Baal Hazor, cf. 2 Sam. 13:23) dominate Samaria's horizon. [**See maps 11 and 18.**]

Though mountainous, Samaria is also interspersed with a number of small plains and open valleys, one of which is located near the juncture of the Carmel and Gilboa inclines, in proximity to the city of Dothan. [**See map 22.**] This plain of Dothan is the largest and most intensively cultivated basin of Samaria, and is where Joseph was sold into captivity (Gen. 37:12–28). Another trough, the long, slender plain of Mikhmetat, runs south from Shechem before it is pinched off by J. Rahwat. [**See map 11.**] It rests astride the water-divide along which the Central Ridge Road winds toward Jerusalem. Laterally dividing western Samaria from Socoh to Shechem is the low-lying valley known as W. Shekhem. Similarly, dividing eastern Samaria from the vicinity of Tirzah to the Jordan valley, one finds the incisive fracture known as W. Far`ah. Combined, these two valleys represent the lowest point of

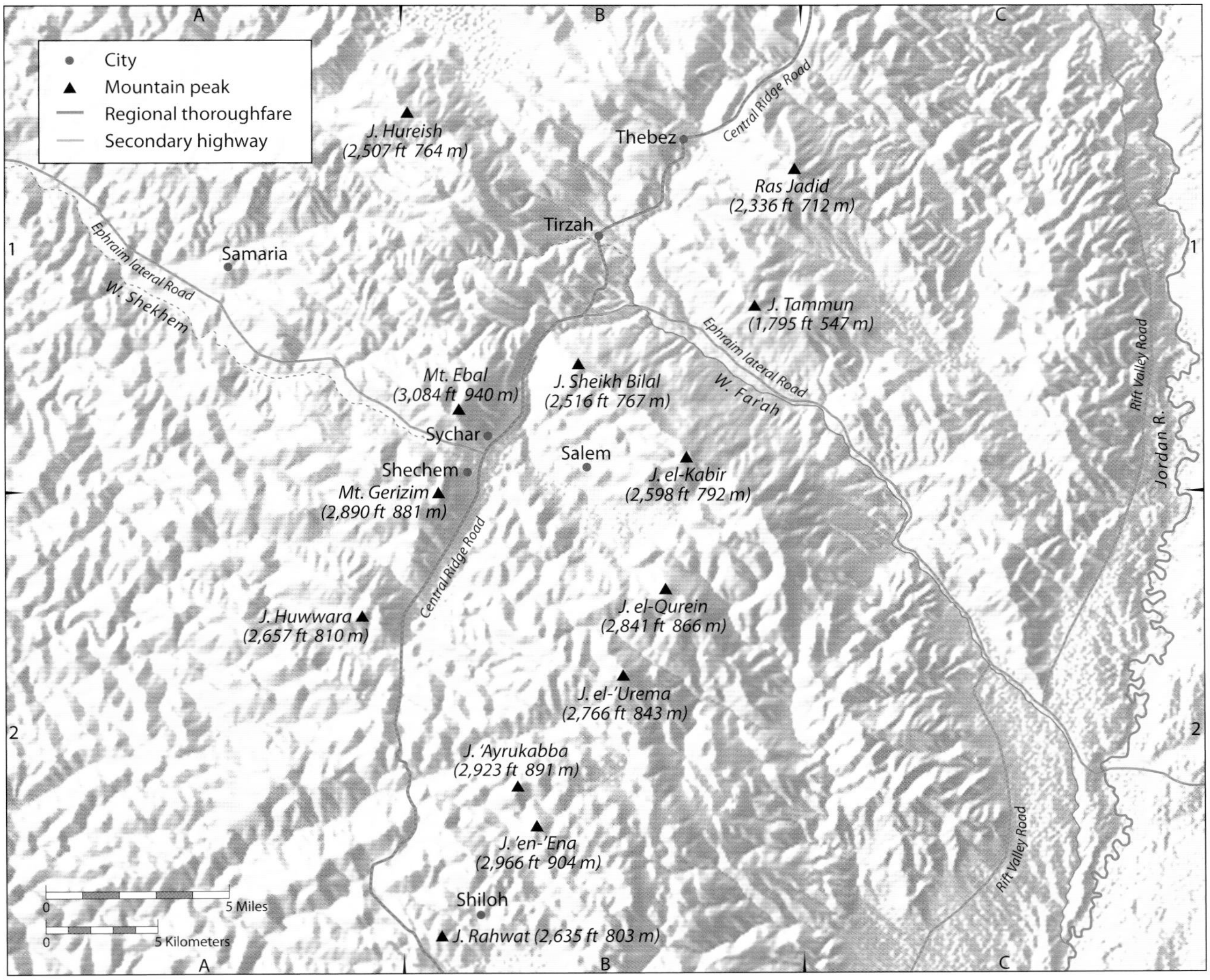

altitude in all of Samaria. They were the easiest and most utilized paths for crossing Samaria's spine, which helps explain why certain places were selected to serve as capital cities of Israel during the days of the divided kingdom (Shechem, Tirzah, Samaria).

Judah. While there is no defined geological boundary separating Samaria and Judah, there is a marked difference in the topography of the two regions. Samaria's larger amounts of rainfall have contributed to much greater erosion and more deeply furrowed wadies. Judah remains more of a high plateau, less dissected because of its drier climate. [**See map 19.**] As one proceeds south in Judah, the landscape becomes harsher and more rugged and sterile. Judah's chief surface features are bare rocks and wide stretches of loose, broken stones, washed free of soil. Only along the watershed in the vicinity of Ramah and between Bethlehem and Hebron do the soils of Judah permit cultivation. Elsewhere, the shallow soil eroding in the winter downpours has largely prevented cultivation.

Only about five miles southeast of Jerusalem, the wilderness of Judah begins (Num. 21:20; 1 Sam. 26:1–2; cf. Mark 1:4). A fearful spectacle of desolation, the wilderness of Judah, also known as the Jeshimon, is a genuine desert. It is a solitary, howling, rough and rocky wasteland, nearly devoid of plants and animals, and virtually without rainfall (Ps. 63:1). Even modern nomadic Bedouin tend to avoid its aridity and rugged terrain. On its eastern edge, the wilderness of Judah plunges steeply, almost vertically, in places as much as 4,500 feet into the Jordan valley below. Between Jericho and the southern end of the Dead Sea, there are more than 20 deep gorges that have been carved out by wadies. [**See map 15.**] Yet those wadies were all too narrow and tortuous to carry significant roadways during the biblical era, and Judah was thereby naturally insulated on its eastern front. The prophet Isaiah heralded a time, however, when even the contorted and convoluted topography of the Judean wilderness will be made straight and flat, and when every rough place will be made smooth (Isa. 40:3–4; cf. 41:18–20; 51:3).

The Judean mountain spine breaks off only slightly less abruptly on the west. A narrow, shallow trough (W. Ghurab, W. Sar) divides the highlands of Judah from a distinct topographic region known as the Shephela ("foothills;" e.g., Deut. 1:7; Josh. 9:1; 10:40; 12:8; Judg. 1:9; 1 Kings 10:27; 1 Chron. 27:28; 2 Chron. 9:27; 26:10; 28:18; Jer. 17:26; 32:44; 33:13; Obad. 19). [**See map 12.**] The Shephela stretches from the Aijalon valley some 35 miles south to the area of T. Beit Mirsim. These foothills cover an area about eight to ten miles wide and, significantly, extend west to the vicinity of what were the Philistine cities of Gezer, Ekron, and Gath. [**See map 57.**] Mainly composed of soft limestone [**map 16**] with a rolling surface sloping westward and intersected by several important and fertile wadies, the Shephela represented an intermediate buffer zone between the Judean spine (occupied by Israelites) and the southern Coastal Plain (occupied by Philistines). Not surprisingly, the area became the scene for a number of biblical episodes of economic warfare between the Israelites and the Philistines (Judg. 15:4–5; 2 Sam. 23:11–12). Actually, it may be that most of the contention between the Philistines and Israelites was occasioned precisely by a desire on the part of both peoples to dominate and exploit the rich agricultural valleys of the Shephela.

The Negeb ("dry ground"; e.g., Gen. 24:62; Num. 13:29; Josh. 15:19; Judg. 1:15) originally denoted the barren wilderness south of Judah (e.g., Josh. 15:2–4; 18:19; 1 Sam. 27:10; 2 Sam. 24:7; cf. note the alluvial fans that stretch from the area of Beersheba as far as Arad [**map 16**]). Over time, the word evolved in its meaning and came to refer to a compass point in the direction of that barrenness ("south"), and hence it came to designate south of almost anywhere (Josh. 11:2; Zech. 14:10; 1 Sam. 30:14).

Today the Negeb (Negev) includes what in the Bible is referred to as the wilderness of Zin (Num. 20:1; 34:3; Josh. 15:1) and the wilderness of Paran (Num. 10:12; Deut. 1:1). The region of the modern Negeb constitutes an adverse environment to human activity or extensive settlement. The area is entirely dependent on rainfall, always scant and uncertain, though the territory does have a few wells in the vicinity of Beersheba (Gen. 26:18–22) and Kadesh-barnea. [**See map 34.**]

Jordan Rift Valley

The dominant geological forces that have sculpted the most eminently characteristic features of the Levant are most apparent in the Jordan Rift Valley. Extending even beyond the Levant, the geological fissure is known as the Afro-Arabian Rift Valley. [**See map 13.**] A sunken block confined by two parallel fault lines begins in southeastern Turkey and extends southward through the Levant as far as the Gulf of Aqaba. From this point, the fracture continues southward on a line that runs parallel to the Red Sea as far as Ethiopia, resulting in the separation of the Arabian Peninsula from Africa. At the base of the Red Sea, the fault line itself splits: an eastern

The elevated tell of Beersheba is located in the biblical Negeb at a strategic junction of several wadies (see right of picture).

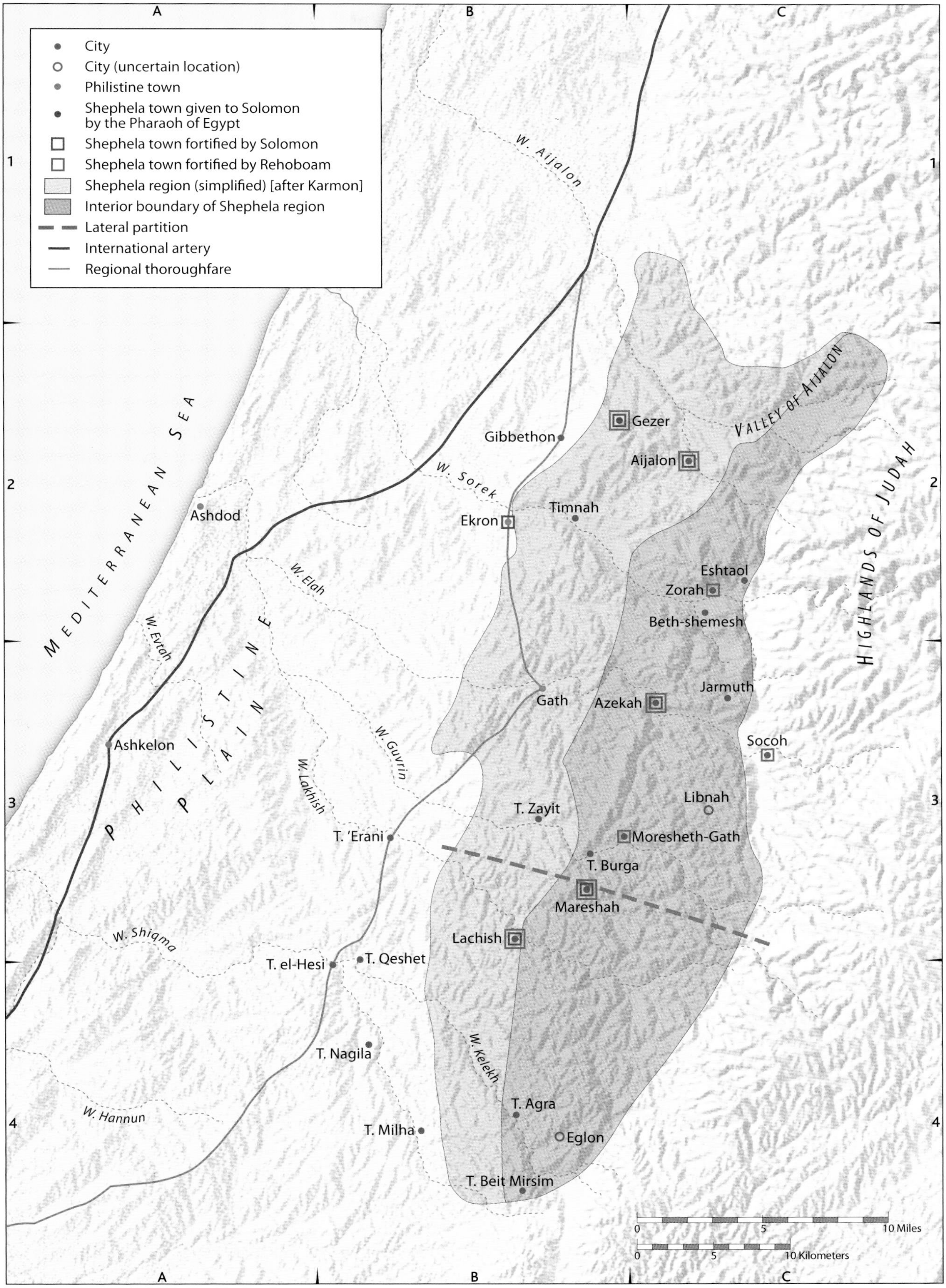
City
City (uncertain location)
Philistine town
Shephela town given to Solomon by the Pharaoh of Egypt
Shephela town fortified by Solomon
Shephela town fortified by Rehoboam
Shephela region (simplified) [after Karmon]
Interior boundary of Shephela region
Lateral partition
International artery
Regional thoroughfare
MEDITERRANEAN SEA
PHILISTINE PLAIN
VALLEY OF AIJALON
HIGHLANDS OF JUDAH
W. Aijalon
W. Sorek
W. Elah
W. Evtah
W. Guvrin
W. Lakhish
W. Shiqma
W. Hannun
W. Kelekh
Gezer
Gibbethon
Aijalon
Timnah
Ekron
Ashdod
Eshtaol
Zorah
Beth-shemesh
Jarmuth
Gath
Azekah
Socoh
Ashkelon
Libnah
T. Zayit
Moresheth-Gath
T. 'Erani
T. Burga
Mareshah
Lachish
T. el-Hesi
T. Qeshet
T. Nagila
T. Agra
Eglon
T. Milha
T. Beit Mirsim
0 5 10 Miles
0 5 10 Kilometers

branch divides the Arabian plate from the Somalian plate and the "Horn of Africa," and extends far into the depths of the Indian Ocean; a western branch begins a diagonal penetration of Ethiopia, Kenya, Uganda, Tanzania, Malawi, and Mozambique. Known in those parts as the "Great African Rift Valley," this geological cleavage has been responsible for creating most of the elongated lakes of East Africa (Turkana, Albert, Edward, Kivu, Tanganyika, Malawi), for shaping Lake Victoria, and for severing the island of Madagascar from continental Africa.[80] Chiseled here into the earth's crust is a single fault line that extends continuously across more than 4,000 miles—60 degrees of latitude, or about one-sixth of the earth's circumference.

This fault line also represents the deepest fissure presently known to exist in the surface of the earth, and the deepest point along the continental gash lies on the shores of the Dead Sea. Here, beside the western shore, a tight succession of secondary faults running immediately parallel to the main fault line has allowed scientists to study and postulate displacement depths. Drill holes have demonstrated vertical displacements ranging up to 11,750 feet, and geophysical testing of the region has given rise to estimates as thick as 23,000 feet. The area surrounding the Dead Sea already lies at an extremely low altitude (-1,380 feet), which means that unconsolidated deposits overlying bedrock are estimated to descend below the level of the Mediterranean to almost 25,000 feet. In other words, a person digging at certain places along the Dead Sea would encounter only sedimentary alluvium down to approximately -24,800 feet, before finally encountering rock stratification.[81]

Fanning out in every direction from this "parent fissure" are scores of secondary fractures that make a geological mosaic of the land; some of these branches have themselves created lateral valleys (Harod, Far`ah, Jezreel). According to seismographic registrations, some 200 to 300 "microquakes" are recorded on a daily basis today in Israel.[82] The vast majority of these, of course, are humanly undetectable. Occasionally, however, a devastating earthquake strikes this land, such as: (1) December 7 and 8, 1267—A quake is reported to have collapsed part of the cliff aligning the Jordan River at Damiya [**map 37**], thereby damming up the downstream flow of the Jordan for some 10 hours;[83] (2) January 14, 1546—An earthquake struck around noontime with its epicenter near the Samarian city of Nablus (Shechem), again stopping the flow of the Jordan River—this time for about two days; (3) January 1, 1837—A severe earthquake with multiple epicenters struck Israel and Jordan. In Galilee, 4,000 citizens of the town of Safed were killed, as were an additional 1,000 in surrounding regions. The entire village of Gush Halav was destroyed. In central Israel, two streets of houses completely disappeared in Nablus, and a hotel collapsed at Jericho, causing additional casualties. Both ends of what is known today as the Allenby Bridge were

The Afro-Arabian Fault Line ***map 13***

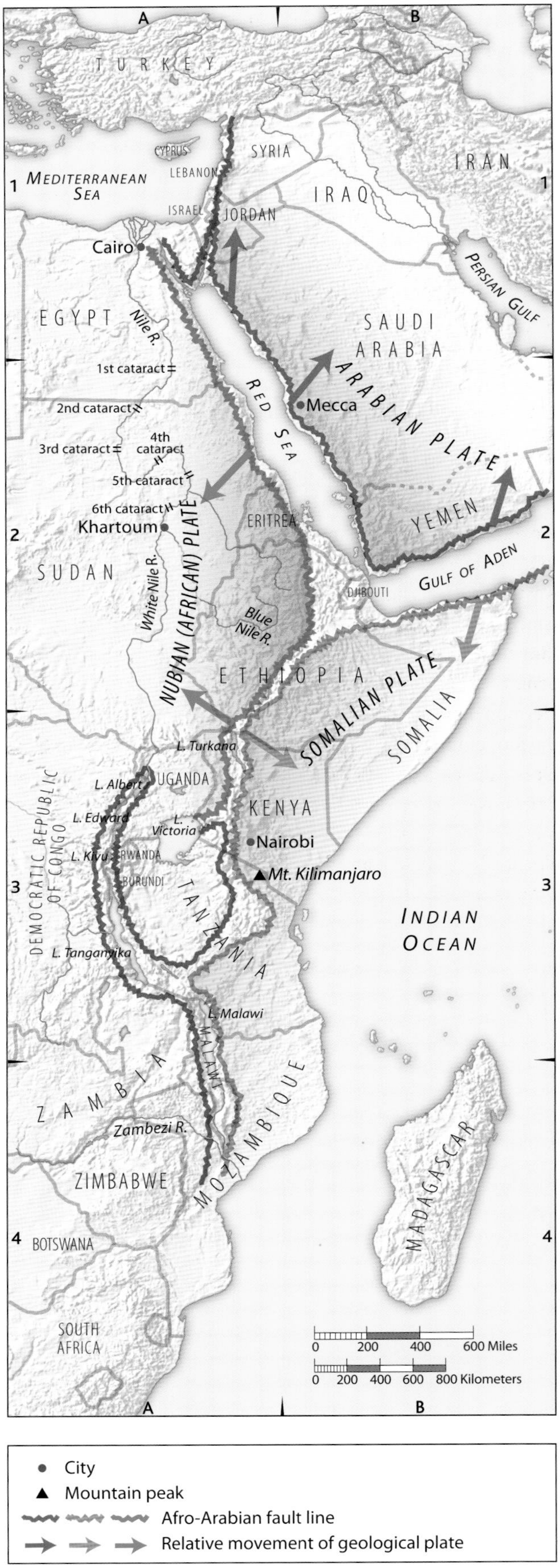

displaced. Even more than 100 miles away, in Amman, much damage was reported from this quake; (4) July 11, 1927—A quake took place in the early afternoon, the epicenter of which apparently was somewhere in the northern end of the Dead Sea.[84] It was reported that this quake collapsed a 150-foot wall of earth near Damiya that took out a roadway and dammed up the Jordan for twenty-one and a half hours (although this was a secondhand report that has been challenged in recent years).[85]

One cannot rule out the possibility that a similar event may have been at work in Israel's crossing the Jordan "on dry ground" (Josh. 3:7–17). [**See map 37.**]

Having surveyed the Jordan Rift Valley as a whole, let us examine its several parts. First, at an altitude of 9,232 feet, Mt. Hermon receives an annual precipitation of 60 inches and remains snow-clad throughout the year (cf. Jer. 18:14). Cascading from its side or percolating from near its base are hundreds of springs and rivulets that join to form the four principal streams of the headwaters of the Jordan. The westernmost—Ayun (N. Bareighit)—emerges near the modern Israeli border town of Metulla and flows almost due south. [**See map 18.**] Not far from there is the largest flow, the river Senir (N. Hasbani), which issues from the western side of Hermon opposite the Lebanese village of Hasbiyya. Rising near the foot of the biblical site of Dan is the river Dan/Leddan (N. Qadi), and emerging from the caves near the modern site of Banyas is the river Hermon (N. Banias). By the time it finally merges to form a single stream near Lake Hula, the water has already descended to an approximate altitude of only 300 feet above sea level.

Continuing its downward course, the water arrives at the Sea of Galilee (Matt. 4:18; 15:29; Mark 1:16; 7:31; John 6:1), known also by other names: Chinnereth (Num. 34:11; Deut. 3:17; Josh. 12:3; 13:27), Gennesaret (Luke 5:1), Tiberias (John 6:1; 21:1), or simply "the Sea" (Luke 5:1; John 6:16). The Sea of Galilee is a fresh-water inland lake measuring approximately 13 miles north-south, eight miles east-west, and about 151 feet in depth. [**See map 14.**] The surface of the sea is at some 695 feet below sea level, making the Sea of Galilee the lowest body of fresh water on earth.

Flanked by the highlands of Lower Galilee on the west and Golan on the east, the Sea of Galilee must have been alive with activity throughout the biblical period. Capernaum, near the passage of the Great Trunk Road, manifests evidence of occupation as early as 8000 B.C., and at least 25 other sites in Lower Galilee were settled by the Early Bronze Age.[86] It was during the Roman period, however, that the human utilization of the region reached its peak. The rabbis stated: "The Lord has created seven seas, but the Sea of Gennesaret is his delight."[87]

The Sea of Galilee also delighted Herod Antipas, who constructed along its shores the city of Tiberias with its many architectural accoutrements of Roman grandeur. Nearby, hot baths were constructed at Hammath, a hippodrome at Magdala (Taricheae), as well as a host of villas, many paved streets, and numerous archways. In New Testament times, the Sea was thus experiencing a period of relative affluence, related

The Sea of Galilee is nestled between Lower Galilee (foreground of picture) and the Golan Heights (background).

in large part to a flourishing fishing industry with an estimated annual catch as high as 2,000 tons. A low-water point in the Sea during the mid-1980s led to the discovery of more than a dozen Roman harbors encircling the Sea of Galilee.[88]

This affluence is reflected in several incidents from the gospels that took place near the Sea. For example, Jesus' parable concerning a rich fool who thought it advisable to tear down his barns and to build still bigger ones was uttered along the shores of the Sea (Luke 12:16–21). His parable of the wheat and tares was predicated upon the affluence of a householder who possessed barns and servants (Matt. 13:24–43). As part of the Sermon on the Mount, traditionally situated in the area just north of Tabgha, Jesus addressed the subjects of giving alms and laying up earthly possessions (Matt. 6:1–14). And his famous question in the vicinity of Caesarea Philippi—"What does it profit a man to gain the whole world and to lose his own soul?"—was addressed to Galilean listeners, some of whom doubtless had great wealth or knew of others who did (Mark 8:27-37; Luke 9:23-25).

A distance of only 65 air miles separates the Sea of Galilee and the Dead Sea, yet the Jordan River twists and meanders for almost 150 miles within this space. (Note on **map 14** a possible change in the Jordan's entry point into the Sea of Galilee and exit point since biblical antiquity.) Here, the sunken Rift valley, sometimes called the Ghor ("depression"), varies in width from two to four miles, though it widens at the Beth-shan and Jericho basins. The Jordan itself courses through the lowest winding bed of the Ghor—through a low and tangled thicket of dense tamarisk, poplar, and oleander vegetation, outstretched thorn bushes, and a scattering of dead driftwood logs (2 Kings 6:2–7). It is sometimes referred to as the "jungle of the Jordan"[89] (Jer. 12:5; 49:19; 50:44; Zech. 11:3).

Several biblical texts suggest that this "thicket" was inhabited by wild animals in antiquity (1 Sam. 17:34–36 [by implication]; 2 Kings 2:24; Mark 1:13). Skeletal remains of various species of wild animals have been exhumed from the valley floor,[90] and modern travelers report seeing lions, bears, leopards, wolves, jackals, hyenas, and a wide variety of waterfowl in the area.[91] In addition, many modern Arabic towns in or near the valley appear to bear the names of wild animals, and the Medeba map (a sixth-century A.D. floor mosaic map—the oldest known original depiction of the land) shows a lion on the prowl in the valley.[92] No evidence of bridges across the Jordan exists until the sixth century A.D., so one must imagine that normal passage during the biblical period was by the demanding and potentially perilous means of swimming (Judg. 6:33; 1 Sam. 13:7; 31:11–13; 2 Sam. 2:29; 10:17; 17:22; 24:5), probably most often at one of the several fords across the river (Josh. 2:7; Judg. 3:28; 12:5–6). [**See map 18.**]

At the end of its journey, the Jordan River emptied into the Dead Sea, or as it is known in the Bible, the Salt Sea (Gen. 14:3; Num. 34:3, 12; Deut. 3:17; Josh. 3:16; 12:3; 15:2, 5; 18:19), the Sea of the Arabah (Deut. 3:17; 4:49; Josh. 3:16; 12:3; 2 Kings 14:25), or the Eastern Sea (Ezek. 47:18; Joel 2:20; Zech. 14:8). The name "Dead Sea" appears in Greek literature from the early first-century A.D.,[93] and it appears to have been introduced into Christian tradition through the work of St. Jerome.[94] With a water surface at approximately 1,380 feet below sea level (and lowering by the year!), the Dead Sea is by far the lowest continental depression on earth. By way of comparison, the great Turfan depression—otherwise the lowest point in elevation in continental Asia—lies at 490 feet below sea level. The lowest point in Africa (the Qattara depression in the Sahara) plunges to a depth of -512 feet. The lowest point in North America (Death Valley in California) rests at 282 feet below sea level.

The Dead Sea is a terminal lake (without access to the oceans) that measures some 10 miles in width, about 50 miles in length, and achieves a depth of slightly over 1,000 feet at one point in its northern basin. [**See map 15.**] By way of sharp contrast, the shallow southern basin is devoid of water today, but almost certainly held a minimum of 10 to 30 feet of water throughout the whole of the biblical era.[95] The Dead Sea's extreme negative elevation creates a vast and extensive catchment basin of approximately 27,000 miles, making it in area the largest hydrological system of the Levant.[96] [**See map 18.**] Before dams were erected and siphon canals were dug in its catchment area during the 20th century,[97] the Dead Sea would have received an estimated total discharge of 97.36 billion cubic feet of water annually (2.757 billion cubic meters), which would have required a daily average of some 193.17 million cubic feet of evaporation (5.47 million cubic meters) in order to maintain an equilibrium of water level. The annual inflow of the Jordan River system alone, before these modern conservation efforts were undertaken, was approximately 47.1 billion cubic feet (1.335 billion cubic meters), which means that for most of biblical antiquity the Lower Jordan must have flowed with an approximate volume of today's Colorado or Susquehanna rivers, whereas today it is but a trickle.

The Dead Sea is also the world's most hypersaline lake. Average ocean salinity is 3.5 percent. The Great Salt Lake is about 18 percent salt, and Shark's Bay, Australia, contains a little more than 20 percent salinity. But several factors combine to create a water salinity in the Dead Sea that ranges between 26 and 35 percent: (1) it is fed by some streams that are unusually saline, flowing through nitrous soil and sulfurous springs; (2) it is contaminated by an infusion of chemical salts found in its underlying fault line (sodium chloride, calcium chloride, potassium chloride, magnesium bromide); and (3) it is exposed to the erosive defilement of Mt. Sedom, a very deep and massively cavernous rock-salt plug that stretches for five miles along its southwestern shore. The high salt content

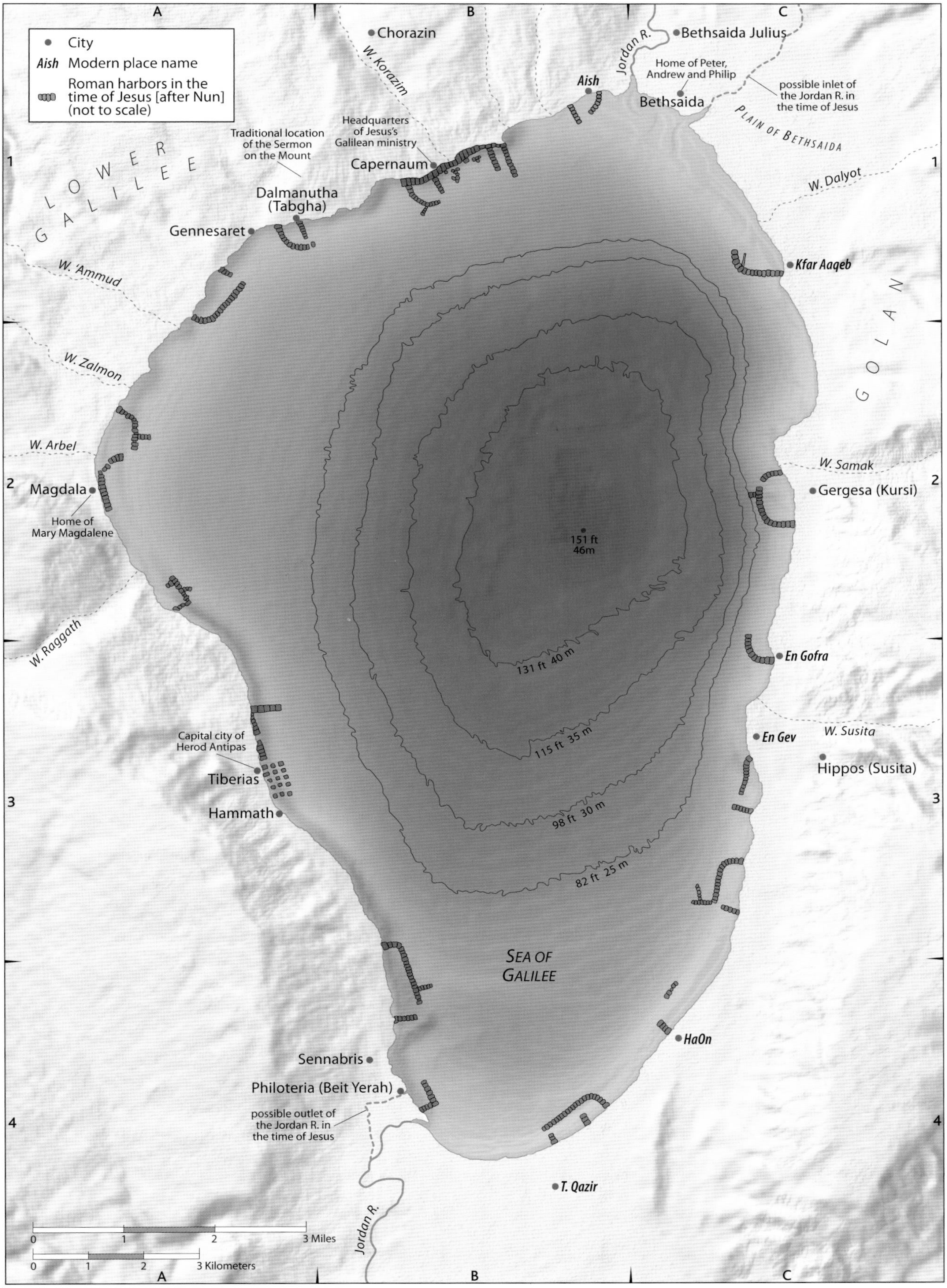
A
B
C
1
2
3
4
City
Aish Modern place name
Roman harbors in the time of Jesus [after Nun] (not to scale)
Chorazin
W. Korazim
Jordan R.
Bethsaida Julius
Home of Peter, Andrew and Philip
Aish
Bethsaida
possible inlet of the Jordan R. in the time of Jesus
Plain of Bethsaida
Traditional location of the Sermon on the Mount
Headquarters of Jesus's Galilean ministry
Capernaum
Lower Galilee
Dalmanutha (Tabgha)
Gennesaret
W. Dalyot
Kfar Aaqeb
W. 'Ammud
Golan
W. Zalmon
W. Arbel
W. Samak
Magdala
Home of Mary Magdalene
Gergesa (Kursi)
151 ft 46m
131 ft 40 m
W. Raggath
En Gofra
Capital city of Herod Antipas
En Gev
W. Susita
115 ft 35 m
Hippos (Susita)
Tiberias
Hammath
98 ft 30 m
82 ft 25 m
Sea of Galilee
HaOn
Sennabris
Philoteria (Beit Yerah)
possible outlet of the Jordan R. in the time of Jesus
T. Qazir
Jordan R.
0 1 2 3 Miles
0 1 2 3 Kilometers

prevents aquatic life in the Dead Sea, aside from a few microorganisms (simple bacteria, green and red algae, protozoa) that have recently been discovered.[98]

At times throughout history, however, the minerals of the Dead Sea have caused the surrounding real estate to increase in value. One commodity prized since at least the Neolithic period[99] is bitumen, a form of petroleum hardened through evaporation and oxidation, and used for sealing and gluing purposes, basket-weaving, medicine, and in the manufacture of mud bricks. Bitumen from the Dead Sea was used as a preservative agent in ancient Egyptian mummies.[100] During the New Testament era, Dead Sea bitumen trade was controlled by the Nabateans, and it has been suggested that Cleopatra's desire to govern the area around the Dead Sea was stimulated by her eagerness to regulate bitumen trade.

Also in high demand was Dead Sea balsam, the most highly prized perfume and medication in the classical world.[101] Galen, the noted second-century A.D. physician affiliated with the famous Asklepeion at Pergamum, is said to have traveled from his home in Asia Minor as far as the Dead Sea for the express purpose of returning with "true balsam."[102] Another Dead Sea mineral, potassium chloride, became popular in the 20th century for use in the manufacture of chemical fertilizer. Meanwhile, bathing in the thermo-mineral springs along the Dead Sea has become a popular treatment for various skin ailments, especially psoriasis.[103] In that sense, perhaps one can say that the Dead Sea has been coming to life in recent times.

Yet in antiquity, the ominous description of the Dead Sea chasm is reflected in the pages of Scripture. The destruction of Sodom and Gomorrah (Gen. 19) transpired in close proximity to this Sea. [**See map 15.**] Though the exact nature of the destruction rained upon the two cities has been variously interpreted either as a volcanic eruption or a spontaneous explosion of subsurface pockets of bituminous soil, karstic salt pillars (known as "Lot's wife") are a frequent phenomenon in the Dead Sea area. It is almost predictable that the howling wilderness surrounding the Dead Sea should have provided a suitable refuge for the fugitive David (1 Sam. 21—31) as well as Qumran Essenes and the disenfranchised Jewish insurgents of the first Jewish rebellion. [**See map 15 for the locations of Dead Sea textual discoveries.**] It was amid similar barrenness that Jesus was confronted with his temptations (Matt. 4:1–11); perhaps such dismal surroundings contributed to the anguish he felt. On the other hand, the prophet Ezekiel (47:1–12; cf. Zech. 14:8) envisioned a time when even the brinish waters of the Dead Sea will be re-created afresh and the stark lifeless character of the water will brim with life.

Beginning with the Sebkha ("salt swamps") south of the Dead Sea, the Great Rift Valley forms a rounded trough that narrows to the Gulf of Aqaba. There it begins to broaden again toward the Red Sea, and the Gulf is flanked by craggy slopes and high cliffs that rise in excess of 2,500 feet. Then again, there are depths in the Gulf of Aqaba not more than a mile away from those cliffs where the water depth exceeds 6,000 feet.[104]

Transjordanian Plateau

The fourth and easternmost physiographical zone is known as the Transjordanian Plateau. The region of the plateau immediately flanks the Arabah and is designated in the Bible as "beyond the Jordan" (Gen. 50:10; Num. 22:1; Deut. 1:5; Josh. 1:14; 1 Sam. 31:7; 1 Chron. 12:37). As a whole, the physical topography of Transjordan is more uniform in character than that of Cisjordan.[105]

Transjordan's high tableland stretches about 250 miles in length (from Mt. Hermon to the Red Sea), is between

The stark Judean Wilderness drops off precipitously down to the Dead Sea. For scale, note a modern road notched into the vertical topography.

The Dead Sea

map 15

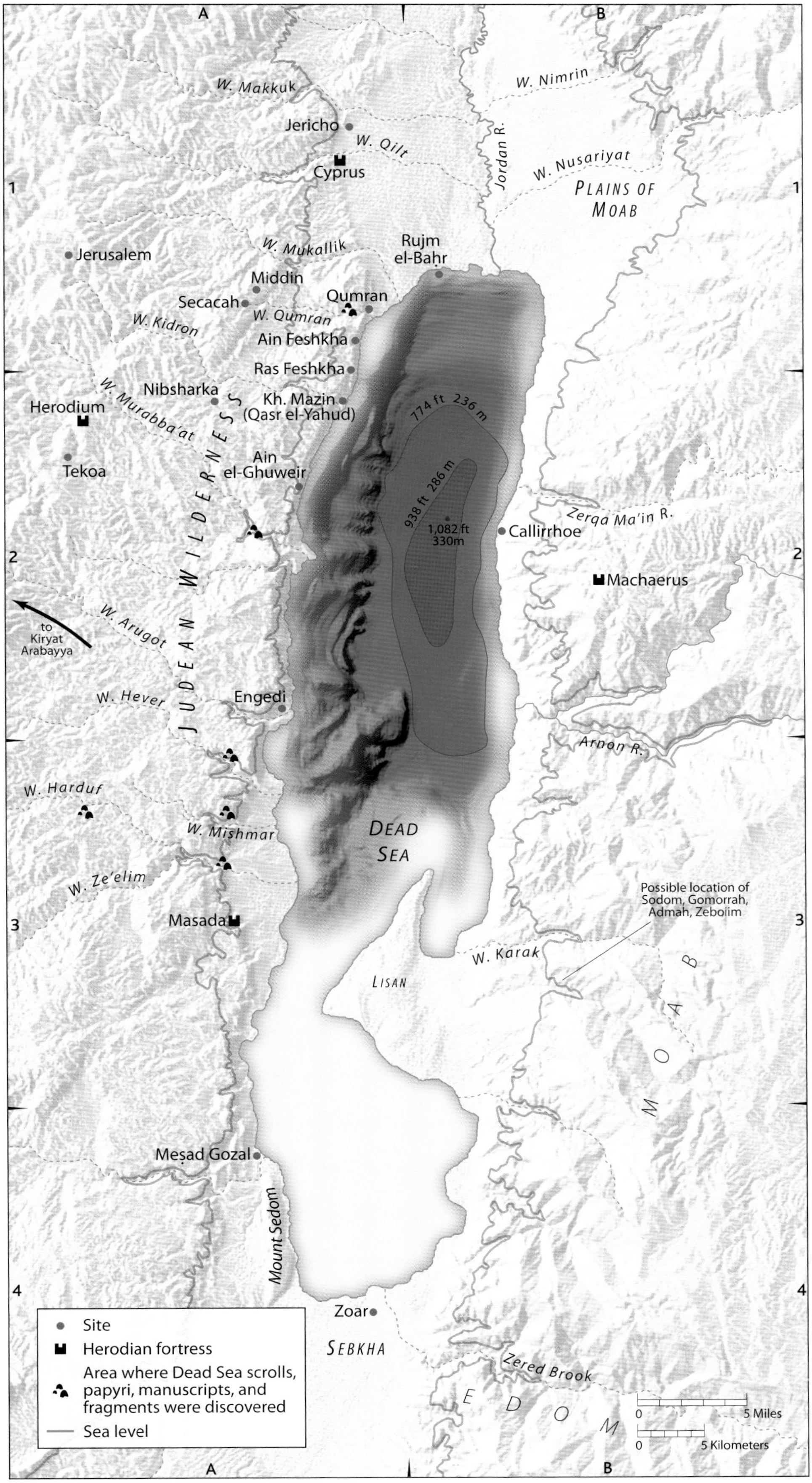

30 and 80 miles in width, and rises to heights of 5,000 feet above the sea. [**See map 8.**] Its significant precipitation has carved four deep, largely lateral gorges, through which run the Yarmuk, Jabbok, Arnon, and Zered rivers. Overlying a sandstone foundation that is exposed in those four cavernous ravines and in a few southern sections, the surface of Transjordan is composed chiefly of limestone in the north, with a thin basalt covering north of the Yarmuk. [**See map 16.**] The highlands continue southward with granite outcroppings that form the eastern wall of the Arabah. In the agricultural season, therefore, the northern regions of Transjordan are fertile, as the better-watered soil can produce large supplies of various grains, especially wheat (cf. Amos 4:1–3). During the Roman period, this region served as a breadbasket for the whole Syro-Palestinian province.

East of the main drainage divide, which lies at a level of about 3,000 feet and at a distance of 15 to 40 miles from the Jordan rift, there develops a rather sudden transition from steppe to the Eastern Desert. Many parts of the Gilead Dome, for example, are rich in brooks and springs with good drinking water, whereas east of the watershed, cisterns are necessary. The seasonal lushness of grain fields gives way to intermittent shallow grasses foraged by the animals of migrating nomads.

It is a destitute land

The land allotted to biblical Israel possesses meager physical and economic resource.[106] It contains virtually no precious metals (small quantities of low-grade copper ore, and a little iron and manganese), and a very limited range of minerals (various Dead Sea evaporates). Natural gas has been discovered in the modern Negeb. Despite repeated claims to the contrary, no substantial fields of petroleum have been found there.[107] The land possesses scant hardwood timber resources, and it does not have a sufficient fresh water supply. (See sections that follow concerning hydrology and forestation.)

THE LAND'S GEOLOGY

The broad outlines of the land's geological history can be reconstructed from rock formations that outcrop primarily in the areas south of the Dead Sea in eastern Sinai, in the walls of the Arabah, in the canyons cut by Transjordanian rivers, and from rocks encountered through modern drilling efforts. [**See map 16.**] This evidence suggests widespread activities of immense proportion and complexity, much too complicated to warrant full discussion here. Nevertheless, because the story of how God prepared this land for his people is intricately linked to the creation of mountains and valleys (Deut. 8:7; 11:11; Ps. 65:6; 90:2; cf. Rev. 6:14), what follows is a brief and simplified sketch of the processes by which this landscape appears to have been fashioned.

> You set the earth on its foundations,
> so that it can never be shaken.
> You covered it with the deep as with a garment,
> the waters stood above the mountains.
> But at your rebuke the waters fled;
> at the sound of your thunder they took to flight.
> The mountains rose, and the valleys sank down
> to the place you appointed for them.
> You set a boundary which they cannot cross,
> so that they might not again cover the earth.
> (Psalm 104:5–9)

This entire region lies along the shattered edge of an ancient landmass upon which rest Arabia and northeast Africa today. Successive layers of sandstone formations were deposited over a platform of metamorphosed igneous (volcanic) rocks—granite, porphyry, diorite, and the like. It would appear that the southern and eastern sectors of the land were exposed to this deposition for lengthier and more frequent periods. Sandstone formations in southeastern Transjordan are measured in thousands of feet, whereas they are much thinner in the north and in Cisjordan.

Later, in what geologists call the "great Cretaceous transgression," the entire region was gradually and repeatedly submerged in water from an ocean, of which the present Mediterranean Sea is but a vestige. Actually a recurring series of transgressions caused by slow movements in the earth's surface, the event deposited several varieties of limestone formations. One result was the greater part of rocks exposed today in Cisjordan, including the Cenomanian, Turonian, Senonian, and Eocene deposits.

As a rule of thumb, Cenomanian deposits are the hardest because they contain the highest concentrations of silica and calcium. They are therefore most resistant to erosion (and thus stand at the highest elevations) but dissolve into higher quality of erosive soils (e.g., red terra rosa soils). [**See map 17.**] They are more impermeable to water, making them a prime source of springs and cisterns, and are better for architectural purposes. By way of contrast, Senonian deposits are the softest and are therefore given to comparatively rapid erosion. They dissolve into chemically poorer soils and are found at lower and flatter elevations. Eocene formations are chalkier and mixed with layers of dark, hard flint, sometimes interlaced with thinly bedded chert of almost pure silica. However, where they contain a high calcium content, as in the Shephela, Eocene limestones weather into brown alluvial soils. Brown alluvium is theoretically less rich than terra rosa, yet it supports a wider range of crops and trees, is easier to till, is less affected by runoff, and thus has deeper and more heavily textured deposits.

In a word, then, from Cenomanian (and also Turonian) formations emerge mountains, sometimes high and precipitous, making them attractive to masons and city-dwellers seeking safety. Eocene formations can erode to form fertile lowlands, making them desirable to farmers and vinedressers, and Senonian deposits weather into flat valleys, which prove to be welcomed by travelers. A comparison of **maps 16 and 27** will show how many of the narrow Senonian troughs have provided roadways in the Levant (e.g., west of Lake Hula to the Sea of Galilee; the ascent of Beth-horon; the Mt. Carmel passes of Jokneam, Megiddo, and Taanach; the moat separating the Shephela from the central spine; and the diagonal trough from Shechem to Beth-shan).

The final act of the great Cretaceous drama included the creation of a large lake, called the Lisan. It inundated the terrain of the Jordan valley lower than 650 feet below sea level—the area from the northern end of the Sea of Galilee to a point about 25 miles south of the present Dead Sea. Formed during a pluvial period in which there was excessively heavy and extended precipitation, this brackish lake was responsible for laying down as much as 500 feet of the sedimentary strata found in the terrain it covered. During the same time, the Transjordanian streams also carved out their deep, spectacular gorges. As the rains gradually diminished and evaporation lowered the level of the Lisan lake, thousands of very thin salt-laden laminations of Lisan marl were gradually uncovered. Alternately mixed with gypsum and dark calcite, these paper-thin strata are the

The Geology of Palestine

map 16

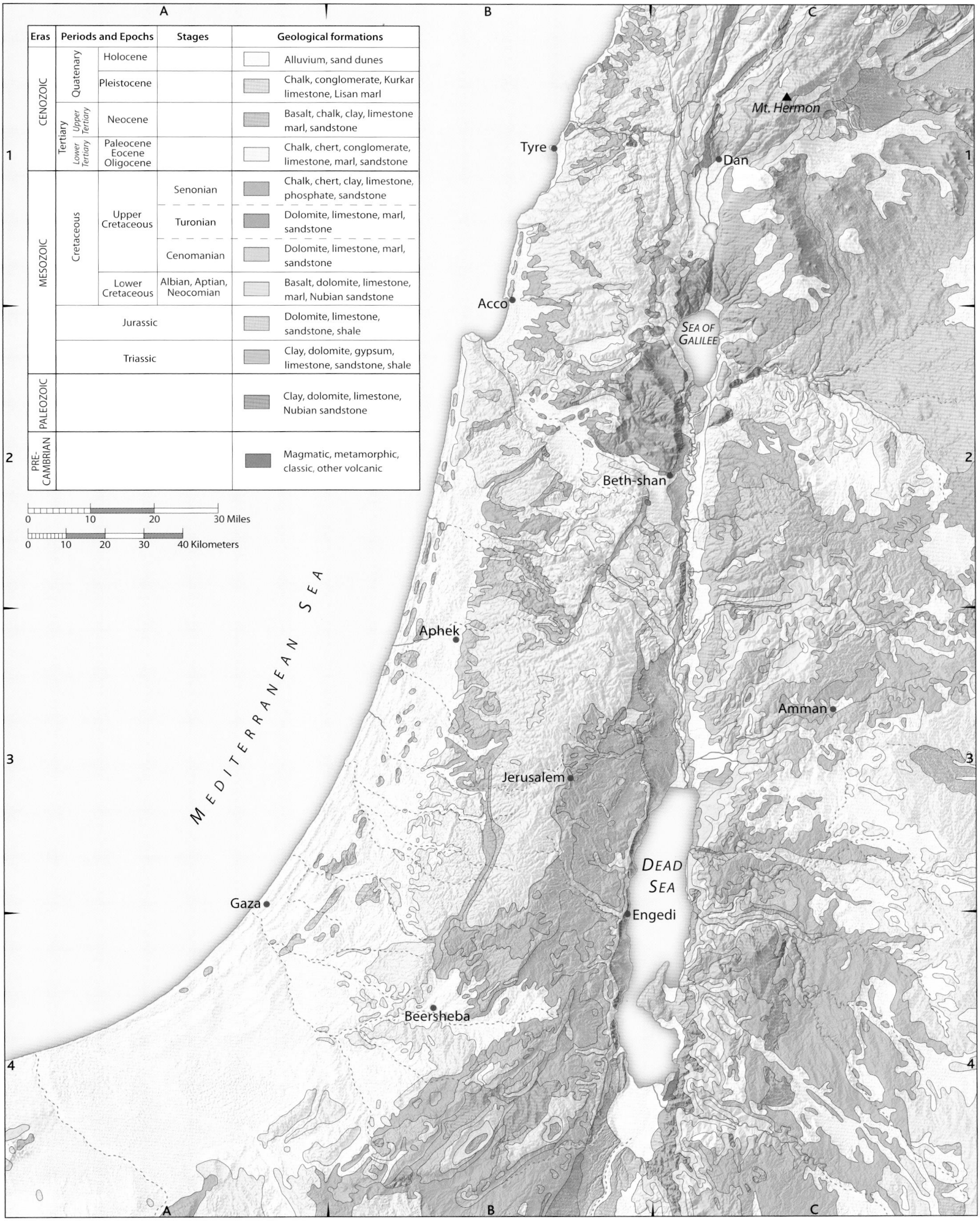
Eras
Periods and Epochs
Stages
Geological formations
CENOZOIC
Quaternary
Holocene
Alluvium, sand dunes
Pleistocene
Chalk, conglomerate, Kurkar limestone, Lisan marl
Tertiary
Upper Tertiary
Neocene
Basalt, chalk, clay, limestone marl, sandstone
Lower Tertiary
Paleocene Eocene Oligocene
Chalk, chert, conglomerate, limestone, marl, sandstone
MESOZOIC
Cretaceous
Upper Cretaceous
Senonian
Chalk, chert, clay, limestone, phosphate, sandstone
Turonian
Dolomite, limestone, marl, sandstone
Cenomanian
Dolomite, limestone, marl, sandstone
Lower Cretaceous
Albian, Aptian, Neocomian
Basalt, dolomite, limestone, marl, Nubian sandstone
Jurassic
Dolomite, limestone, sandstone, shale
Triassic
Clay, dolomite, gypsum, limestone, sandstone, shale
PALEOZOIC
Clay, dolomite, limestone, Nubian sandstone
PRE-CAMBRIAN
Magmatic, metamorphic, classic, other volcanic
0 10 20 30 Miles
0 10 20 30 40 Kilometers
A
B
C
1
2
3
4
Mt. Hermon
Tyre
Dan
Acco
SEA OF GALILEE
Beth-shan
MEDITERRANEAN SEA
Aphek
Amman
Jerusalem
DEAD SEA
Gaza
Engedi
Beersheba

predominant characteristic of the southern rift and northern Arabah nowadays. This pluvial period also deposited a thick accumulation of shale on the Coastal Plain and created the ridges of kurkar that align the Mediterranean's shoreline. More recent deposits include layers of sandy alluvium (from water erosion) and loess (from wind erosion), both commonly characteristic of the contemporary Coastal Plain.

THE LAND'S HYDROLOGY

It is no coincidence that the chief god of Egypt (Amon-Re) was a solar deity, as was the head of the Mesopotamian pantheon (Marduk).[108] In contrast, the great god of Canaan (Baal) was a rain/fertility god. Herein lies a story with profound and far-reaching consequences for anyone wishing to live in Canaan, a story that controlled much of the Canaanite worldview and at times came to absorb Israelite thinking as well. The story is a direct reflection of certain hydrological realities in this land.

Simply stated, it never needs to rain in Egypt or Mesopotamia. Each of those ancient lands was endowed with the rich heritage of a great river. From the Nile and Euphrates, Egyptian and Mesopotamian civilizations respectively drew their sustenance and life, irrigated their crops, and watered their flocks and herds. Each of these rivers offered a vast supply of fresh water, more than ever could have been consumed by the societies they fed and sustained. As long as there was sufficient precipitation hundreds of miles away in the mountains of Ethiopia and Uganda (for the Nile) and the rugged highlands of eastern Turkey (for the Euphrates), it never needed to rain in Egypt or much of Mesopotamia. And in reality, it scarcely ever did! Survival in those parts depended upon nourishment from rivers that could be tapped and utilized in the greenhouse-like environment created along their banks by the warmth of the sun.

In Canaan, by way of sharp contrast, survival depended precisely upon rainfall. In this land, there were no great rivers, and what meager riverine resources did exist were incapable of meeting the inhabitants' needs. Certainly the Jordan River coursed through the land, but south of the Sea of Galilee it lay at such a low altitude and was always so heavily laden with chemicals that its potential nourishment was essentially lost to Canaanite society. Amid the historical trend of civilizations emerging along the banks of rivers, the Jordan stands as a conspicuous exception.[109]

Apart from the Jordan, Canaan possessed only a trickle of fresh groundwater. [**See map 18.**] The Jarkon River, which rises from springs near Aphek and flows into the Mediterranean just north of Joppa, produced sufficient dampness in antiquity to force travel to its inland side, but not until the 20th century were its resources finally tapped. The Kishon River, which drains part of the Jezreel valley before being emptied into the Mediterranean in the Acco Plain, is little more than a brook for much of the year. And the Harod River, which enters the Jordan opposite Beth-shan, flows from a single spring at the foot of Mt. Gilboa. So it was that the Canaanites, and even the covenant community of God, would in this land experience survival or death, crop success or failure, fertility or drought, precisely as a consequence of storms that might deposit their rainfall upon a land that was otherwise incapable of sustaining human existence.

It is a recurring, even formulaic, pattern for the authors of Scripture to sermonize that faith produces blessing whereas faithlessness results in condemnation. Perhaps nothing more forcefully underscored this pattern than rainfall dependence. For example, near to the inception of Israel's national existence at Sinai, the people were instructed about the consequences of faith: "If you . . . observe my commandments . . . then I will give you rains in their season, and the land shall yield its increase . . . but if you will not hearken to me . . . I will make your heavens like iron and your earth like brass . . . and your land shall not yield its increase" (Lev. 26:3–20). Later, as the people were about to embark on their mission of settling Canaan, they were given one of the most vivid and complete descriptions of that land's hydrological properties. "The land which you are going to enter to take possession of is not like the land of Egypt, from which you have come, where you sowed your seed and watered it with your foot [referring either to a kind of water-lifting device operated by foot power or to irrigation sluice gates that could be raised by foot to permit waters to flow into secondary channels], like a garden of vegetables; but the land which you are going over to possess is a land of hills and valleys, which drinks water by the rain from heaven, a land which the Lord your God cares for; the eyes of the Lord your God are always upon it, from the beginning of the year to the end of the year" (Deut. 11:10–12). The biblical author then proceeded to contrast faith and fertility (vv. 13–17). His message was, in effect, that if the Israelites obeyed God's commands, he would send both the former and latter rains so that the people could gather in grain, wine, and oil. But should their hearts prove faithless, in anger God would shut up the heavens and there would be no rain. It seems clear, then, that fertility in that land became a function of faith, and that life itself in that particular terrain was imperiled by lack of rainfall, with its ensuing drought and famine.

Moreover, both of the previous texts clearly sound a note that is echoed in many other passages, in each section and genre of biblical literature: it is God who benevolently sustains life in the land of promise by bestowing the blessing of rainfall (e.g., Deut. 28:12; 2 Chron. 7:13–14; Job 5:10; 28:25–26; 36:27–28; Pss. 65:9–13; 135:7; 147:8, 18; Isa. 30:23–25; Ezek. 34:26; Hos. 6:3; Amos 9:6; Zech. 10:1; Mal. 3:10; Matt. 5:45; Acts 14:17; Heb. 6:7). Similarly, it is within God's sovereign prerogative to withhold rain as a sign of his displeasure and judgment (e.g., Deut. 28:22–24; 1 Kings 8:35–36; 17:1; 2 Chron. 6:26–27; Job 12:15; Isa. 5:6; Jer. 3:3; 14:1–6; Amos 4:7–8;

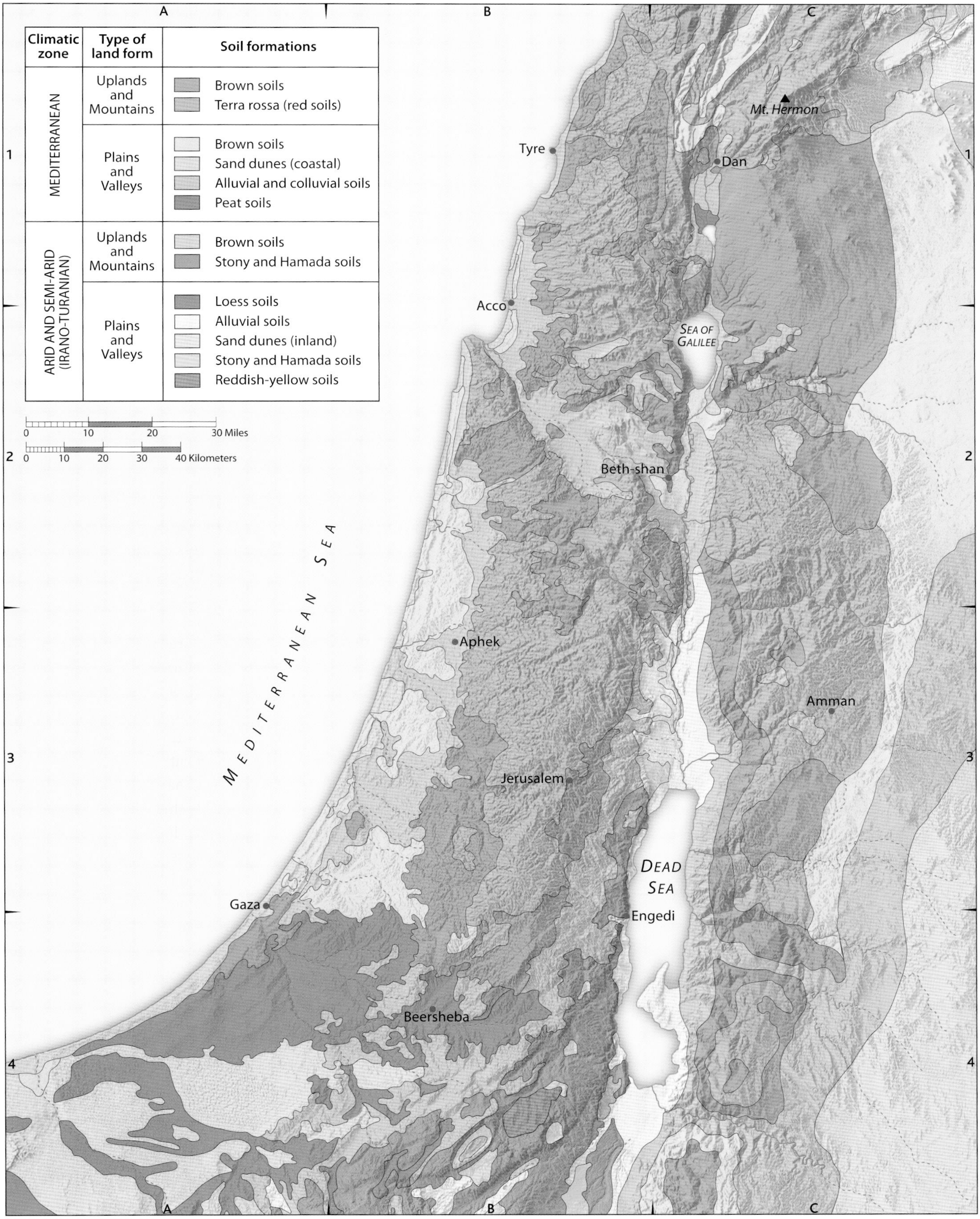
A
B
C
1
2
3
4
Climatic zone
Type of land form
Soil formations
MEDITERRANEAN
Uplands and Mountains
Brown soils
Terra rossa (red soils)
Plains and Valleys
Brown soils
Sand dunes (coastal)
Alluvial and colluvial soils
Peat soils
ARID AND SEMI-ARID (IRANO-TURANIAN)
Uplands and Mountains
Brown soils
Stony and Hamada soils
Plains and Valleys
Loess soils
Alluvial soils
Sand dunes (inland)
Stony and Hamada soils
Reddish-yellow soils
0 10 20 30 Miles
0 10 20 30 40 Kilometers
Mt. Hermon
Tyre
Dan
Acco
SEA OF GALILEE
Beth-shan
MEDITERRANEAN SEA
Aphek
Amman
Jerusalem
DEAD SEA
Gaza
Engedi
Beersheba

Zech. 14:17).[110] It appears that this theological reality was employed by authors of Scripture precisely because of the dynamic hydrological implications that would have been all too evident to anyone attempting to survive in Canaan. For the ancient Israelite, rainfall was a providentially conditioned factor.[111]

At times in Israel's history, God became so displeased with their behavior that he withheld from them both rain *and dew* (e.g., 1 Kings 17:1; Hag. 1:10–11; cf. Gen. 27:39; 2 Sam. 1:21; Isa. 26:19; Hos. 14:5; Job 29:19).[112] Certainly few North American or European farmers ever experience crop success primarily because of the presence of dew. Yet in ancient Israel where water was scarce and unavailable except from the heavens, crop growth in certain seasons depended entirely upon the formation of dew. This was especially true when grapes and figs were ripening in the early autumn just prior to the start of the "former rains."[113] Under normal circumstances, the Coastal Plain south of Gaza, the central Jezreel valley (Judg. 6:36–40), the heights of Mt. Carmel, and the western Negeb all experience about 250 dew nights annually.[114]

Some scholars have even asserted, with good reason, that the interconnection between precipitation, faith, and life may best explain why the Israelites, having crossed the Jordan River and taken up residence in Canaan, could so quickly and completely apostatize. Perhaps no generation of Israelites living before the time of Christ had experienced the element of divine miracle in a more convincing manner than those who participated in the settlement of their land. Yet their children and grandchildren became quickly and thoroughly enamored of the god Baal and of Canaanite Baalism (Judg. 6:25–32; 1 Sam. 4:5–8; 1 Kings 16:32–33; 19:10–14), and their syncretism became the dismally recurring theme of the book of Judges. That later generation let the prophetic exhortations go unheeded, and they soon found themselves to be functional Canaanites—people who sought to guarantee a sufficient rainfall through the practices of the fertility cult.

Canaanite Baalism was committed to a cyclical (not a linear) worldview, in which the phenomenal world, namely the forces of nature, were personified. So proponents of Baalism could not appreciate that the seasons of the year were rhythmic and mechanically regular. Such seasonal variation and recurrence was perceived in terms of cosmic struggles. When the dry springtime season commenced with its ensuing cessation of rainfall and death of vegetation, they wrongly inferred that the god of sterility (Mot) had slain his opponent, Baal. Conversely, when the autumn early rains began to fall so that seeds could be planted and crops later harvested, Baalism again mistakenly inferred that the god of fertility (Baal) had been resurrected and restored to prominence.

Moreover, Canaanite Baalism's failure to perceive that seasonal variation was governed by the inevitability of natural law led to the belief that the outcome of cosmic struggles was in doubt and could be humanly manipulated. Accordingly, when the Canaanites wished their deities to perform certain actions, they believed they could persuade them by performing the same actions themselves in a cultic setting, a practice known today as "sympathetic magic." For them, the ongoing triumph of Baal was tantamount to having assured, enduring fertility. This desire gave rise to the sacred prostitute, a male or female sacred personage whose actions were thought integral to anticipate, induce, and participate in Baal's intercourse with the land. (They perceived rainfall as Baal's semen.) According to Canaan's fertility worship, when Baal triumphed, women would be fertile, flocks and herds would reproduce in abundance, and fields would be standing full of grain.

The prophets, beginning with Moses, inveighed against the wholesale adoption of this abomination (Deut. 4—26; cf. Jer. 2:7–8, 22–23; 11:13; Hos. 4:12–14; Mic. 1:7). Yet despite all warnings, the hydrologic reality of the land apparently led the Israelites to suppose that they too needed Canaanite rites to survive in a place that was so rainfall dependent (1 Sam. 12:2–18; 1 Kings 14:22–24; 2 Kings 23:6–7; 2 Chron. 15:16; Jer. 3:2–5; Ezek. 8:14–15; 23:37–45). Israel soon began to attribute the good gifts of the land to Baal, not Yahweh (Isa. 1:3–9; Jer. 2:7; Hos. 2:5–13), and eventually the Israelites went so far as to call Yahweh "Baal" (Hos. 2:16). The recurring biblical theme of "playing the harlot" represented profoundly more than just theological metaphor (Judg. 2:17; 8:27, 33; 1 Chron. 5:25; Ezek. 6:9; Hos. 4:12; 9:1; cf. Deut. 31:16; 1 Kings 14:24; 2 Kings 23:7). Moreover, in the end, the adoption of this degeneracy contributed to Israel's defeat and exile (e.g., 1 Chron. 5:26; 9:1; Ps. 106:34–43; Jer. 5:18–28; 9:12–16; 44:5–30; Ezek. 6:1–7; 33:23–29).

It is highly probable that the characteristic expression most commonly used in the Bible to describe Israel's inheritance— "a land flowing with milk and honey"—likewise addresses this issue of rainfall dependence. Modern westerners are apt to see in this metaphor a connotation of lush fertility and abundance, of a veritable paradise or luxuriant Garden of Eden, but the expression paints quite another picture. To begin with, the "principle of first reference" may be germane to this metaphor: when the expression first arises in the canon and the history of Israel, it is employed specifically to contrast Israel's life in Egypt with what life would be like in Canaan (Ex. 3:8, 17). And whereas the metaphor is also used to describe the land of God's covenant with Israel (Deut. 6:3; 31:20; Josh. 5:6; Jer. 11:5), later Scripture also employs the metaphor to rehearse this sharp contrast between Egypt and Canaan (e.g., Deut. 11:9–12; 26:8–9; Jer. 32:21–23; Ezek. 20:6). The text of Deuteronomy 11:8–17 is particularly insightful in this regard: here the land of milk and honey is a place that will be conditionally fertile as a function of faith, contrasted with the assured fertility of Egypt.[115]

The commodities involved also seem to point away from the notion of lush fertility (cf. Isa. 7:15–25). The word for "milk"

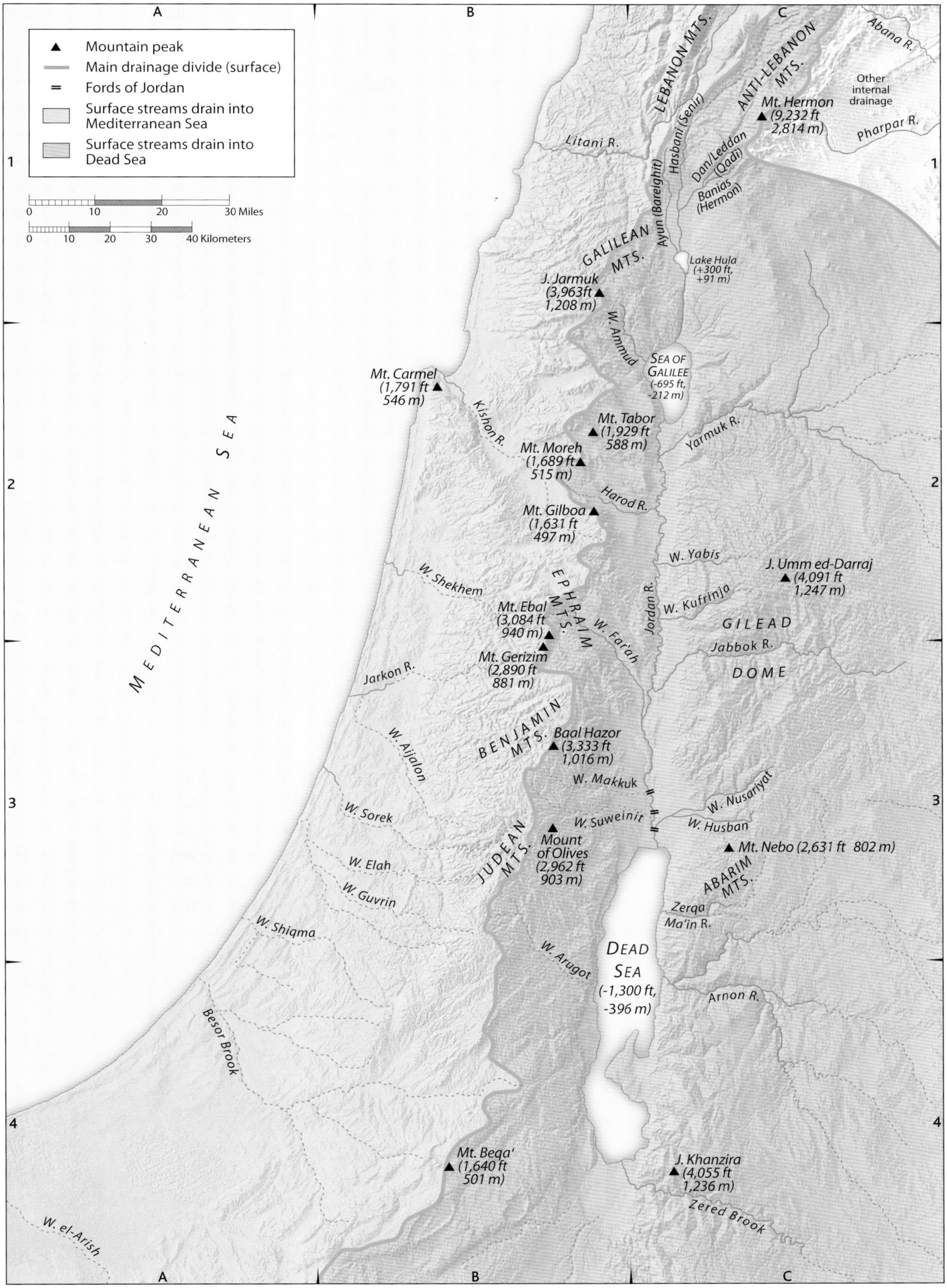
Mountain peak
Main drainage divide (surface)
Fords of Jordan
Surface streams drain into Mediterranean Sea
Surface streams drain into Dead Sea
0 10 20 30 Miles
0 10 20 30 40 Kilometers
LEBANON MTS.
ANTI-LEBANON MTS.
Abana R.
Other internal drainage
Mt. Hermon (9,232 ft 2,814 m)
Pharpar R.
Litani R.
Hasbani (Senir)
Dan/Leddan (Qadi)
Banias (Hermon)
Ayun (Bareighit)
GALILEAN MTS.
Lake Hula (+300 ft, +91 m)
J. Jarmuk (3,963ft 1,208 m)
W. Ammud
SEA OF GALILEE (-695 ft, -212 m)
Mt. Carmel (1,791 ft 546 m)
Kishon R.
MEDITERRANEAN SEA
Mt. Tabor (1,929 ft 588 m)
Yarmuk R.
Mt. Moreh (1,689 ft 515 m)
Harod R.
Mt. Gilboa (1,631 ft 497 m)
W. Yabis
J. Umm ed-Darraj (4,091 ft 1,247 m)
W. Shekhem
EPHRAIM MTS.
Jordan R.
W. Kufrinja
Mt. Ebal (3,084 ft 940 m)
W. Far'ah
GILEAD
Jabbok R.
DOME
Mt. Gerizim (2,890 ft 881 m)
Jarkon R.
BENJAMIN MTS.
Baal Hazor (3,333 ft 1,016 m)
W. Ajjalon
W. Makkuk
W. Nusariyat
W. Sorek
W. Suweinit
W. Husban
Mt. Nebo (2,631 ft 802 m)
JUDEAN MTS.
Mount of Olives (2,962 ft 903 m)
W. Elah
ABARIM MTS.
W. Guvrin
Zerqa Ma'in R.
W. Shiqma
DEAD SEA (-1,300 ft, -396 m)
W. Arugot
Arnon R.
Besor Brook
Mt. Beqa' (1,640 ft 501 m)
J. Khanzira (4,055 ft 1,236 m)
Zered Brook
W. el-Arish
A
B
C
1
2
3
4

(*ḥālāb*) is used commonly to refer to the milk of goats and sheep (Ex. 23:19; Deut. 14:21; 1 Sam. 7:9; Prov. 27:26–27), very rarely of cows (Deut. 32:14), and never of camels. The word for "honey" (*dᵉbaš*) is occasionally taken to refer to a syrup or jam made from grapes or dates, or secreted from certain trees, but in this context almost certainly must refer to bees' honey. The word is used specifically with bees (*dᵉbôrâ*, cf. Judg. 14:8–9), and it appears with several different words for honeycomb (Prov. 24:13; Song of Songs 4:11; cf. 1 Sam. 14:25–27; Ps. 19:10; Prov. 16:24; Song of Songs 5:1). Early Egyptian literature describes Canaan as having its own supply of honey,[116] an important observation in light of the well-established fact that domestic beekeeping was known quite early in Egypt.[117] Archaeological excavations in 2007 at the modern site of Rehov/Rehob, just south of Beth-shan [**map 44**], came upon unmistakable evidence of domestic beekeeping in Canaan, radiometrically dating to the period of Israel's united monarchy. In addition to honey, traces of beeswax and parts of bees' bodies have been extracted from the apiary, and the rows of beehives found there thus far are thought to have been able to produce as much as 1,000 pounds of honey annually.[118]

The commodities referenced in the metaphor describing the land must be goats' milk and bees' honey: both items are products of identical topographic and economic conditions (Isa. 7:15–25; Job 20:17) and of uncultivated grazing areas. Neither is the product of cultivated farmland. Accordingly, one should conclude that the commodities of milk and honey are pastoral in nature, not agricultural. The land, therefore, is being described as a pastoral realm.[119]

The force of this final observation may be felt when one contrasts milk and honey with the commodities from Egypt cited in the Bible (Num. 11:4–9). As the people of Israel were moving through the desert, they became disenchanted with their monotonous daily diet of manna, and they reflected longingly on their former diet in Egypt (fish, cucumbers, melons, leeks, onions, and garlic). What they got hungry for, in addition to fish, were commodities that could be planted and harvested. In other words, while in Egypt, Israelites ate primarily an agricultural diet, and the notion of pastoralism is nowhere to be found in this text. Egypt seems to be portrayed primarily as an agricultural place of the farmer, whereas the land of Israel's inheritance is portrayed primarily as a pastoral place of the shepherd. This is not to say that shepherds were not present in Egypt (cf. Gen. 46:34), nor that farmers were not found in Canaan (cf. Matt. 22:5); it is to suggest that Egypt was a *predominantly* agricultural environment, whereas Canaan was predominantly pastoral in character. In moving from Egypt to a "land flowing with milk and honey," Israel would experience a dramatic change of environment and lifestyle.

This probably also explains why the Bible contains very little mention of farmers, cows, and herds. Yet it is filled with pastoral references:

- Shepherds (1 Sam. 17:40; 1 Kings 22:17; Ps. 23:1; Isa. 13:20; 40:11; Jer. 31:10; Ezek. 34:2; Amos 3:12; Zech. 10:2; John 10:11; Heb. 13:20; 1 Pet. 5:4);
- Sheep/lambs/goats (Ex. 12:3–5; Josh. 7:24; 1 Sam. 8:17; 16:19; 2 Sam. 7:8; Neh. 3:1; Ps. 44:11; Isa. 13:14; Jer. 50:6; Zech. 13:7; Matt. 12:11; 25:32–33; John 1:29, 36; 21:15–16; Acts 8:32; Rev. 5:12; 21:22);
- Wolves (Isa. 11:6; 65:25; Matt. 7:15); and
- Flocks (Judg. 5:16; 1 Sam. 17:34; Job 24:2; Song of Songs 4:1; Isa. 40:11; Jer. 6:3; 51:23; Ezek. 34:12; Zeph. 2:14; 1 Pet. 5:2).

Accordingly, to say the land "flowed with milk and honey" served three primary purposes. The phrase (1) described the distinctively pastoral character of Israel's new environment; (2) contrasted that environment with Israel's previous lifestyle in Egypt; and (3) instructed them that fertility/survival in their new land would be a function of faith and a consequence of obedience. The Israelites would no longer be Egyptian subjects living in Egypt, but neither were they supposed to become Canaanite subjects living in Canaan. They were to be God's people who must live lives of faith in this unusual rainfall-dependent place of his choosing (sometimes referenced as geo-piety).

In light of the harsh hydrologic realities of the land, the need for conserving meager water supplies would have reigned supreme in Israel. So it is that the Bible is replete with references to water and related items with both positive and negative applications. We find mention of:

- Wells (Gen. 21:19; 26:18–22; Jer. 6:7; John 4:6–26);
- Cisterns (2 Chron. 26:10; Isa. 36:16);
- Fountains (Jer. 9:1; Zech. 13:1);
- Springs (Gen. 16:7; Judg. 7:1; Prov. 5:15–16);
- Water as a vehicle for conveying spiritual truth (Isa. 12:3–4; Rev. 22:17); and
- Water to symbolize *blessing* (Num. 24:6–7; Isa. 41:17–20; 44:3–5), *joy* (Isa. 35), *delight* (Ps. 1:1–3), and even *eschatological perfection* (Isa. 43:19–21; Jer. 31:10–14; Ezek. 47:1–12; Zech. 8:12; 14:8; Rev. 22:1–2).

On the other hand, the absence of water quickly resulted in a torrid and parched land (Pss. 63:1; 143:6). The resulting imagery was especially eloquent:

- Dried-up rivers (Ezek. 30:12; Nah. 1:4);
- Poisonous water (Jer. 23:15);
- Clouds without water (Prov. 25:14; Jude 12);
- Springs turned to dust (Ps. 107:33);
- Parched springs (Hos. 13:15);
- Dry fountains (Jer. 51:36);
- Polluted fountains (Prov. 25:26);
- Empty cisterns (Gen. 37:24; cf. 1 Sam. 13:6; Jer. 41:9); and
- Broken cisterns (Jer. 2:13).

Precipitation in Palestine

map 19

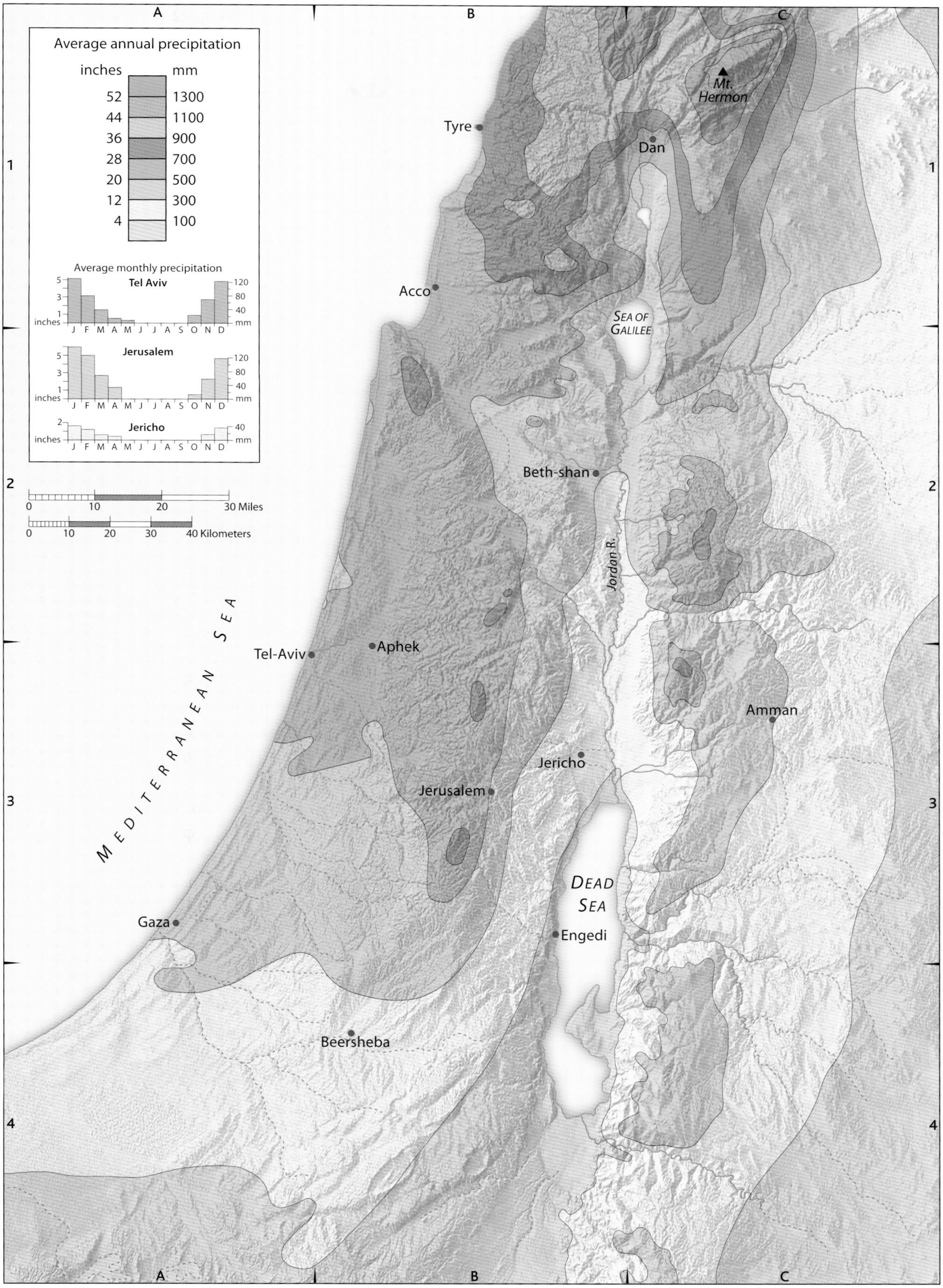
A
B
C
1
2
3
4
Average annual precipitation
inches
mm
52
1300
44
1100
36
900
28
700
20
500
12
300
4
100
Average monthly precipitation
Tel Aviv
Jerusalem
Jericho
J F M A M J J A S O N D
inches
mm
0
10
20
30 Miles
0
10
20
30
40 Kilometers
Mt. Hermon
Tyre
Dan
Acco
SEA OF GALILEE
Beth-shan
Jordan R.
MEDITERRANEAN SEA
Tel-Aviv
Aphek
Amman
Jericho
Jerusalem
DEAD SEA
Gaza
Engedi
Beersheba

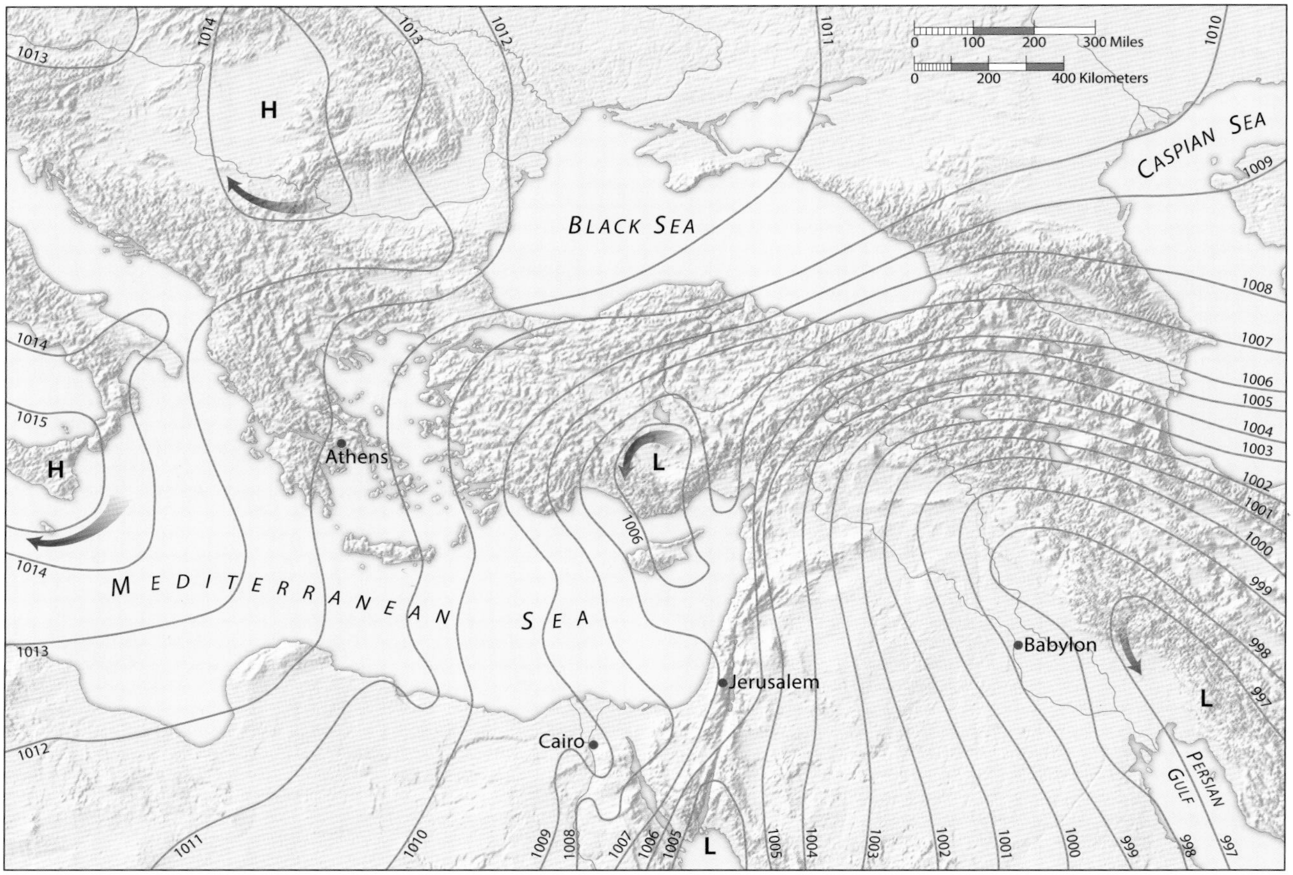

During the New Testament era, Greek and Roman hydrotechnologies partially relieved the dire water situation for some major cities. The Roman Empire was particularly effective in conveying water, sometimes across many miles, from its source(s) into principal urban areas. Refined technology created both open and enclosed aqueducts—water channels that may have included various forms of piping (stone, terra-cotta, lead, bronze, and even wood). Some of the conduits were built above ground and others were constructed underground.[120]

In addition to the massive architectural demands of construction, these systems also required considerable skill and sophistication in planning. The Romans took advantage of gravitational force, even across long distances of uneven or hilly terrain. They inserted vent pipes at certain intervals to reduce problems of water pressure or air pressure and to enable workers to clear out silting. They also used siphons to enable water to travel uphill to a repository above an adjoining valley, but below the level of the water source. Along with a network of aqueducts, the Romans created many open canals, sluice gates, sewers, dams, and water reservoirs.[121] As a result, most Roman urbanites enjoyed public baths, latrines, and fountains. Some had swimming pools and even dishwashing.[122] In Palestine, in particular, the ritual bath (*mikveh*) was introduced.

THE LAND'S CLIMATE

Like other places in the world,[123] this land's climatological realities were and are largely determined by a combination of four factors: (1) terrain configuration, including altitude, ground cover, angle of relief, and so forth; (2) locational relationship to larger bodies of water or continental landmasses; (3) direction and effect of principal air currents; and (4) latitude, which determines the length of daylight and darkness.

The land, situated between 29 and 33 degrees north latitude and dominated by prevailing westerly (oceanic) winds, has a climate marked by two sharply divided and well-defined seasons. Summer is a hot/dry period that runs from approximately mid-June to mid-September; winter is a warm/wet period extending between October and mid-June. It is a place of sea breezes, desert winds, semi-desert terrain, maximum solar radiation throughout most of the year, and seasonal variations of temperature and relative humidity. As such, its climate is quite similar to certain parts of the state of California, as expressed in the graph on the next page.

The word that most aptly characterizes the land's summer season is "stability." During summer, the jet stream (that allows for the depression and convection of air masses and produces storms) is forced northward to the vicinity of the Alps by the equatorial movement of the sun toward the northern hemisphere. As a consequence, a stationary high-pressure

The Atmosphere of the Middle East in Winter

map 21

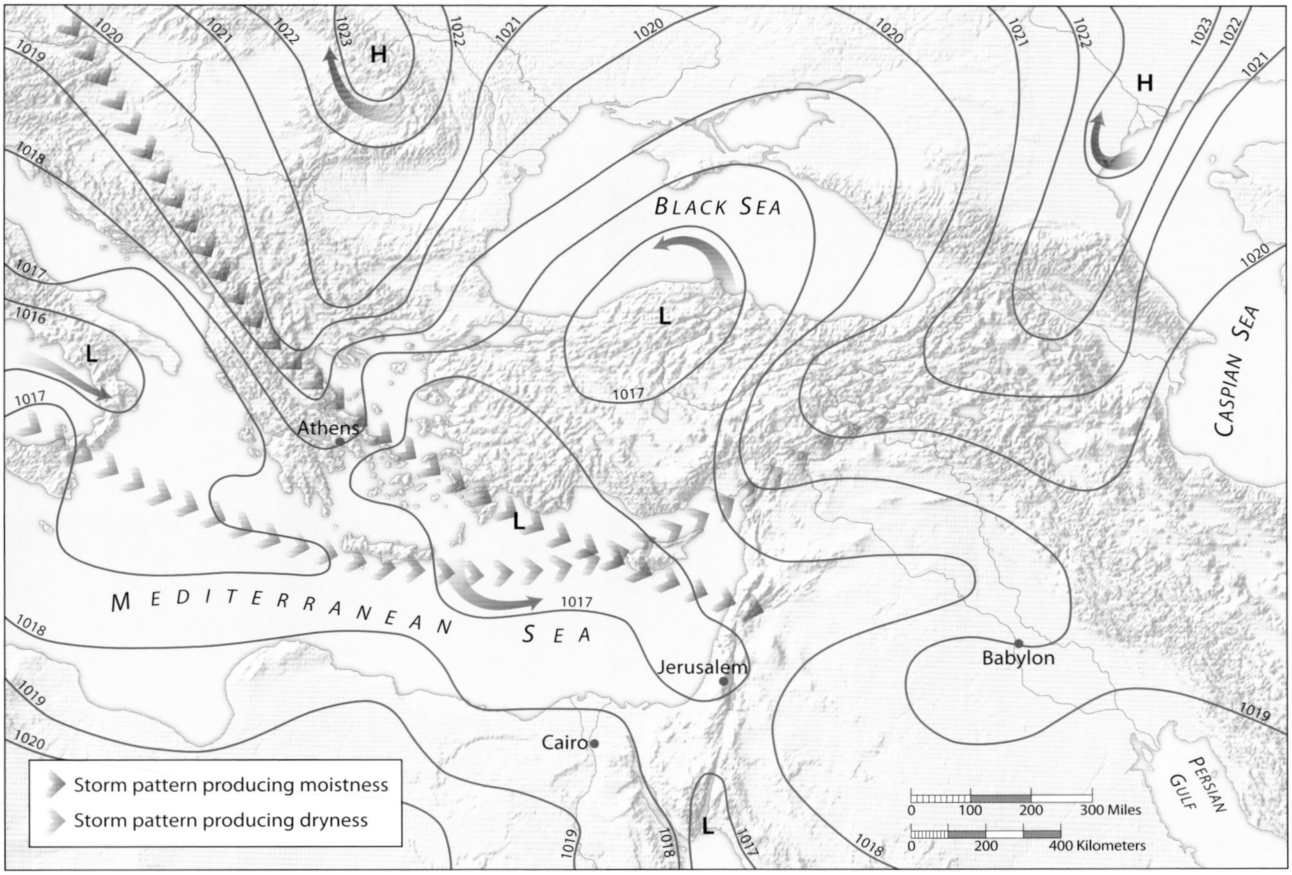

cell develops over the Azores, together with a monsoonal low over Iran and Pakistan, resulting in basically north-south isobars (barometric pressure lines) over Palestine. [**See map 20.**] A thermal barrier results that produces uniformly clear daylight conditions and prevents the formation of rain clouds, in spite of extremely high relative humidity. The summer features consistently fine weather, regular westerly breezes, daytime heat, and almost complete drought. Summer air masses, slightly cooled and moistened as they pass over the Mediterranean, condense to form some dew, which can nourish summer growth. But summer storms are most unexpected (1 Sam. 12:17–18).

On the other hand, the winter season is characterized by the word "instability." In winter, upper air masses take advantage of the equatorial path of the sun toward the southern hemisphere and become infused with extremely cold polarized air. The mixing of those air masses can create a number of dominant high-pressure currents [**map 21**], any one of which can collide unpredictably with the air that meanders through the Mediterranean depression:

1. The Asian high is a direct flow of polar air that can be as high as 1036 millibars. It sometimes traverses over the entire Syrian Desert and strikes the land of Israel from the east with a blast of freezing air and frost (Job 1:19).

Palestine environmental analogue	Tel Aviv	Jerusalem	Jericho
California environmental analogue	Azusa	Davis	Palm Springs
Mean temperature during coldest month (January)	55° F.	47° F.	57° F.
Mean temperature during warmest month (August)	81° F.	75° F.	88° F.
Maximum temperature	115° F.	107° F.	120° F.
Minimum temperature	37° F.	26° F.	36° F.
Precipitation: April through October	1.7 in.	1.3 in.	0.6 in.
Precipitation: December through February	15.3 in.	12.3 in.	3.8 in.
Annual Precipitation	20.8 in.	15.9 in.	5.0 in.
Average relative humidity	79%	69%	54%

2. The Balkan high, in the wake of a severe Mediterranean depression, can capture the moisture of a cyclonic storm and strike Israel from the west with rain, snow, and hail. This type of system is generally responsible for depositing rain and snow in the Levant (2 Sam. 23:20; 1 Chron. 11:22; Job 37:6; Ps. 68:14; Prov. 26:1).
3. A somewhat less intense Libyan high can be attracted toward the Negeb and carry dust storms that turn into rain.

The Mediterranean trough itself is a relatively stationary depression through which move about 25 cyclonic storms in an average winter season. An influx of warmer air takes about four to six days to cross the Mediterranean and to collide with one of these fronts. Should these depressions run a more southerly course, they tend to be deflected north of Cyprus and deposit their precipitation across eastern Europe. Such a course leaves the Levant deprived of its considerable moisture [**map 21**] and produces drought that at times has led to famine.[124] But when they take a northerly—and far more favorable—course, they tend to be propelled farther south by a secondary low over the Aegean, and they strike the Levant with storms that can last two to four days (Deut. 11:11; 1 Kings 18:43–45; Luke 12:54). The winter, then, is the rainy season (Ps. 29:1–11; Song of Songs 2:11; Acts 27:12; 28:2) that includes both the "early and latter rains" (Deut. 11:14; Job 29:23; Ps. 84:6; Prov. 16:15; Jer. 5:24; Hos. 6:3; Joel 2:23; Zech. 10:1; James 5:7).[125] The days of heaviest rainfall coincide with the period of the coldest weather, in December through February (Ezra 10:9, 13; Jer. 36:22), when the precipitation often includes snow and hail.[126]

Generally speaking, precipitation increases as one proceeds north. Elat on the Red Sea receives one inch or less annually; Beersheba in the Negeb gets about eight inches; Nazareth in the hills of Lower Galilee receives some 27 inches a year; J. Jarmuk in Upper Galilee gets approximately 44 inches; and Mt. Hermon receives nearly 60 inches of precipitation. [**See map 19 for averages at Tel Aviv, Jerusalem, and Jericho.**] Precipitation also tends to increase toward the west.

Brief transitional periods occur at the turning of the seasons, one between late April and early May, and another between mid-September and mid-October. During such times, a hot sweltering air mass, popularly known today as a "sirocco" or "hamsin," may strike Palestine from the Arabian Desert.[127] This condition produces torrid heat and parched dryness, not unlike the Santa Ana winds of California. Known in the Bible as "an east wind" (Ex. 10:13; Isa. 27:8; Jer. 18:17; Ezek. 19:12; Hos. 12:1; 13:15) or "a south wind" (Luke 12:55), a sirocco can sometimes persist for more than a week, withering delicate vegetation and causing more than a little irritation to humans and beasts. The biblical east winds could blight grain (Gen. 41:6), dry up the sea (Ex. 14:21), bring death and destruction (Job 1:19), blow men away (Job 27:21), wreck ships (Ps. 48:7; Ezek. 27:26), and make people faint and lose their senses (Jon. 4:8). By way of contrast, "a north wind" nourished and invigorated life (Job 37:22; Prov. 25:23). The Sumerian word for "north wind" literally means "a favorable wind."

THE LAND'S FORESTATION

Where the land received adequate rainfall, ancient Palestinian forestation included standing woodlands of oak, pine, turpentine, almond, and carob species (Deut. 19:5; 2 Sam. 18:6; 2 Kings 2:24; Eccles. 2:6; Isa. 10:17–19). More commonly, however, the land was covered by the thicket brush and shrubby plants (maquis) typical of the Mediterranean basin (Josh. 17:15; 1 Sam. 22:5; Hos. 2:14). Based on a wide sampling of pollen analyses as well as from plant and seed remains derived from sediment cores, Palestinian indigenous forestation in high antiquity was most likely rather dense and sometimes impassable, except in the southern and southeastern regions that bordered on desert.[128]

Present evidence indicates, however, an ever-increasing destruction of that forestation and vegetation by the ravages of humankind, beginning as early as around 3000 B.C. But three periods stand out as particularly ruinous: (1) the early Iron Age (1200–900 B.C.); (2) the late Hellenistic and Roman periods (c. 200 B.C.–A.D. 300); and (3) the last 200 years.

The first of these cycles of destruction most affects the biblical story of forestation and land use. The land of Palestine in the early Iron Age experienced a massive and enduring encroachment by humans upon its landscape, triggered largely by a substantial wave of new immigrants and the introduction of iron implements. Palestine's woodlands began to disappear before society's domestic, industrial, and imperialistic needs.

In the domestic realm, for instance, large tracts of land had to be cleared to make way for human settlement and the production of food (Josh. 17:14–18). Vast amounts of timber would have been required in the construction and ornamentation of homes (2 Kings 6:1–7; Jer. 10:3). It is estimated that each household would have required one to two tons of firewood annually (Josh. 9:21–27; Isa. 44:14–17; Ezek. 15:1–8; Mark 14:54).[129] And the grazing of transient flocks of sheep and goats would have uprooted seasonal forestation that was succulent but not deeply rooted.

Humankind's settlements in turn would have enlisted the support of certain industries, many requiring vast wood resources that surely damaged Palestine's delicate ecological balance. Wood was burned in baking kilns and industrial hearths. It was required for the production and glazing of glass and in the manufacturing of lime, plaster, bricks, terra-cotta pipes and drains, baking utensils, iron tools, and writing tablets. (Some writing was actually placed *on* wooden tablets.) Certain wood by-products were industrially useful as water solvent, in tanning and dyeing, and in medicine. Much wood was used for the quarrying of mountainsides and the damming of streams. More was transformed into charcoal for the mining, smelting, and forging of metals.[130] Large quantities were also consumed during sacrifices at Palestinian temples. Finally, additional areas of forestation would have been devoured through ancient imperialism, either in the production of military implements (Deut. 20:19–20), in wanton wartime activities (2 Kings 3:25; Ps. 83:14–15; Isa. 10:15–19; Jer. 6:4–8), or in the payment of compulsory tribute.[131]

The effects of deforestation were dramatic and permanent. There is considerable evidence that the accompanying disturbance of Palestinian topsoils led directly to greatly accelerated wind and water erosion, with a subsequent loss in potential fertility of the thinly coated hillsides. Some soil conservationists estimate that more than three feet of soil and subsoil have been irretrievably swept off the Central Mountain Spine as a result of Iron Age deforestation, which resulted in the exposure of bare bedrock over substantial portions of that terrain. Once the topsoils were severely marred or destroyed, the predominantly unproductive subsoils were unable to regenerate forestation. Compelling evidence exists of climatic fluctuations during the period of biblical Israel, but very little evidence of substantial or radical climate change.[132] The area's rampant deforestation, with its subsequent deterioration and displacement of fertile topsoil, has nevertheless caused a gradual and inexorable degradation of the land's natural environment. The landscape has been altered for the worst, and even modern reforestation efforts have yet to prove completely successful.

Ironically enough, the activities of the Israelites themselves must have contributed significantly to this diminished capacity of early Iron Age Palestinian land resources. The Bible's portrait of Palestinian forestation seems to comport with this evidence. While there is frequent mention of certain kinds of vintage varieties of trees that are more conducive to marred and erosive soil conditions (olive, fig, sycamore, acacia, almond, pomegranate, terebinth, myrtle, balsam), the Bible makes scant reference to hardwood trees required for architectural purposes (oak, cedar, fir, cypress, pine). And mention of the latter varieties were often in regard to other locations—frequently Bashan, Mt. Hermon, or Lebanon (Judg. 9:15; 1 Kings 4:33; Ps. 92:12; Isa. 40:16; Ezek. 27:5–6; Zech. 11:2). To be sure, Lebanon's seemingly inexhaustible supply of timber was celebrated in the ancient world; it was imported into Egypt as early as the Old Kingdom period and thereafter.[133] Numerous Mesopotamian and Assyrian kings traveled there to obtain cedar. Assyrian kings in particular often boasted that one of their supreme accomplishments was scaling the heights of Lebanon and cutting down its massive timbers (Isa. 14:8).

Because of Palestine's virtual lack of hardwood resources, David found it necessary to conclude a treaty with Hiram, king of Tyre, when he undertook his construction projects in Jerusalem (e.g., 2 Sam. 5:11; 1 Chron. 14:1). Solomon was obliged to ratify that pact when he began *his* numerous architectural enterprises (1 Kings 5:1–18; 7:2–12; 2 Chron. 2:1–16; 9:10-28). Phoenicians from Tyre supplied Solomon with both the raw materials and the technology to build his merchant fleets (1 Kings 10:22; cf. Ezek. 27:5–9, 25–36). Throughout the monarchy period, construction on even a modest scale entailed securing of hardwoods from outside sources, as Jehoash and Josiah discovered (2 Kings 12:12; 22:6). On one occasion timber being used to construct a town in the northern kingdom was carried off as an act of aggression, in order to build towns in Judah (2 Chron. 16:6).

The availability of local hardwoods had not improved by the post-exilic period. As part of Cyrus's decree permitting Jews to return to their land to rebuild their temple, the Persian monarch granted them a sum of money with which they were to secure timber in Lebanon (Ezra 3:7). It is suspected, however, that when that timber arrived in Jerusalem, it was squandered instead for use on private dwellings (Hag. 1:8, cf. v. 4). Later, as Nehemiah sought release from his royal appointment in an attempt to improve living conditions around Jerusalem, he secured letters from king Artaxerxes enabling him to obtain timber for the reconstruction of the city walls and gates (Neh. 2:4–8). Still later, wood necessary for Herod's massive architectural undertaking at Caesarea Maritima had to be imported, probably from Italy.[134] And even as late as the 19th century, when Charles Warren needed wooden planks to continue his archaeological work at Jerusalem, he discovered that wood was still among the scarcest and most expensive commodities in Palestine.[135]

CITIES IN THE BIBLICAL WORLD

Factors that Influence Location

A number of geographical conditions influenced the sites of urban settlements in the biblical world. Generally speaking, there were five major factors that could be determinative in this regard: (1) water accessibility; (2) availability of natural resources; (3) regional topography; (4) local topography; and (5) natural lines of communication. These factors were not necessarily mutually exclusive, so more than one could sometimes play a role in determining a given city's exact location.

Foremost among these factors was the consideration of water accessibility, especially before the introduction of aqueducts, siphons, and reservoirs. Although it could be rightly argued that water was central to all settlement in an otherwise arid environment, some cities appear to have been positioned *exclusively* on this basis. Two examples are Damascus (situated at the eastern foot of the Anti-Lebanon Mountains, on a vast oasis fed by the effusive Abana and Pharpar rivers [2 Kings 5:12]) and Tadmor (located in a

Major Cities of Palestine

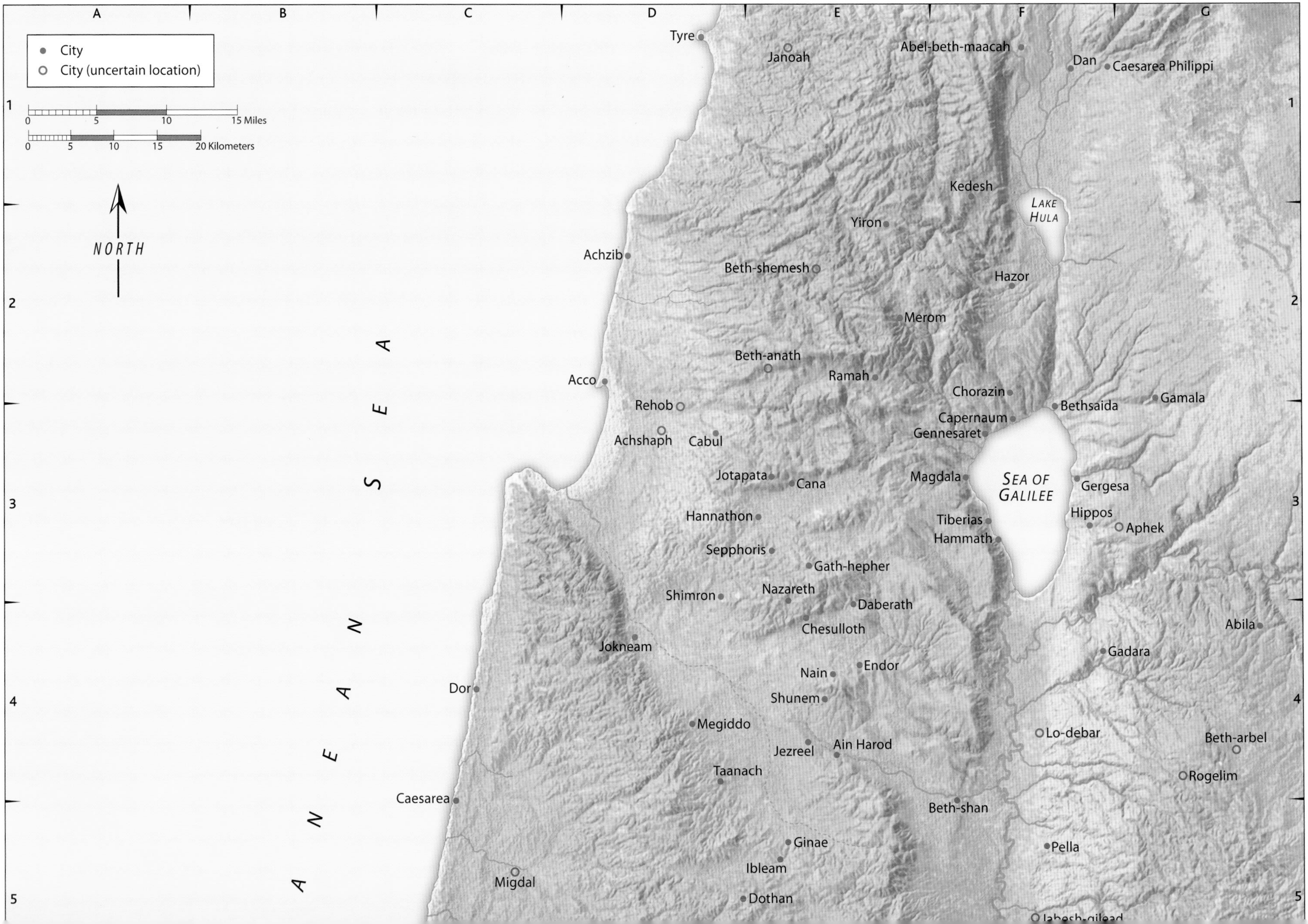

M E D I T E
Samaria
Gerasa
Zarethan
Zaphon
Sychar
Shechem
Succoth (T. Deir 'Alla)
Penuel
Mahanaim
Pirathon
Aphek
Ebenezer
Gath-rimmon
Tappuah
Mizpah
Adam
Lebonah
Shiloh
Joppa
Ono
Arimathea
Gilgal
Timnah-serah
Jordan R.
Jazer
Jogbehah
Beth-dagon
Lod
Gophna
Ophrah
Amman
Modiin
Bethel
Ai
Gittaim
Lower Beth-horon
Beth-nimrah
Mizpah
Michmash
Gilgal
Jamnia
Gibbethon
Gezer
Shaalbim
Upper Beth-horon
Jericho (OT)
Gibeon
Ramah
Geba
Jericho (NT)
Shittim
Emmaus
Aijalon
Beeroth
Gibeah
Kiriath-jearim
Beth-haram
Heshbon
Timnah
Wells of Nephtoah
Baal-peor
Bezer
Ekron
Zorah
Eshtaol
Jerusalem
Bethany
Beth-jeshimoth
Ashdod
Beth-shemesh
City of Salt
Nebo
Jarmuth
Medeba
Gath
Azekah
Bethlehem
Socoh
Ashkelon
Libnah
Adullam
Almon-diblathaim
Moresheth-gath
Tekoa
Beth-guvrin
Keilah
Mareshah
Beth-zur
Dead Sea
Ataroth
Lachish
Jahaz
Kedemoth
Hebron
Gaza
Eglon
Dibon
Mephaath
Ziph
Aroer
Engedi
Debir
Carmel
Ziklag
Gerar
Eshtemoa
Mattanah
A
B
C
D
E
F
G
6
7
8
9
10

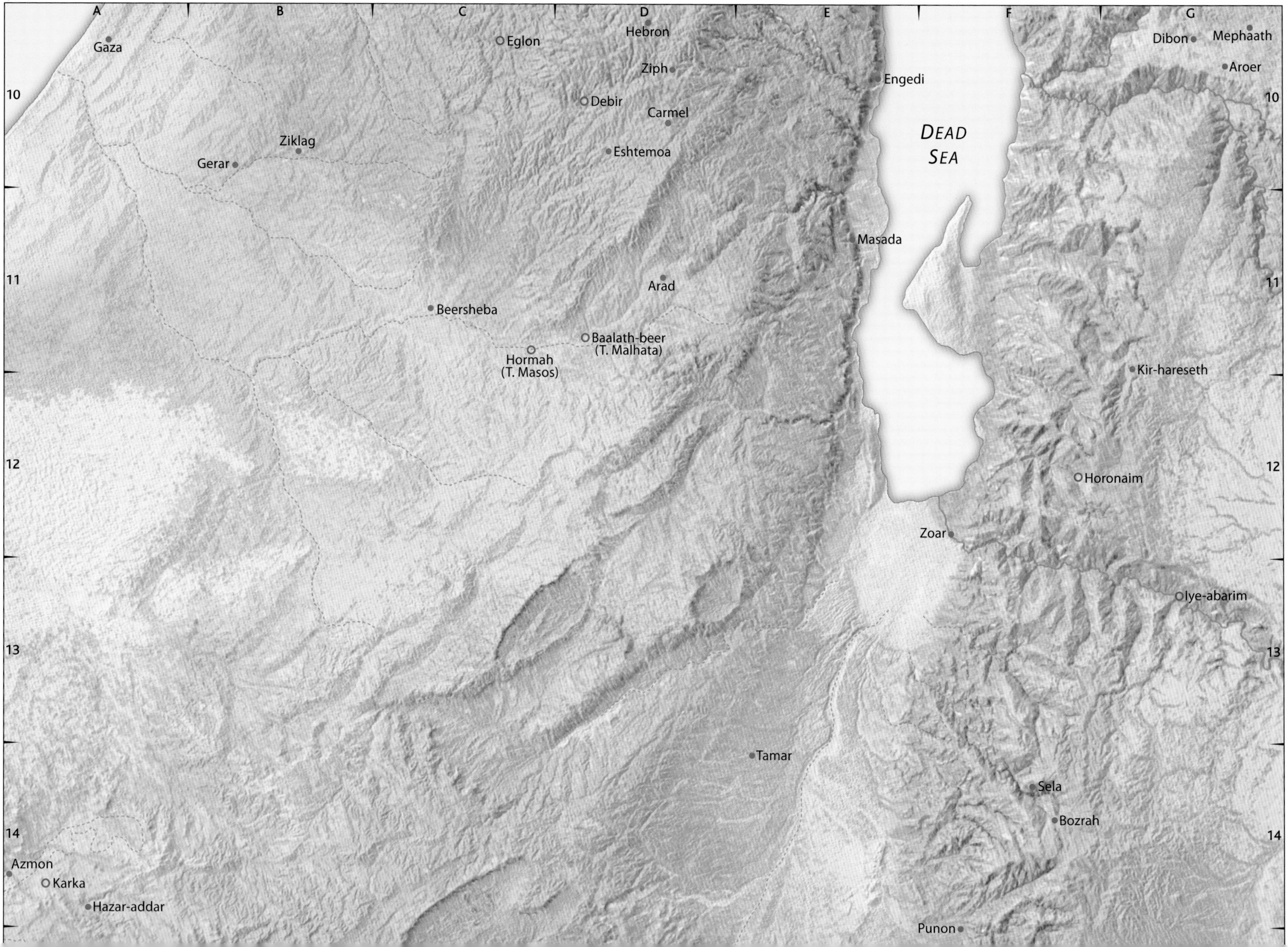
A
B
C
D
E
F
G
10
11
12
13
14
Gaza
Eglon
Hebron
Ziph
Debir
Carmel
Eshtemoa
Ziklag
Gerar
Engedi
DEAD SEA
Masada
Arad
Beersheba
Baalath-beer (T. Malhata)
Hormah (T. Masos)
Dibon
Mephaath
Aroer
Kir-hareseth
Horonaim
Zoar
Iye-abarim
Tamar
Sela
Bozrah
Azmon
Karka
Hazar-addar
Punon

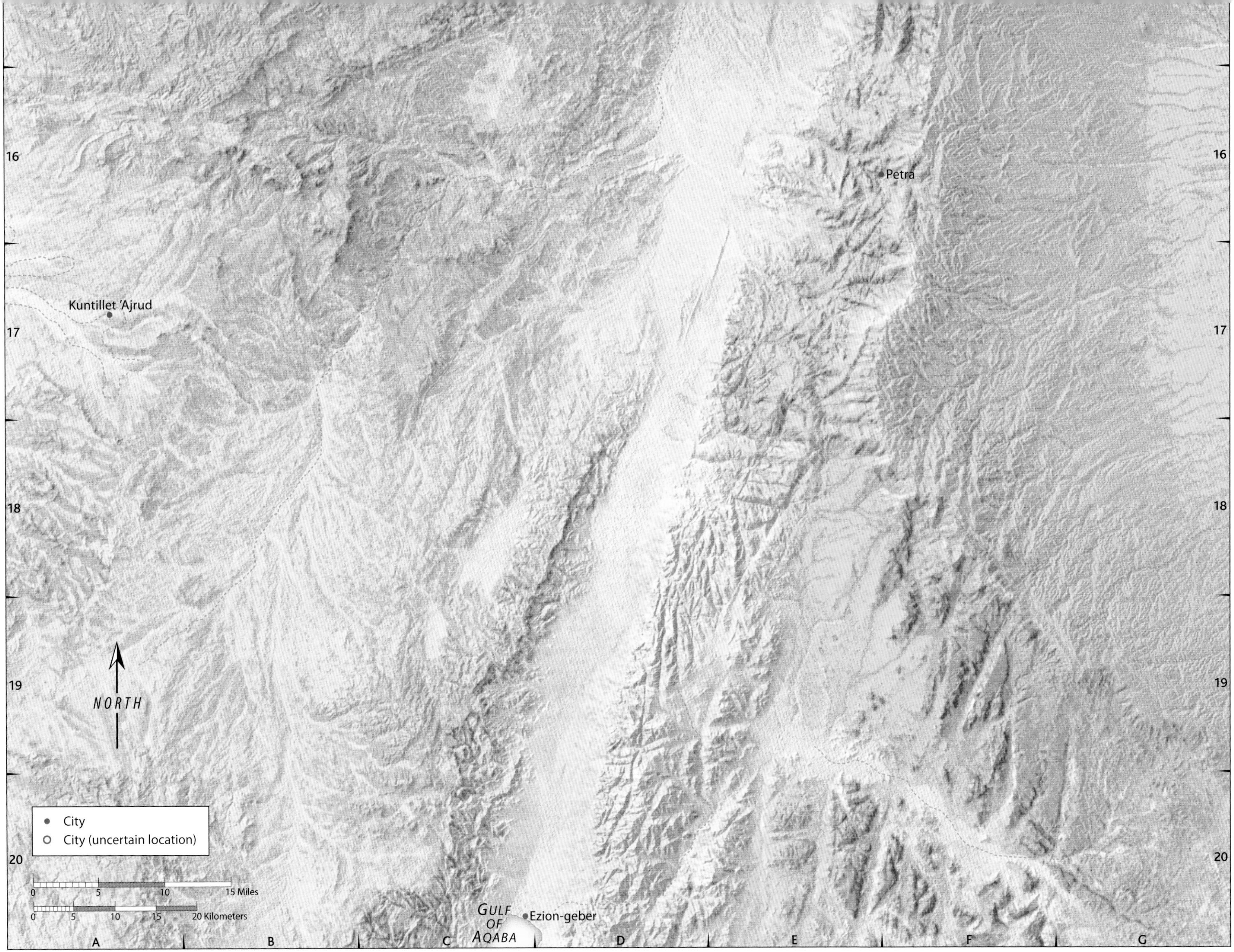
Petra
Kuntillet 'Ajrud
NORTH
City
City (uncertain location)
0 5 10 15 Miles
0 5 10 15 20 Kilometers
GULF OF AQABA
Ezion-geber
A
B
C
D
E
F
G
16
17
18
19
20

lush and prolific oasis in the middle of the Eastern Desert). Owing to the available supply of fresh water at such locations, settlements long before the dawn of biblical history have been found at these sites, and they represent some of the oldest continuously occupied settlements in the biblical world.

Other cities were positioned to be in close proximity to natural resources. A prime illustration is the location of Jericho, one of the earliest settlements of ancient Canaan. Old Testament Jericho was built adjacent to an exceptionally large spring, yet it is also likely that the city was established there because that spring was situated near the Dead Sea and its bitumen resources. Bitumen was a highly prized commodity with numerous uses. The Dead Sea was one of the few known sources of the commodity in high antiquity, so its bitumen was collected and transported throughout Egypt and much of the Fertile Crescent. Consequently, an economic motivation first brought into the area a colony of laborers and soon resulted in the founding of a settlement nearby. Similarly, the location of the city of ancient Sardis, situated near the base of Mt. Tmolus and adjacent to the Pactolus stream, was surely determined by the discovery of gold there, creating legendary wealth in that locale.[136] Coins made of a gold-silver alloy are known to have been minted at Sardis as early as the seventh century B.C.[137]

Some cities were situated in accordance with regional topography. We have already seen how Megiddo was positioned to dominate a strategic intersection at a pass in the Mt. Carmel range. Likewise, the town of Beth-horon was situated to govern the main approach from the west into the interior of the mountains of Judah and Jerusalem. [**See maps 27 and 91.**] Regional topography also explains the location of Corinth, a sprawling seaport city strategically situated on a narrow three-and-one-half-mile isthmus of land separating the Aegean Sea and the Adriatic Sea, and forming the only link between the Greek mainland and the Peloponnesian peninsula.[138]

Still other cities were located in conformity with the principle of local topography. Jerusalem was surrounded on every side except the north by deeply carved valleys that plunged more than 200 feet. Masada was a lofty isolated mesa encompassed by precipitous rock cliffs in excess of 600 feet at places. Samaria straddled a 300-feet-high isolated hill that was engulfed by two steep valleys. As a consequence of local topography, these cities were commonly rather resistant to attacks, or they fell to opponents only after a protracted period of siege.[139]

Finally, urban settlements may have been positioned along natural lines of communication. A classic illustration of this criterion is Hazor, a heavily fortified emplacement, a provincial capital (Josh. 11:10), and a 200-acre tell that was among the largest of Canaan. The city's location was dictated by the course and trajectory of the Great Trunk Road. Throughout antiquity Hazor served as the port of entry into Palestine and points south, and it is often referenced in secular literature in connection with trade and transportation.[140] In the same way, lines of communication are most likely the determining factor for where the cities of Gaza and Rabbah/Amman came to be situated. Also, several towns west of Pella on the Via Egnatia (Herakleia, Lychnidos, and Clodiana) are very unlikely ever to have developed aside from the existence and location of the major roadway. And there are places along the Persian Royal Road (such as Diyarbekir and Pteria) that owe their prominence, if not their very existence, to the placement of that ancient highway.

Because the factors dictating their placement remained rather constant, towns and cities in the biblical world usually experienced an amazing degree of continuity of settlement. Even when a site was destroyed or abandoned for a long period, later settlers were almost always attracted by the same factor(s) that had been determinative in the original choice of the site. The subsequent settlers were glad to make use of earthen ramparts, portions of walls still standing, beaten earth floors, fortifications, storage pits, or wells. As succeeding settlements rose and fell, and towns were often literally built one on top of another, the platform mound (tell) on which they rested (Josh. 11:13; Jer. 30:18; 49:2) grew ever higher, with steeper slopes along its perimeter, thus rendering the site increasingly defensible. When such a pattern was frequently repeated, as in the case of Lachish, Megiddo, Hazor, or Beth-shan, the occupational debris could reach heights of 70 to 100 feet.[141]

Proper Identification of Ancient Cities

This leads to the issue of site identification, which is crucial to the concerns of a Bible atlas. Continuity of settlement is useful, yet sound identification of biblical places is not possible in every case due to insufficient documentary evidence and/or a limited knowledge of geography. Many names have not been preserved to the present time, and even when a place name has survived or has been resurrected and applied to a site in modern times, attempts at identification may be fraught with problems. There are cases in which a particular name has undergone a location shift. Old Testament Jericho is not at the same site as New Testament Jericho, and neither site corresponds to modern Jericho. Similar location shifts are known to have occurred with Shechem, Arad, Beersheba, Beth-shan, Beth-shemesh, Tiberias, and elsewhere.[142]

Name shifts may also occur from one culture or period of time to another. Old Testament Rabbah became New Testament Philadelphia, which in turn became modern Amman. Old Testament Acco became New Testament Ptolemais, which in turn became Acre to the Crusaders. Old Testament Shechem became New Testament Neapolis, which evolved into modern Nablus. And in some instances a name change occurred *within* a Testament (e.g., Luz/Bethel,

Kiraith-Arba/Hebron, Kiriath-sepher/Debir, and Laish/Dan). Analysis of these cases often demands an intimate familiarity with the cultural succession and linguistic interrelationships between several epochs of Palestinian history. Even then, site identification often remains elusive.

There is also the problem of homonymy: more than one site may bear the same name. Scripture knows of an Aphek ("fortress")[143] in Lebanon (Josh. 13:4), in the Sharon Plain (1 Sam. 4:1), in Galilee (Josh. 19:30), and in Golan (1 Kings 20:26-30).[144] There is a Socoh ("thorny place")[145] in the Shephela (1 Sam. 17:1), in Judah (Josh. 15:48), and in the Sharon Plain (1 Kings 4:10).[146] As illustrated here, homonymy normally occurs because place names are generic in meaning: Hazor means "enclosure," Bethlehem means "granary," Migdal means "tower," Abel means "meadow," Gibeah means "hill," Kadesh means "cultic shrine," Ain means "spring," Mizpah means "watchtower," Rimmon means "pomegranate," and Carmel means "vineyard of God." Not unexpectedly, therefore, more than one biblical location is associated with each of these names. Knowing exactly when to posit another case of homonymy can always be problematic in creating a Bible atlas. Another dimension of the same vexed issue occurs when one and the same name may alternately apply to a town and to a surrounding province or territory, as in the case of Samaria (1 Kings 16:24, but 1 Kings 13:32), Jezreel (1 Kings 18:45–46, but Josh. 17:16), Damascus (Gen. 14:15, but Ezek. 27:18), or Tyre (1 Kings 7:13, but 2 Sam. 24:7).

Despite these difficulties, the scientific identification of biblical sites is generally predicated on three considerations: archaeological attestation, uninterrupted tradition, and literary/topographic analysis.[147] The first of these, which is the most direct and conclusive, identifies a given city through an inscription exhumed from the site. Although numerous specimens of this sort occur in Syro-Mesopotamia, they are relatively scarce within Palestine. Such documentation has been found in the cities of Gezer, Arad, Beth-shan, Hazor, Ekron, Lachish, Taanach, Gibeon, Dan, and Mephaath.

Regrettably, most place names cannot be identified by inscriptional evidence, so one of the other considerations must be employed. The first of these, name survival, can apply where the name of a site has remained lexically the same and the identity of a site has never been lost. The criterion is fairly conclusive, although it applies in very few cases: Jerusalem, Hebron, Bethlehem, and Nazareth. Many modern sites with biblical names cannot offer that kind of uninterrupted traditional support. Consequently, this raises

As at many other locations, the Roman theater of Amman/Philadelphia is situated against a natural recess at the foot of a hill/mountain.

Major Archaeological Sites of the Biblical World

map 25

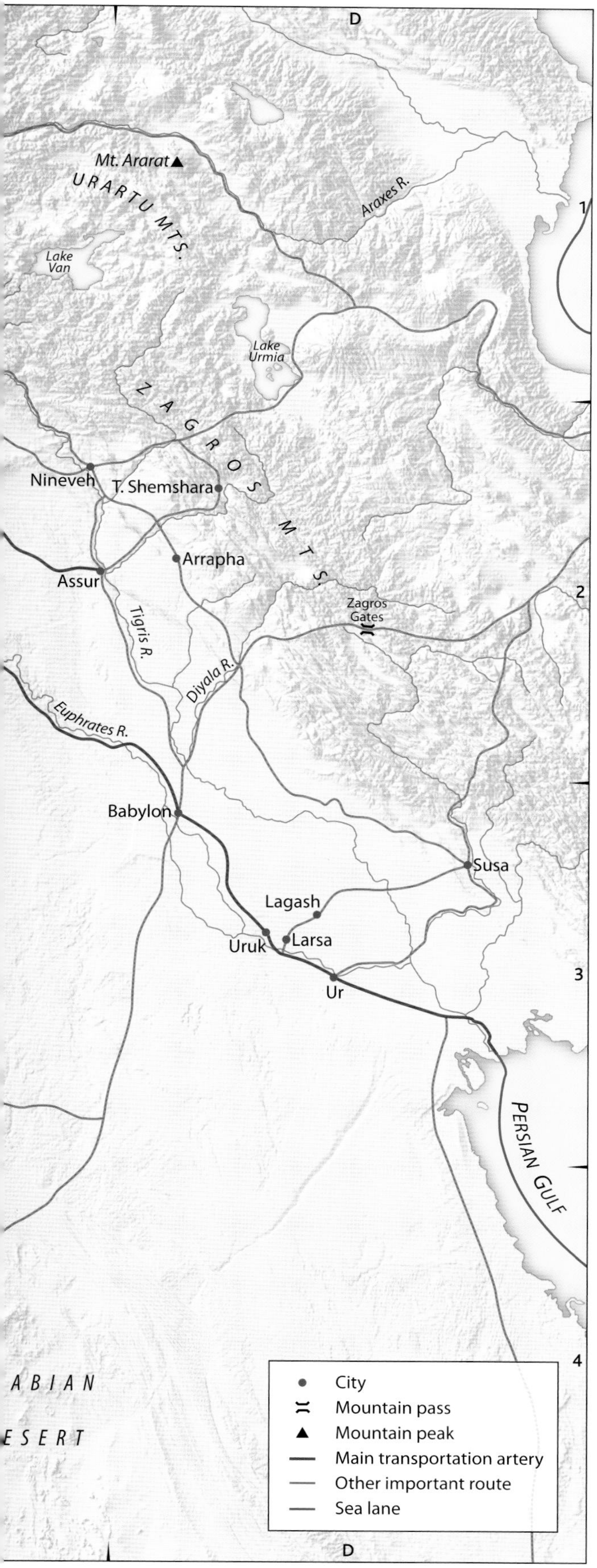

Geographical determinism refers to largely unchanging physiographic and/or hydrologic factors in the ancient biblical world that determined routes followed by caravans, migrants, or armies. These passageways remained relatively unaltered throughout extended periods of time (except where temporarily or partially contravened by geopolitics or in isolated cases of unlawful movement). In general, it would appear that the lowland areas offered the least hindrance to human movement and the most scope for the development of transportation networks or the deployment of troops. By contrast, deeply incised canyons cut by sometimes raging rivers were an impediment to travel to be avoided. If unavoidable, they were to be forded at places offering a minimum of difficulty. The quagmire of disease-infested swamps, the sterility and blazing heat offered by desert zones, and the badlands of congealed lava were formidable obstacles to be shunned at any cost. Densely forested mountain slopes, often with twisting gorges, were consistently navigated at passes, however narrow or hazardous those passes might have been. Alternatively, where mountain ridges could be straddled for great distances without the interruption of gorges or valleys, they tended to be employed for travel in all periods. The need to commute between copious sources of fresh water was a prerequisite for travel during all eras. So even though we do not possess an ancient map of the biblical world, the location of main roads can still be logically inferred with a high degree of probability, especially when the principle of geographical determinism can be augmented with other lines of evidence.

Literary documentation often helps delineate a highway with greater specificity. This evidence may derive from the Bible, extra-biblical ancient sources, classical writers, early travel itineraries, medieval geographers, or more recent travel pioneers. Some literary sources attempt to survey a portion of land or an itinerary route using both distance and direction; they cite the distance between two or more known points in a way that can be reconstructed only by presupposing a particular intermediate course. At times these sources may describe a route in terms of intervening natural terrain (along a certain bank of a given river; near a canyon, ford, tar pit, or oasis; adjacent to a named canal, island, or mountain; etc.) or a noteworthy point of interest along the way. Towns along a route may be described as forming part of a particular district or as being contiguous to a given province, sharing common grazing lands, sending communications via fire signals, or coming simultaneously under the control of a certain king. Approximate distances between towns, together with a presumed route, may be inferred from texts that speak of a king or a courier taking his daily rations at point A on day one, at point B on the next, at point C on the third day, and so on. An army or caravan may be given a prescribed number of days' rations in order to undertake a particular journey, or a specific trip is said to have taken a stated number of days to complete.

As a group, literary sources were not composed for the purpose of enabling someone to trace out the course of completely ascertainable highways. They are extremely wide-ranging sources. The geographical details they provide are many, varied, and occasionally mistaken. They do not offer the same degree of detail for all regions within the biblical world. Still, their cumulative value is critical because they often supply precise details upon which a road can be plausibly reconstructed, or they will give a nuance that can be gainfully employed when combined with other lines of evidence.

In addition to geographical determinism and literary documentation, *archaeological attestation* can help reconstruct ancient roadways. Identifying an ancient city by discovering its name in archaeological data exhumed from the site helps to clarify literary texts that mention the place and to provide a fixed geographical point. Because Laish/Dan (T. el-Qadi) was positively identified from an inscription excavated at the site, greater specificity is automatically conferred upon journeys like those of Abraham (Gen. 14) or Ben-hadad (1 Kings 15; 2 Chron. 16). Even when the name of an ancient town remains unknown, it is helpful when archaeological remains bespeak the type of occupation the site may have experienced. A palace unearthed, for instance, may allow for the inference that a royal or provincial capital was involved, whereas a small but heavily fortified site may suggest a garrison or fortress town. A discernible sequence of a similar type of site, such as the string of New Kingdom Egyptian fortresses discovered southwest of Gaza, may enable one to trace out the probable regional course of a roadway. On a wider scale, archaeology may disclose settlement patterns during particular periods of time. For example, many Middle Bronze sites within Canaan appear to have been adjacent to established transportation arteries, whereas this does not appear to have been the case for Early Bronze settlements. Similarly, a cluster of Middle Bronze settlements aligned the banks of the upper Habur River in Syria, whereas no such concentration is known immediately before or after this era.

This kind of information is useful if settlement patterns can be linked to causes of movement to the area. So if these Middle Bronze sites can be ascribable to migrations, and if emigration locations are known, the archaeological evidence might presuppose certain routes that were capable of sustaining domesticated animals with pasturage and migrants with food, while at the same time virtually eliminating other routes. There were, of course, many possible climatological or sociological factors that produced migrations in antiquity, but the fact remains that people and animals had to eat off the land as they moved.

Sometimes movement to sites might be archaeologically linked to trade. Perhaps objects are recovered that are foreign to where they were found (Egyptian scarabs, Mesopotamian cylinder seals, etc.) or trading commodities may be discovered that were not native to the entire Fertile Crescent (tin, amber, cloves, silk, cinnamon, etc.). Reconstructing highways would then take into account the geographical source of these objects or commodities, the dates of passage from one point to another, and where markets and intermediate storehouses were located. Where such trade was carried on for extended periods (such as the Baltic amber route from Europe, the silk route from southeast Asia, or the spice route from western Saudi Arabia), somewhat fixed commodity routes can be established. Often this kind of archaeological evidence can be nuanced by literary documentation, as in the case of tin itinerary texts that spell out itinerary stations across the Fertile Crescent during the Middle Bronze Age.

Another possibility is that movement to new sites can be linked archaeologically to military invasion, perhaps due to the discovery of a monumental victory stela or a destruction layer that can be synchronized with an earthen rampart constructed against the exterior of a city wall. The demands of military strategy, troop maintenance, and material procurement were such that some areas would be nearly immune to any army. Scholars on a quest to trace out ancient roads and highways have recently benefited from supplementing their archaeological attestation with aerial photographs or satellite imagery that can detect rudiments or even short segments of roadways that have not become completely obliterated.[152]

A fourth line of evidence for reconstructing ancient roadways is *Roman milestones*, although erecting guideposts along roads predates the Roman period (Jer. 31:21).[153] To date, between 450 and 500 Roman milestones have been found in modern Israel, and nearly 1,000 have been discovered across Asia Minor.[154] Milestones inside modern Israel date as early as A.D. 69; specimens dating as early as A.D. 56 are known from modern Lebanon. On the other hand, milestones from Asia Minor tend to date to a later Roman period, and it does not appear that most roads there were paved before the "Flavian dynasty," which began with Vespasian in A.D. 69—a harsh fact that is well to bear in mind when considering the difficulty of commuting through Asia during the time of the apostle Paul.

These milestones usually mark precisely the location of Roman highways, which frequently followed the course of much earlier roadways. Locations and inscriptions of milestones can give evidence that certain towns were linked in the same sequence as recorded in earlier literature. For example, some 25 milestones representing 20 different mile-stations have been discovered along a stretch of Roman coastal road between Syrian Antioch and New Testament Ptolemais. Inasmuch as some of the same towns located along that highway were said to have been visited by king Shalmaneser III on the return of his campaign in Israel (841 B.C.) [**map 76**], the milestones indicate the probable roadway employed by the Assyrian monarch. In this case, this inference is explicitly confirmed by the discovery of Shalmaneser's victory monument carved into a cliff alongside the mouth of the Dog River, just south of the Lebanese city of Byblos.[155] Similarly, these same milestones enable one to configure the opening phases of Sennacherib's famous third campaign (701 B.C.) [**map 77**], in which the Assyrian boasts that he "shut up Hezekiah in Jerusalem like a bird in a cage." Likewise these stones allow one to trace out the course through Canaan taken by Ramses II, Tiglath-pileser III, Esarhaddon, Alexander the Great, Cambyses II, Cestius Gallus, Vespasian, and the Pilgrim of Bordeaux.

Difficulties of ancient travel

Modern North Americans accustomed to an interstate highway system or Europeans who have sped along the Autobahn may find it difficult to comprehend the notion of biblical travel. Today travel entails such "harsh realities" as rich Corinthian leather, double wishbone suspension, burled walnut interior, and sound and temperature surround systems. A wide array of amenities and services are immediately accessible at about every third interstate exit. Most long-distance highways are smoothly paved, well lighted, clearly marked, and securely patrolled. Hundreds of horsepower carry us along in comfort and speed. When we stop at night, we can rather easily get a private room with utilities, a bed, cable TV, Internet service, and private bath with hot and cold water. We can quickly find a wide array of food service already prepared for us. We can carry with us special music and reading, pictures of relatives, credit cards, and fresh changes of clothing. We can almost instantly fax, text message, email, or telephone friends back home. And we don't give much attention to danger of communicable disease issues or to lack of access to medicines.

How starkly different was travel in the biblical era. In antiquity, even international arterial highways were sometimes mere narrow winding paths that were clogged by mud or marsh after winter rains, or dusty and rutted throughout the many months of oppressive, searing heat. Certain places along those roadways required travelers to navigate difficult, almost impassable terrain. Travel could include facing the hazards of water shortage, life-threatening weather, wild beasts of prey, or bandits.

Such difficulties and perils help explain why most international travel in antiquity was undertaken by caravans. Numbers provided *some* protection against alien elements and agents. Considerable evidence from Mesopotamia and Asia Minor indicates that caravans were generally large and almost always escorted by security guards armed for their tasks. The caravaneers were expected to stay strictly on the preordained route. It was not uncommon for caravans to include as many as 100 to 200 donkeys, sometimes carrying priceless commodities (cf. Gen. 37:25; Judg. 5:6–7; 1 Kings 10:2; Job 6:18–20; Isa. 21:13; 30:6; Luke 2:41–45).[156] Private caravans are attested only rarely in antiquity. Wealthy travelers were in a position to buy slaves to serve as armed guards (Gen. 14:14–15), but poorer people either moved in groups or attached themselves to a governmental or commercial entourage headed for a particular destination. Evidence also shows that considerable travel took place under the cover of darkness; nocturnal movement would offer escape from the oppressive heat of the midday sun and would lessen likelihood of detection by brigands and bandits. It may even be that travel at nighttime contributed directly to the wide diffusion of moon-cult worship, the most prevalent form of religion across the Fertile Crescent.

Another consideration of overland travel during biblical times was the limited headway possible per day. To be sure, distances might vary due to factors of dissimilar terrain, different purposes of travel, number and kind of persons in a given travel party, type of equipment being transported, and variation of season. Accordingly, the ancient world was not unfamiliar with exceptional distances covered in a single day. Herodotus made a famous statement about messengers traveling along the Persian Royal Road at great speeds.[157] Tiberias rode some 500 miles in 72 hours to be at the bedside of his dying brother Drusus.[158] And Roman postal couriers in the Roman period are said to have averaged almost 100 miles per day.[159] But these were rare exceptions in the biblical world, and they should be acknowledged as such!

The evidence is generally uniform and mutually corroborating that a one-day journey in the biblical world incorporated a distance of 17 to 23 miles, with slightly higher averages when traveling downstream by boat.[160] Similar daily averages continued to be the norm in later classical, Arab, and medieval itineraries, from Egypt to Turkey, and even to Iran. As recently as 100 years ago, some itineraries and travel accounts document similar meager daily averages.

A number of biblical episodes depict the same limited headway related to travel:

- Abraham sighted Mt. Moriah (almost certainly in the vicinity of Jerusalem) during the third day of his trip from Beersheba (Gen. 22:4), and the two sites are separated by some 50 miles;
- David and his men arrived from Aphek at Ziklag on the third day (1 Sam. 30:1), and again, the two sites are separated by just over 50 miles;
- Kadesh-barnea (Ain Qadeis) was an 11-day journey from Horeb (near or at J. Musa) via the road by Mt. Seir[161] (Deut. 1:2), and some 190 miles separate the two places;
- A march from Jerusalem via the "way of Edom" to the capital city of Moab (Kir-hareseth) lasted seven days, and the approximate distance involved in that route was about 115 miles (2 Kings 3:5–10);

⊠ II Augusta

XXX Ulpia ⊠

◇ I Minerva ⊠

◇ XXII Primigenia ⊠

VIII Augusta ⊠

Rhine R.

X Gemina ⊠ XIV Gemina ⊠ I Adriutrix ⊠

II Adriutri

ATLANTIC
OCEAN

◇ Loire R.

A L P S

Po R. Ravenna

Rhone R.

Salona

ADRIATIC SEA

VII Gemina ⊠

Douro R.

Ebro R.

PYRENEES

GULF
OF LION

CORSICA

Rome
Ostia Merinum Dyrrh.

Misenum
Puteoli

Brundisium

Tagus R.

BALEARIC ISLANDS

SARDINIA

TYRRHENIAN
SEA

IONIA
SEA

•Emerita

M E D I T E R

Guadalquivir R.

Caesarea
Mauretania

Carthage

SICILY

Rhegium

R A N E A

Tangier

⊠ III Augusta

MALTA

SYRTIS MINOR

Leptis
Magna

SYRTIS MAJOR

S A H A R A

D E S E R T

- • City
- ⬡ Site of wonder of the ancient world
- ☀ Site of Roman lighthouse
- ⛴ Home port of Roman imperial fleet
- ⊠ Location of Roman legion at the time of Trajan
- — Principal nautical trade routes in the Greco-Roman world
- ← Major wind currents (summer season)
- ← Major water currents

Commodities moved/traded within the Roman empire

◆ Copper	◇ Glass	◇ Grain
◆ Brass	◆ Textiles	◆ Horses
◆ Iron	◆ Wine	◆ Timber

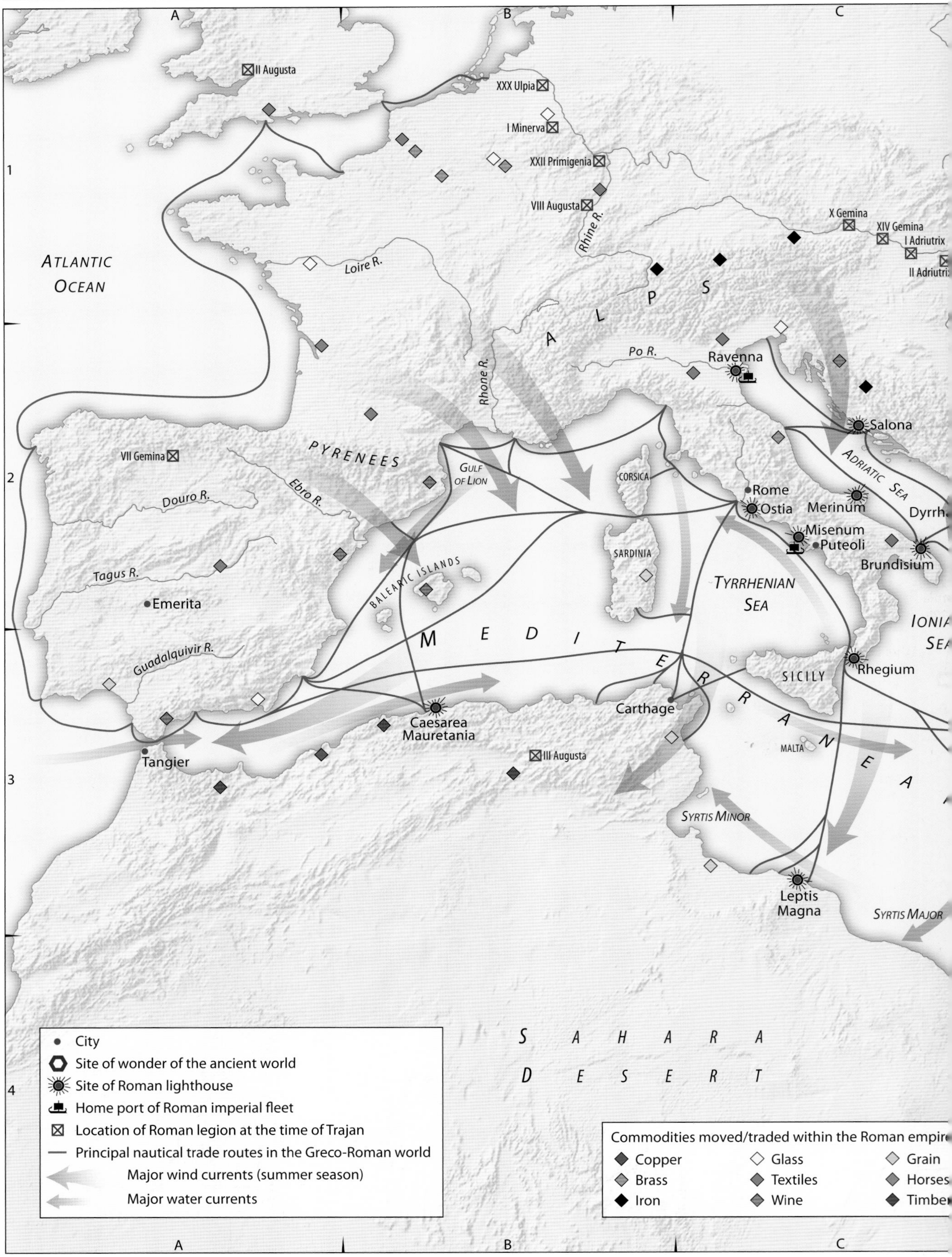

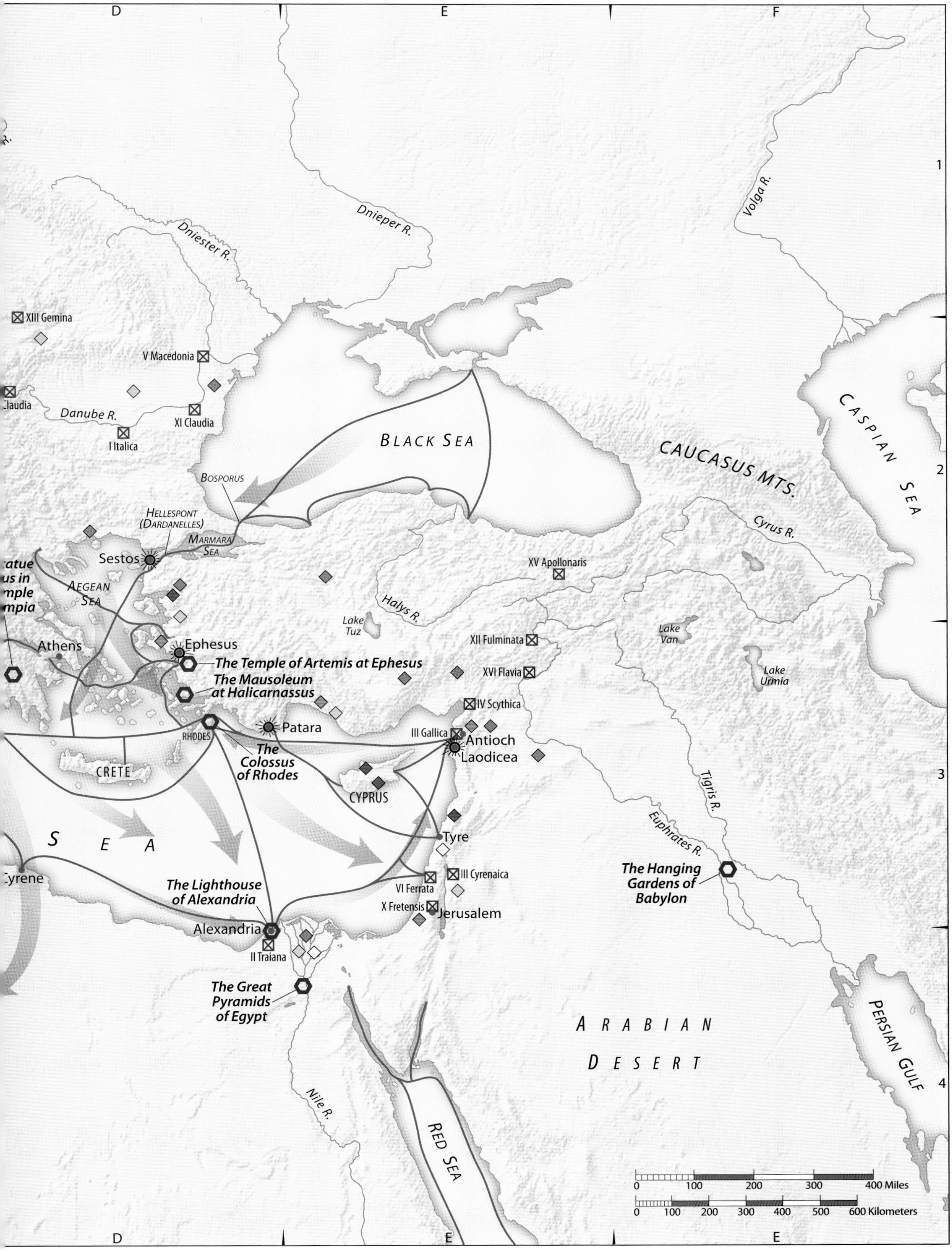
D
E
F
1
2
3
4
Dnieper R.
Dniester R.
Volga R.
XIII Gemina
V Macedonia
Claudia
Danube R.
XI Claudia
I Italica
BLACK SEA
BOSPORUS
CASPIAN SEA
CAUCASUS MTS.
HELLESPONT (DARDANELLES)
MARMARA SEA
Sestos
AEGEAN SEA
Cyrus R.
XV Apollonaris
Halys R.
Lake Tuz
Lake Van
Lake Urmia
XII Fulminata
XVI Flavia
Athens
Ephesus
The Temple of Artemis at Ephesus
The Mausoleum at Halicarnassus
IV Scythica
Patara
III Gallica
Antioch
Laodicea
RHODES
The Colossus of Rhodes
CRETE
CYPRUS
Tigris R.
Euphrates R.
SEA
Tyre
III Cyrenaica
VI Ferrata
X Fretensis
Jerusalem
The Hanging Gardens of Babylon
The Lighthouse of Alexandria
Alexandria
II Traiana
The Great Pyramids of Egypt
ARABIAN DESERT
PERSIAN GULF
Nile R.
RED SEA
0 100 200 300 400 Miles
0 100 200 300 400 500 600 Kilometers

- Ezra's Jewish caravan is said to have departed the Babylonian frontier (whether at Hit or at Awana) on the 12th day of the first month (Ezra 8:31), and it arrived in Jerusalem on the first day of the fifth month (Ezra 7:9), which means that the journey lasted a little more than three and one-half months.[162] Given the probable route traversed by Ezra and his compatriots (8:22, 31—the more dangerous shortcut past Tadmor?; **map 81**), they traveled about 900 miles in a little more than 100 days, but the size and makeup of his caravan might have mitigated against greater daily averages. Alternatively, had they followed the longer course of the Euphrates as far as Imar, and proceeded from there along the Great Trunk Road past Damascus (the normal route), a more typical daily average would have obtained.

Similar distances hold true in the New Testament as well.[163] On one occasion, Peter journeyed 40 miles from Joppa to Caesarea and arrived at his destination on the second day (Acts 10:23–24). The urgency of the apostle's mission allows for the inference that he took a direct route and made no intermediate stops. (Cornelius later stated that his ambassadors had journeyed round-trip between Joppa and Caesarea in four days [Acts 10:30].) On another occasion Paul was hurriedly taken to Caesarea via Antipatris by military escort in two days' time (Acts 23:23–32), a distance of about 65 miles according to the roads the soldiers most likely followed. According to Josephus, it was possible to travel between Galilee and Jerusalem, by way of Samaria (a distance of some 70 miles), in three days' time.[164]

The location of major roadways

The Great Trunk Road

What was unquestionably the most important highway in the biblical world is here called the Great Trunk Road.[165] This highway passed from Egypt to Babylonia and to frontiers beyond, and vitally linked every part of the Fertile Crescent in all periods. [**See map 25.**] The road began in Memphis (Noph), near the base of the Nile delta, and passed the Egyptian towns of Ra`amses and Sile [**map 33**] before arriving at Gaza, a fortified emplacement on the edge of Canaan. Gaza was an extremely important Egyptian provincial capital and often served as a launching pad for Egyptian campaigns throughout the Levant. This southwestern sector of the highway, known by Egyptians as the "way(s) of Horus," was of paramount importance to Egyptian security. [**See map 34.**]

From Gaza the highway stretched to Aphek/Antipatris, situated at the springs of the Jarkon River; this effusion constituted a serious obstacle to movement and forced most traffic to its inland (east) side. [**See map 27.**] Continuing in a northward direction, the roadway skirted the menacing sand dunes and seasonal marsh of the Sharon Plain until it inevitably confronted the barrier of Mt. Carmel. Several passes through Mt. Carmel afforded passage from the Sharon Plain to the Jezreel valley. [**See map 10.**] The shortest of these, known today as the Aruna Pass (N. `Iron), was the most frequently utilized. The northern end of this narrow pass, where it opened onto the Jezreel, was dominated by the installation city of Megiddo.

At Megiddo, the highway broke into at least three branches. One led to the Mediterranean shoreline at Acco, and then ran northward along the Sea as far as Syrian Antioch. A second branch from Megiddo stretched diagonally across the Jezreel valley on a line created by a volcanic causeway. It passed between Mt. Moreh and Mt. Tabor as far as the vicinity of the Horns of Hattin where it veered east, traversed the Arbel Pass with its sheer cliffs, and finally burst onto the plain along the northwestern shoreline of the Sea of Galilee.[166] A third option from Megiddo turned eastward, following the contours of the northern flanks of Mt. Carmel and Mt. Gilboa before arriving at the strongly fortified garrison city of Beth-shan. This section probably ran along the edge of the valley during the dry season, but took to higher ground to avoid marshy conditions during the winter months. At Beth-shan, the Trunk Road took a sharp northern turn and proceeded along the Jordan valley as far as the southern end of the Sea of Galilee, where the highway skirted the Sea on the west side as far as Gennesaret, near Capernaum. [**See map 14.**] During the New Testament era, many travelers would have crossed the Jordan just north of Beth-shan and made their way across the Yarmuk valley and the Golan plateau as far as Damascus.

From Gennesaret, the Great Trunk Road proceeded up the west flank of the Upper Jordan and approached the preeminent fortress city of Hazor, which guarded Canaan's northernmost sectors. Near Hazor, the roadway turned northeast in the direction of Damascus, hugging the outliers of the Anti-Lebanon range and attempting to avoid the basaltic land surfaces of the upper Golan and the Hauran. [**See map 16.**] From Damascus, it continued a northward trek around the eastern slopes of the Anti-Lebanon as far as the city of Hamath, on the Orontes River. Here it struck out on a more directly northern course, passing Ebla and arriving at Aleppo, where it made a sharp bend east toward the Euphrates. Arriving on the river at the site of Imar, the highway then essentially followed the course of the Euphrates flood plain to a point just north of Babylon, where the river could more easily be forded. Continuing southward from there, the highway transected Babylonia, passing Uruk and Ur before finally arriving at the head of the Persian Gulf.

The King's Highway

Another major roadway that intersected Bible lands was known in the Old Testament as the King's Highway (Num. 20:17; 21:22)[167] and outside the Bible as Trajan's Highway (Via Nova Traiana). It was the emperor Trajan who converted this route from a road into a bona fide highway in the second

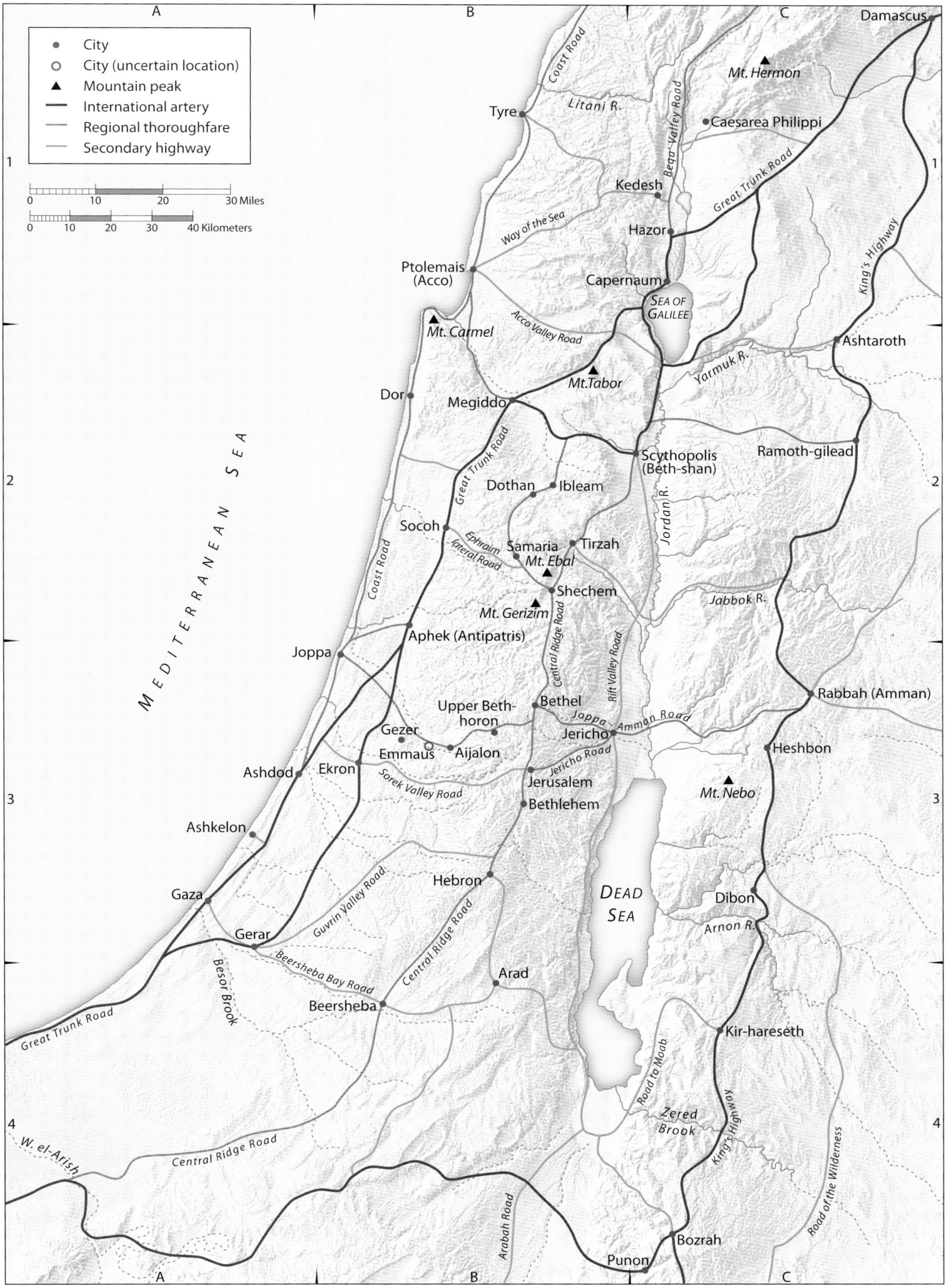
City
City (uncertain location)
Mountain peak
International artery
Regional thoroughfare
Secondary highway
0 10 20 30 Miles
0 10 20 30 40 Kilometers
A
B
C
1
2
3
4
Damascus
Mt. Hermon
Coast Road
Litani R.
Beqa' Valley Road
Tyre
Caesarea Philippi
Kedesh
Great Trunk Road
Hazor
Way of the Sea
King's Highway
Ptolemais (Acco)
Capernaum
Sea of Galilee
Mt. Carmel
Acco Valley Road
Ashtaroth
Yarmuk R.
Mt. Tabor
Dor
Megiddo
Scythopolis (Beth-shan)
Ramoth-gilead
Mediterranean Sea
Dothan
Ibleam
Jordan R.
Socoh
Ephraim lateral Road
Samaria
Tirzah
Mt. Ebal
Shechem
Jabbok R.
Mt. Gerizim
Central Ridge Road
Aphek (Antipatris)
Joppa
Rift Valley Road
Bethel
Rabbah (Amman)
Upper Beth-horon
Joppa–Amman Road
Gezer
Jericho
Emmaus
Aijalon
Heshbon
Jericho Road
Ashdod
Ekron
Jerusalem
Mt. Nebo
Sorek Valley Road
Bethlehem
Ashkelon
Hebron
Dead Sea
Gaza
Guvrin Valley Road
Dibon
Arnon R.
Gerar
Besor Brook
Beersheba Bay Road
Arad
Beersheba
Kir-hareseth
Road to Moab
Zered Brook
W. el-Arish
Road of the Wilderness
Arabah Road
Bozrah
Punon

A large gymnasium and courtyard at Sardis is flanked to the west (left of picture) by the remains of a sizeable Jewish synagogue. Between the area of the synagogue and the modern road may be found a vestige of the Persian Royal Road, which ran from Susa in Elam some 1,650 miles west and ended at Sardis.

century A.D. The highway stretched north from the Gulf of Aqaba near Ezion-geber and essentially rode the watershed of Edom and Moab, passing the cities of Petra, Bozrah, Kir-hareseth, Dibon, and Heshbon before coming to Amman.[168] [**See map 34.**] It made its way from Amman across the Gilead and Bashan plateaus to Damascus, where it joined the Great Trunk Road.

The Old Assyrian Caravan Road

Used to carry Assyrian economic and military interests into Asia Minor, the Old Assyrian Caravan Road is known from the early second millennium B.C.[169] From any of the cities that successively served as the Assyrian capital, this highway most likely swept westward as far as the vicinity of the J. Sinjar, where it veered due west and arrived at the base of the Habur River triangle. The roadway then followed the course of one of its streams past T. Halaf to a place near modern Samsat, where the Euphrates could more easily be forded. From there, the roadway cut through a major pass in the Taurus mountains (due west of Malatya), passed through the Elbistan Plain, and eventually arrived at the strategic Hittite city of Kanish. An extension of the roadway then proceeded to cross the central Anatolian plateau, past what later became the sites of Derbe, Lystra, Iconium, and Antioch in Pisidia. Along its descent to the Aegean coasts, the highway intersected places later incorporated as Laodicea, Philadelphia, Sardis, and Pergamum. From Pergamum, the road ran essentially parallel with the Aegean coast and came to the city of Troy, situated on the threshold of Europe.

The Persian Royal Road

For the Persian Royal Road, **see the commentary at map 86.**

Travel by Sea

Sea travel on the Mediterranean appears not to have varied much during the Old Testament period. Late Bronze Age ships with a capacity in excess of 200 tons are known from Ugarit and T. el-Amarna, and Phoenician vessels crossed the entire breadth of the Mediterranean during the early Iron Age. [**See map 63.**] Much early nautical activity would have taken place not far from the mainland or between intermediate islands, and apparently sailors often cast anchor at night. The distance between daily anchorage points was approximately 40 miles (e.g., Acts 16:11; 20:6, 14–15).[170]

Early seafarers often preferred to make anchor at promontories or islets lying near the coastline (Tyre, Sidon, Byblos, Arvad, Athlit, Beirut, Ugarit, Carthage, etc.); islands could be used as a natural breakwater and the inlet as a kind of harbor. The advent of the Roman imperium brought with it an enormous expansion in the type, size, and quantity of nautical vessels, and routes were developed across the entire Mediterranean world and beyond. [**See map 26.**] Before the end of the first Christian century, a combination of a widely deployed legionary force, a standing imperial naval fleet, and the need to move vast quantities of commodities to sometimes far-reaching points within the empire meant that large numbers of both merchant and military vessels were plying distant waters. The long-distance routes thus created the need to construct an entire network of imperial lighthouses and enlarged coastal harbors with enormous warehouse storage facilities.

CHAPTER 2

The Historical Geography of the Land

GARDEN OF EDEN

God created for the first couple a place to live, a place that included trees, rivers, and animals, a place that came to be known as "Eden" (Gen. 2:4b–15). The high drama of this arresting account has fascinated young and old readers alike, has prompted sober and profound reflections for philosophers and theologians, and has inspired many a poet's pen and artist's brush. But when one attempts to reconstruct the geographical setting of this biblical text and locate Eden, he discovers much that remains shrouded in obscurity at a number of levels.

The verb from which "Eden" derives never occurs unambiguously in the Old Testament.[1] Other nouns homonymous to Eden do occur in the Old Testament, relating to (1) a person's name (2 Chron. 29:12; 31:15), (2) delightful/precious things (2 Sam. 1:24; Ps. 36:8; Jer. 51:34), or (3) a region or territory in Mesopotamia (2 Kings 19:12; Isa. 37:12; Ezek. 27:23; Amos 1:5).[2] Yet it remains difficult to ascertain the precise nuance of a given noun unless its cognate can be found outside the Bible, in ancient Near Eastern literature, in rather clear and revealing contexts.

In the case of "Eden," a cognate word (*edinu*) appears in Akkadian/Sumerian, where it designates a plain or a steppe land, presumably located somewhere in Mesopotamia.[3] In Ugaritic, and more recently in Aramaic, a similar word (*ʿdn*) seems to denote a place that is fertile and well-watered.[4] Fortunately the Akkadian citation is found in a lexical text aligned with its Sumerian equivalent, and an Aramaic attestation is found in an Aramean/Akkadian bilingual text, where the corresponding word in the Akkadian panel[5] also denotes a sense of abundance or lavishness. Accordingly, this evidence is often taken to suggest that Eden should be located in a relatively fertile segment of the steppe land in or near Mesopotamia.

It is commonly understood that the biblical account is written from the perspective of Canaan. So Eden's location *in the east* (Gen. 2:8) also points in the direction of Mesopotamia. Eden is further described as a "garden" (2:15) where one could find a river (2:10) and streams/springs to water the ground (2:6). Given Canaan's meager water supply, it is perhaps predictable that the biblical writer should have borrowed an Akkadian term to describe a watery condition that was alien to his own environment. An initial observation placing Eden somewhere in the Mesopotamian plain at a fertile location is reinforced by two other facts: (1) two of the rivers named in the narrative—the Tigris and Euphrates—are known to have coursed through Mesopotamia; and (2) the biblical name attached to each of these rivers corresponds precisely to its name in Mesopotamian literature.[6]

Fanciful attempts to locate the garden of Eden in Ethiopia, Australia, India, Pakistan, Egypt, Germany, Sweden, Mongolia, the Americas, Africa, the Seychelles Islands, the Far East, the Indian Ocean, at the equator, at the North Pole, or elsewhere need not detain us. No more plausible are those efforts that interpret the narrative to portray four rivers thought in antiquity to have encircled the entire globe. Such a hypothesis assumes the passage is legendary in character and/or that the biblical writer was ignorant of his world. Nor does our initial observation comport with an allegorical interpretation among the early church (e.g., Origen) according to which Eden was a paradise of the soul. They associate the four rivers with the virtues of prudence, courage, justice, and self-mastery, creating a paradise of divine perfection—but one that lay beyond geographical and historical realms.[7]

But even after accepting a Mesopotamian locale for the garden, it remains problematic to identify the first two rivers—Pishon and Gihon. They are not attested elsewhere in ancient literature, aside from a few passing references in later Jewish writings.[8] Their names bear no resemblance to any river names known in that region today, and the words themselves suggest that they may be descriptions of a river's *movement* rather than a river's name. (Pishon means "to cascade/gush," and Gihon means "to bubble/percolate.")[9] Yet it has been fashionable since as early as the first century A.D. to equate the Pishon with the Ganges River and the Gihon with the Nile, though alternative identities for the Pishon include the Indus or Danube rivers, and an alternative for the Gihon is the Gihon spring at Jerusalem.[10] Jerome should be credited with introducing into Christian tradition the identification of the four rivers as the Tigris, Euphrates, Ganges, and Nile.

Attempts to identify the Pishon and Gihon on the basis of their assumed relationships with the descendants of Havilah and Cush are also frustrated (Gen. 2:11, 13). In the case of Havilah, the Old Testament designates at least two such clans (Gen. 10:7, 29), neither of which can be demonstrably located inside Mesopotamia. [**See map 31.**] Similarly, Cush in the Bible normally designates a section of the Sudan [**map 31**], though in at least one text (Gen. 10:8) the term may refer to the Kassites, a dynasty of people who occupied a sector of Babylonia for much of the second millennium B.C.

Neither does the mention of gold and bdellium in Havilah (Gen. 2:12) aid in a geographical quest. Gold in antiquity was found in faraway places like India and Egypt, but was also rather common throughout much of Mesopotamia and not isolated to any one region. As for bdellium, even its translation remains in doubt: the word could refer to a precious stone

The Garden of Eden

map 28

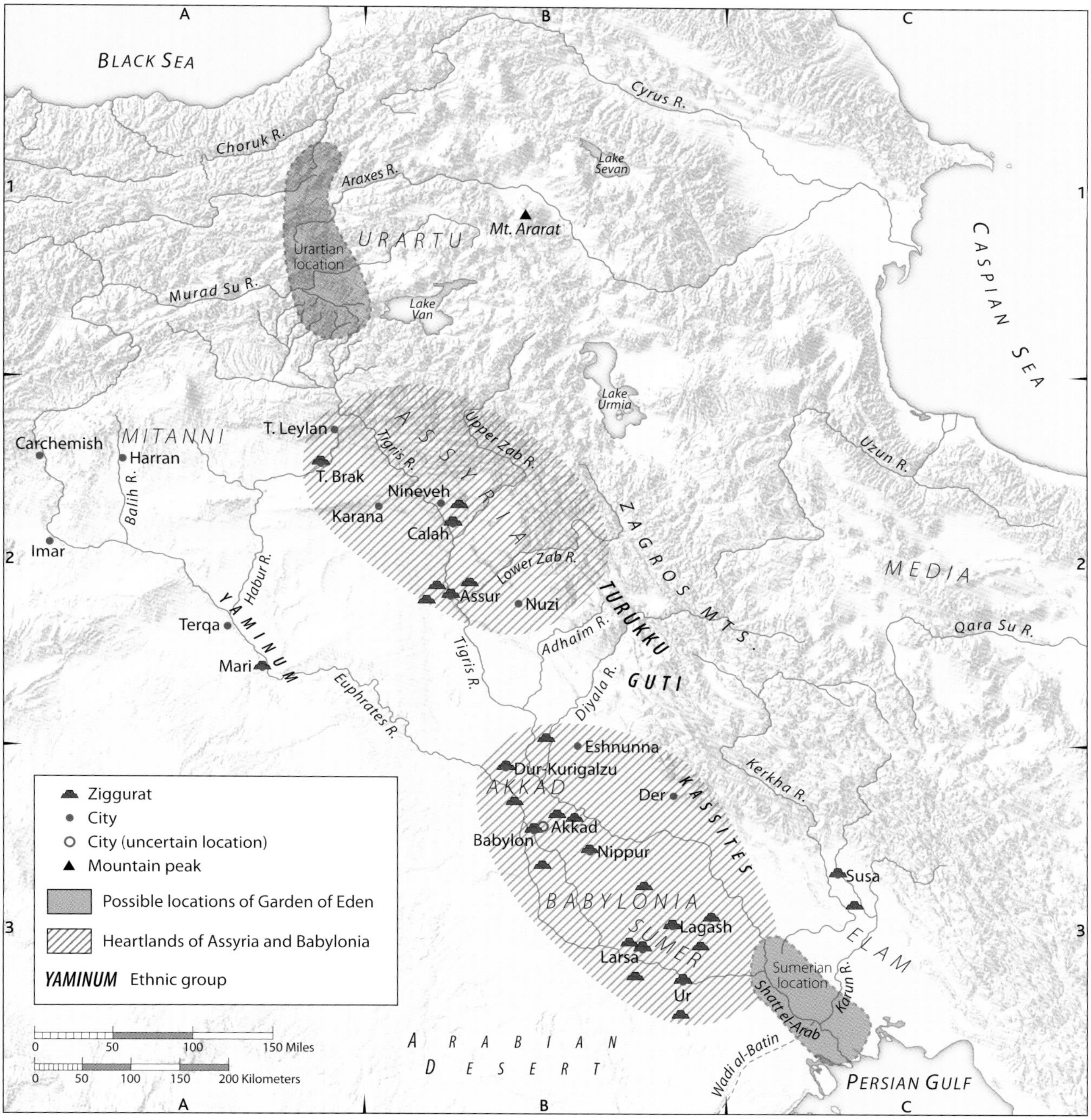

such as a ruby or crystal, or perhaps an apothecary aromatic, such as a kind of gum-resin.[11]

The map shows a northern (Urartian) and a southern (Sumerian) environment in which the garden may have been situated. One rather cogent argument in favor of each of these viewpoints can be presented. The Urartian view seeks support from Genesis 2:10, which states that a river went out to water the garden and then diverged to become four branches. Urartian proponents argue that this text requires locating Eden at a place from which rivers radiate outward. Part of the Tigris's headwaters and one of the main sources of the Upper Euphrates (Murad Su) emerge from the Urartian highlands, west of Lake Van near the modern town of Batman, Turkey, just over a half-mile from each other. In the same general region are the headstreams of the Araxes and Choruk rivers. Advocates of a northern hypothesis often equate these rivers with the Pishon and Gihon.[12]

Proponents of the Sumerian view seek support from Genesis 2:12b, which associates the Pishon River with the place of the "onyx stone." The word "onyx" in the Bible is regularly qualified by the addition of the word "stone" (Ex. 25:7; 28:9; 35:9, 27; 39:6; 1 Chron. 29:2), which is otherwise rare for minerals in the Old Testament. The one mineral in the Mesopotamian world that was regularly hyphenated with the word "stone" is known today as lapis lazuli, an expensive deep-blue stone commonly used for royal or official decoration throughout Mesopotamia and beyond. (Note the inclusion of the onyx as part of the decoration of the high priest's attire [Ex. 28:20; 39:13].)

If the word translated "onyx" were actually specifying lapis lazuli,[13] a Sumerian viewpoint would be greatly enhanced, since there was only one known source of this mineral in antiquity—Afghanistan. Lapis was imported into Mesopotamia via established southern arteries of transportation,[14] but apparently not from the north. Akkadian texts make mention of the "lapis lazuli river," which is identified either with the Kerkha River, the Karun River, or a portion of the Lower Tigris just above its confluence with the Euphrates.[15] However, the expression is never employed with a river in central or northern Mesopotamia. Hence a Sumerian location for the Pishon River is advanced by some scholars and, in such a scenario, the most likely candidate for the Gihon is either the Karun River, the Kerkha River, or the Wadi Batin (known to have been a true river in antiquity, flowing across the Arabian Desert and emptying its waters into the Shatt el-Arab waterway just north of the Persian Gulf).[16]

In the 16th century, John Calvin introduced a modification of the Sumerian viewpoint into Christian theology, though his exegesis was substantially borrowed from Augustinus Steuchus, an Old Testament scholar who was also the papal librarian at the time.[17] Steuchus asserted that the "four heads/branches" (Gen. 2:10b) referenced both the point where the rivers emerged from the ground *and* the point where they emptied into the sea.[18] Picking up on this, Calvin argued that the entities were really four separate branches of a single river inside Eden, with the two upper streams flowing downward from their sources into the garden and the two lower streams flowing out of the garden and downward into the Persian Gulf.[19] Calvin pictured what amounts to an upper Euphrates and a lower Euphrates, and an upper Tigris and a lower Tigris, with a confluence point in the middle of the map where their waters commingled for a short distance. At that point, according to the Reformer, there was an island on which Eden was located. Despite Calvin's inaccurate geographical analysis and even forced exegesis, his location of Eden persisted prominently in the history of commentaries and Protestant Bibles for more than 200 years.

One additional caution is warranted. Some Bible atlases[20] and other cartographic sources,[21] when describing earlier events in the Bible, refer to an "ancient shoreline" that extended the Persian Gulf northward about 125 miles almost as far as Ur, thus inundating (and effectively eliminating!) the so-called Sumerian location of Eden. Derived from scientific investigation published around 1900 but perhaps going back conceptually as early as the first century A.D.,[22] this theory is based on the geological assumption that there was a gradual one-way delta advance from the area of Ur (and Samarra on the Tigris) to the present shoreline [**map 23**], coming about over time exclusively as the result of sedimentation laid down by the Tigris and Euphrates rivers. Assuming that, the theory then made further uniformitarian assumptions having to do with dating and distance and asserted that this "ancient shoreline" should be dated to approximately 5000–4000 B.C.

More recent geological and paleo-climatological research has demonstrated conclusively that such previous assumptions were quite premature and are no longer tenable. We know today that worldwide mean sea levels around 5000 to 4000 B.C. were *lower* than present levels, generally by approximately three meters.[23] Offshore human habitational ruins from that period, now inundated by water, are known in the upper Persian Gulf,[24] indicating that the ancient coastline of the Persian Gulf extended farther south at that time, not farther north.[25]

In fact, sedimentation from the Tigris and Euphrates rivers, though widespread and heavy from the vicinity of Samarra (Tigris) and Ramadi (Euphrates) almost as far as the point where the rivers join to form the Shatt el-Arab waterway, is virtually nonexistent beyond that point south for the next 100 miles as far as the current shoreline of the Persian Gulf.[26] Accordingly, the southern/Sumerian view of Eden must not be dismissed from consideration purely on the basis of this sort of outmoded geographical reasoning.

THE TABLE OF NATIONS

Genesis 10 is sometimes called the "Table of Nations" and has been the subject of countless studies and commentaries. Few Old Testament texts have been more widely analyzed. Yet significant and diverse questions remain concerning its structure, purpose, and outlook. What is clear is that the Table may be subdivided into three sections: (1) the 14 descendants of Japheth (vv. 2–5); (2) the 30 descendants of Ham (vv. 6–20); and (3) the 26 descendants of Shem (vv. 21–31). Each section concludes with a formula summarizing the preceding narrative (vv. 5b, 20, 31) in terms of families (genealogy/sociology), languages (linguistics), lands (geographical territories), and nations (politics). The Table ends with verse 32, which summarizes all the entries in the list.

But there are a myriad of ways to understand these respective terms and interpret what the various subdivisions represent. For example, the sections have been classified according to:

- *Biology*—The chapter presents a verbal description of the family tree of Noah, perhaps based on similar genealogical tables unearthed in Mesopotamian archaeology.
- *Climate*—The names of Noah's sons are assigned a weather-related meaning. For example, Ham is construed to mean "hot," so the Hamites are classified as those nations who live nearest the equator.[27]
- *Apologetics*—The chapter is designed to demonstrate that the Hebrews (Eberites) were related to the major nations of the world.
- *Ethnology*—The chapter presents a complete anthropological register of humankind.
- *Mathematics*—The significance of the symbolic values of seven and ten is evident throughout the Old Testament. So the "70" nations of the descendants of Noah represent the dispersal of the whole of humanity.
- *Sociopolitics*—The nations have been classified according to their degree of friendship with or animosity toward the Israelites.
- *Geography*—The Table puts into verbal form the contents of an early map of the world. Early efforts at mapmaking are attested as early as the late third millennium B.C.[28]

It must also be emphasized that the names in Genesis 10 are presented in a dissimilar manner: the context may be that of a nation (e.g., Elam, v. 22), a people (e.g., Jebusites, v. 16), a place (e.g., Asshur, v. 22), or even an individual (e.g., Nimrod, vv. 8–9). A failure to appreciate this mixed arrangement found in the Table has led to numerous unwarranted conclusions. For example, it should not be assumed that all the descendants of any of Noah's sons lived in the same locality, spoke the same language, or even belonged to one particular race. A glance at the map shows the first of these conclusions to be untenable. The descendants of Ham, for example, reside in Africa, Canaan, Syria, and Mesopotamia. But neither can the text be interpreted in a purely linguistic manner: the Elamite language (Shem) is a non-Semitic language, whereas Canaanite (Ham) bears all the earmarks of a Semitic dialect. Attempts to trace all existing languages back to three parent groups are ultimately frustrated because the earliest written forms are pictographic in nature, and such symbolic forms are not conducive to precise linguistic classification. Moreover, anthropologists have not yet achieved consensus regarding what constitutes a proper definition of "race," thus further weakening any conclusions about racial groups represented in the Table.

THE FOURTEEN DESCENDANTS OF JAPHETH

1. **Gomer.** Gomer is mentioned in cuneiform sources as Gimirrai and in classical texts as Cimmeria, referring to a nomadic people living in north-central Turkey. After being defeated by the Assyrian monarchs Esarhaddon and Ashurbanipal,[29] they conquered Gugu/Gog of Luddi (Gyges of Lydia; cf. Ezek. 38:2) and colonized that area of Cappadocia. According to Herodotus[30] they were displaced by the Scythians and eventually settled in the area around Lake Van. The Behistun trilingual inscription equates the Gimirrai with the Saka/Scythians,[31] and Josephus states that the Greeks referred to the descendants of Gomer as Galatians.
2. **Magog.** Magog is associated with Tubal and Meshech in Ezekiel 38:2, and with Gomer and Togarmah in Ezekiel 38:6, all of which on other grounds must be situated in central or western Turkey. Josephus equated Magog with the Scythians (people known to have lived in the vicinity of the Black Sea). Magog in the Bible is sometimes explained as a derivation of Akkadian *mā(t) gog(i)*, "land of Gog," whose invading army is referenced by the prophet Ezekiel (38:14–23) as a threat to the people of Israel.[32]
3. **Madai.** Both here and elsewhere in the Old Testament (2 Kings 17:6; 18:11; Isa. 13:17; 21:2; Jer. 25:25; 51:11, 28), the Madai refers to the Medes, an Indo-European people who in the eighth century B.C. carved out a domain across most of present-day Iran, building their capital city at Ecbatana. They participated in the overthrow of the Assyrian Empire in the late seventh century B.C. [**map 79**], allowing them to expand their kingdom westward.[33]

4. **Javan.** This name occurs frequently in Akkadian literature from the 8th century B.C. onward as a reference to the Ionian Greeks of the western coast of Asia Minor.[34] Biblical texts also associate Javan with Elishah/Cyprus and connect it with islands or trade within the Mediterranean Sea (Isa. 66:19; Ezek. 27:13; Joel 3:6). In the aftermath of Alexander the Great and his accomplishments, Javan came to designate all of Greece in both secular and biblical literature.
5. **Tubal.** The Tubal, or Tabali, are a people group linked to Anatolia in the vicinity of modern Caesarea (Mazaca). [**Refer to map 112.**] Tubal is normally listed together with Meshech in the Old Testament texts where they occur (e.g., Ezek. 27:13; 38:2; 39:1) as well as in Herodotus, where both names are mentioned as part of the 19th satrapy of Persia.[35]
6. **Meshech.** Known as the Mushki/Mushkaya in first-millennium B.C. Akkadian texts,[36] this is a people located in eastern Asia Minor, in the area later known as Phrygia. [**See map 112.**] Herodotus placed the Meshech in eastern Asia Minor, and Josephus equated them with the Cappadocians. Others allege a linkage between the Mash people (#9 under the descendants of Shem) and possibly with the Masha, one of the contingents of Sea Peoples mentioned in the time of Ramesses III and earlier in Hittite texts. The Masha also apparently hail from eastern Asia Minor.
7. **Tiras.** One of the Sea Peoples groups joining the Libyans to fight against Pharaoh Merneptah in his fifth year was the Tursha.[37] Since the Sea Peoples almost certainly originated in the Aegean area, and since others in the line of Japheth are independently known to have come from central or western Turkey, it has been fairly common to equate the Tiras and the Tursha, an equation that is both etymologically possible and historically plausible. On the basis of a reasonable proximity in both space and time, some scholars also wish to equate the Tursha—and thus the Tiras—with the (E)truscans who lived in the area of Lydia until around the ninth century B.C.
8. **Ashkenaz.** Various sources locate Ashkenaz in an area north of Mesopotamia. Beyond the Genesis 10 and 1 Chronicles 1 citations, the only other biblical reference to Ashkenaz is found in Jeremiah 51:27, where the armies of Ararat, Minni, and Ashkenaz join forces to wage war against Babylon. The location of Ararat (Urartu) is well established in the north of Lake Van, and the kingdom of Minni/Mannai must be situated in the vicinity of Lake Urmia, based on its attestation in Elamite, Babylonian, and Assyrian sources.[38]
9. **Riphath.**[39] This is an uncertain location. Josephus equates the Riphateans with the Paphlogonians,[40] a people known to have occupied a territory between the south edge of the Black Sea and the province of Bithynia. Riphath's close connection in the biblical text with the better known Gomer, Ashkenaz, and Togarmah could lead to a similar conclusion.
10. **Togarmah.** In Ezekiel's oracle describing the allies of Gog/Gyges (Ezek. 38), Beth-togarmah ("the house/dynasty of Togarmah") is listed, together with Meshech, Tubal, and Gomer (vv. 3–6; cf. Gen. 10:2–3; Ezek. 27:12–13), which indicates a northerly direction. This is confirmed in verse 6, where Beth-togarmah is further defined as being located in the "uttermost parts of the north."[41]
11. **Elishah.** This name doubtlessly refers to the island of Cyprus.[42] The name Alashiya is frequently attested in ancient literature, including Hittite, Akkadian, West Semitic, Ugaritic, and Egyptian.[43]
12. **Tarshish.** Tarshish refers to the coastal region of southern Spain. [See commentary at **map 63**.]
13. **Kittim.** Kittim represents the Hebrew spelling of Greek *Kítion*, a well-attested Phoenician city located near the southeastern coast of Cyprus, just south of Larnaca.[44] Kittim is associated in some biblical texts with ships (Num. 24:24; Dan. 11:30) or coastlands (Jer. 2:10; Ezek. 27:6). Kittim and Elishah both appear in the Table, just as both also appear in Ugaritic and Phoenician. It is quite probable that Elishah represented the island of Cyprus as a whole, whereas Kittim designated only the city of Kition and its immediate environs. However, the name Kittim underwent a degree of evolution in some of its later uses.[45]
14. **Rodanim.** This entry is written Dodanim in Genesis and Rodanim in 1 Chronicles. The Samaritan Pentateuch reads Rodanim in Genesis, and the *LXX* and some Hebrew manuscripts read Rodanim in both Genesis and Chronicles. Accordingly, Rodanim has been adopted by most commentators and is used here to designate the island of Rhodes. Sometimes a Dodanim reading, referring to the Danunim people who in antiquity resided in coastal Syria north of Tyre, is given consideration. However, a more plausible alternative view[46] equates Dodanim with the residents of Dodona, famed site of an ancient oracle of Zeus in western Greece.

THE THIRTY DESCENDANTS OF HAM

1. **Cush.** The land of Cush lies to the south of Egypt (Ezek. 29:10), upstream of the First Cataract of the Nile, in an area also known in antiquity as Nubia.[47] Cush is often rendered as Ethiopia in both the *LXX* (e.g., Isa. 11:11; 18:1) and by classical writers.
2. **Seba.** This is an uncertain entry. In the few biblical texts where Seba is found, it is associated with Egypt and Ethiopia/Cush (e.g., Isa. 43:3; 45:14), which points to a location in Africa. In the former of these texts, Seba is read by the *LXX* as *Soēnē* (Aswan), which also underscores an African locale, to the south of Egypt and probably not too far from Cush. It is improbable, therefore, that one should confuse Seba son of Cush (Gen. 10:7a; 1 Chron. 1:9a) with Sheba son of Raamah (Gen. 10:7b; 1 Chron. 1:9b). The

The Table of Nations

map 29

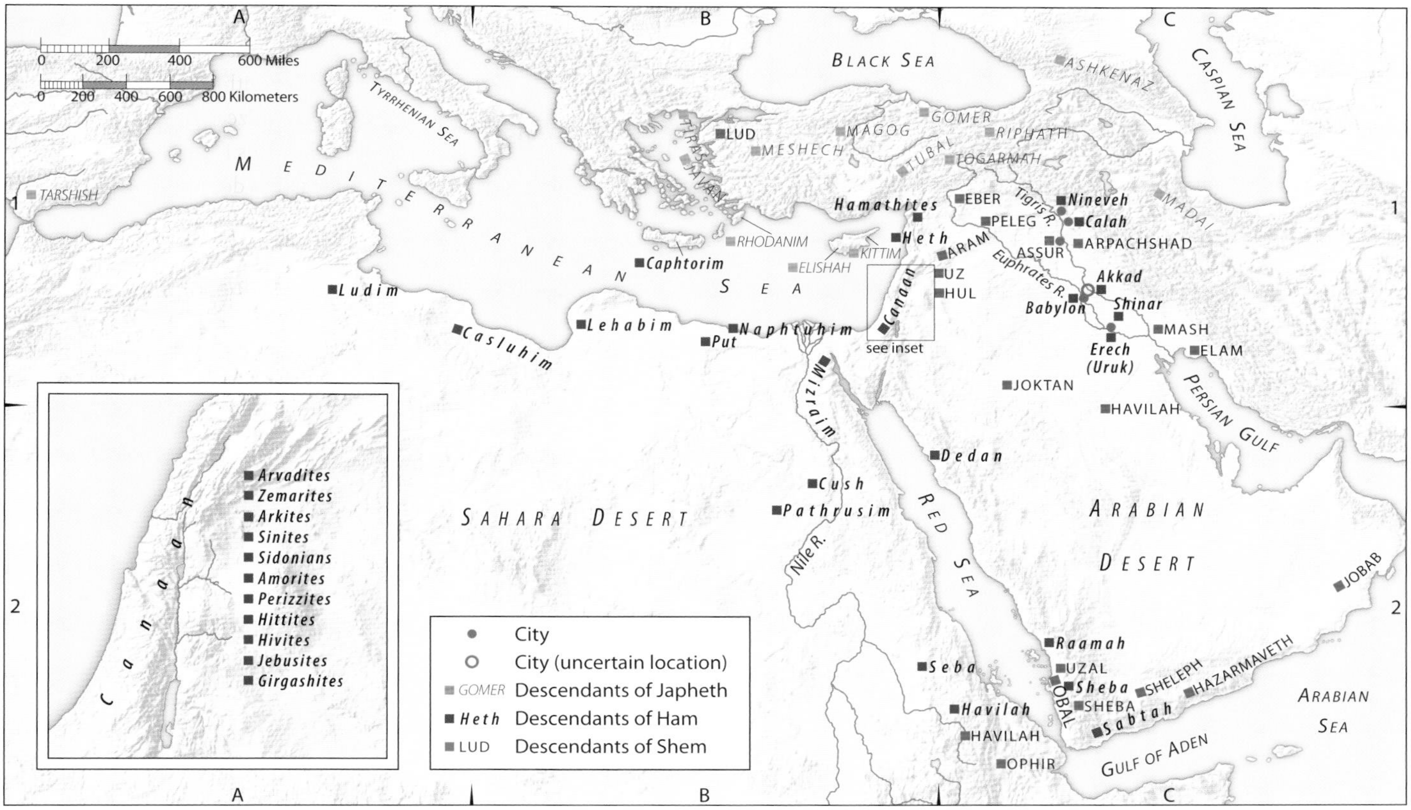

two entities are clearly distinguished in Psalm 72:10 and, unlike Seba, Sheba is consistently located in Arabia, not Africa. (See Sheba [#7] below.) Josephus located Seba along the Nile at the city of Meroe between the Fifth and Sixth Cataracts. [**See map 63.**] Strabo positioned the site farther east, along the edge of the Red Sea coast, a location also supported by modern scholarship.[48]

3. **Havilah.** This too is an uncertain entry. Beyond the Hamite genealogy, Havilah occurs elsewhere only in Genesis 2:11 and 25:18, and 1 Samuel 15:7. In the last two texts, Havilah is associated with "Shur, which is east of Egypt." If this qualification references *both* Havilah and Shur, then Havilah would have to be situated somewhere in the Arabian peninsula, probably along its western perimeter, but the Hebrew syntax is ambiguous. At least one scholar has sought Havilah in the eastern Arabia peninsula.[49]
4. **Sabtah.** Although Josephus located Sabtah on the Nile in the vicinity of Meroe, it is fairly commonly held today that the term designates Shabwat of Sabean inscriptions and Sabatah of Greek texts.[50] Sabtah would then be Sabota, capital city of modern Hadramaut, identified by Strabo as a place of myrrh.
5. **Raamah.** The location and even the name of this entry are uncertain.[51] The name may be associated with the city Ragmatum, known from Old South Arabian texts and one Minaean text to have been situated in the Nejrān oasis, located in extreme southwest Saudi Arabia, just north of its border with Yemen. Ragmatum was an important station along the incense route between interior Yemen and the Mediterranean Sea. Other scholars seek to equate Raamah with the place-name [*Rģm*], known from a Minaean inscription to have been situated in the Ma`īn region of northern Yemen, not too far from the Nejrān oasis. Such a placement of Raamah makes it almost certain that the name should not be related to the city Rhegama,[52] situated in the extreme east of Saudi Arabia, on the Persian Gulf.
6. **Sabteca.** This place is unknown.[53] Based on the *LXX* rendition of Sabteca (*Sabathaka*), several places situated on ancient trade routes in modern Hadramaut, including Shabaka and Shubaika, have been suggested.[54]
7. **Sheba.** Biblical references to Sheba underscore its fame as a trading center, utilizing camels (Isa. 60:6) and exporting such commodities as gold, spices, frankincense, and precious stones (Ps. 72:15; Isa. 60:6; Jer. 6:20; Ezek. 27:22). Some of these same commodities were conveyed by the queen of Sheba when she visited Solomon in Jerusalem (1 Kings 10:1–13; 2 Chron. 9:1–12). As early as Strabo, the famous Sabean kingdom has been known to center at Ma'rib, in eastern Yemen, and it is here that one should locate Sheba.[55] Therefore, Hamite Seba should not be confused with Sheba.[56]
8. **Dedan.** Biblical texts indicate that Dedan was situated near the border of Edom (Ezek. 25:13; cf. Jer. 49:8, where

people from neighboring Dedan are living in Edom). Like Sheba, the site of Dedan is closely linked to caravans and trade in the Bible (Isa. 21:13; Ezek. 27:15,[57] 20; 38:13). Dedan is confidently located at the oasis of al-Ula, in the western Arabian Desert, on the major trade route from Yemen and Mecca north toward Amman and Jerusalem, about 175 miles north-to-northwest of Medina.[58] One notes again the close connections between various Hamite descendants and major trading routes across the Arabian Desert.

9. **Nimrod.** Nimrod is said to be a heroic king who ruled in the land of Shinar (Sumer and Babylonia)[59] over the cities of Babel (Babylon), Erech (Uruk), and Akkad. [**See map 23.**] From there he traveled to Assyria and built Nineveh, Rehoboth-Ir (perhaps a suburb or a quarter of Nineveh), Calah (Nimrud), and Resen[60] (perhaps an irrigation system or a source of water for Nineveh). Nimrod has been identified with various figures and heroes from antiquity, including Sargon the Great, Naram-Sin (warlike grandson of Sargon), Tukulti-Ninurta I (Assyrian monarch who succeeded in capturing Babylon and carrying off the statue of Marduk), Amenhotep III, or Gilgamesh (cunning hunter in Sumerian literature).
10. **Mizraim.** Mizraim represents the land of Egypt. The word "Egypt" is never found in the Hebrew Old Testament, but is of Greek derivation. As in other ancient literatures the nation was commonly called Mizri/Muṣri.[61] The Egyptians called their country either the "black land" (a reference to the dark alluvial soil deposited by the Nile) or "the two lands" (because of the geographic duality of Upper Egypt and Lower Egypt).
11. **Ludim.** This is an uncertain entry. The genealogy of Ham includes a people known as the Ludim (Gen. 10:13; 1 Chron. 1:11) and the descendancy of Shem makes reference to a Lud (Gen. 10:22; 1 Chron. 1:17 [the *–îm* ending is a plural indicator]).[62] Similarly, some prophetic texts make reference to Lud(im) in the context of oracles against Egypt, where Lud(im) is clearly linked with other places known to have been in North Africa (Jer. 46:9; Ezek. 30:5). Another text relates the term with the islands of the Mediterranean world and adjacent regions (Isa. 66:19).[63] In Ezekiel 27:10 the reference is geographically ambiguous and could designate either an African or a Mediterranean location. Accordingly, it is preferable to locate the Ludim somewhere in North Africa, near the other descendants of Mizraim, and to differentiate between the Hamite Ludim and the Shemite Lud/Lydians. (See below: Descendants of Shem #4.)
12. **Anamim.** This appears to be an otherwise unknown entity. Because of their association in the Table with groups such as the Pathrusim and Caphtorim, it has been proposed that the Anamim represented a people from the North African vicinity of Cyrene[64] [**map 86**], which also fits well with the homeland of other offspring of Mizraim.
13. **Lehabim.** This name occurs only in the Table and in the synoptic genealogy of 1 Chronicles 1. It is reasonable to consider Lehabim as an alternate spelling of Lubim, referring to people customarily equated with the ancient Libyans.
14. **Naphtuhim.** This is an uncertain entry. Because the Naphtuhim are located in the Table between the Lehabim (Libyans) and the Pathrusim (people of Pathros, in Upper Egypt), scholars have tended to locate the Naphtuhim in the vicinity of the Egyptian Delta (part of Lower Egypt).
15. **Pathrusim.** Biblical texts explicitly place Pathros/Pathrusim "in the land of Egypt" (Jer. 44:1, 15; cf. Ezek. 29:14; 30:14), so there can be no doubt that this is the Hebrew equivalent of the Egyptian name for the administrative district of Upper (southern) Egypt. (Paturisi means "those of the Southland.")
16. **Casluhim.** This is an extremely uncertain entry. A possible relationship existed between the Casluhim and the Philistines. Because the name is elsewhere unknown and because the *LXX* renders the word as Chasmoniem, some scholars speculate that this term designates the Nasamonians,[65] a group of nomadic Libyans who lived near the North African coast in the vicinity of the Gulf of Sidra, known today as Syrtis Major. [**See map 112.**] The suggestion that the Casluhim are somehow related to the Tjekker, one of the Sea Peoples who attacked Egypt in the time of Ramesses III, is extremely unlikely on several grounds.
17. **Caphtorim.** The identity of Caphtor/Caphtorim has been vigorously debated for at least 30 years, and it is widely accepted today that the term designates the island of Crete.
18. **Put.** The Old Testament location of Put is often associated with other African localities (Jer. 46:9; Ezek. 30:5; Nah. 3:9) and the word is rendered *Libyes* (Libya) in all non-genealogical passages of the *LXX*. (Whether the term corresponds to Put or Ludim is uncertain.) Accordingly, Put is almost certainly an area west of the Nile Delta, in the eastern stretches of modern Libya. The name should not be confused with Punt of Egyptian texts, which was located south of Egypt along the west coast of the Red Sea.
19. **Canaan.** Canaan designates the land and one of the people groups who lived west of the Jordan River (Num. 13:29; Deut. 11:29–30). When Israel was on the threshold of crossing the Jordan and settling in Canaan, the land was occupied by the Canaanites, the Hittites, the Hivites, the Perizzites, the Girgashites, the Amorites, and the Jebusites (Josh. 3:10; cf. Deut. 7:1; Acts 13:19). All of these people groups are listed in the Table of Nations. (Both the antiquity and attestation of the name, as well as the boundaries, were discussed in Chapter One.)
20. **Sidon.** Sidon is a main city of the ancient Phoenicians, situated on the Mediterranean coast about 25 miles north of Tyre. [**See map 25.**]

21. **Heth.** Certain people in the Old Testament are described as the "sons of Heth" (Gen. 23:5), "the daughters of Heth" (Gen. 27:46), or "the Hittites" (Gen. 23:10b). They appear to have lived in a section of what was to become the territory of Judah, in the vicinity of Hebron (Gen. 23; cf. Gen. 49:29–30; 50:13). The Old Testament and cuneiform literature also attest to a geographic/ethnic entity in upper Syria, north of Damascus, known as Hittites/Hatti, a group of city-states that existed during the first half of the first millennium B.C. It is improbable that these "neo-Hittite kingdoms," as they are known in contemporary literature, were related biologically to the "sons of Heth." It is more certain that the sons of Heth should in no way be linked to the better-known Indo-European ethnic group from the second millennium B.C. who created the "Hittite Empire" in Asia Minor that continued to exist until its demise around 1200 B.C.
22. **Jebusite.** Included in the "seven nations" of Canaan (Deut. 7:1), Jebusites in the pre-monarchy period lived in the hill country of Canaan (Num. 13:29) and more specifically in the area around Jerusalem (Jebus as it was known at that time). David seized the city from the Jebusites and made it the capital of his domain (2 Sam. 5:6–10).
23. **Amorite.** The Amorites/Amurru are well known from Akkadian literature between the late third millennium B.C. and the neo-Assyrian period. The Sumerian equivalent of Amurru [*mar.tu*] is found along the upper edge of a cuneiform map from Nuzi, dating to about 2300 B.C., where it functions unambiguously as one of the four cardinal compass points: "wind of the west." Therefore, from a Mesopotamian perspective, Amorites are "westerners." Groups of Amorites/Amurru tend to be located in literature along the entire Levant, in Syria, Lebanon, and Canaan. In the Old Testament, the term appears to be used somewhat equivocally, marking those who lived in the central hill country (Num. 13:29; Josh. 10:5–6), but also delineating Transjordanian kings/realms (Deut. 4:46, in Heshbon; 4:47, in Bashan; cf. 31:4; refer also to Num. 21:13, at the Arnon River; Judg. 10:8, in Gilead).
24. **Girgashite.** Nothing beyond a very general localization can be established for the Girgashites, whose name appears in the Old Testament only on the roster of the "seven nations" of Canaan's pre-Israelite population. Somewhat plausible is the suggestion made by certain scholars that the name could be related to the Gergasenes/Gerasenes/Gadarenes (Matt. 8:28; Mark 5:1),[66] though employing a text from as late as the Greek era to locate an Old Testament name is methodologically precarious.
25. **Hivite.** The Hivites (or "Hivvites") represent another one of the "seven nations" of Canaan's pre-Israelite population, but nothing more specific or certain can be gleaned from the biblical texts that mention this people. Hivites in the Old Testament may be related to Gibeon (Josh. 11:19), Shechem (Gen. 34:2), or the area adjacent to Mt. Hermon (Josh. 11:3; Judg. 3:3). A few scholars identify the Hivites with the Horites, presumably the Hurrians known to have existed in second-millennium B.C. northern Mesopotamia and even at points farther west and south.[67] A direct

Remains of the Jebusite wall of Jerusalem, dating to the 18th century B.C.

connection between Hiv(v)ites and Ammia (in Lebanon, presumably near the city of Byblos)[68] is possible, but tenuous on present evidence. Yet in light of other entries in the Table also said to have descended from Canaan—Sidonians, Arkites, Sinites, Arvadites, Zemarites, and Hamathites—it cannot be fully dismissed.

26. **Arkite.** Scholars since the time of Josephus have linked the Arkites with the site of I/Arqata,[69] a coastal town in Lebanon situated about 12 miles northeast of Tripolis. [**See map 4.**]
27. **Sinite.** The Sinites should be associated with Siyannu, a city-state attested in literature from Ugarit and Assyria. Siyannu was situated along the Syrian seacoast between Ugarit and Arvad.[70]
28. **Arvadite.** The Arvadites correspond to an ancient entity known as Arvad [**map 70**], the northernmost city in the Phoenician homeland. Arvad appears to have been the northernmost descendant of Canaan listed in the Table and is preserved to this day in the name Ruad, a small island located just off the Mediterranean coast about 55 miles north of Byblos.
29. **Zemarite.** Ancient literature is replete with references to Sumra/Sumur/Simirra, a place that must be situated south of Arvad and near the Mediterranean shoreline.[71] Biblical Zemarites should be related to this documentation. Classical literature includes the site Simyra, situated at T. Kazel, immediately north of the mouth of the Eleutheros River (N. el-Kabir), adjacent to the modern Syrian-Lebanese border. [**See map 4.**] This location serves more or less as the biblical border of Canaan.
30. **Hamathite.** The Hamathites are related to the frequently attested city on the Orontes River, modern Hama, located approximately 105 miles north of Damascus. [**See map 23.**]

THE TWENTY-SIX DESCENDANTS OF SHEM

1. **Elam.** This famous domain of Elam, with Susa as its capital city, lay to the east of southern Mesopotamia and near the Persian Gulf. The name is known as early as the third millennium B.C.,[72] and it is regularly attested in later literature down to the neo-Babylonian period.[73]
2. **Asshur.** The domain of Asshur adopted its name from its first capital city. [**See map 75.**]
3. **Arpachshad.** This is an uncertain entry, and speculation has taken several forms. Josephus connected Arpachshad with the Chaldeans, an identity later embraced by others[74] because the last three letters of the Hebrew word could also spell Chaldeans and because Chaldea would otherwise be absent from the Table. Another view equates the entry with Babylon.[75] Based also on sound similarity, Arpachshad has also been related to the commonly attested site of Arrapha (Kirkuk),[76] located near to ancient Nuzi.
4. **Lud.** As early as Josephus the Ludim were related to the Lydians of Asia Minor. As indicated previously, it is highly unlikely that the Hamite "Ludim" should be confused with the Shemite "Lud," the latter being situated in North Africa. The name Lud(u) occurs in Akkadian literature where it unambiguously references a region of Asia Minor[77] and there is no compelling reason to reject this viewpoint. Yet because such a position would separate Lud at a far distance from other Shemite entries in the Table, some seek alternatives geographically closer to Mesopotamia.
5. **Aram.** This entry in the Table makes reference to the Arameans and their homeland stretching between Damascus and territory just east of the Upper Euphrates River. Biblical patriarchs appear to have had an especially close relationship with the Arameans, particularly with those who lived between the Euphrates and the Habur rivers in an area known in the Old Testament as Aram-naharaim (Gen. 24:10; cf. Gen. 25:20; and see Deut. 26:5). The area of Aram also became known as "Assyria" by the middle of the first millennium B.C.,[78] a name that was abridged to Syria by the Greeks.
6. **Uz.** This is an uncertain entry because biblical citations of Uz are mixed geographically, even assuming they all reference one and the same entity. For example, Lamentations 4:21 associates Uz with Edom (cf. Gen. 36:28), which has led some scholars to look southward toward the land of Edom. On the other hand, Genesis 22:21 links Uz with Nahor and Aram, which suggests a more northerly locale. Josephus located Uz in the region of Trachonitis and Damascus. [**See map 6.**]
7. **Hul.** This is a basically unknown entry. Because Hul follows in sequence after Aram and Uz, one might conjecture that it should be located somewhere within greater Aram. Josephus located Hul in Armenia, which seems geographically out of place with Aram and his known descendants.
8. **Gether.** This is an unknown entry. Again, given its place amid the Aramean descendancy, one might conjecture a location near to or within greater Aram. In this connection, it has been suggested that this is a reference to the land of Geshur.[79]
9. **Mash.** Despite much speculation, this remains another unknown entry.
10. **Shelah.** This is yet another unknown entry. One should not attempt to connect this entry in the Table to the third son of Judah (Gen. 38:5; 46:12; Num. 26:20), as the two words have a different final Hebrew letter. Only coincidentally are their names spelled the same in English.
11. **Eber.** Cognate to the word "Hebrew," this entry may plausibly be related to the Eberites (the Hebrews), which suggests an ethnic association with the Israelite forebears. Such an understanding would promote the idea that Eber should be situated in the same general vicinity as others of

the patriarchs' immediate kin: Nahor, Harran, and Paddan-aram. Alternatively, this root occurs in Akkadian where it means to cross over water. This word can also occur in a phrase (*eber nāri*) that designates an official region of upper Syria, known as "Beyond [west of] the River [the Euphrates]." On either of these suggestions, Eber would be positioned in rather close proximity to the upper Euphrates.

12. **Peleg.** This too is an uncertain entry. One text does refer to a Palga people who lived near the Habur River in upper Mesopotamia,[80] a location that comports well with the placement of Eber. Later geographers reference a site, Phaliga, in this same location. Alternatively, late-Babylonian references to the city of Palkatta (Fallujah, a town on the Euphrates in southern Iraq) would seem to be too far south to be relevant here.
13. **Joktan.** Here again uncertainty prevails. Joktan is presented as the father of the remaining thirteen groups in the Table, some of which are thought to be located in the southern Arabian peninsula and lend themselves to Arabic etymologies. None is clearly situated in another geographical context. Speculation on Joktan, therefore, tends to center in modern Saudi Arabia.
14. **Almoded.** This entry defies classification, as it does not appear outside the Bible. Perhaps this entry should be understood as "al-moded," an Akkadian reference to an individual identified as "the beloved one."
15. **Sheleph.** The equivalent of this name does occur in various literatures from antiquity, but with various possible locations including the town known as Šalab/pi in southern Mesopotamia and the northeastern Arabian peninsula where the Salapeni tribe appear to have lived. More promising are references in Sabean inscriptions and in Arab geographic treatises to a South Arabian tribe or tribes, named as al-Salif and al-Sulaf,[81] and located in the southern quarter of the Arabian peninsula, in modern Yemen.
16. **Hazarmaveth.** This descendant of Joktan should be identified with modern Hadramaut, a frankincense-producing region located along the Arabian coast within southern Yemen.[82]
17. **Jerah.** A town called J/Iarih existed near the confluence of the Euphrates and Balih rivers. Such a location, however, does not fit well with that of the other descendants of Joktan. Because "Jerah" is cognate to a common Semitic word for "moon,"[83] it seems likely that Jerah should be related in some way with moon cult worship, which was ubiquitous in antiquity across the central and southern stretches of the Arabian peninsula. Its exact location is unknown.
18. **Hadoraim.** This is an uncertain entry. Attempts have been made to equate this name with a similar name (*Dauram*) found in several Sabean inscriptions and normally located in west central Yemen, near its capital city of San`a. The location fits quite nicely with other known descendants of Joktan.
19. **Uzal.** The name Uzal is fairly common in South Arabic sources, where it is said to have been the original name for San`a, capital city of modern Yemen.[84] This is the most likely location for biblical Uzal. Other possibilities include a site/region known as Izalla (perhaps Mt. Izalla [Mons Izalla][85] between the Habur triangle and the upper Tigris River [the modern Tur Abdin range]). Ezekiel 27:19 indicates Uzal as a source of prime wine, which would allow for the Tur Abdin site or somewhere in the mountains of Lebanon.[86] None of these locales, however, fits well with what is otherwise known about the descendants of Joktan.
20. **Diklah.** This is an unknown entity. The name in Hebrew means a "date-palm," and hence any place that would be particularly noted for this product might qualify.
21. **Obal.** This entry almost certainly corresponds to `Ubal, a place in western Yemen, between Hodeida on the Red Sea coast and the capital city of San`a.[87] More than one tribe/clan by this name is found in Sabean inscriptions.
22. **Abimael.** This is an unknown entry. Whether the name means "my father is truly God" or "Father is God," nothing is known by which this place can be identified.
23. **Sheba.** See previous comments under Hamite Sheba, which cannot be distinguished from its homonym.[88]
24. **Ophir.** For a discussion of this name, refer to the commentary accompanying **map 63**.
25. **Havilah.** See previous comments at Hamite Havilah, which cannot be distinguished from its homonym.[89]
26. **Jobab.** The location of this entry remains in dispute. It has been argued that Jobab must be related to a Sabean tribe of a similar name, located near Mecca in the western Arabian peninsula.[90] A group known as the Iobaritae, located in the southeastern corner of the Arabian peninsula (modern Oman), has also been the basis of speculation but is geographically less likely.

THE MIGRATION OF THE PATRIARCHS

The book of Genesis portrays both the migrations and wanderings of the patriarchs. The patriarchal migrations in Genesis commenced when Abraham moved as part of his father's clan from Ur of the Chaldeans to the city of Harran[91] (Gen. 11:31–32). The location of Harran can be firmly established at modern Haran, situated near the Balih River about ten miles southeast of Urfa (Edessa) and some four miles north of the modern Turkish-Syrian border. Modern excavations indicate its first inhabitants may have lived there as early as around 8000 B.C., and the site is amply attested in cuneiform texts from the third, second, and first millennia B.C. The place was later known by the Romans as Carrhae.

Yet the location of Ur of the Chaldeans continues to remain in some dispute. Since the archaeological work and publications of Leonard Woolley in the early 20th century, it has been fashionable to equate "biblical Ur" with the famous Sumerian capital of the Third Dynasty of Ur (T. Muqayyar), located on the lower Euphrates about 65 miles upstream of its confluence with the Tigris. [**See map 28.**] Initially this view seemed logical because of the obvious name similarity, because of the complexity and spectacular finds of the site, and because both the Sumerian Ur and the city of Harran flourished during the second millennium B.C. as prime centers of moon-cult worship. A form of moon-cult religion is clearly attested in patriarchal ancestry: the names of Terah (Gen. 11:24–26), Laban (Gen. 24:29), Milcah (Gen. 11:29), and Sarai (Gen. 11:29) may all be related to the worship of the moon (Josh. 24:2). According to this view, the initial leg of Abraham's migration took him from one center of moon-cult worship to another such center.

Subsequent investigation, however, has brought Woolley's view into some question. Uncertainty prevails, in the first place, because the Bible never refers merely to "Ur," but always to "Ur *of the Chaldeans*" or "Ur *in the land of the Chaldeans*" (Gen. 11:28, 31; 15:7; Neh. 9:7; cf. Acts 7:4). Such a consistent qualification could suggest that biblical writers were endeavoring to distinguish the place of Abraham's emigration from the famous contemporary metropolis with the same name (just as a resident of Paris, *Illinois*, might have to qualify where he lives to avoid confusion with the more famous French city). In the many attestations of Woolley's, it is never so qualified; Ur is associated with the Sumerians, not the Chaldeans, until the seventh century B.C.

The need to distinguish the name Ur may be strengthened further when grappling with the meaning of "Chaldeans." Any interpretation points to a *northern* Mesopotamian location. No sure trace of the Chaldeans exists in southern Babylonia before the early ninth century B.C., which is after the conclusion of the patriarchal era. Earlier than that date, one must look to northern Mesopotamia to find references to Chaldeans. In addition, the word translated "Chaldeans" is *kaśdîm* in Hebrew. Scholars identify this word with "Chaldeans" either on grounds

Mudbrick "beehive" houses characterize the architecture of the site of Harran.

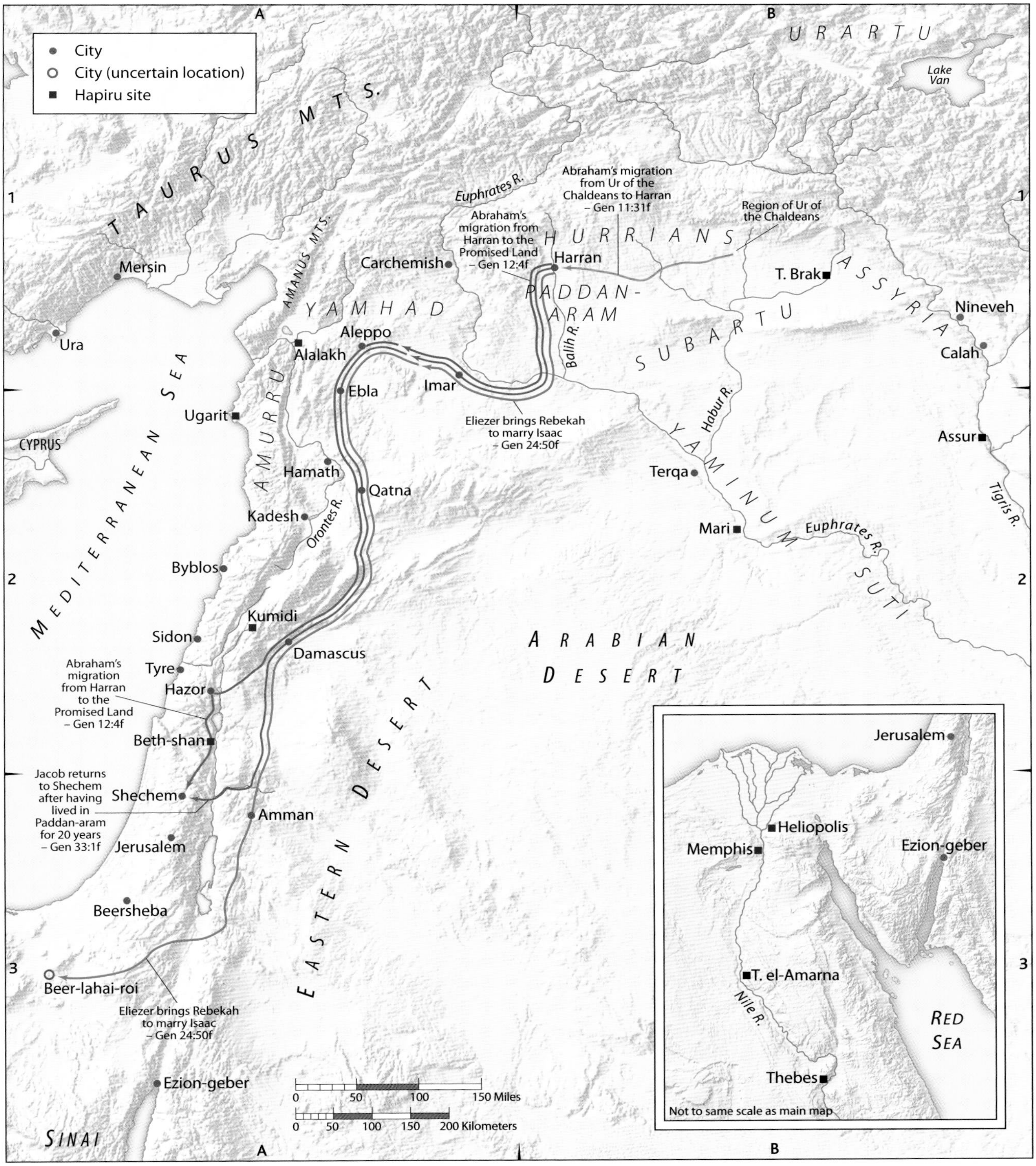

of phonetics or phonology. If *kaśdîm* were to be related to the patriarchal ancestor Chesed (Gen. 22:22), the phrase would be understood to mean, "Ur of [the land/region of] Chesed." Even so, one would draw the same conclusion, since Chesed's descendants are said to have settled in Paddan-aram—in northern Mesopotamia (Gen. 24:10).

Moreover, where Mesopotamian cultural influences appear to be reflected in the lives of the patriarchs (levirate marriage, dimorphic tribalism, genealogical inheritance, population makeup, etc.), it is northern Mesopotamian literature that ordinarily provides the cultural parallels.[92] Southern Babylonian influence, as far as we now know, is almost totally lacking in the patriarchal narratives.

Mesopotamian literatures do attest to the presence of several second-millennium B.C. cities known as "Ur(a/u)" or its linguistic equivalent, which must be situated somewhere in or near the north of Mesopotamia. On the basis of significant archival accounts,[93] we can assert with confidence the existence of a second-millennium B.C. "northern" Ur located either (1) somewhere in close proximity to the Mediterranean coast, or (2) somewhere inland between the upper Habur River and the Tigris River near Nineveh.[94] It is probable that there were more than two northern sites with this name, but it is not possible there were fewer than two sites. Of course, whether any of these sites correspond to the biblical Ur of the Chaldeans remains an open question, and the location near the Mediterranean must be considered a very remote possibility. In light of these considerations, some scholars[95] seek Ur of the Chaldeans somewhere in the north of Mesopotamia, and not at Woolley's noted southern site. This viewpoint is depicted on the accompanying map.

THE WANDERINGS OF THE PATRIARCHS

A study of the patriarchal wanderings presents us with two overriding conclusions. The first is that the patriarchs lived in tents as pastoral semi-nomads on seasonal pasturelands. The places in Canaan visited by patriarchs received between ten and thirty inches of annual rainfall, which is ideally suited for the grazing of flocks and herds. The patriarchs did not normally settle in towns. (Lot was an exception.) They did not tend to farm. (Genesis 26:12 is probably an exception.) They seem not to have owned land, except for a few modest burial sites at Mamre/Hebron (Gen. 23:2–20; cf. 25:9–10; 35:27; 49:29–32; 50:13), Shechem (Gen. 33:19; cf. Josh. 24:32), and where Rachel was buried (Gen. 35:16–20). [**See map 32.**]

The second conclusion is that the patriarchs must have arrived in Canaan during an era when the land was relatively free from external political control. Abraham and his clan appear to have moved from one place to another without political interference, and yet the size of his entourage (Gen. 14:14) suggests that his movements would certainly otherwise have been detected by provincial political authorities. Such a scenario coincides with the historical profile of Canaan during the latter part of the Middle Bronze Age (1850–1550 B.C.) when Canaan and Syria were vitally involved together and shared a common material culture. But by the Late Bronze Age (1550–1200 B.C.), the strong Egyptian domination and the formation of larger political entities led to much more cultural differentiation, which undoubtedly would have made free traffic and ethnic migration much more difficult.

Several other aspects of the patriarchal narratives point toward a Middle Bronze Age setting. For instance, the 20 shekels of silver paid by the Amalekite traders for Joseph (Gen. 37:28) represented the average price paid for a slave during the Middle Bronze Age.[96] At the same time, a variety of patriarchal social customs also fit well into a Middle Bronze Age social milieu:

- A father could explicitly prohibit a prospective son-in-law from taking other wives (Gen. 31:50);
- A female slave was often given as part of a dowry at the point of marriage (Gen. 16:1–6; 30:1–13);
- A man without male offspring could resort to adoption (Gen. 15:2–6) or polygamy to obtain a son (Gen. 16:1–6);
- A barren wife could provide male offspring by way of a handmaiden (Gen. 30:1–8); and
- Inheritance rights of the firstborn were normally respected (Gen. 25:5–6, 32–34; 43:33–34; 49:3–4).

The term "Habiru" is frequently employed in cuneiform and Egyptian literatures between the 21st and 12th centuries B.C. to denote various groups of peoples who often lived on the fringes of society and were sometimes portrayed as a threat to local cities and rulers.[97] "Habiru" is similar to "Hebrews"—the term that described the patriarchs of Genesis (Gen. 14:13; 39:14, 17; 40:15; 41:12; 43:32) before the adoption of a more common designation, "children of Israel" (e.g., Ex. 1:1, 7). Because the patriarchs were presented as living on the fringes of society, and because name similarity is sometimes converted into name identity, some scholars believe the patriarchal Hebrews should be equated with the Habiru of ancient secular texts. However, a glance at the map demonstrates how geographically unviable is such a conclusion. Habiru appear in texts throughout the whole of Mesopotamia, in addition to places as far flung as Susa in the east, Hattusha in the north, and Thebes in southern Egypt, distantly beyond anything imaginable of the patriarchal Hebrews.

In summary, though no individual or group mentioned in the book of Genesis is otherwise known from antiquity, the patriarchal journeys do present an accurate historical picture of that age.

ABRAHAM IN PALESTINE

In some respects, God's "call" upon Abraham (Gen. 12:1–3) carried with it many of the same consequences as his "curse" upon Cain (Gen. 4:12–16): each person was directed to forsake every form of security known to his world and go live in another place.

Abraham abandoned his land, clan, and family at Harran and proceeded toward the land his descendants would eventually inherit (Gen. 12:4–5). Upon arriving in the central highlands of Canaan, the great patriarch built an altar at the city of Shechem and worshiped God (Gen. 12:6–7). From there he moved southward to encamp near Bethel and Ai (Gen. 12:8) [**1**]. But Abraham also discovered rather harsh realities in this new place: the land was dominated at the time by Canaanites (Gen. 12:6b), and it was caught in the grip of a famine (Gen. 12:10), thus forcing him to travel on to Egypt, presumably by way of the central roadway that passed Hebron and Beersheba [**2**].

When the famine came to an end, Abraham and his entourage retraced their steps via the Negeb and returned to his former campsite near Bethel/Ai, where they again took up residence (Gen. 13:3–4) [**3**]. But before long Abraham experienced yet another conflict—this time an internal one. There was apparently an insufficient amount of grazing lands to support the flocks of Abraham and his nephew Lot, which resulted in Lot's departure to the better-watered Jordan plain and residence in the town of Sodom (Gen. 13:11–12; cf. 14:12) [**4**]. Meanwhile, Abraham moved south and came to settle by the oaks of Mamre, at Hebron (Gen. 13:18) [**5**], where he constructed yet another altar to the Lord.

Some time thereafter, five cities situated in the Valley of Siddim (Sodom, Gomorrah, Admah, Zeboiim, and Zoar) rebelled against their Mesopotamian overlords (Gen. 14:1–4). Responding to this challenge, the Mesopotamian monarchs led their armies toward Canaan and, along the way, assaulted the Transjordanian lands of the Rephaim, Zuzim, Emim, and Horites as far as El-paran (Gen. 14:5–6) [**6**]. Passing El-paran, the enemy kings turned toward Enmishpat (Kadesh-barnea), where they subdued some Amalekites (14:7a) before

Situated at the point where W. Shekhem joins the Central Ridge Route is biblical Shechem (modern Nablus).

vanquishing the Amorites at Tamar (14:7b) [7]. This action would have allowed the Mesopotamian kings to turn their attention toward their real foes: the cities of the Valley of Siddim (Gen. 14:8–11) [8].

The wording of Genesis 13:10–11 has led some people to seek the cities near the northern end of the Dead Sea and the mouth of the Jordan River. However, it is much more prevalent to argue that these cities must have been situated toward the southern end of the Dead Sea based on the fact that the name of one of them (Zoar) is located in that region on the sixth-century Medeba mosaic map. [**See map 15.**] Furthermore, many Early Bronze Age graves containing thousands of human skeletal remains have been found near the southeastern shore of the Dead Sea—hypothesized by some writers to be related to events surrounding Sodom and Gomorrah.[98]

A very early Christian tradition that became quite prevalent in early medieval maps was to locate Sodom and Gomorrah *beneath* the waters of the Dead Sea basins, particularly the southern basin.[99] However, the lowering of the level of the Dead Sea in the 20th century has resulted in the exposure of dry land in the southern basin, and no archaeological remains have been discovered to support this supposition.

A Mesopotamian victory was swift and decisive. The cities of the Jordan plain were defeated. Some of their citizens, including Lot, were carried away as far north as the city of Dan (Gen. 14:12) [9]. When informed of this calamity, Abraham immediately led some of his men in pursuit of Lot's captors, overtaking them near Dan and successfully routing them as far as Damascus and even beyond (Gen. 14:13–15) [10]. As he returned from his mission and came near to the Valley of Shaveh, Abraham was met by the king of Salem, Melchizedek, with whom the patriarch shared the spoils of victory (Gen. 14:17–24) [11].

Abraham is said to have journeyed south from there toward the Negeb and eventually came to Gerar (Gen. 20:1) [12]. During his years there, the long-awaited promise of a son was finally realized (Gen. 21:2–3). But when a problem over water rights arose with the king of Gerar (Gen. 21:25), Abraham moved inland to Beersheba (Gen. 21:31, by implication) [13]. This location apparently served as the patriarch's home until his death, when he was taken and buried beside Sarah in the cave near Hebron (Gen. 25:8–10).

Abraham in Palestine

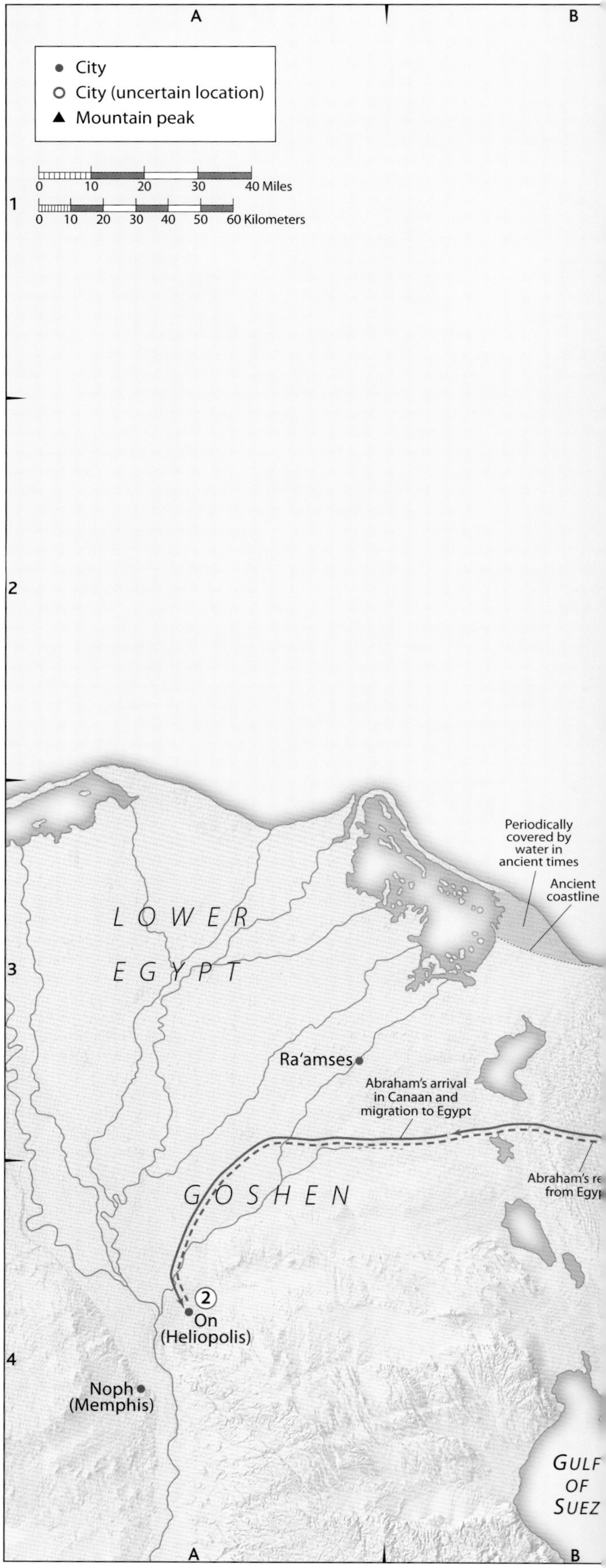

C
D
E
to Hobah
Damascus
10
Mt. Hermon
Litani R.
Abraham's pursuit of enemy kings
Dan
9
Course taken by enemy kings in Genesis 14
Abraham's return from battle
1
Hazor
MEDITERRANEAN SEA
SEA OF GALILEE
Karnaim
REPHAIM
Ashtaroth
Kishon R.
Yarmuk R.
Megiddo
Ham
Jordan R.
ZUZIM
Samaria
Shechem
1
Jabbok R.
Jarkon R.
Aphek
2
Lot's departure from Abraham
Bethel
1 3
Ai
Jericho
Ekron
Ashdod
VALLEY OF SHAVEH
Salem
4
11
Kiriathaim
Hebron
5
Gaza
Dibon
Abraham's final journey to Beersheba
12 Gerar
DEAD SEA
Arnon R.
EMIM
Besor Brook
Abraham's return from Egypt
13
2
Beersheba
NEGEB
Abraham's arrival in Canaan and migration to Egypt
Possible location of Sodom, Gomorrah, Admar, Zeboiim
W. el-Arish
Zoar
8
Zered Brook
3
Hagar fled here from Sarah – Gen 16:14f
Isaac lived here after Abraham's death – Gen 25:11f
AMORITES
VALLEY OF SIDDIM
7 Tamar
Beer-lahai-roi
EASTERN
AMALEKITES
HORITES
Punon
7
Kadesh-barnea (En-mishpat)
DESERT
WILDERNESS OF SHUR
Petra
Course taken by enemy kings in Genesis 14
4
WILDERNESS OF PARAN
6 El-paran
GULF OF AQABA
C
D
E

THE PATRIARCHS IN PALESTINE

The patriarchs of Genesis spent their lives in the Promised Land within the southern half of the Central Mountain Spine. Only on brief occasions did their travels take them temporarily beyond that realm—the exception being when Jacob left Canaan for a lengthy stay in his ancestral homeland in northern Mesopotamia (Gen. 28:10—33:20). [**See map 30.**] But while living in the land, the patriarchs are said to have taken up residence, built altars, and worshiped the Lord in Shechem, Bethel, Hebron/Mamre, and Beersheba. They and their wives were buried in that same area, either in the family burial plot at Mamre/Hebron, at Shechem, or at the burial spot of Rachel.

As Jacob was returning to Canaan from his twenty years in the household of Laban (Gen. 31:41), he arrived at the Jabbok River. There he was informed that his brother Esau was en route to meet him, thus triggering a night of wrestling (Gen. 32:6–7, 22–30). The narration of chapter 32 (at the end of his sojourn) forms a fitting sequel to that of chapter 28 (at the beginning of his sojourn). Both texts describe Jacob being alone at night, faced with a crisis, meeting "angels of God" (28:12; 32:1), and assigning a new name to a place (Bethel, 28:19; Penuel, 32:30).

The location of the Transjordanian sites of Mahanaim and Penuel is uncertain, beyond being situated adjacent to the Jabbok gorge. Mahanaim was allotted to the tribe of Gad (Josh. 13:26) but was on the border with Manasseh (Josh. 13:30). [**See map 40.**] The town was a levitical city (Josh. 21:38–39) [**map 41**], a royal residence for Ishbaal (2 Sam. 2:8, 12), and a temporary refuge for David when he fled from Absalom (2 Sam. 17:24–27). On the map, Mahanaim has been placed tentatively at the site of T. er-Reheil, where the main north-south road from Damascus approaches the Jabbok River and intersects with a secondary road running westward toward the Jordan. [**See map 27.**] Penuel must have been nearby, though it was situated between Mahanaim (Gen. 32:1) and Succoth (33:17), possibly at T. edh-Dhahab esh-Sharqia.

After his return from Mesopotamia, Jacob journeyed from his residence at Bethel to be with his father, Isaac, at Hebron/Mamre (Gen. 35:1, 27). But as the caravan was traveling along the road, the time came for Rachel to give birth to Benjamin. She died during the childbirth and was buried there (Gen. 35:16–20). Since the fourth Christian century, travelers and pilgrims have visited a "tomb of Rachel" on the north edge of Bethlehem, along the road from Jerusalem. The site was designated presumably on the basis of an editorial comment in Genesis 35:19.[100] But a later text (1 Sam. 10:2) makes clear that Rachel was buried at "the border of [the tribe of] Benjamin, at Zelzah." Although Zelzah is an unknown site not otherwise attested, the context of this reference is fairly clear. In the search for his father's lost asses, Saul traveled from his home at Gibeah (T. el-Ful [1 Sam. 10:26]), northward across the hill country of Ephraim, back around into the territory of Benjamin (1 Sam. 9:4), and finally to Ramah, Samuel's hometown (er-Ram [1 Sam. 9:5, 10]). On his return from Ramah to Gibeah, he is said to have passed by Rachel's tomb (1 Sam. 10:2).

In yet another text, the prophet Jeremiah (31:15) directly linked the "weeping of Rachel" to the town of Ramah, also located inside the territory of Benjamin. So while the exact location of Rachel's tomb remains in some dispute, a placement at Bethlehem has very little to commend it. It may be pertinent in this regard to recall the exact wording of the Genesis narrative. Rachel is said to have been buried "along the way/road to Ephrath [Bethlehem]" (Gen. 35:19; cf. 48:7b), "while they were still a good distance away [lit. "a distance of the land"][101] from Ephrath" (Gen. 35:16; cf. 48:7a).

Whatever the case, as Jacob continued his journey from Rachel's burial place toward Hebron/Mamre, he came to the Tower of Eder (Migdal-eder [Gen. 35:21]), located possibly in the vicinity of Salem or Bethlehem.

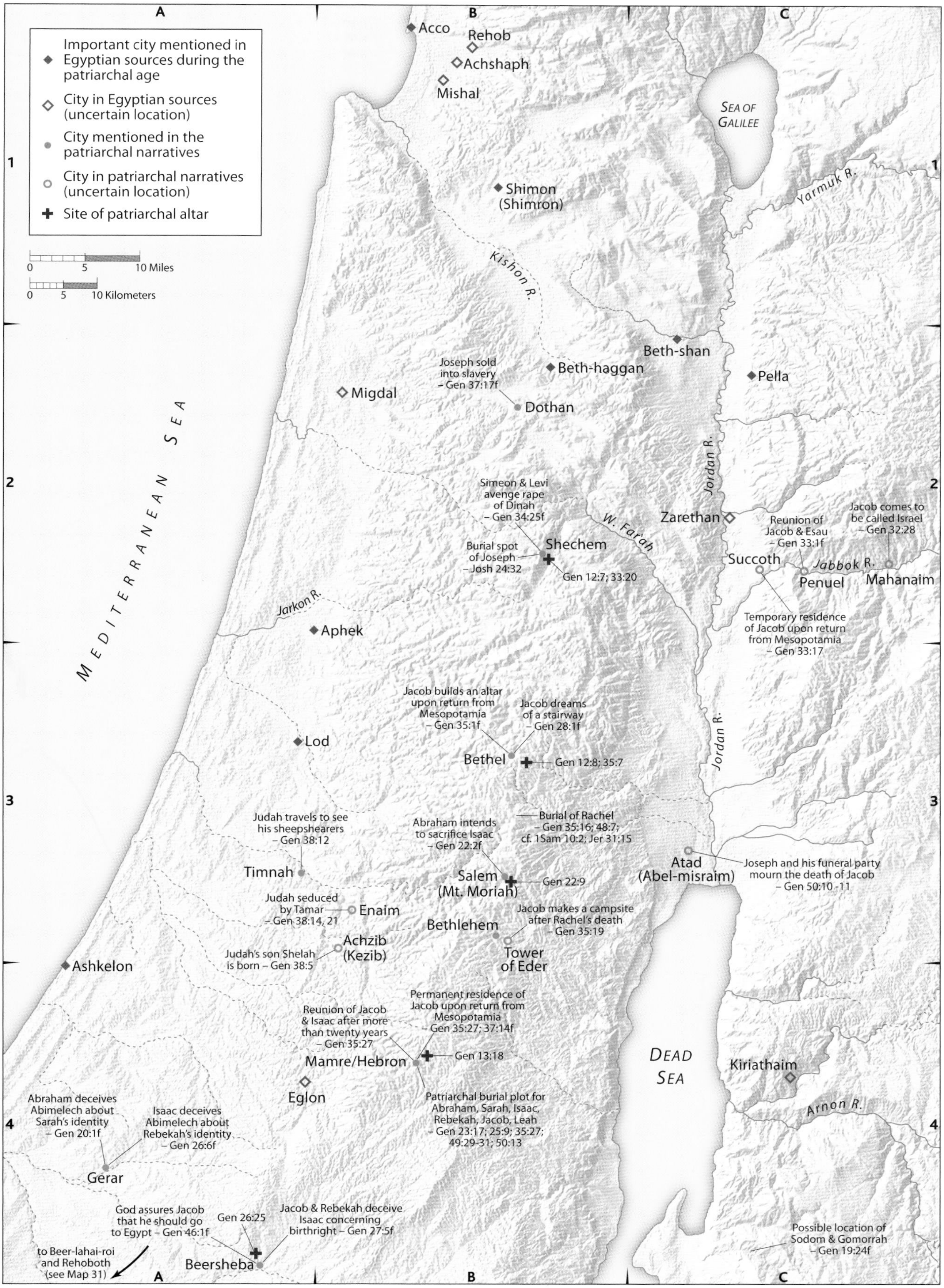
A
B
C
1
2
3
4
Important city mentioned in Egyptian sources during the patriarchal age
City in Egyptian sources (uncertain location)
City mentioned in the patriarchal narratives
City in patriarchal narratives (uncertain location)
Site of patriarchal altar
0 5 10 Miles
0 5 10 Kilometers
Acco
Rehob
Achshaph
Mishal
SEA OF GALILEE
Shimon (Shimron)
Yarmuk R.
Kishon R.
Beth-shan
Beth-haggan
Pella
Joseph sold into slavery – Gen 37:17f
Migdal
Dothan
MEDITERRANEAN SEA
Jordan R.
Simeon & Levi avenge rape of Dinah – Gen 34:25f
W. Far'ah
Zarethan
Reunion of Jacob & Esau – Gen 33:1f
Jacob comes to be called Israel – Gen 32:28
Burial spot of Joseph – Josh 24:32
Shechem
Gen 12:7; 33:20
Succoth
Jabbok R.
Penuel
Mahanaim
Jarkon R.
Aphek
Temporary residence of Jacob upon return from Mesopotamia – Gen 33:17
Jacob builds an altar upon return from Mesopotamia – Gen 35:1f
Jacob dreams of a stairway – Gen 28:1f
Lod
Bethel
Gen 12:8; 35:7
Jordan R.
Burial of Rachel – Gen 35:16; 48:7; cf. 1Sam 10:2; Jer 31:15
Judah travels to see his sheepshearers – Gen 38:12
Abraham intends to sacrifice Isaac – Gen 22:2f
Atad (Abel-misraim)
Joseph and his funeral party mourn the death of Jacob – Gen 50:10-11
Timnah
Salem (Mt. Moriah)
Gen 22:9
Judah seduced by Tamar – Gen 38:14, 21
Enaim
Jacob makes a campsite after Rachel's death – Gen 35:19
Bethlehem
Achzib (Kezib)
Judah's son Shelah is born – Gen 38:5
Tower of Eder
Ashkelon
Permanent residence of Jacob upon return from Mesopotamia – Gen 35:27; 37:14f
Reunion of Jacob & Isaac after more than twenty years – Gen 35:27
Gen 13:18
Mamre/Hebron
DEAD SEA
Kiriathaim
Eglon
Patriarchal burial plot for Abraham, Sarah, Isaac, Rebekah, Jacob, Leah – Gen 23:17; 25:9; 35:27; 49:29-31; 50:13
Abraham deceives Abimelech about Sarah's identity – Gen 20:1f
Isaac deceives Abimelech about Rebekah's identity – Gen 26:6f
Arnon R.
Gerar
God assures Jacob that he should go to Egypt – Gen 46:1f
Gen 26:25
Jacob & Rebekah deceive Isaac concerning birthright – Gen 27:5f
Possible location of Sodom & Gomorrah – Gen 19:24f
to Beer-lahai-roi and Rehoboth (see Map 31)
Beersheba

THE ROUTE OF THE EXODUS

There can be no doubt that an Israelite exodus from Egypt occurred. However, a number of significant historical and geographical questions remain concerning events prior to and surrounding the exodus. The geographical questions will receive the most attention here, but perhaps a passing historical footnote is first in order.

THE HISTORICAL BACKGROUND

From as early as Egypt's "Middle Kingdom," in the late 12th Dynasty (c. 1800 B.C.), increasing numbers of Asiatic people came to Egypt and took up residence primarily in and around the eastern Nile delta.[102] The Egyptians came to call these people *heqaw khasut*, an expression that meant "rulers of foreign lands," but which referred more specifically to the rulers from Canaan who spoke a West Semitic dialect.[103] We use the Greek version of the term to describe such people: *Hyksos.*

Throughout the 18th century B.C., Egyptian strength decreased as Hyksos numbers continued to increase numerically. The Hyksos's distinctive architectural structures, pottery forms, and various Canaanite social and religious practices reflect a relative strength and a growing independence. They are credited with introducing into Egypt several forms of military technological innovation, including the horse-drawn war chariot, the composite bow, and the battering ram,[104] which would have made them an even more imposing military force and self-determining political entity. Eventually, around 1640 B.C. or thereabouts, the Hyksos became strong enough to seize control of almost all Egypt, forming what is known in Egyptian history as Dynasties 15 and 16.[105]

The Hyksos established their headquarters at Avaris/T. el-Dab`a, on the easternmost (Pelusium) branch of the delta, and flourished there for about 100 years. [**See map 33.**] The city's independence during this period is also reflected in its broad commercial reach, stretching across the eastern Mediterranean, the Levant, and Mesopotamia, and as far south as Nubia.

The Hyksos capital city of Avaris was plundered by the Egyptians around 1560 B.C. Not long afterward, the Hyksos were expelled from Egypt by native princes, and the so-called "New Kingdom" period of Egyptian history was inaugurated. A concerted—even passionate—effort was mounted by the pharaohs of the New Kingdom period to rid a reunified Egypt of any trace of Hyksos influence. Numerous military campaigns were even launched into Canaan and Syria against the Hyksos and, in due course, against their Asiatic allies, especially the Arameans and the Mitannians. [**See map 44.**]

Biblical, historical, and archaeological data seem to indicate that it was a Hyksos monarch before whom Joseph stood as an interpreter of dreams (Gen. 41:14–37) and who later ceded a choice parcel of land (Goshen) to Joseph's family (Gen. 47:5–6). This theory could explain how Joseph—a non-Egyptian—was able to experience such a meteoric political rise to the position of vice-regent in a country that normally exhibited a xenophobic and sometimes contemptuous mentality toward foreigners. Similarly, the pharaoh warmly received the *Semitic* family of Joseph *from Canaan* (Gen. 47:1–11) and bequeathed to them a prominent piece of real estate in which to live—a gesture more suggestive of a monarch who was himself a Semite from Canaan than of a native Egyptian. This theory is consistent with the fact that those who made their descent with Jacob were able to prosper and multiply in Egypt, and for a time they became strong enough to represent a potential threat to a pharaoh.

Continuing with such a theory, the "new king over Egypt who did not know Joseph" (Ex. 1:8) would then have been one of the native Egyptian pharaohs of the New Kingdom era. As such, he would be determined to regain absolute political control over the eastern delta as part of the Hyksos purge, resolutely refusing to recognize the ongoing legitimacy of the Goshen land grant. Furthermore, discerning in the Israelites a multitude that might well be inclined to form an alliance with his Hyksos enemies in war (both having come to Egypt from Canaan), this new king acted preemptively to enslave God's people (Ex. 1:9–11).

These are broad if defensible generalizations, to be sure, but beyond this it seems hazardous to speculate concerning the identity of a specific pharaoh who promoted Joseph, of a particular king who enslaved the Israelites, or of the monarch of Egypt at the time of the exodus. No unambiguous data exist upon which a definitive claim can be made in this regard.

THE GEOGRAPHIC SETTING

The biblical narratives locate the starting point of the Israelite exodus from Egypt at the city of Ra`amses (Num. 33:3; cf. Ex. 1:11; 12:37), from which they journeyed first to Succoth (Ex. 12:37; cf. Num. 33:5), then to Etham (Ex. 13:20; cf. Num. 33:6), and finally to Pi-hahiroth at the body of water (Ex. 14:2; cf. Num. 33:7–8). [**See map 33.**] Of these places, only the location of Ra`amses is known beyond doubt. Today we know that biblical Ra`amses was situated at T. el Dab`a/Qantir. Construction started there around 1290 B.C. by Pharaoh Seti I, but the city was greatly enlarged and splendidly expanded by Pharaoh Ramses II adjacent to the remains of the Hyksos city of Avaris.[106]

Biblical Ra`amses became a vast sprawling metropolis, covering an area of at least six square miles over the space of some 2,500 acres. The city contained an extensive array of royal and religious buildings. Most were constructed of mud-brick (Ex. 1:14; 5:7–8, 16–19), an architectural form not previously known in the delta, even though stone in that region would have been at a premium. Ra`amses also included a large fortified military citadel,[107] a spacious temple complex in which archaeologists even found gold dusting waste on the floor from the gilding work on royal furnishings,[108] an extensive horse and chariot complex capable of stabling more than 450 horses, dozens of chariot parts,[109] an immense industrial area for bronze production, and many workshops and mud-brick storage facilities (Ex. 1:11). A factory was discovered where glazed blue tiles were manufactured for use in the palatial estates of pharaohs. In the immediate environs of this installation were found certain ostraca that actually bear the name "Ra`amses."[110] And a cuneiform tablet has only very recently been found, which appears to confirm the site as Ramses's royal residence.[111] Without doubt, then, this was the locale from which the Israelites began their journey.

The Israelites leave Egypt *map 33*

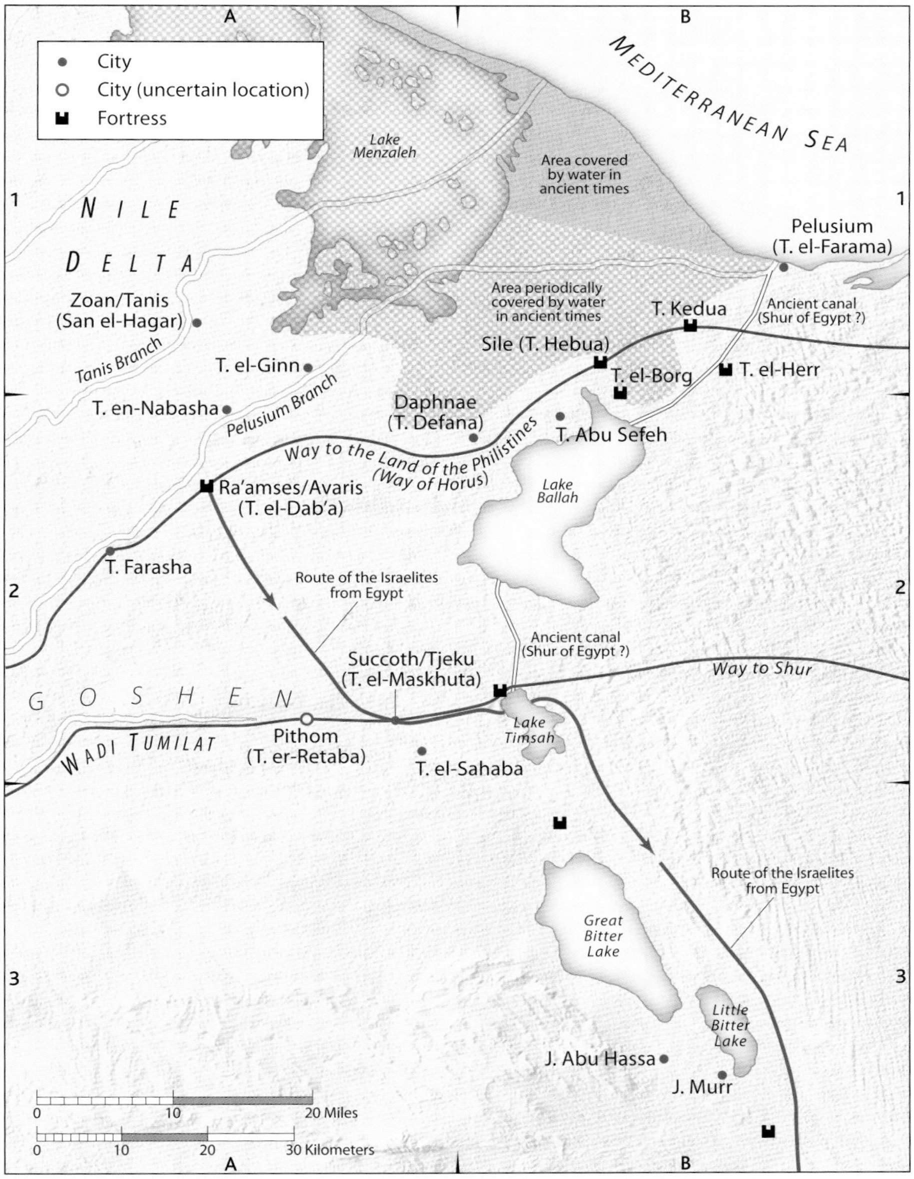

Departing Ra`amses, the Israelites came to Succoth (Ex. 12:37; Num. 33:5). Scholars have long acknowledged Succoth to be the Hebrew phonetic equivalent of the Egyptian *Tjeku*, a term found on monuments and inscriptions at two sites in the Wadi Tumilat. The W. Tumilat is a fertile valley that extends directly east from the delta as far as modern Ismalia and Lake Timsah. It has served as a major transportation corridor in antiquity [**see map**] and in modern times, and the valley contains a number of sites dating to the Hyksos and New Kingdom periods that manifest Canaanite artifacts.

The two largest sites in the W. Tumilat are T. el-Maskhuta (about eight miles west of Ismalia) and T. er-Retaba (another eight miles or so west of Maskhuta). [**See map 33.**] These happen to be the two places where the term *Tjeku* is attested in Egyptian literature and are often equated with biblical Succoth and Pithom. But which is which?

A 13th-century Egyptian text indicates that Pithom was located west of Tjeku/Succoth.[112] Some scholars have sought Tjeku/Succoth at T. el-Maskhuta[113] and believe the actual name Succoth may be reflected in the modern name Maskhuta. If so, then T. er-Retaba becomes an excellent candidate for the location of biblical Pithom (Ex. 1:11), though this is less certain.

From Succoth, the departing Israelites are said to have proceeded to Etham, on the edge of the wilderness/desert (Ex. 13:20; Num. 33:6). Unlike Succoth and Pithom, both of which have a transparently Egyptian etymology, the derivation of Etham is uncertain. But given the trajectory inherent in a trip from T. el-Dab`a/Ra`amses to T. el-Maskhuta/Succoth en route to the body of water, combined with the additional qualification that Etham was "on the edge of the wilderness/desert," Etham must have been situated east of T. el-Maskhuta/Succoth, probably along the main road heading east toward the wilderness of Shur. The word *Etham* may derive from an Egyptian place name—*Ḥwt-Itm* (a variant of the word for Atum, the sun god of Heliopolis),[114] located in the W. Tumilat.

From Etham, the Israelites arrived at Pi-hahiroth, which is described in Exodus as being "between Migdol and the sea, in front of Baal-zephon" (Ex. 14:2) and in Numbers as "facing/opposite Baal-zephon, where they encamped at Migdol" (Num. 33:7). Wherever this place is, it must have been immediately adjacent to the body of water through which Israel crossed on "dry ground," since in Exodus the Israelites are said to have been encamped there "by the sea" (14:2b) and in Numbers their departure from Pi-hahiroth has them immediately passing "through the sea into the wilderness" (Num. 33:8).

It is debated whether the name Pi-hahiroth is of Egyptian origin (*pi(r)-hahiroth* means "house of Hathor" [an Egyptian sky goddess]) or Semitic origin (meaning "to dig/cut" and implying a location along a canal). In the latter regard, the map portrays the vestige of an ancient canal, only recently discovered, that stretched northward from Lake Timsah as far as the Mediterranean shoreline. Portions of this canal measure some 230 feet across at ground level, about 65 feet wide at the bottom, and nearly ten feet deep. The canal was doubtless operational at the time of the Israelite departure from Egypt, irrespective of which date of the exodus one adopts. Scholars have concluded that, though it may also have had navigational or irrigational purposes, its primary purpose in antiquity was as a military wall of defense.[115]

Another indication that Pi-hahiroth may have been related to some sort of defensive military obstruction is its connection in both exodus accounts to Migdol (Ex. 14:2; Num. 33:7). The Egyptian word *maktar* reflects the Semitic word *migdol*, which means "fortress." Numerous references to Maktar/Migdol are found in Egyptian literature, and sites known as Maktar/Migdol were established in various locations. [**See map 33.**] One site is in the extreme eastern sector of the Wadi Tumilat,[116] probably quite near modern Ismalia. If the Israelites were proceeding in an eastward direction past T. el-Maskhuta via the W. Tumilat, it is predictable that they would have come to this "Maktar/Migdol."

At the very outset of the exodus journey, the Bible records that Israel was forbidden from taking "the Way to the Land of the Philistines" (Ex. 13:17). We now know that this preeminent Egyptian military route—"the Way(s) of Horus"—was protected by a whole series of Egyptian military installations between Sile and Gaza.[117] Had it not been an established route, the divine prohibition would seem to have been unnecessary. Additionally, a 13th-century B.C. Egyptian text[118] tells of an Egyptian officer in pursuit of fugitives who had passed through Ra`amses, Tjeku/Succoth, and Maktar/Migdol—in that order—and had then turned north, presumably toward Canaan. The likelihood that both Israel and the Egyptian officer passed three identically named sites in the very same sequence, within only a few days' time, is too great to be coincidental. The evidence strongly suggests that the fugitives, the Egyptian officer, and the Israelites were all following the same well-known and well-traveled transportation corridor, and—in the case of the Israelites—not some out-of-the-way alternative in an attempt to avoid detection by the pharaoh and his forces.

The map shows three such transportation arteries radiating eastward from the delta. From north to south these are: (1) "the Way to the Land of the Philistines"; (2) "the Way to Shur" (Gen. 16:7); and (3) a roadway later known as the "Darb el-Hajj" (a pilgrimage road from Egypt to Mecca). As was stated above, the northernmost option had been divinely eliminated (Ex. 13:17). Of the two remaining choices, it seems significant that the fugitives mentioned in the Egyptian papyrus, having cleared the Maktar/Migdol of Seti and making their way into the desert, turned *north*. This fact creates a very strong likelihood that they were traveling on the quicker and more direct exit ("the Way to Shur") and that they had not gone as far south as the Darb el-Hajj. So "the Way to Shur" would appear to be the most likely established route followed by the Israelites. [**See map 34.**]

The Israelites Beside the Sea

The Israelites arrived at a body of water where they would be rescued and the Egyptian army would be drowned. The Greek Old Testament (*LXX*) identifies the body of water as *erythrá thálassa* ("Red Sea"), which has led many people to imagine that Israel must have been positioned at the body of water that we now know as the Red Sea. However, in the classical world when the *LXX* was translated, the expression *erythrá thálassa* could designate not only what on a modern map would be called the Red Sea, but also the Persian Gulf, the Indian Ocean, and/or related waters . . . or even all of those bodies of water combined.[119] It appears, then, that the *LXX* translators employed the expression *erythrá thálassa* in a manner consistent with its usage elsewhere in the classical period (Acts 7:36; Heb. 11:29). There was a classical "Red Sea," just as there is a modern "Red Sea," but those two bodies of water are not coextensive and should not be confused.

On the other hand, the Hebrew Old Testament identified the body of water where the Israelites stopped as *yam sûf* ("sea of reeds/papyrus"). This same word *sûf* is used to refer to reeds/papyrus that grew along the Nile. Moses' mother put her son in a basket and placed it among the *sûf* (Ex. 2:3, 5). In the same way, prophetic literature also references a kind of water plant. After being cast from the ship, Jonah declared that *sûf* ("seaweed"?) got wrapped around his head (Jon. 2:5). Isaiah writes that Egypt's rivers and canals will dry up; its reeds and *sûf* ("rushes"?) will rot away (Isa. 19:6). It is all but certain that *sûf* was borrowed from an Egyptian word, *ṯwf(y)*, attested in the New Kingdom era, that meant "reeds/papyrus,"[120] and should be rendered accordingly in the expression *yam sûf* here in Exodus. It is of interest to note in passing that Luther's heavy reliance upon the Hebrew text at this point led him to translate the expression with the German *Schilfmeer* ("sea of reeds").

The word *t̠wf(y)* in Egyptian often designated a region where papyrus marshes and pasturelands were found together. With the probable route created by the locations of Ra`amses, Succoth/Tjeku, and Migdol/Maktar, it seems most plausible that the divine crossing of the "sea" (Ps. 77:19–20) took place at or near Lake Timsah, where the established transportation artery ("the Way to Shur") intersected a line of lakes. [**See map 33.**] Even while striving to be fiercely biblical at this point, it is impossible to draw certain geographical conclusions from this part of the investigation.

But although the Bible supplies precious few geographical and logistical details concerning the miraculous crossing, what *is* clear, but often overlooked, is the fact that the crossing apparently took place during a very short time span. The chronology of the event seems to be as follows:

1. The Egyptians were bearing down upon the Israelites when "night fell" (Ex. 14:10–20; v. 20b);
2. As Moses stretched forth his hand, there arose a strong east wind that divided the waters "all through the night" and enabled the passage of the Israelites (Ex. 14:21–22; cf. 15:8, 10);
3. By the "morning watch" (as the morning light was just beginning to appear), the Egyptians' chariots were already getting clogged in the mire (Ex. 14:23–25); and
4. At "sunrise" (Ex. 14:26–28; v. 27b) the flooding waters drowned the Egyptians in the sea.

It appears the Israelites commenced their crossing after sunset, and yet by the first light of a new day the pursuing Egyptians were already attempting to traverse the sea. This suggests persuasively that the entire Israelite crossing could not have extended beyond about eight hours at the most.[121] The Israelites had just been emancipated from slavery and had left Egypt hurriedly with their flocks and herds (Ex. 12:38). Simply to move from one side of a body of water to the other, in such a short amount of time with little more efficiency of movement than a slightly organized mob, would have required a miracle on a magnitude far greater than the one portrayed by Cecil B. DeMille, medieval art, or contemporary Christian literature. It is not inconceivable that a corridor of land as wide as several miles was required to accommodate the logistics and timing of the Israelite crossing. It is no wonder, then, that later biblical writers repeatedly cite the exodus event when seeking to establish a paradigm of God's absolute sovereign might (Pss. 66:5–6; 78:13; 106:11; Isa. 51:9–10; 63:12–14) or when providing a rationale for believing that Yahweh is the only true God of history (Num. 23:22; 24:8; Josh. 2:10–11; 9:9–10).

Having been delivered at the water, Israel was next directed to set out on a course for Mt. Sinai. Few Old Testament geographical questions have been more vigorously debated than the location of Mt. Sinai. Today the sacred mountain is sought in any one of three principal regions: (1) somewhere in northwest Saudi Arabia or south Jordan; (2) somewhere in the northern Sinai peninsula; or (3) somewhere in the granite highlands of the southern Sinai.

Searching for Mt. Sinai in Saudi Arabia/South Jordan

Advocates of the Saudi Arabian/Jordanian hypothesis make three biblical points. First, having earlier fled from a pharaoh who was seeking to take his life, Moses took up residence in the land of Midian and became the son-in-law of a priest there (Ex. 2:15–16; 18:1). Second, the Bible is replete with references to what appears to have been volcanic or earthquake activity associated with the establishment of the Sinaitic covenant (Ex. 19:18; 24:17; Deut. 4:11–12; 5:22–26; 9:10, 15; 10:4; Judg. 5:5; Ps. 68:8; Hag. 2:6). And third, the apostle Paul explicitly located Mt. Sinai *in Arabia* (Gal. 4:25).

According to this viewpoint, the land of Midian was situated exclusively in the terrain east of the Gulf of Aqaba. It is further asserted that

Nestled below the lower stretches of J. Musa ("the mountain of Moses") is the Greek Orthodox monastery of St. Catherine.

the geological structure of mountains within the Sinai itself is not conducive to either volcanic or seismic activity, or at least not to recent activity. And finally, this view argues that it represents the only principal option for locating the holy mountain inside Arabia. Individuals who subscribe to this theory will most likely locate Mt. Sinai either at Petra, J. Baqir, J. al-Lawz, J. Manifa, or Ḥalā el-Bedr. [**See map for locations.**]

Objections to each of the three arguments for the Saudi Arabian/Jordanian location have seriously eroded their cogency. Biblical tradition links Moses to the Kenites (Judg. 1:16; 4:11) as well as the Midianites. One cannot assert that the nomadic Midianites, or their sub-tribe the Kenites, were confined exclusively to only one region prior to the Greco-Roman period. Midianites resided within the territory of Moab (Gen. 36:35; 1 Chron. 1:46), in the Mishor tableland of Transjordan (Josh. 13:21), in the wilderness areas east of Moab and Ammon (Judg. 7:25) or northern Sinai (1 Kings 11:18), and even (perhaps seasonally) inside Canaan itself (Judg. 6:1–6; 7:1).

The volcanic/seismic argument is no more decisive, for several reasons. First, although it is admitted that no recent volcanic activity is attested within Sinai itself, seismic evidence shows that the area of the Gulf of Aqaba has been quite active in this regard.[122] As recently as 1982 the Sinai peninsula experienced a major earthquake (measuring more than six points on the Richter scale). But second, the phenomenological language in the relevant biblical texts could be reflective of weather conditions surrounding Mt. Sinai *at the time* (Ps. 68:8–10). Alternatively, it is possible to understand the language of these texts in a dynamic sense as a vivid underscoring of an appearance of God—a theophany.[123] Other theophanic passages in the Old Testament employ similar terminology without presupposing volcanic/earthquake activity (2 Sam. 22:8–16; Pss. 18:7–15; 89:5–18; 97:1–5; 104:31–32).

The question of "Arabia" requires additional elucidation. If one uses the term today, it might refer to either Saudi Arabia or the entire Arabian peninsula. Similarly, ancient references to "Arabia" could denote different terrains.[124] In fact, the classical world generally gives attestation to at least five distinct regions known as "Arabia."[125] Accordingly, it is essential for the modern interpreter to understand that the apostle Paul (Gal. 4:25) was accurately reflecting the geographical truth of *his* world—not ours! So while none of the three principal viewpoints concerning the location of Mt. Sinai can claim exclusive geographical support from Paul's statement, neither are any of them eliminated by virtue of his declaration.

Searching for Mt. Sinai in the Northern Sinai Peninsula

Advocates of the northern Sinai hypothesis also attempt to anchor their argumentation in the Bible as they locate Mt. Sinai at J. Sin Bisher, J. Magharah, J. Helal, J. Yeleq, J. Kharif,

The Route of the Exodus

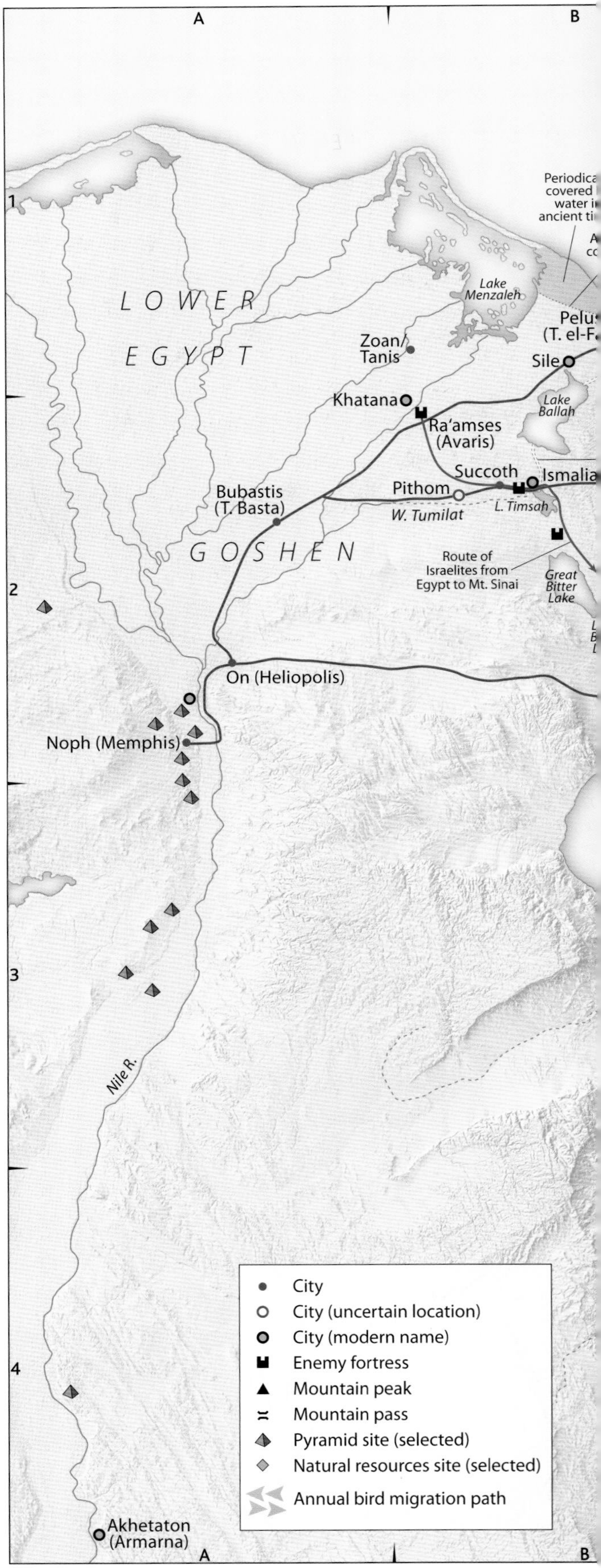

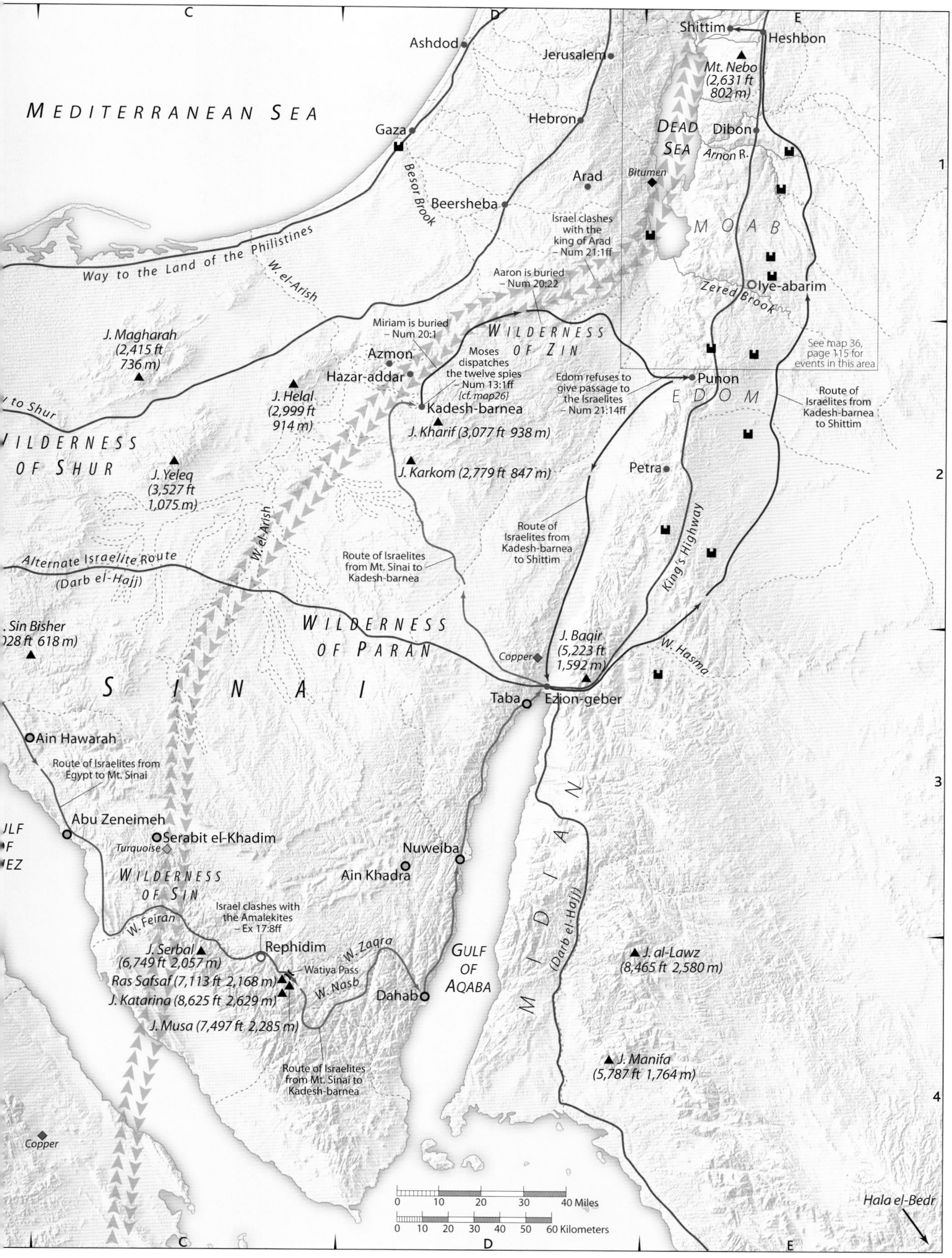
C
D
E
1
2
3
4
MEDITERRANEAN SEA
Ashdod
Jerusalem
Shittim
Heshbon
Mt. Nebo (2,631 ft 802 m)
Gaza
Hebron
DEAD SEA
Dibon
Arnon R.
Besor Brook
Arad
Bitumen
Beersheba
Israel clashes with the king of Arad – Num 21:1ff
MOAB
Way to the Land of the Philistines
W. el-Arish
Aaron is buried – Num 20:22
Iye-abarim
Zered Brook
Miriam is buried – Num 20:1
WILDERNESS OF ZIN
J. Magharah (2,415 ft 736 m)
Azmon
Moses dispatches the twelve spies – Num 13:1ff {cf. map26}
Hazar-addar
Edom refuses to give passage to the Israelites – Num 21:14ff
Punon
See map 36, page 115 for events in this area
EDOM
Route of Israelites from Kadesh-barnea to Shittim
J. Helal (2,999 ft 914 m)
Kadesh-barnea
J. Kharif (3,077 ft 938 m)
Way to Shur
WILDERNESS OF SHUR
J. Yeleq (3,527 ft 1,075 m)
J. Karkom (2,779 ft 847 m)
Petra
Route of Israelites from Kadesh-barnea to Shittim
W. el-Arish
King's Highway
Alternate Israelite Route (Darb el-Hajj)
Route of Israelites from Mt. Sinai to Kadesh-barnea
WILDERNESS OF PARAN
Sin Bisher
028 ft 618 m)
J. Baqir (5,223 ft 1,592 m)
Copper
W. Hasma
SINAI
Taba
Ezion-geber
Ain Hawarah
Route of Israelites from Egypt to Mt. Sinai
Abu Zeneimeh
Serabit el-Khadim
Turquoise
ULF
F
EZ
Nuweiba
Ain Khadra
WILDERNESS OF SIN
MIDIAN
Israel clashes with the Amalekites – Ex 17:8ff
W. Feiran
(Darb el-Hajj)
J. Serbal (6,749 ft 2,057 m)
Rephidim
W. Zagra
GULF OF AQABA
J. al-Lawz (8,465 ft 2,580 m)
Ras Safsaf (7,113 ft 2,168 m)
Watiya Pass
J. Katarina (8,625 ft 2,629 m)
W. Nasb
Dahab
J. Musa (7,497 ft 2,285 m)
Route of Israelites from Mt. Sinai to Kadesh-barnea
J. Manifa (5,787 ft 1,764 m)
Copper
0 10 20 30 40 Miles
0 10 20 30 40 50 60 Kilometers
Hala el-Bedr

J. Karkom, or Kadesh-barnea itself. [**See map for locations.**] To begin with, Moses' request of the pharaoh was to go into the wilderness a distance requiring three days of travel (Ex. 5:3; cf. 3:18; 8:27). Proponents of the northern Sinai viewpoint deduce therefore that Mt. Sinai could not have been separated from Goshen by much more than a three-day march. Second, two biblical references to the arrival of quail are cited (Ex. 16:13; Num. 11:31–32), and residents of northern Sinai are still easily able to capture exhausted quail that have just completed a protracted leg in their annual migration between southern Europe and Arabia. Third, the Israelite victory over the Amalekites at Rephidim is said to decisively favor a northern location (Ex. 17:8–13), since this is the region where the Amalakites are otherwise encountered in the Bible. And fourth, certain Old Testament poetic passages are said to support a northern location (Deut. 33:2; Judg. 5:4; Hab. 3:3, 7).

Taken as a whole, these arguments appear rather impressive, but individually they can be regarded as inconclusive. The three-day proposal presupposes a literal interpretation of the expression "three days," which could be just as likely a loose period of time or an example of oriental bargaining.[126] It also requires that the destination involved in Moses' request was Mt. Sinai, though that is never stated in the text. The nearest proposed destinations to Sinai are 75 miles from the Goshen area—too great a distance to cover in a three-day period. Annals from this general period indicate the Egyptian army could cover about 15 miles per day. The Israelites, encumbered with women, children, flocks, and herds (Ex. 12:37–38; 34:3), would not travel nearly as far. The average daily distance maintained today by a group of Bedouin moving through that terrain is about six miles.[127] And a total of *eight* intermediate encampments were named between Israel's deliverance at the sea and their arrival at Mt. Sinai (Num. 33:8–15).

The journey from Goshen to Mt. Sinai took place in the springtime (Ex. 13:3–6: the month of Abib corresponds to March/April),[128] and the trek from Mt. Sinai to Kadesh-barnea occurred about one year later, also during the springtime (Num. 9:1; 10:11). Anyone who seeks to interpret the two quail narratives (Ex. 16:13; Num 11:31–35) in terms of natural phenomena, therefore, is obliged to relate them to the *spring* migration of the birds. In point of fact, perhaps as many as one billion migrating birds, from as many as 350 different species, fly annually over the Sinai peninsula in their northward spring migrations.[129] [**See map for path of annual migrations.**] Yet as might be imagined, the vast majority of these birds land near the peninsular (the southern) shore rather than points farther north. A northern landing is more suggestive of an autumnal migration.[130] Thus, given the explicit seasonal indication of both "quail" narratives, those events would most convincingly be located somewhere in the south of the Sinai peninsula, not another 150 miles or so to the north.

The location of the encounter between the Israelites and Amalekites at Rephidim (Ex. 17:8–16) remains something of a geographic mystery, especially in light of the narrative in 1 Samuel 15. Elsewhere in the Old Testament the Amalekites seem to be found primarily in northern regions. They were located in the land of Edom (Gen. 36:16), the area around Kadesh-barnea (Gen. 14:7), the Negeb (Num. 13:29), the terrain just south of Judah (1 Sam. 27:8), the hill country of Ephraim (Judg. 12:15), near Ziklag (1 Sam. 30:1–2), and even as far west as the territory of Shur (1 Sam. 15:7). There are also accounts of Amalekites being in league with Moabites (Judg. 3:12–14) and Midianites (Judg. 6:33; 7:12). Given this wide territorial distribution, their highly mobile lifestyle, and the fact that they are sometimes said to have employed camels for transportation (Judg. 6:5; 7:12), the Amalekites are commonly regarded as a nomadic people. Their movements, though widespread, tended to be connected with deserts and desolate wastelands.[131] Therefore, this argument does not appear to decisively favor a northern Sinai location.

Concerning the texts in Deuteronomy, Judges, and Habakkuk that seem to equate Mt. Sinai with Seir, Paran, Teman, and Edom, one must bear in mind that their transparently poetic structure includes elements of Hebrew parallelism. On the same grounds, therefore, one might with equal justification attempt to argue that Paran must be equated with Seir, Teman, or Edom, which of course is absurd. Furthermore, the passages represent specimens of a theophany:[132] they each reflect the reality that the God of Israel, a divine warrior, can rescue his people from oppression. The common denominator of Sinai, Seir, Paran, Teman, and Edom in these texts is simply that they are all located in the same general southward direction from Canaan.

In addition, a number of biblical texts suggest that Mt. Sinai was separated from the area of Kadesh-barnea by a great distance. In the Israelite itinerary between Mt. Sinai and Kadesh (Num. 33:16–36), some 20 intermediate stations are recorded, and that itinerary may be *selective* in nature (Deut. 1:1). Deuteronomy 1:2 stipulates that there was an 11-day march between Horeb/Sinai and Kadesh-barnea.[133] Similarly, the text of 1 Kings 19:8 indicates that it took Elijah 40 days to travel from Beersheba to Mt. Sinai. Though the amount of time for travel differs from text to text, these biblical narratives concur that Mt. Sinai was separated from Kadesh-barnea by a considerable distance—a conclusion that is fatal to the contention that Mt. Sinai should be located somewhere in northern Sinai.

Searching for Mt. Sinai in Southern Sinai

Advocates of the southern Sinai viewpoint are apt to seek out Mt. Sinai at J. Serbal, Ras Safsaf, J. Katarina, or J. Musa. [**See map for location.**] This position also has a long and very rich tradition: more than 2,500 Nabatean inscriptions have been found near Serbal, dating as early as the second and third

Christian centuries. Such inscriptions are usually invocations for a safe journey and may be indicative of a pilgrimage route.[134] Additionally, coins from the fourth century have been found in the vicinity.[135]

Christian tradition dating back to the early Byzantine era has revered the site of J. Musa ("mountain of Moses"), which is surprising in several respects. Ten other mountain peaks in southern Sinai are loftier than J. Musa, making them more likely choices if the selection were merely random or based on altitude or appearance. In fact, the contours of its surrounding topography make the summit of J. Musa almost invisible from the surrounding plains and render the mountain distinctly unimpressive. Yet a small band of Christian ascetics was living at J. Musa by the time of Roman persecutions in the third century[136] and a monastery existed at the foot of the mountain by the early fourth century.[137]

The tradition of associating J. Musa with Mt. Sinai deserves additional credence because it runs counter to the Byzantine tendency of locating sacred shrines at places that were easily accessible to Christian pilgrims. And unlike so many early Christian sites in the Levant, Mt. Sinai is associated not with the New Testament, but with the God of the Old Testament and with the prophets Moses and Elijah. It stands at the very edge of Christian tradition.

As further evidence for a southern location, certain sites along the Israelite itinerary to Mt. Sinai (Ex. 15:22—19:1) and between Mt. Sinai and Kadesh-barnea (Num. 21; 33; Deut. 1) are suggestive of some modern place names, and the location of three intermediate stations necessarily presupposes a southern route. But a note of caution must be sounded. Since most of the southern Sinai has never been permanently occupied, one must not claim that all, most, or even many of the intermediate stations in the itinerary can be located today with geographic precision. Some of the place names are said to have been assigned by the Israelites as they were passing through (e.g., Marah [Ex. 15:23], Massah, and Meribah [Ex. 17:7]). Obviously, names rendered under such circumstances would never have become fixed.

However, Ezion-geber (Num. 33:35) was indisputably located in the vicinity of modern Eilat (cf. 1 Kings 9:26), most likely at the adjacent island site of Jezirat Fara'un.[138] Likewise, Di-zahab (Deut. 1:1) seems to be reflected in the modern town Dahab, as the names are phonetic equivalents and both have to do with places of gold.[139] Moreover, the name of the largest and most luxuriant oasis in southwestern Sinai (Feiran) appears to have been retained in classical and Byzantine sources.[140] Beyond these fairly safe correlations, some scholars suggest that the station Jotbathah (Num. 33:33), listed as the second stop northward before Ezion-geber en route to Kadesh-barnea, should be identified with the modern oasis at Taba, located some seven miles south of Ezion-geber along the Red Sea shoreline.[141]

It seems that the location of Ezion-geber itself would make the northern Sinai route impossibly circuitous. For how does one explain a trip from J. Kharif, J. Karkom, J. Helal, J. Yeleq, or even from J. Sin Bisher to Ezion-geber, if the destination of the itinerary is Kadesh-barnea? By the same token, if either of the other identifications (Feiran, Di-zahab) could be demonstrated beyond cavil, the Saudi Arabian/Jordanian thesis would also be rendered geographically incoherent. Therefore, the traditional, southern Sinai hypothesis appears to be the most probable one. It seems to have the most to commend it and there is nothing fatal to militate against it.[142]

Continuing the Israelites' Route

Based on this conclusion, it is possible to reconstruct a plausible Israelite route to Mt. Sinai, then on to Kadesh-barnea, and finally on to Shittim. At the point they were rescued from Egypt, it is likely the Israelites followed the coastal road east of the Gulf of Suez the whole way south to the mouth of the W. Feiran, along which there was a succession of oases and wells to provide water.[143]

An alternative route via W. Matalla could have taken them inland at a point just south of modern Abu Zeneimeh, passing Serabit el-Khadim and then proceeding on a southeast diagonal to a junction with the W. Feiran near Rephidim. However, this is an extremely problematic alternative, both historically and geographically.[144] On the other hand, the W. Feiran (also known in its upper stretches as the W. Sheikh) is a rather broad, continuous, gently rising passageway through otherwise rugged and somewhat precipitous granite terrain, the whole way to the Watiya Pass. Bending south through the Watiya Pass, the Israelites would have emerged directly into the er-Raha plain, located just north of J. Musa.

Later, when leaving Mt. Sinai for Ezion-geber and points beyond, the W. Nasb would have represented an excellent choice. By following the course of this single, continuous, gently descending wadi to the point of its outlet near modern Dahab, the Israelites would have passed a network of oases,[145] the most prominent of which was Bir Nasb. With comparative ease they would have been able to pass through the mountain barrier that runs longitudinally along the eastern peninsula and flanks the Gulf of Aqaba. And then, when they reached the Gulf, they could have trekked northward between the mountain and the Gulf, again past a number of oases, including Nuweiba—the largest and most prolific oasis in all of eastern Sinai—until finally they arrived at Ezion-geber.

From there, the Israelites most likely proceeded in a northwesterly direction, along the course of a roadway known today as Darb al-Ghazza, toward Kadesh-barnea (Ain Qadeis). It was from Kadesh-barnea that twelve men were dispatched to enter Canaan and spy it out (Num. 13). [**See map 35.**] When the majority of the men presented a faithless, negative report, which was adopted by the community of Israel (Num. 14:1–10), that generation was officially disqualified from entering and possessing the land, and Israel remained more or less stationary at Kadesh for perhaps 35 years or more (cf. Deut. 1:46).[146]

When the Israelites eventually departed from Kadesh and were en route to Shittim, they were refused passage by the king of Edom at Punon, a pass through the mountains of Edom across to the "King's Highway" (Num. 20:14–17). This necessitated a detour through more than 175 miles of rather imposing landscape, which is possibly what precipitated the so-called "bronze serpent" incident (Num. 21:4–9). Skirting the entire Edomite territory took Israel once again by way of the "Red Sea" (Num. 21:4) and Ezion-geber (Deut. 2:8), and then along the desert fringes that flanked a series of Edomite and Moabite military fortresses, probably utilizing a road later called the "Pilgrims' Highway."[147] Finally, they approached the King's Highway for a second time (Num. 21:22). Once again they were refused passage, this time by Sihon, an Amorite monarch. A battle ensued in which Sihon was defeated (Num. 21:23–30), thus paving the way for the Israelites finally to complete the circuitous third leg of their journey, as the wanderers passed by Dibon, Heshbon, and arrived at Abel-shittim ("the meadow/pasture of Shittim" [Num. 33:45–49]), or Shittim, as the place is normally known in the Old Testament (Num. 25:1; Josh. 2:1).

The Journey of the Spies ***map 35***

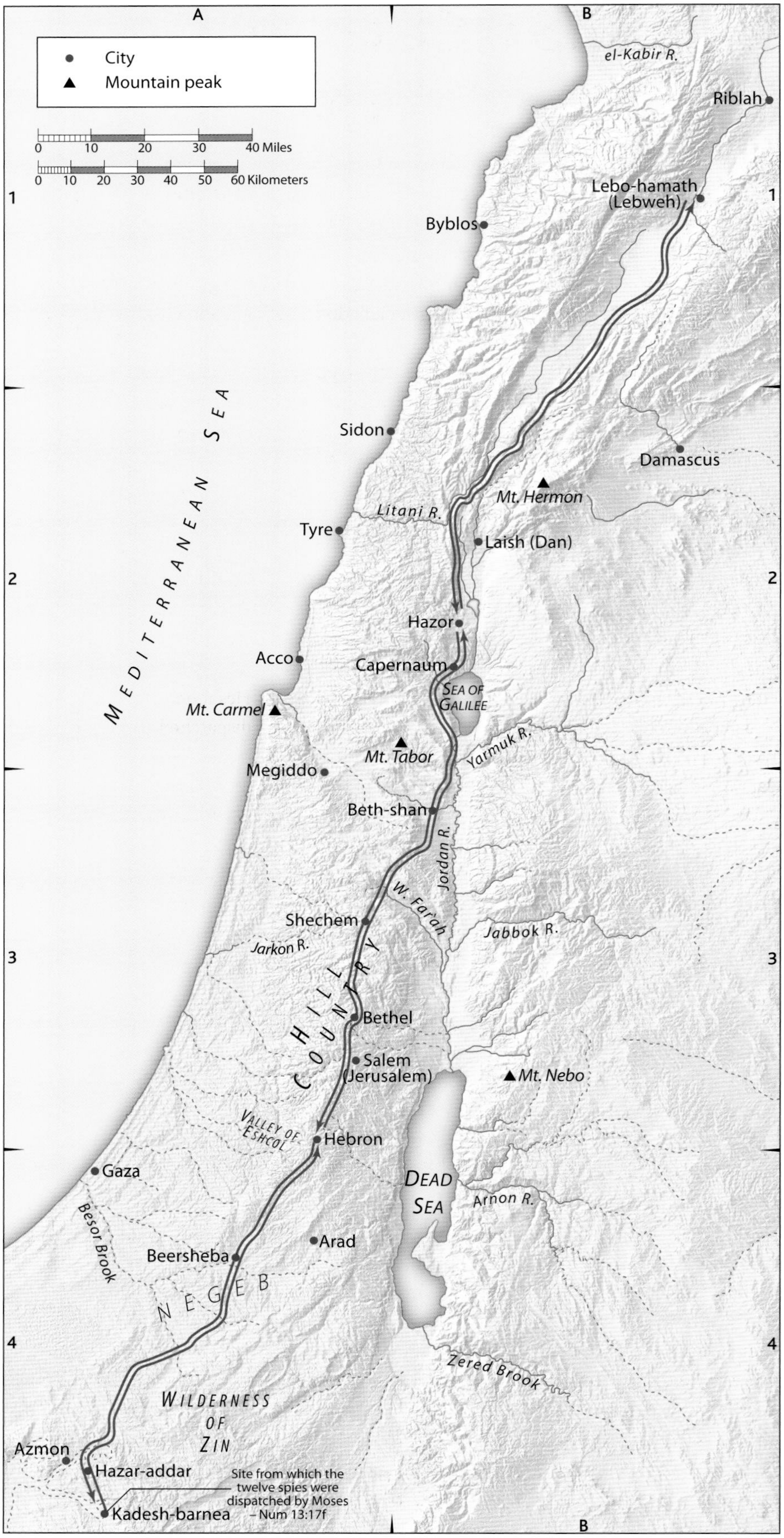

ISRAEL'S OCCUPATION OF TRANSJORDAN

Transjordan was somewhat sparsely populated at the point of Israel's entry into the land, yet appears to have been occupied by Edomites, Moabites, Ammonites, Amorites, and other tribes. The first three of these groups were portrayed as being distantly related to Israel (Gen. 19:37–38; 36:1, 9; Deut. 2:2–23). Apparently there were no confrontations between those groups and the Israelites at first. The formidable Amorite kingdoms of Sihon and Og, however, presented a different challenge.

The realm of Sihon extended east of the Jordan River, from the Jabbok River in the north as far south as the capital city of Heshbon, including a region of numerous cities and towns. At the time of the exodus, however, Sihon had extended his domain even farther south to the Arnon River (Judg. 11:18–20), thus encroaching on Moabite territory. According to the biblical narrative, the Israelite itinerary brought them into the wilderness of Kedemoth and the site of Mattanah (Num. 21:18–19). Entering the territory of Sihon, a message requesting safe passage was delivered to the Amorite monarch (Num. 21:21–22; Deut. 2:26–29). Sihon adamantly refused and instead mustered his troops and led them to Jahaz. A battle ensued in which his forces were routed and Sihon himself was slain (Num. 21:23–26; Deut. 2:32–36). As a result, Israel gained control of the territory between the Arnon River and the area of Heshbon.

Following this victory, a contingent of Israelite troops was dispatched northward against other Amorites living at Jazer (Num. 21:32); the troops captured that city and proceeded farther north in the direction of Bashan. These maneuvers must have concerned Og, for this king of Bashan marched his army to Edrei, a fortress city that protected his southern frontier (Num. 21:33–35; Deut. 3:1–11; cf. Josh. 12:4). But the Israelite army again prevailed, destroying Og and capturing his territory of sixty cities and many unwalled villages. Therefore, most of the rest of Transjordan—from Heshbon as far north as Mt. Hermon, was subdued before the Israelite force, which now returned to bivouac on the plains of Moab, opposite Jericho.

The victories over Sihon and Og were of great significance. Geographically, the Transjordanian territory captured between the Arnon and Mt. Hermon would be allotted to the Israelite tribes of Reuben, Gad, and East Manasseh (Josh. 13:8–33). [**See map 40.**] Theologically, the two victories would later be recounted as a reminder of Israel's covenantal identity and God's covenant-keeping fidelity (Deut. 29:7–9; Neh. 9:22; Pss. 135:11; 136:19–20). And strategically, these victories had the effect of planting fear in the hearts of some of the remaining peoples living nearby, even before any further conflict ensued (Josh. 2:10; 9:10).

It was doubtless this disturbing chain of events that prompted Balak, king of Moab, to solicit the services of Balaam, a seer from faraway Upper Mesopotamia (Num. 22:1–6; cf. Deut. 23:4). The king desired to secure from Balaam a powerful oracle that would significantly diminish the threat Israel appeared to be. When finally beckoned, Balaam was taken several times to high peaks in the vicinity of Mt. Nebo (Num. 22:41; 23:14, 28). From such an elevated vantage point overlooking the plains of Moab and the Israelites below, Balaam repeatedly tried to deliver his curse. Yet he was unable and instead pronounced a blessing upon Israel (Num. 22—24).

Israel's Occupation of Transjordan *map 36*

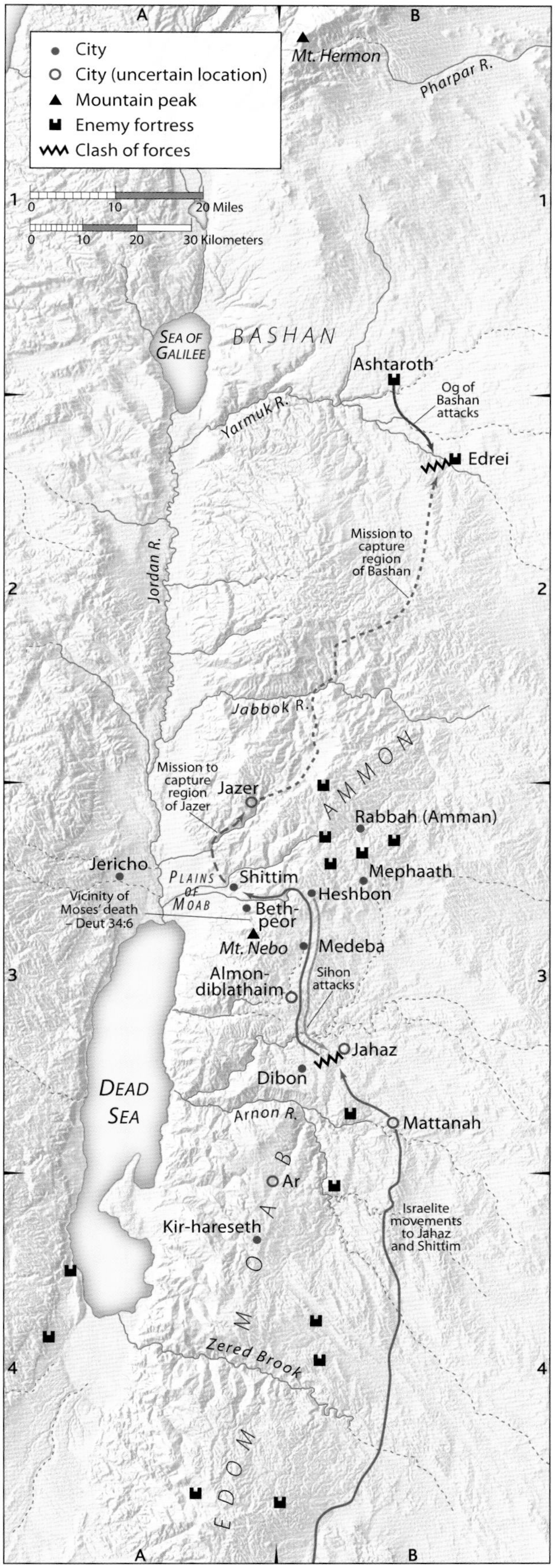

THE BATTLES OF JERICHO AND AI/BETHEL

Israel's campaign that allowed them to enter and possess the land is frequently called the "biblical conquest," but is actually a composite of four battles described in the book of Joshua: (1) Jericho (Josh. 6); (2) Ai/Bethel (Josh. 7—8); (3) Gibeon-Makkedah (Josh. 9—10); and (4) Hazor (Josh. 11). Yet the roster of all kings and territories subjugated by Joshua's forces (Josh. 11:16–23; 12) indicates that more than just four battles were involved [**map 42**], so the "conquest narratives" must be selective in character. These four battles were chosen from a wider ranger of conflicts to be included in the text because they contain significant historical information and because they contribute in a foundational way to the overall theological strategy developed in and through this book.

The book of Joshua is laid out in a way that demonstrates a legitimate succession of God's authority and power. This would have been a sorely needed message in the immediate aftermath of the death of Moses. The early chapters (1—5) contain a recurring formula central to this theology. At times the people affirmed to Joshua: "Just as we obeyed Moses in all things, so we will obey you" (1:17; 4:14). At other times God declared to Joshua: "As I was with Moses, so I will be with you" (1:5; 3:7; 6:27). And like his predecessor, Joshua was commanded: "Remove your sandals from your feet, for the place where you are standing is holy" (5:15; cf. Ex. 3:5). Prior to crossing the Jordan River to occupy the land to the west, Joshua had prepared the people of Israel emotionally (1:10–11), strategically (2:1–24), domestically (4:4–7), and spiritually (5:2–7). And in a way again reminiscent of his mentor, Joshua dispatched men to "search out the land" (2:1; cf. Num. 13:17).

At the appropriate moment, Joshua led a new generation through divided waters "on dry ground" (Josh. 3:17; 4:18, 22; cf. Ex. 14:22, 29; 15:19). Not only did he reproduce the magnitude of the miracle of his predecessor, he did so at precisely the same time in the calendar year (Josh. 4:19–23; cf. Ex. 12:3). Such actions could accomplish nothing less than to accredit Joshua and highlight him as the bona fide successor of Moses.

The crossing of the Jordan occurred during the time of harvest (Josh. 4:19—"the tenth day of the first month"), when the river was at flood stage (Josh. 3:15; 4:18; 1 Chron. 12:15). Before the construction of numerous dams in the 20th century, the Jordan's flood stage in springtime would have entailed a flow of approximately ten to twelve feet in depth at Jericho, spread out over an area estimated to have been as much as a mile in width.[148] In this instance, we are told that the Jordan's waters were restrained at Adam (T. ad-Damiyya), situated adjacent to the east bank, some 23 air miles north of the Dead Sea. At a place just below the confluence of the Jordan and Jabbok rivers and a restriction in the width of the Ghor [**map 9**], landslides are known to have temporarily blocked the flow of the river.[149] [**See Chapter 1 commentary, pp. 50–51.**]

After safely crossing the river, the Israelites took up temporary residence at the site of Gilgal (Josh. 5:8–12; 9:6; 10:6), located at a place that must be in close proximity to Jericho (Josh. 4:19) and the fords of the Jordan (2 Sam. 19:15). Wherever Joshua's temporary headquarters was situated (T. el-Mefjir?), the site should not be confused with another Gilgal located in the hill country of Samaria, perhaps near Bethel (2 Kings 2:1–4). [**See maps 54 and 72.**]

From Gilgal the people of Israel undertook the first of their forays: the conquest of Jericho. Though Old Testament Jericho (T. es-Sultan) covered a mere six acres, a combination of factors made the place a desirable initial target. The town had been built at the largest and most copious oasis in all of eastern Canaan, and the scarcity of water in that land explains why the site was occupied from as early as 9000 B.C. Additionally, Jericho was situated strategically at the intersection of at least three roadways [**map 27**], providing lateral access into the highlands of Bethel and/or Jerusalem and longitudinal access into the Jezreel Valley and Galilee. [**See map 115** where a Roman legion had been strategically placed at Jericho.] Jericho represented a gateway to the East, providing effective control of the fords of the Jordan and their necessary linkage back to the Plains of Moab.

It might be that not all the soldiers crossed the river with Joshua. Moses had consented to the request of the tribes of Reuben, Gad, and East Manasseh who desired Transjordanian inheritance, but he stipulated that all the fighting men from those tribes should join with their brothers in the contests that still awaited Israel (Num. 32:29). Yet when Joshua crossed the river, only some 40,000 men from those tribes accompanied him (Josh. 4:12–13). The tribes of Reuben and Gad alone were reckoned to have more than 90,000 fighting men (Num. 1:20–21, 24–25), but the idea that they reneged on their promise to Moses appears untenable in light of the hearty recommendation Joshua later gave them (Josh. 22:1–9). It seems clear that some Israelites, especially women and children (Josh. 1:12–15; Deut. 3:18–22), temporarily remained behind in safety. Those people would have provided a supply line to the Israelite forces and, combined with their flocks and herds, would have needed military protection provided by some of the fighting men from each of the tribes. Failure to seize Jericho would threaten to sever this supply line.

But Joshua was victorious at Jericho and next set his sights on the central highlands. He decided to deploy a minor force to capture the town of Ai, possibly a temporary military outpost of Bethel located near the city on the east side (Josh. 7:2; 8:12; cf. Gen. 13:3–4). Historically, biblical Ai has been placed at the site of et-Tell, based principally on the more certain placement of Bethel (Beitin) and the description of Eusebius in his *Onomasticon*.[150] However, et-Tell manifests no evidence of human occupation at the time of the biblical conquest, so a few scholars have sought Ai elsewhere, either at Kh. Nisya, Aiath, or Kh. el-Maqatir.[151] [**See locations on map.**] While none of these alternatives can be dismissed out of hand, no compelling reason exists to embrace any of them or to confer upon them an air of probability. Other sites beyond Ai are mentioned in conjunction with Israel's settlement in Canaan and in Transjordan that also yield no evidence of human occupation at the time of Israel's settlement. A reasonable approach in such circumstances is to keep one's judgment suspended until additional evidence is exhumed or other more decisive data become available. As the oft-cited and time-honored aphorism reminds us, "Absence of evidence is not evidence of absence."

The minor force dispatched to capture Ai was bitterly defeated, and the first Israelite casualties of the conquest were recorded (Josh. 7:2–5). After the sin of Achan (the cause of the defeat) had been revealed and addressed, Joshua prepared a systematic strategy for attacking Ai/Bethel. First, a large ambush force was secretly deployed between Ai and Bethel (Josh. 8:3–4). From Gilgal, it is likely that this force took up its position by traversing the W. Qilt and the W. Suweinit to the end, which would have placed it immediately south of Bethel but in a well-concealed position. Then, in plain view of the occupants of Ai, Joshua led his main force up close to the town, encamping overnight on the north side of Ai, with a ravine separating them from the city (Josh. 8:10–11). Such a vivid description of the topography permits one to identify Joshua's route as the W. Makkuk. A main branch of this wadi system flanks the north side of et-Tell, and from the summit of the site one has practically a bird's-eye view down the descent of W. Makkuk in the direction of Jericho.

The following morning, Joshua's force feigned retreat down the wadi toward the Jordan valley, but not before a small ambush force had been stationed north of Ai (Josh. 8:12–13). Supposing the maneuver to have been a repeat of the earlier skirmish, the commander of Ai ordered his men to chase the Israelites back down the wadi. But at Joshua's predetermined signal, both ambush forces came forward

The Battles of Jericho and Ai/Bethel *map 37*

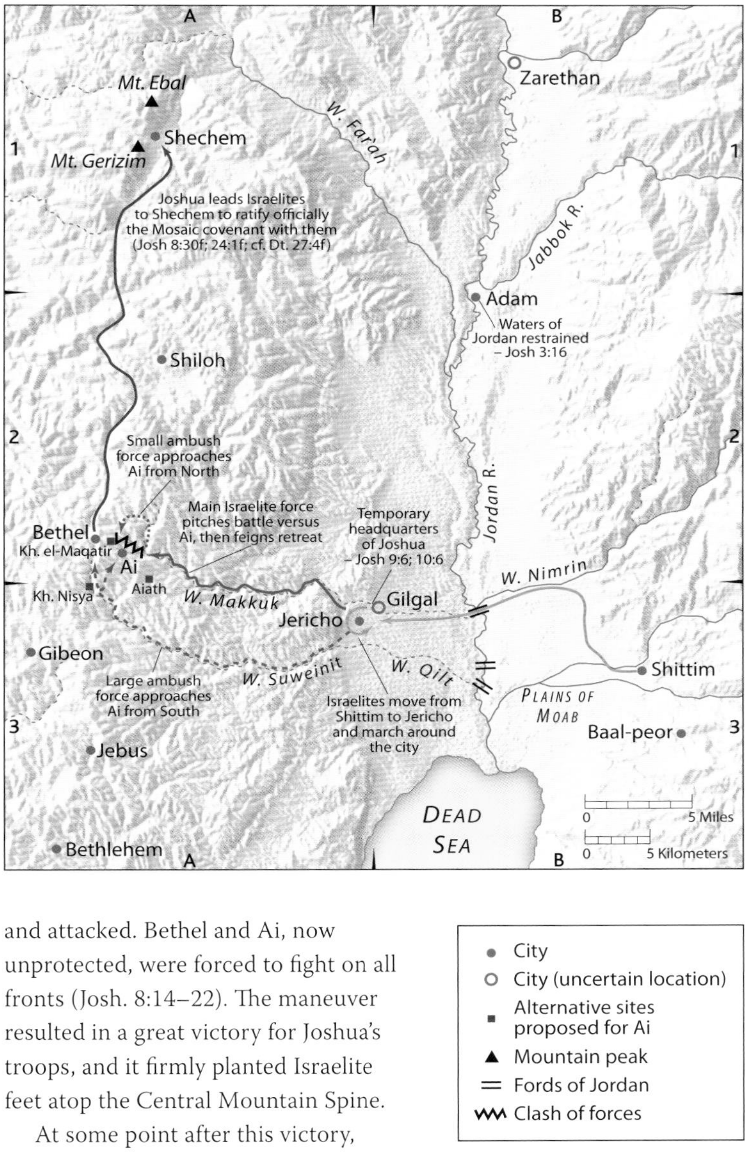

and attacked. Bethel and Ai, now unprotected, were forced to fight on all fronts (Josh. 8:14–22). The maneuver resulted in a great victory for Joshua's troops, and it firmly planted Israelite feet atop the Central Mountain Spine.

At some point after this victory, Joshua led the people of Israel to Shechem, flanked by Mt. Ebal in the north and by Mt. Gerizim in the south. In a manner reminiscent of Mt. Sinai (Ex. 19:1–2) Joshua constructed there an altar of uncut stones (Josh. 8:30; cf. Ex. 20:25; Deut. 27:5–6), made burnt offerings and peace offerings (Josh. 8:31; cf. Ex. 20:24), and officially ratified the terms of the Mosaic covenant with a new generation (Josh. 8:32; 24:1–28; cf. Deut. 27:1–26). Again, Joshua was portrayed as the legitimate successor of Moses, the great lawgiver. And geographically, such a movement from Bethel to Shechem presupposes other settlement activities that must have been inherent, though we learn nothing of the details from the Bible.

THE BATTLE OF GIBEON

The subjugation of Jericho and Ai/Bethel paved the way for the Israelites to make significant inroads into the central highlands of Canaan. But the action also provoked the widespread consternation of kings west of the Jordan in Canaan (Josh. 9:1–2), who apparently formed some kind of coalition against Israel. As a consequence, citizens of four towns in the vicinity of Gibeon (el-Jib), a city situated between Bethel/Ai and Jerusalem, must have realized their vulnerability.

Though described as inhabitants of Gibeon, they are also called "Hivites" (Josh. 9:7) or "Amorites" (2 Sam. 21:2), which is doubly intriguing in the story line: Hivites were not only part of this Canaanite coalition against Israel (Josh. 9:1b), but also had been identified on several occasions as one of the groups in Canaan with whom the Israelites must *not* make a treaty (Ex. 34:11–12; Deut. 7:1–2). Rather, the Hivites were to be overthrown (Ex. 23:23–24; Deut. 20:17; cf. Josh. 3:10). Yet the Gibeonites devised a cunning scheme to deceive Israel into making a treaty with them (Josh. 9:3–15).

When the Amorite kings of the cities of Jerusalem, Hebron, Eglon, Lachish, and Jarmuth discovered the treachery of the Hivites, they determined to attack them immediately (Josh. 10:1–5) [**1**]. Apparently outclassed militarily, the Hivites from Gibeon took advantage of their treaty with Joshua and summoned his assistance. Joshua and his troops set out from Gilgal on a forced march through the night (10:7–9) and arrived at Gibeon by dawn [**2**]. The Amorites were thrown into a panic as the battle ensued, fleeing west by the way of the ascent at Beth-horon and Aijalon. They made their way to Azekah and Makkedah, where the kings of the five Amorite cities were captured and killed (10:10–27). This action across the central and southern Shephela led the Israelites into collateral missions against the nearby towns of Libnah (Kh. el-Beida?), Lachish (T. ed-Duweir/T. Lachish), Eglon (T. Eton?), Hebron (T. er-Rumeidah), and finally "turning back" to Debir (Kh. Rabud?) [**3**], before returning to their temporary headquarters at Gilgal (Josh. 10:15, 29–43).

Included in this narrative is Joshua's prayer for the sun to "stand still" at Gibeon and for the moon "to be still" at the valley of Aijalon (Josh. 10:12–14). Few Old Testament texts have excited greater interest or evoked more diverse opinion. Several critical questions have been posed as a result of this text. First, is it possible to discern when in the calendar year the event occurred, based on the presumption of when an observer at Gibeon might have been able to behold the moon over the valley of Aijalon and the sun overhead—"in the midst of the sky" (10:12b–13)? Several authors have followed this line of reasoning and have speculated on dates such as February 12, July 22, October 25, or October 30.[152] Perhaps such an approach collapses under the weight of its own presuppositions and mutually exclusive conclusions. In any event, this methodology offers nothing definitive and cannot be employed advantageously.

A second critical question has to do with the nature of the prayer itself. Was Joshua asking the sun to stop *moving* or to stop *shining*? Did he feel he and his troops needed *time* or *shade*? If it were the former, the rationale for the prayer was likely that the forces of Israel were so dramatically routing their Amorite foes that, with the aid of some additional time in the day, they could summarily vanquish them right then. (Agamemnon made a similar request to Zeus while routing his enemies in the *Iliad.*) If it were the latter, the rationale may have been that the Israelite army, having undertaken a steep uphill march from Gilgal to Gibeon throughout the preceding night—a distance of some 15 miles involving a climb in excess of 3,000 feet in altitude—was therefore not as vibrant and energized as the Amorite forces at the commencement of the battle and was in desperate need of relief from the oppressive heat of the sun.

Both verbs in question, translated "to be still/silent" and "to stay/stop," are used elsewhere in the Bible in either of these senses: "be motionless" (1 Sam. 14:9; Gen. 19:17; 2 Kings 4:6) and "be silent/quiet" (Ezek. 24:17; Amos 5:13; Job 32:16). Moreover, both words are found in Akkadian literature in astronomical contexts, which has led a number of scholars to render these verbs "to be obscured/eclipsed" and to picture a solar eclipse (cf. Hab. 3:11).[153] While this view is consistent with one meaning of the verbs involved, it poses other inherent problems. To begin with, between the years 1500–1000 B.C., only three solar eclipses are known to have occurred that were observable in central Palestine.[154] None of the dates comes even remotely close to what would be required of an early exodus/Late Bronze Age time frame, although two could work satisfactorily in a late exodus/Iron Age settlement scheme. A further difficulty may lie in the fact that an obliteration of the sun's rays may actually have adversely affected an Israelite pursuer while benefiting an Amorite enemy who wished to avoid detection and capture. Finally, the eclipse view offers no explanation whatsoever for the role of the moon in the episode. The admittedly poetic text describes the action of the moon in verse 13a by employing the very same verb that describes the action of the sun in verse 13b. But solar eclipses and lunar eclipses cannot occur simultaneously; solar eclipses occur only at the time of new moon and lunar eclipses take place only at the time of full moon. So this question remains somewhat unresolved. We're still unsure if Joshua was requesting *time* or *shade*.

The Tribal Distribution of the Land

map 40

City
City (uncertain location)
Capital city
Mountain peak
Leah tribal allotment
Territory ceded to Simeon
Zilpah (Leah) tribal allotment
Rachel tribal allotment
Bilhah (Rachel) tribal allotment
0 10 20 30 Miles
0 10 20 30 40 Kilometers
MEDITERRANEAN SEA
ARAM
Damascus
Mt. Hermon
Pharpar R.
Ijon
Dan
Litani R.
Tyre
ASHER (Josh 19:24f)
NAPHTALI (Josh 19:32f)
Yiron
Kedesh
Achzib
Merom
Hazor
EAST MANASSEH (Josh 13:29f)
Beth-anath
Acco
Achshaph
Capernaum
Chinnereth
Cabul
ZEBULUN (Josh 19:10f)
SEA OF GALILEE
Hannathon
Rimmon
Golan
Ashtaroth
Bethlehem
Daberath
Jabneel
Yarmuk R.
Helkath
Chesulloth
Jokneam
Sarid
Mt. Tabor
En-haddah
Dor
Megiddo
Mt. Moreh
Endor
Edrei
Shunem
ISSACHAR (Josh 19:17f)
Lo-debar
Jezreel
Taanach
Ramoth-gilead
En-gannim
Beth-shan
Dothan
Ibleam
Jabesh-gilead
Socoh
MANASSEH (Josh 17:1f)
Jordan R.
Tirzah
Gerasa
Samaria
Mt. Ebal
Shechem
Succoth
Penuel
Mahanaim
Pirathon
Mt. Gerizim
Jabbok R.
Jarkon R.
Micmethath
Janoah
GAD (Josh 13:24f)
Gath-rimmon
Aphek
Tappuah
Joppa
Shiloh
Jehud
Timnah-serah Inheritance of Joshua – Josh 19:50
EPHRAIM (Josh 16:5f)
Jazer
DAN (Josh 19:40f)
Lod
Upper Beth-horon
Bethel
Beth-nimrah
Rabbah (Amman)
Gibbethon
Gittaim
Mizpah
Naarath
Gilgal
Gezer
Shaalbim
BENJAMIN (Josh 18:11f)
Jericho
Shittim
Aroer
AMMON
Jabneel
Aijalon
Baalath
Timnah
Gibeon
Adummim
Beth-hoglah
Heshbon
Bezer
Ashdod
Zorah
Jerusalem
Ekron
Chesalon
Kiriath-jearim
Mt. Nebo
Beth-shemesh
Medeba
Gath
Bethlehem
Jahaz
Ashkelon
REUBEN (Josh 13:15f)
Mareshah
Beth-zur
Lachish
Hebron Inheritance of Caleb – Josh 15:13
Kedemoth
Gaza
Eglon
DEAD SEA
Dibon
JUDAH (Josh 15:1f)
Engedi
Aroer
Arnon R.
Gerar
Eshtemoa
Ziklag
Bethul
Ashan
Kabzeel
Arad
Sharuhen
Beersheba
MOAB
Hazar-shual
Baalah
Hormah
Kir-hareseth
SIMEON (Josh 19:1f)
Eltolad
Ezem
EASTERN DESERT
Zered Brook
Tamar
EDOM
Bozrah
A
B
C
1
2
3
4

THE LEVITICAL CITIES AND CITIES OF REFUGE

As part of the territorial distribution process, members from the tribe of Levi traveled to Shiloh where the question of their inheritance was addressed separately and in considerable detail. Levi was given no fixed independent *tribal* allotment (Josh. 13:14, 33; 14:3b–4; 18:7; cf. Josh. 21). Instead, a total of 48 cities and their surrounding pasturelands were given to them by lot and settled according to their family lines (Josh. 21:41; cf. Num. 35:7).

Biblical genealogies accord Levi a total of three sons: Gershon (or Gershom), Kohath, and Merari (Gen. 46:11; Ex. 6:16; Num. 3:17; 26:57; 1 Chron. 6:16; 23:6). However, because the genealogy of Kohath included Aaron and Moses, the so-called "Aaronic line" was given further elaboration and priestly prestige in the biblical record (1 Chron. 6:2–15). As a result, the Joshua 21 narrative and the 1 Chronicles 6 synoptic text divided the Levites into *four* identifiable families rather than three, and the classification of cities was laid out in an essentially clockwise rotation, starting in Judah:

- Thirteen cities in the tribes of Judah and Benjamin were given to the group of Kohathites who were descendants of Aaron (Josh. 21:4, 13–19; 1 Chron. 6:54–60);
- Ten cities were given to other Kohathites who were not of the Aaronic line, located within the tribal allotments of Dan, Ephraim, and Manasseh (Josh. 21:5, 20–26; 1 Chron. 6:61, 66–70);
- Thirteen cities were given to the Gershonites, all situated northward from the Jezreel valley but on both sides of the Jordan River (Josh. 21:6, 27–33; 1 Chron. 6:62, 71–76); and
- Twelve cities were given to the Merarites, most of which were positioned inside the Transjordanian territories of the tribes of Gad and Reuben (Josh. 21:7, 34–40; 1 Chron. 6:63, 77–81).

A comparison of this map with **maps 42 and 43** makes clear that some levitical cities were located in territory that lay *beyond* the realm of Israel's permanent control and did not come under Israelite aegis until the days of David or Solomon (e.g., Gezer, Taanach, Ibleam, Nahalal, and Rehob [Judges 1]). Moreover, a few levitical cities located *within* the area of Israel's permanent control do not manifest clear archaeological evidence of occupation until the days of Israel's monarchy (e.g., Golan, Mephaath, Heshbon, Eshtemoa[?]).[160] This may be suggestive of an editorial penchant for detail and recordkeeping of the sort that manifests itself clearly in the monarchy period. Or this list of cities—like the territorial allotments found just before it in chapters 13—19 [**map 40**]—may reflect an ideal/utopian outlook upon what was theoretically allocated and was in due course to occur within Israel's body politic.[161]

Given the pivotal and influential standing of priests, particularly in Israel's pre-monarchical history, it is perhaps surprising that certain cities related to early priestly activities were *not* identified as levitical cities and were not included on this list. Excluded were places like Bethel (Gen. 12:8; 35:7) and Beersheba (Gen. 26:23), where Israel's patriarchs are first said to have erected altars in Canaan and worshiped Yahweh. Missing are Gilgal (Josh. 4:19), Shiloh (Josh. 18:1; 19:51; Judg. 18:31; 1 Sam. 2:14b; 4:4), and Bethel (Judg. 20:26), where the ark of the covenant was housed in early Israel. Absent are Ramah and Mizpah of Benjamin (1 Sam. 7:15–17), places associated with the seer Samuel who offered sacrifices for the people of Israel (1 Sam. 9:9), anointed Saul and David (1 Sam. 10:1; 16:13), and played a seminal role in Israel's pre-monarchic ecclesiastical order (1 Sam. 7:9; 9:13; 10:8; 16:1–5).

Finally, six levitical cities were also demarcated as "cities of refuge/asylum" (Josh. 20:2; Num. 35:6). This was a land where justice was largely administered at the local level. The shedding of blood "polluted the land" and needed to be avenged (Num. 35:33–34)—the responsibility of either the nearest of kin or a representative of the elders of a given city designated as an "avenger of blood" (Num. 35:12; Deut. 19:6, 12; Josh. 20:3, 5, 9).[162] Therefore, the notion of protecting the genuinely innocent needed also to be addressed.

From as early as the Sinai legislation, Israel maintained a clear distinction between premeditated murder (Ex. 21:12, 14–15) and innocent killing (Ex. 21:13). Consequently, provision was made to create a "safe space" in this regard (Num. 35:6, 9–15; Deut. 4:41–43; 19:1–10) through these six cities set apart by Joshua for the administration of justice in the event of a killing that was accidental (*bišgāgâ,* "by mistake") or unintentional (*biltî-da`at,* "without knowledge"). The individual responsible for the killing would have recourse to justice. Since all six of these places were levitical cities, occupied by those charged with the priestly duties of worship and instruction in the law (Num. 1:47–54; 3:5–10; Deut. 10:8; 33:8–10), it is reasonable to assume that the teachings of the Sinai covenant would have been known in this regard and practiced in those places.

Three cities of refuge were selected on either side of the Jordan River, positioned at easily accessible locations. [See the roads on **map 27** and note the comment in Deuteronomy 19:3a.] The six locations within different regions of Israel's domain (Josh. 20:7–9) provided fairly even access to all of the tribes. [See locations of Kedesh (T. Qedesh) in Naphtali, Shechem (T. el-Balata) in West Manasseh, Hebron (J. er-Rumeida) in Judah, Golan (Sahm el-Jaulan) in East Manasseh, Ramoth-gilead (T. ar-Ramith) in Gad, and Bezer (Umm al-`Amad) in Reuben.]

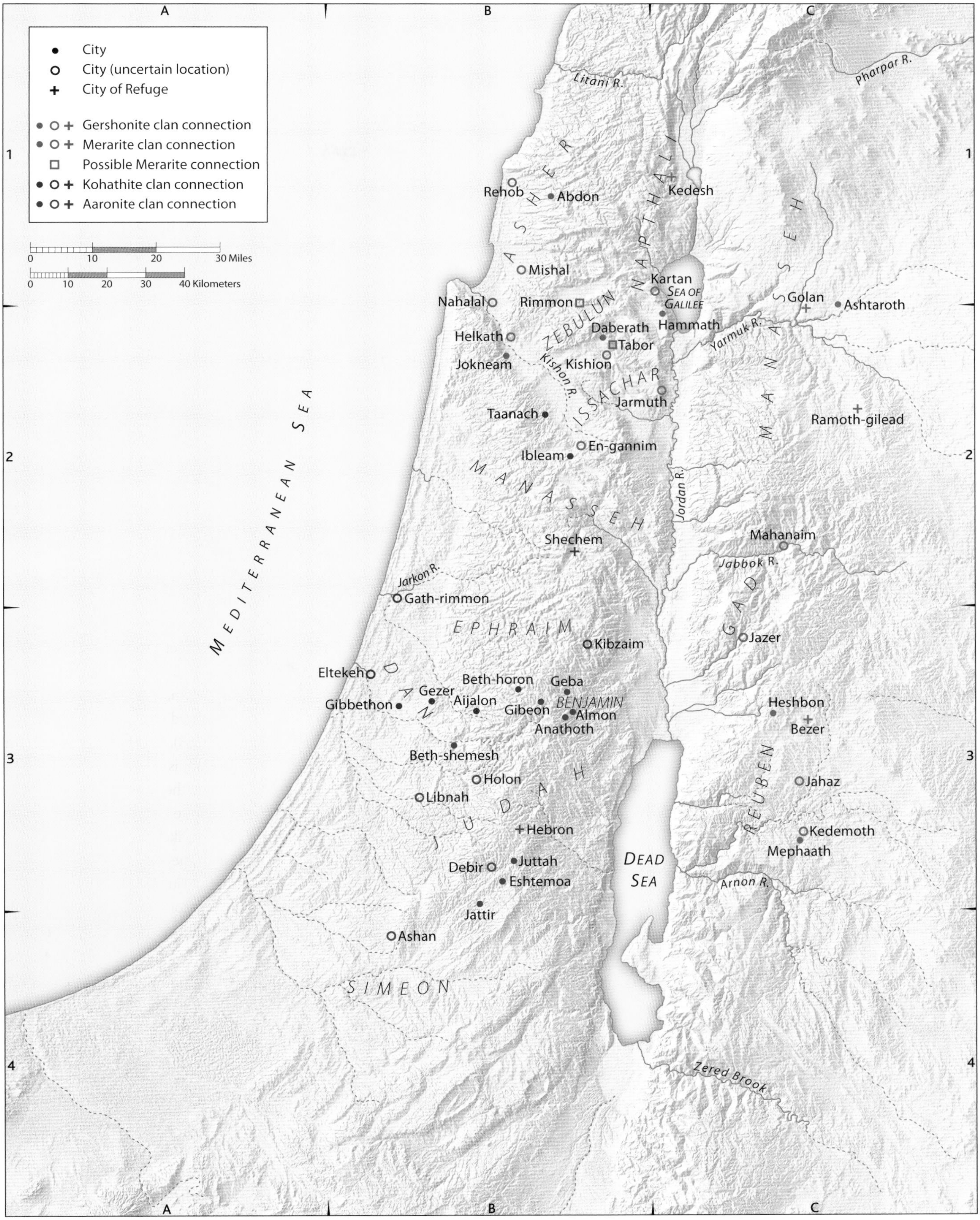
City
City (uncertain location)
City of Refuge
Gershonite clan connection
Merarite clan connection
Possible Merarite connection
Kohathite clan connection
Aaronite clan connection
0 10 20 30 Miles
0 10 20 30 40 Kilometers
A
B
C
1
2
3
4
Litani R.
Pharpar R.
ASHER
NAPHTALI
Rehob
Abdon
Kedesh
Mishal
Kartan
SEA OF GALILEE
Nahalal
Rimmon
ZEBULUN
Hammath
Golan
Ashtaroth
Daberath
Tabor
Yarmuk R.
Helkath
Jokneam
Kishon R.
Kishion
ISSACHAR
Jarmuth
MANASSEH
Taanach
Ramoth-gilead
En-gannim
Ibleam
MEDITERRANEAN SEA
Jordan R.
Shechem
Mahanaim
Jabbok R.
Jarkon R.
Gath-rimmon
EPHRAIM
GAD
Kibzaim
Jazer
Eltekeh
DAN
Beth-horon
Geba
Gezer
Aijalon
BENJAMIN
Gibbethon
Gibeon
Almon
Anathoth
Heshbon
Bezer
Beth-shemesh
REUBEN
Holon
Jahaz
Libnah
JUDAH
Hebron
Kedemoth
Mephaath
DEAD SEA
Debir
Juttah
Eshtemoa
Arnon R.
Jattir
Ashan
SIMEON
Zered Brook

AN ANALYSIS OF ISRAEL'S SETTLEMENT OF PALESTINE

Although at first glance the book of Joshua seems to portray a conquest that was lightning quick, confrontal in nature, and highly successful, a closer look at all the details suggests another verdict. It is true enough that Israel is described as having experienced a string of stunning successes at Jericho, Ai, Gibeon, and Hazor. However, it is also true that near the end of Joshua's life there remained huge tracts of Canaan still to be possessed, including:

1. The territories of Philistia (Ekron, Gath, Ashdod, Ashkelon, Gaza), Phoenicia (Acco, Tyre, Sidon, Gebal [Byblos]), Geshur, and Maacah (from Mt. Hermon southward) (Josh. 13:1–13; Judg. 3:1–3);
2. Strategic cities in the Jezreel valley (Megiddo, Taanach, Ibleam, Endor, and Beth-shan) and the coastal plain (Dor, Aphek, and Gezer) (Josh. 13:4; 16:10; 17:11–12; cf. Judg. 1:27, 29); and
3. The city of Jerusalem (Josh. 15:63; cf. Judg. 1:21).

Judges 1 continues the grim story of unconquered lands by adding that vast stretches of the Phoenician plain (Ahlab, Rehob, Achzib, Beth-shemesh, Acco, and Nahalal), as well as the major pass from the coastal plains into the Judahite heartland (Shaalbim, Aijalon, Har-heres [Beth-shemesh]), still remained outside Israel's control. [**See map 42.**]

A number of significant geographical factors emerge concerning the manner and extent of Israel's settlement. First, it seems that wherever the Philistines or their allies could maneuver iron chariots—in the Philistine plain (Judg. 1:19) or in the Jezreel valley (Josh. 17:16)—the Israelites were unable to take the terrain. But where that advantage was neutralized by the rugged mountain highlands of Canaan's interior, and in rugged Transjordan, Israel was able to carve out its nascent settlement. An especially striking example of this may be seen near the Jezreel valley, where the lowland sites of Taanach, Ibleam, and Beth-shan could not be taken, and yet the intermediate but higher site of Jezreel was seized.

Second, there is no Israelite record of Egyptian interference during the time of its settlement, which is puzzling indeed since Canaan formed part of the Egyptian kingdom at the time, and the Israelite settlement took place during a period of relative military strength in Egypt. Perhaps this lack of reference to Egyptian presence can be explained geographically. Late Bronze Age tablets from T. el-Amarna make it clear that the Egyptians had a strong interest in internal affairs in Canaan at that time, yet many of their campaigns there appear to center on the Great Trunk Road and its contiguous lowland cities (Gaza, Aphek, Megiddo, Beth-shan, Hazor). Even in those cases where a given campaign was conducted *in* Canaan, and not merely through Canaan (e.g., Thutmosis III, Amenhotep II, Seti I) [**map 44**], pharaohs did not wander far from that arterial roadway. Before the time of Merneptah, they did not seem to show much interest in the central Canaanite highlands. At the same time, Israel was unable to gain a sizeable foothold in areas adjacent to the Great Trunk Road. Geographically speaking, then, one might suggest that Egyptian and Israelite interests in Canaan at that time were mutually exclusive to a large extent, which might explain why Egypt appears to have remained uninvolved in local politics during the time of the Israelite settlement.

Third, one can observe across the central highlands on this map a rather close geographical correlation between the territory permanently controlled by ancient Israel and what is known today as the "West Bank" of the country of Jordan. During its Six-Day War of June 1967, modern Israel seized essentially the same central highland areas of Samaria and Judah that ancient Israel acquired during the biblical settlement. Here is poignant illustration of how geographic factors may dictate where and how history occurs, the advances of modern military technology notwithstanding.

RECENT INTRIGUING DISCOVERIES

Moreover, just after the Six-Day War, the State of Israel undertook a massive project of comprehensively surveying and mapping land as far east as the Jordan River. While this undertaking was motivated primarily for political, strategic, and military purposes, the newly captured territory had also been a prime area of ancient Israelite settlement, and hence modern Israeli archaeologists were also enlisted into the project. Accordingly, what in archaeological terms is known as "extensive surveying" or "emergency surveying" was begun throughout the new territory in late 1967, and the first volume of results was published a few years later.[163]

Subsequent surveys in over a dozen regions[164] have yielded remarkable, even stunning results. They have uncovered hundreds of brand-new, small, circular or elliptical-shaped camplike settlements dating to the early Iron Age (c. 1225–1150 B.C.). The new sites appear suddenly and without any traces of burning or destruction, and many appear to have been abandoned by approximately 900 B.C. They are small (most less than two acres in size), simple (architecturally and aesthetically unsophisticated), open (unwalled), and dull (use of utilitarian, undecorated pottery wares of a domestic variety rather than luxury or imported items). The sites are mostly located in the hills—areas that were largely unoccupied in the Late Bronze

Age. They exhibit no pattern of urbanization, with essentially no city walls, city gates, or public buildings such as a palace or temple. They show no sign of central political authority, and the inhabitants appear to have been economically poor. Some sites are attested only by unplastered storage pits for grain, earthen floors, and foundations of huts. They apparently used shallow graves but no grave goods.[165] The sites reflect a pastoral preoccupation, with significant faunal remains and a fair amount of living space given over to the care of sheep and goats (that were apparently brought in at night and given enclosed space inside the housing area). A more-or-less uniform house size with open and easy access from room to pillared room[166] seems to indicate an egalitarian mentality and non-hierarchical ideology, quite unlike what is known to have been common in Canaan in the preceding period and what is seen from the eight century B.C. onward. No shrines were found at the sites, and almost no weapons or pig bones were exhumed. All of this evidence unmistakably demonstrates that the new sites represent something far more than the mere evolutionary redistribution of the basic Late Bronze Age population groups from a sedentary to a pastoral mode of existence.

More than 700 such early Iron Age sites have been discovered to date,[167] which can provide a fairly comprehensive basis for formulating early Iron Age demography. Such a demographic analysis indicates that the population of Canaan tripled between around 1200 B.C. and 1000 B.C., and then more than doubled again by 800 B.C. The great number of sites and increase in population is baffling. One must speculate as to who these settlers were and where they had come from.[168]

Could there be any evidentiary connection between these sites and pre-monarchic Israel? Could these new settlers have been "Israelites" or in some way related to early Israel? Such a notion offers a rather convincing degree of plausibility for six reasons:

1. In many respects, the material culture of these new sites is strikingly distinctive from what immediately preceded in the Late Bronze era. In terms of ceramic assemblages and domestic architecture (the so-called "four-room" or "pillared" house, in contrast to the "courtyard" houses characteristic of the Late Bronze Age),[169] there are strong links of cultural continuity between the early Iron sites and the later Iron II sites (c. 800 B.C.). And the inhabitants of the Iron II sites are almost universally identified as "Israelites," by which scholars are referring to the Israelites of the Bible.
2. An arresting geographic correlation exists between the locations of these new sites and where, according to the Bible, the ancient Israelites settled in Canaan (Josh. 11:16–20; 13:1–7; 17:1–18; Judg. 1). [**See map 42.**] In addition to the Transjordan, Israel came to settle precisely in the highlands of Samaria, Judah, the Negeb, and eastern Galilee, but they were unable to settle along the coastal plains or in some inland valleys.
3. While these new sites and their immediate environs have thus far yielded a scant number of written documents, the few early Iron texts that have been found deserve comment.[170] While these texts are still being analyzed linguistically and historically, and more clarity will surely emerge over the next several years, it can be said that these documents are written in a simple archaic, alphabetic script, sometimes called "Canaanite/Old Hebrew." It is unmistakably the same script used by "Israelites" just a few years later.[171]
4. The type of woodlands that dominated the central highlands of Canaan is ideally suited for pig production,[172] and several species of pigs/swine were native to the region,[173] so the absence of pig bones is significant.[174] In fact, pig bones are found in the central highlands, sometimes in large quantities, both *before* and *after* these early Iron settlements,[175] whereas they almost disappear in the highlands *during* the early Iron period but are found precisely at that point in time in areas adjacent to the highlands. Coastal sites in particular show a transition from Late Bronze consumption of sheep/goats to an early Iron consumption of pigs/cattle, but by virtue of the pottery at these sites, they are indisputably Philistine settlements.[176] The Israelites were said to have occupied one end of the Sorek valley (Beth-shemesh) during the early Iron Age, and the Philistines occupied the interior and opposite end of the same valley (Timnah, Ekron). The presence of pig bones at Timnah and Ekron and the absence of pig bones at Beth-Shemesh provide a compelling index of ethnic distinction, at a minimum. Several sociocultural reasons are postulated for why people migrating out of a desert culture into a more sedentary life might not consume swine (cost, ignorance of the option, limited usefulness, cultural prejudice, pigs unsuited for a rural setting), but one must not overlook the taboo of the Old Testament itself as a plausible explanation for this distinction. Israel's dietary laws forbade the consumption of swine or any other "unclean" animal (Deut. 14:8; Lev. 11:26–27). Pigs were raised in substantial numbers across Canaan in certain periods, a fact which suggests that their disappearance in the central highlands during the early Iron period was a function of ethnicity and/or culture, not environment or ecology.[177]
5. Ancient Israel is often described in a basically "pastoralist" mode of existence, with flocks and herds, much like the occupants of the newly discovered settlements. The Bible consistently presents the notion of a group of Israelite forebears who entered Canaan from elsewhere, having been emancipated from slavery a generation earlier and having lived in a desert environment in the meanwhile. Such a socioeconomic reality comports well with settlements that lack

City
City (uncertain location)
Capital city
City of Refuge
Mountain peak
Area permanently controlled by ancient Israel
Modern boundary of the West Bank of Jordan
City not captured according to Joshua 17 or Judges 1
City beyond area of Israelite permanent control
City within area of Israelite permanent control
City whose king is said to have been defeated by Israel (Joshua 12)
0 10 20 30 Miles
0 10 20 30 40 Kilometers
Damascus
Mt. Hermon
ARAM
PHOENICIA
Ahlab
Litani R.
Tyre
Dan
MAACAH
Kitron
Great Trunk Road
Rehob
Beth-shemesh
Kedesh
Achzib
Hazor
J. Jarmuk
Merom
Beth-anath
BASHAN
King's Highway
Acco
Achshaph
SEA OF GALILEE
GESHUR
Mt. Carmel
Aphek
Nahalal
Golan
Ashtaroth
Harosheth-hagoiim
Yarmuk R.
Shimron
Mt. Tabor
Jokneam
Endor
Dor
Megiddo
Edrei
Mt. Moreh
Jezreel
Ramoth-gilead
Taanach
Beth-shan
Ibleam
Hepher
Jabesh-gilead
Bezek
Socoh
MEDITERRANEAN SEA
Tirzah
Mt. Ebal
Mahanaim
Succoth
Shechem
Mt. Gerizim
Jarkon R.
Tappuah
Jabbok R.
Aphek
Joppa
Shiloh
Jogbehah
Jordan R.
AMMON
Jazer
Rabbah (Amman)
Bethel
Gezer
Ai
Mizpah
Jericho
Heshbon
Shaalbim
Gibeon
Aijalon
Ashdod
Ekron
Jerusalem
Bezer
Beth-shemesh (Har-heres)
Mt. Nebo
Gath
Jarmuth
Bethlehem
Jahaz
Geder
Ashkelon
PHILISTIA
Libnah
Adullam
Lachish
Hebron
DEAD SEA
Makkedah
Mephaath
Gaza
Eglon
Dibon
Debir
Engedi
Aroer
Gerar
Arnon R.
Ziklag
Arad
Besor Brook
Beersheba
MOAB
Great Trunk Road
AVVITES
Kir-hareseth
Hormah
to Shihor
King's Highway
EASTERN DESERT
Zered Brook
WILDERNESS OF ZIN
EDOM
Bozrah

City
City (uncertain location)
Capital city
City of Refuge
Mountain peak
Area permanently controlled by ancient Israel
Modern boundary of the West Bank of Jordan
Main cities occupied by the Philistines (Joshua 13:3)
City said to have been set on fire or burned by Israel
City whose population is said to have been destroyed by Israel
City said to have been placed under a sacred ban by Israel
0 10 20 30 Miles
0 10 20 30 40 Kilometers
A
B
C
1
2
3
4
Damascus
Mt. Hermon
ARAM
Ahlab
Litani R.
Tyre
PHOENICIA
Dan
MAACAH
Kitron
Great Trunk Road
Rehob
Beth-shemesh
Kedesh
Achzib
Hazor
J. Jarmuk
Merom
Beth-anath
BASHAN
King's Highway
Acco
Achshaph
GESHUR
Sea of Galilee
Aphek
Mt. Carmel
Nahalal
Golan
Ashtaroth
Harosheth-hagoiim
Shimron
Yarmuk R.
Mt. Tabor
Jokneam
Endor
Dor
Megiddo
Mt. Moreh
Edrei
Jezreel
Taanach
Beth-shan
Ramoth-gilead
Ibleam
Hepher
Jabesh-gilead
Bezek
Socoh
Tirzah
Mt. Ebal
Mahanaim
Succoth
Shechem
Mt. Gerizim
Jarkon R.
Jabbok R.
Tappuah
Aphek
MEDITERRANEAN SEA
Joppa
Shiloh
Jordan R.
Jogbehah
AMMON
Jazer
Bethel
Ai
Rabbah (Amman)
Gezer
Mizpah
Gibeon
Jericho
Heshbon
Shaalbim
Aijalon
Ashdod
Ekron
Beth-shemesh (Har-heres)
Jerusalem
Bezer
Mt. Nebo
Gath
Bethlehem
Jarmuth
Jahaz
Ashkelon
Libnah
Geder
Adullam
PHILISTIA
Hebron
Lachish
DEAD SEA
Makkedah
Mephaath
Gaza
Eglon
Dibon
Debir
Engedi
Aroer
Arnon R.
Gerar
Ziklag
Arad
Besor Brook
Great Trunk Road
Beersheba
MOAB
Kir-hareseth
AVVITES
Hormah
to Shihor
EASTERN DESERT
King's Highway
Zered Brook
WILDERNESS OF ZIN
EDOM
Bozrah

cultural sophistication and are small and comparatively impoverished. Some of the biblical place names from this era may relate to a settlement pattern: Gibeah ("hill"), Ramah ("high place"), Hazor ("enclosure"), Mahaneh-dan ("settlement of Dan"), and Gilgal ("circle [of stones?]"). At the same time, a new type of place name not earlier attested begins to appear on the Canaanite map, one containing the theophoric element "Baal" (and see names hyphenated with Baal in the Old Testament: Baal-berith, Baal-gad, Baal-hermon, Baal-meon, Baal-peor, Baal-perazim, Baal-zebub, etc.). Here is further suggestion that the new sites were not being occupied by Late Bronze Age residents.

In the same vein, while it is clear that the early Israelites forcefully took certain towns (Jericho, Ai, Hazor), this probably did not represent their normal method of entering into their tribal allotments and settling down over the course of time. Whatever else we learn from the books of Joshua and Judges about the occupation of their land, it is clear that the early Israelites functioned basically as a tribal social organization that lacked the sort of national identity found, for example, in the office of a king. Few political structures existed, and tribal/clan ties were the center of social focus. Early Israelites tend to be depicted as depending on themselves—on their own crops and their own flocks/herds—for material necessities and survival. Early on, an essentially egalitarian mentality is clearly reflected in their settlement narratives. (For example, "There was no king in Israel in those days, and everyone did what was right in his own eyes" [Judg. 21:25]. Yet by around 800 B.C. and thereafter, clear evidence exists of social stratification inside Israel (Isa. 3:14–15; Hos. 12:8; Amos 2:6–8; 3:15; 4:1; 5:11; 6:4; Mic. 2:1–12). The same socioeconomic pattern is observed in the contemporaneous early Iron settlements.[178]

6. Finally, this scheme represents a rather convincing chronological fit. An *ethnic* entity known as "Israel," located somewhere inside Canaan, was explicitly referenced in a poetic victory stela dated early in the reign of the Egyptian pharaoh Merneptah (1213–1203 B.C.).[179] [**See map 44.**] The text reads as follows:

> "Canaan has been plundered with every sort of woe
> Ashkelon has been carried off
> Gezer has been seized
> Yenoam has been made nonexistent
> Israel has been wasted, its seed is not
> Hurru has become a widow [because] of Egypt."[180]

EGYPT CAMPAIGNS INTO CANAAN

Egyptian pharaohs from as early as the Old Kingdom period (c. 2700–2160 B.C.)[181] undertook military campaigns into Asia to protect substantial political and commercial interests on their northern front. We learn of perhaps as many as 40 such campaigns from various stelae, annals, papyri, topographic lists, inscribed war-panel scenes, tomb paintings, and other kinds of texts. Most were against Hittite, Aramean, or Mitannian antagonists.[182] Yet because the great majority of these were land campaigns, Canaan/Palestine also became involved in these maneuvers as an unwitting transportation corridor and buffer zone.

On a few occasions, however, the battle appears to have been pitched *within* Canaan or directed primarily against Canaanite targets. These skirmishes—with one exception (Shishak)—tended to occur on or near Egypt's transportation/communication lifeline to Mesopotamia [**map 25**] and may have had a commercial rationale.

THUTMOSIS III

One such occasion was in the 22nd year of Thutmosis III (1457 B.C.), when a Syro-Canaanite coalition gathered at the strategically situated city of Megiddo.[183] To meet this challenge, Thutmosis led his army north to Gaza, the seat of Egyptian administration in Canaan that often served as a military base or launching pad for Egyptian campaigns into Asia.[184]

From Gaza, the pharaoh marched north past Aphek and Socoh, and came to Yaham. At this point an important tactical decision was required. One option was for the Egyptian army to proceed farther north through either a western pass in the Mt. Carmel range that emerged onto the Jezreel Valley at Jokneam or an eastern pass that entered the valley near Taanach. [**See map 10.**] A second option was to proceed directly north past Aruna through the so-called "Aruna pass" (W. `Ara). The generals reporting to Thutmosis argued for the first option, knowing that the central pass was an extremely narrow passageway that would force the Egyptian army into the potentially vulnerable position of being spread out over a distance of more than ten miles as it moved north toward Megiddo.

Instinctively calculating that his opponents would think like his own generals, Thutmosis embraced the second option instead. A small secondary force was dispatched through each of the other passes, but his main army set out past Aruna and came directly to the vicinity of Megiddo. His tactical instinct proved to be correct. The Syro-Canaanites had in fact deployed their troops near the western and eastern passes, but not at the central pass. Realizing their near-fatal miscalculation, the coalition forces quickly retreated to Megiddo. The Egyptian army found it necessary to lay siege to the city for some seven months, but finally forced their enemies to capitulate.[185]

AMENHOTEP II

About 40 years later, Amenhotep II undertook a campaign into Canaan during his ninth regnal year (1419 B.C.), which seems to have been directed against local Canaanite insurgents.[186] Following the same route as Thutmosis before him,

The high, heavily fortified tell of Megiddo is strategically situated between the Jezreel/Esdraelon Valley (foreground of picture) and Mt. Carmel (background) near the "Aruna pass" (W. `Ara).

Amenhotep also marched north past Gaza, Aphek, Socoh, and came to Yaham, where he halted temporarily to engage in some side clashes in the direction of the Sharon plain from which much booty was seized. The main thrust of his expedition, however, took him through the "Aruna pass," along the Jezreel valley, and eastward into Lower Galilee and to the town of Anaharath (T. Rekesh?). Amenhotep vanquished the town in less than a week, turned back past Megiddo, and eventually returned to Memphis.

SETI I

Several documents relate to a campaign undertaken by Seti I early in his reign, perhaps around 1289 B.C., in part against Canaanite targets.[187] Seti also traveled north via the Great Trunk Road, passed Megiddo, and then turned east. He undertook a major attack on the dominant city of Beth-shan and a few of its suburbs before launching an assault on the Galilean town of Yenoam.[188] From Yenoam, Seti plausibly backtracked as far as Megiddo, but then he continued his campaign in a northward direction along the coast. He marched past the Phoenician cities of Tyre and Ullaza before turning inland to arrive at Kadesh on the Orontes, in Syria.

MERNEPTAH

A ten-foot slab of black granite was originally inscribed with a record of the building activities of pharaoh Amenhotep III and set up in what was presumably his mortuary temple in west Thebes. This slab was later appropriated by pharaoh Merneptah; he had the reverse side engraved with his celebrated victory over the Libyans and installed the stela in his own mortuary temple nearby.

At the bottom of the slab, seemingly as an afterthought because of unused space remaining, Merneptah's scribes appended a short poem commemorating his triumph over forces in Canaan. The text mentions that he had vanquished the cities of Ashkelon, Gezer, and Yenoam, and that he had laid waste to "Israel."[189] This is the most ancient extra-biblical reference to the "Israel" of the Bible, and the only such reference known before the eighth century B.C. [**See maps 42 and 43.**]

Remnants of Merneptah's presence in Canaan at about this time have been discovered at various places within the land. An ivory chain with two cartouches bearing his name was exhumed from a late-13th-century B.C. stratum at Gezer; a Merneptah cartouche on an ivory tusk was discovered in a 13th-century B.C. stratum of the Ekron temple complex; and the late-13th-century B.C. Papyrus Anastasi III contains an entry dated to Merneptah's third year, which makes reference to "wells of Merneptah" located "on the mountain range"—presumably of Canaan[190] (Josh. 15:9; 18:15 [reading "the wells of Merneptah" (Lifta?) instead of the redundant "the wells of the water of Nephtoah"]). Based on this literary and archaeological evidence, a plausible if conjectural campaign itinerary for Merneptah into Canaan, probably around his fourth year (1208 B.C.), would have taken him to sites including Gaza, Lachish, Ekron, Gezer, Yenoam, and perhaps Lifta.

SHISHAK

A campaign of pharaoh Shishak (Shoshenq I) to Canaan may be inferred from the Bible (1 Kings 14:25–28; 2 Chron. 12:2–12) and from a battle relief of Shishak found at Karnak, Egypt. [**See map 67 for discussion.**] Neither of these sources provides an exact itinerary, so the campaign must be conjecturally reconstructed.

Based on Shishak's own record, he appears to have taken a distinct route and approached many different cities than his predecessors, so perhaps his motivation also differed. Whatever the case, it seems that Shishak led his army as far north as Gaza, where it split. One Egyptian contingent traveled east past Yurza and Gerar and marched across the entire Negeb. It appears from Shishak's battle registers that he was quite preoccupied with the Negeb; his scribes made repeated references to the Negeb or to places located there (e.g., Arad, Ezem, and perhaps Kadesh-barnea).[191] We now know of more than sixty tenth-century B.C. fortresses that were located across the length and breadth of the Negeb,[192] built as caravan fortresses presumably for commercial and/or military purposes, perhaps by Solomon.[193] [**See also map 64.**] Many of these were either destroyed or abandoned near the end of the tenth century B.C., an event attributed by many scholars to Shishak's campaign.[194]

Shishak's other military contingent apparently traveled north from Gaza into the heart of Palestine. The following sites listed in Shishak's victory panels, over which he claimed victory, may be relevant to a reconstructed itinerary: Gezer (register #12), Aijalon (#26), Beth-horon (#24), Kiriath-jearim (#25), Gibeon (#23), Gophna (#64), Tappuah (#39), Tirzah (#59), the Jordan River (#150), Adam (#56), Succoth (#55), Penuel (#53), Mahanaim (#22), Rehob (#17), Beth-shan (#16), Shunem (#15), Taanach (#14), and Megiddo (#27). [**See also map 67.**]

These data suggest that, from the vicinity of Ekron and Gezer, Shishak took an inland route or routes as far as the area of Gibeon and Jerusalem, where he maneuvered northward. In due course he went east across the Jordan River and along the Jabbok River valley for a distance. Afterward, he must have retraced his steps back to the west side of the Jordan and marched as far north as the mouth of the Jezreel valley, near Beth-shan. He apparently veered west and eventually made his way to the preeminent site of Megiddo. (A portion of a Shishak victory stela was discovered there.) It is possible he may have made a quick foray from Megiddo into Galilee and southern Phoenicia. It also appears that from Megiddo he began his homeward journey, passing the sites of Aruna, Yaham, and Socoh along the way.

Egypt Campaigns into Canaan

map 44

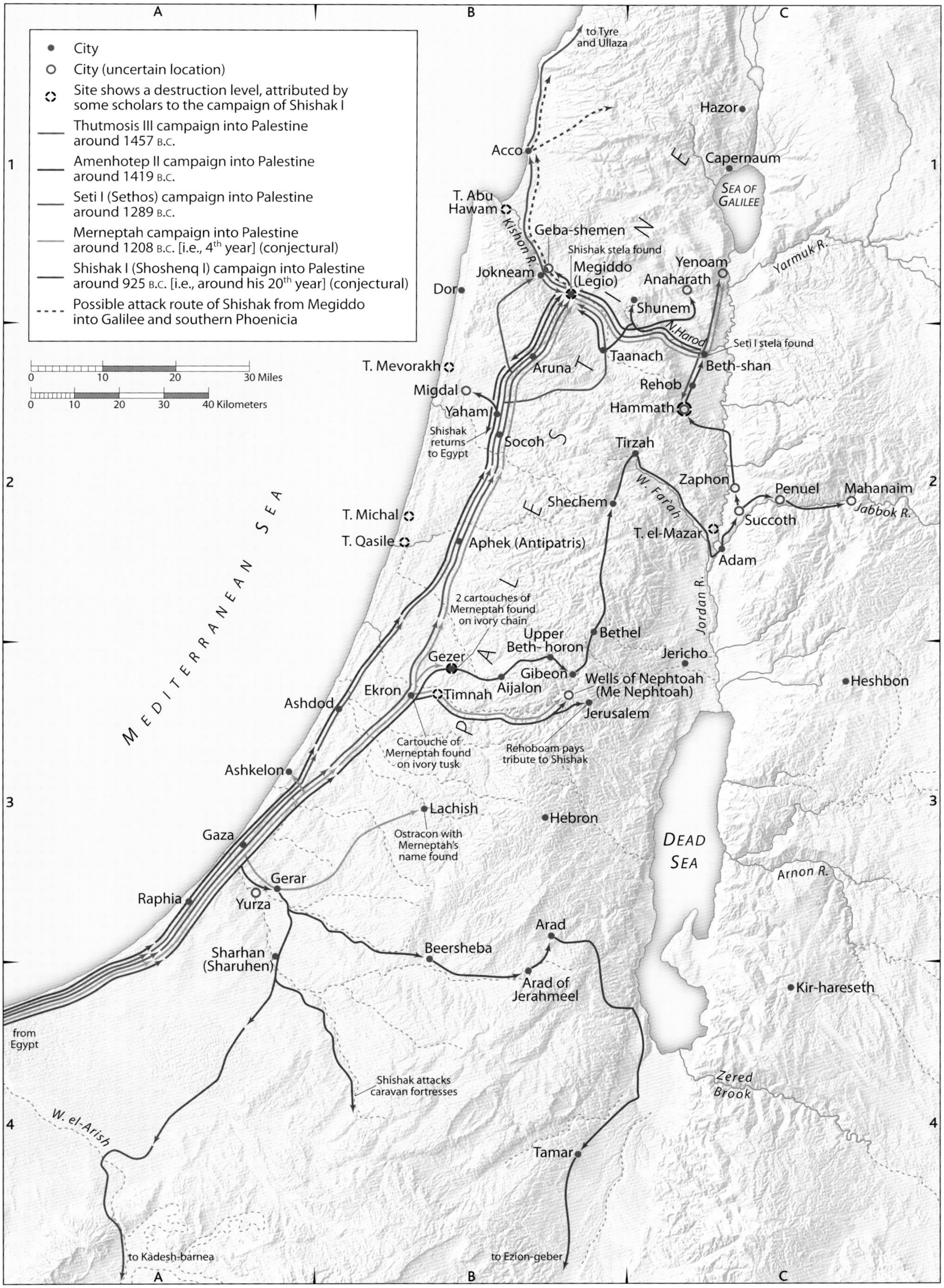

A
B
C
City
City (uncertain location)
Site shows a destruction level, attributed by some scholars to the campaign of Shishak I
Thutmosis III campaign into Palestine around 1457 B.C.
Amenhotep II campaign into Palestine around 1419 B.C.
Seti I (Sethos) campaign into Palestine around 1289 B.C.
Merneptah campaign into Palestine around 1208 B.C. [i.e., 4th year] (conjectural)
Shishak I (Shoshenq I) campaign into Palestine around 925 B.C. [i.e., around his 20th year] (conjectural)
Possible attack route of Shishak from Megiddo into Galilee and southern Phoenicia
0 10 20 30 Miles
0 10 20 30 40 Kilometers
to Tyre and Ullaza
Hazor
Acco
Capernaum
Sea of Galilee
T. Abu Hawam
Kishon R.
Geba-shemen
Shishak stela found
Megiddo (Legio)
Jokneam
Yenoam
Yarmuk R.
Anaharath
Dor
Shunem
N. Harod
Seti I stela found
Taanach
Beth-shan
T. Mevorakh
Aruna
Rehob
Migdal
Hammath
Yaham
Shishak returns to Egypt
Socoh
Tirzah
W. Far'ah
Zaphon
Penuel
Mahanaim
Jabbok R.
Shechem
Succoth
T. Michal
T. el-Mazar
T. Qasile
Aphek (Antipatris)
Adam
Mediterranean Sea
Galilee
Palestine
Jordan R.
2 cartouches of Merneptah found on ivory chain
Bethel
Upper Beth-horon
Gezer
Jericho
Gibeon
Wells of Nephtoah (Me Nephtoah)
Heshbon
Ekron
Timnah
Aijalon
Ashdod
Jerusalem
Cartouche of Merneptah found on ivory tusk
Rehoboam pays tribute to Shishak
Ashkelon
Lachish
Hebron
Gaza
Ostracon with Merneptah's name found
Dead Sea
Gerar
Arnon R.
Raphia
Yurza
Arad
Beersheba
Sharhan (Sharuhen)
Arad of Jerahmeel
Kir-hareseth
from Egypt
Shishak attacks caravan fortresses
Zered Brook
W. el-Arish
Tamar
to Kadesh-barnea
to Ezion-geber
1
2
3
4

THE ERA OF THE JUDGES

The era of the Israelite judges was one of charismatic leadership during which the Spirit of God would equip a man or woman for particular service (Judg. 3:10; 6:34; 11:29; 13:25; 14:6; 15:14). Unlike the institution of king that would later arise in Israel, the authority of judges was non-hereditary and not dependent on social status. The judges included a prophet (4:4), a farmer who was self-described as the "least of the least" (6:11, 15), a soldier (11:1), and a pleasure seeker (16:1, 4). Aside from tribal infrastructures there was no bureaucratic apparatus. The individuals involved were sometimes characterized by a close relationship to God, and occasionally their exploits were accompanied by the public performance of miracles. At other times, neither holiness nor wonder-working was apparent in their lives. Though coming from different tribes and divergent regions, the judges arose from territory occupied by early Israel or from immediately adjacent areas. [**Compare maps 42 and 43.**]

What *is* apparent in the book of Judges is the cyclical formula repeatedly recited there:

1. Israel rebels (3:7, 12a; 4:1a; 6:1a; 10:6; 13:1a);
2. Israel is oppressed by outside powers (3:8; 3:12b; 4:2; 6:1b; 10:7; 13:1b);
3. Israel repents (3:9a; 3:15a; 4:3a; 6:7; 10:10);
4. God raises up a judge (3:9b; 3:15b; 4:6b; 6:14; 11:29);
5. Israel is delivered (3:10; 3:15b–29; 4:14–24; 7:19–8:21; 11:29–40); and
6. Israel has a period of peace (3:11a; 3:30b; 5:31b; 8:28b; cf. 2:11–23).

This kind of programmatic recurrence might suggest that "oppression" was a static category, but oppressions could assume a number of forms. Philistine imperialism was a military oppression as faced by Samson and Shamgar. Oppression could take a political shape, as when Deborah and Barak went up against certain temporarily dispossessed Canaanites who had been able to regroup and retake land previously claimed by Israel. The powerful Midianites imposed economic oppression by seasonally plundering the Israelites' crops at harvest time . . . until Gideon was called to defeat them.

Nor must we imagine that all judges functioned in the same way. Deborah's judgeship was essentially judicial in character; the judgeships of Gideon and Jephthah were principally military in nature; Samson's bears sociological earmarks. Not much is known about the judgeships of Shamgar, Tola, Jair, Ibzan, Elon, and Abdon, thus giving rise to the expression "minor judges." In some cases we know the town where

The prominent 30-acre site of Lachish dominates the southern Shephela. Parts of the outer revetment wall are visible (just beyond the modern road), as well as the more well-defined perimeter wall that encircles the summit.

The Era of the Judges

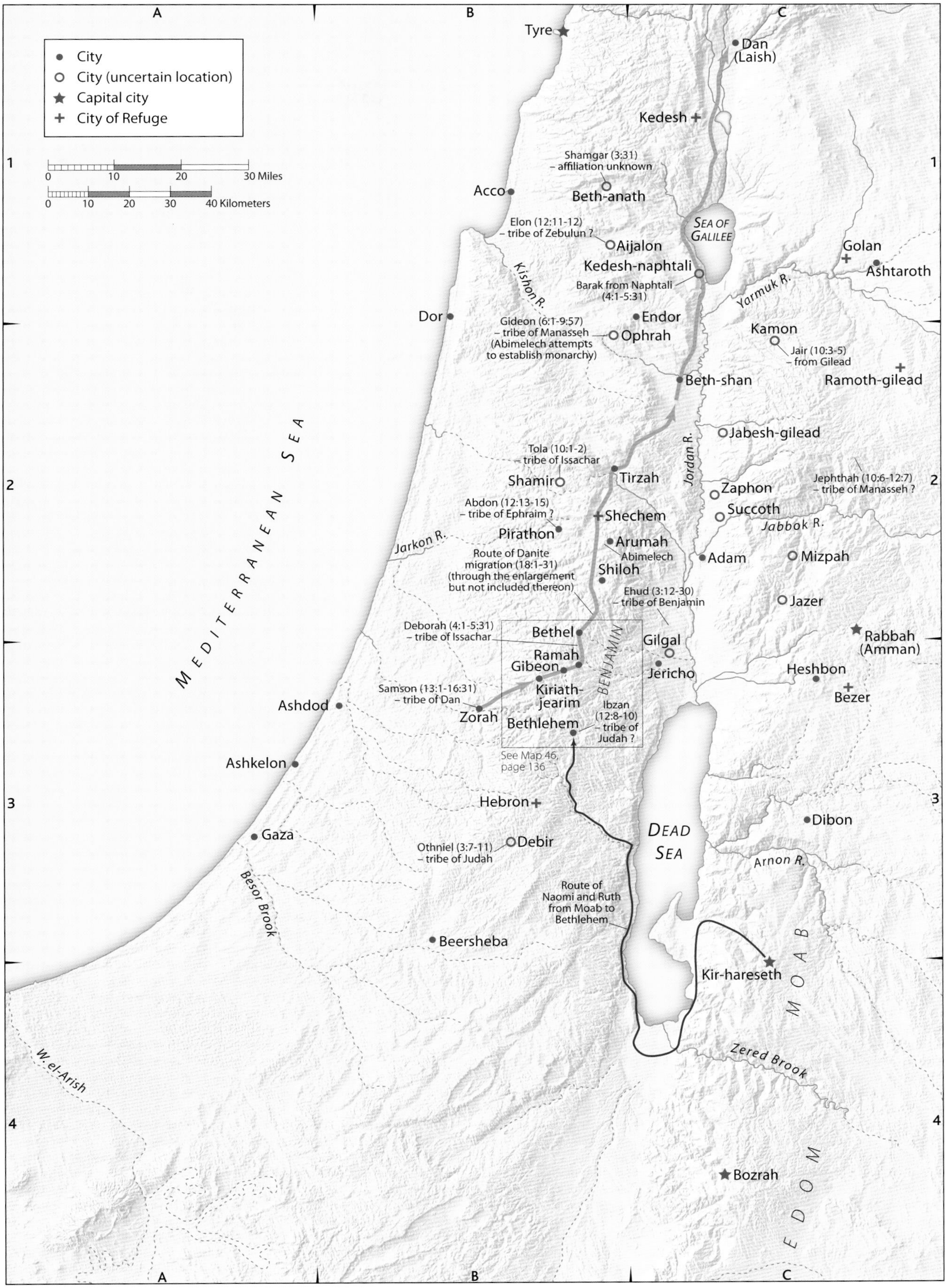

A
B
C
City
City (uncertain location)
Capital city
City of Refuge
0 10 20 30 Miles
0 10 20 30 40 Kilometers
1
2
3
4
Tyre
Dan (Laish)
Kedesh
Shamgar (3:31) – affiliation unknown
Beth-anath
Acco
Sea of Galilee
Elon (12:11-12) – tribe of Zebulun ?
Aijalon
Kedesh-naphtali
Barak from Naphtali (4:1-5:31)
Golan
Ashtaroth
Yarmuk R.
Kishon R.
Dor
Gideon (6:1-9:57) – tribe of Manasseh (Abimelech attempts to establish monarchy)
Endor
Ophrah
Kamon
Jair (10:3-5) – from Gilead
Beth-shan
Ramoth-gilead
Mediterranean Sea
Jabesh-gilead
Tola (10:1-2) – tribe of Issachar
Jordan R.
Shamir
Tirzah
Zaphon
Jephthah (10:6-12:7) – tribe of Manasseh ?
Abdon (12:13-15) – tribe of Ephraim ?
Shechem
Succoth
Jabbok R.
Pirathon
Jarkon R.
Arumah
Abimelech
Route of Danite migration (18:1-31) (through the enlargement but not included thereon)
Shiloh
Adam
Mizpah
Ehud (3:12-30) – tribe of Benjamin
Jazer
Deborah (4:1-5:31) – tribe of Issachar
Bethel
Benjamin
Gilgal
Rabbah (Amman)
Ramah
Gibeon
Jericho
Heshbon
Samson (13:1-16:31) – tribe of Dan
Kiriath-jearim
Bezer
Ashdod
Zorah
Bethlehem
Ibzan (12:8-10) – tribe of Judah ?
See Map 46, page 136
Ashkelon
Hebron
Dead Sea
Dibon
Gaza
Othniel (3:7-11) – tribe of Judah
Debir
Arnon R.
Besor Brook
Route of Naomi and Ruth from Moab to Bethlehem
Beersheba
Kir-hareseth
Moab
Zered Brook
W. el-Arish
Bozrah
Edom

minor judges lived and/or were buried, their tribal affiliation, the length of their tenure, or something of their progeny, but little more can be gleaned from the accounts.

It may be useful to observe that, with a few exceptions, the major judges are presented to us in a south-to-north geographical sequence. At the same time, they appear in a deteriorating pattern of personal character. Not only is the institution of judge portrayed as being powerless to prevent recurring apostasy in Israel, but also the judges themselves seem to be increasingly involved in many of the same unsavory tendencies that characterized the general population at that time.

Perhaps the common denominator of all Israelite judges is that they represented dominant figures in a society that was otherwise highly decentralized, chaotic if not anarchistic beyond the tribal level, and decadent to the core. The two concluding episodes of Judges (Micah and his priest, and the Levite and his concubine [Judg. 17—21]) trumpet loudly the refrain of Israel's total decadence, exemplified domestically (17:1–4a; 19:24–25), morally (19:22–23, 25; 20:13b; 21:20–21), politically (17:6; 18:1; 19:1; 21:25), religiously (17:4b–7, 12; 18:4, 30), and culturally (19:11, 15, 18).

The Israelites Attack Gibeah ***map 46***

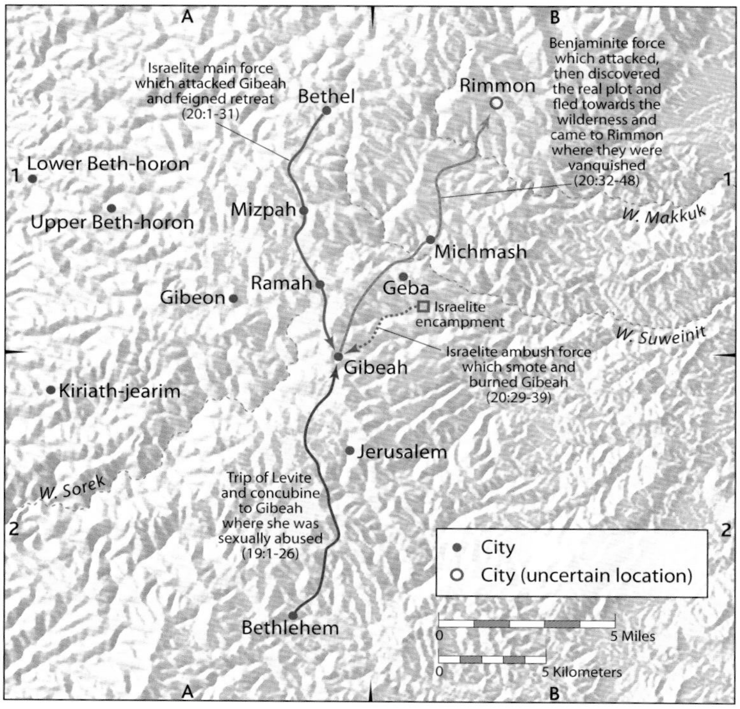

Such repulsive stories often "turn the stomach" of modern readers. Yet that may have been their precise intention, in the context of biblical theology. One observes that the victim in both stories hailed from the town of Bethlehem, which was located inside the tribal allotment of Judah (Mic. 5:2). [**See map 40.**] The victim in both stories was victimized in "the hill country of Ephraim" (17:8b; 19:1b) and in one instance, more specifically at the town of Gibeah (19:16), which was located inside the tribal allotment of Benjamin (19:14b; cf. 1 Sam. 13:15). Moreover, Israelite hostility was directed against the tribe of Benjamin in the second story (20:13b–16), with similar hostility directed against their allies, the inhabitants of the town of Jabesh-gilead (T. Abu Kharaz?), located on the east side of the Jordan River (21:8–12). And finally, one observes inside these stories the motif of a concubine/wife who had returned to her father's house and needed to be retrieved by her husband (19:2b–9; cf. 20:4).

Not much later in Scripture we discover that David's hometown was Bethlehem in Judah (1 Sam. 17:12), whereas the Benjaminite Saul hailed from the town of Gibeah, in the hill country of Ephraim (1 Sam. 10:26; 11:4; Isa. 10:29b). The close connection between the tribe of Benjamin and the otherwise insignificant town of Jabesh-gilead across the Jordan unmistakably evokes the memory of Saul. Jabesh-gilead was the location of the only military victory won by Saul personally, recorded in the Bible at the inception of his reign (1 Sam. 11:1–11), and it is where he was buried (1 Sam. 31:11–13; cf. 2 Sam. 2:4b–7; 21:12). But beyond its role in these two pivotal events of Saul's career, and in the story of the Levite and his concubine, Jabesh-gilead is virtually unknown in biblical tradition. Similarly, the notion of a concubine/wife who had returned to her father's house and needed to be retrieved by her husband is conspicuously reminiscent of the story of David and Michal (1 Sam. 18:27b; 2 Sam. 3:12–16).

Consequently, it appears that these two stories at the end of Judges may also play a profound and deeply theological role: here is where one encounters the recurrent formula eliciting the very institution of monarchy itself. ("There was no king in Israel in those days, and everyone did what seemed right in their own eyes" [17:6; 18:1; 19:1; 21:25; cf. Deut. 12:8b; Gen. 36:31b].) In other words, this refrain advances an explanation for why Israel repeatedly experienced apostasy and societal decadence.

In terms of biblical theology, anointing a king seemed to offer the prospect of ending this dismal pattern. Yet upon closer examination, perhaps the two stories are suggestive not so much of kingship in general, but are rather a plea for a certain type of monarchy. Decadent stories such as these, taking place within the tribe of Benjamin, should have made one more wary of a Benjaminite king as represented by the person of Saul and more confident to embrace a Judean monarchy as embodied in the person of David. Accordingly, a case can arguably be made that the book of Judges was designed as an apologetic for a *Davidic* monarchy.[195]

OTHNIEL, EHUD, AND SAMSON

OTHNIEL

First in the list of judges is Othniel, Caleb's nephew from the tribe of Judah (Judg. 1:13; 3:9; cf. Josh. 15:17). Othniel also became Caleb's son-in-law as a reward for capturing the city of Debir, also known as Kiriath-sepher (Josh. 15:13–16; Judg. 1:11–12). Both the personal and national identity of Israel's adversary during the judgeship of Othniel, however, continues to vex biblical scholarship. "Cushan-rishathaim" (Judg. 3:8b, 10) means "Cushan of double-wickedness"—hardly a name given by a parent at birth or adopted by an individual as a surname. It may be, therefore, that the biblical writer intended to assign a pejorative connotation to this oppressor.[196]

The national identity of Cushan-rishathaim is also uncertain. Was he a Mesopotamian or an Edomite ruler? He is said to have been king of Aram-naharaim ("Aram of the two rivers" [Judg. 3:8b, 10]), a geographical expression that elsewhere in the Bible designated a section of northern Mesopotamia (Gen. 24:10; Deut. 23:4). However, oppressors in the book of Judges normally did not travel from such faraway lands, and the Hebrew letters comprising the word Aram [*'rm*] are sometimes confused with the letters for the word Edom [*'dm*] (e.g., 2 Kings 16:6 [twice]; 2 Chron. 20:2; Ezek. 16:57; 27:16; cf. 1 Sam. 21:7 [*LXX*]). Therefore, some scholars propose that Cushan-rishathaim actually hailed from Edom. Inasmuch as the graphically similar Hebrew letters *r/d* are often confused in the biblical text, the reading "Edom" could be obtained without difficulty. However, no support in the Hebrew text or in the versions for "Edom" in this particular passage is adducible. And even if "Edom" was mistakenly rendered "Aram," such a reading requires one to ignore "naharaim." That word lacks apparent meaning with Edom and is never elsewhere hyphenated with Edom in the Bible or in ancient Near Eastern literature.

Alternatively, a more attractive theory presents itself if one bears in mind that Hebrew was originally written without vowels or spaces between words. The vowel-less and undivided letters translated "Aram-naharaim" [*'rmnhrym*] should perhaps have been split *after*, not before, the letter *n*.[197] The result is then *'rmn hrym*, which would be translated "mountainous fortress/fortification."[198] The word *'rmn* ("fortress") *is* elsewhere used of Edom, an apt description of its elevated and impregnable mountain fortifications (Isa. 34:13; Amos 1:12b). Furthermore, the only other biblical occurrence of the name Cushan is found in a poetic text (Hab. 3:7) where a place near Edom is envisaged and where Mesopotamia is certainly not in the picture.[199] Nevertheless, though contextually workable, this explanation is far from certain. So the map presents two possible routes for Othniel: one that he might have used against a Mesopotamian foe [**1a**] and another if his enemy were from Edom [**1b**].

The Judgeships of Othniel and Samson *map 47*

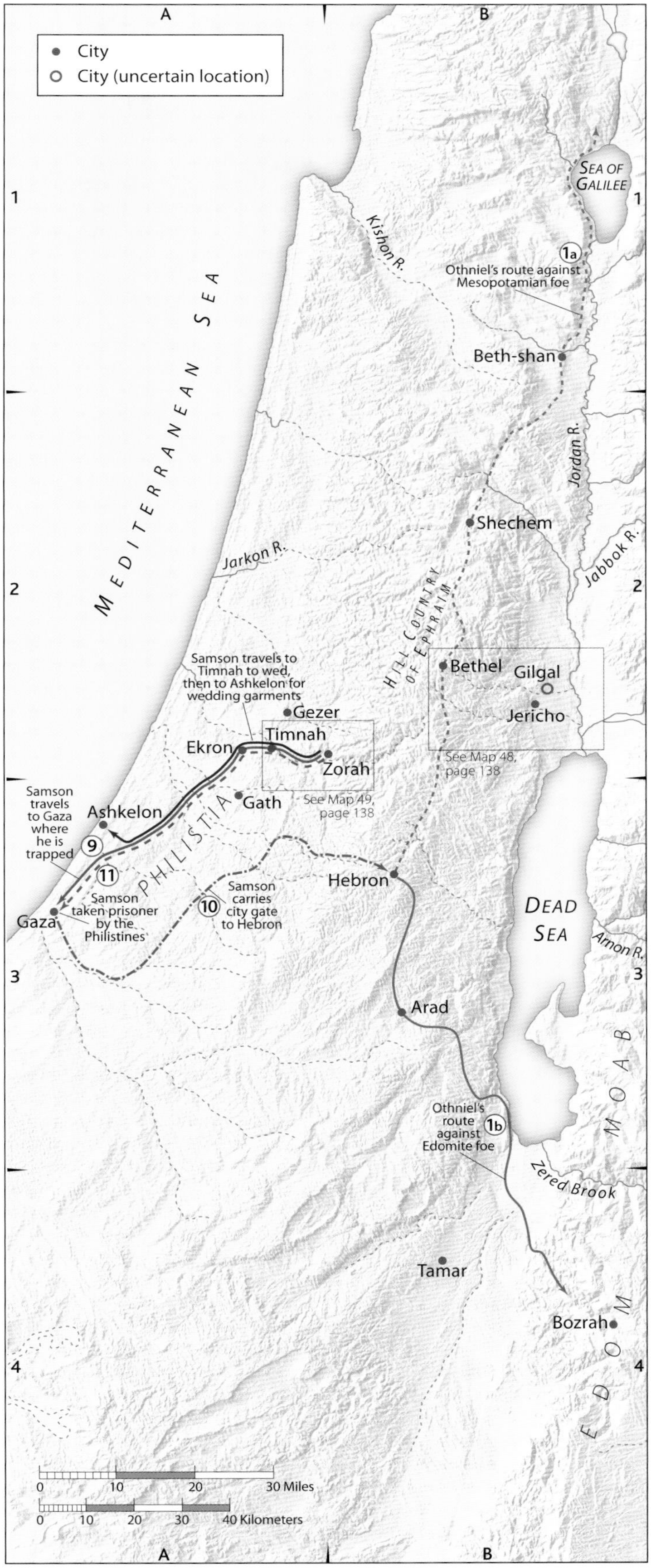

The Judgeship of Ehud *map 48*

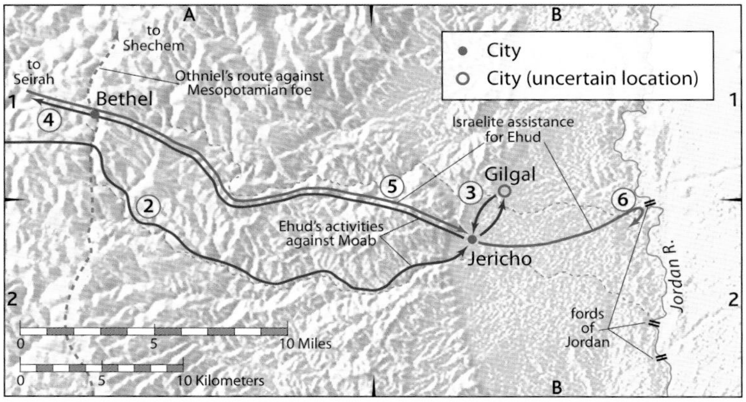

The Judgeship of Samson *map 49*

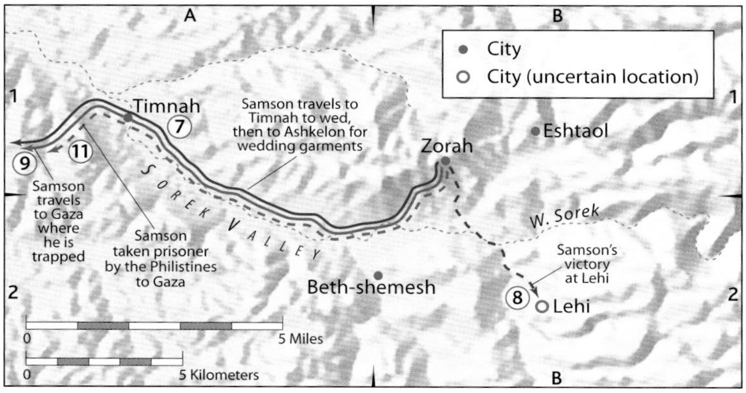

EHUD

Ehud's call from God was precipitated by a Moabite/Ammonite/Amalekite confederated invasion that culminated in a protracted oppression that included an enemy occupation of the "city of palms" (Judg. 3:12–14). The Hebrew word for palms is *tāmār*, so Ehud's skirmish is sometimes placed just south of the Dead Sea at the city of Tamar (Judg. 1:16; 1 Kings 9:18; Ezek. 47:19; 48:28). Caution is needed, however, because the "city of palms" is also one explicit description for the city of Jericho (Deut. 34:3; 2 Chron. 28:15). Also, Ehud's route to the city of palms placed him in close proximity to the town of Gilgal—an uncertain location, but one that cannot be situated to the south of the Dead Sea. Furthermore, the pivotal role played by the men of the "hill country of Ephraim" at the "fords of the Jordan" (Judg. 3:27–28) forces one to locate the Ehud episode *north* of the Dead Sea and in relatively close proximity to the Jordan River. Nor does Joshua's curse on Jericho (Josh. 6:26; cf. 1 Kings 16:34) require that *Moabites* could not have taken up residence at that location.

Ehud used the occasion of taxpaying to exploit the vulnerability of the Moabite king, Eglon [**2**]. As the delegation he led started home from paying the tribute, Ehud returned alone to the king with the enticement of a secret message [**3**]. Later, having assassinated Eglon, Ehud fled toward Seirah [**4**] where, in the "hill country of Ephraim" (3:27), he summoned Israelite assistance. The men who responded followed him to Jericho [**5**], while others passed over to the fords of the Jordan [**6**] and prevented the Moabites from fleeing toward their homes.

SAMSON

In several respects, Samson stands as a perplexing and enigmatic figure. As a judge, he had no following and ultimately was unsuccessful in his bid to end the Philistine oppression. (At the conclusion of his story cycle, notice an absence of reference to an enemy being defeated and to Israel enjoying rest.) As a person, Samson displayed a tacit disregard for the values of his parents and the spiritual training inherent in his Nazirite heritage. He was impulsively sensual and verbally vulgar, and the spiritual catharsis linked with his death does little to modify this basic assessment. If the book of Judges were written to show a decentralized judgeship that was powerless to prevent recurring apostasy, arguing instead for the office of king, it is perhaps understandable that the Samson cycle should stand as the book's final judgeship narrative. In unprecedented proportions, Samson epitomizes the innate tendencies of his own subjects.

Samson's problems with the Philistines began when he saw a girl from Timnah (T. Batash) and demanded that his parents arrange for their marriage [**7**]. Subjected to the enticement of her charms, however, Samson lost the contest of his wedding riddle, which necessitated a trip to Ashkelon to secure garments for his wedding party (Judg. 14:1–20). But the woman was given in marriage to another, causing Samson in due course to burn out the Philistine wheat fields, probably in the Sorek valley not too far from his native town of Zorah (Judg. 15:1–8). The Philistines retaliated by assaulting the men of Judah, who immediately dissociated themselves from Samson and attempted to hand him over to the Philistines at the town of Lehi (15:9–13). But Samson easily broke out of the ropes that bound him and used an ass's jawbone to exact vengeance upon his foes for a second time [**8**] (15:14–17).

Later, Samson went to Gaza where he stayed with a harlot [**9**]. Thinking that they surely had their enemy trapped in their city, the men of Gaza sought to prevent Samson's departure. But in the middle of the night, Samson simply went through the Gaza city wall, taking city gate and bars with him, and he fled to the Hebron area (16:1–3) [**10**]. Samson's love affair with Delilah would ultimately bring him back to Gaza, but in the inglorious manner of a blind slave of the Philistines [**11**] (16:4–22). Not satisfied with his imprisonment in Gaza, the Philistines decided to publicly taunt their human trophy. So it was that this final judge of Israel had opportunity to avenge himself against his enemies for a third time, though in this instance he also paid for it with his own life (16:23–31).

THE JUDGESHIP OF DEBORAH AND BARAK

Deborah was a prophet and a judge (Judg. 4:4–5) whose judgeship has been uniquely transmitted in two forms: recounted in prose (Judg. 4) and celebrated in poetry (Judg. 5). She may have hailed from the tribe of Issachar (5:15a). In her position of authority she summoned Barak, a resident of Kedesh-Naphtali (Kh. Qedesh?), to command Israel's forces against a cruel Canaanite oppression that had lasted for 20 years (4:3b). In contrast to the other major judges, Deborah's judgeship related to indigenous elements from within Canaan, and in this case Israel's forces were also obliged to face an imposing military force that included hundreds of iron chariots.

The narrative identifies the antagonist as Jabin, "king of Canaan" from Hazor (T. el-Qedah). Jabin's field commander—Sisera—was dwelling at the decisive moment with his chariot force at a place called Harosheth-hagoiim (Judg. 4:2–3), an unknown entity not otherwise attested in ancient literature. If the word refers to a city, the ruins of Kh. el-Harbaj, situated some eight miles southeast of modern Haifa along the Kishon River, would be a candidate.[200] As another option, the first element of the name—Harosheth—is thought to derive from an Akkadian word for *plantation*, allowing the possibility of a "plantation," a "forest," or even a "region/plain."[201] All one can say with some confidence is that Harosheth-hagoiim must have been a geographical entity situated in close proximity to the Kishon River. When mobilized for battle, Sisera's army mustered at the Kishon (4:13), presumably not too far from Megiddo (5:19b). After the battle at Mt. Tabor, retreating from Barak's courageous pursuit, Sisera arrived again at Harosheth-hagoiim (4:16), where his chariots became ensnared in the waters of the Kishon and his army was destroyed (Judg. 5:21; cf. Ps. 83:9).

Barak's untrained and ill-equipped militia (5:8b) included men from the tribes of Naphtali, Zebulun, Benjamin,

Flanked by portions of the Jezreel/Esdraelon valley, the isolated hill of Mt. Tabor was the scene of Barak's victory over the Canaanite forces of Sisera.

The Judgeship of Deborah and Barak

map 50

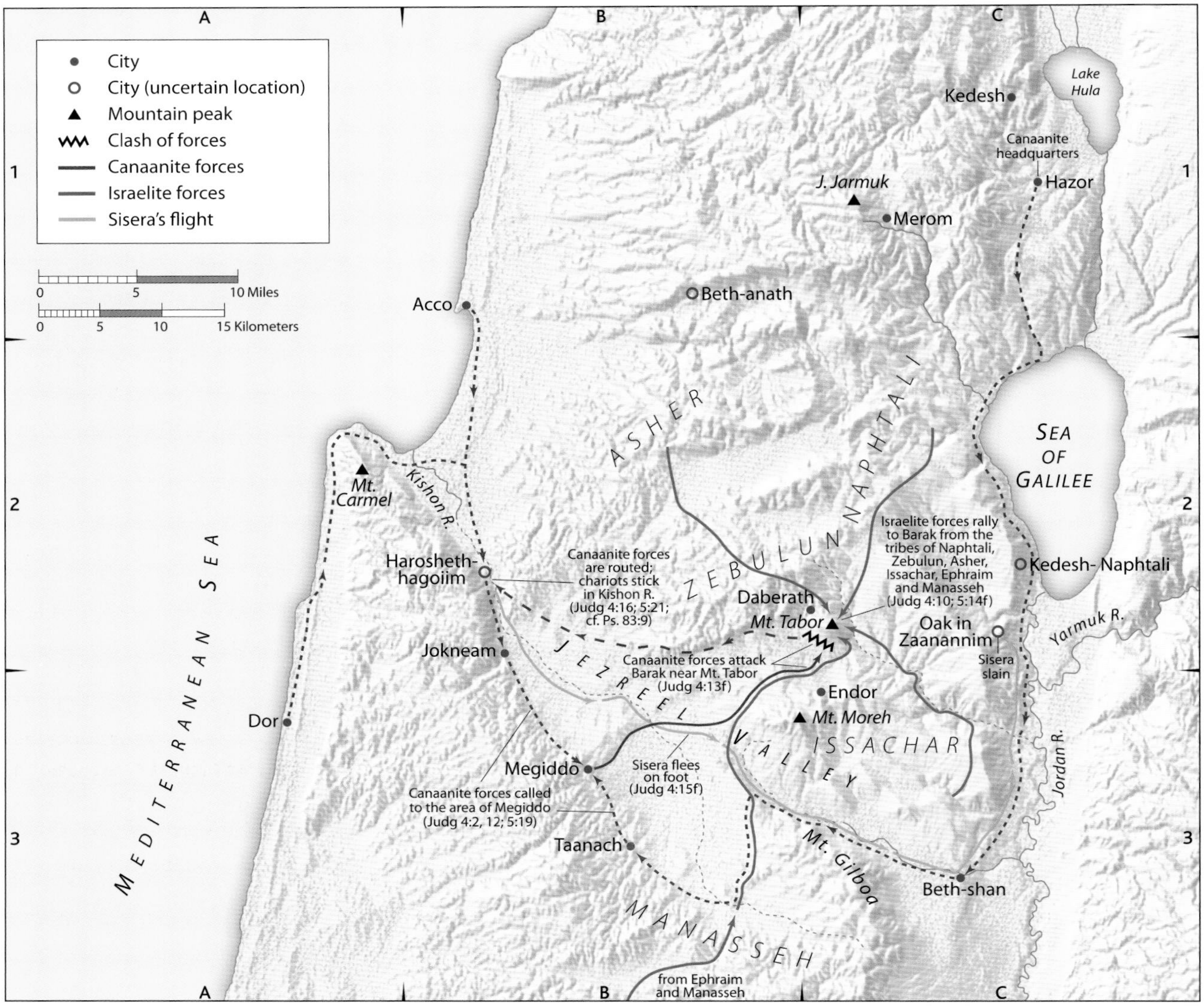

Issachar, Ephraim, and probably Manasseh (4:6, 10; 5:14–15). Arrayed at the heights of Mt. Tabor, Barak's forces attacked at Deborah's command, charging down the mountain toward the Canaanite army (4:12–14). Sisera's disheveled troops were quickly caught in the swollen waters of the Kishon.[202] Sisera sought to escape by abandoning his chariot and fleeing the battlefield on foot. He ran east, coming in due course to a place in the southern section of the tribe of Naphtali near Kedesh-Naphtali (Judg. 4:11b), identified as the Oak in Zaanannim (Josh. 19:33). Ironically, he found treachery rather than safety in the tent of an *ally* (Judg. 4:17–22).

Barak's victory during Deborah's judgeship enabled the Galilean tribes in particular to be temporarily free of a decades-old Canaanite yoke and to regain territory previously held by Israel. Even though Hazor suffered massive destruction in the 13th century B.C., recent archaeological investigations have shown that the site was reoccupied in the 12th century B.C., though it was very small in size and consisted mostly of minor architectural features.[203] At the same time, because this victory involved tribes from both the north and south sides of the Jezreel valley, it may have given Israel a new measure of control over this productive agricultural environ, if only briefly (Judg. 6:3–5).

THE JUDGESHIPS OF GIDEON AND JEPHTHAH

The judgeships of Gideon and Jephthah involved confrontation with two Transjordanian foes—Midianites and Ammonites—who seem to have been rather well-established by the Iron Age.[204] The Midianites played a vital role in spice and incense trade from the interior of Arabia by capitalizing on the widespread domestication of the camel as a new means of commerce.[205] But the camel also offered a new tactic of warfare (Judg. 6:5; 7:12; 8:21, 26). Gideon's night attack (Judg. 7:17–23) may have been designed to neutralize the superiority and mobility of the enemy. The blaring of 300 well-positioned ram's horns in a nocturnal setting would have caused camels to panic and stampede, and the torches could have been used to set ablaze both the Midianites' tents and their sensibilities. The text envisages a Israelite rout that covered considerable territory, from Mt. Moreh (Judg. 7:1) approximately 170 miles southeast as far as Karkor (Qarqar?), an important caravan site in the W. Sirhan, deep into the Eastern desert (Judg. 8:8–10) [**map 62**], by way of the towns of Succoth (T. Deir `Alla?, 8:5) and Penuel (T. ad-Dahab al-Garbi?, 8:8).

During the same period, the Ammonites succeeded in fortifying their borders with a series of massive fortresses to the west and south of their capital Rabbah/Amman.[206] From there they were emboldened to launch strikes against Gilead and even against the regions of Judah, Benjamin, and Ephraim (Judg. 10:8b–9), causing the desperate elders of Gilead to turn to Jephthah, an outcast who earlier had been expelled from his father's household because of the circumstances of his birth (Judg. 11:1–3). Jephthah had fled to the land of Tob (et-Taiyiba?), east of the city of Ramoth-gilead, where he had proven himself an effective fighter and had surrounded himself with a small army of wanton mercenaries. It was doubtless with some fear and intimidation that the elders appealed to Jephthah for deliverance. But as the result of some adroit negotiations, Jephthah accompanied them to Mizpah of Gilead (Kh. Jel`ad?) where he was officially installed as the "head and commander" over all of Gilead (Judg. 11:4–11).

Jephthah was less successful in his negotiations with the Ammonites, however, and was obliged to levy troops from the tribes of Gad and East Manasseh to engage in hostilities at various Ammonite towns around Mizpah and as far south as Aroer and Abel-keramim (Judg. 11:15–33). Ironically, the men of Ephraim were indignant that they had not being included in Jephthah's call to arms (Judg. 8:1). Feeling slighted and deprived of their share of the spoils, they "crossed over [the Jordan River and came] to Zaphon" (not "northward" as found in *AV* and *RV* translations) where they forced Jephthah into a civil war that ended in an Ephraimite defeat (Judg. 12:1–6).

Unfortunately for Transjordanian Israel, this internal conflict may have facilitated the Ammonites' ability to recover from losses suffered at the hands of Jephthah. Early in Saul's reign (1 Sam. 11:1–4) a confederated Ammonite army was able to lay siege to the town of Jabesh-gilead. [**See also map 54.**]

The Judgeship of Gideon *map 51*

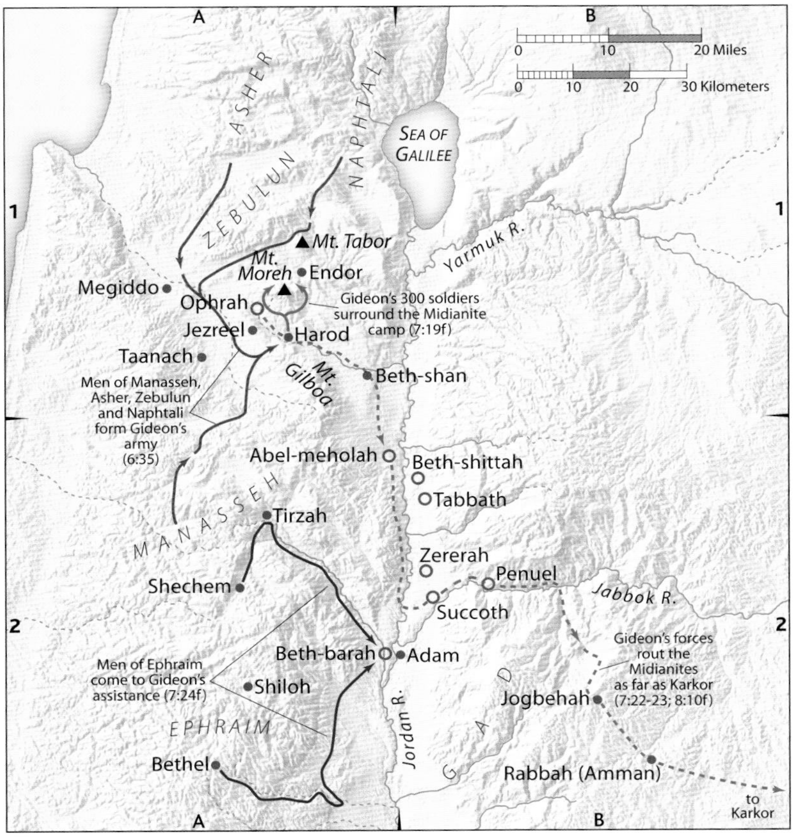

- ● City
- ○ City (uncertain location)
- ▲ Mountain peak
- - - - Gideon's forces
- —— Men of Manasseh, Asher, Zebulun, and Naphtali
- —— Men of Ephraim

The Judgeship of Jephthah

map 52

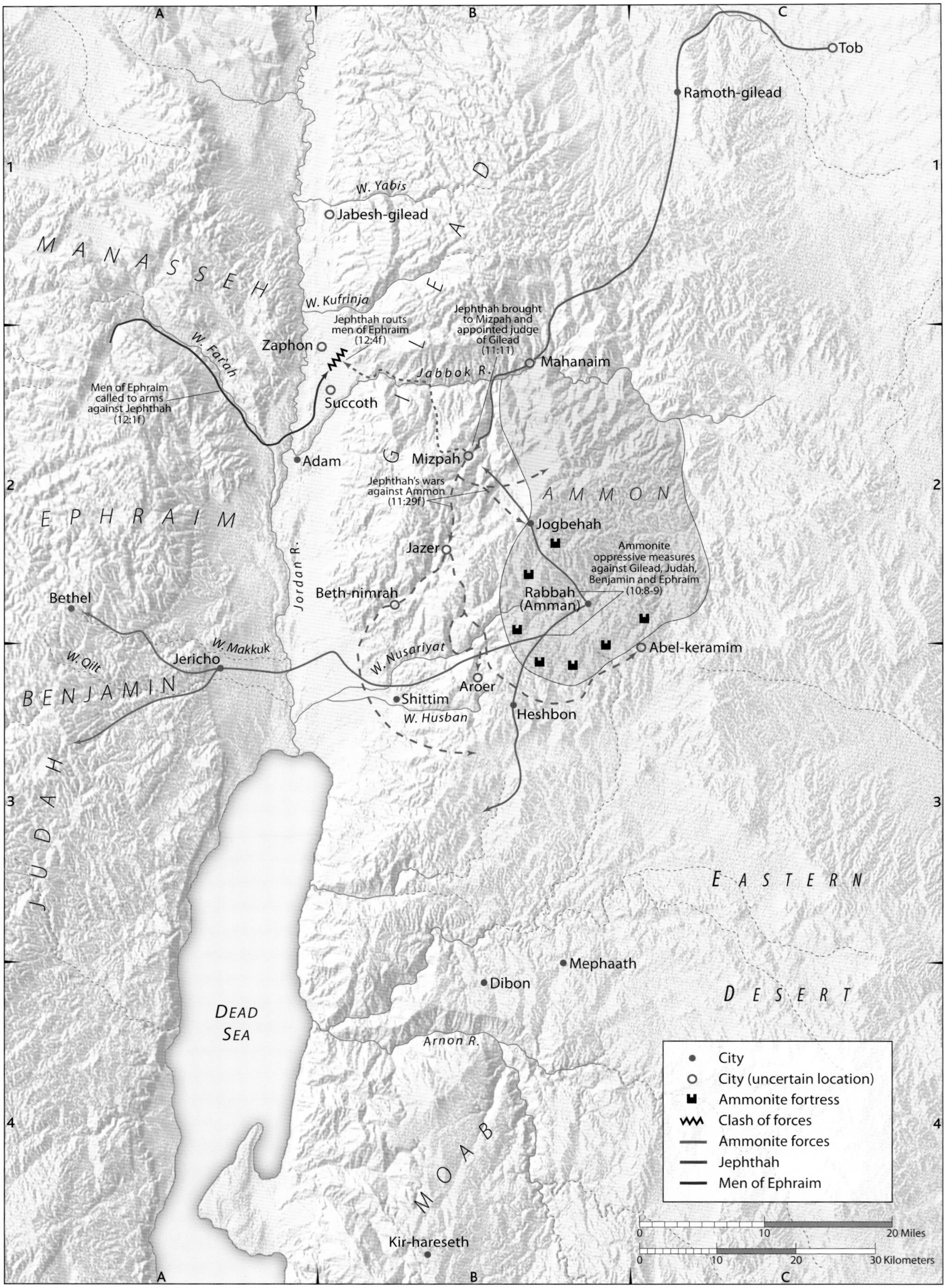

A
B
C
Tob
Ramoth-gilead
W. Yabis
Jabesh-gilead
M A N A S S E H
G I L E A D
W. Kufrinja
Jephthah routs men of Ephraim (12:4f)
Jephthah brought to Mizpah and appointed judge of Gilead (11:11)
Zaphon
Mahanaim
W. Farah
Jabbok R.
Men of Ephraim called to arms against Jephthah (12:1f)
Succoth
Adam
Mizpah
Jephthah's wars against Ammon (11:29f)
A M M O N
E P H R A I M
Jogbehah
Jazer
Ammonite oppressive measures against Gilead, Judah, Benjamin and Ephraim (10:8-9)
Jordan R.
Beth-nimrah
Rabbah (Amman)
Bethel
W. Makkuk
W. Qilt
Jericho
W. Nusariyat
Abel-keramim
B E N J A M I N
Aroer
Shittim
Heshbon
W. Husban
J U D A H
E A S T E R N
Mephaath
Dibon
D E S E R T
DEAD SEA
Arnon R.
M O A B
Kir-hareseth
City
City (uncertain location)
Ammonite fortress
Clash of forces
Ammonite forces
Jephthah
Men of Ephraim
0
10
20 Miles
0
10
20
30 Kilometers
1
2
3
4

THE MOVEMENTS OF THE ARK

The Philistines, and even the Israelites in a sense, were a foreign people who had come to homestead in Canaan at approximately the same time. The Israelites gained control of the central mountainous highlands, while the Philistines dominated the coastal plains of southwest Canaan. [**See maps 42 and 43.**] It was inevitable that tensions between these two groups should arise, particularly as they both sought to expand and exploit the rich and productive agricultural valleys of the Shephela that lay between them. [**See map 12.**]

During the time of Samuel, tensions gave way to open hostilities and Israel suffered a defeat at the town of Aphek (T. Afeq), on the edge of the coastal plain (1 Sam. 4:1b–2). Realizing the gravity of their situation, the elders of Israel decided to move the ark of the covenant. Already imbibing in Canaanite theology with its propensity for magic and the use of local gods, the elders had come to believe that the physical presence of God in a battle would magically guarantee victory. Thus the ark was dispatched from Shiloh (Kh. Seilun) to the Israelite camp at Ebenezer (Izbet Sartah?). It was accompanied by Hophni and Phinehas, the two sons of Eli, the ranking priest of the Lord (4:3–4). The shouting and rejoicing that took place as the ark entered Israel's encampment was so great that it was overheard by the Philistine forces stationed across the plain at Aphek. Also Canaanite in their theological persuasions (2 Sam. 5:21a; 1 Chron. 14:12a), the Philistines immediately realized the implications of this event. They sought to inspire their warriors "to acquit themselves like men and fight courageously," for they now supposed that they must fight against both Israel's army *and* Israel's God (1 Sam. 4:5–9).

Philistine fervor won the day, producing an outcome of catastrophic defeat for Israel. Its army was decimated. Hophni and Phinehas, who had borne the ark, were killed. Most humiliating of all, Israel's sacred ark was captured by the Philistines [**1**]. Moreover, archaeological evidence seems to indicate that the shrine city of Shiloh itself was destroyed at this time,[207] presumably by the Philistines who were emboldened to capitalize on their victory and to press into Canaan's central highlands (Ps. 78:60; Jer. 7:12–15; 26:6–9). What *is* clear is that Shiloh no longer played a significant role as a sanctuary city and that the Philistines were able to establish garrisons at other places in the central highlands not far from Shiloh, including Gibeah, Geba, and Bethlehem (1 Sam. 10:5; 13:3–4; cf. 2 Sam. 23:14; 1 Chron. 11:16).

The triumphal Philistines carried the captured ark like a trophy to the city of Ashdod, where it was placed in the temple of Dagon [**2**], the Philistine patron deity (cf. Judg. 16:23; 1 Chron. 10:10).[208] But the Philistines' ecstasy was short-lived. Within days Dagon had fallen and broken into pieces before

The Movements of the Ark *map 53*

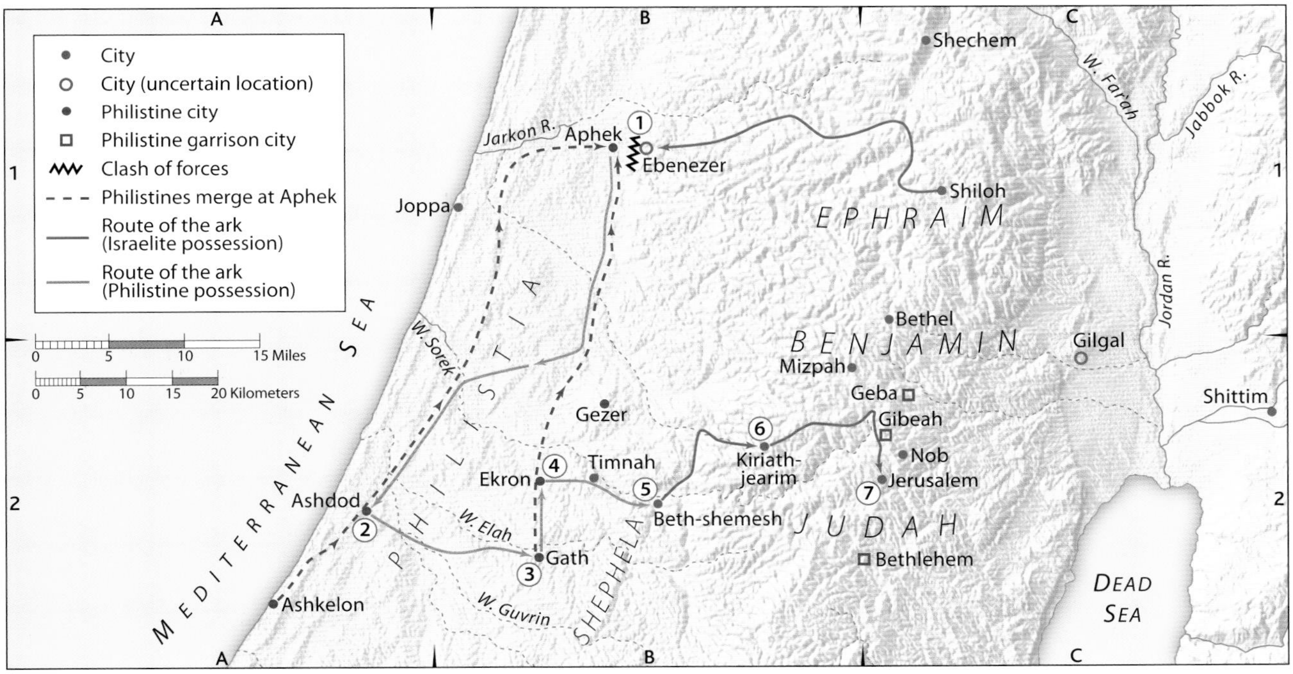

the ark, and an outbreak of "tumors" (possibly the bubonic plague)[209] was reported throughout the whole Ashdod district (1 Sam. 5:1–6). In an attempt to avoid further calamity, it was decided to transport the ark inland to the Philistine city of Gath (Ṭeṣ-Ṣafi), but again an epidemic ensued [**3**]. They moved the ark once more to their city of Ekron (T. Miqne), with the same result [**4**].

Finally, the Philistines recognized that the time had come to attempt to placate the ire of the Israelite deity (1 Sam. 5:7–12). They placed the ark, accompanied by a "guilt offering," on a cart drawn by two cows and sent it up the Sorek valley, past Timnah, in the direction of Israel, thus ending their seven-month ordeal (6:1–12). The ark returned to Israelite hands as it arrived at harvest time in the fields outside the levitical city of Beth-shemesh (T. er-Rumeilah), where it was received by some Levites (6:13–16) [**5**].

Here again, possession of this object in Israelite religion was cause for great rejoicing, and a sacrifice of thanksgiving was offered to Yahweh. But when some of the citizens of Beth-shemesh dared to look inside the holy ark, a great number of them were slain, possibly with their oxen.[210] After this unfortunate incident (6:17—7:2), the ark was taken by the Israelites and stored in the highland town of Kiriath-jearim (T. Qiryat Yearim) [**6**].

The ark of the covenant remained at Kiriath-jearim for a number of years, until the time of David (2 Sam. 6:1–5; 1 Chron. 13:6–8; 2 Chron. 1:4), although it may have been taken again on occasion into Israelite conflict (1 Sam. 14:18). In David's initial enthusiasm to transfer the ark to his new capital of Jerusalem, he neglected to transfer it in the prescribed manner, and misfortune again surrounded this object (2 Sam. 6:6–9; 1 Chron. 13:9–12). But after three months, another mission properly transported the ark to its residence in the holy city (2 Sam. 6:10–19; 1 Chron. 15:2–15) [**7**].

It seems reasonable to conclude that, with a few brief exceptions (2 Sam. 11:11; 15:24; cf. 2 Chron. 35:3), the ark stayed in Jerusalem for the balance of its existence. It was eventually transferred into the Solomonic Temple (1 Kings 8:1–8) where it remained until Babylonian troops under Nebuchadnezzar systematically demolished the city and the Temple in 586 B.C. But what happened to the ark at that time is a matter of widely divergent opinion, and early Judaism suggests at least four possible responses. Perhaps it was (1) carried away to Babylonia and stored there during the captivity, together with the other holy vessels of the Temple (2 Chron. 36:10; Ezra 1:7–10; 5:14–15; 6:5);[211] (2) secretly concealed under the Temple complex itself;[212] (3) taken by the prophet Jeremiah and hidden away on Mt. Nebo;[213] or (4) destroyed by the Babylonian soldiers as part of their ravaging of the Temple. Additionally, a Samaritan tradition alleges that the ark was hidden on Mt. Gerizim.[214]

The prophet Jeremiah was presumably present in Jerusalem at the time and may even have been an eyewitness to the Temple's destruction. Yet his only pertinent comment in this regard was that the ark "would not again come to mind, be remembered, be missed, or be remade" (Jer. 3:16), which is regrettably too ambiguous to be helpful. There are no post-exilic references to the ark in the Old Testament, and the only two New Testament citations of the ark (Heb. 9:4–5; Rev. 11:19) are also unhelpful.

In 63 B.C., the Roman general Pompey summarily overwhelmed the Maccabean militia, capturing Judea and Jerusalem[215] and claiming the right to enter the sacred precincts of the Temple and see all that had been unlawful for men to behold.[216] [**See also map 93**.] Pompey apparently examined many holy objects—including the golden candlestick, the golden table, numerous vessels and spices, and the treasury—yet there is no indication that he saw an "ark." In fact, the historian Tacitus explicitly records that the Holy of Holies was completely empty at the time. Assuming the accuracy of these accounts, some scholars have concluded that Judaism's post-exilic worship forms and the institution of synagogue rendered the ark superfluous. Some have even related Pompey's experience of finding the Holy of Holies empty to a proverb that eventually spread throughout much of the Roman Empire that branded the Jews as "atheists"[217]—an unfortunate mischaracterization of Judaism that may have contributed to needless repression from several different quarters in antiquity.

THE WARS OF KING SAUL

If the book of Judges had demonstrated how Israel was vulnerable to enemy attack at the tribal level, the debacle at Ebenezer [**map 53**] vividly underscored the same reality, but on a national scale. So a delegation of elders went to Samuel, requesting that Israel become like its neighbors and have a king appointed (1 Sam. 8:1–6). Ostensibly their request was predicated upon Samuel's old age and his sons' corruption, but ultimately their motivation was to create a monarchy. They wanted to secure a *national* leader who would lead their army against enemy threats that might arise and who would prevent another calamity similar to the loss of the ark (8:19–20).

In one sense, their request for kingship was quite unremarkable. After all, such an institution becoming part of Israel's experience in the land of promise had already been addressed (Deut. 17:14–17). The only stipulations were that the individual chosen must not be a foreigner and, almost as a foil for the reign of Solomon, the king must not multiply horses, wives, and wealth. In this particular situation, however, the elders' request for monarchy was tantamount to a repudiation of theocracy. Still, God told Samuel to accede to their request.

Samuel complied with the request, yet he declared, perhaps prophetically from the vantage point of Solomon's reign, that the appointment of a king in Israel would also entail four undesirable results. The king would (1) conscript a standing army (1 Sam. 8:11b–12a; 1 Kings 9:22b); (2) confiscate land and redistribute it to his own servants (1 Sam. 8:14; 1 Kings 4:7–19); (3) impose heavy taxation (1 Sam. 8:15, 17a; 1 Kings 12:4); and (4) enforce mandatory state labor (1 Sam. 8:12b–13, 16; 1 Kings 5:13–18; 9:15–19).

Throughout Saul's reign, the mound of Beth-shan (right side of picture) was retained in Egyptian hands; at his death, Saul's remains were impaled on the city wall of Beth-shan. Also pictured here are the extensive ruins of the New Testament city, known in that period as Scythopolis.

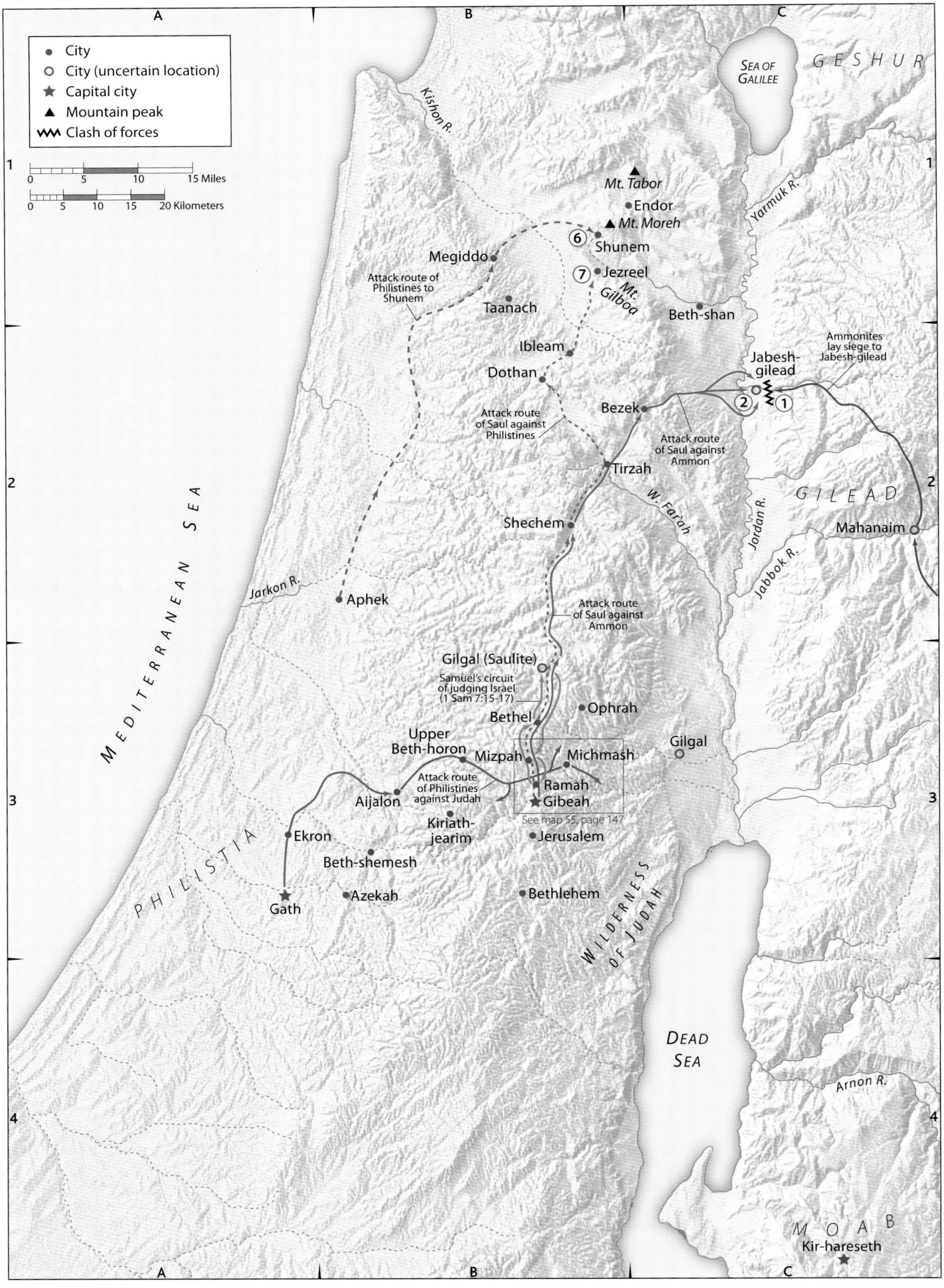
City
City (uncertain location)
Capital city
Mountain peak
Clash of forces
0 5 10 15 Miles
0 5 10 15 20 Kilometers
Sea of Galilee
Geshur
Kishon R.
Mt. Tabor
Endor
Mt. Moreh
Shunem
Megiddo
Jezreel
Mt. Gilboa
Attack route of Philistines to Shunem
Taanach
Beth-shan
Yarmuk R.
Ibleam
Dothan
Jabesh-gilead
Ammonites lay siege to Jabesh-gilead
Bezek
Attack route of Saul against Philistines
Attack route of Saul against Ammon
Tirzah
W. Farah
Gilead
Mediterranean Sea
Shechem
Jordan R.
Mahanaim
Jabbok R.
Jarkon R.
Aphek
Attack route of Saul against Ammon
Gilgal (Saulite)
Samuel's circuit of judging Israel (1 Sam 7:15-17)
Ophrah
Bethel
Upper Beth-horon
Mizpah
Michmash
Gilgal
Attack route of Philistines against Judah
Ramah
Gibeah
Aijalon
Kiriath-jearim
See map 55, page 147
Ekron
Jerusalem
Philistia
Beth-shemesh
Gath
Azekah
Bethlehem
Wilderness of Judah
Dead Sea
Arnon R.
Moab
Kir-hareseth

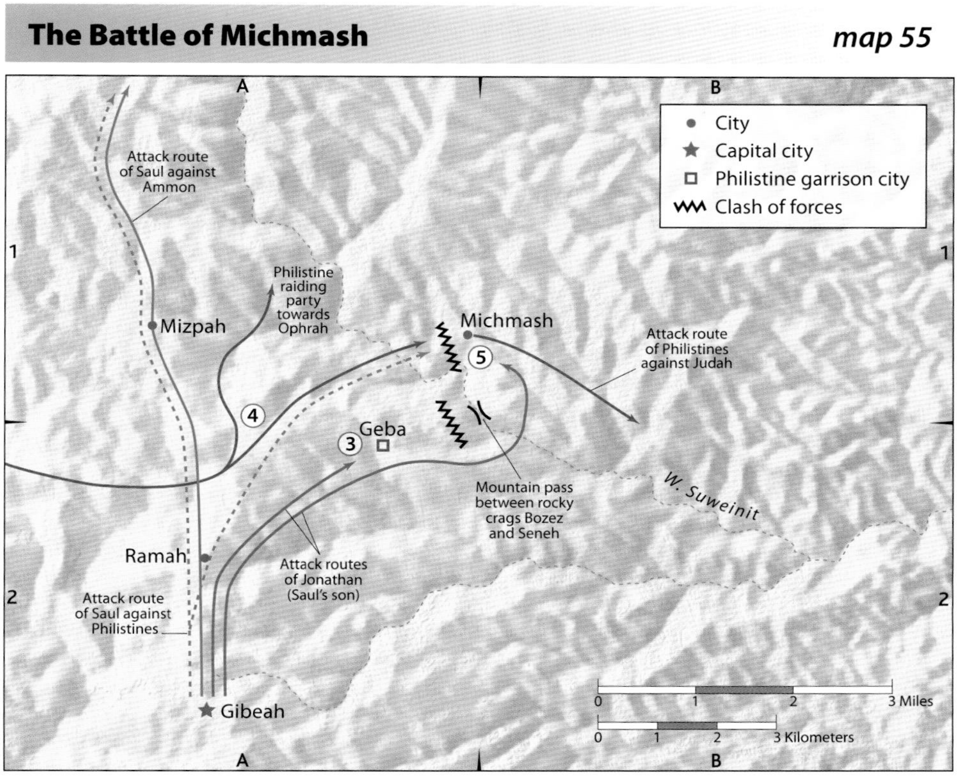

Saul was selected as Israel's first king, but his appointment did not win immediate or unanimous approval (1 Sam. 10:27; 11:12). When the Ammonite forces of Nahash laid siege to the town of Jabesh-gilead (T. Abu Kharaz?), however, Saul's moment of opportunity had arrived (11:1–4) [**1**]. Mustering his army at Bezek (Kh. Ibziq), Saul undertook a night march across to Jabesh-gilead, where he divided his forces into three companies and engaged the Ammonites on multiple fronts, from just before sunrise until the heat of the day (11:6–11) [**2**]. Saul displayed some brilliant strategy in liberating the people of Jabesh-gilead and, as a result, his appointment was acclaimed nationally (11:14–15). Unfortunately for him, this was to be the only biblically detailed military success he would accomplish.

The lingering menace of the Philistines had not yet been addressed. When Jonathan, Saul's son, made a raid on their garrison at Geba [**3**], the mighty enemy of the west retaliated by moving thousands of horses, chariots, and infantrymen into a position to assault Michmash (Kh. el-Hara el-Fawqa). Simultaneously, the Philistines dispatched raiding parties toward Ophrah, Beth-horon, and into the valley of Zeboim (probably down the W. Suweinit from Michmash in the direction of the Jordan River [13:15b–23]) [**4**]. Saul's "army" simply dissolved before such an imposing sight, and again it was Jonathan who exhibited courage. He and his armor-bearer stealthily passed over to the Philistine camp outside Michmash, confronted the uncircumcised enemies, and routed them westward through the pass at Aijalon (14:1–31a) [**5**]. With the temporary reprieve provided by Jonathan's raid, Saul apparently felt at liberty to engage in limited warfare against other opponents: Moab, Ammon, Edom, Zobah, and Amalek (14:47–48). [**See map 56.**]

But before too many years the consolidated Philistine forces regrouped and pitched their tents in the Jezreel valley at Shunem (Solem), at the foot of Mt. Moreh (28:4a) [**6**]. Such a hostile move would have effectively severed Saul's kingdom from north to south. Moreover, it would have made it impossible for Saul to maintain even a semblance of control over the Great Trunk Road. Consequently, Saul responded to this challenge by leading his army, for one last time, as far as Mt. Gilboa (28:4b; cf. 29:1), across the valley from Shunem, where the scene for a major confrontation in the Jezreel valley had been set [**7**]. [For the battle of Mt. Gilboa**, see map 59.**]

THE KINGDOM OF SAUL

Several aspects of both the kingship and the kingdom of Saul are shrouded in uncertainty. As for his kingship, neither his age when he began to reign nor the length of his reign can be determined with finality.[218] And as for the extent of his kingdom, that information is nowhere delineated in the Bible. Nevertheless, we do know that Saul hailed from the tribe of Benjamin (1 Sam. 9:1–2) and lived in the town of Gibeah (T. el-Ful), which also served as his capital city throughout his reign (10:26). Justification for a theoretical demarcation of Saul's kingdom may be derived from several other facts.

1. At Saul's death, his son Ishbosheth was taken by Saul's commander-in-chief to the Transjordanian town of Mahanaim (T. ed-Dhahab el-Garbi?) and installed there as the successor to his father. Allegiance was paid to Ishbosheth by Gilead, Ashur,[219] Jezreel, Ephraim, and Benjamin (2 Sam. 2:8–9), which means that Saul's nascent realm had included territories on both sides of the Jordan River.
2. While the tribe of Judah did not follow Ishbosheth (2 Sam. 2:10b), there is biblical evidence that Saul himself had enjoyed considerable support from Judah and the eastern Shephela. He would have passed through the territory of Judah in order to wage war on the Amalekites and the Edomites (1 Sam. 14:47–48) and presumably to get to the Elah valley where his forces engaged the Philistines (1 Sam. 17:2; **map 57**). In addition, David feared for his parents' safety in Judah (1 Sam. 22:3–4) and for his own life while living there (1 Sam. 27:1). David's fears were assuredly well justified, as Saul was able to pursue him relentlessly across Judean territory. [**See map 58.**] On at least two occasions Judeans from deep inside Judah betrayed David and showed allegiance to Saul (1 Sam. 23:19; 26:1).
3. A summary about Saul's exploits includes the statement that he fought wars against Moab, Ammon, Edom, Zobah, Philistia, and Amalek (1 Sam. 14:47–48). [**See red lines and arrows on map.**] While such an attenuated statement cannot provide indication of why, when, or precisely where those engagements took place, it is suggestive of what might be called the "outer limits" of Saul's realm.

Taken as a whole, these observations suggest that the heart of Saul's kingdom had been forged by his own countrymen, the Benjaminites, together with people from the highland territories of Ephraim, West Manasseh, and Gilead. He had the capability of mustering Israel's army at the site of Bezek in Manasseh (1 Sam. 11:8) and felt compelled to respond when the Gileadite town of Jabesh-gilead was attacked (11:5b–7). [**See map 54.**] Saul's considerable influence was clearly felt throughout most of Judah, and, based on his warfare against the kings of Zobah, it is likely to have extended through the highlands of Galilee as well.

On the other hand, it is quite certain that Saul's kingdom did not include either Philistia or the coastal plains farther north where an unmistakable Phoenician influence is represented archaeologically. It is equally apparent that Saul was unable to maintain permanent control over the Jezreel valley, where especially the massive Egyptian site of Beth-shan was never lost to Israel,[220] indicating that Megiddo, the crucial transportation link from Beth-shan south into Philistia and Egypt, would also have remained beyond the absolute control of Saul. [**See map 59.**] Likewise, Saul's hold on the Jordan valley was probably fluid and tenuous. Evidence at several towns adjacent to the valley, especially at the site of Zarethan (T. es-Saidiya?), but also at nearby Succoth (T. Deir `Alla?) and elsewhere, reveals a conspicuous Philistine presence in the early 10th century.[221] Finally, the biblical text makes clear that the area of Jebus/Jerusalem was only incorporated into Israel during the days of David (2 Sam. 5:6–16).

As a result, the kingdom of Saul may essentially be divided into three sectors: (1) most of the highland terrain between the Jezreel valley and south as far as Beersheba and the borders of Amalek; (2) much of the Galilean highlands north of the Jezreel and including the enclave at Dan (1 Sam. 3:20; 2 Sam. 3:10); and (3) the Transjordanian territories of Gilead and the Mishor, excluding both Ammon and Moab.

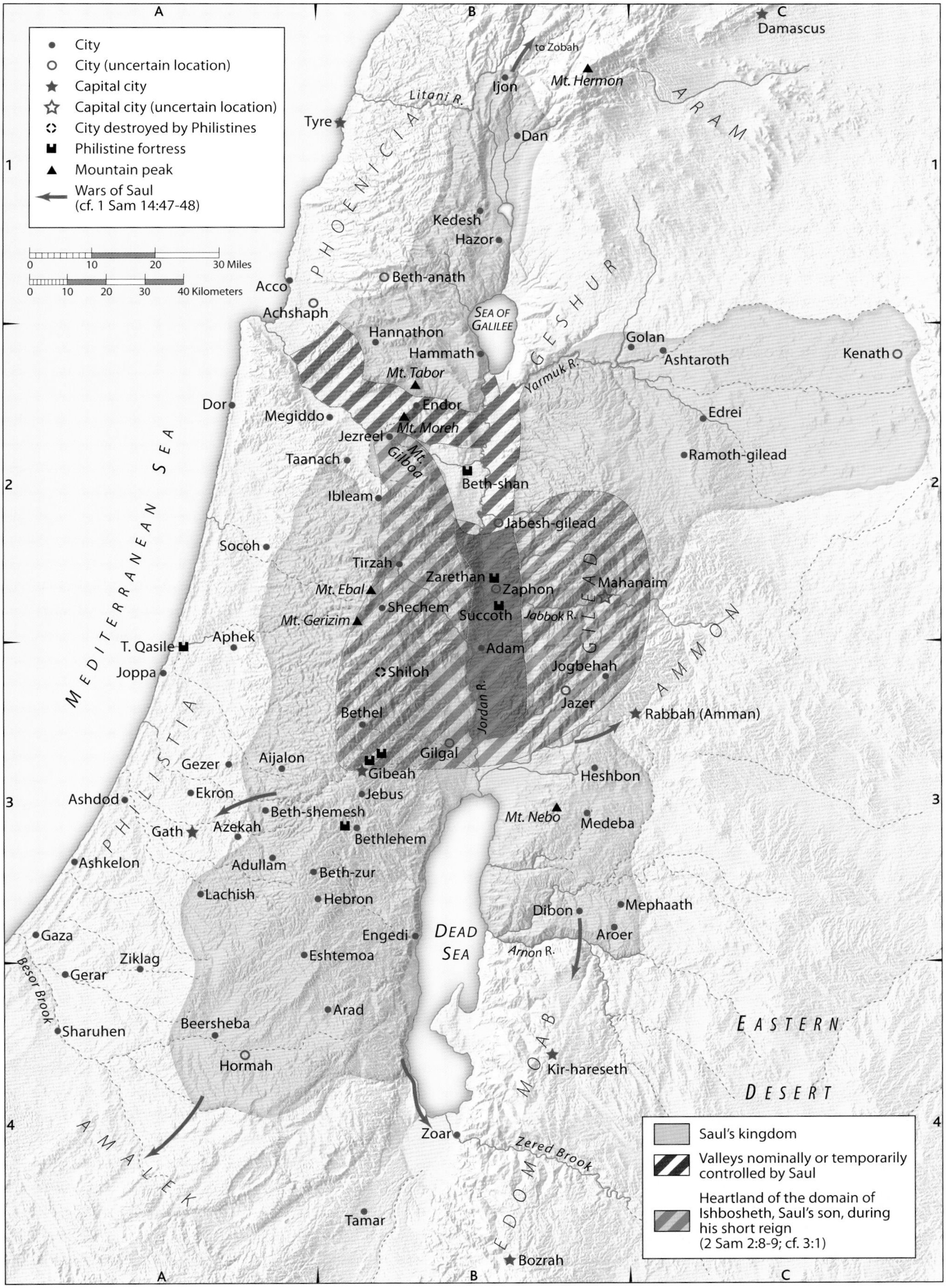
City
City (uncertain location)
Capital city
Capital city (uncertain location)
City destroyed by Philistines
Philistine fortress
Mountain peak
Wars of Saul
(cf. 1 Sam 14:47-48)
0 10 20 30 Miles
0 10 20 30 40 Kilometers
Saul's kingdom
Valleys nominally or temporarily controlled by Saul
Heartland of the domain of Ishbosheth, Saul's son, during his short reign
(2 Sam 2:8-9; cf. 3:1)
Damascus
to Zobah
Mt. Hermon
Ijon
Litani R.
Tyre
Dan
ARAM
PHOENICIA
Kedesh
Hazor
Beth-anath
Acco
Achshaph
SEA OF GALILEE
GESHUR
Hannathon
Hammath
Golan
Ashtaroth
Kenath
Mt. Tabor
Yarmuk R.
Dor
Endor
Megiddo
Mt. Moreh
Edrei
Jezreel
Mt. Gilboa
Taanach
Ramoth-gilead
Beth-shan
Ibleam
Jabesh-gilead
MEDITERRANEAN SEA
Socoh
Tirzah
Zarethan
Zaphon
Mahanaim
Mt. Ebal
GILEAD
Shechem
Succoth
Jabbok R.
Mt. Gerizim
Aphek
T. Qasile
Adam
AMMON
Joppa
Shiloh
Jogbehah
Jazer
Jordan R.
Bethel
Rabbah (Amman)
PHILISTIA
Gilgal
Gezer
Aijalon
Gibeah
Heshbon
Ekron
Jebus
Ashdod
Beth-shemesh
Mt. Nebo
Gath
Azekah
Medeba
Bethlehem
Ashkelon
Adullam
Beth-zur
Lachish
Hebron
Dibon
Mephaath
DEAD SEA
Gaza
Engedi
Aroer
Ziklag
Eshtemoa
Arnon R.
Gerar
Besor Brook
Arad
EASTERN DESERT
Sharuhen
Beersheba
MOAB
Hormah
Kir-hareseth
AMALEK
Zoar
Zered Brook
EDOM
Tamar
Bozrah
A
B
C
1
2
3
4

DAVID AND GOLIATH

In what was doubtless the most celebrated of the numerous agricultural conflicts that Israel and Philistia waged for control of the Judahite Shephela, David faced Goliath in the Elah valley (1 Sam. 17:1–54; cf. 2 Sam. 21:18–22; 1 Chron. 20:5–8). As was observed in Chapter One, cities along the eastern stretches of the Shephela tended to reflect a Judahite orientation throughout the Iron Age; those along the western fringes manifested a distinctly Philistine geopolitical bent. In this particular instance, the Philistines appear to have made the first move. They gathered at the town of Socoh "in Judah" (Kh. Abbad [2 Chron. 28:18]), not to be confused with Socoh in the Judean hill country (Kh. Shuweikah [Josh. 15:48]), located about 10 miles southwest of Hebron. The mention of the Philistine encampment "between Socoh and Azekah" (1 Sam. 17:1) is a clue that the Philistines probably occupied the rolling crests aligning the *south* side of the Elah valley.

Unwilling to allow such aggression to go unchallenged, Saul and his army moved into position and pitched their battle line "on the hills on the other side" of the Elah (the slopes aligning the *north* side of the Elah). The valley separated the two camps (1 Sam. 17:1–3). For 40 days the Philistine hero Goliath would go out into the Elah valley and taunt the terrified army of Saul, challenging them to send forth a single combatant to face him (17:16). Such representative warfare was elsewhere known in the ancient world.[222]

David was dispatched from Bethlehem by his father to take provisions and to see how things were faring for three of his older brothers who were in Saul's army. He apparently arrived on the scene about the time Goliath began one of his bellicose actions of intimidation, and he responded with faith and courage. David saw not a giant but an uncircumcised Philistine defying the army of the Lord. One may have hurled invectives, but the other hurled a smooth stone with great precision and sagacity. That day David's opponent was slain with a slingshot.

This stunning victory is often dismissed as an allegory or a piece of historiographical exaggeration. Yet, given the nature of warfare at the time, the narrative might better be taken as an illustration of the remarkable skill that ancient slingers often possessed and the trust they put in such a weapon. Use of the sling in warfare is amply attested in both the art and literature of ancient Assyria, Babylonia, and Egypt from as early as the mid-second millennium B.C., and it continued to be employed by armed troops of the neo-Hittite city-states, Persia, Greece, and Rome.[223]

Seeing that their champion had been vanquished, the Philistines immediately scattered and fled in the direction of home. Some took flight down the valley toward Gath, while others headed in the direction of Ekron. But they were pursued by now emboldened Israelite soldiers, and many fell all along the way (17:51–54).

David and Goliath ***map 57***

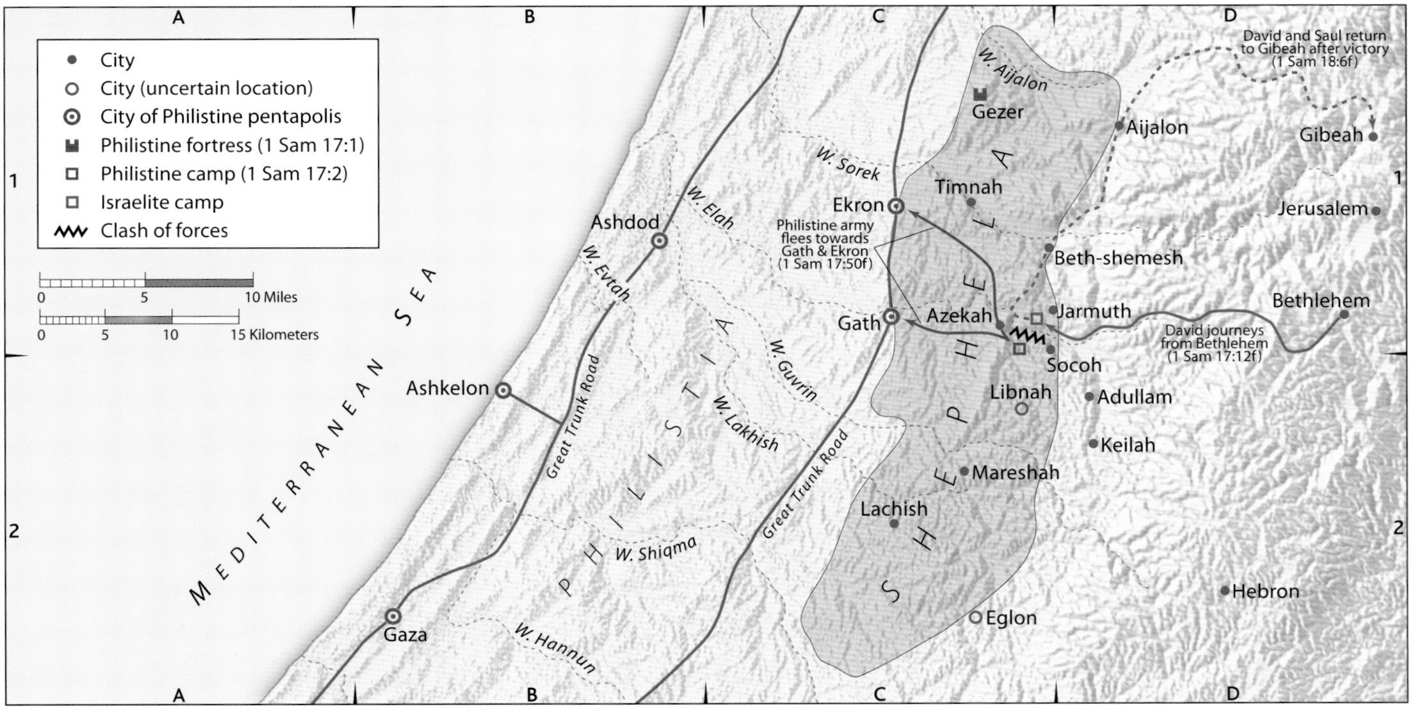

THE EXPLOITS OF KING DAVID

David had a thirty-three-year reign at Jerusalem (2 Sam. 5:5b), which became the nerve center of a kingdom stretching at least as far south as the "river of Egypt" (W. el-Arish) and the Red Sea, and as far north as Kadesh on the Orontes, Tadmor in the desert, and the fringes of Hamath (2 Sam. 8:3, 9–12; 1 Chron. 13:5). [**See map 62.**] His conversion of the city included considerable building and expansion (2 Sam. 5:9–11; 1 Chron. 11:8–9; 15:1a). [**See map 93.**] Eventually he brought the ark of the covenant within its walls (2 Sam. 6:1–19; 1 Chron. 15:3–16:36), thereby merging for the first and only time in Israel's history its political and religious capitals. David aspired to make permanent this arrangement, to enshrine Yahweh in Jerusalem forever by building him a temple there (2 Sam. 7; 1 Chron. 17). But he had been a man who shed blood in battle, so the execution of his dream was reserved for one of his sons (1 Chron. 28:3; cf. 1 Chron. 22:9–10).

The flat terrain in the vicinity of Timnah offered the Philistines western access into Judah.

David's main military exploits are associated with the earlier portion of his reign. His army faced major confrontations with the Philistines, Arameans, Edomites, and the Ammonite-Aramean alliance, in addition to what seem to have been minor skirmishes against the Moabites (2 Sam. 8:2; 1 Chron. 18:2) and the Amalekites (2 Sam. 8:12; 1 Chron. 18:11).

Not long after David had seized Jerusalem, the Philistines twice attempted to crush their former vassal (2 Sam. 5:17–21, 22–25; 1 Chron. 14:8–12, 13–16) by proceeding up the Sorek valley to the valley of Rephaim, immediately west of Jerusalem [**1**]. In at least one of those incursions, the Philistines appear to have been supported by troops from their nearby garrison at Bethlehem (cf. 2 Sam. 23:13–16). Responding to the first of those attacks, David directly confronted his antagonists at the town of Baal-perazim, repelling them back down the valley and capturing some statues of their gods that had been abandoned during their retreat (2 Sam. 5:20–21; 1 Chron. 14:11–12; cf. 1 Sam. 4:4–5, 11). In the second instance, he flanked their assault and attacked them from the rear, driving them north past Gibeon and Upper Beth-horon as far as Gezer (2 Sam. 5:22–25; 1 Chron. 14:13–16) [**2**].

With his western front relatively secure, David turned his attention toward Transjordanian opponents. It was inevitable that Zobah should collide with Israel's monarchy. The Aramean city-state encompassed much of central Lebanon along Israel's northern frontier. Not only did it possess valuable minerals, rich vineyards, and grain fields, but also its kings at times displayed aggressive tendencies (2 Sam. 10:6–8). David launched a successful strike against Zobah, even though its king Hadadezer received support from Damascus (2 Sam. 8:3–8; 1 Chron. 18:3–8). David carried off spoil from the Zobahite towns of Berothai, Tibhath, and Cun [**3**]. This victory also precipitated a friendship treaty between David and the powerful kingdom of Hamath in the north (2 Sam. 8:9–12; 1 Chron. 18:9–11). [**See map 62.**]

The Battle of the Valley of Rephaim *map 60*

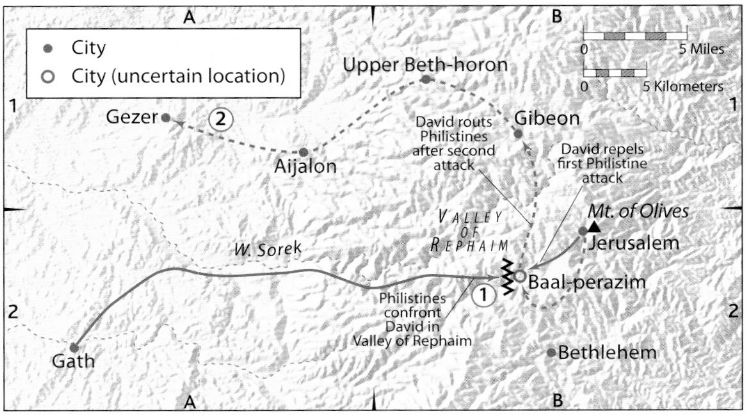

After returning to Jerusalem, David learned of a threat posed by the Edomites, who had descended from the heights of their stronghold, and who were encamped in the valley of Salt, near the southern end of the Dead Sea. (Perhaps they had come from the ancient capital of Edom, Bozrah [Buseirah] on the King's Highway, though no evidence of this site's occupation as early as the 10th century B.C. is currently known.) Acting swiftly, David led his troops into the valley and decisively crushed the enemy (2 Sam. 8:13b–14; 1 Chron. 18:12–13a) [**4**]. And as he had done earlier at Damascus (2 Sam. 8:6; 1 Chron. 18:6), David posted military garrisons at various places around Edom (2 Sam. 8:14; 1 Chron. 18:13) to ensure his control over important arterial transportation routes in areas nearer the northeastern and southeastern fringes of his domain. This victory also should have gone a long way toward paving Davidic control as far south as the Gulf of Aqaba. [**See map 62.**]

David's problems with the Ammonites arose just after the death of their king, Nahash, whom Saul had apparently succeeded in holding in check (1 Sam. 11:1–11). When Nahash died, his son (Hanun) took over, and David sent a delegation to bear condolences. But Israel's ambassadors were publicly disgraced at the court in Rabbah (2 Sam. 10:1–5; 1 Chron. 19:1–5). Sensing that David would likely retaliate for such humiliating treatment of his men, Hanun quickly secured the services of a large mercenary force from Zobah, Beth-rehob, Maacah, and Tob, who marched south toward Rabbah. Meanwhile the Ammonite army drew up in battle array at the entrance of its capital city.

To meet the challenge, Joab—David's army general—divided the Israelite soldiers into two companies. He courageously led a contingent of special troops against the Aramean mercenaries, while the remainder of the army was placed in the charge of Abishai and commanded to attack the Ammonites (2 Sam. 10:6–14; 1 Chron. 19:6–15) [**5**]. The resulting dramatic Israelite victory effectively incorporated the kingdom of Ammon into David's nascent domain. [**See also map 62.**]

Soon after this defeat, and perhaps with some desperation, Hadadezer of Zobah solicited forces from as far away as the Euphrates River and attempted an all-out attack on David, marching as far south as Helam, just northeast of Ramoth-gilead. Alerted to this new threat, David once again led his troops into Transjordanian territory. He won a brilliant victory, roundly defeating the Arameans and capturing many of their horses and chariots. Such a triumph extensively broadened the northern horizons of David's kingdom, as Hadadezer's vassals were obliged to conclude a peace treaty with David (2 Sam. 10:15–19; 1 Chron. 19:16–19) [**6**].

A final episode that illustrates both the extent and the consolidation of David's kingdom is his census of the people (2 Sam. 24). Dispatched under the leadership of Joab, a census team journeyed across the Jordan River and began their work at the city of Aroer (Arair), near the border of Moab on the north bank of the Arnon River. Then they traveled north to the levitical city of Jazer (Kh. Jazzir?), near the Ammonite frontier, and on through Gilead and Galilee before arriving at Dan. From Dan the census takers went out to the Mediterranean Sea by Sidon and began a southward trek, passing the "fortress of Tyre" (Ushu?) and the coastal cities of the Hivites and Canaanites. They concluded their cycle at the Judahite city of Beersheba [**8**]. Having spent nearly ten months on their mission, the group returned to Jerusalem and reported to the king (2 Sam. 24:1–9). One might say that this census demonstrated closure of a geopolitical circle left open since the days of Israel's first occupation of the land, incorporating especially coastal territories that had not been permanently settled by Israel at that time. [**See maps 42 and 43.**]

God had promised David that one of his sons would build a temple in Jerusalem (2 Sam. 7:12–16; 1 Chron. 17:11–14). It is strikingly ironic, therefore, that in his waning years when David might have cherished that expectation for one of his offspring, he became instead the object of intrigue and beleaguered insurrection that stemmed from *his own sons*. His eldest surviving son was Absalom, born to a wife who had been an Aramean princess of Geshur (2 Sam. 3:3; 1 Chron. 3:2a). Absalom spent three years in exile with his maternal grandfather after murdering his half-brother Amnon in retaliation for the rape of Absalom's sister Tamar (2 Sam. 13:37–39). When he later returned to Jerusalem, Absalom spent some four years listening to the grievances of his father's subjects, gaining their favor, and establishing a power base that included even some of David's personal counselors (2 Sam. 14:21–24; 15:1–12). When the opportunity seemed to be advantageous, Absalom attacked Jerusalem and succeeded in accomplishing what no foreign power could have imagined—expelling David from his own capital city (2 Sam. 15:13–37).

But David was no stranger to being hunted down, and he craftily fled across the Jordan River (2 Sam. 16:1–14) where he sought refuge in the secluded highlands around Mahanaim. He received supplies and assistance from the towns of Lo-debar, Rogelim, and Rabbah (2 Sam. 17:27–29) [**7**]. Meanwhile, back in Jerusalem, to signify the finality of his coup, Absalom publicly engaged in sexual relations with his father's concubines (2 Sam. 16:22; cf. 12:11). Unfortunately for him, Absalom's delay in the royal city would provide David with sufficient time to prepare a counteroffensive. When Absalom and his troops finally arrived, a battle ensued during which Absalom was slain by Joab in the forest of Ephraim (2 Sam. 18:1–15). Absalom's usurpation of power had been short-lived indeed! But in David's final hours, yet another of his sons, Adonijah, attempted to usurp the kingship. The title was reserved for another, however, and David ordered Zadok to anoint Solomon (1 Kings 1:5–10, 32–40).

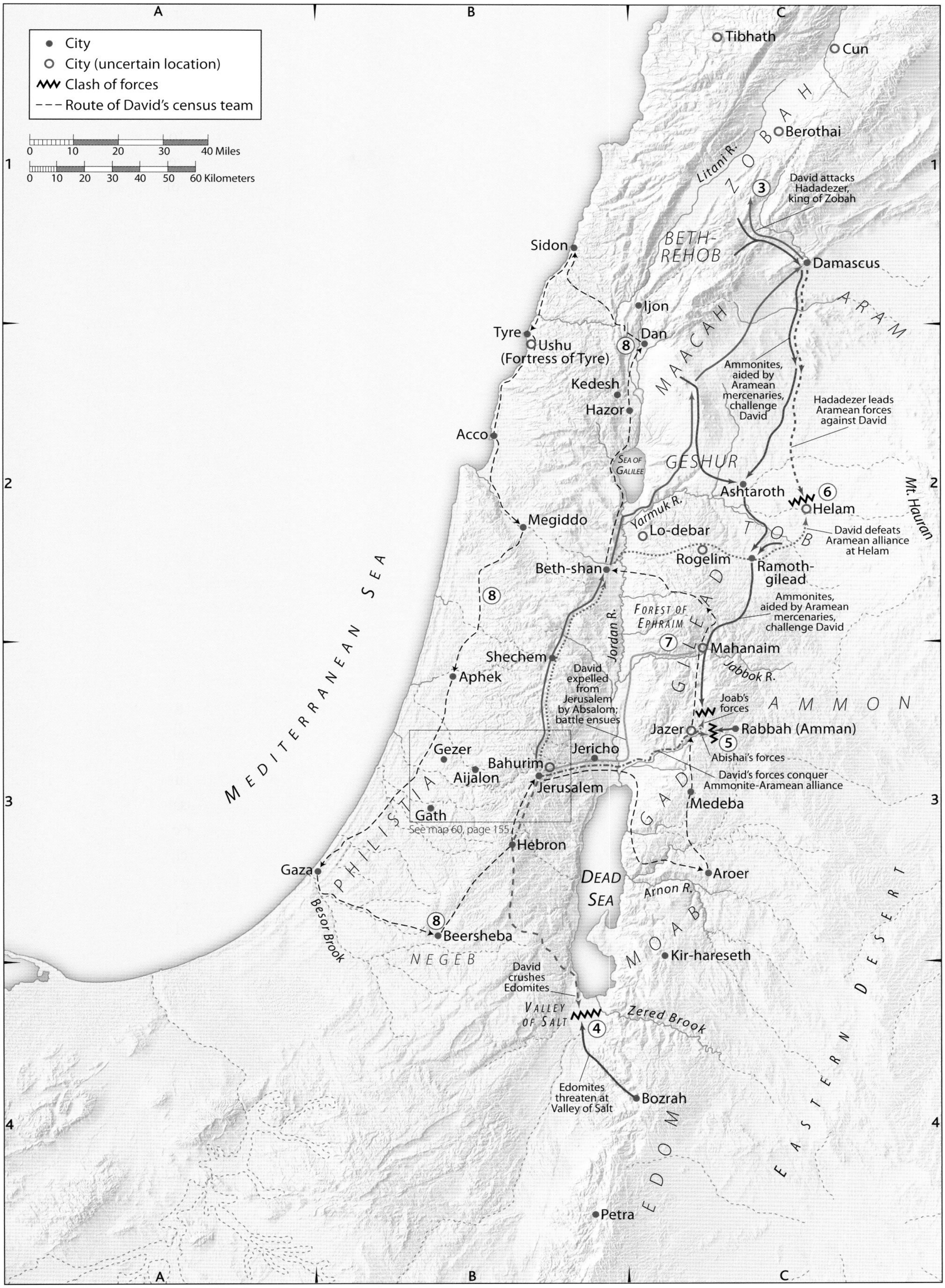
City
City (uncertain location)
Clash of forces
Route of David's census team
0 10 20 30 40 Miles
0 10 20 30 40 50 60 Kilometers
Tibhath
Cun
ZOBAH
Berothai
Litani R.
David attacks Hadadezer, king of Zobah
BETH-REHOB
Sidon
Damascus
ARAM
Ijon
MAACAH
Tyre
Ushu (Fortress of Tyre)
Dan
Kedesh
Hazor
Ammonites, aided by Aramean mercenaries, challenge David
Hadadezer leads Aramean forces against David
Acco
Sea of Galilee
GESHUR
Ashtaroth
Helam
Mt. Hauran
Yarmuk R.
Megiddo
Lo-debar
TOB
David defeats Aramean alliance at Helam
Rogelim
Ramoth-gilead
Beth-shan
MEDITERRANEAN SEA
Forest of Ephraim
GILEAD
Ammonites, aided by Aramean mercenaries, challenge David
Jordan R.
Mahanaim
Shechem
Jabbok R.
Aphek
David expelled from Jerusalem by Absalom; battle ensues
Joab's forces
AMMON
Jazer
Rabbah (Amman)
Gezer
Jericho
Abishai's forces
Bahurim
Aijalon
David's forces conquer Ammonite-Aramean alliance
Jerusalem
GAD
Medeba
Gath
See map 60, page 155
PHILISTIA
Hebron
Gaza
Dead Sea
Aroer
Arnon R.
Besor Brook
MOAB
Beersheba
NEGEB
Kir-hareseth
David crushes Edomites
Valley of Salt
Zered Brook
EASTERN DESERT
Edomites threaten at Valley of Salt
Bozrah
EDOM
Petra
A
B
C
1
2
3
4

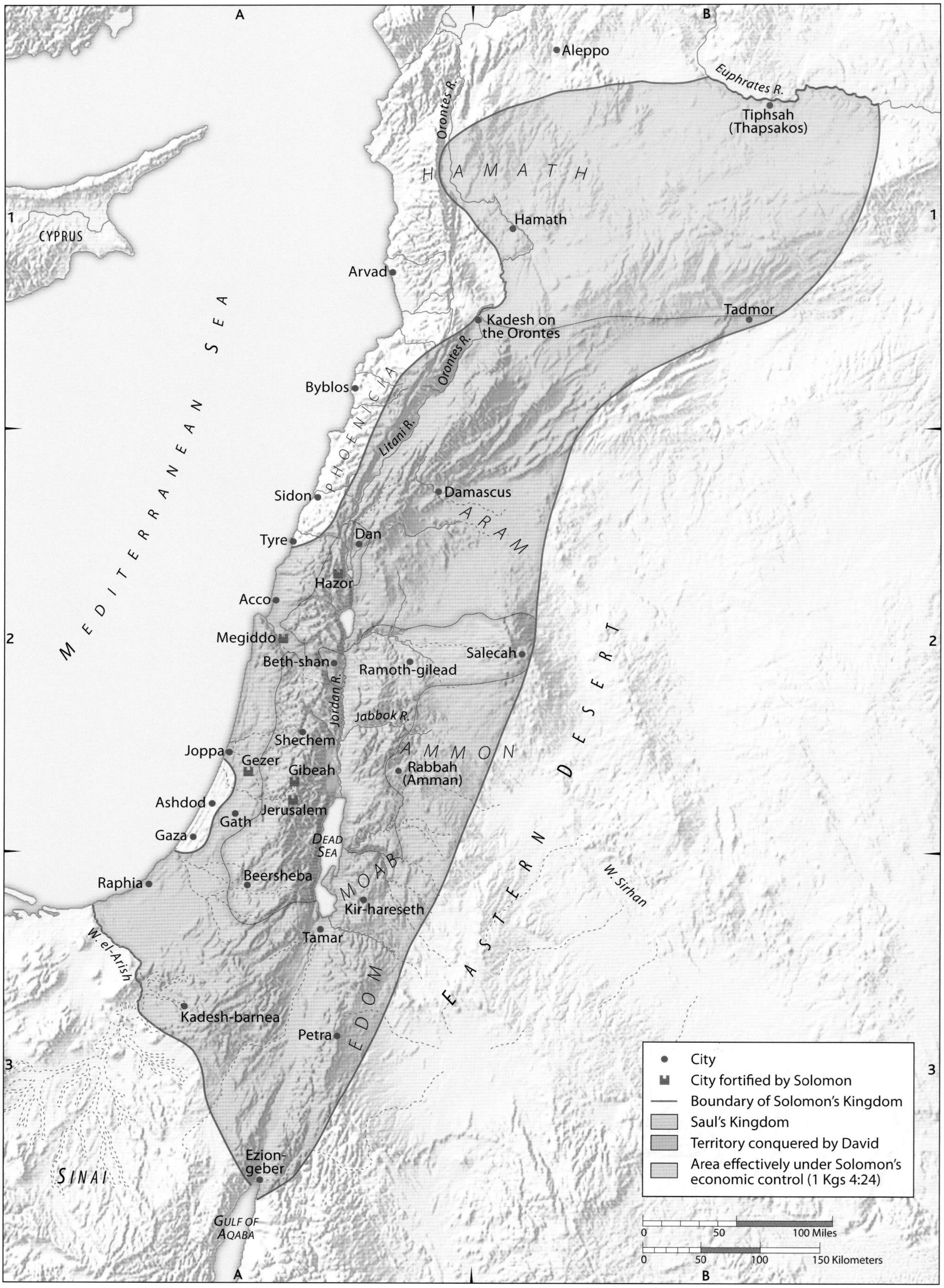
A
B
Aleppo
Euphrates R.
Tiphsah
(Thapsakos)
Orontes R.
H A M A T H
Hamath
1
CYPRUS
Arvad
Tadmor
Kadesh on
the Orontes
M E D I T E R R A N E A N S E A
Orontes R.
Byblos
P H O E N I C I A
Litani R.
Sidon
Damascus
A R A M
Tyre
Dan
Hazor
Acco
2
Megiddo
Salecah
Beth-shan
Ramoth-gilead
Jordan R.
Jabbok R.
Shechem
A M M O N
E A S T E R N D E S E R T
Joppa
Gezer
Gibeah
Rabbah
(Amman)
Ashdod
Jerusalem
Gath
Gaza
Dead
Sea
W. Sirhan
Raphia
Beersheba
MOAB
Kir-hareseth
W. el-Arish
Tamar
EDOM
Kadesh-barnea
Petra
3
City
City fortified by Solomon
Boundary of Solomon's Kingdom
Saul's Kingdom
Territory conquered by David
Area effectively under Solomon's economic control (1 Kgs 4:24)
Sinai
Ezion-
geber
Gulf of
Aqaba
0 50 100 Miles
0 50 100 150 Kilometers

SOLOMON'S INTERNATIONAL TRADING NETWORKS

Solomon inherited a kingdom that was secure and extensive. His accession to the throne was not seriously challenged by others, but he nevertheless moved quickly and decisively against Adonijah, Abiathar, Joab, and Shimei (1 Kings 2:13–46). In an effort to guarantee external security, Solomon married wives from many nations around Israel (1 Kings 11:1–8), including the daughter of an Egyptian pharaoh (1 Kings 3:1; 9:16). This marriage undoubtedly paved the way for chariots to be imported from Egypt (1 Kings 10:29; 2 Chron. 1:17; 9:28),[226] just as his renewed control of Hamath (2 Chron. 8:3–4) made it possible to import horses from Kue/Cilicia (1 Kings 10:28; 2 Chron. 1:16).

Solomon also led Israel into a brief period of vast commercial expansion. The location, extent, and consolidation of his domain [**map 62**] meant that he was in control of the main trading arteries connecting Egypt, Asia, Arabia, and the Mediterranean [**map 64**], which brought lucrative benefits to his court (1 Kings 10:14–15; 2 Chron. 9:13–14). It is conceivable that Solomon's domination of those routes occasioned the visit from the queen of Sheba, who wished to gain trade access for her Arabian commodities into the Mediterranean world and beyond (1 Kings 10:1; 2 Chron. 9:1). At the same time, he revived the alliance with Hiram of Tyre, providing for large quantities of cedar and cypress trees to be imported into Israel in exchange for certain staple commodities not found in abundance in Phoenicia (1 Kings 5:10–11; 2 Chron. 2:15–16).

Solomon's league with Hiram came at the dawn of Phoenician commercial and maritime expansionism into the Mediterranean world. Historical notices in the Bible seem to speak of two nautical partnerships between Hiram and Solomon: one joint merchant fleet on the Red Sea that sailed to the destination port of Ophir (1 Kings 9:26–28; 2 Chron. 8:17–18; 9:10–11), and another one on the Mediterranean that sailed as far as Tarshish (1 Kings 10:22; 2 Chron. 9:21). The text indicates that the Red Sea operation, whatever its nature, focused almost exclusively on exploiting the gold resources of Ophir (located either in East Africa or on the Arabian peninsula), while the royal fleet on the Mediterranean would return from Tarshish with more varied cargoes. The biblical chroniclers indicate that voyages to Tarshish would return every three years (1 Kings 10:22b; 2 Chron. 9:21b); we are not told with what frequency the vessels sailed the Red Sea.

A number of influential historians today regard Hiram's partnership with Solomon on the Red Sea as a reliable tradition,[227] yet many of the same authorities view any such nautical enterprise on the Mediterranean with skepticism, perceiving that the biblical historians were engaging in hyperbole, describing in imaginative and exaggerated style a "golden age" of Solomon. A great many scholars conflate all these biblical texts into a single maritime activity and locate that activity on the Red Sea, based on literary-critical grounds and/or the strength of one synoptic text describing the failed nautical venture of Jehoshaphat. (See below.) As a consequence, a very broad spectrum of contemporary scholarship embraces the notion that the biblical expression "the ships of Tarshish" represents either a general poetic designation of the Sea or a certain type of nautical vessel of oceangoing quality.

TARSHISH: A REAL LOCATION

Yet there is evidence to justify an alternative viewpoint: (1) that there existed on the Mediterranean Sea an Iron Age site or sites, known by the Phoenicians, Assyrians, and Israelites as "Tarshish"; and (2) that early Phoenicians were navigating a wide sweep of the Mediterranean by the 10th century B.C. and occupied on at least one occasion a site known as "Tarshish." This evidence is sufficient to challenge the generally accepted understanding of Tarshish described previously, and may even be sufficient on its own to accord these narratives a prima facie case of historical plausibility.

An examination of the numerous biblical citations of the word "Tarshish" reveals four semantic fields:

- Four times as a personal name (e.g., Gen. 10:4; 1 Chron. 7:10);
- Seven times as a jewel or precious stone (e.g., Ex. 28:20; Ezek. 1:16);
- Ten times as an element in the expression "the ship(s) of Tarshish" (e.g., Isa. 2:16; Ezek. 27:25); and
- Fourteen times as a place name (e.g., 2 Chron. 20:36; Isa. 66:19; Jon. 4:2).

As a place name in the Bible, Tarshish is often associated with the city of Tyre (Isa. 23:1, 10–15), the port of Joppa (Jon. 1:3), the island of Cyprus or other islands/coastlands (Ezek. 27:7; Isa. 23:6; Ps. 72:10),[228] the region of Ionia (Isa. 66:19; Ezek. 27:12), or other places unequivocally located in the Mediterranean world (Isa. 23:10; Ezek. 27:12–13). Biblical citations of Tarshish are sometimes governed by verbs like "going to" (2 Chron. 9:21; 20:36–37), "fleeing to" (Jon 1:3; 4:2), or "crossing over to" (Isa. 23:6). The word sometimes contains a feature of the Hebrew language often associated with proper names (and especially with place names) designed to indicate motion or show direction.[229]

Solomon's International Trading Networks

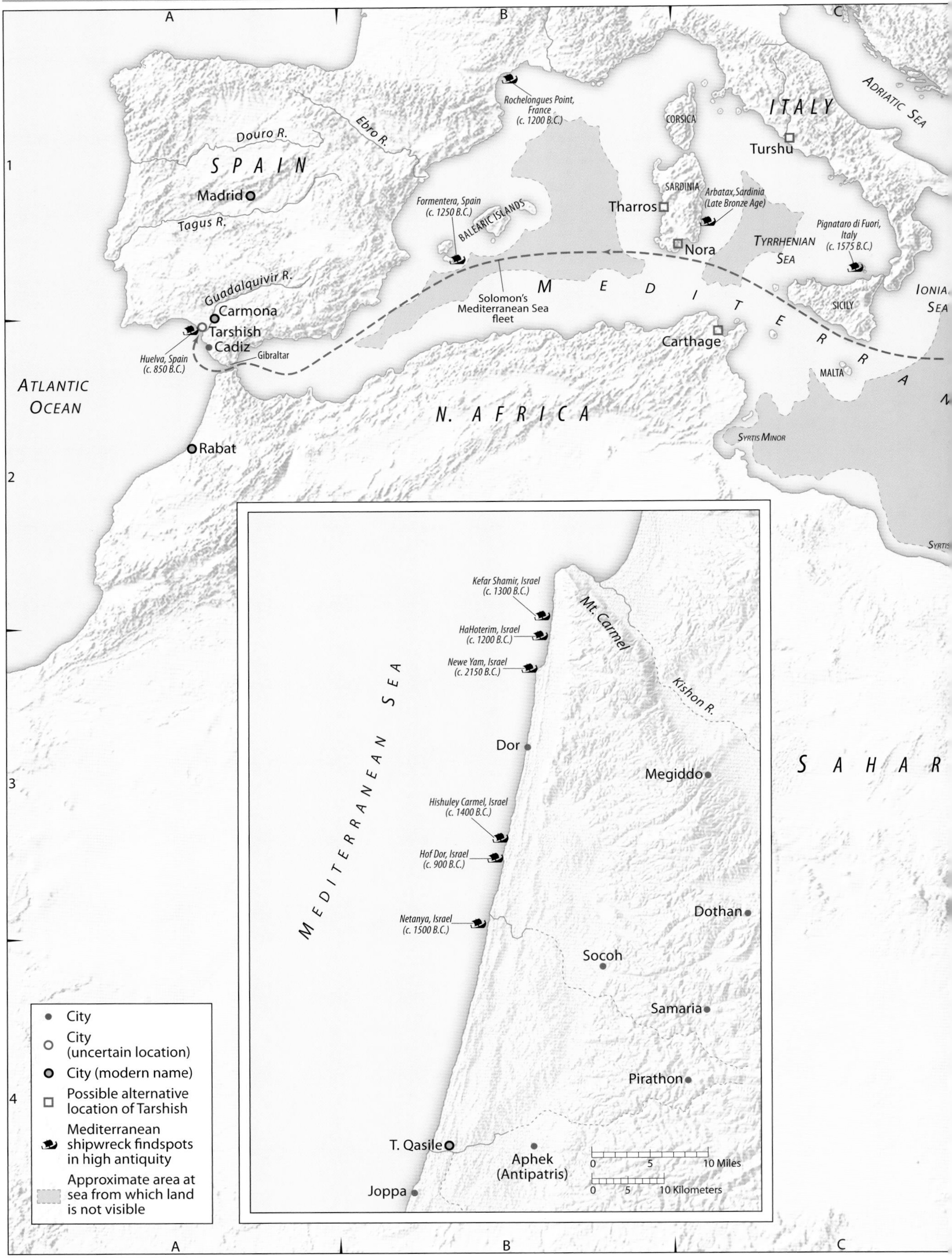

SPAIN
Madrid
Douro R.
Ebro R.
Tagus R.
Guadalquivir R.
Carmona
Tarshish
Cadiz
Gibraltar
Huelva, Spain (c. 850 B.C.)
Atlantic Ocean
Rabat
N. AFRICA
Rochelongues Point, France (c. 1200 B.C.)
Formentera, Spain (c. 1250 B.C.)
BALEARIC ISLANDS
Solomon's Mediterranean Sea fleet
MEDITERRANEAN
CORSICA
SARDINIA
Tharros
Arbatax, Sardinia (Late Bronze Age)
Nora
ITALY
Turshu
Adriatic Sea
Tyrrhenian Sea
Pignataro di Fuori, Italy (c. 1575 B.C.)
SICILY
Ionian Sea
Carthage
MALTA
Syrtis Minor
SAHARA
Mediterranean Sea
Kefar Shamir, Israel (c. 1300 B.C.)
HaHoterim, Israel (c. 1200 B.C.)
Newe Yam, Israel (c. 2150 B.C.)
Mt. Carmel
Kishon R.
Dor
Megiddo
Hishuley Carmel, Israel (c. 1400 B.C.)
Hof Dor, Israel (c. 900 B.C.)
Netanya, Israel (c. 1500 B.C.)
Dothan
Socoh
Samaria
Pirathon
T. Qasile
Aphek (Antipatris)
Joppa
0 5 10 Miles
0 5 10 Kilometers
City
City (uncertain location)
City (modern name)
Possible alternative location of Tarshish
Mediterranean shipwreck findspots in high antiquity
Approximate area at sea from which land is not visible

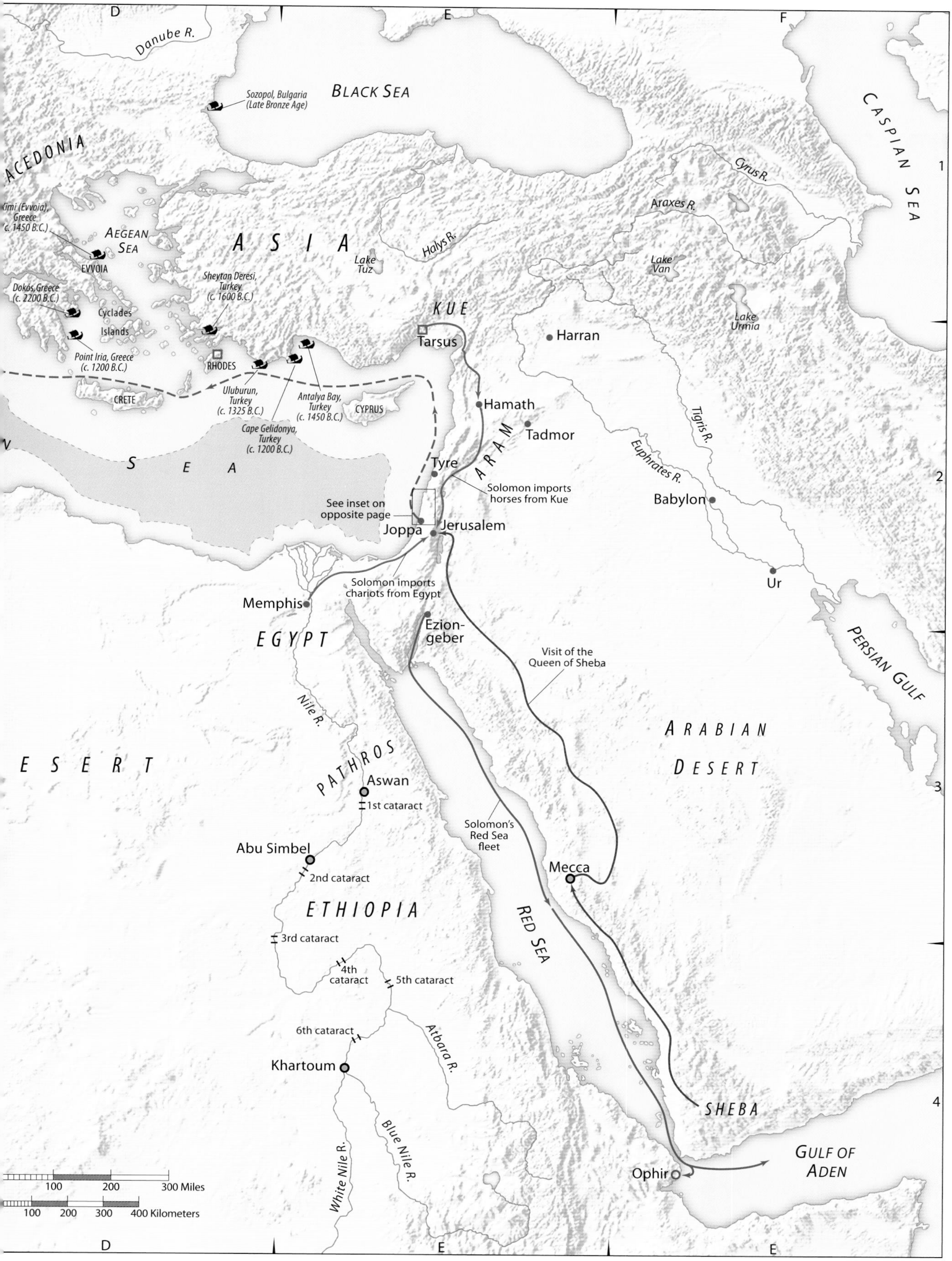

Danube R.
BLACK SEA
Sozopol, Bulgaria (Late Bronze Age)
CASPIAN SEA
ACEDONIA
Cyrus R.
Araxes R.
Kimi (Evvoia), Greece (c. 1450 B.C.)
AEGEAN SEA
EVVOIA
ASIA
Lake Tuz
Halys R.
Lake Van
Dokós, Greece (c. 2200 B.C.)
Sheytan Deresi, Turkey (c. 1600 B.C.)
Cyclades Islands
KUE
Lake Urmia
Tarsus
Harran
Point Iria, Greece (c. 1200 B.C.)
RHODES
CRETE
Uluburun, Turkey (c. 1325 B.C.)
Antalya Bay, Turkey (c. 1450 B.C.)
CYPRUS
Cape Gelidonya, Turkey (c. 1200 B.C.)
Hamath
Tadmor
ARAM
Tigris R.
Euphrates R.
SEA
Tyre
Solomon imports horses from Kue
Babylon
See inset on opposite page
Joppa
Jerusalem
Ur
Solomon imports chariots from Egypt
Memphis
Ezion-geber
EGYPT
Visit of the Queen of Sheba
PERSIAN GULF
Nile R.
ARABIAN DESERT
ESERT
PATHROS
Aswan
1st cataract
Solomon's Red Sea fleet
Abu Simbel
Mecca
2nd cataract
ETHIOPIA
RED SEA
3rd cataract
4th cataract
5th cataract
6th cataract
Atbara R.
Khartoum
SHEBA
Blue Nile R.
White Nile R.
GULF OF ADEN
Ophir
100 200 300 Miles
100 200 300 400 Kilometers
D
E
F
1
2
3
4

A similar conclusion must be drawn in regard to the three extra-biblical references to "Tarshish." An eight-line Phoenician dedicatory inscription exhumed from the archaeological site of Nora on the south coast of the island of Sardinia is dated paleographically to the ninth century B.C.[230] The text of the 40-inch limestone stela refers to a military force under the direction of a Phoenician named Milkûtôn that had arrived safely in Sardinia from Tarshish and was looking forward to living there in peace.[231] This unambiguous reference to a place name known by the Phoenicians as "Tarshish" requires its placement somewhere in or immediately adjacent to the western Mediterranean Sea.[232] It is equally clear from the stela that this Tarshish was occupied by a Phoenician military force, lending strong support to the supposition that Phoenicians were involved in the western Mediterranean in systematic activities by the ninth century B.C.

A second attestation of the name occurs in a seventh-century B.C. Akkadian inscription of king Esarhaddon discovered in Assur.[233] This alabaster slab was apparently designed to extol some of Esarhaddon's greatest architectural and political accomplishments. It declares that the Assyrian king, having vanquished Tyre, an "island in the middle of the sea" (cf. Ezek. 27:32), proceeded to conquer Egypt, Pathros, and Nubia. Later in the text, Esarhaddon's scribe concludes:

> "All of the kings in the middle of the sea—from Yadanana [Cyprus] and Yaman [Ionia, the area of later Greek settlement in and around the Aegean Sea] as far as Tarshish—fell at my feet and presented me with heavy tribute."[234]

Here again, this inscription makes plain that Assyrians knew of a geographical place called "Tarshish" that was situated indisputably somewhere in the Mediterranean. And if one assumes a logical westward progression in Esarhaddon's pronouncement (from Cyprus, to Ionia, to Tarshish), a location for Tarshish somewhere west of the Aegean Sea would be required. Isaiah's writing (66:19) also juxtaposes Tarshish and Ionia, and Ezekiel's lamentation over Tyre (Ezek. 27) makes adjoining mention of Cyprus (27:6), Ionia (27:13), and Tarshish (27:12).

A third extra-biblical text mentioning Tarshish, an Old Hebrew ostracon, was recently published from a private collection.[235] A late seventh-century B.C. document based on paleographic analysis, this five-line pottery fragment is of unknown provenance and uncertain authenticity. The document speaks of an individual who commands that "three shekels of silver from Tarshish" be donated to the house of Yahweh. In addition to the authenticity question, this text is also the least helpful in our locational quest, though it does clearly mark Tarshish as a geographical name and a place that apparently was a source of silver. Accordingly, a cogent argument can be advanced from both biblical and Near Eastern literatures that "Tarshish" consistently denoted the name of an ancient site or sites that must have been situated somewhere in the Mediterranean world.

THE SHIPS OF TARSHISH

How is one to understand the biblical expression "the ship(s) of Tarshish"? May it be construed generically to denote a certain type or quality of seaworthy vessel, without regard to any possible geographical designation? The ancient world was certainly familiar with nautical expressions of a generic type, such as "ships of the sea," "ships of trade," "deep-going ships," "planked ships," "ships of reeds," "ships with battering rams," "ships with sails," "ships of [a particular deity]," "ships of [a particular king]," "ships of [a particular people]," and others.

But in vivid contradistinction to all of these is the expression "the ship(s) of X," where X is otherwise known to have been a *geographical* entity. Early Akkadian literature describing the seafaring merchants of Ur and Eridu is replete with references to "the ship(s) of Magan," "the ship(s) of Meluhha," or "the ship(s) of Dilmun." While the exact location of some of these places may remain in doubt, the "X" element refers indisputably and without exception to a specific geographic locale. At the same time, Mesopotamian literature occasionally refers to "the ship(s) of Akkad," "the ship(s) of Assur," "the ship(s) of Mari," or "the ship(s) of Ur." Similarly, Egyptian texts make mention of "the ship(s) of Punt," "the ship(s) of Byblos," "the ship(s) of Kittim/Cyprus," or "the ship(s) of Keftiu/Crete." In all these instances the "X" element represents a known geographical entity whether the expression originally designated the destination point or the provenience of the respective vessels.[236]

Of course, an original geographical designation may occasionally shift, but it does so over time. Two examples: Dilmun was apparently originally situated in what is today eastern Saudi Arabia,[237] but was shifted geographically in the Ur III period to the island of Bahrain; and Meluhha, though originally situated somewhere near the Indus Valley, was shifted to Nubia by the advent of the neo-Assyrian period.[238] "The ship(s) of Meluhha" in literature came to designate a completely different geographical arena. Likewise, an original designation may evolve in its meaning and even become obscured, as when a "ship of Meluhha" or a "ship of Dilmun" was later called a *magillu*-ship (a kind of boat) or a *mabba*-ship (a seagoing vessel). "Ship of Byblos" eventually became a generic expression for any seagoing vessel, and "ship of Keftiu/Crete" came to denote Mediterranean travel to many different destinations.[239] However, in *all* these situations there appears to have been a historical antecedent that originally related to the location of a given ship's destination or provenience. In other words, whenever the expression "the ship(s) of [a place name]" is applied to a different geographical arena or applied generically, it appears without exception to be only a *derivative* application, not a *native* application.

It is improper to argue, then, that "the ship(s) of Tarshish" *originally* designated some kind of generic oceangoing vessel or that the phrase must be interpreted as such even in its earliest usages in the Bible. That perspective flies in the face of documentation and appears to represent an assertion that must stand without the benefit of evidentiary support from antiquity.

This basic understanding is necessary to properly understand 2 Chronicles 20:36–37 (cf. 1 Kings 22:48), a passage that unmistakably places "the ship(s) of Tarshish" on the Red Sea and is the lynchpin text for a "generic" interpretation of Tarshish in the Bible. However, the statement is contained entirely within the summary conclusion of Jehoshaphat's reign, which must not be underestimated or too easily dismissed.

The reigns of Israelite and Judahite kings are summarized in the biblical text with an astonishing degree of uniformity. Each summarizing formula begins with a standard introduction and a reference to an annalistic written account, followed in sequence by: (1) a statement about sleeping with one's ancestors; (2) an identification of one's burial site; and (3) a declaration of legitimate succession. With arresting consistency, this pattern appears in the case of 18 of the 19 kings of Israel and 15 of the 19 kings of Judah. (The exceptions generally come toward the end of the series when the kingdoms are in turmoil due to assault from without.) This pattern is the same whether the king was from the north or the south, whether recorded in Kings or Chronicles, whether citing a standard secondary source or an unusual source, whether the reign was short or covered decades, whether the king was militarily strong or weak, and whether the king was assessed by the biblical historians in positive or negative terms.

Admittedly, there are instances when not all elements of this pattern are present, as when a reference is omitted to sleeping with one's ancestors (e.g., Amon), naming one's burial place (e.g., Jehoash), or identifying one's successor (e.g., Ahab). In just a few cases more than one element may be missing. However, almost without exception this standard formula is not interrupted by the *insinuation of additional material.* And even in those few instances where an additional element may appear, it represents either a general summary of a given king's life of warfare ("there was continual war all his days") or a description of unusual circumstances relating to a given king's death (mention of a foot disease that killed Asa, a conspiracy that killed Joash or Amaziah, or a brief explanation of Josiah's or Shallum's untimely demise).

In contrast to this consistent pattern stands the unique summary record of Jehoshaphat. It is precisely into the *middle* of the Jehoshaphat formula—immediately after reference to a

Relief of a Phoenician vessel.

secondary source (2 Chron. 20:34b) and immediately before reference to his sleeping with his ancestors, being buried in Jerusalem, and being succeeded by Jehoram (2 Chron. 21:1)—that one finds statements having to do with his building a fleet of ships of Tarshish to go to Tarshish, including Ahaziah's possible partnership with him in the effort and the wrecking of his fleet at Ezion-geber.

One must be wary about foundationally anchoring an assertion of a single nautical enterprise on a text that, in point of fact, may be an exegetical outlier.[240] Given the four generations between Solomon and Jehoshaphat and the estimated interval of some 90 years between their alleged nautical ventures, it is possible that the Jehoshaphat text may represent an evolutional attestation of the expression "ships of Tarshish" rather than reflecting its native original geographical designation. Whatever the case, caution is advised against allowing this one text to dictate and categorically redefine the meaning of the expression "the ship(s) of Tarshish." It is the only known text in antiquity, biblical or otherwise, explicitly to locate the *site* of Tarshish, not just the ships of Tarshish, some place other than on the Mediterranean Sea.

EVIDENCE FOR 10TH-CENTURY B.C. PHOENICIAN TRADE ON THE MEDITERRANEAN

A case is sometimes made that the upheaval associated with the end of the Late Bronze Age was actually fortuitous for Phoenicia's trade and politics. The destruction of the Hittites and the neutralization of significant city-states across North Syria and the Syrian coast ended any further serious threat from the north, and the death of Ramses III appears to have led to an eclipse of Egypt's nautical endeavors in the south. Meanwhile, Mycenaean trading networks into the Levant and their maritime stranglehold on the mid-Mediterranean came to an end around 1200 B.C., and Assyria was unable to sustain its expansionism as far west as the Mediterranean until the ninth century B.C. [**See map 75.**] As a result, Phoenician coastal cities were momentarily no longer at the mercy of passing imperial armies or competitive naval interests. Phoenicians began to sail farther west rather freely.[241]

The map shows the extent of land visibility from Tyre and the Phoenician coastland across the entire span of the Mediterranean, although the Phoenicians are credited with navigating the open seas at night.[242] No fewer than 19 ancient shipwrecks in the greater Mediterranean world can be dated to the approximate time of Hiram and Solomon or earlier. [**See map for locations and dates.**] A few include Phoenician materials and all are found in waters where land is visible.[243] Discussions addressing the date of Phoenician westward expansion often include elements that may lack sufficient modal clarity or precision of dating,[244] so the story is most likely greater than told here, but it cannot be less.

Phoenicians were undoubtedly present at several places across Cyprus by the 11th century B.C., as amply demonstrated by inscriptional, stratified pottery, and perhaps even architectural evidence.[245] They may even have colonized the island by the end of the 10th century B.C.[246] Phoenician evidence across Crete dates perhaps as early as the late 11th century B.C. and, in any event, not later than the 10th century B.C.[247] Sardinia has produced three early Phoenician texts that range in dates from the 11th to the ninth century B.C.[248] All are monumental in nature and strongly suggestive of a Phoenician *presence* there rather than merely an article of trade or something with an heirloom quality.

Evidence for a Phoenician presence in coastal Spain dates to the end of the 10th century B.C. or the beginning of the ninth century B.C. In 1998 at the modern city of

The dreary terrain of Timnah, site of Solomon's copper mines.

Huelva, on the Atlantic coast of Spain north of the mouth of the Guadalquivir River, a huge site now thought to have been an ancient Phoenician emporium was accidentally uncovered.[249] To date, more than 3,000 pieces of distinctly Phoenician pottery of various types have been discovered *in situ* (undisturbed), together with vestiges of goods from all over the Mediterranean, including Italy, Sardinia, Greece, and Cyprus.[250] The Phoenician materials are largely of a domestic nature, rather than luxury or prestige articles, which may be taken to suggest the presence of a full-fledged settlement and not merely of a transit station for trade. Reliable radiocarbon tests conducted on several bone samples yielded a mean calibrated age of 930–830 B.C.[251] These Phoenician finds, the oldest of their kind in the western Mediterranean, are strongly suggestive of an *ongoing* Phoenician presence in Spain. In the words of the Spanish excavators, they are "remarkably close in date to Hiram and Solomon . . . only a difference of a few decades, if any."[252]

This kind of evidence may reveal when Phoenicians first engaged in systematic settlement in Spain, but it begs the question: When did Phoenicians first *arrive* there? Is it more logical to assume that the earliest Phoenician settlements in coastal Iberia were founded on impulse by seamen passing that way for the first time around 930–900 B.C., or by traders/merchants who after perhaps as many as two to three generations had developed the need for more permanent stations and not just offshore moorings? Scholars are in agreement that the earliest Phoenician pre-colonial contacts in the west would have left little or no recognizable material traces.[253] Students of Mycenaean or Greek colonization in the Mediterranean describe what they call a "phased development" that lasted a few generations.[254] It seems altogether reasonable to make the same sort of claim for the process of Phoenician colonization.

The existence of Phoenicians in the middle and western Mediterranean by the 10th century B.C. is supported by writing and both nautical and terrestrial archaeological discovery. While the evidence points overwhelmingly to a motivation of mercantilism, which would be consistent with the biblical verdict, the dynamics and modalities of their activities are not well known. Moreover, direct proof of any Judahite participation in Mediterranean Sea trade is still lacking.[255] Yet while many internal complexities still require elucidation, given the unambiguous presence of Phoenicians across the Mediterranean by the 10th century B.C., it seems reasonable to accord a level of plausibility to the Tarshish narratives in this regard.

Solomon's Domestic Initiatives — map 64

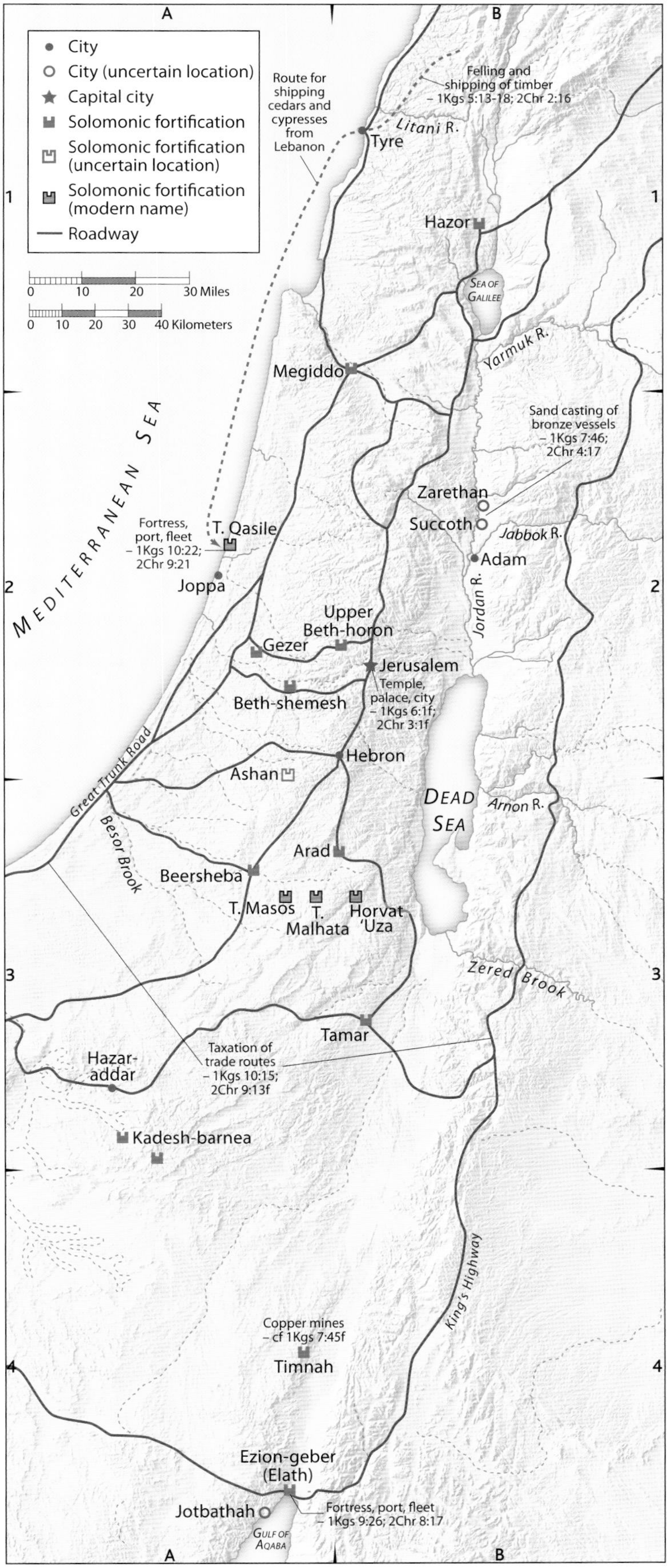

SOLOMON'S DOMESTIC ADMINISTRATION

Solomon's vast standing army and momentous building projects required larger revenue sources than apparently even his commercial ventures could supply. Consequently, the king was obliged to impose increasingly heavy taxes upon the population of Israel, which seems to be a realization of what Samuel had predicted when he replied to the Israelites' original request to have a king (1 Sam. 8:11–22).

One such measure to deal with a revenue shortfall involved dividing Israel into 12 administrative districts, each with a provincial governor and an obligation to furnish provisions for the royal bureaucracy and harem in Jerusalem for one month of the year (1 Kings 4:7–19). Two of the provincial governors were Solomon's own sons-in-law, a detail that both authenticates the historical value of the roster and may at the same time suggest the stringent demand for enforcement that existed out in the districts. Whatever the case, such a system must have been an extremely irritating policy to Solomon's subjects. For one thing, it was grossly unfair: the entire territory of Judah appears to have been exonerated from its demands. In addition, this measure represented a very heavy economic strain by adding to the already demanding forced labor of tens of thousands of Israelites in Solomon's various building enterprises (1 Kings 4:6b; 5:13–18).

Solomon later appointed the industrious Jeroboam as governor over one of these districts (1 Kings 11:28), a position Jeroboam apparently attempted to exploit to his own political advantage (1 Kings 11:26–40). Despite having to flee to Egypt to avoid Solomon's ill intentions, Jeroboam returned to Israel at Solomon's death and was enlisted to help renegotiate this levy with Solomon's son and successor, Rehoboam (1 Kings 12:1–4). When that effort failed, the people in the north realized that Solomon's heavy taxation system would continue for another generation (1 Kings 12:13–16; 2 Chron. 10:6–15) and the monarchy fractured.

Rehoboam, apparently not sensing how strongly they felt, dispatched his savvy cabinet officer in charge of forced labor in an attempt to enforce the despised levy. But the administrator was brutally stoned to death by the citizens of the north (1 Kings 12:18), thus officially bringing both the levy and the united monarchy to an abrupt and unceremonious end. Jeroboam soon was made the first king of the ten northern tribes.

Even with an equivalent number of Israelite tribes and calendar months, Solomon for some reason had avoided what would appear to have been a very natural way of apportioning the new levy. It has been argued that Solomon's redistricting criterion was related to whether or not certain territories had been incorporated into Israel at the point of its original settlement.[256] Yet it seems preferable to conclude that Solomon was motivated by a more contemporary political agenda, attempting to further obliterate cherished tribal boundaries and centralize royal power in Jerusalem.[257]

This was especially true for districts 1, 3–5, and 8–10, divided in a few cases *across* natural geographical and/or historic tribal boundaries. [**Compare map 40.**] A noticeable exception was district 11, which conformed more or less to the territorial allotment of the tribe of Benjamin. One wonders, in fact, whether Solomon's measure might have been designed to be particularly repressive to the descendants of Saul. Consider the disproportionately small size of that district, the presumed small population (cf. Num. 1:36–37), and the fact that the rugged topography of the Benjaminite hill country would have made agricultural efforts all the more stressful. Whatever his purpose may have been, Solomon's division of the administrative districts seems to have included a conscious effort to rid Israel of its treasured tribal heritage and to solidify further the monarchistic ideal.

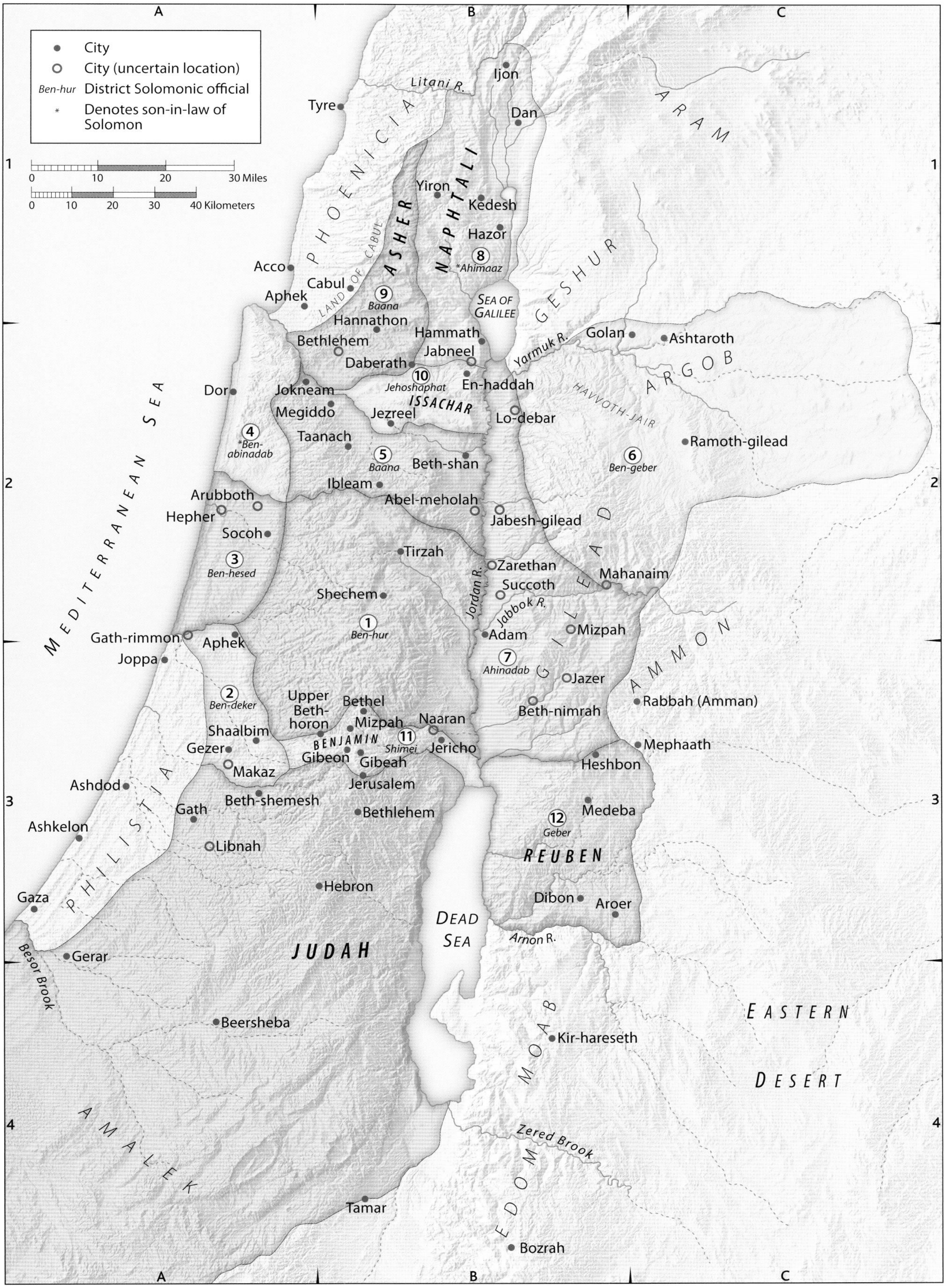
City
City (uncertain location)
Ben-hur District Solomonic official
* Denotes son-in-law of Solomon
0 10 20 30 Miles
0 10 20 30 40 Kilometers
A
B
C
1
2
3
4
Litani R.
Ijon
Dan
Tyre
PHOENICIA
ARAM
NAPHTALI
ASHER
LAND OF CABUL
Yiron
Kedesh
Hazor
8
*Ahimaaz
Acco
Cabul
Aphek
9
Baana
SEA OF GALILEE
GESHUR
Hannathon
Hammath
Bethlehem
Jabneel
Daberath
Yarmuk R.
Golan
Ashtaroth
ARGOB
10
Jehoshaphat
En-haddah
ISSACHAR
Dor
Jokneam
Megiddo
Jezreel
Lo-debar
HAVVOTH-JAIR
MEDITERRANEAN SEA
4
*Ben-abinadab
Taanach
5
Baana
Beth-shan
Ramoth-gilead
6
Ben-geber
Ibleam
Arubboth
Abel-meholah
Hepher
Jabesh-gilead
Socoh
GILEAD
Tirzah
3
Ben-hesed
Zarethan
Jordan R.
Mahanaim
Succoth
Shechem
Jabbok R.
1
Ben-hur
Mizpah
Gath-rimmon
Aphek
Adam
Joppa
7
Ahinadab
AMMON
Jazer
2
Ben-deker
Upper Beth-horon
Bethel
Beth-nimrah
Rabbah (Amman)
Mizpah
Naaran
Shaalbim
BENJAMIN
11
Shimei
Jericho
Gezer
Gibeon
Mephaath
Gibeah
Heshbon
Makaz
Ashdod
Jerusalem
Beth-shemesh
Gath
Bethlehem
Medeba
Ashkelon
12
Geber
Libnah
REUBEN
PHILISTIA
Hebron
Gaza
Dibon
Aroer
DEAD SEA
Arnon R.
Gerar
JUDAH
Besor Brook
MOAB
Beersheba
EASTERN
Kir-hareseth
DESERT
AMALEK
Zered Brook
EDOM
Tamar
Bozrah

THE MONARCHY DIVIDES

Despite all his greatness and wisdom, Solomon brought his once-extensive realm to the threshold of economic ruin and political collapse with his abuse of power and wealth. Even before his death, Edomites were asserting themselves in the south of his kingdom (1 Kings 11:14–22) and Arameans were contesting his rule in the northernmost sectors (1 Kings 11:23–25). Closer to home, the northern tribes of Israel were keenly feeling the strain of increasing alienation (1 Kings 11:26–40). [**See map 65.**] The wise king bequeathed to his son Rehoboam a kingdom that was teetering on the brink.

For his part, Rehoboam seems to have done little to forestall the inevitable. When a delegation of northern citizens met him at Shechem and appealed to have their tax burdens lightened, the new monarch responded by attempting to impose even heavier burdens (1 Kings 12:1–15). It was a desperate gamble for Rehoboam, perhaps one that he was forced to take. But it also ignited the flames of anarchy and tribal secession (1 Kings 12:16; cf. 2 Sam. 20:1b).

What became the northern kingdom is often called the "ten northern tribes," a legitimate denotation based on the declaration of the prophet Ahijah to Jeroboam (1 Kings 11:30–35) who was promised ten parts of what had been Solomon's kingdom. One part was to be reserved for Rehoboam because of the faithfulness of his grandfather David. But given the fact that Israel was comprised of 12 tribes and that Ahijah's garment was torn into 12 pieces, not 11 pieces, this imprecision of arithmetic calls for some comment. If there were ten tribes that formed the northern kingdom, and the tribe of Judah represented the southern kingdom (cf. 1 Kings 12:20), what tribal entity was unaccounted for in Ahijah's computation?

While it is geographically and politically true that the territory of the tribe of Simeon was absorbed into the tribe of Judah (2 Chron. 15:9; Josh. 19:1–9 [but see 15:26–32, 42]; cf. Neh. 11:26–30) [**map 40**], it is hard to see how the 12th piece of Ahijah's garment could have represented the marginalized tribe of Simeon. However, the disintegration of the monarchy also resulted in the simultaneous and doubtless painful shredding of the tribal fabric of Benjamin. For example, the Benjaminite city of Jerusalem remained within the realm of Rehoboam and all his Judahite dynastic descendants until the Babylonian forces of Nebuchadnezzar destroyed the capital city. But Jeroboam erected one of his two golden calves in the Benjaminite city of Bethel, which remained an Israelite cultic institution throughout the entire existence of the ten northern tribes and continued even after the Assyrian destruction of Israel in 722 B.C. (2 Kings 23:15–17). While it is true that Rehoboam is said to have mustered the tribes of Judah and Benjamin *against* Israel (1 Kings 12:21–23; 2 Chron. 11:1–3, 23), it is no less true that the Benjaminite cities of Ramah, Geba, and Mizpah (1 Kings 15:17, 22–23; 2 Chron. 16:1–6) became places of contention *between* Israel and Judah (cf. 1 Kings 16:34, where a man from Bethel rebuilt the Benjaminite town of Jericho). [**See map 67.**] The Bible records several hostile actions between Israel and Judah inside the territory of Benjamin during the early days of the divided monarchy (e.g., 1 Kings 15:16–22; 2 Chron. 13:2b–7; 16:1–10), which points both to a fluctuating geographical border between the two kingdoms and a fractured and atomistic tribal fallout for the Benjaminites. In this sense one might say that the 12th piece of Ahijah's garment was itself torn asunder as a result of the breach in the monarchy.

In reality three nations were created from what had been Solomon's territorial domain: (1) Judah, the southern kingdom; (2) Israel (including the Transjordanian tribes), the northern kingdom; and (3) Aram with its city-states of Damascus, Hamath, and Qatna. [**See map 62.**] At the same time, the territories of Ammon, Moab, and Edom were emboldened to disavow loyalties to either Judah or Israel, and Phoenicia continued to maintain the political independence it had enjoyed as far back as the time of David and Solomon. Politically, both Judah and Israel were left weak and relatively defenseless. In fact, between the disintegration of Solomon's monarchy (c. 930 B.C.) and the destruction of Samaria (722 B.C.) and Jerusalem (586 B.C.), the political history of both kingdoms was largely one of humiliating foreign assaults and plundering. [**See maps 68, 76, 77, and 80.**]

The territory of the southern wilderness was periodically contested by Judah and Edom during the days of the divided monarchy. Judah's reach temporarily extended southward in the first part of the ninth century B.C., during the rule of Jehoshaphat (1 Kings 22:47–48; 2 Chron. 20:35–36) and Jehoram (2 Kings 8:20–22), and then again for a brief moment in the first half of the eighth century B.C., during the reigns of Amaziah (2 Chron. 25:11–13; cf. 2 Kings 14:7; Amos 1:11–12) and especially Uzziah (2 Kings 14:22; 2 Chron. 26:2–10). [**See map 74.**] But for the most part these were temporary forays that did not lead to sustained occupation. The Edomites, however, increasingly asserted their lasting presence upon this landscape (e.g., 2 Kings 16:6; 2 Chron. 28:17; cf. Isa. 63:1–6; Jer. 49:7–22). Clear evidence exists of Edomite occupation of most of the wilderness, even as far north as the biblical Negeb, by the eighth century B.C. and beyond.[258] And, of course, the forging of an Edomite imprint upon this land by the early

Legend:
- • City
- ○ City (uncertain location)
- ★ Capital city
- ✚ Sanctuary city
- □ Seaport
- ▲ Mountain peak
- — International artery

Scale:
0 10 20 30 40 Miles
0 10 20 30 40 50 60 Kilometers

Byblos

Beirut

PHOENICIA

Sidon

Litani R.

Tyre

▲ *Mt. Hermon*

✚ Dan

★ Damascus

Great Trunk Road

A R A M

Kedesh

Hazor

Acco □

SEA OF GALILEE

King's Highway

MEDITERRANEAN SEA

Mt. Carmel ▲

Kishon R.

Mt. Tabor ▲

Dor □

Megiddo

Yarmuk R.

Ashtaroth

Mt. Hauran

Edrei

Ramoth-gilead

Taanach

▲ Beth-shan

Mt. Gilboa

Ibleam

Jordan R.

Jabesh-gilead ○

Samaria ★

Tirzah ★

Mt. Ebal ▲

Penuel

Succoth ○ ○

Mahanaim ○

Mt. Gerizim ▲ Shechem

Jabbok R.

Aphek

Joppa □

Shiloh

I S R A E L

A M M O N

Gezer

Bethel ✚

Jericho

Rabbah (Amman) ★

Ashdod □

Aijalon

Jerusalem ★

Heshbon

Gath ★

Bethlehem

Mt. Nebo ▲

Medeba

Ashkelon □

Mareshah

P H I L I S T I A

Great Trunk Road

Besor Brook

Gaza

DEAD SEA

Hebron

J U D A H

Arnon R.

M O A B

Dibon

Beersheba

Kir-hareseth ★

Zered Brook

Region perodically contested by Edom and Judah

E A S T E R N

W. el-Arish

Bozrah ★

Punon

D E S E R T

Kadesh-barnea

E D O M

King's Highway

W I L D E R N E S S

post-exilic period is reflected in its regional name at that time—Idumea [**map 85**], from which Herod the Great would emerge in due course.

On the economic front, the division of the monarchy produced a strange irony. Rehoboam had sought to sustain the economic advantages Judah had gained during the latter days of Solomon, but the schism actually created economic advantages for Israel. Whatever natural resources and access to international trade this land possessed would now be largely controlled by the northern kingdom. Most of the larger cities were in Israel, as were the only seaports; and the arterial Great Trunk Road and King's Highway, a potential economic bonanza, intersected the northern kingdom but skirted Judah. Such economic advantages may help explain why foreign powers conquered Israel more than 125 years before Judah.

Israel's first king, Jeroboam, was quick to capitalize on Israel's earlier traditions in order to legitimize his own authority. He astutely sought to establish a headquarters at Shechem (1 Kings 12:25), the spot where Abraham had first built an altar and worshiped Yahweh on the soil of Canaan (Gen. 12:6–7), where the bones of Joseph had been buried (Gen. 50:25; Ex. 13:19; Josh. 24:32), and where the nation of Israel had officially ratified its covenantal relationship with Yahweh (Josh. 8:30–35; 24:1–28). Yet Shechem proved to be an unfortunate tactical choice for a capital city because it was situated in a vale between Mt. Ebal and Mt. Gerizim—vulnerable to both north-south and east-west attacks. It appears that Jeroboam moved the capital from Shechem to Tirzah early in his reign (1 Kings 14:17; cf. 15:21). About 35 years after Jeroboam's reign ended, King Omri purchased a high, isolated, and relatively defensible hill that he converted into the third and final capital of the northern tribes—the city of Samaria (1 Kings 16:24).

Jeroboam bequeathed a permanent legacy to his realm by exploiting another aspect of Israel's tradition. He created sanctuary cities at Dan and Bethel, easily accessible places on either end of his kingdom, and instituted an official religion around two golden calves (1 Kings 12:25–33). Transparently seeking to emulate the earlier religious expression of Moses' brother Aaron at Mt. Sinai, he presented his calves to the people with an almost identical call to worship (1 Kings 12:28b; cf. Ex. 32:4, 8). Jeroboam's action would characterize Israel throughout the remainder of its pre-exilic existence. Biblical historians summarize reign after reign in the north with words such as "he walked in the ways of Jeroboam and in his sin" (1 Kings 15:34; 16:19, 26; 22:52), "he did not turn away from the sin of Jeroboam" (2 Kings 10:29; 13:11; 14:24; 15: 18, 24, 28), "he clung to the sin of Jeroboam" (2 Kings 3:3), or "he considered it trivial to commit the sin of Jeroboam" (1 Kings 16:31). Only three of Jeroboam's 18 successors lack such a statement: Elah and Shallum had short reigns, and Hoshea was the final king, for whom a formal summary statement is not recorded. Moreover, the theological verdict at the time of Samaria's destruction, and the concept of exile itself, is specifically tied to Jeroboam's sin (2 Kings 17:21–23).

In the south, the majority of Judahite kings are said either to have worshiped idols or not to have opposed idolatry (1 Kings 14:23–24; 15:14a; 22:43; 2 Kings 12:3; 14:4; 15:4, 35; 16:4; 23:5; 2 Chron. 24:18; 28:2–3; 33:3–7). It is a curious fact, then, that only three kings in the north were explicitly associated with Baal (Ahab, Ahaziah, and Joram). Moreover, Jehu even engaged in a systematic purge of Baal and Baalism in Israel (2 Kings 10:1–28), and yet he retained Jeroboam's calves (2 Kings 10:29–31). Perhaps it is fair to state that Jeroboam's religion, like Aaron's before it, bears the earmarks of perverted Yahwism. The problem was not idolatry, the importing of false religion, but rather apostasy, the subverting of true religion.

Partially-reconstructed altar of Rehoboam at Dan.

REHOBOAM'S FORTIFIED CITIES

Solomon's heavy taxation system was both brutal and unjust. As an administrator in that system (1 Kings 11:28), Jeroboam must have heard many of the complaints firsthand, and it appears that he might have attempted to exploit this situation to his own political advantage. Apparently sensing Jeroboam's potential threat, Solomon sought to kill him (1 Kings 11:40), so Jeroboam fled to Egypt where he was given asylum by a pharaoh named Shishak (Shoshenq I). Earlier Solomon had enjoyed a close, personal relationship with an Egyptian king (1 Kings 9:16–17a). But now that Jeroboam had been called back from Egypt to become the first king of the "northern kingdom" (1 Kings 12:1–16; 2 Chron. 10:1–16), Rehoboam might well have suspected that loyalties had shifted and may have anticipated some sort of aggressive action out of Egypt.

It appears probable that in preparation for such an invasion, or perhaps in its immediate aftermath,[259] Rehoboam created a fortified defense line designed to impede any unwanted traffic into Judah from the south and west (2 Chron. 11:5–12)—ironically, not from the *north*. Some 15 of the more strategic points in the Judean hill country and the eastern Shephela were fortified by the Judahite king and manned by his forces, as every convenient access into Jerusalem was effectively blockaded. What amounted to a perimeter wall of defense was created for Judah.[260]

Sure enough, in his fifth year, Rehoboam's worst fears were fully realized as Shishak invaded his land, carrying off much treasure from the Jerusalem temple (1 Kings 14:25–28; 2 Chron. 12:2–12). Because of certain precisely dated events that are recorded both in Assyrian literature and in the Bible [**map 70**], biblical dates during this period can be very exact—within a margin of not more than ± one year. We can say with confidence that the Bible dates Shishak's campaign as the fifth year of Rehoboam—926 or 925 B.C.,[261] depending on when during that year the campaign was launched.

Here the story shifts from Jerusalem some 650 miles south to the Great Temple complex at Karnak, in upper Egypt. Probably the most extravagant and ornate religious edifice ever built, and certainly the largest, Karnak contained 250 acres of temples, chapels, courts, majestic pylons, granite obelisks, flagstaffs, inscribed and painted columns and wall panels, hypostyle halls, long avenues of ram-headed or human-headed sphinxes, and colossal statues—all loudly proclaiming the stately and magnificent grandeur that once was Egypt.[262]

Featured among the ornaments of greatness in this complex are "triumphant battle reliefs" that visually depict and verbally describe Egyptian military campaigns against Asiatic enemies. At least 17 such victory reliefs are found at Karnak.[263] The Shishak (unfinished) triumphal battle relief of his campaign into Asia appears on the southern exterior wall of the hypostyle court between pylons II and III, just east

Rehoboam's Fortified Cities *map 67*

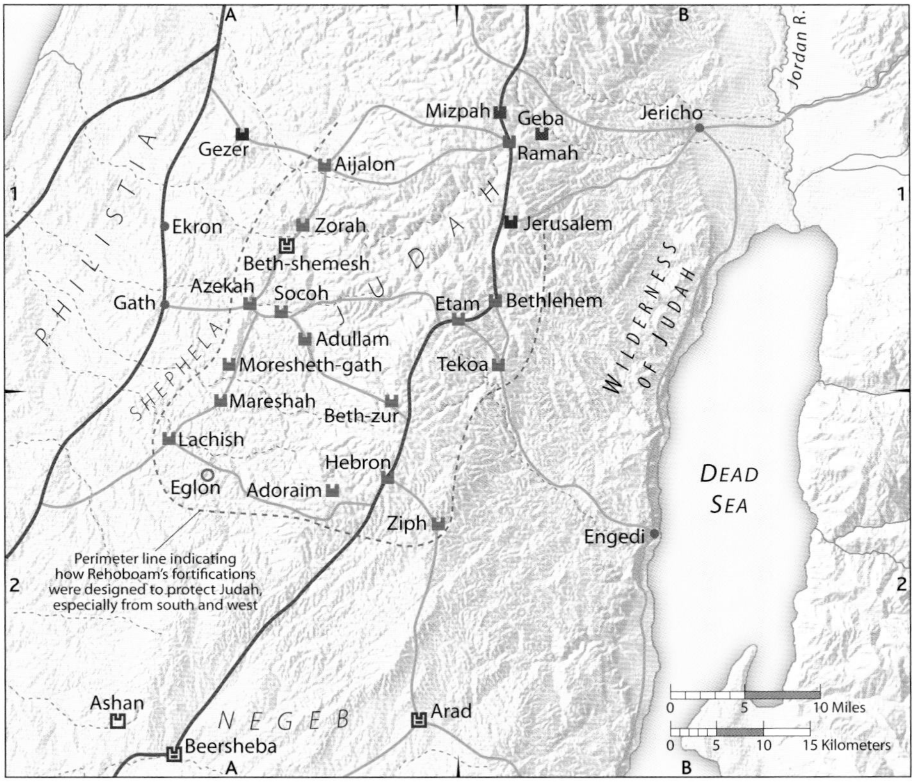

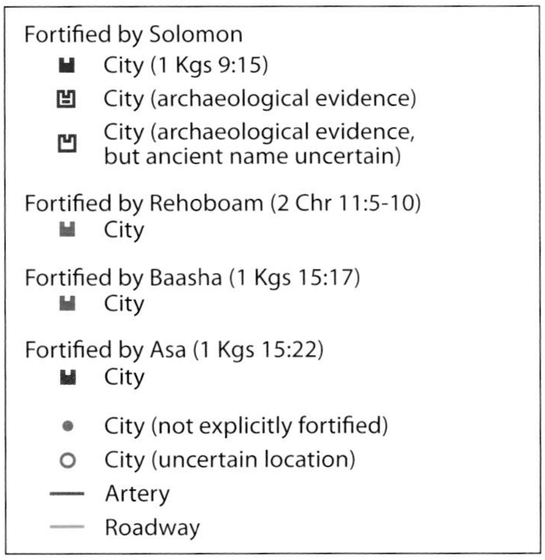

Fortified by Solomon
City (1 Kgs 9:15)
City (archaeological evidence)
City (archaeological evidence, but ancient name uncertain)
Fortified by Rehoboam (2 Chr 11:5-10)
City
Fortified by Baasha (1 Kgs 15:17)
City
Fortified by Asa (1 Kgs 15:22)
City
City (not explicitly fortified)
City (uncertain location)
Artery
Roadway

of the Ramses III temple. This is the only known campaign into Canaan Shishak ever made, so we can affirm with a fair degree of confidence that he was celebrating here at Karnak what was being simultaneously lamented in Jerusalem during the days of Rehoboam.

Further bolstering this contention is another fact. The large limestone slabs required for much of Egypt's colossal architecture, including at Karnak, were cut from the royal quarry at Jebel es-Silsileh/Kheny (about 80 miles south of Karnak, midway between Edfu and Elephantine). [**See map 86.**] A stone inscription was discovered at this quarry that mentions Shishak and describes his monumental construction at the great Karnak temple. The text dates when the slabs earmarked for Shishak's construction were quarried. This date, entirely free and independent from biblical chronology, conforms precisely to when Shishak's campaign was dated in Jerusalem by the biblical historians.[264]

Finally, a hieroglyphically inscribed victory stela containing the full and unique cartouche of Shishak was uncovered (unfortunately in an unstratified context) among the ruins of Megiddo, one of the cities conquered by Shishak according to his Karnak relief [#27]. Add to that evidence more than a dozen sites in Canaan and dozens of fortresses in the highlands of the modern Negeb that manifest a 10th-century destruction level attributed by many authorities to the campaign of Shishak.[265]

Yet some scholars appear prepared to go to any lengths to demolish this precise and cogent synchronism and to dispute other evidence. They challenge both the historicity of Shishak's campaign[266] and the historicity of the biblical narratives. One scholar argues that the equivalence between the biblical name Shishak and the pharaonic name Shoshenq is apparent, but misleading—that "Shishak" is actually a "pet" name of Ramses II.[267] This claim has been soundly rebutted.[268] More generally, it has become somewhat fashionable for scholars to aver that what the Bible attributes to the reign of Rehoboam is actually a literary creation from a later period in time. Again, there is much evidence to the contrary.[269]

Archaeological evidence is not at all decisive against Rehoboam. Known fortifications along Judah's southern and western perimeter fit very well with his reign.[270] The absence of fortifications situated *north* of Jerusalem also comports better with what is known about the period of Rehoboam (1 Kings 12:21–24; 2 Chron. 11:1–4). Later in the monarchy period, Abijah pressed northward from Jerusalem into Benjamin and captured the towns of Bethel, Jeshanah, and Ophrah (2 Chron. 13:4, 19) [**map 66**], and still later Asa repelled Baasha's advances at Ramah, building Judean fortifications at Mizpah and Geba (1 Kings 15:16–22; 2 Chron. 16:1–6). [**See map 67.**] Thereafter, the boundary between Judah and Israel stretched across the Benjamin plateau, and it was no longer adjacent to Jerusalem.

Furthermore, if this were a story more or less manufactured hundreds of years after the fact by Jewish scribes living in Babylonian exile, or still later in Canaan after the exile, they would have had no way of knowing about a pharaoh with a particular name and certainly no way of knowing how, when, or even if he attacked Jerusalem. It is sometimes alleged that such chroniclers journeyed the 1,300 miles or so round-trip between Jerusalem and Karnak just to study and copy Shishak's reliefs,[271] but there is no evidence. Had they made the journey, it is highly unlikely that they could have gained access into what would have been a "royal/sacred precinct" into which not even the *Egyptian* general public was permitted access.[272] Even if they did go to Karnak, were somehow admitted, and could read hieroglyphics, one would then have to imagine that their record of the details would very closely parallel that of Shishak's Egyptian scribes. However, the two accounts differ quite dramatically in detail: nothing at Karnak identifies Rehoboam as the antagonist; there is no mention of "Israel" or "Judah"; the city of Jerusalem does not even appear in Shishak's list of conquered towns;[273] and the biblical account focuses on the city of Jerusalem alone, while most of the known place names in Shishak's registers come from what would have been the ten northern tribes rather than Judah. Finally, there is nothing on the relief that dates the event with the precision found in the biblical narratives. To have retrieved that chronological information, the alleged chroniclers would also have had to travel farther south to visit the Silsileh quarry and have had the good fortune of finding Shishak's stela there. Even so, the event would have been dated to Shishak, whereas their biblical account dates the event to Rehoboam.

In the same way that the details of Shishak's campaign and topographical information could only have been based on intelligence gathered during the actual campaign—indicating some sort of on-site scribal activity at that time in Egypt—so the biblical account of the campaign indicates that scribes must have been active in Jerusalem during the same era. As early as David (2 Sam. 8:16; 20:24) and Solomon (1 Kings 4:3), a cabinet-level post of "royal scribe" is said to have been created within Israel.[274] At the same time, several external annalistic sources come to be referenced beginning at this point in the Bible.[275]

We may not know who wrote the book of Kings or the book of Chronicles or exactly when or how they were composed, yet the numerous external sources provide compelling reason to believe that Israel's later scribes could gain access to earlier source materials recounting historical events as early as the time of David and Solomon and the united monarchy.[276] A classic example is found in their factual account of a pharaoh named Shishak who undertook a military campaign against a Judean king named Rehoboam—in the fifth year of the latter, which corresponds to the 21st year of the former—and returned to Egypt with some of the wealth of Jerusalem as a result.[277]

JUDAH AND JERUSALEM BESIEGED

After Solomon's monarchy was fractured and the kingdoms of Israel and Judah were created, both nations were weak and militarily vulnerable. Isaiah graphically lamented, "Your country lies desolate, your cities are burned with fire; foreigners devour your land in your very presence; it is a heap, as overthrown by strangers. And the daughter of Zion is left like a hut in a vineyard, like a shack in a cucumber field, like a besieged city" (Isa. 1:7–8). The psalmist expressed a similar lament: "Even boars [unclean animals (foreigners)] from the thicket ravage [the land], all the wild creatures of the field devour it" (Ps. 80:13).

In fact, the history of Judah and Jerusalem throughout the divided monarchy period largely revolved around a series of foreign assaults and plundering. The "kingdom" was militarily pregnable from virtually every direction. [**See map 68.**] Perhaps as expected, it was assaulted by the major forces of the later Iron Age world: Egypt, Assyria, and Babylonia. But sadly and humiliatingly it also fell victim to minor and insignificant players of the period (e.g., Arabia and Edom).

Almost immediately after the schism, Pharaoh Shishak invaded with some 1,200 chariots and 60,000 infantry (1 Kings 14:25; 2 Chron. 12:2) [**1**]. [**See map 69.**] And for the first few generations after Solomon, hostilities repeatedly erupted between Israel and Judah over their exact boundary line. At issue ultimately was the alignment of the tribe of Benjamin, which was claimed, in effect, by both kingdoms. [**See map 66.**] During the days of Abijah, Jeroboam laid an ambush near Bethel (2 Chron. 13:13) [**2**]. Later, in the time of Asa, king

Situated near southern Judah, the early Iron Age fortress site of Arad dominates the plains of the eastern Negeb. A square citadel was fortified with casemate walls and featured a temple shrine remarkably similar in design to the description of the Temple in Jerusalem.

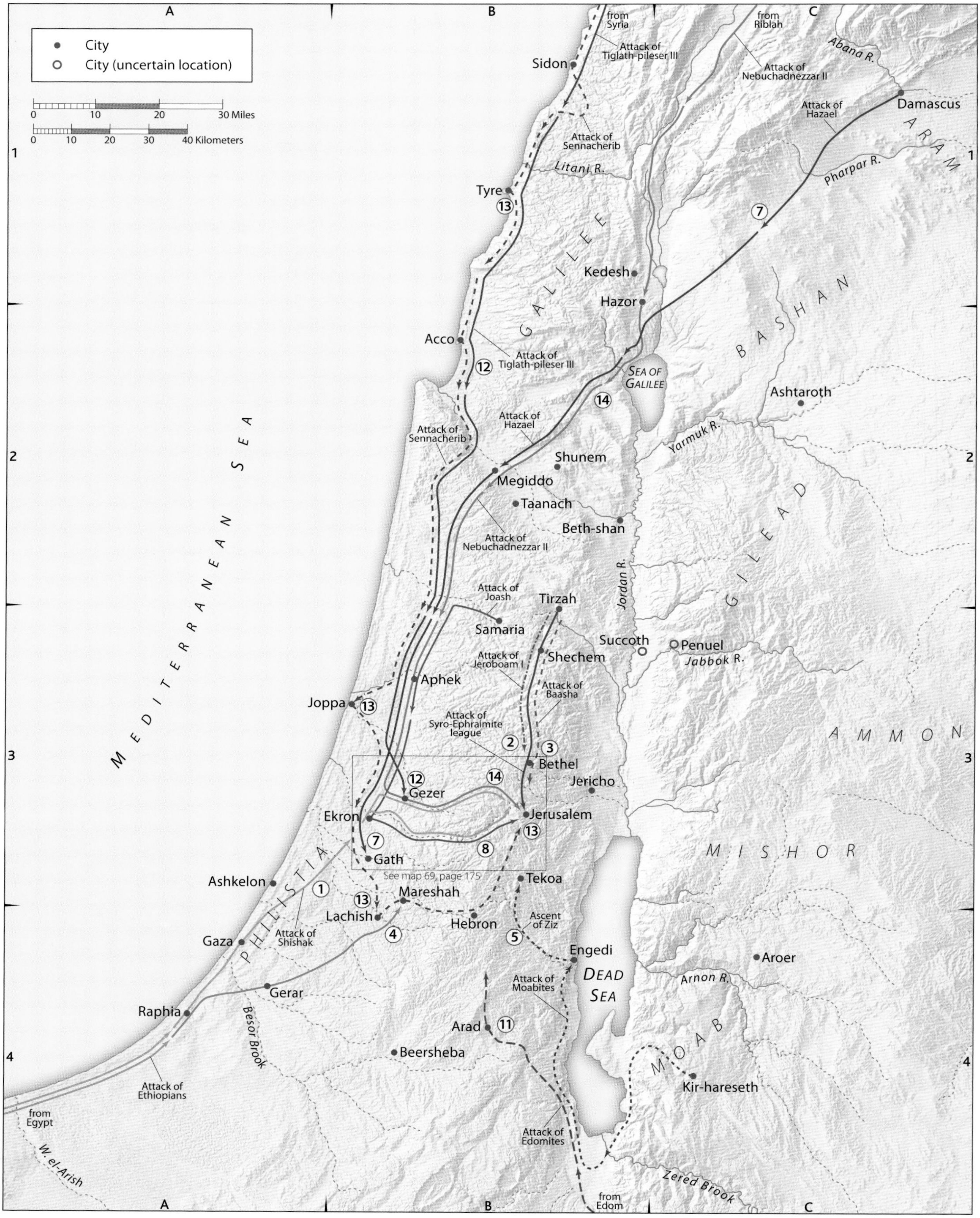

City
City (uncertain location)
0 10 20 30 Miles
0 10 20 30 40 Kilometers
A
B
C
1
2
3
4
from Syria
Attack of Tiglath-pileser III
from Riblah
Attack of Nebuchadnezzar II
Sidon
Abana R.
Damascus
Attack of Hazael
Attack of Sennacherib
ARAM
Litani R.
Pharpar R.
Tyre
13
7
GALILEE
Kedesh
Hazor
BASHAN
Acco
12
Attack of Tiglath-pileser III
SEA OF GALILEE
14
Ashtaroth
Attack of Sennacherib
Attack of Hazael
Yarmuk R.
MEDITERRANEAN SEA
Shunem
Megiddo
Taanach
Beth-shan
GILEAD
Attack of Nebuchadnezzar II
Jordan R.
Attack of Joash
Tirzah
Samaria
Succoth
Penuel
Attack of Jeroboam I
Shechem
Jabbok R.
Aphek
Attack of Baasha
Joppa
13
Attack of Syro-Ephraimite league
2
3
AMMON
Bethel
12
14
Jericho
Gezer
Ekron
Jerusalem
13
7
8
MISHOR
Gath
See map 69, page 175
Ashkelon
Tekoa
1
Mareshah
PHILISTIA
13
Lachish
Hebron
Ascent of Ziz
Attack of Shishak
4
5
Gaza
Engedi
Aroer
DEAD SEA
Gerar
Attack of Moabites
Arnon R.
Raphia
Besor Brook
Arad
11
MOAB
Beersheba
Kir-hareseth
Attack of Ethiopians
from Egypt
Attack of Edomites
W. el-Arish
Zered Brook
from Edom

The Vulnerability of Judah and Jerusalem

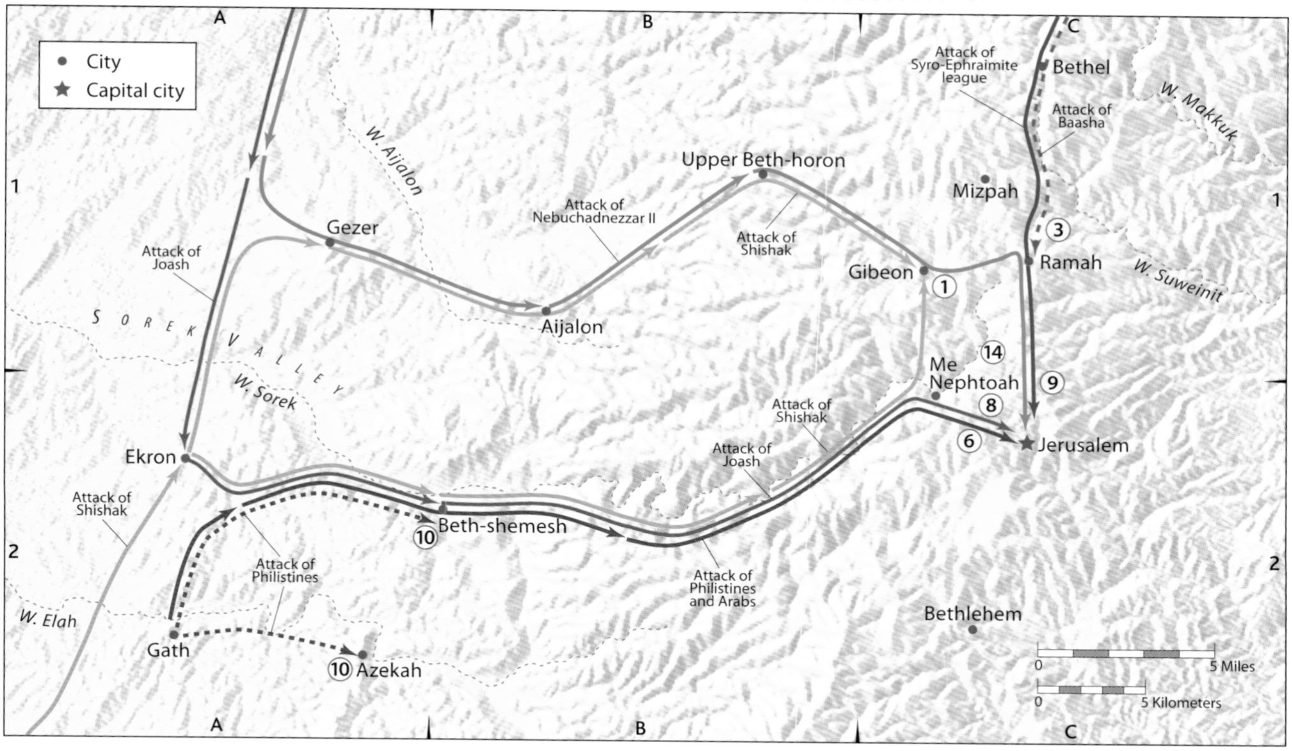

Baasha of Israel was able to press southward as far as Ramah, just five miles from Jerusalem, though he was later repelled (1 Kings 15:16; 2 Chron. 16:1) [**3**].

Judah gained a temporary reprieve when king Asa decisively defeated an Ethiopian league headed by Zerah (2 Chron. 14:9–15; 16:8). In that case, the battle lines were set at the city of Mareshah, about 25 miles southwest of Jerusalem, and the Ethiopians were routed as far as Gerar [**4**]. Later, during the days of Jehoshaphat, a Moabite alliance moved through Edom to Engedi, and then followed the Ascent of Ziz as far as the town of Tekoa, where it was finally repulsed by Jehoshaphat's forces (2 Chron. 20:1–26) [**5**].

But Judah's fortunes worsened dramatically beginning with Jehoram's reign. Not only was Edom able to repudiate Judahite lordship for a time (2 Kings 8:20–22), but also a confederation of Philistines and Arabs launched an attack on Jerusalem and carried away some spoil from the royal city (2 Chron. 21:16–17) [**6**].

Jehoash was faced with the force of the growing Aramean city-state of Damascus (2 Kings 12:17–18; cf. 10:32–33). Hazael, king of Damascus, came south and captured the Philistine city of Gath [7]. With that victory in hand, Hazael set his sights on Jerusalem. Jehoash bribed him by sending him the gold of the Temple treasury, once again sparing Jerusalem.

Warfare between Israel and Judah was renewed during the time of Judah's Amaziah. He hired some Israelite mercenaries in preparation for a military operation against Edom, but at the urging of an unnamed prophet, he discharged them before actually going into battle (2 Chron. 25:5–10; cf. 2 Kings 14:7). The outraged mercenaries proceeded to loot and murder on their way back home. After Amaziah returned in triumph over the Edomites, he challenged Joash (Israel's king) to account for the mercenaries' behavior. Not intimidated, Joash warned Amaziah to back off, which the Judahite refused to do. So they met in battle at the town of Beth-shemesh. Amaziah's army was soundly defeated, and he was taken captive. Joash's troops ascended to Jerusalem where they broke down part of the city wall and carried off hostages and precious booty before returning home to Samaria (2 Kings 14:8–14; 2 Chron. 25:17–24) [**8**].

This sort of grim political refrain for Judah was muted early in the eighth century B.C. as both Judah and Israel experienced something of a renaissance under the leadership of Israel's Jeroboam II and Judah's Uzziah. [**See map 74.**] Seizing upon the advantage that his father had gained against Aram at the citadel of Aphek (2 Kings 13:17, 24–25), Jeroboam II restored some of Israel's borders that had existed in the days of David and Solomon (2 Kings 14:25). Only scant information about these gains is provided, though the prophet Amos does refer to capturing the towns of Lo-debar and Karnaim, and to establishing a border from Lebo-hamath to the Sea of the Arabah (Dead Sea) (Amos 6:13–14). [**See map 74.**]

Uzziah's exploits were no less impressive (2 Kings 14:22; 2 Chron. 26:6–15). [**See map 74.**] He demolished the walls of the Philistine cities of Gath, Jabneh (unknown location), and Ashdod. He drove south and restored to Judahite control the city of Elath on the Red Sea. He is said to have constructed numerous fortresses in the wilderness and to have received tribute from the Ammonites. But regrettably, with all their newly discovered influence that led to some wealth, Israel and Judah reverted to their old ways. Their renaissance soon faded.

The kingdom of Judah was severely tested during the days of Ahaz. Just a few years before Ahaz ascended to the throne (around 738 B.C.), Assyrian king Tiglath-pileser III (nicknamed "Pul" in the Bible and in Assyrian texts) [278] had come west and received tribute from a number of city-states in Syria (e.g., Carchemish, Malatya, Hamath, Damascus, Byblos, and Tyre). [**See map 75.**] Included in the list of those who paid tribute was "Menahem of Samaria"[279] (2 Kings 15:19–20). And just four years later, in what was probably Ahaz's first year as king, the Assyrian marched as far south as Gaza, where he set up a base of operations near the river of Egypt (W. el-Arish).[280] In response to such repeated moves by the Assyrian that deep into Syria and Canaan, a number of apprehensive city-states attempted to forge an anti-Assyrian coalition. Known today as the Syro-Ephraimite league because of the dominant participation of King Rezin of Syria and Pekah of Israel (Isa. 7:2), that coalition apparently sought the participation of Ahaz.

When he refused, the league turned against Ahaz, drove an army to Jerusalem, and attempted a palace takeover (2 Kings 15:37; 16:5; Isa. 7:1, 5–6). Ahaz survived, but it appears that his opponents succeeded in capturing many prisoners and carrying off substantial booty (2 Chron. 28:5–6, 8) [**9**]. Ahaz contemplated appealing directly to Assyria for military support. The prophet Isaiah urged him not to do so, predicting that the league would be destroyed within a relatively short period of time (Isa. 7:1–9). But Ahaz's preoccupation with threats from the north had made him more susceptible to plundering from the west and south. The Philistines moved to recover some cities of the Shephela (2 Chron. 28:10) [**10**], while the Edomites were emboldened to invade southern Judah itself (2 Kings 16:6; 2 Chron. 28:17) [**11**]. Pressed to the limit, Ahaz resorted to the unthinkable: he rejected the reassuring counsel of Isaiah, dug deep into Jerusalem's treasury, and appealed directly for assistance to none other than Tiglath-pileser himself (2 Kings 16:7–9; 2 Chron. 28:16–19).

Never one to miss an opportunity for imperialism, Tiglath-pileser almost immediately marched his army from Sidon, past Tyre, Acco, and the Carmel mountain range, as far south as the fortress of Gezer, which he assaulted and captured[281] [**12**]. [**See maps 76 and 77.**] The following year Tiglath-pileser invaded Galilee and Gilead, capturing many cities and initiating for the first time inside Israel a policy of deportation (2 Kings 15:29). During this time, Hoshea murdered King Pekah of Israel, assumed his office, and apparently demonstrated his loyalty to Tiglath-pileser by paying him tribute[282] (2 Kings 15:30; 17:1–4). Thus Ahaz had set into motion a chain of events that, within less than ten years, would bring the imposing and violent military machine of Assyria to the doorstep of Samaria, Israel's capital. [**See maps 76 and 77.**]

Hezekiah came to the throne of Jerusalem when the Assyrian empire was reaching its zenith under Sennacherib. But when the Assyrian ruler became preoccupied with a menace in his neighboring Babylonia, Hezekiah decided to rebel (2 Kings 18:7b). This may have laid the foundation for an all-out campaign to the west, apparently the only one undertaken by Sennacherib in that direction. His army marched through the coastal cities of Lebanon before razing a number of Canaanite municipalities, including Acco, Joppa, Ekron, and especially Lachish[283] (2 Kings 18:13; 2 Chron. 32:1; Isa. 36:1) [**13**]. [**See also maps 76 and 77.**] From Lachish, Sennacherib turned his attention toward Jerusalem. He claimed to have taken out some 46 cities within Judah and to have seized over 200,000 prisoners. Continuing to boast, he made reference to "Hezekiah the Judean," saying that "he was locked up inside Jerusalem, like a bird in a cage," and that he "was surrounded by earthworks that made it even unthinkable to him to exit his city."[284] Hezekiah was obliged to pay a huge sum in tribute (2 Kings 18:14–17), but his city was miraculously delivered from annihilation. Sennacherib returned to Nineveh where, some 20 years later, he was assassinated in a palace coup headed by one of his own sons—Adrammelech (cf. 2 Kings 19:36–37; Isa. 37:37–38).[285]

But by the time the Babylonian kingdom had arisen some 100 years later, the limits of God's mercy had been reached. Judah persisted in its evil ways, and the prophet Jeremiah even predicted that the Babylonians would become God's agents to bring about Judah's demise (Jer. 19; 21:3–6). So it was that the Babylonian military hoards of Nebuchadnezzar plundered Judah several times [**map 80**], eventually demolishing Jerusalem, its wall, the palace, and the Temple. And many of Jerusalem's elite were carried away into Babylonian exile (2 Kings 24:1–4; 25:27; 2 Chron. 36:6–7; Jer. 52:28–30) [**14**].

THE BATTLE OF QARQAR

In the sixth year of his reign, Shalmaneser III of Assyria fought a battle against a coalition of 12 western kings, headed by Irhuleni of Hamath and including Ben-hadad II of Damascus and Ahab of Israel.[286] Although the kingdom of the Israelite monarch was far from the center of Shalmaneser's campaign, Ahab exercised control over trade routes from Egypt and Arabia to the north and must have felt threatened by the growing Assyrian expansionism. [**See map 75**.] The battle took place at Qarqar (T. Qarqur),[287] a large and impressive ancient fortress site located on the east bank of the mid-Orontes River, northwest of Hamath. The fortress protected Hamath and the more southerly city-states against an enemy approaching from the north.

The principal source of information concerning this significant battle is Shalmaneser's famous "Monolith Inscription," which was uncovered with a relief figure of the king himself[288] at the modern town of Kurkh (Turkey), located approximately 75 miles northeast of Harran. According to the inscription, Shalmaneser set out from Nineveh in the spring of his sixth year, marching across upper Mesopotamia and receiving tribute at a number of cities, including Pitru (Ausheriya?), Sahlala (T. Sahlan), and presumably Harran. He proceeded from the Balih River over to the Euphrates, forded it at flood stage (probably in June), and exacted taxes from other municipalities, including Carchemish and Melit (Malatya). He then turned south and marched toward Halab/Aleppo, where he received still more tribute and offered sacrifices to the storm god Hadad. From there Shalmaneser penetrated into the realm of Irhuleni and eventually arrived at the city of Qarqar, where—in the summer of 853 B.C.—he pitched his battle line against the confederation.

The relative military strength of Israel in the confederation is evidenced by the observation that Ahab supplied 2,000

The Battle of Qarqar *map 70*

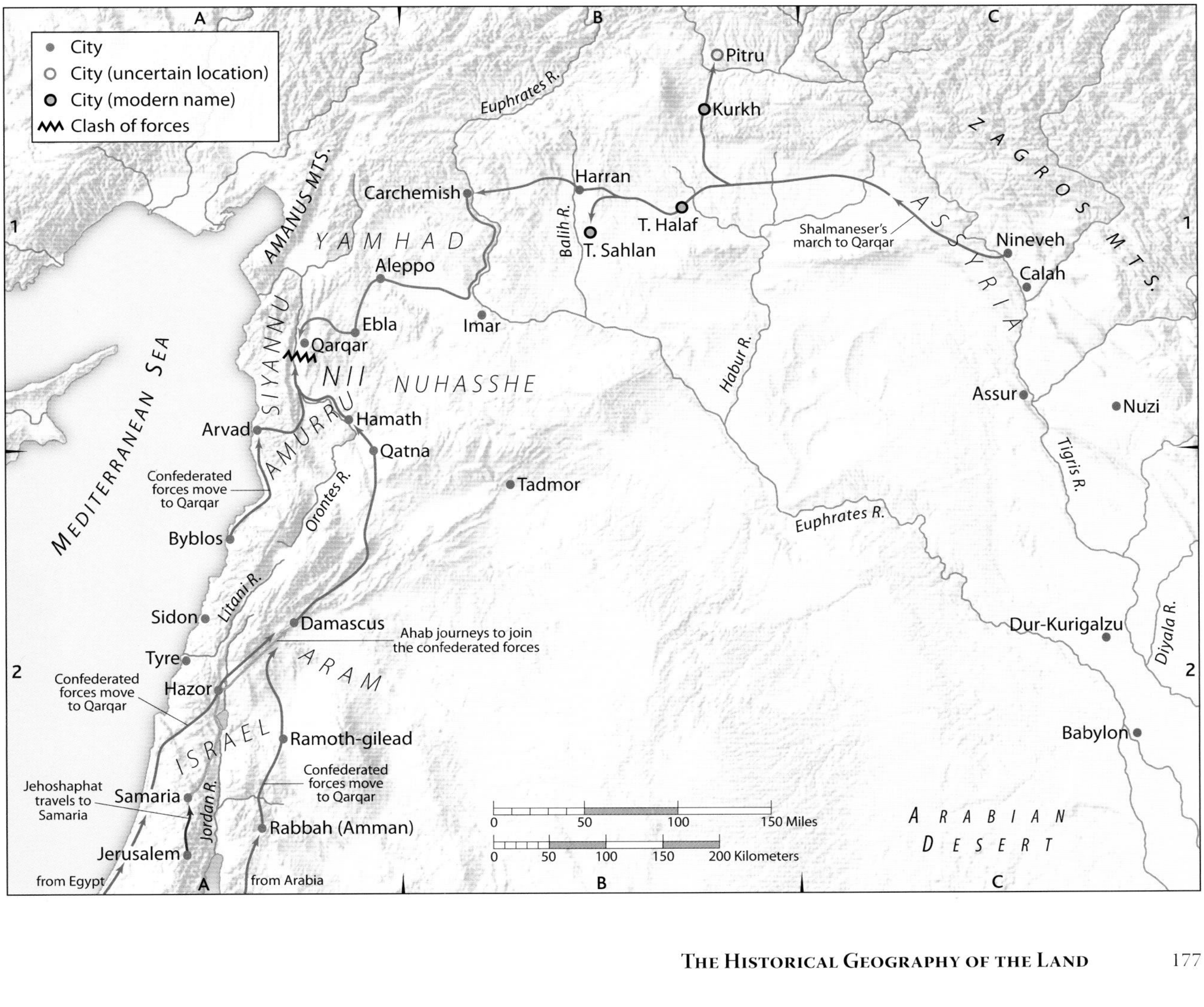

chariots (more than half the total chariot force) and 10,000 soldiers (at least one-sixth of the total infantry). And the fact that forces from faraway Egypt and Arabia were included among the confederation while Moab and Edom were absent may reflect that the latter were Ahab's vassals at that point in time. [**See map 66.**]

Despite the numerous inscriptions of Shalmaneser III that celebrate Qarqar as a stunning Assyrian triumph, the outcome of this confrontation remains very much in doubt today. The fact that Shalmaneser found it necessary to return and again confront a similar western confederation led by the kings of Hamath and Damascus in years 10, 11, and 14 of his reign[289] provides strong indication that the coalition achieved at least a stalemate at Qarqar.

Although the battle of Qarqar is not mentioned directly in the Bible, it is of supreme importance for Old Testament studies. During the period in question, Assyrian dates can be fixed with a margin of error of only one year. Owing to documentary records of this battle, one is able to establish the earliest known exact synchronism between Israelite and Assyrian history and, on that basis, begin to reconstruct the backbone of an Old Testament chronology.

Assyrian records make it possible to date the battle of Qarqar to the year 853 B.C. (± one year).[290] Whatever the outcome at Qarqar, the temporary reduction of the Assyrian threat renewed the conflict between temporary allies Ben-hadad II and Ahab (1 Kings 22:1–36; cf. 20:1–34). One wonders, in fact, if perhaps Ben-hadad was emboldened to renew his contest with Ahab because the latter had suffered disproportionately high casualties at Qarqar (2 Kings 13:7). Equally telling is the fact that Ahab apparently felt the need to enlist the military forces of Judah in his fight against Ben-hadad (1 Kings 22:1–4). In this regard, it is noteworthy that Moab attempted to regain its independence from Israel upon the death of Ahab (2 Kings 3:4–5).[291] In any event, the importance of the Ahab/Ben-hadad renewed confrontation lies in the fact that it must have taken place within the same calendar year of Ahab's reign as did the battle of Qarqar.

This assertion can be sustained on the strength of other evidence. Four inscriptions concur that Shalmaneser III boasted how, in his 18th year, he crossed the Euphrates River for the 16th time and in the course of his campaign there received tribute from "Jehu, man of Bit-Humri" ("house of Omri").[292] [**See maps 76 and 77.**] Shalmaneser's 18th year manifestly corresponds to the year 841 B.C. (± one year).[293] In other words, Shalmaneser claims to have encountered Ahab in his sixth regnal year and Jehu in his 18th year.

Ahab was succeeded by Ahaziah, who was officially accorded two years of reign (1 Kings 22:51). Ahaziah was followed in turn by Joram,[294] whose length of reign was 12 years before he was murdered by his successor, Jehu (2 Kings 3:1). On the surface, this seems to imply that the reigns of Ahab and Jehu were separated by approximately 14 (2 + 12) years. It has been demonstrated, however, that Israel's kings in that era followed an Egyptian pattern of ancient chronology called a "nonaccession" (antedating) system, according to which a king began to count his first regnal year from the very day he ascended to the throne. The new king's first year, therefore, corresponded to his accession year, and his second year was figured as commencing with the beginning of the new calendar year, even if the new year should have begun only weeks after the new king's accession to the throne. Each king was credited with a whole year for any part of which he reigned.[295] This means, then, that the supposed 14 years that separated Ahab and Jehu must actually be collapsed into an interval of only 12 years: Ahab's last year would have corresponded to Ahaziah's accession (first) year, and Ahaziah's last year would have been coeval with Joram's accession year.

Some scholars have attempted to argue that the battle of Qarqar need not have taken place in the final year of Ahab's reign, that the Israelite king might have continued to live for another three or four years after fighting at Qarqar.[296] Yet the only way that king Jehu could have paid Assyrian tribute in Shalmaneser's 18th year (841 B.C.), as noted on numerous Assyrian artifacts, is for Ahab to have died during Shalmaneser's sixth year (853 B.C.)—the date of the battle of Qarqar. Therefore, this date has become a cardinal datum point for the reconstruction of an Old Testament chronology, especially as related to the united monarchy and divided monarchy periods.

THE EXPLOITS OF JEHU AGAINST THE HOUSE OF AHAB

The turf warfare between Aram and Israel that had claimed the life of Ahab (1 Kings 22:34–35; 2 Chron. 18:33–34) continued in a series of confrontations during the reign of his son, Joram (2 Kings 6:9—8:28). In one of those border clashes, Joram was wounded at Ramoth-gilead and retreated west to Jezreel to receive medical assistance. While there, Joram was visited by Ahaziah, king of Judah, who had fought as his ally on the northeastern front (2 Kings 8:28–29; 9:16; 2 Chron. 22:5–6).

Also involved in the battle at Ramoth-gilead was a veteran military commander named Jehu who was renowned as a charioteer. As a younger soldier, Jehu had apparently been among Ahab's bodyguards (2 Kings 9:25–26; cf. 1 Kings 21:1–24) and had overheard the prediction of doom Elijah pronounced on the line of Ahab and Jezebel. Years later, having been anointed as king of Israel by a servant of the prophet Elisha, and in the absence of Joram, Jehu moved with alacrity to be publicly acclaimed king by the remainder of the Israelite army (2 Kings 9:4–13).

Wasting no time, Jehu drove his chariot from Ramoth-gilead to Jezreel. His surprise arrival quickly resulted in the deaths of both Joram and his mother, Jezebel (2 Kings 9:24–26, 30–37). King Ahaziah fled south toward Beth-haggan (Jenin), was pursued, and was wounded while riding in his chariot near Ibleam. He managed to escape to Megiddo, where he later died in uncertain circumstances (2 Kings 9:27–29; 2 Chron. 22:9).[297] As Jehu continued in the direction of Samaria, he encountered some of Ahaziah's kinsmen near Beth-eked (Kefr Ra'i?) who were headed north to Jezreel, apparently to join Ahaziah's hospitality mission (and who were unaware of recent developments there). When told of their intentions, Jehu ruthlessly had them executed (2 Kings 10:12–14; 2 Chron. 22:8–9).

Having already received the humble submission of the political authorities in the city of Samaria, Jehu continued to slaughter the biological line of Ahab. As a final step, Jehu entered what was now his own capital city, where he engaged in a massacre against Baal and Baal worshipers in Israel (2 Kings 10:1–11, 18–27). With unbridled enthusiasm and callous resolve, Jehu brought the house of Ahab to an end and began his own dynasty. It was destined to become the longest-lasting dynasty in the history of the northern kingdom, continuing until the time of Zechariah (2 Kings 15:8–12; cf. 10:30).

The Exploits of Jehu against the House of Ahab *map 71*

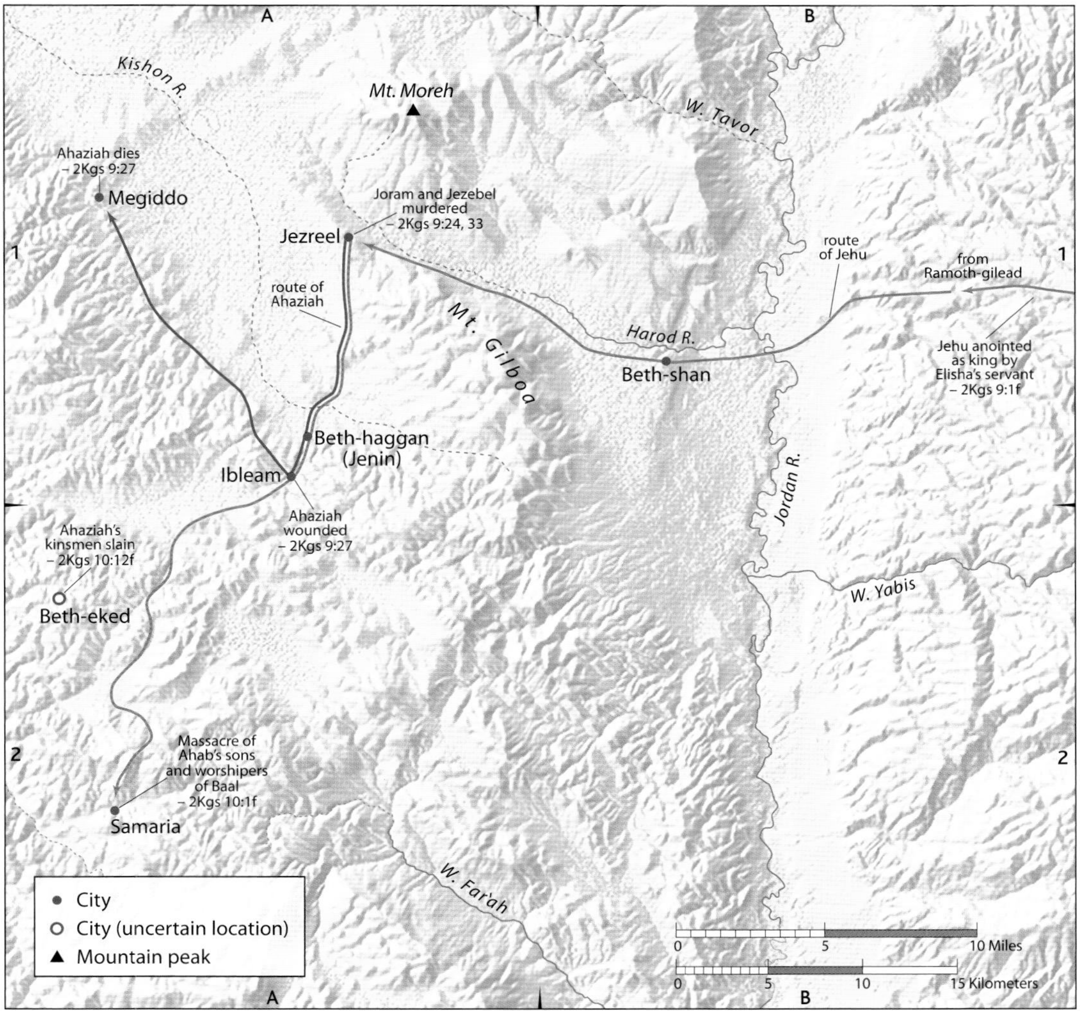

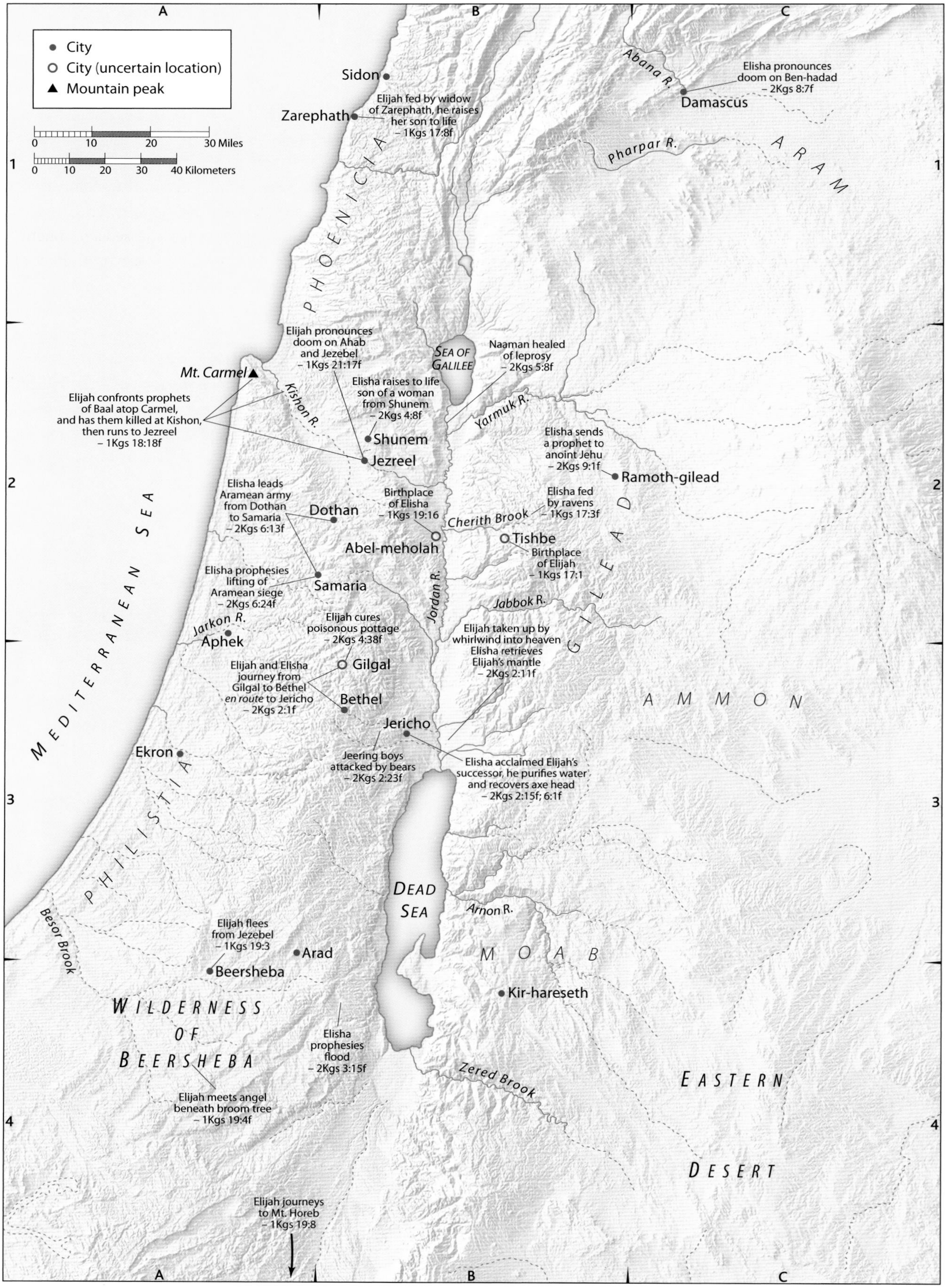
City
City (uncertain location)
Mountain peak
0 10 20 30 Miles
0 10 20 30 40 Kilometers
A
B
C
1
2
3
4
Sidon
Zarephath
Elijah fed by widow of Zarephath, he raises her son to life – 1Kgs 17:8f
Damascus
Elisha pronounces doom on Ben-hadad – 2Kgs 8:7f
Abana R.
Pharpar R.
ARAM
PHOENICIA
Elijah pronounces doom on Ahab and Jezebel – 1Kgs 21:17f
SEA OF GALILEE
Naaman healed of leprosy – 2Kgs 5:8f
Mt. Carmel
Kishon R.
Elisha raises to life son of a woman from Shunem – 2Kgs 4:8f
Elijah confronts prophets of Baal atop Carmel, and has them killed at Kishon, then runs to Jezreel – 1Kgs 18:18f
Yarmuk R.
Shunem
Jezreel
Elisha sends a prophet to anoint Jehu – 2Kgs 9:1f
Ramoth-gilead
Elisha leads Aramean army from Dothan to Samaria – 2Kgs 6:13f
Dothan
Birthplace of Elisha – 1Kgs 19:16
Elisha fed by ravens – 1Kgs 17:3f
Cherith Brook
Abel-meholah
Tishbe
Birthplace of Elijah – 1Kgs 17:1
GILEAD
MEDITERRANEAN SEA
Elisha prophesies lifting of Aramean siege – 2Kgs 6:24f
Samaria
Jordan R.
Jabbok R.
Jarkon R.
Aphek
Elijah cures poisonous pottage – 2Kgs 4:38f
Elijah taken up by whirlwind into heaven Elisha retrieves Elijah's mantle – 2Kgs 2:11f
Elijah and Elisha journey from Gilgal to Bethel en route to Jericho – 2Kgs 2:1f
Gilgal
Bethel
AMMON
Jericho
Ekron
Jeering boys attacked by bears – 2Kgs 2:23f
Elisha acclaimed Elijah's successor, he purifies water and recovers axe head – 2Kgs 2:15f; 6:1f
PHILISTIA
DEAD SEA
Arnon R.
Besor Brook
Elijah flees from Jezebel – 1Kgs 19:3
Arad
MOAB
Beersheba
Kir-hareseth
WILDERNESS OF BEERSHEBA
Elisha prophesies flood – 2Kgs 3:15f
Zered Brook
EASTERN DESERT
Elijah meets angel beneath broom tree – 1Kgs 19:4f
Elijah journeys to Mt. Horeb – 1Kgs 19:8

ISRAEL'S PROPHETS

With the foundation of Israel's monarchy came the virtual eclipse of the office of priest. In the initial years, when Samuel proclaimed that Saul had been deposed from his kingly office (1 Sam. 13:13–15; cf. 15:24–29), the priest's separation from the king was tantamount to the separation of God. Saul seems to have been powerless to respond. Only two generations later, however, king Solomon had already garnered sufficient authority to oust Abiathar from his priestly office and to banish him to his hometown (1 Kings 2:26–27)—ample illustration of the uncontested authority that the Israelites soon conferred upon their newly created office of king.

Along with the virtual demise of the priestly office came a concomitant new tendency in Israel toward apostasy and idolatry; levitical religion ceased to be the central focus around which the life of Israel would revolve. And although the prophetic institution had formally existed previously and certainly did not arise merely from national impulse, it was largely this set of historical circumstances that served as the occasion for God to raise up another cycle of prophets. It is fair to state that the office of prophet obtained a more theocratic and public profile. Prophets could advise kings concerning policy or rebuke them concerning sin, while also warning the populace about the abomination of the Canaanites.

Categorization of Israel's prophets is a difficult task, for they came from a diversity of background, tribe, class, and educational distinction. Unlike priests, prophets did not receive their office by birthright, nor did they act according to pattern or prescription (Isa. 20:1–4; Jer. 13:1–7; 27:1—28:16; Ezek. 4:4–17; 5:1–4; Hos. 1:2–9). Some were officers of the state (Isaiah) while others were political outcasts (Elijah, Jeremiah). Some functioned as individuals (Amos) while others functioned within prophetic schools (Elisha). Some uttered predictions (Micaiah) while futuristic prophecy played no role in the lives of others (Nathan, Jonah). Some performed miracles (Elijah) while others did not (Malachi). Some occupied their office for decades (Isaiah, Jeremiah) while others, as far as we know, functioned in that capacity for only months (Haggai). What Israel's prophets *did* share was a common belief, vision, and function. Each had a distinct call of God to the office, each possessed a prophetic awareness of history, and each functioned as a proclaimer of the Word of God.

Israel's Prophets ***map 73***

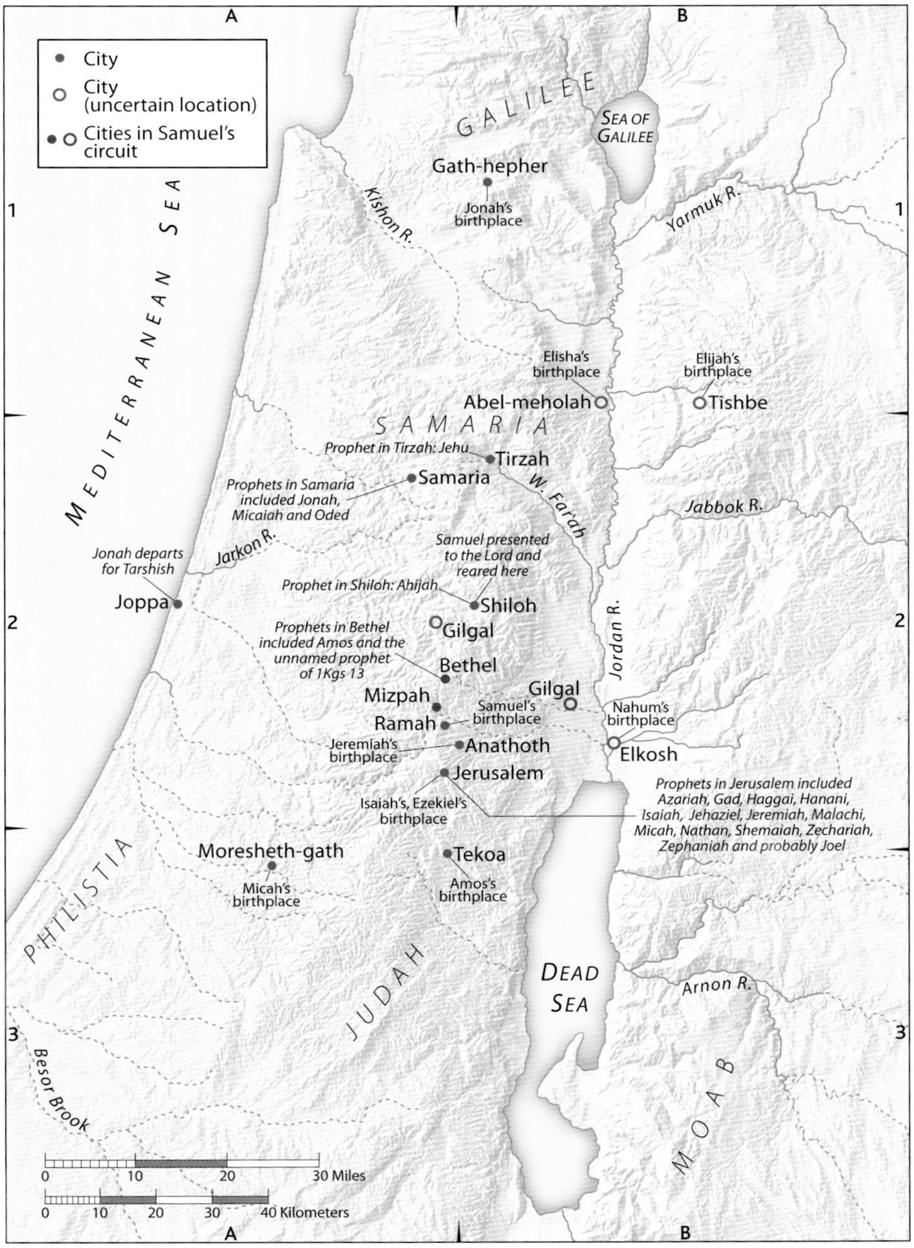

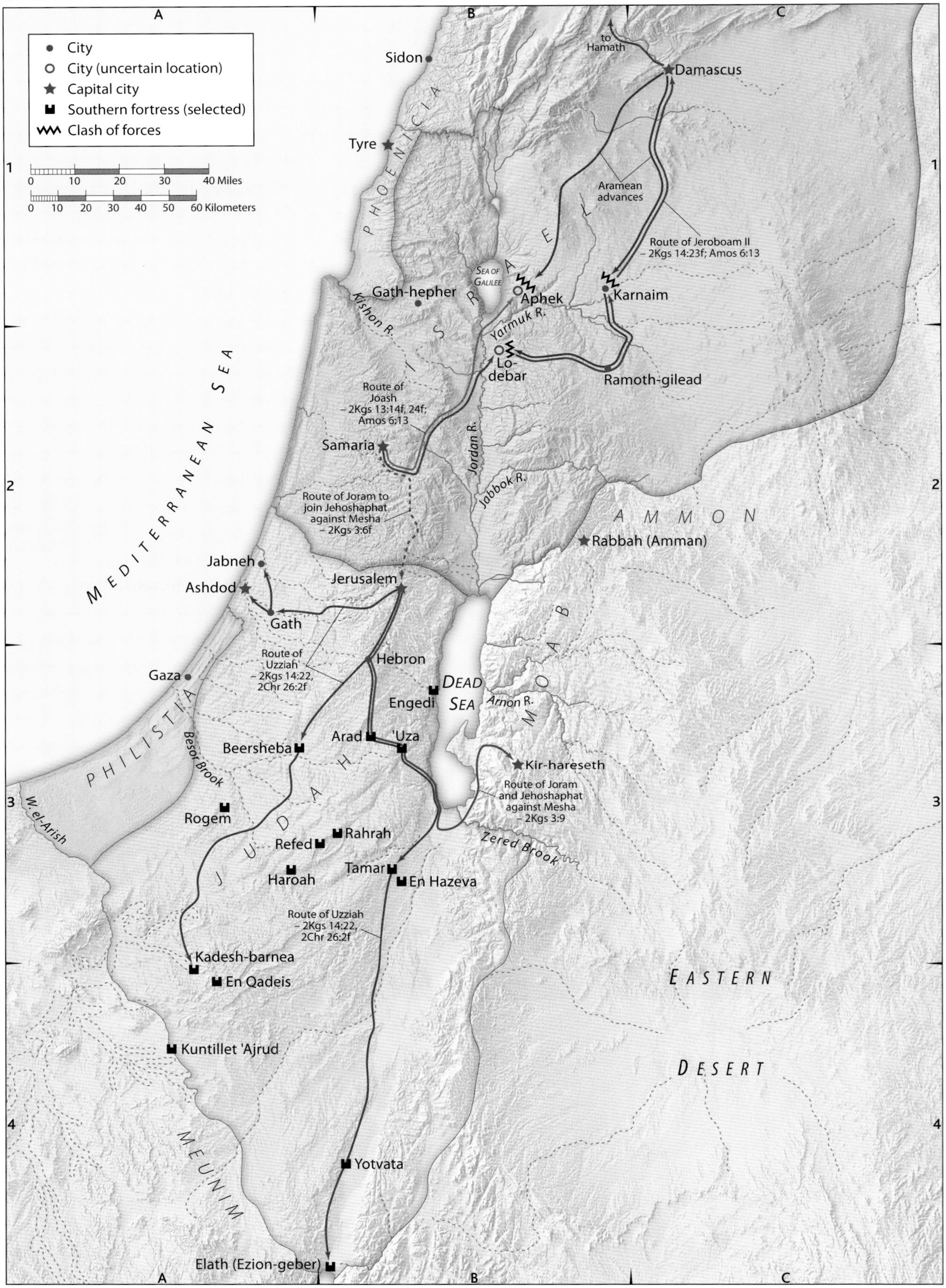

City
City (uncertain location)
Capital city
Southern fortress (selected)
Clash of forces
0 10 20 30 40 Miles
0 10 20 30 40 50 60 Kilometers
to Hamath
Damascus
Sidon
Tyre
PHOENICIA
ISRAEL
Aramean advances
Route of Jeroboam II – 2Kgs 14:23f; Amos 6:13
SEA OF GALILEE
Aphek
Karnaim
Gath-hepher
Kishon R.
Yarmuk R.
Lo-debar
Ramoth-gilead
MEDITERRANEAN SEA
Route of Joash – 2Kgs 13:14f, 24f; Amos 6:13
Samaria
Jordan R.
Jabbok R.
Route of Joram to join Jehoshaphat against Mesha – 2Kgs 3:6f
AMMON
Rabbah (Amman)
Jabneh
Ashdod
Jerusalem
Gath
MOAB
Route of Uzziah – 2Kgs 14:22, 2Chr 26:2f
Hebron
Gaza
DEAD SEA
Engedi
Arnon R.
PHILISTIA
Besor Brook
Arad
'Uza
Beersheba
Kir-hareseth
Route of Joram and Jehoshaphat against Mesha – 2Kgs 3:9
W. el-Arish
Rogem
JUDAH
Rahrah
Refed
Zered Brook
Haroah
Tamar
En Hazeva
Route of Uzziah – 2Kgs 14:22, 2Chr 26:2f
Kadesh-barnea
En Qadeis
EASTERN
Kuntillet 'Ajrud
DESERT
MEUNIM
Yotvata
Elath (Ezion-geber)
A
B
C
1
2
3
4

THE ASSYRIAN EMPIRE

The term "Assyria" designating a unified territorial state first appeared in the historical record during the reign of Ashur-uballit I, around the year 1350 B.C.[298] At that time people from the city of Assur decided to capture the city of Nineveh and throw off a Mitanni yoke, which had lasted a little more than 100 years.[299] From that time until the Assyrian city of Assur collapsed in 614 B.C., what might be called the "heartland of Assyria" was never lost by the Assyrians. [**See map 79.**]

Assyria's heartland in the days of Ashur-uballit I comprised the plains that straddled the middle Tigris from a point just north of Nineveh, where the Mesopotamian steppe gives rise to higher mountains, to a place along the river just west of Eshnunna, where again a chain of mountains interrupts the plain. A tablet in the Amarna archive[300] sent from Ashur-uballit I to the Egyptian pharaoh and addressed to a "brother" (equal) suggests the presence of a unified territorial state in northeastern Mesopotamia. Adad-nirari I added lands from Babylon to Mitanni, located in the upper Habur River basin, which meant that the imperial border also extended as far west as the Euphrates River. By the reign of Tukulti-ninurta I, the land of Assyria arched essentially from Babylon to Carchemish, on the upper Euphrates, but after his death Assyria fell into internal decline until the ninth century B.C.

After a period of stagnation, a renaissance of Assyrian imperialistic aggression began during the time of Ashurnasirpal II. His actions included frequent (almost annual) campaigns eliciting tribute, wholesale and massive deportations, and the conversion of countries into Assyrian provinces ruled by Assyrian governors—the type of havoc described in the Bible. [**See map 78.**] This Assyrian monarch made significant incursions into the Zagros mountains in the east, conquered Nairi, and began to make inroads into what was at that time the powerful kingdom of Urartu, a sustained rival of Assyria with its elevated and imposing capital city of Tushpa on the shore of Lake Van. Later Shalmaneser III gained control of the major Phoenician coastal cities (Arvad, Byblos, Tyre, and Sidon), areas of inland Syria (e.g., Carchemish, Hamath, and Damascus), and southern Lebanon. Shalmaneser also managed to keep the Urartian foes in the north at bay as Assyrian annual campaigns now began to gain ascendancy.

Tiglath-pileser III continued and even expanded Assyrian aggression by establishing vassal treaties and implementing massive deportations. He seized Sumer, effectively neutralized the powerful kingdoms of Urartu and Kummuhu in the north, and gained ground in vicinity of Damascus and Bashan. Sargon II successfully fought major wars in Canaan, Phrygia, Urartu, Babylonia, and along the Median frontier in the east. Sennacherib wrested much of Judah from the hands of king Hezekiah and destroyed the city of Babylon. Later, Esarhaddon gained temporary control of Elam, seized Transjordania, and extended Assyria's dominion into Lower Egypt by sacking Memphis. The empire reached its maximal territorial extent under Ashurbanipal, who solidified Assyrian control of Elam, captured most of the region of Lydia, and seized Thebes in Upper Egypt. If one is to believe his boast, he claimed to have carried back to Nineveh (some 1,440 miles) two huge obelisks, each weighing an estimated 170 tons, as trophies of his triumph.[301]

Over the course of its existence, Assyria's empire builders created four successive capital cities. The first capital city was Assur, chosen by Assur-uballit I (c. 1350–875 B.C.). Assyrian resurgence during the time of Ashurnasirpal II manifested itself in the erection of a huge and magnificent new capital city at Calah/Nimrud (c. 875–720 B.C.), built over the remains of what had been a small village.[302] During the reign of Sargon II, a third capital city was constructed at

The upper Euphrates river at Carchemish, site of an important Assyrian administrative center. The river could be more easily forded at Carchemish, and so Assyrian monarchs regularly crossed here into the Levant.

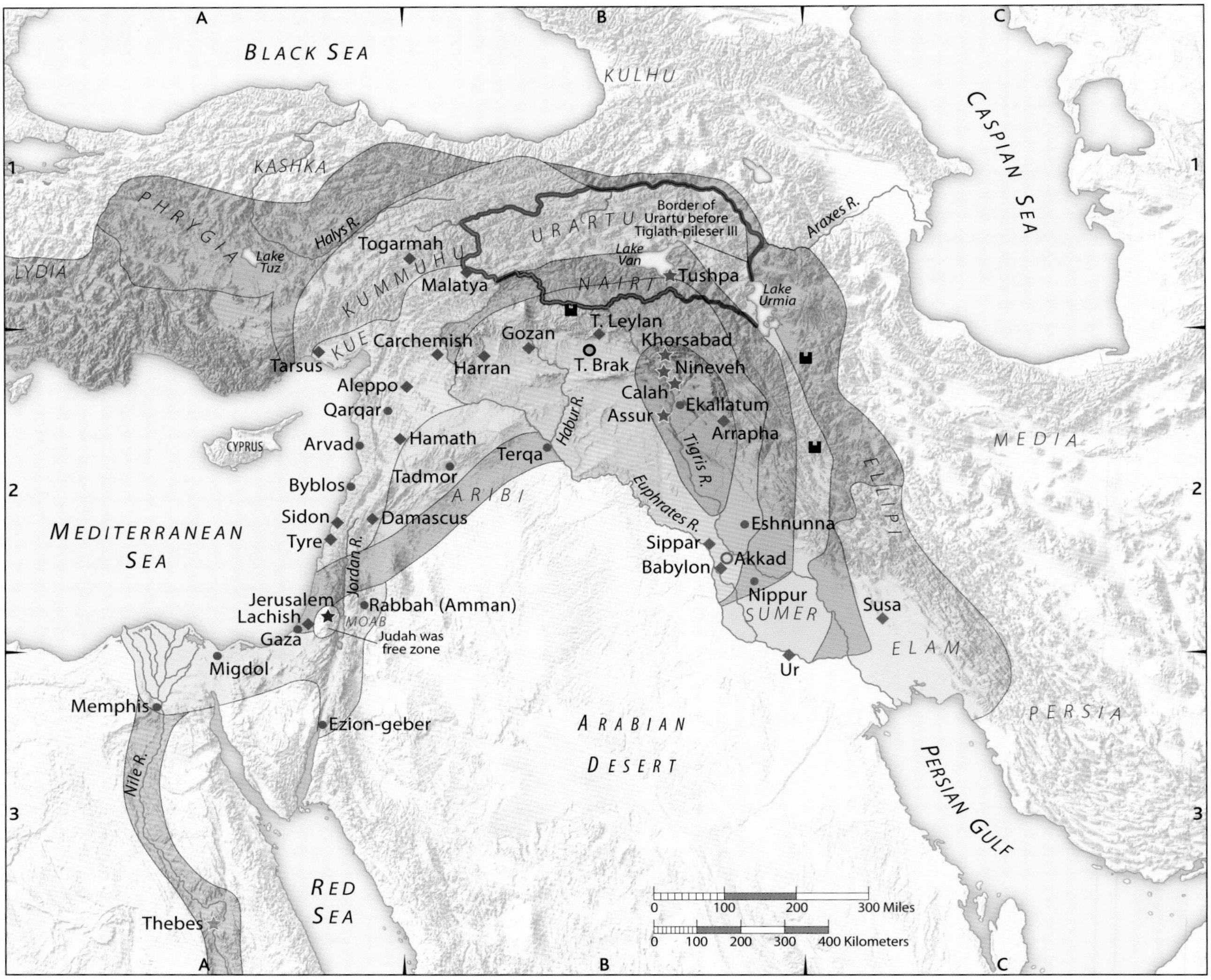

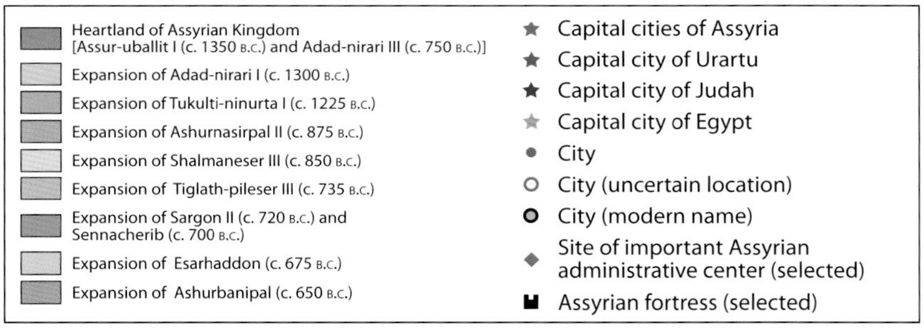

Khorsabad/Dur-Sharrukin ("the fortress of Sargon," c. 720–700 B.C.). Finally, the capital city was moved by Sennacherib to his greatly expanded city of Nineveh (c. 700–612 B.C.), though this city shows evidence of existence as early as the seventh millennium B.C., followed by a succession of occupation until the time of Sennacherib.

A final observation may be relevant and helpful here: no names of actual biblical characters living before the time of the divided monarchy have thus far been attested unambiguously in ancient secular literature, nor is there mention of secular notables in the earliest biblical narratives.[303] It is surely significant to note *when* biblical figures (usually kings) began to have their names etched onto secular documentation and, coincidentally, when foreign monarchs began to appear by name in the biblical record. It is precisely when the Assyrians experienced their renaissance in the ninth century B.C. and began to march west as far as Canaan—when for the first time they came into direct political contact and even military conflict with Israel's divided kingdom. At that point, references to actual biblical characters begin to appear in secular annals and on slabs and other artifacts. No less significant is the appearance of actual names of Assyrian royalty in the biblical testimony at exactly that same time. And from that point forward until the collapse of the Assyrian Empire, *every* Assyrian monarch—without exception—is mentioned by name in the Bible![304]

THE ASSYRIAN CAMPAIGNS AGAINST ISRAEL AND JUDAH

As previously noted, Assyrian expansion westward brought their powerful army onto Israelite soil. [**See map 70; cf. map 75.**] In the year 841 B.C., Shalmaneser III journeyed west by way of Damascus, marched across northern Israel as far as Beth-arbel (Hos. 10:14) and even on to Mt. Hauran. He also traveled west of the Sea of Galilee as far as the vicinity of Megiddo (perhaps where Jehu paid tribute) and Mt. Carmel.[305] From there he began a trek north, past Tyre and Sidon, as far as the mouth of the el-Kabir River [**map 4**], where he carved a victory monument of his campaign on a nearby cliff.[306]

Some 45 years later, another Assyrian monarch—Adad-nirari III—turned westward and subdued several political entities across North Syria, ultimately entering Israelite territory. In this case the Assyrian boasted that he received

Assyria's Earlier Campaigns against Israel

map 76

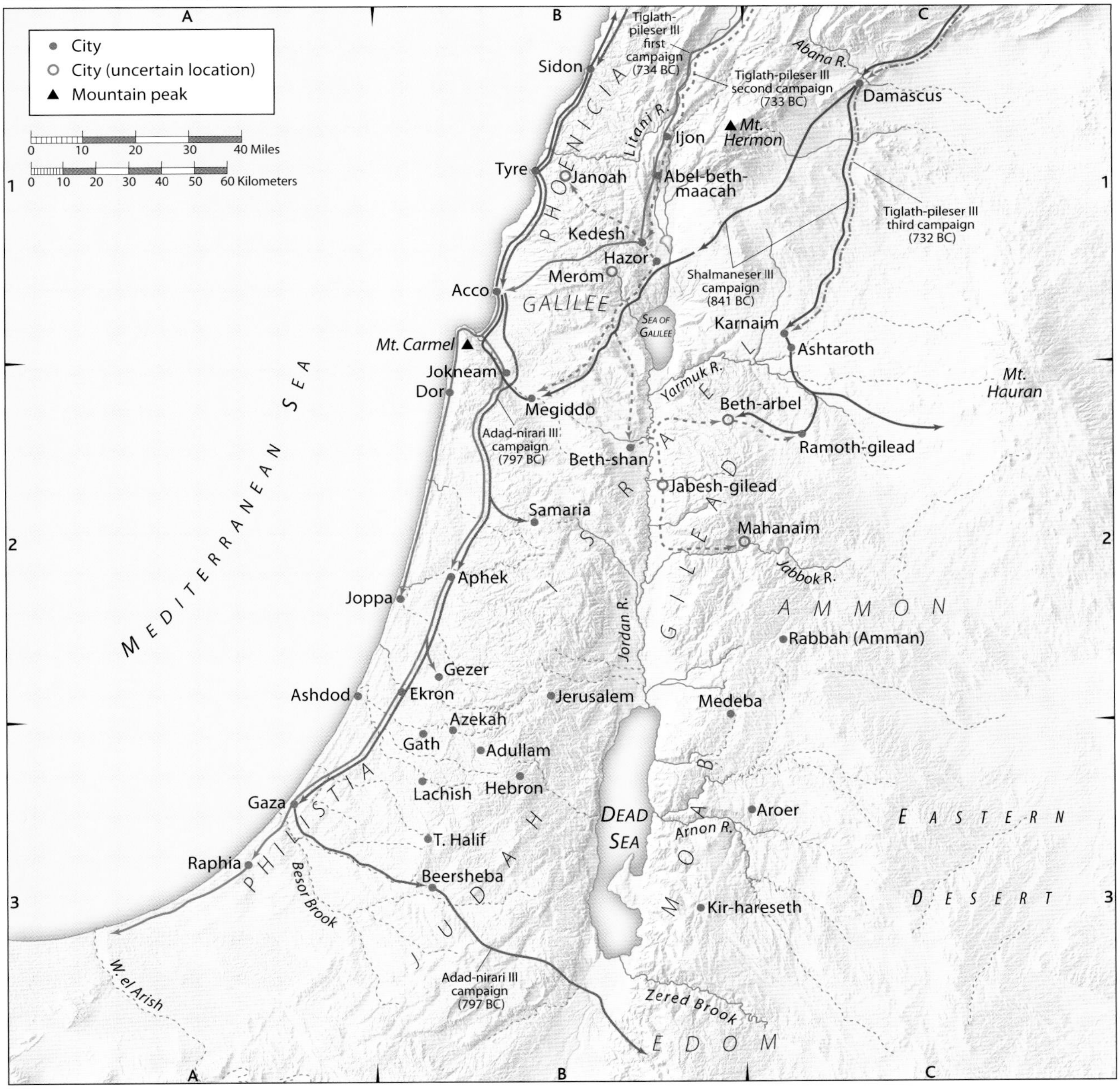

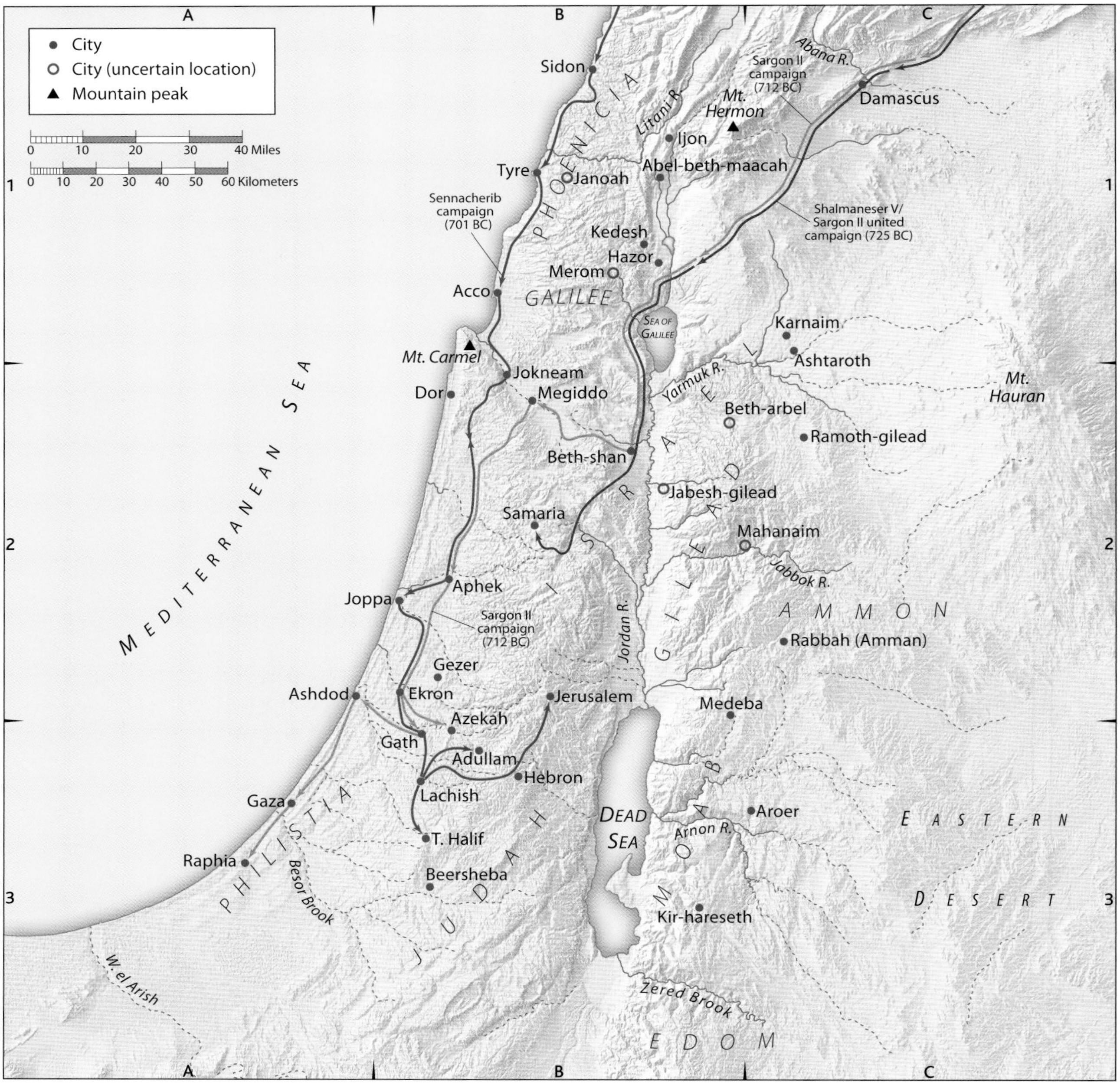

tribute from various Phoenician cities (Arvad, Sidon, and Tyre) and Mansuate, a province in the vicinity of Damascus. Then he received tribute from "Joash the Samarian,"[307] presumably at Samaria.[308] From there he is said to have moved on to subdue the territories of Philistia and Edom.

Data on the several western campaigns of Tiglath-pileser III into Canaan are considerable and diverse in nature, understandably leading to varied interpretations. It seems preferable to interpret the data in the following manner:

1. In 734 B.C. Tiglath-pileser III marched south past the coastal cities of Sidon, Tyre, and Acco, and arrived at the Mt. Carmel range. Continuing south along the coastal plains, he laid siege to the city of Gezer, which fell in due course. [**See map 68.**] From there the Assyrian marched into Philistia, to Gaza, and on to the river of Egypt (W. el-Arish) where he established a base of military operations.[309]
2. The following year Tiglath-pileser marched directly against the city of Damascus,[310] perhaps as a result of a Judahite request for intervention (2 Kings 16:7–9; 2 Chron. 28:16–20), and came more directly against the northern kingdom itself. This time he marched into Galilee, capturing such towns of Ijon (T. ed-Dibbin), Abel-beth-maacah (T. Abil el-Qamh), Hazor, Kedesh, and Janoah (Yanuh?). Tiglath-pileser is said to have conquered the "entire region of Naphtali" (2 Kings 15:29; cf. Isa. 9:1),[311] and to have deported perhaps as many as 13,500 Israelite captives to upper Mesopotamia. [**See map 81.**] He apparently crossed

Palestine after the Fall of the Northern Kingdom

map 78

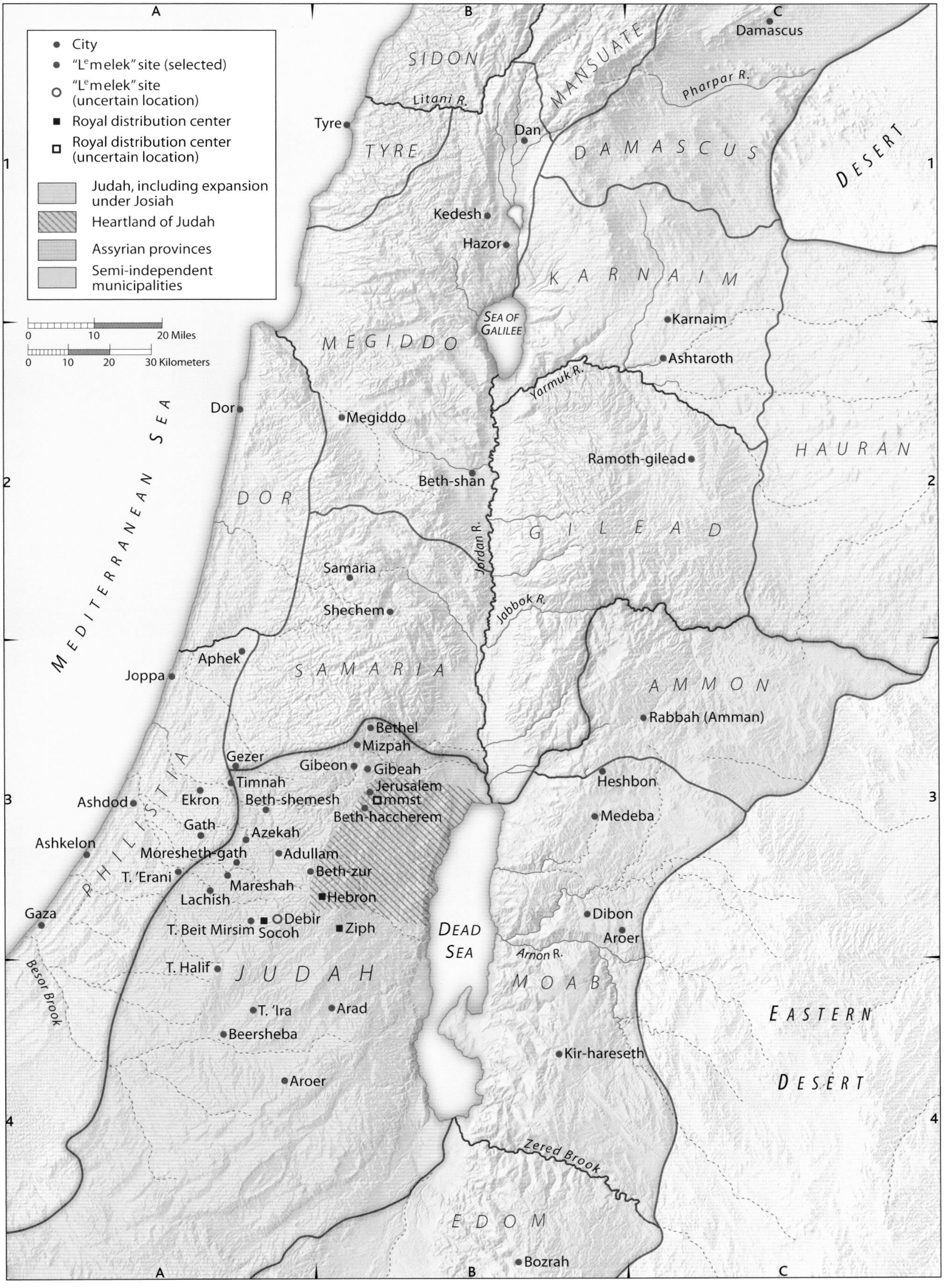

City
"Lᵉmelek" site (selected)
"Lᵉmelek" site (uncertain location)
Royal distribution center
Royal distribution center (uncertain location)
Judah, including expansion under Josiah
Heartland of Judah
Assyrian provinces
Semi-independent municipalities
0 10 20 Miles
0 10 20 30 Kilometers
SIDON
Litani R.
Tyre
TYRE
MANSUATE
Damascus
Pharpar R.
DAMASCUS
DESERT
Dan
Kedesh
Hazor
KARNAIM
SEA OF GALILEE
Karnaim
Ashtaroth
MEGIDDO
Yarmuk R.
Dor
Megiddo
MEDITERRANEAN SEA
HAURAN
Ramoth-gilead
Beth-shan
DOR
Jordan R.
GILEAD
Samaria
Shechem
Jabbok R.
Aphek
Joppa
SAMARIA
AMMON
Rabbah (Amman)
Bethel
Mizpah
Gezer
Gibeon
Gibeah
Timnah
Jerusalem
mmst
Heshbon
Ashdod
Ekron
Beth-shemesh
Beth-haccherem
PHILISTIA
Gath
Azekah
Medeba
Ashkelon
Moresheth-gath
Adullam
T. 'Erani
Beth-zur
Mareshah
Lachish
Hebron
Gaza
Debir
T. Beit Mirsim
Socoh
Ziph
DEAD SEA
Dibon
Aroer
Arnon R.
Besor Brook
T. Halif
JUDAH
MOAB
T. 'Ira
Arad
EASTERN DESERT
Beersheba
Kir-hareseth
Aroer
Zered Brook
EDOM
Bozrah
A
B
C
1
2
3
4

the Jordan River on this occasion and marched as far east as Ramoth-gilead (T. Ramith),[312] annexing portions of the Gilead region (1 Chron. 5:6, 26) and again engaging in deportation. It was perhaps in this moment of crisis that Hoshea struck down Israelite king Pekah and then paid his allegiance to the Assyrian (2 Kings 15:30; 17:3b), averting the annihilation of Israel, at least temporarily.

3. It appears that Tiglath-pileser's earlier actions left Damascus completely isolated. Accordingly, in 732 B.C. the Assyrian monarch successfully focused on this target.[313] He must also have ventured as far south as Ashtaroth because that city is thought to be referenced and depicted in an Assyrian limestone relief found at Nimrud.[314]

Isaiah's pronouncement of doom against Damascus (Isa. 7:1–9) was now realized, but the destruction of Samaria awaited another Assyrian monarch.[315] In that regard, the Assyrian army of Shalmaneser V came west in the year 725 B.C. and laid siege to several cities of Phoenicia and Israel, including the capital city of Samaria (2 Kings 17:1–41 [esp. vv. 4–6]; 18:9–12). For three years the Israelite capital city was able to resist capitulation,[316] but in August or September 722 B.C., Samaria fell to the Assyrian army[317] and deportation was yet again imposed. [**See map 81.**]

Both the Old Testament (2 Kings 17:3b–6; 18:9–12) and the Babylonian Chronicle[318] attribute this event to the reign of Shalmaneser. However, Shalmaneser's successor, Sargon II, takes credit for victory over Samaria in at least eight different inscriptions.[319] We know that Shalmaneser V died in 722 B.C., in the month of December,[320] and that Sargon immediately assumed the throne. So we can be assured that Shalmaneser was still at the helm of the ruthless Assyrian military machinery when the city of Samaria fell in the summer of 722 B.C., even though there is now evidence to suggest that some of Sargon's claims may relate to a further campaign against Samaria he conducted in the year 720 B.C.[321] Whatever the case, Isaiah's prediction had run full circle.

Sargon II found it necessary to return to Canaan several times after his 720 B.C. assault of Samaria. His expedition of 712 B.C. is of particular importance, not least because it seems to be the cause for the only biblical citation of the king. In this instance Sargon marched south and quelled a serious anti-Assyrian coalition, apparently having spread from Philistia to towns in Judah, Edom, and Moab,[322] which were perhaps acting in partnership with Egypt. Several Sargon texts indicate that this seditious activity was centered in Ashdod, so the Philistine city was singled out for particularly harsh reprisal (Isa. 20:1), though the Assyrian also confronted other towns in the vicinity, including Gaza, Raphia, Samaria, Ekron, and Gath.[323]

Yet another Assyrian campaign against this land was conducted by Sennacherib in 701 B.C.[324] He marched south, capturing the seacoast cities of Arvad, Byblos, Sarepta, Sidon, Tyre, Achzib, and Acco without a fight. He also asserted that he quickly seized a number of towns that had belonged to the king of Ashkelon (Joppa) as well as the city of Ekron (T. Miqne).

At some point in this campaign, Sennacherib faced an Egyptian/Cushite coalition that had traveled north to aid the people of Ekron (2 Kings 18:21–24; Isa. 36:6–9). The ensuing battle took place in the plain of Eltekeh, between Joppa and Ekron. The question is *when* Sennacherib faced this inveterate foe. It seems definitely to have taken place prior to when his army arrived in Jerusalem and probably after he had conquered Ekron,[325] but beyond that it remains unclear.

A reasonable argument can be made that it was from Lachish that the Assyrian army went out to clash with Egypt. For one thing, Lachish was a significant city and the scene of a decisive military victory prominently commemorated by Sennacherib in wall reliefs found in his royal palace at Nineveh.[326] [**See also map 81.**] For another, Lachish became Sennacherib's headquarters from where he challenged Hezekiah in Jerusalem (2 Kings 18:14, 17; Isa. 36:2; 37:8; 2 Chron. 32:9). Having dispatched the Egyptians, Sennacherib then set his sights on the realm of "Hezekiah the Judean" and his capital city of Jerusalem. He made threats and boasts [**map 68**], and Hezekiah paid an enormously heavy price in tribute (2 Kings 18:14–16), yet Sennacherib was denied his ultimate objective. In the words of Isaiah, God had pierced the king's nose with his hook, placed a bit in his mouth, and turned him back toward Nineveh (2 Kings 19:28; Isa. 37:29).

THE BATTLE OF CARCHEMISH

The Assyrian Empire reached its zenith during the time of king Sennacherib. During his rule an era of *Pax Assyriaca* ("Assyrian peace")[327] was fully realized. By the time Assyrian hordes descended upon Jerusalem in 701 B.C. (2 Kings 18:13—19:37; 2 Chron. 32:1–23; Isa 36:1—38:22), the ruthless and imposing imperial colossus had already conquered a territory roughly the size of modern Europe. Yet Assyrian imperialistic power was reaching its natural limits because of the demands of governing such an expanse. Sennacherib and his immediate successors are noted as much for their administrative, domestic, and literary achievements as for their prowess on the battlefield.

Sennacherib was responsible for the celebrated grandeur of the city of Nineveh with its walls stretching almost two and a half miles in length, 15 metal city gates, ornate palace, numerous temples, public housing, armory, large plantation with a cotton plant, zoological gardens, and many other features. Great engineering skill is reflected in the construction of his new capital. The Tebiltu River joined the Tigris right at Nineveh. A dam built on the Tebiltu prevented erosion of the tell on which the city was built, led to the agricultural recovery of what had been marshland, and provided water for a network of canals Sennacherib dug throughout the district.

Efforts to locate new sources of building materials led to the discovery of a new, copious supply of fresh water in the mountains near modern Bavian. To bring this source of drinking water to his capital, Sennacherib constructed a stone channel more than 50 miles long. In what was clearly one of the earliest efforts in civil engineering, he built a stone aqueduct that spanned a branch of the Gomer River at the modern city of Jerwan, permitting the new supply of water to continue its southward course toward Nineveh.[328]

Two generations later, Sennacherib's grandson Ashurbanipal channeled literature and learning into Nineveh with the establishment of a large royal library. Embodying more than 25,000 texts and fragments, and representing virtually every phase of Mesopotamian society, the library of Ashurbanipal remains one of the most important sources of Akkadian literature.[329]

Perhaps it was a preoccupation with cultural advancement that made the once mighty Assyrian Empire such easy prey. Within slightly more than a decade (626–612 B.C.), Assyrian

The Battle of Carchemish *map 79*

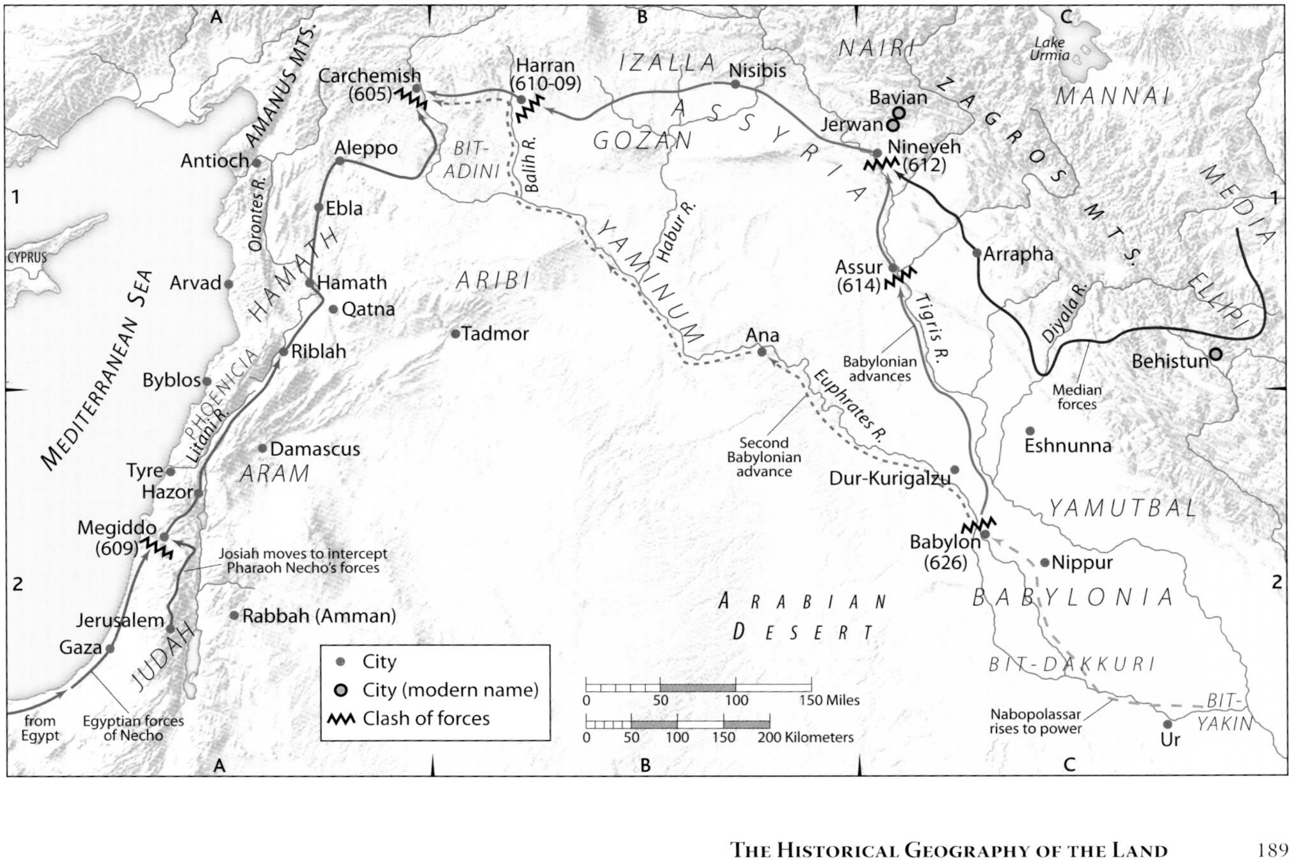

dominance both at home and abroad came to an abrupt end. The individual largely responsible for this rapid demise was Nabopolassar, a Chaldean prince from the region of Bit-Yakin (near the confluence point of the Tigris and Euphrates rivers) who would become the father of Nebuchadnezzar. Having already confederated several diverse political forces within Babylonia, Nabopolassar wrested the city of Babylon from Assyrian control in 626 B.C. Using that city as his command base, the Chaldean gained control of the whole of Babylonia within four years.[330]

After a few years, Nabopolassar set his sights on Assyria itself. Unfortunately for Assyria, king Cyaxares and the Medes decided to enter this struggle at the same time. Though Nabopolassar was unsuccessful in his initial attempt to overthrow the city of Assur, the former capital city was subsequently crushed and its citizens massacred in the year 614 B.C., presumably by Median forces. Nabopolassar and Cyaxares met near Assur to conclude a formal political alliance confirmed by a marriage between their two dynasties, so it was a Medo-Babylonian coalition that waged war against the Assyrians for a time.[331] Leading this new confederation, Nabopolassar marched against the citadel at Nineveh later in 614 B.C., and then in 612 B.C., after a short siege, he was able to destroy this last bastion of Assyrian imperialism.[332] Two years later Nabopolassar's confederated army marched via Izalla and expelled the Assyrians from the precincts of Harran. They rapidly retreated west to the very edge of Mesopotamia, at Carchemish.[333]

Somewhat unexpectedly, Pharaoh Necho II endeavored at that moment to come to the aid of the retreating Assyrians (2 Kings 23:29–30; 2 Chron. 35:20–22). Intending to lead his Egyptian army to Carchemish, Necho drove northward through Canaan. It was at that point that Josiah, king of Judah, unwisely sought to interject himself into the shifting balance of political power. He had no affinity whatsoever for Assyrian aggression, and he sought to intercept the northward march of Necho at the strategic pass of Megiddo (2 Kings 23:8–20; 2 Chron. 34:6–7).[334] But Josiah's effort proved both fruitless and fatal: being greatly outclassed in manpower and technology, his army was decimated, and Josiah himself was slain in the battle (2 Kings 23:29–30; 2 Chron. 35:20–24).

As a parenthetical aside, the reigns of Necho II (610–595 B.C.) and Josiah (640–609 B.C.) represent a very narrow margin of chronological overlap. This synchronism is therefore very precise and quite remarkable, in view of the fact that the computation of Egyptian chronology and biblical chronology for this period is based on completely independent and unrelated criteria.

Josiah's untimely death at the hands of the Egyptians carried profound psychological implications for the covenant community living in Jerusalem at the time, since the messianic hopes they had pinned on their king had falsely led them to believe that Jerusalem would remain secure amid the political turmoil all around. But Josiah's death signaled a new wave of Egyptian presence in Jerusalem (2 Kings 23:31–37), a presence that influenced quite seminally the pro-Egyptian/pro-Babylonian factionalism that had come to dominate political life during the last 20 years of Judah.

Meanwhile, Babylonian forces now under the command of crown prince Nebuchadnezzar laid siege to the city of Carchemish in 607 B.C., where for the next two years they repelled every effort on the part of the Assyrian-Egyptian coalition to regain Mesopotamian turf. Finally, in 605 B.C., in one of the supreme turning points of Near Eastern history, the two armies collided in full-scale confrontation. Nebuchadnezzar inflicted a sweeping defeat on his foes,[335] and one of the most long-lasting and remarkable civilizations of the ancient world perished as a result (Isa. 14:24–27; Nah. 2:1–10; Zeph. 2:13).

Historians often point out a strange irony in the wake of this event. In the first Christian century, Assyria finally reemerged into history as a Parthian territory known as Adiabene.[336] One of its early rulers, Izates, converted to Judaism, was circumcised, and decreed that the royal house should follow suit.[337] The allegiance of the Adiabenians to the newly founded Jewish state was demonstrated during the Roman War (A.D. 66–73) when their troops fought alongside the Jews in their quest for freedom.[338]

JERUSALEM FALLS TO BABYLONIA

The first native Babylonian ruler mentioned by name in the Old Testament (2 Kings 20:12; Isa. 39:1) was Merodach-baladan II, a Chaldean prince from the tribe of Bit-Yakin. [**See map 79.**] He was also the only Babylonian to become king of Babylonia twice,[339] and for a dozen years around 700 B.C. he succeeded in loosening Babylonia from the grip of Assyrian domination.[340] After reestablishing himself as king in Babylon around 703 B.C., Merodach-baladan sought to incite rebellion elsewhere in Assyria's empire. This was likely his motive in sending a delegation to Hezekiah in Jerusalem (2 Kings 20:12–19; Isa. 39:1–8; cf. 2 Chron. 32:31).

King Hezekiah welcomed the Babylonian emissaries and ushered them into the royal treasury to see the wealth of his domain. This was most likely his way of demonstrating to the Babylonians that he represented a worthy ally, one who was quite capable of mustering an army. But when Isaiah learned of what Hezekiah had done, the prophet warned that it had been a fatal maneuver on the king's part—one that would certainly give the Babylonian monarchs an economic incentive to return to Jerusalem, and one that would eventually send Judeans into Babylonian captivity (2 Kings 20:14–18; Isa. 39:3–7). Isaiah's distrust of Merodach-baladan appears to have been well founded; recently discovered documents from Assyria disclose that the Babylonian monarch was a notorious traitor.[341]

Confirming Isaiah's prediction to Hezekiah and according to the biblical record, king Nebuchadnezzar conducted four campaigns between 605 and 582 B.C. that would bring the Babylonian monarch and/or his army to the city of Jerusalem. The first of these campaigns was occasioned by the outcome of the Battle of Carchemish. Following their triumph in May-June 605 B.C. [**map 79**], Nebuchadnezzar's army vigorously pursued Egyptians who were hastily retreating southward toward home and overtook them at the city of Hamath, inflicting many more casualties.[342] However, upon learning of his father's death, Nebuchadnezzar immediately returned from the battlefield to Babylon where, on September 7, 605 B.C., he was installed and officially recognized as the uncontested successor and true king of Babylon.

Wasting no time, however, Nebuchadnezzar returned to the battlefront in the autumn of 605 B.C. and forced all of "the land of Hatti" (Syro-Palestine) to appear before him and pay heavy tribute.[343] While this statement in the Babylonian Chronicle may be a little exaggerated,[344] it doubtless included the powerful city-states of Damascus and Tyre [**1**]. Nebuchadnezzar's southward march against his Egyptian enemy brought a contingent of his army to the threshold of the city of Jerusalem, where king Jehoiakim became his vassal (2 Kings 24:1; cf. Jer. 25:1–2) and doubtless paid him tribute. It is also possible that some Judahite citizens, perhaps including Daniel, were carried off into Babylonian captivity at this point (Dan. 1:3–7) [**2**]. Perhaps because of its Egyptian

Bull from the Ishtar Gate of Nebuchadnezzar II at Babylon (copy in Istanbul).

affiliation, the city of Ashkelon was singled out for particularly harsh treatment during this campaign[345] [**3**]. Nebuchadnezzar's forces now controlled everything north from the border of Egypt (2 Kings 24:7).

About five years later, in December of 599 B.C., Nebuchadnezzar again mustered his troops and marched into "the land of Hatti." This time the precipitating event appears to have been Jehoiakim's refusal to pay the annual tribute owed (2 Kings 24:1). This campaign appears to have been directed almost exclusively against Jerusalem. According to the Babylonian Chronicle, on the second day of the month Adar (which corresponds to March 16, 597 B.C.), following a siege of the city, Nebuchadnezzar succeeded in seizing Jerusalem, capturing its king, and appointing there a king of his own choice.[346] Relating this report to the biblical data, it seems that the Babylonian siege lasted for three months (2 Chron. 36:9; Ezek. 40:1), which may have corresponded to the three-month tenure of king Jehoiachin, who appears to have been both seated and unseated by Nebuchadnezzar (2 Kings 24:8; cf. Jer. 52:28). This would mean that the captured Judahite king mentioned in the Chronicle is most likely Jehoiachin, who was subsequently placed in fetters and deported to Babylon (2 Kings 24:12; 2 Chron. 36:10).[347]

Obscurity continues to surround the end of Jehoiakim's life. Like Jehoiachin, he was also taken prisoner by Nebuchadnezzar (2 Chron. 36:6), but he apparently died or was assassinated while still in the Jerusalem area. We do know that this monarch was deprived of the privileged burial plot customarily accorded Davidic royalty (Jer. 22:19).

In any event, Jerusalem fell to Nebuchadnezzar on exactly March 16, 597 B.C. [**See map 93.**] After that, Mattaniah (Jehoiachin's uncle, whom Nebuchadnezzar renamed Zedekiah) was enthroned as a Babylonian puppet, and a massive deportation involving more than 10,000 Judahites occurred. Ezekiel was among this group (Ezek. 40:1). The Babylonian's second campaign had rendered Judah weak and relatively defenseless, and Zedekiah's heartland seems to have reduced in size considerably. [**See map 78.**] Troops from the Edomite kingdom apparently seized the opportunity at that time to do a bit of plundering themselves (Lam. 4:21–22; cf. Ps. 137:7–8). A letter from that period discovered at the southern Judahite town of Arad[348] refers to the effectiveness of Edomite assaults [**4**].

Nebuchadnezzar's third biblically recorded campaign to Palestine appears to have been brought about by Zedekiah's insubordination and subsequent realignment with Egypt (2 Kings 24:20b—25:2). As a result, the Babylonian military commenced the systematic destruction of many cities of Judah, including Beth-shemesh, Lachish, Beth-zur, Beth-haccherem, and Engedi [**5**]. Archaeological excavation at these sites amply attests to the ferocity of Nebuchadnezzar's onslaught. City after city capitulated until, in addition to Jerusalem, only the major cities of Azekah and Lachish remained in Judean hands (Jer. 34:7). But the situation apparently grew even grimmer. Fire signals, the form of communication between remaining towns, could no longer be seen at Azekah—that city had fallen[349] [**6**]. Only Lachish was left in the Shephela [**7**], but not for long. The destruction layer remaining there is especially intense. Chemical analysis of samples found outside the city's main gate revealed ground mixed with human blood. Felled trees had been stacked along the perimeter of the wall and set aflame; the fire apparently became so intense that even mortar melted in the wall and solidified again at the base.[350] Gaping holes in the walls can still be seen today. With the fall of Lachish, only Jerusalem remained!

In January 587 B.C., Nebuchadnezzar's forces laid siege to Jerusalem (2 Kings 25:1).[351] The city was encased within a massive siege wall for a prolonged period of time, and both severe famine and pestilence soon followed (2 Kings 25:3; Jer. 52:6; cf. Jer. 38:2). Fecal matter excavated from toilets inside Jerusalem indicate that residents of the city were starving, reduced to eating dandelions or uncooked meat, which resulted in tapeworms and other intestinal parasites.[352] Finally, on July 19, 586 B.C., after holding out for some 18 months,[353] Jerusalem fell to Nebuchadnezzar's onslaught (2 Kings 25:1–3; 2 Chron. 36:11–21; Jer. 52:4–7) [**8**]. With all hope now gone, Zedekiah unsuccessfully attempted to escape into Transjordan [**9**]. Apprehended near Jericho, the monarch was captured and eventually deported to Babylon (2 Kings 25:5–7; Jer. 52:8–11; cf. Jer. 39:5). This time Nebuchadnezzar decided to extend his fury to the city and even to the Temple. Approximately one month after the city fell (2 Kings 25:8–9; Jer. 52:12–14; cf. 2 Chron. 36:19; Jer. 39:8)—on August 16, 586 B.C.—the Solomonic Temple was destroyed by fire. Its treasures were either pillaged or carried off to Babylon. The city walls were demolished, the palace burnt, and the remainder of the city looted and plundered. And once again, Judean citizens were deported into Babylonian captivity (2 Kings 25:11; 2 Chron. 36:20; Jer. 39:9; 52:15). Nebuchadnezzar appointed a certain Gedeliah as governor of Judah (2 Kings 25:22; Jer. 40:5–7), and he established a headquarters slightly north of the demolished Jerusalem, at Mizpah.

A fourth biblically recorded Babylonian campaign to Jerusalem took place in 582 B.C. (Jer. 52:30) in response to the murder of Gedeliah (2 Kings 25:25; Jer. 41:2–3). Only a few sketchy details are known about this mission, aside from the fact that another 745 Judean citizens were deported to Babylon.

Jerusalem Falls to Babylonia

map 80

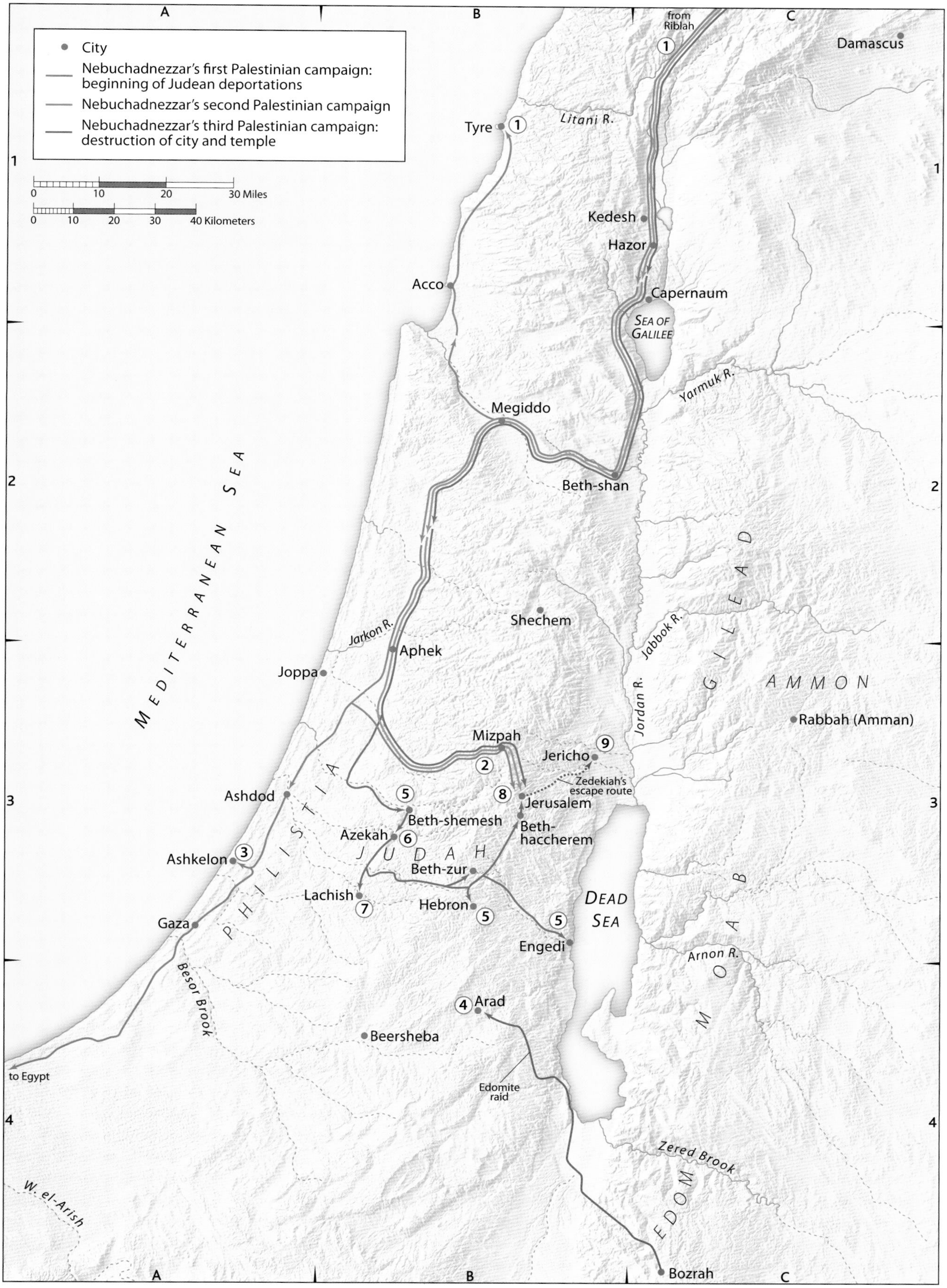

City
Nebuchadnezzar's first Palestinian campaign: beginning of Judean deportations
Nebuchadnezzar's second Palestinian campaign
Nebuchadnezzar's third Palestinian campaign: destruction of city and temple
0 10 20 30 Miles
0 10 20 30 40 Kilometers
A
B
C
1
2
3
4
from Riblah
Damascus
Tyre
Litani R.
Kedesh
Hazor
Acco
Capernaum
SEA OF GALILEE
Yarmuk R.
Megiddo
Beth-shan
MEDITERRANEAN SEA
Shechem
Jarkon R.
Aphek
Joppa
Jabbok R.
Jordan R.
GILEAD
AMMON
Rabbah (Amman)
Mizpah
Jericho
Zedekiah's escape route
Jerusalem
Ashdod
Beth-shemesh
Beth-haccherem
Azekah
JUDAH
PHILISTIA
Ashkelon
Beth-zur
Lachish
Hebron
DEAD SEA
Gaza
Engedi
Arnon R.
MOAB
Besor Brook
Arad
Beersheba
to Egypt
Edomite raid
Zered Brook
W. el-Arish
EDOM
Bozrah

JEWISH DEPORTATIONS AND RETURNS

In the ancient world the ill-treatment of deportees and prisoners was common. Sometimes their hands or other body parts were severed. At other times, as depicted here, ropes were placed around their necks and subjects were obliged to undertake forced marches to faraway destinations.

The concept of mass deportation as employed by the Neo-Assyrians and Neo-Babylonians might be described as an ancient form of ethnic cleansing, even though its primary motivations had more to do with governmental administration, military conscription, and socioeconomics. Ancient documents reveal that, beginning with the Assyrian imperialist Tiglath-pileser III (744–727 B.C.), kings regularly used this mechanism to inflict punishment, maintain peace, populate cities, recruit skilled and unskilled workers, and build armies. Forty-three documented cases clearly enumerate the number of deportees, revealing that more than 1.2 million individuals were thrust from their homelands and deported to faraway locations. Taking the known figures at face value, and extrapolating from the fact that two-thirds of the deportation texts either do not provide a complete number of deportees or provide no number at all, scholars estimate that perhaps as many as 4.5 million persons may have been uprooted and deported during the Assyrian period alone.[354]

The texts indicate that no sector of the Middle East was immune to this phenomenon. Deportations occurred in Egypt, across the entire Levant (Samaria, Judea, Aram, Syria, various Phoenician seacoast cities), Asia Minor (Mushku), northern Mesopotamia (Bit-Adini, Izalla, Nairi, Urartu), eastern Mesopotamia (Manna, Media, Elam), southern Mesopotamia (Chaldea, cities of Nippur, Babylon, Uruk, Sippar, Cutha), and the desert (Aribi). Likewise, people from all political and socioeconomic strata were susceptible to deportation: members of royal families and high officials of the court, understandably, but also tradesmen, soldiers, and slaves.

The Old Testament documents a series of Israelite and Judean deportations:

1. Two deportations occurred during the reign of Tiglath-pileser III:
   - A Galilean deportation of an undisclosed number of people to Assyria in conjunction with his 733 B.C. campaign (2 Kings 15:29); and
   - A Transjordanian deportation of an unspecified number to scattered sites in the year 732 B.C. (1 Chron. 5:26) [**map 76**].
2. A wholesale deportation to several sites took place under Shalmaneser V as a consequence of the destruction of the city of Samaria and the demise of the northern kingdom in 722 B.C. (2 Kings 17:6; 18:11) [**map 77**].
3. Four deportations to Babylon are documented during the reign of Nebuchadnezzar [**map 80**]:
   - 605 B.C.—A small and specially chosen group including members of the royal family and young elites who possessed extraordinary gifts and promise (Dan. 1:3–7);
   - 597 B.C.—10,000 Judeans, among them high governmental officials, men with military prowess, and 1,000 craftsmen and smiths (2 Kings 24:14–16; cf. Jer. 52:28);

Jewish Deportations and Returns

map 81

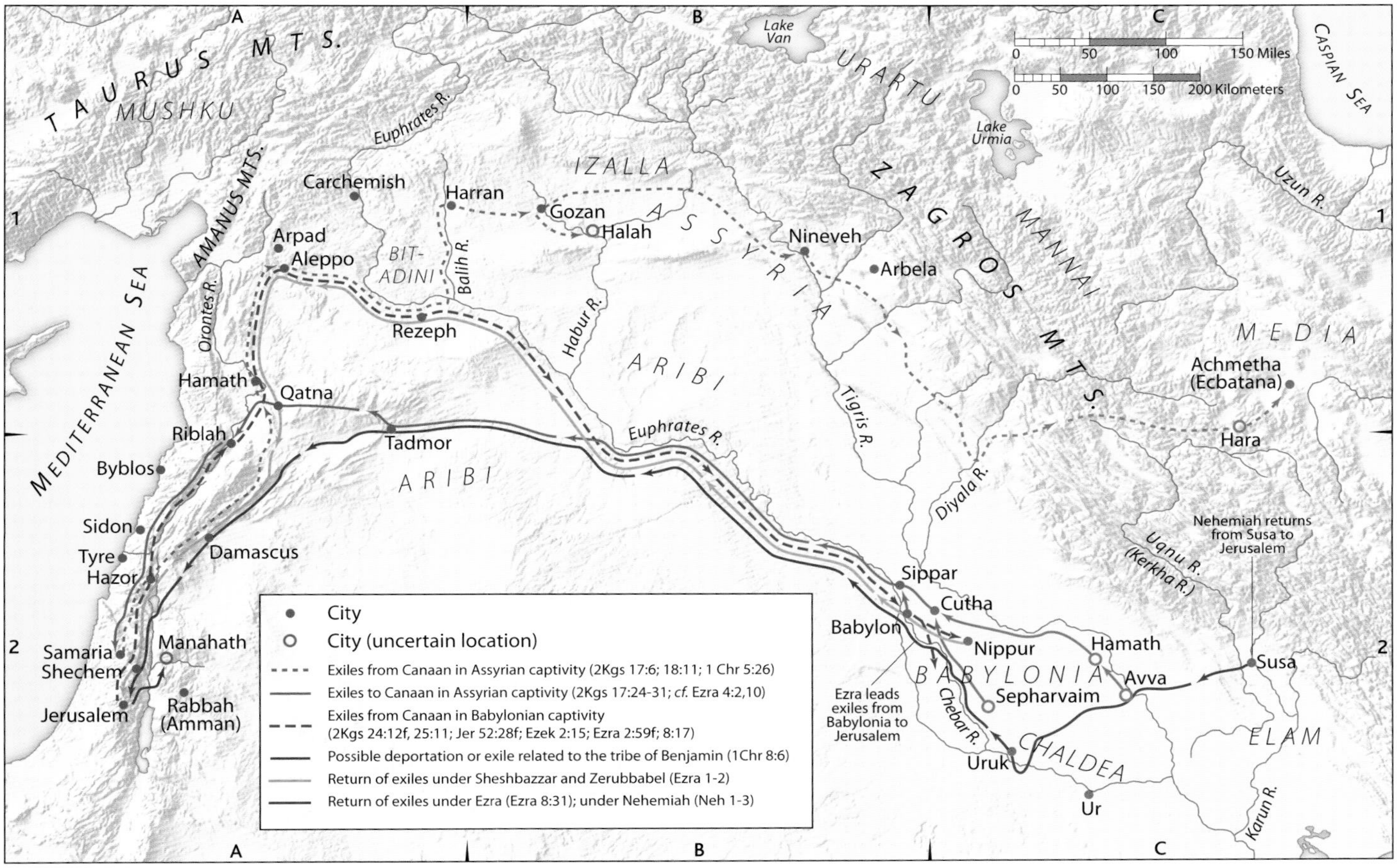

- 586 B.C.—Following the destruction of Jerusalem, a group of unknown size that included some of the poorest people of Judah (2 Kings 25:11–12; 2 Chron. 36:20; Jer. 39:9; 52:15; cf. Jer. 52:29); and
- 582 B.C.—A small number of Judean citizens (Jer. 52:30).

While the Bible only refers to Babylonia generally when describing the destination of Nebuchadnezzar's deportations, Assyrian deportations provide more specific details.[355] Israelites were scattered to such northern Mesopotamian sites as Gozan (T. Halaf), the Habur River, and Halah (Halahhu?), as well as to the "cities of the Medes" (2 Kings 17:6; 18:11; 1 Chron. 5:26).[356] At the same time, people from Babylonia were deported *into* Samaria,[357] from such southeastern cities as Babylon, Cutha (T. Ibrahim), Avva (Ama on the Tigris River?), Hamath (Amati near Avva?), and Sepharvaim (Bit-Amukani?) (2 Kings 17:24, 30–31).[358] Unlike the Assyrians in Samaria, the Babylonians did not repopulate Judah with peoples from elsewhere. Therefore, the post-exilic province of Judah avoided an equivalent of the "Samarian problem" (Ezra 4:1–24) that eventually became a "Samaritan problem" (John 4:9b) farther north.

When Cyrus emancipated the city of Babylon and issued his decree of clemency [**map 85**], some 50,000 Jewish people chose to return to Judea in 538 B.C. under the leadership of Zerubbabel (Ezra 1—2; cf. Hag. 1—2). About 80 years later (458 B.C.), Ezra led back another group probably smaller than the first contingent (Ezra 8:1–14, 31). In this instance his group had no military escort (Ezra 8:22), which most likely means that he used the more dangerous if less traveled desert road past the oasis at Tadmor.[359] Finally, around the year 444 B.C., Nehemiah returned from Susa to Jerusalem with a small cadre of people, but with letters from the king permitting repair of Jerusalem's dilapidated city walls and gates (Neh. 1—3).

THE BABYLONIAN KINGDOM

Nabopolassar's Medo-Babylonian confederation succeeded in driving the Assyrians from Nineveh in 612 B.C. [**map 79**], setting into motion a chain of events that would lead inescapably to the collapse of Assyria. At that time, the brilliant strategist directed his efforts toward acquiring as much as possible of what had been the Assyrian Empire. He stationed garrisons of troops near Nineveh and Calah, and farther north in the Izalla region. When his strenuous efforts to grab land north of Izalla in Urartu were rebuffed by the Scythians, Nabopolassar had to be content with gaining Kue.[360]

Thus was forged the Babylonian kingdom. More properly speaking, this was the Neo-Babylonian (Chaldean) kingdom, in contrast to the Old Babylonian kingdom of Hammurapi. Within a remarkably brief period, Babylon controlled nearly all that had taken Assyria centuries to subjugate. The Babylonian triumph at Carchemish [**map 79**] opened the gates of the Levant and Egypt to Nebuchadnezzar [**map 80**], though he appears to have maintained a tenuous hold at best on Egypt, which was constantly fomenting revolt (2 Kings 25:22–26; Jer. 40:7–41:18; Ezek. 29:6–21).

Meanwhile the Medes were preoccupied with extending their control northward. Cyaxares overran the kingdom of Urartu and pushed into Asia Minor where he met the

Bird's-eye view illustration of Babylon.

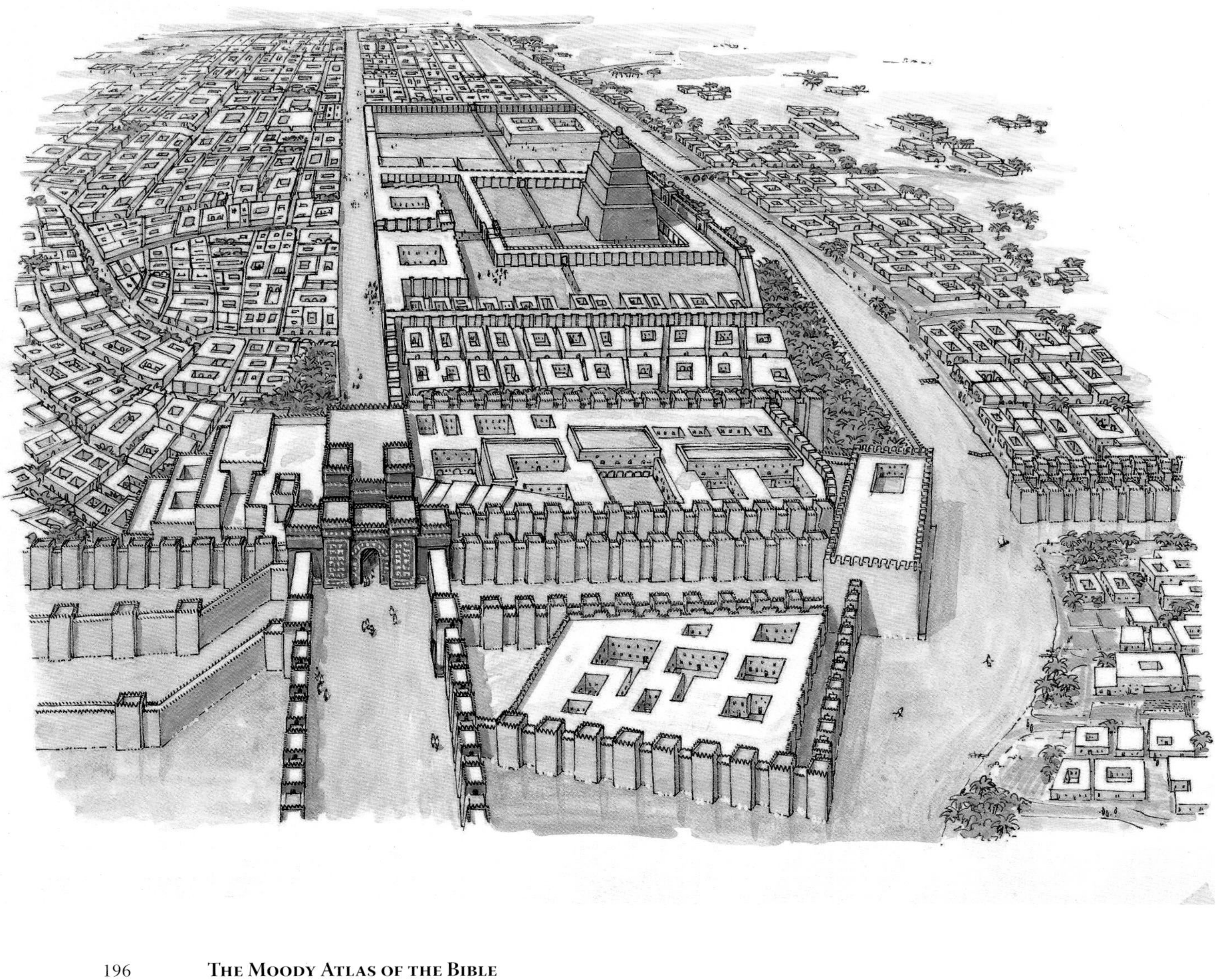

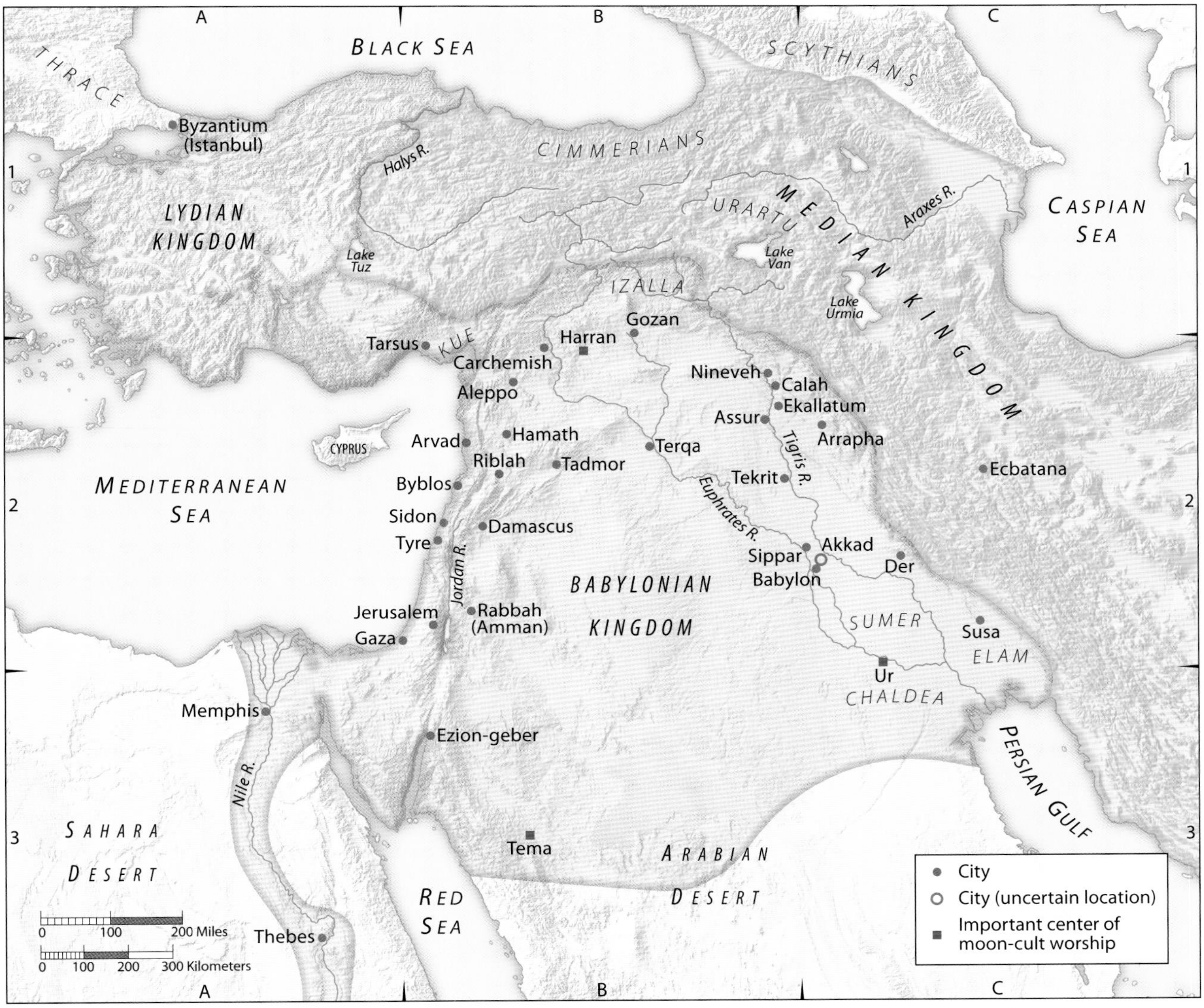

Lydians in five years of protracted battle. Those forays culminated in a treaty between Media and Lydia. A boundary was established at the Halys River in a treaty that was negotiated by Nabonidus, an ambassador of Nebuchadnezzar.[361] However, a son of Nabonidus, Belshazzar (Dan. 5:22), would meet the Medians under less pleasant circumstances when Cyrus the Mede was hailed as a liberator in Babylon.[362] Shortly thereafter, dispossessed peoples, including the Jews, would be permitted to return to their homelands. [**See map 86.**]

JEREMIAH IS TAKEN TO EGYPT

> "The Lord determined to tear down the walls of the daughter of Zion," Jeremiah mourned. "He marked it off with a measuring line and did not withhold his hand from destroying; he caused ramparts and walls to lament, they languish together."
> (Lam. 2:8)

Nebuchadnezzar's military machine penetrated the walls of Jerusalem on July 19, 586 B.C., and began their systematic demolition and conflagration of the city and Temple (2 Kings 25:9–10; 2 Chron. 36:19–21; Jer. 52:13–14). King Zedekiah, who earlier had been enthroned by Nebuchadnezzar, fled under the cover of darkness, attempting to find refuge in the Transjordanian highlands. He was apprehended near Jericho and taken to Riblah, Nebuchadnezzar's headquarters in Syria, from where he was eventually exiled to Babylonia. Along with Zedekiah, many others from Jerusalem were deported to Babylon (2 Kings 25:4–11; Jer. 39:4–9; 52:15).

In Zedekiah's place the Babylonian authorities installed a certain Gedaliah as governor of Judah (2 Kings 25:22; Jer. 40:5, 12). An inscribed seal dating to around 600 B.C., found at Lachish, mentions a "Gedaliah, overseer of the royal palace."[363] Whether or not its owner was the same individual as the new governor, it is clear that the newly appointed governor had previously held high office in the administration of Zedekiah. Though not a descendant of David, Gedaliah ruled Judah temporarily. His headquarters was at Mizpah because Jerusalem had been razed and was uninhabitable (cf. Lam. 2:8–13). But just as the governor's efforts to restore Judah were beginning to succeed (2 Kings 25:23–24; Jer. 40:7–12), nationalist fervor resurfaced when a small band of fanatics murdered Gedaliah. Fearing swift and harsh Babylonian reprisal, many people from Judah began to flee to Egypt (2 Kings 25:25–26). When Jeremiah opposed such a move (Jer. 42:7–22), he was forcibly taken, along with his scribe, Baruch, to the city of Tahpanhes in Egypt (Jer. 43:7). Undaunted, Jeremiah continued to warn refugees that they should not feel secure because Nebuchadnezzar's pestilence and destructive zeal would surely come to Egypt as well (Jer. 43:8–44:30).

Warnings such as these surely contributed to the establishment of Jewish colonies much farther upstream along the Nile. [**See map 106.**] Whatever the case, Jewish colonization in Egypt became rather widespread during the Persian period, and Jeremiah sent oracles to his expatriates as far away as Pathros, in Upper Egypt (Jer. 44:1).

One important military colony in the land of Pathros was located about 500 miles south of Tahpanhes, on an island at the first cataract of the Nile, opposite the town of Syene (modern Aswan; cf. Ezek. 29:10; 30:6). [**See map 63.**] Dozens of Aramaic papyri dating to the fifth century B.C. have been found on that island, known today as Elephantine but then as Yeb (Abu in Egyptian). Those extremely important texts are contemporary with biblical Ezra and Nehemiah, and they provide the earliest extra-biblical documentation addressing the socioeconomic and political life of a post-exilic Jewish community in or outside Palestine. They also provide valuable and even surprising insight into Jewish religious life away from Jerusalem's Temple and priesthood.[364]

Jeremiah Is Taken to Egypt

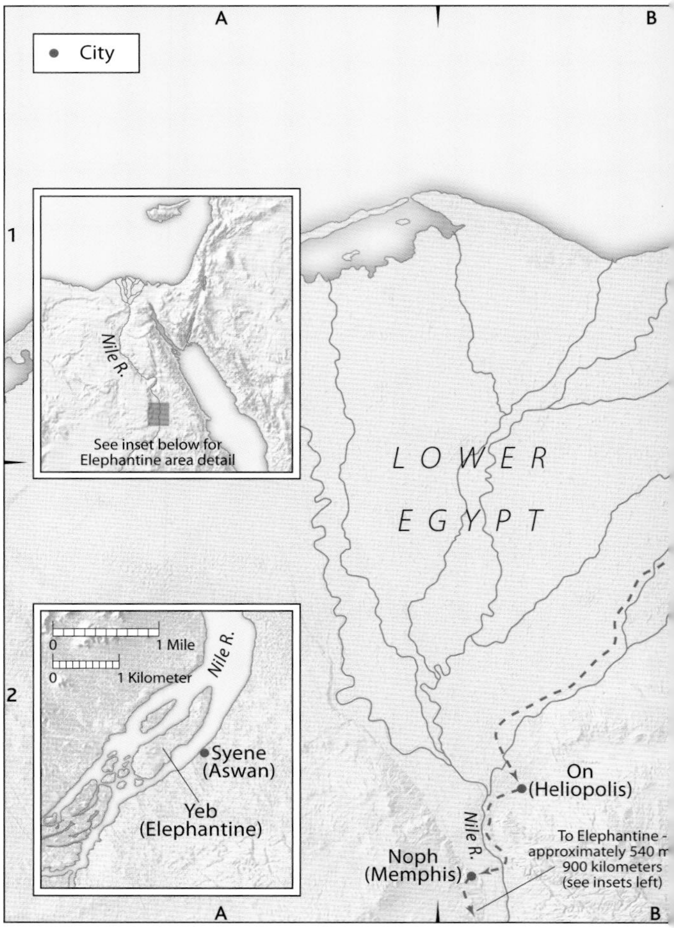

Lying in the midst of the upper Nile river is the lush green island of Elephantine, where a Jewish colony was founded during the days of Ezra and Nehemiah.

map 83

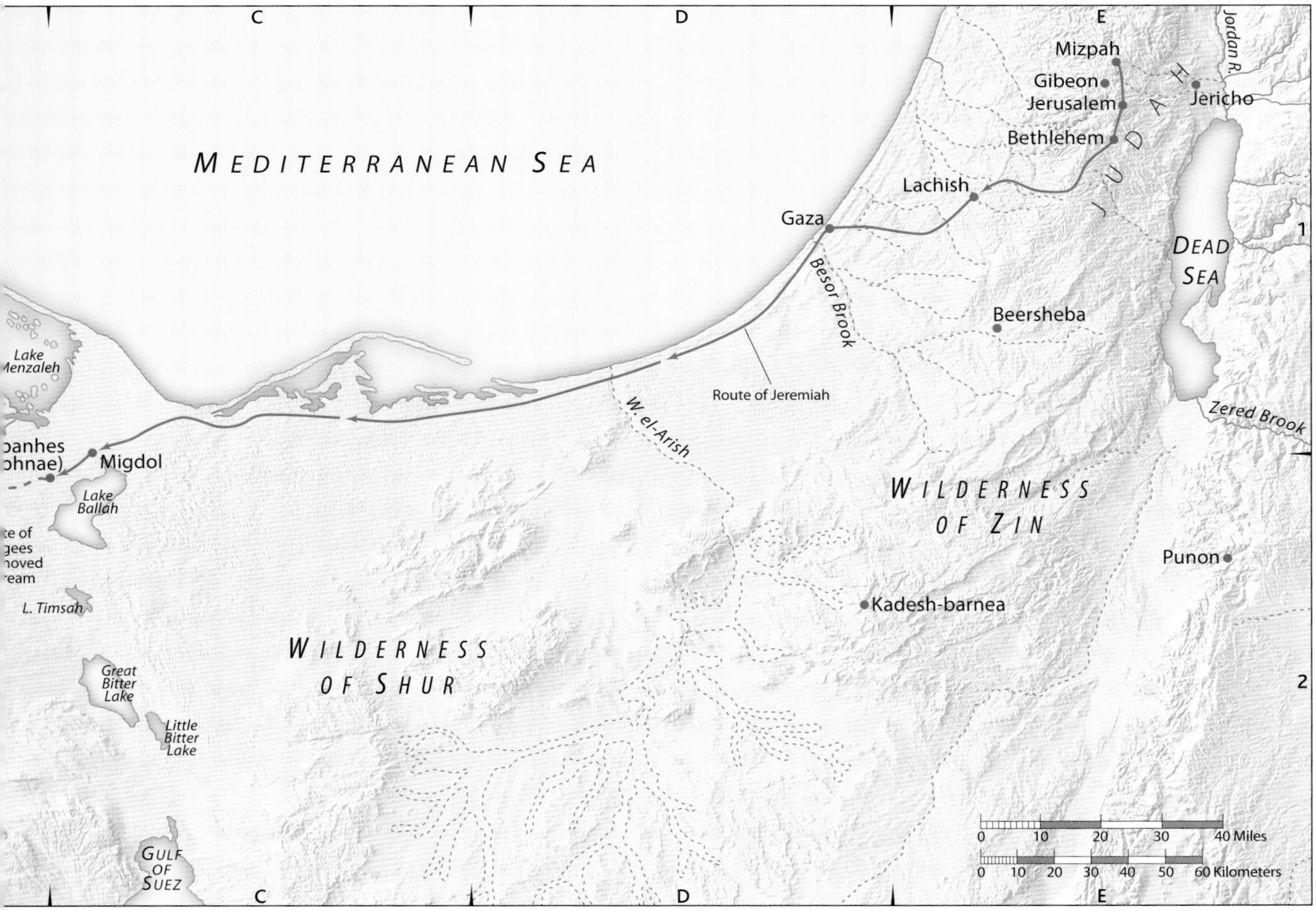

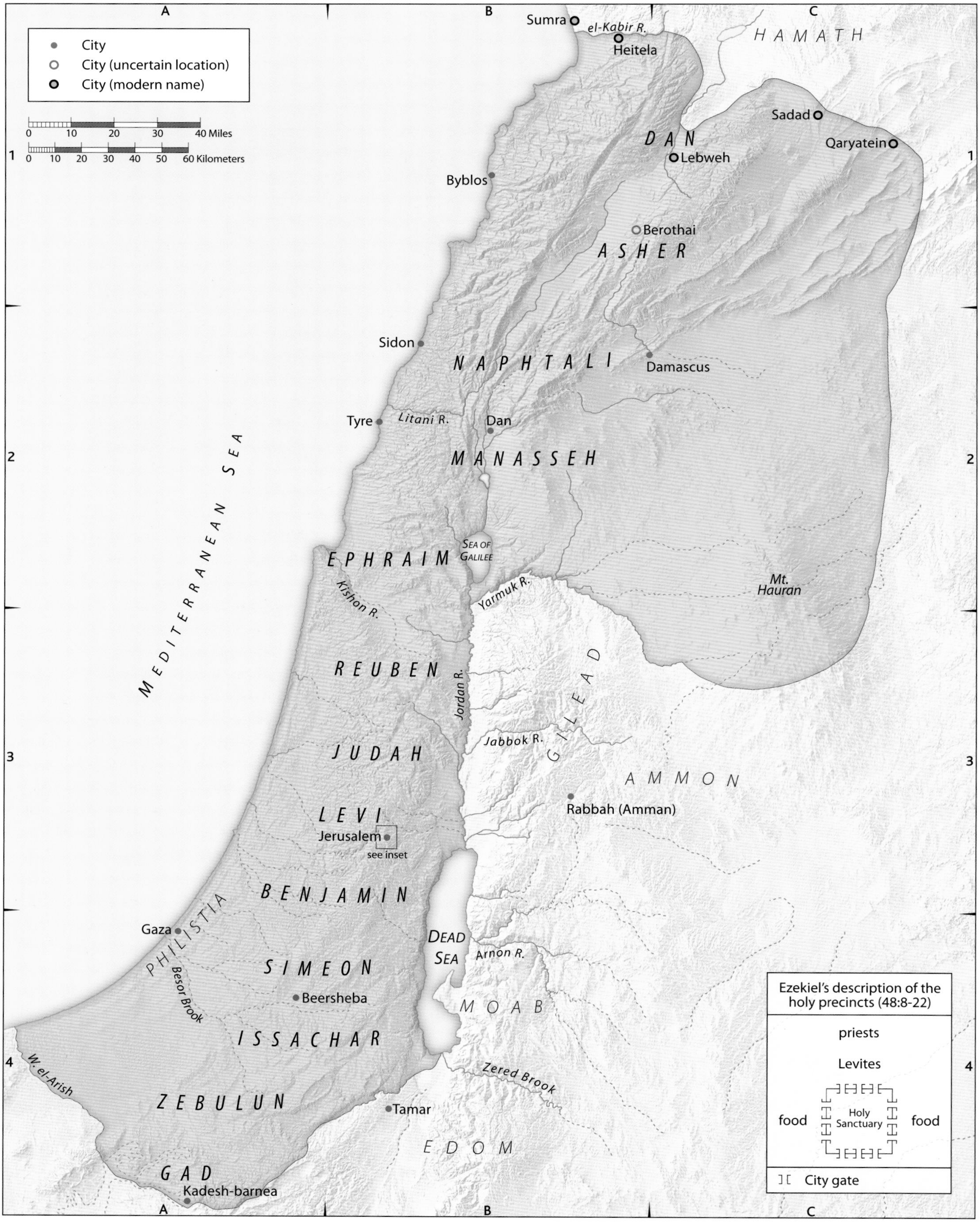

Legend:
- • City
- ○ City (uncertain location)
- ◎ City (modern name)

0 10 20 30 40 Miles
0 10 20 30 40 50 60 Kilometers

HAMATH

Sumra ○
el-Kabir R.
Heitela ◎

Sadad ◎

DAN
Lebweh ○

Qaryatein ◎

Byblos ●

Berothai ○

ASHER

MEDITERRANEAN SEA

Sidon ●

NAPHTALI

Damascus ●

Tyre ● Litani R. Dan ●

MANASSEH

SEA OF GALILEE

EPHRAIM

Kishon R.

Yarmuk R.

Mt. Hauran

REUBEN

Jordan R.

GILEAD

Jabbok R.

AMMON

JUDAH

LEVI

Rabbah (Amman) ●

Jerusalem ●
see inset

BENJAMIN

Gaza ●

PHILISTIA

DEAD SEA

Besor Brook

SIMEON

Arnon R.

● Beersheba

MOAB

ISSACHAR

Zered Brook

W. el-Arish

ZEBULUN

● Tamar

EDOM

GAD
Kadesh-barnea

Ezekiel's description of the holy precincts (48:8-22)

priests

Levites

food Holy Sanctuary food

][City gate

JUDEA AFTER THE EXILE

The year 539 B.C. is one of the most pivotal dates in the history of the ancient Near East. First, Semitic influence that had dominated the landmass of the Fertile Crescent for thousands of years—Akkadians, Amorites, Old-Babylonians, Assyrians, Phoenicians, Chaldeans (Neo-Babylonians)—came to an end. A succession of new non-Semitic forces—Persians, Greeks, Parthians, Romans—came to solidify western Asia. Second, the seizure of the city of Babylon by the forces of Cyrus II (the Great) on October 12, 539 B.C.,[365] meant that Jewish exiles, along with other dispossessed peoples, could finally return to their own homelands.

The year following his capture of Babylon, Cyrus issued his now-celebrated decree of clemency. He declared: "I sought the welfare of the city of Babylon and all its sacred centers. As for the citizens of Babylon upon whom a corvée had been imposed, which was not god's will, I relieved their weariness and freed them from its service." He continued: "From [the cities of] Nineveh, Asshur, Susa, Akkad, Eshnunna, Zabban, Meturnu, Der as far as the border of the Guti—whose sacred temples beyond the Tigris River had lain in ruins for a long time—I returned to their places; I let them [i.e., their gods] dwell in permanent shrines. As for all their people, I gathered them together and returned them to their [former] dwellings."[366] (See Ezra 1:1–4; 6:1–5; 2 Chron. 36:22–23.)

Almost immediately a group of approximately 50,000 Jewish refugees set out for Judea with Sheshbazzar, whom Cyrus had appointed provincial governor (Ezra 1:8; 5:14) [**map 81**] and Zerubbabel, possibly his nephew (1 Chron. 3:18) and successor (Neh. 12:1; Hag. 1:1). At any rate, Zerubbabel was a direct descendant of Jehoiachin (1 Chron. 3:17–19) who stood in Davidic dynastic succession. God's pre-exilic royal "signet ring" (Jehoiachin) had been rejected, torn off from his finger, and thrown to the Babylonians (Jer. 22:24), but the post-exilic royal "signet ring" (Zerubbabel) was chosen by God, restored, and had endured beyond the Babylonians (Hag. 2:23). For this community continuing to wonder about the ongoing viability and status of the Davidic covenantal promises, it would have been enormously assuring and theologically

The Cyrus Cylinder. This baked-clay cylinder records the fall of Babylon.

Judea after the Exile

map 85

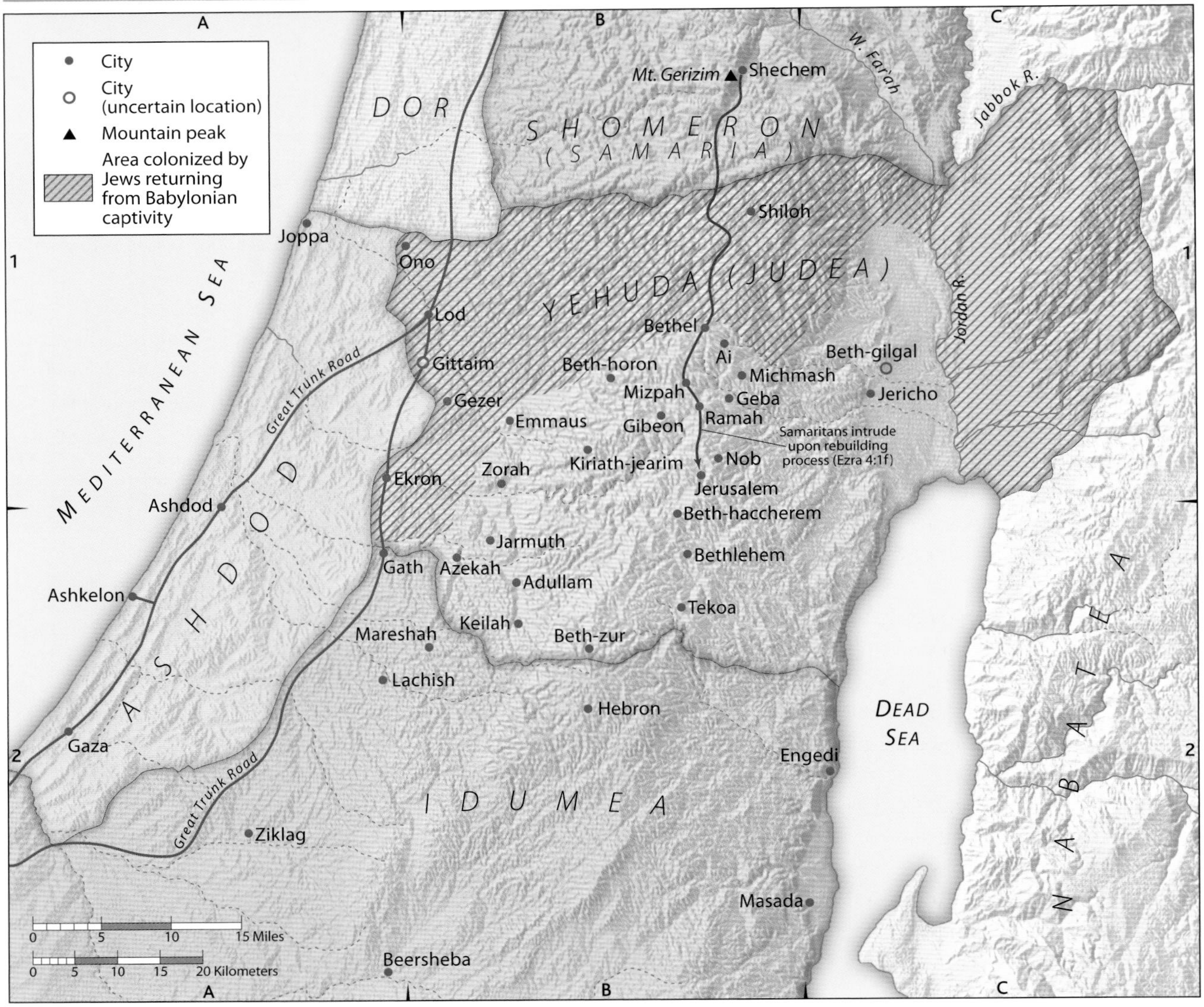

important to discover that God's covenant was alive and well (Matt. 1:12–13; Luke 3:27)!

For reasons that are not completely clear, most returnees (other than leaders) colonized areas *around* Jerusalem, especially northern sectors, but did not occupy the city itself. Important in this context were places like Beth-gilgal, Michmash, Bethel, Mizpah, Emmaus, Gittaim, Hadid, and especially Ono and Lod. Also significant were Beth-haccherem, Jarmuth, Keilah, and Beth-zur in the south (Ezra 2:21–35; Neh. 6:2–3; 7:6–38; 11:25–35; 12:27–29). Nehemiah (11:1–2) describes later measures taken to bring ten percent of the population inside the holy city to live, while the remaining nine-tenths could remain in the suburbs.

THE CAMPAIGN OF ALEXANDER THE GREAT AGAINST PERSIA

Philip II of Macedonia was one of the greatest reformers in all of Greek history. Before his mysterious death at Pella in 336 B.C., Philip had transformed Macedonia into a strong, centralized monarchy with a standing army equipped with new revolutionary tactics (such as an infantry phalanx armed with spears measuring almost 20 feet in length). Philip's army had dominated all the city-states of mainland Greece except Sparta, and had conquered all of coastal Thrace to the Black Sea. Philip had built for himself a power base upon which he intended to wrest Asia Minor from Persia. His noteworthy achievements are overshadowed only by those of his extraordinary son, Alexander III ("the Great").[373]

As a 21-year-old claimant to the Macedonian throne, Alexander set out in the spring of 334 B.C. His treasury was empty and his troops (largely mercenary) numbered only around 35,000 or 40,000.[374] Yet he had a very ambitious, even audacious mission: to demolish the entire Persian Empire, not just those neighboring parts in Asia Minor. And in what is arguably one of the most remarkable achievements in the annals of military history, Alexander summarily accomplished his entire mission, and more, in a span of just eleven years.

He crossed the Hellespont, the narrow watercourse separating the continents of Europe and Asia, and became the first Macedonian monarch to set foot on Asian soil. Almost immediately, and with some theatrics, he burned all his ships so his men would realize they had no escape and would fight like heroic champions. Following a short stop at Troy where he sacrificed to the goddess Athena and walked off with the armor of Achilles, Alexander personally led his troops in a narrow victory over part of the Persian army at the Granicus River.[375] Following this initial battle, Alexander deliberately

The Cilician Gates (Gülek Pass) represented the arterial passageway from Asia into Syria and Mesopotamia in antiquity, conveying armies, merchants, pilgrims, and other caravaneers.

The Greek Empire

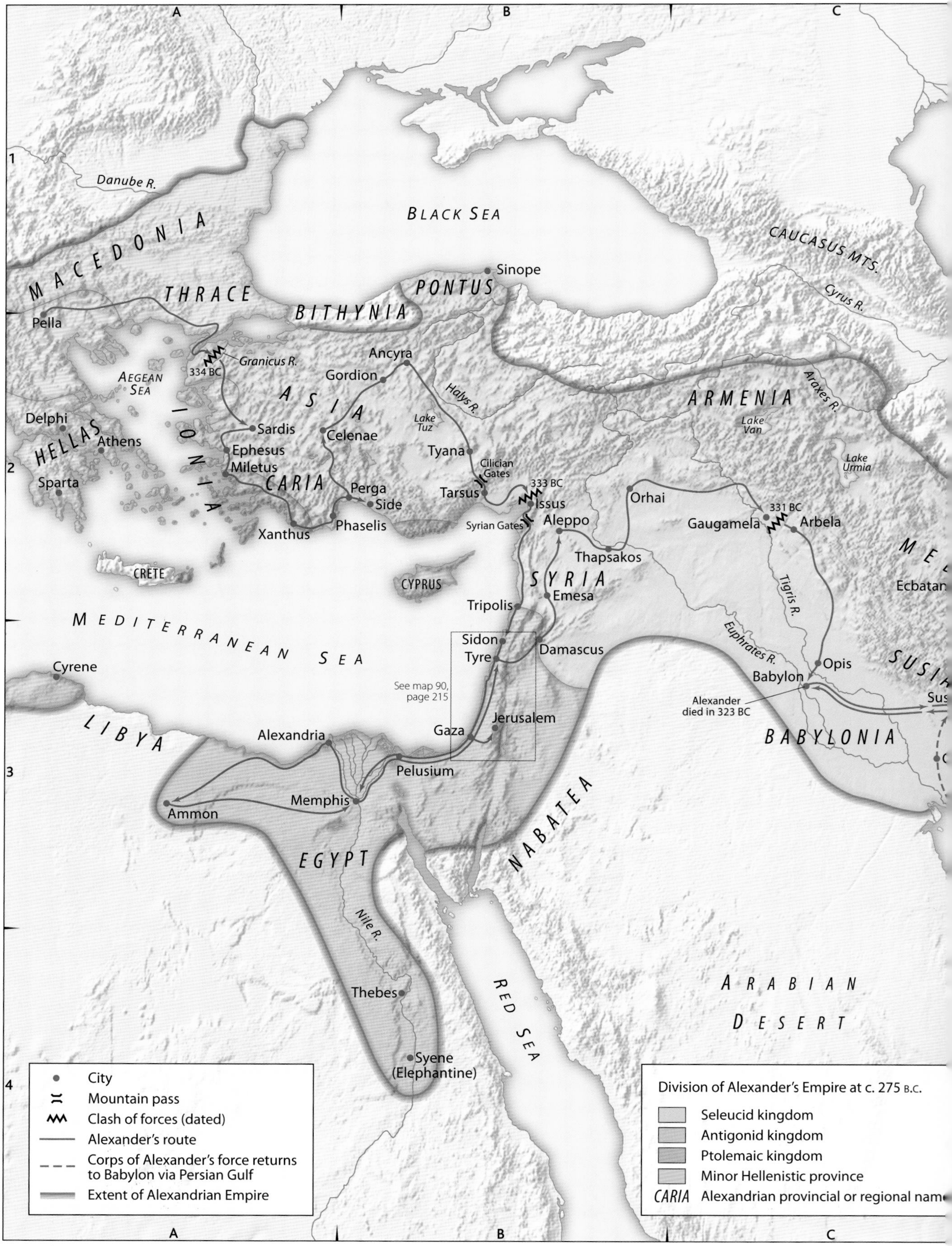

A
B
C
1
2
3
4
Danube R.
BLACK SEA
CAUCASUS MTS.
Cyrus R.
MACEDONIA
THRACE
BITHYNIA
PONTUS
Sinope
Pella
Granicus R.
334 BC
AEGEAN SEA
Ancyra
Gordion
ASIA
Halys R.
Araxes R.
ARMENIA
Lake Van
Lake Urmia
Lake Tuz
Delphi
HELLAS
Athens
IONIA
Sardis
Celenae
Ephesus
Miletus
Sparta
CARIA
Tyana
Cilician Gates
333 BC
Tarsus
Perga
Side
Issus
Orhai
331 BC
Gaugamela
Arbela
Xanthus
Phaselis
Syrian Gates
Aleppo
Thapsakos
CRETE
CYPRUS
SYRIA
Emesa
Tigris R.
Ecbatan
Tripolis
MEDITERRANEAN SEA
Sidon
Tyre
Damascus
Euphrates R.
Opis
Cyrene
Babylon
See map 90, page 215
Alexander died in 323 BC
Jerusalem
LIBYA
Alexandria
Gaza
BABYLONIA
Pelusium
Memphis
Ammon
NABATEA
EGYPT
Nile R.
RED SEA
Thebes
ARABIAN DESERT
Syene (Elephantine)
City
Mountain pass
Clash of forces (dated)
Alexander's route
Corps of Alexander's force returns to Babylon via Persian Gulf
Extent of Alexandrian Empire
Division of Alexander's Empire at c. 275 B.C.
Seleucid kingdom
Antigonid kingdom
Ptolemaic kingdom
Minor Hellenistic province
CARIA Alexandrian provincial or regional name

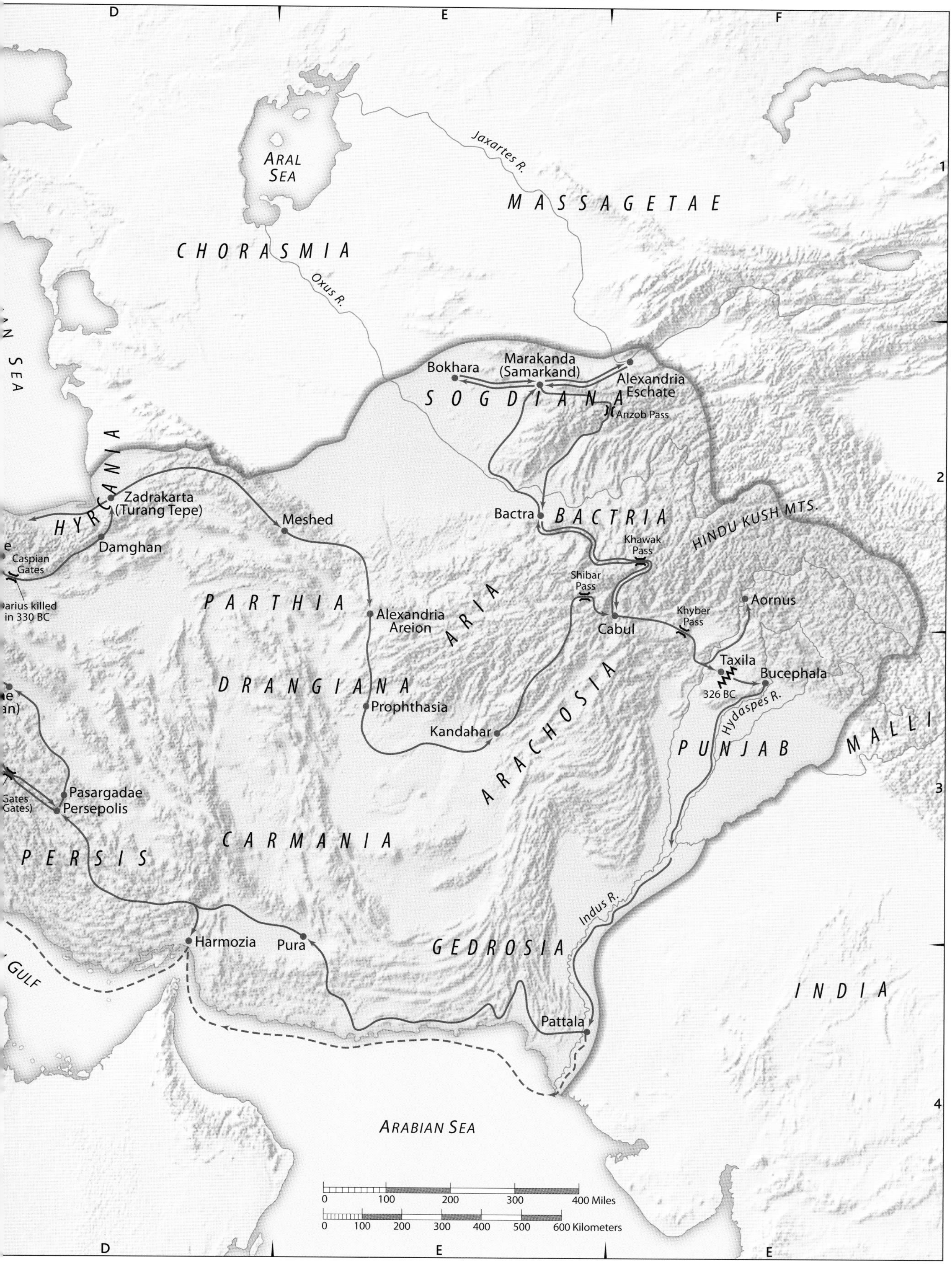
ARAL SEA
CHORASMIA
MASSAGETAE
Jaxartes R.
Oxus R.
Bokhara
Marakanda (Samarkand)
Alexandria Eschate
SOGDIANA
Anzob Pass
HYRCANIA
Zadrakarta (Turang Tepe)
Damghan
Caspian Gates
Meshed
Bactra
BACTRIA
HINDU KUSH MTS.
Khawak Pass
Shibar Pass
Cabul
Khyber Pass
Aornus
Taxila
Bucephala
326 BC
Hydaspes R.
PARTHIA
Alexandria Areion
ARIA
DRANGIANA
Prophthasia
Kandahar
ARACHOSIA
PUNJAB
MALLI
Pasargadae
Persepolis
PERSIS
CARMANIA
Harmozia
Pura
GEDROSIA
Indus R.
Pattala
INDIA
GULF
ARABIAN SEA
0 100 200 300 400 Miles
0 100 200 300 400 500 600 Kilometers
D
E
F
1
2
3
4

pressed south rather than pursuing the retreating Persians eastward. He received the submission of the cities of Sardis, Ephesus, Miletus, Halicarnassus, Xanthus, Phaselis, Perga, and Side,[376] thus gaining uncontested control over the Ionian and Carian coastlands and major ports—and denying the Persian fleet any bases for counterattack.

Alexander then turned inland, overpowering the Phrygians and capturing the city of Gordion, where he found provisions and chose to winter his troops.[377] Then in the summer of 333 B.C., Alexander marched across western Cappadocia, through the Cilician Gates, and on to the site of Issus on the Mediterranean coast. There one of the most pivotal battles in all of biblical antiquity took place. [**See map 89**.]

After his defeat at Issus, Darius, the Persian leader, was on the defensive but undaunted. He fled east from Issus to Babylon to regroup for another day.[378] Once again, Alexander chose not to pursue his retreating enemy. A brilliant strategist, he instead marched south through Syria. Dividing his army, he dispatched one small contingent to seize Damascus [**map 88**], while he personally led the majority of his troops past Sidon to Tyre. After a seven-month siege of that island stronghold, Alexander succeeded in constructing a stone and wooden causeway out to Tyre and capturing the city in August 332 B.C.[379] With the fall of Tyre, Phoenicia's loyalty to Darius and its ties to the Persian fleet were crushed, and Alexander was now free to move against other targets. His army's southward procession past Acco, Dora, Strato's Tower, and Samaria was more or less unimpeded. [**See map 88.**] But the strongly fortified Gaza offered resistance for two months in late 332 B.C., until finally Alexander's troops were able to breach its walls and capture the citadel.[380] With Gaza's demise, no further military obstacles separated the Macedonian from his African objective.

Josephus tells us, however, that instead of marching directly into Egypt, Alexander made his way to Jerusalem, was greeted by the high priest, and was ushered into the Temple where he offered sacrifices to God.[381] Thereupon, according to Josephus, Alexander was shown a copy of the book of Daniel, which declared that a Greek should destroy the Persian Empire, and Alexander believed himself to be the one indicated.[382] Seeing that Alexander had honored the Jews by visiting Jerusalem, a delegation of Samaritans came to the outskirts of Jerusalem to curry his favor by inviting him to visit their shrine atop Mt. Gerizim.[383] He promised them a visit on his return trip from Egypt. [**See map 88**.] Since this brief chapter in Alexander's life is told only by Josephus but is not found in other classical writings, it is difficult to assess the story's historical essence. It is certainly reasonable to assume that Jewish leaders from Jerusalem would have been subject to the same kind of requirements of submission to Alexander's rule that are elsewhere commonly known throughout the empire, and the Greek king offered sacrifices at different temples and to different deities throughout his nascent kingdom. Furthermore, the part of the episode having to do with the Samaritans, related perhaps to Alexander's eventual antipathy toward them, is elsewhere reported by classical writers, which may lend additional credence to the story.[384]

From Jerusalem, Alexander marched into Pelusium, where throngs of Egyptian citizens met him and hailed him as a liberator. He sailed upstream to Memphis, where the Persian satrap surrendered and the Egyptian priesthood hailed him as the pharaoh. From Memphis, Alexander continued to the Mediterranean shoreline where he founded a city that still bears his name.[385] Afterward he proceeded into the Libyan desert to visit the site of the prominent oracle of Ammon, identified by the Greeks as Zeus, the most powerful of all Greek deities. The leading priest of the oracle greeted Alexander as the "son of Ammon," and his historians began to identify Alexander as "son of Zeus."[386]

Occupying Egypt had assured Alexander that his southern flank was now secure, so in the spring of 331 B.C., the general departed Egypt, via Palestine, Tyre, and Damascus. [**See map 88.**] He set his sights once again directly on Darius, this time in Mesopotamia, where his second and final encounter with the Persian would take place. By this time Darius had conscripted a very sizeable army[387] and had marched north from Babylon to a carefully selected battle site just west of the city of Arbela. The spacious plain of Gaugamela offered Darius ideal fighting conditions for his huge cavalry force, his specially prepared war chariots, and even his elephants. In fact, Darius had been at Gaugamela leading his army in war games for some time before the arrival of Alexander.[388]

The two armies collided in full-scale conflict on October 1, 331 B.C.[389] Darius's hopes were soon dashed. As at Issus, the prowess of Alexander personally against the center of the Persian army forced Darius to abandon his forces and flee, this time in the direction of Ecbatana and the Caspian Sea. The heartland of Darius's empire was now Alexander's for the taking, and in very rapid succession the capital cities of Babylon, Susa, and Persepolis all capitulated to the Macedonian.[390] Perhaps even more significant for his mercenaries, Alexander's capture of Susa and Persepolis also meant that the vast accumulated treasures of 200 years of Persian imperial rule, estimated to have been a few thousand tons of precious metals and coins, were now completely in the hands of the Greek army.[391]

Departing Persepolis in April 330 B.C., Alexander set out on a direct course toward Ecbatana, the only remaining Persian capital, where Darius was holed up. Unable to assemble yet another coalition against the Macedonian, Darius fled Alexander's fast approach with the intention of traveling east to Bactria. But the Persian monarch got only as far as the vicinity of the Caspian Gates where, in July, he was assassinated by a few of his former princes from the east.[392] Learning of the death of this last Achaemenid king while en route to the Caspian Gates, Alexander immediately assumed the role of his successor and defender of Achaemenid legitimacy against all other claimants.

For various military, political, and perhaps even scientific reasons,[393] Alexander decided to continue his push eastward against Bactria and Sogdiana. Crossing the Hindu Kush mountains, he launched an Indian campaign toward the Ganges River. In 326 B.C. he fought an Indian prince about 40 miles east of the Indus River on the famous route through the Khyber Pass, near classical Taxila, where he won a decisive victory despite his opponent's use of war elephants.[394] But when Alexander attempted to plunge still deeper into the Indian interior, his troops mutinied at the Hydaspes River, and he was forced to turn back.[395] Alexander returned via the Indus River valley to the Arabian Sea, where he commissioned a naval force under his admiral Nearchus to sail the Persian Gulf to Mesopotamia.[396] Meanwhile, he and his army trekked across the forbidding plains of Baluchistan past Persepolis to Susa in early 324 B.C.[397] In early 323 B.C. he made his way back to Babylon, where he began preparations for a full-scale invasion of Arabia. But Alexander fell ill toward the end of May, and in mid-June 323 B.C., he died at age 32, presumably of a fever.[398]

The political power play that predictably ensued in the immediate aftermath of Alexander's death was both chaotic and bloody. By around 275 B.C., the number of important rivals had been reduced to three, and the breakup of the Greek Empire was effected. One of Alexander's generals, Seleucus I (and his dynasty), took control of Mesopotamia, Syria, most of Asia Minor, and points east to the border of India. Another of his generals, Ptolemy I Soter (and his dynasty), grabbed Egypt, Cyrene, Palestine, Phoenicia, Cyprus, several Mediterranean islands, and some coastal parts of southern Asia Minor. Meanwhile, the Antigonid dynasty ruled the territory around Alexander's homeland in the vicinity of Pella. This alignment would soon change for Palestine, however, and in a most dramatic and profound way.

When the Ptolemaic hold on Palestine was lost to the Seleucids in 200 B.C. at the battle of Panias, Hellenization of the upper strata of Jewish society was officially inaugurated. Ensuing tensions gave rise inevitably to Jewish factionalism: the more progressive Jews embraced Hellenistic ideology, but the more traditional viewed it as a threat to their ancestral religion. When Antiochus IV Epiphanes ascended to the Seleucid throne in 175 B.C., efforts towards Hellenization would reach their climax. [See map 91.]

Alexander Marches through Palestine ***map 88***

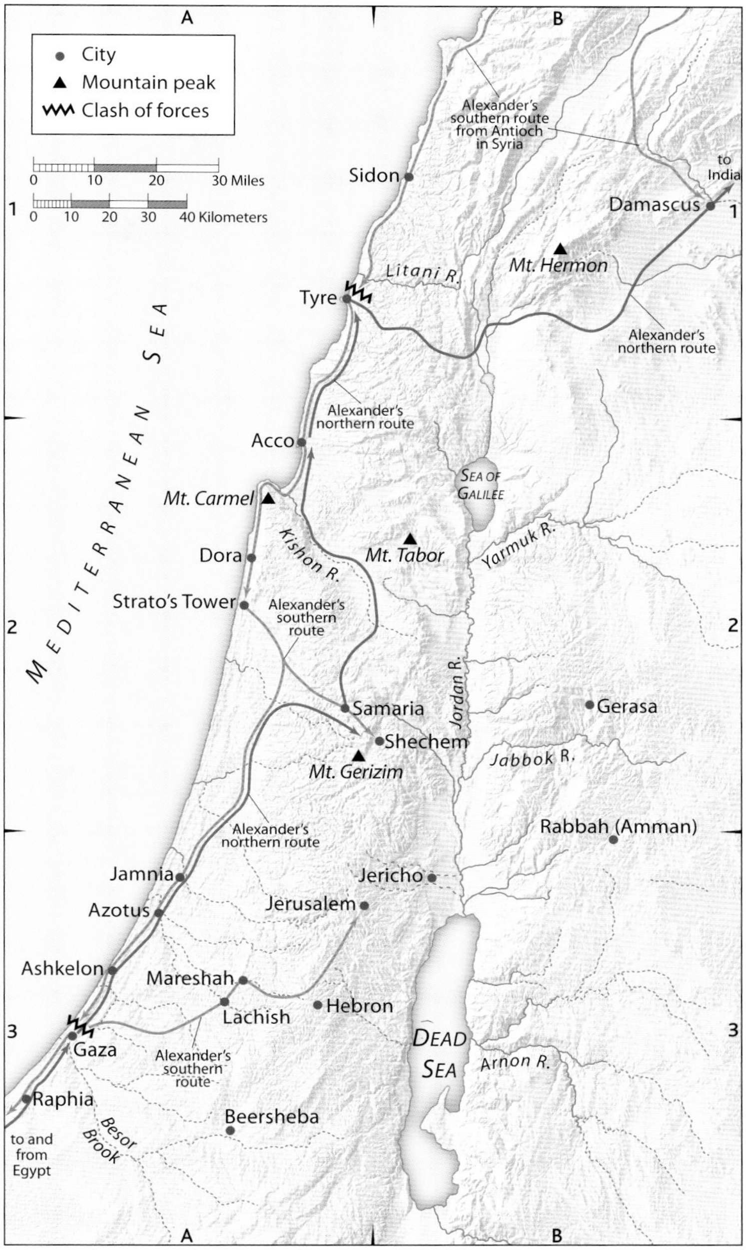

THE BATTLE OF ISSUS

The Aleian plain and the Issus plain comprise a narrow, fairly isolated, horseshoe-shaped lowland. They lie adjacent to the sea and are hemmed in by the Taurus mountain range in the north and west and the Amanus mountains in the east. Access in and out of these plains would have been extremely difficult, except at three passes: (1) a northwestern gate, known today as the Gülek Pass and in antiquity as the Cilician Gates;[399] (2) a northeastern gate, known today as the Bahçe Pass and in antiquity as the Amanus Gates;[400] and (3) a southern gate, known today as the Belen Pass and in antiquity as the Syrian Gates.[401]

Alexander the Great set out from Gordion in the summer of 333 B.C. [**map 87**], marching southeast across Galatia and western Cappadocia as far as the city of Tyana (Aurelia Antoniniana). From there he was able to travel on what later would become the Via Taurus, and thus he negotiated the Taurus range via the Cilician Gates.[402] Upon taking control of Cilicia and the town of Tarsus, Alexander unwisely plunged into the water of the Cydnus River, which was extremely cold from the melting snow of the Taurus.[403] By the time his army had arrived on the Mediterranean coast at Soli, he had contracted cramps and a severe chill that developed into a tropical fever. In rather short order, Alexander slipped into a coma, with his life in peril [**1**].

It was apparently during the few months Alexander was near death that Darius III set out from Babylon with his vast Persian imperial army, comprised of light infantry, heavy infantry, cavalry, charioteers, archers, and slingers—a total estimated to be 300,000, or maybe even twice that many.[404] Potential numerical exaggeration notwithstanding, this army must have been quite large and awe-inspiring. It was well fed and very well paid. Accompanying the military host was a resplendent retinue of some 600 mules and 300 camels carrying an imperial treasury, 365 richly dressed royal concubines, the royal chariot of the Persian deity Ahuramazda, an array of silver altars bearing the Persians' "sacred fire," numerous priests and other noncombatants, and part of Darius's own royal family. Sending his treasury and the bulk of his supply train on to Damascus, Darius took up a position at Sochi, a town of uncertain location that must have been situated somewhere near the Amuq plain not too far east of the Syrian Gates [**2**].

Alexander had largely recuperated by early October when he learned of Darius's encampment at Sochi. He immediately moved his forces across the Aleian plain as far as the town of Issus, where he left his sick and wounded soldiers. Convinced that Darius would attack via the Syrian Gates, and wishing to utilize that confined space to neutralize the Persian's vast numerical superiority, Alexander marched with his troops as far south as the town of Myriandrus, prepared his camp for battle, and dispatched scouts to reconnoiter the Pass [**3**].

Underestimating the severity of Alexander's illness, Darius apparently misread the Greek's delay at Soli as cowardice. He also overestimated his own army's abilities in the face of a numerically inferior adversary. Learning of Alexander's southward advance from Issus, Darius was advised to remain out in the Amuq plain and pitch the battle there in a wide-open terrain ideally suited to his army's size. He rejected that counsel and decided instead to lead his forces on a flanking maneuver some 50 miles north. He hoped to enter the Issus plain unopposed through the Amanus Gates, sever Alexander's logistical and supply line in the direction of Anatolia and Greece, and surprise the Macedonian from the rear. It was an extremely daring and shrewd move that indeed outwitted Alexander and gave Darius an advantage—temporarily. Darius brought his hordes down into Issus where he mutilated or massacred Alexander's men left there, and then he pitched his battle line along the north bank of the Pinarus River [**4**].

Perhaps unaware of the presence of the Amanus Gates, Alexander was surprised beyond belief by reports of Darius's cunning and skillful maneuver.[405] He required scouts to confirm such news before he would move his army away from Myriandrus and the Syrian Gates. They verified that the Persian army had in fact already pitched its battle line behind Alexander near the Pinarus, so the Macedonian was obliged to turn his army around and quickly march northward, establishing his own battle line somewhere between the so-called "pillar of Jonah" and the south bank of the Pinarus [**5**].

For Darius, the advantage of surprise soon paled into a disadvantage of space. From the onset of the battle, it was clear that Darius had made a major miscalculation. The coastal plain between the Amanus foothills and the sea near the Pinarus is less than three miles wide. Darius possessed almost infinitely superior numbers and technology, yet his brash tactical decision left him little opportunity to deploy that superiority effectively. Perhaps unwittingly on both of their parts, Darius had played right into Alexander's hands.[406] Almost before the battle had been completely joined, Darius and his army realized the imminence of defeat [**6**]. They attempted to retreat and escape into the lofty Amanus mountains. Alexander and his cavalry pursued them for some 25 miles east, inflicting many more casualties as a result of paths clogged by great numbers of retreating Persians. Classical sources report Persian losses as high as 110,000 men[407] [**7**].

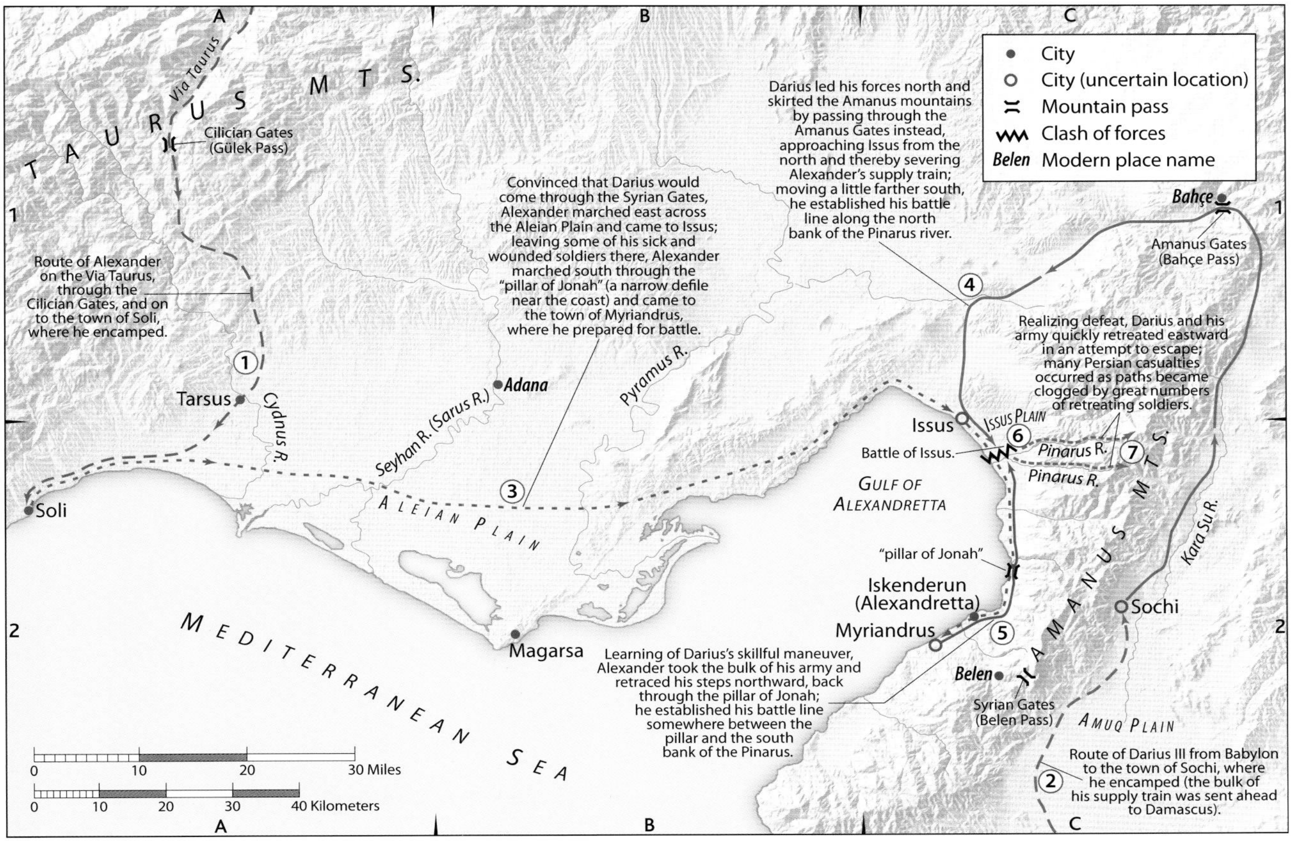
City
City (uncertain location)
Mountain pass
Clash of forces
Belen Modern place name
TAURUS MTS.
Via Taurus
Cilician Gates (Gülek Pass)
Route of Alexander on the Via Taurus, through the Cilician Gates, and on to the town of Soli, where he encamped.
Tarsus
Cydnus R.
Soli
Convinced that Darius would come through the Syrian Gates, Alexander marched east across the Aleian Plain and came to Issus; leaving some of his sick and wounded soldiers there, Alexander marched south through the "pillar of Jonah" (a narrow defile near the coast) and came to the town of Myriandrus, where he prepared for battle.
Adana
Seyhan R. (Sarus R.)
Pyramus R.
ALEIAN PLAIN
Magarsa
MEDITERRANEAN SEA
Darius led his forces north and skirted the Amanus mountains by passing through the Amanus Gates instead, approaching Issus from the north and thereby severing Alexander's supply train; moving a little farther south, he established his battle line along the north bank of the Pinarus river.
Bahçe
Amanus Gates (Bahçe Pass)
Realizing defeat, Darius and his army quickly retreated eastward in an attempt to escape; many Persian casualties occurred as paths became clogged by great numbers of retreating soldiers.
Issus
ISSUS PLAIN
Battle of Issus.
Pinarus R.
GULF OF ALEXANDRETTA
"pillar of Jonah"
Iskenderun (Alexandretta)
Myriandrus
AMANUS MTS.
Kara Su R.
Sochi
Belen
Syrian Gates (Belen Pass)
AMUQ PLAIN
Learning of Darius's skillful maneuver, Alexander took the bulk of his army and retraced his steps northward, back through the pillar of Jonah; he established his battle line somewhere between the pillar and the south bank of the Pinarus.
Route of Darius III from Babylon to the town of Sochi, where he encamped (the bulk of his supply train was sent ahead to Damascus).
0 10 20 30 Miles
0 10 20 30 40 Kilometers

Following the rout, Alexander returned to the battle scene at Issus, claimed control of Darius's royal chariot and imperial insignia, took a bath in Darius's large bathtub, donned a Persian robe, and feasted at a banquet off Persian gold plates. The next morning Alexander met Darius's mother, wife, princesses, and the royal heir. It was only a matter of days until Alexander's troops had occupied Damascus, retrieved the Persian war chest, and were paid for the first time in months. Alexander decided against the immediate eastward pursuit of Darius. Instead, by marching south across Syria and Phoenicia, he effectively neutralized any residual influence of Persian naval efforts along ports on the eastern Mediterranean. Moreover, a southward march would also give him Egypt and provide protection on his southern flank. He would set off to face Darius another day. [**See commentary with map 87.**]

Military academies and textbooks carefully scrutinize the strategic and tactical aspects of the battle of Issus. The conflict is commonly viewed as one of the most important military engagements in the history of humankind. Beyond that, however, the battle of Issus represents a seminal turning point in Near Eastern history.

For one thing, Alexander's victory at Issus enabled him to travel to Egypt where he would be hailed as "pharaoh," and in the process he also marched across Judea and came to Jerusalem. [**See map 88.**] Far more importantly, with the coming of Alexander, "Hellenism"—both as a mentality and a worldview—began to assume a prominent role in this region. Hellenism entailed the introduction of Greek language, government, taxation, education, coinage, city planning, entertainment, architecture, religion, and pantheon. The Hellenistic concept of cultural osmosis and a "world culture" featured equality and uniformity. Being separate from society was thought to be dangerous. So an array of distinctive problems and responses arose within Judaism.[408] One can confidently state that Hellenism greatly accelerated the process of the rise of Jewish sectarianism (Sadducees, Pharisees, Essenes, Nazarenes, Minim, Zealots), which, at its core, represented varying and competing responses to the fundamental challenge of this new worldview. Varying degrees of acculturation also produced a corruption of the Jerusalem priesthood,[409] which led ultimately to the Maccabean revolt and paved the way for the arrival of Rome into Jerusalem and Judea. [**See map 94.**]

Of course, rigid definitive attempts to explain ancient historical reality are notoriously tenuous, at times even woefully simplistic. The cause-effect lines are rarely entirely straightforward or simple. Nevertheless, it is fair to argue that the New Testament world of Judaism, Jewish sectarianism, and early Christianity—perhaps even including the language in which some of those literatures would be written—are all quite likely to have taken a different shape if Darius had been victorious at Issus.

HELLENISTIC CITIES IN PALESTINE

Alexander the Great and his immediate successors established many cities and towns throughout their domains in strategic localities or along arterial roadways—often on the sites of former Achaemenid administrative centers. Erecting a new city (*polis* in Greek) became a key means of spreading Hellenistic culture, settling and providing for former soldiers, and maintaining a degree of local political control.[410]

Ptolemy I Soter and his dynasty began to occupy Palestine and parts of Jordan around 301 B.C. in the aftermath of the battle of Ipsus. He created and fortified the cities of Ptolemais (Acco) and Philadelphia (Rabbah-Amman) as major Ptolemaic administrative centers, which acted in concert with the Ptolemaic administrative headquarters in Alexandria. As part of the same process, certain towns in Palestine (e.g., Dora, Joppa, Samaria, and Ascalon) were granted municipal rights by the Ptolemies, which entailed a fair measure of political autonomy in those places. During the reign of Ptolemy II Philadelphia in particular (285–246 B.C.), some cities were established and named for royal family members: Berenice-Pella and Berenice-Elath were named after one of his daughters, and Philoteria (Beth-yerah) was named after his sister. [**See map 91.**]

When the Ptolemaic hold on Palestine was lost to the Seleucids in 200 B.C. as a result of the battle of Panias, one might say that efforts towards Hellenization—including city building—assumed an even more defined cast. Like Alexander the Great, the Seleucid rulers were of Macedonian origin and were especially fond of naming cities after themselves. Dozens of classical cities bear the name Alexandria, Seleucia, or Antiochus, including cities in Palestine (e.g., Seleucid Demos [Gaza], Antiochia [Jerusalem, Hippos], and Antiochia Seleucia [Gadara]).

The oval-shaped Roman forum at Gerasa/Antiochia-on-Chrysorrhoas ("Antioch on the Golden river") is adjoined to the colonnaded *cardo maximus* street.

Hellenistic Cities in Palestine

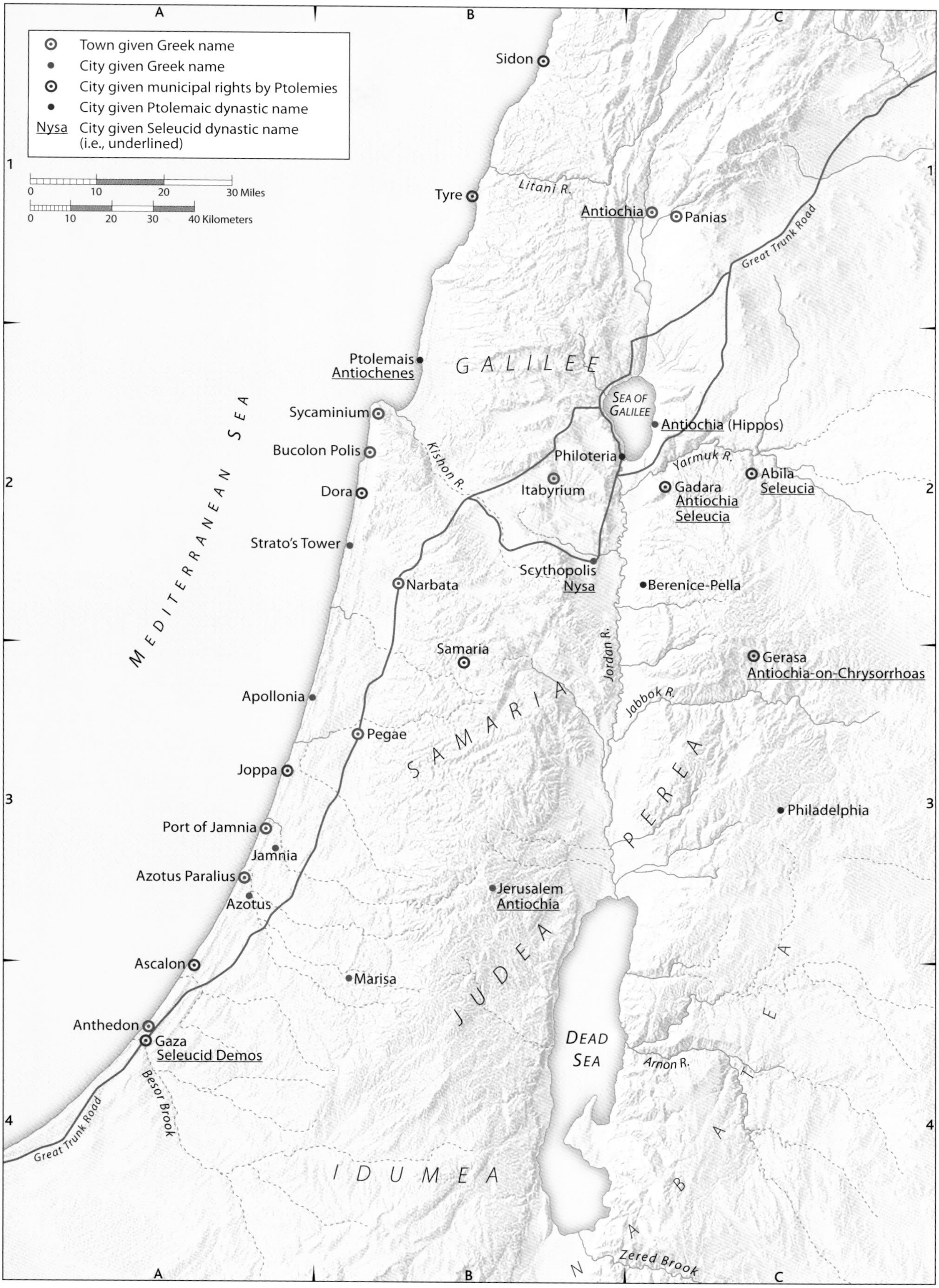

Town given Greek name
City given Greek name
City given municipal rights by Ptolemies
City given Ptolemaic dynastic name
Nysa City given Seleucid dynastic name (i.e., underlined)
0 10 20 30 Miles
0 10 20 30 40 Kilometers
Sidon
Tyre
Litani R.
Antiochia
Panias
Great Trunk Road
Ptolemais
Antiochenes
GALILEE
SEA OF GALILEE
Antiochia (Hippos)
Sycaminium
Bucolon Polis
Kishon R.
Philoteria
Yarmuk R.
Abila
Seleucia
Dora
Itabyrium
Gadara
Antiochia
Seleucia
Strato's Tower
Scythopolis
Nysa
Narbata
Berenice-Pella
MEDITERRANEAN SEA
Samaria
Jordan R.
Gerasa
Antiochia-on-Chrysorrhoas
Apollonia
Jabbok R.
SAMARIA
Pegae
Joppa
PEREA
Philadelphia
Port of Jamnia
Jamnia
Azotus Paralius
Azotus
Jerusalem
Antiochia
Ascalon
Marisa
JUDEA
Anthedon
Gaza
Seleucid Demos
DEAD SEA
Arnon R.
Besor Brook
Great Trunk Road
IDUMEA
NABATEA
Zered Brook

THE MACCABEAN REVOLT

Alexander's sudden death in 323 B.C. plunged much of his kingdom into a period of bloody intrigue and uncertainty as his former generals fought for a share of the territorial spoils. However, life in Judea appears not to have been adversely affected—at least for a short time. Numerous documents from the reign of Ptolemy II Philadelphia (285–246 B.C.) are particularly helpful in this regard. One such text speaks of an aide to the finance minister of Ptolemy II (named Zenon) who traveled throughout much of Judea and parts of Transjordan. He reported broad support for Ptolemaic rule, especially among Jerusalem's elite,[411] and generally peaceful conditions in more remote territory. Landowners in Judean villages and farms in secluded areas were largely free from Ptolemaic interference.[412] Both land and sea trade between Judea and Egypt remained active.[413] Jewish coins minted in Jerusalem and Judea during that time often bore the image of Ptolemy I and his wife.[414] The Letter of Aristeas, also written during the time of Ptolemy II, reports on the release of thousands of Judean prisoners who were free to return home after having been taken captive to Egypt. The same document also describes how 72 Jewish scholars from Judea were sent to Alexandria by the Jerusalem aristocracy for the purpose of translating the Jewish law from Hebrew into Greek, a translation that became known as the "Septuagint."[415] Little evidence indicates that Judea was being thoroughly Hellenized during the Ptolemaic period.[416] **[See map 90.]**

By way of contrast, two new realities forcefully began to impress themselves upon people living in Palestine toward

At the foot of Mt. Hermon (right side of picture) and adjacent to the headwaters of the Hermon/Banias River (left side of picture) lies the site of Panias, renamed Caesarea Philippi during the days of the New Testament. The huge cave at the bottom of Mt. Hermon was believed in the classical world to be where the daughter of Demeter had been carried off by Hades (Pluto), god of the underworld. It was here Jesus declared Peter to be "the rock" against which "the gates of Hades would not prevail."

The Maccabean Revolt

map 91

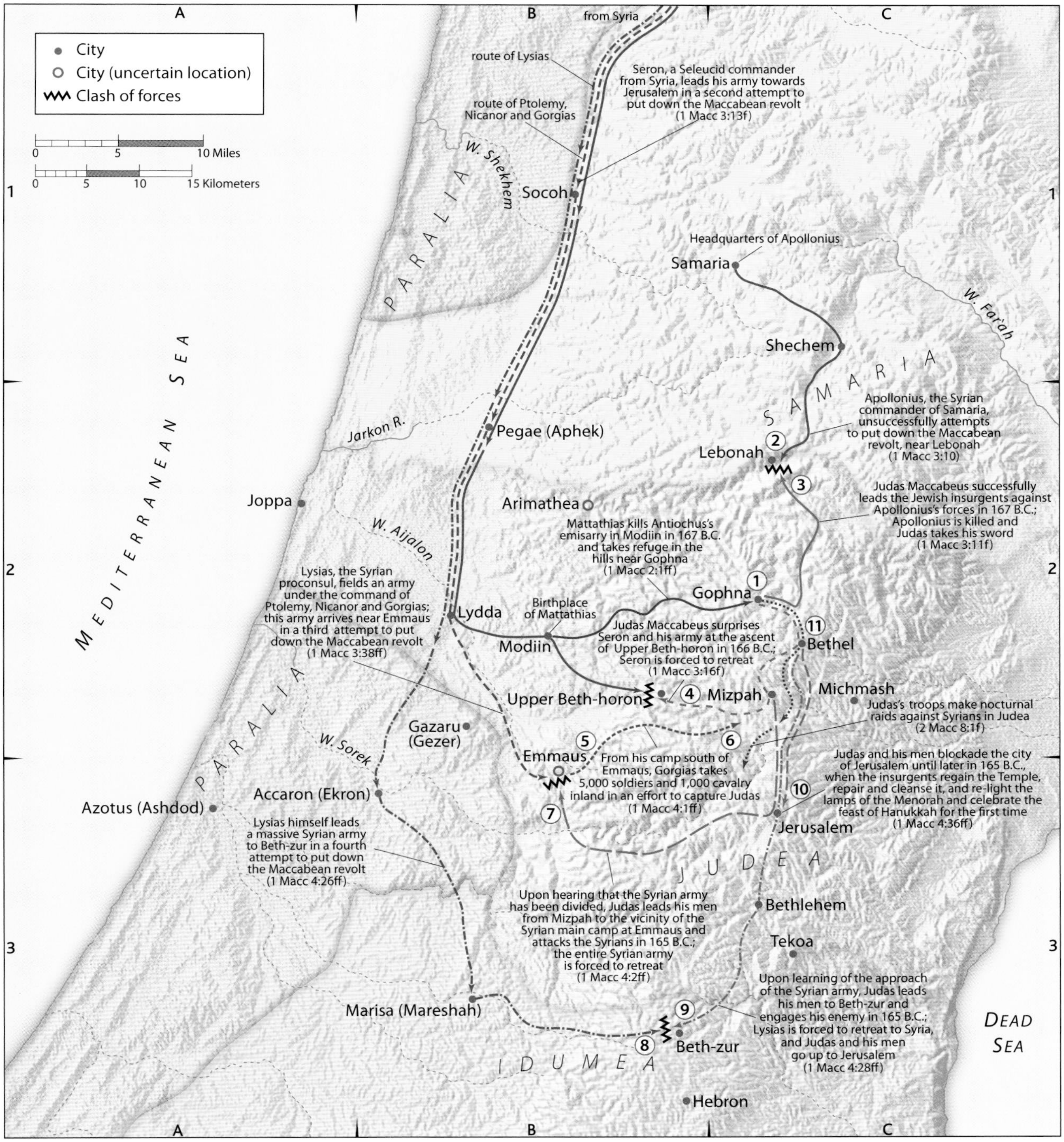

the end of the third century B.C. The first of these was geographic centrality. Palestine had often been conquered by outsiders (Egyptians, Assyrians, Babylonians, etc.), yet because the region was geographically removed from the respective seats of power, it had managed to remain more or less on the political sidelines. Now, however, the terrain of Palestine became a central, signaled battlefield as Ptolemies from the south and Seleucids from the north fought a number of wars for control of the territory. An ascending Seleucid power culminated in the battle of Panias in the year 200 B.C., when a Ptolemaic hold of Palestine was lost to Antiochus III Megas (223–187 B.C.) and the land was incorporated into Seleucid Syria.

The advent of Seleucid control of Palestine brought a second new reality into sharp focus: forced Hellenization. Hellenistic culture presented many deep challenges to post-exilic Judaism. It became the vehicle for introducing the Greek *polis* ("city"), which in turn manifested many new architectural forms (agoras, baths, theaters, and such) and vexing concepts (Greek language, deities, education, coinage,

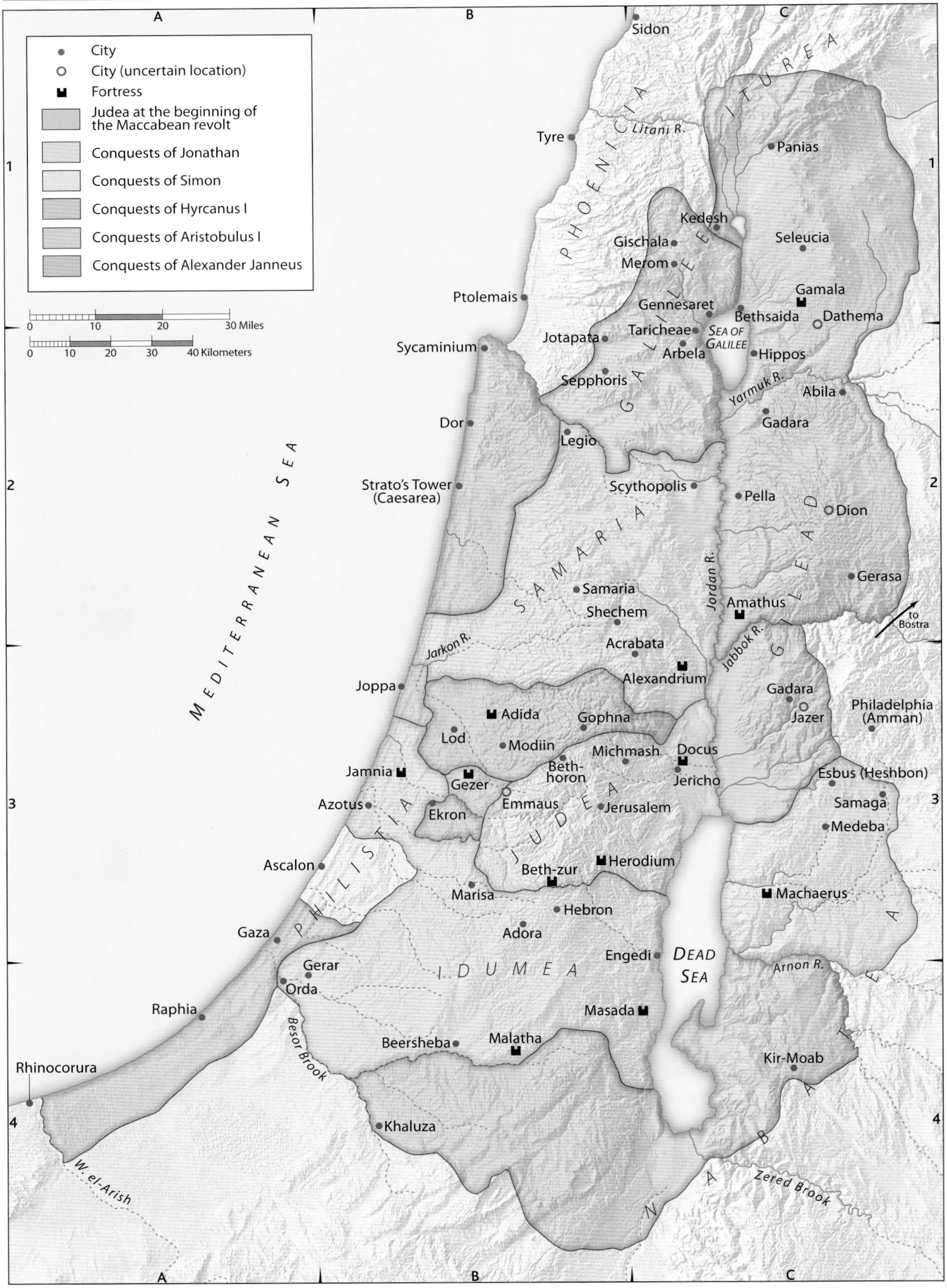
City
City (uncertain location)
Fortress
Judea at the beginning of the Maccabean revolt
Conquests of Jonathan
Conquests of Simon
Conquests of Hyrcanus I
Conquests of Aristobulus I
Conquests of Alexander Janneus
0 10 20 30 Miles
0 10 20 30 40 Kilometers
MEDITERRANEAN SEA
PHOENICIA
ITUREA
GALILEE
SAMARIA
GILEAD
JUDEA
PHILISTIA
IDUMEA
NABATEA
Sidon
Tyre
Litani R.
Panias
Kedesh
Gischala
Merom
Seleucia
Ptolemais
Gamala
Gennesaret
Bethsaida
Dathema
Jotapata
Taricheae
Sea of Galilee
Arbela
Hippos
Sycaminium
Sepphoris
Yarmuk R.
Abila
Gadara
Dor
Legio
Strato's Tower (Caesarea)
Scythopolis
Pella
Dion
Jordan R.
Gerasa
Samaria
Shechem
Amathus
to Bostra
Jarkon R.
Acrabata
Jabbok R.
Alexandrium
Joppa
Adida
Gophna
Gadara
Jazer
Philadelphia (Amman)
Lod
Modiin
Michmash
Docus
Jamnia
Gezer
Beth-horon
Jericho
Esbus (Heshbon)
Emmaus
Azotus
Ekron
Jerusalem
Samaga
Medeba
Ascalon
Herodium
Beth-zur
Marisa
Machaerus
Hebron
Gaza
Adora
Engedi
Dead Sea
Gerar
Arnon R.
Orda
Raphia
Masada
Besor Brook
Beersheba
Malatha
Kir-Moab
Rhinocorura
Khaluza
W. el-Arish
Zered Brook
A
B
C
1
2
3
4

and entertainment). It created a structure for imposing city taxes, temple taxes, and state-owned industries. At its heart, Hellenism represented a competing worldview to Judaism—one that featured equality and uniformity, and where being separate from the dominant culture was thought to be dangerous.

The issue came to a head during the reign of Antiochus IV Epiphanes (175–164 B.C.), who constructed at Jerusalem a gymnasium and converted the city into a Hellenistic *polis*, to be known as Antiochia.[417] In 168 B.C. he erected a fortress in Jerusalem called the Akra, and deployed a Syrian legion there.[418] The following year Antiochus issued further coercive edicts against distinctive Jewish customs and ceremonies, which were carried out with severity in Jerusalem—including banning of circumcision and Sabbath observance and burning of copies of the law. The Temple was desecrated and its treasures confiscated. The worship of Yahweh was abolished, an altar and statue of the Olympian Zeus was installed in the sacred precinct, and pagan sacrifices including a pig were offered there.[419] Antiochus's motivations have been much discussed, but the outcome of his actions is quite clear.

Outraged at such a flagrant perversion, a priest named Mattathias from the town of Modiin, some 18 miles northwest of Jerusalem, resolutely refused to offer the prescribed heathen sacrifices. Instead, he killed Antiochus's emissary, demolished the pagan altar, and fled for his life with his sons into the hills of Gophna.[420] When word of his brave action spread throughout Judea, thousands of insurgents, later to be known as the Hasidim ("pious ones"), openly revolted against Syria under the capable leadership of a son of Mattathias—Judas, nicknamed Maccabeus ("mallet-headed"). Mattathias was a direct descendant of a leading priest known as Hasmonias who ultimately hailed from Jerusalem, so the movement that began at Modiin is often identified as Hasmonean, one that resulted in a Hasmonean state[421] [**1**].

Judas led his well-trained band of armed rebels to successive victories. He crushed an initial attempt to put down the revolt by Apollonius [**2**], a Syrian commander stationed at Samaria, apparently near Lebonah[422] [**3**]. Apollonius was killed in the conflict, and Judas took possession of his sword, which he used in his future battles. A second attempt to quell the uprising was led by Seron, a Seleucid commander from Syria [**4**]. He also met defeat as the Syrian troops were climbing the ascent of Upper Beth-horon.[423] Seron's army was forced to retreat, and he may have been killed in the foray.[424] A third attempt was staged by Lysias, a relative of Antiochus IV and the Syrian proconsul, who fielded an army of battalion size under the commands of Ptolemy, Nicanor, and Gorgias. This consolidated army marched as far south as the vicinity of Emmaus [**5**], and a contingent under the command of Gorgias went farther inland in an attempt to capture Judas [**6**]. Upon hearing that the Syrian army had been divided, Judas led his men from Mizpah, skirting Gorgias's forces, and approached the main camp at Emmaus [**7**]. It was a convincing Maccabean victory. The entire Syrian army was forced to retreat northward.[425] Finally, Lysias himself led out a massive Syrian army from Syrian Antioch to vanquish this revolt. His army marched to the area of Beth-zur, in northern Idumea, where the battle was pitched [**8**]. But Judas learned of the approach of this army, led his men to Beth-zur, and again successfully engaged the enemy [**9**]. Lysias and his entire army were forced to retreat back to Syria.[426]

Thereupon, Judas and his men marched north to Jerusalem where they blockaded the city for a time and beat back several attempts to relieve the Seleucid legion inside the Akra [**10**]. Finally, a truce was declared. The Hasidim were permitted to occupy the Temple hill, to cleanse the Temple of pagan objects, and to reinstitute sacrifices to Yahweh. Some three years after Antiochus profaned the Temple, its lamps were again lit in the name of Yahweh in 164 B.C. This occasion is solemnly memorialized every year in the Feast of Hanukkah.[427]

With religious purity now within view, Judas set out to achieve political freedom as well. He undertook military expeditions in every direction.[428] In the north, his guerrillas experienced victories at Scythopolis and east at Dathema. Farther north, he invaded the territory of the Itureans. On one occasion Judas led his men on a three-day march into the Hauran district to relieve the Jewish population inside the city of Bostra. The Maccabean army was able to march eastward against the Nabateans as far as Jazer. In the south, the Idumean cities of Hebron and Marisa fell to Judas. And on the coastal plain, Judas's forces razed the cities of Azotus and Joppa. His attempt to gain political freedom was far-reaching, for Judas actually set into motion a chain of events that would culminate a century later with the Roman troops of Pompey being hailed in Jerusalem as liberators.

But meanwhile, a Jewish state was created by Judas's successors. His two brothers—Jonathan (161–142 B.C.) and Simon (142–134 B.C.)—extended the Judean heartland from the Mediterranean Sea to the eastern desert. [**See map 92.**] The torch was then carried by a son of Simon, John Hyrcanus I (134–104 B.C.), who incorporated both Samaria and Idumea into Judea. Then came the brief reign of Aristobulus I (104–103 B.C.), who subjugated Galilee. He was followed by his brother, Alexander Janneus (103–76 B.C.), whose exploits took him as far afield as the plain of Dor, northern Gilead, much of northern Nabatea, and the threshold of Egypt. In time, however, one of Alexander's sons (John Hyrcanus II) would be obliged to submit to Pompey's Roman domination.

JERUSALEM THROUGH THE AGES

Jerusalem enjoys a sacred mystique with the Jew, Muslim, and Christian alike. It was the place of Judaism's first Temple, the place where Christians believe Jesus died and was resurrected, and the place where Muslims believe Mohammad ascended to heaven. Shrines for all three religions coexist there, and prayer at or for Jerusalem is a prominent theme, especially within Judaism and Islam. Jerusalem is a city long leavened by divine decrees.[429] Perhaps no other place on the planet has drawn more attention, captivated more religious pilgrims throughout history, or so uniquely influenced the world's thought and literature.

THE NAME

It is a little surprising, then, that the meaning of the city's name has eluded certainty, thereby inviting a veritable kaleidoscope of etymological speculation, ranging from "sacred rock" to "complete cloudburst." Perhaps one reason is the astonishing realization that the word "Jerusalem" is attested only rarely in high antiquity. We might expect the city to have appeared in the Mari tablets—a vast Middle Bronze Age archive of nearly 25,000 documents envisioning a broad geographical horizon stretching from the edge of Iran (Susa) as far west as Crete, and spanning virtually all of the Fertile Crescent. [**See map 23.**] And we know of numerous annals, papyri, and wall panels that describe dozens of Egyptian military campaigns through Canaan, in which the names of at least 250 cities are listed.[430] But "Jerusalem" never explicitly appears in any of this literature.[431]

Temple Mount of Jerusalem looking northeast, which features the Dome of the Rock (gold dome) and the el-Aqsa mosque (silver-domed edifice just inside the southern wall). Beyond its rectangular design lie the Mount of Olives and Gethsemane (right side of picture), the Kidron valley (between the Mt. of Olives and the Temple Mount), an archaeological park (between the southern wall and the street), and the Western/Wailing Wall (large open space just outside the south-central portion of the western wall).

No less striking, the Babylonian Chronicle of Nebuchadnezzar II,[432] which officially documented the fall of Jerusalem to the Babylonians, supplies extended chronological detail and precision but only geographical ambiguity. This Chronicle merely recorded that Nebuchadnezzar seized "the city of Judah" (*āl Yaḫudi*), but it does not mention "Jerusalem."

The earliest known citations of Jerusalem[433] date to around the 19th or 18th centuries B.C. under an Egyptian form probably transliterated *[U]rušalimum*, *[Yu]rušalimum*, or even *Rušalimum*.[434] In the 14th century B.C., the name of the city appears some seven times in three letters from T. el-Amarna, normally written ^{URU}*Urusalim*^{ki}.[435] Still later, the city is attested in the two late-eighth-century B.C. Sennacherib/Hezekiah inscriptions under the form ^{URU}*Ursalimmu*.[436]

This somewhat limited and linguistically diverse evidence suggests that "Jerusalem" may be comprised of two Semitic elements—*uru* ("city") and *šalem* (a divine name). Hyphenating place names by incorporating divine elements was a common phenomenon in the ancient Near Eastern world, and the god Shalem is known to have been a member of the Canaanite pantheon.[437] Moreover, the Old Testament makes clear that Jerusalem was not originally an Israelite city (2 Sam. 5:6–10). Accordingly, it seems plausible to postulate that the name Jerusalem was originally understood to mean "the city of [the god] Shalem."[438]

In the Hebrew Old Testament, Jerusalem is normally written *y^{e}rûšālayim* (e.g., Josh. 10:1), whereas in the Aramaic portions the name is rendered *y^{e}rûš^{e}lēm* (e.g., Dan. 5:2). Here the word seems to combine the elements *yārâ* ("to found") with *šālēm* (a divine name), thus yielding "the foundation of [the god] Shalem" or "Shalem has founded." The eloquence of this alteration is reflected in the word "found[ation]," perhaps indicating the permanent home of Shalem. From this, one may surmise that

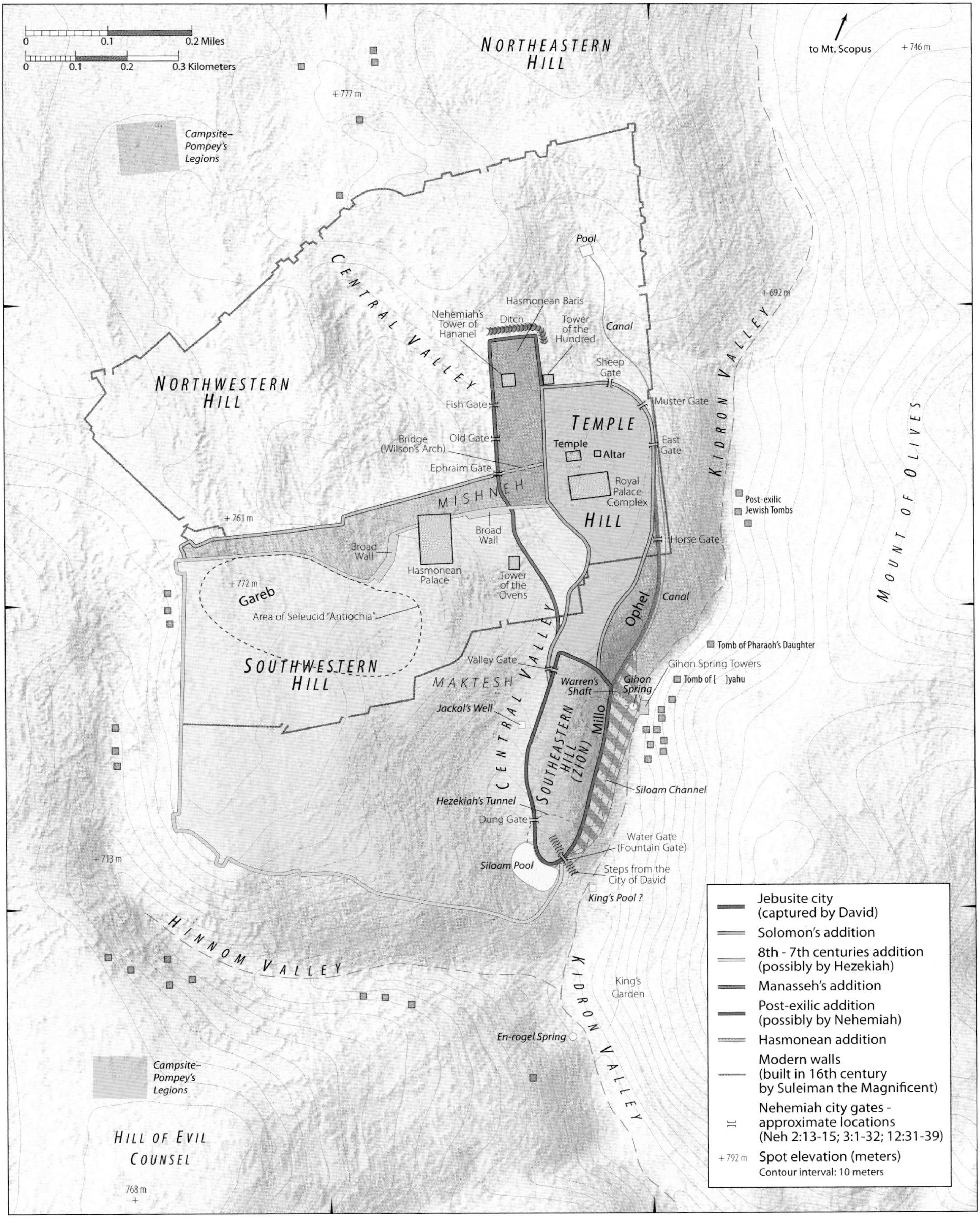
0 0.1 0.2 Miles
0 0.1 0.2 0.3 Kilometers
NORTHEASTERN HILL
to Mt. Scopus
+ 746 m
+ 777 m
Campsite–Pompey's Legions
Pool
CENTRAL VALLEY
Hasmonean Baris
Nehemiah's Tower of Hananel
Ditch
Tower of the Hundred
Canal
+ 692 m
KIDRON VALLEY
Sheep Gate
NORTHWESTERN HILL
Fish Gate
Muster Gate
TEMPLE
Bridge (Wilson's Arch)
Old Gate
Temple
Altar
East Gate
MOUNT OF OLIVES
Ephraim Gate
Royal Palace Complex
MISHNEH
Post-exilic Jewish Tombs
+ 761 m
HILL
Broad Wall
Broad Wall
Horse Gate
Hasmonean Palace
Tower of the Ovens
+ 772 m
Gareb
Area of Seleucid "Antiochia"
Ophel
Canal
Tomb of Pharaoh's Daughter
SOUTHWESTERN HILL
Valley Gate
Gihon Spring Towers
MAKTESH
Warren's Shaft
Gihon Spring
Tomb of [ ]yahu
Jackal's Well
SOUTHEASTERN HILL (ZION)
Millo
Siloam Channel
Hezekiah's Tunnel
Dung Gate
Water Gate (Fountain Gate)
+ 713 m
Siloam Pool
Steps from the City of David
King's Pool ?
HINNOM VALLEY
KIDRON VALLEY
King's Garden
En-rogel Spring
Campsite–Pompey's Legions
HILL OF EVIL COUNSEL
768 m
Jebusite city (captured by David)
Solomon's addition
8th - 7th centuries addition (possibly by Hezekiah)
Manasseh's addition
Post-exilic addition (possibly by Nehemiah)
Hasmonean addition
Modern walls (built in 16th century by Suleiman the Magnificent)
Nehemiah city gates - approximate locations (Neh 2:13-15; 3:1-32; 12:31-39)
+ 792 m Spot elevation (meters)
Contour interval: 10 meters

Shalem had probably become the patron deity of the city and had given his name to it.

In the New Testament, Jerusalem translates the two Greek words *'Ierousalēm* (e.g., Rom. 15:19) and *Hierosolyma* (e.g., Matt. 2:1). The former is simply the Greek transliteration of the Aramaic form; the latter reflects the word *hieros* ("holy"), which represents a classic instance of a Hellenistic paronomasia (pun),[439] but which corresponds neither to the Semitic root meaning nor to the city's historical reality. Besides Jerusalem, the city has been called Salem/Solyma, Jebus, Zion, Moriah, Ariel, the City, Aelia Capitolina, El-Quds, and Bait el-Makdis.

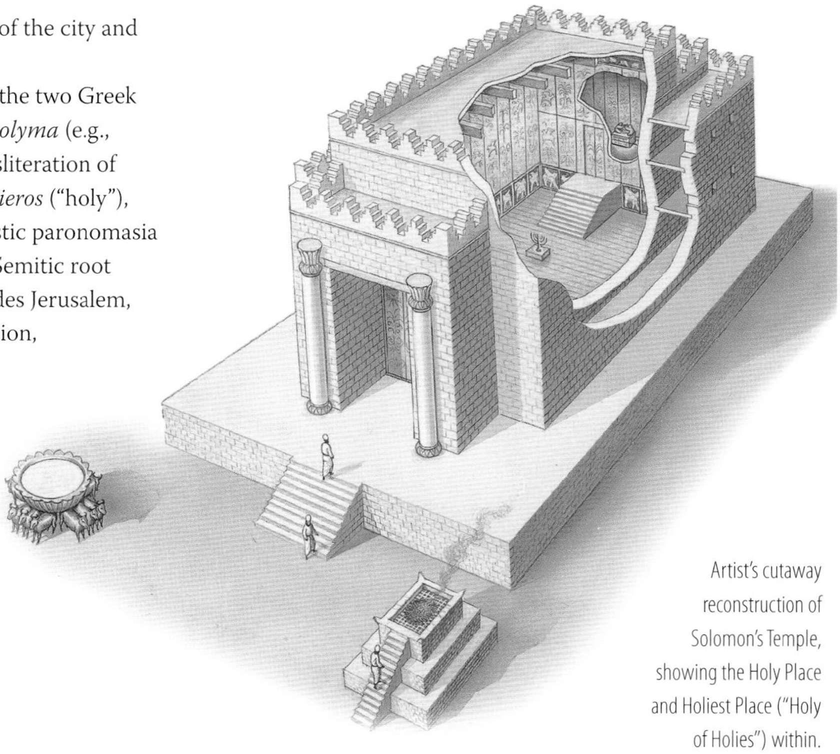

Artist's cutaway reconstruction of Solomon's Temple, showing the Holy Place and Holiest Place ("Holy of Holies") within.

TOPOGRAPHY

Like Rome, Jerusalem is a city set on hills. A cluster of five hills comprises its denuded quadrilateral landmass roughly one mile long and one-half mile wide. It is bordered on all sides except the north by deep ravines. Skirting the city on the west and south is the Hinnom valley (Greek *Gehenna*), and hedging Jerusalem on the east is the Kidron valley (the valley of Jehoshaphat [Joel 3:2, 12]).[440] A third (Central) valley—known since the days of Josephus as the Tyropoeon ("cheesemakers") valley—stretches from the modern Damascus Gate in the north to the vicinity of the Siloam Pool in the south, where it converges with the Kidron. These three ravines are connected by a number of lateral valleys, originally segmenting the configuration of the terrain and creating discreet hills.

Three hills lie east of the Central valley:

- Historically known as the Southeastern hill, this southernmost of the three was the site of earliest occupation, undoubtedly because of its direct and more convenient water access, the Gihon spring. This was the Jebusite city conquered by David, also known in the Old Testament as Zion (not to be confused with modern Mt. Zion). [**See map 97.**] The narrow ridge of Old Testament Zion is no more than 60 yards across at the top and encompasses only about eight acres. Today this area lies completely outside the modern (16th-century) walls of the city.
- The Temple hill lies immediately north of Zion, dominated today by the sacred spot on which rests the Muslim Dome of the Rock. Some scholars associate this hill with the site of Araunah's threshing floor (2 Sam. 24:18–19)[441] and others aver it to be the location of Moriah (Gen. 22:2; 2 Chron. 3:1).[442] (Jerusalem does lie some 50 miles from Beersheba, which makes possible the arrival of Abraham there on the third day [Gen. 22:4], but it is a curiosity that someone should have carried wood from the desert environs of Beersheba to the more wooded country around Jerusalem.) The Temple hill is separated from the third crest on the east of the Central valley by "St. Anne's valley," a lateral depression that extends east to St. Stephen's Gate. [**See map 97.**]
- North of this depression is the Northeastern hill, which was occupied and named Bezetha ("the new city") during the Roman period when practical necessity dictated that a third northern wall be constructed to accommodate a growing population. [**See map 94.**]

To the west of the Tyropoeon (Central) valley stand the two remaining hills:

- What is historically known as the Southwestern hill was called by Josephus the "Upper City,"[443] a reference to its higher elevation. Today the Southwestern hill roughly corresponds to the Armenian Quarter. It is occupied by the citadel of David (constructed upon the foundations of Herod's towers), the Church of St. James, the traditional (though clearly mistaken!) site of David's tomb, the traditional site of the "Upper Room," and the Dormitian Abbey. [**See maps 95 and 97.**] Part of this hill in Old Testament times included the Gareb (cf. Jer. 31:39), commonly regarded by Protestants until near the end of the 19th century as the place of Calvary.[444]
- The remaining hill to the west is known as the Northwestern hill, which generally corresponds to the Christian quarter today. It is dominated by the Church of the Holy Sepulchre and the Church of the Redeemer. [**See map 97.**]

Jerusalem is a city not only *set on* hills, but also *surrounded by* hills. East of the city rises the lofty summit of the Mount of Olives; south lies the heights of the Mount of Offense and the Hill of Evil Counsel. Mount Shalmon, Givat Ram, and Mount Menuhot rise in the west, while the northern horizon is dominated by the summit of Mount Scopus and French Hill. The reality of Jerusalem's hills nestled among even higher surroundings is meaningfully reflected in the words of the Psalmist: "as the mountains surround Jerusalem, so the Lord surrounds his people, from now and for evermore" (Ps. 125:2).

Jerusalem lay geographically central to the land. It was astride the summit of the central mountain spine and adjacent to the central ridge road that connects Beersheba, Hebron, and Bethlehem with Shechem and points north. [**See map 27.**] The lateral roadway through the Judean mountains eastward (Jericho road) could not pass south of the city, being blocked by the Dead Sea and the sheer cliffs of the Judean wilderness. The only natural possibility for this route was through the saddle of land from Jericho in the direction of Jerusalem, westward from there through the Aijalon pass, and out into the plains. Thus, Jerusalem was positioned immediately adjacent to the natural crossroads of Judea.[445]

Water has always been in meager supply at Jerusalem. The only natural source of permanent water was the Gihon spring, located along the Kidron valley near the Jebusite fortress conquered by David. Hezekiah's tunnel was cut through nearly 1,800 feet of hard limestone, allowing the waters of the Gihon to pass through the interior of the hill of Zion to the Siloam pool, inside the city walls (2 Kings 20:20; 2 Chron. 32:3, 30; cf. Isa. 22:9–11).[446] An "upper pool" (2 Kings 18:17; Isa. 36:2), presumably on the north side of the Temple complex, may also have been a source of water. Another small spring (En-rogel) once lay farther south where the Kidron and Hinnom valleys converge (Josh. 15:7). Due to the lowering of the water table, however, this spring ceased to percolate and was subsequently converted into a well. These three sources were clearly insufficient to sustain a sizeable population, so an entire network of cisterns, reservoirs, and water conduits for supplemental supply had to be devised. During the New Testament period, a number of aqueducts, constructed by Herod and others, carried substantial supplies of water to Jerusalem from points south and west.[447]

EXPLORATIONS AND EXCAVATIONS

No Palestinian city can boast of more excavations, yet most of Jerusalem's archaeological returns have been substantially fragmentary and chronologically incoherent.[448] Contributing factors include the city's dense contemporary population, its sacral character, and the surprisingly late arrival of modern archaeological technology. While an impressive number of explorations and excavations have been undertaken *at* Jerusalem, never has there been a systematic excavation *of* Jerusalem. Nevertheless, a history of the city's excavations revolves primarily around the axes of five creative periods, accompanied by a host of other very commendable efforts.

Modern exploration at Jerusalem appears to date from the surveying of Johann Van Kootwijck (1598–1599),[449] but it was the research of Edward Robinson that inaugurated Jerusalem's first creative epoch.[450] Robinson made a series of topographic surveys that have profound significance even today, and his activities mark the advent of a flood of new literature. This American scholar dared to challenge the time-honored axiom that ecclesiastical traditions provided the primary source for reconstructing the city's history. Instead, he sought to reconstruct Jerusalem's history on the basis of the unsuspecting evidence of the stones, thereby signaling for the holy city the advent of the archaeological method.[451]

The old city of Jerusalem viewed from the Mount of Olives.

A second creative period commenced in 1865 when the Palestine Exploration Fund launched its first archaeological mission to Jerusalem thanks to the philanthropic contribution of Lady Burdett-Coutts of London, who wished to improve the sanitary conditions and water supply of the city. Between 1867 and 1870, this modest venture was expanded as Captain (later "Sir") Charles Warren carried out extensive excavations around the Temple area, on the Southeastern hill, and in the Tyropoeon valley. Of special interest was his unearthing of a section of an ancient wall near the southeastern sector of the Temple. While conducting more extensive research within Hezekiah's tunnel, Warren discovered an alternate, archaic shaft connecting the Gihon with a plateau of the Southeastern hill. The cartographic materials amassed by Warren and his predecessor, Charles Wilson, remain an invaluable source of much contemporary topographic research.

In the wake of the much-publicized discoveries of Wilson and Warren came the discovery of the now famous late-eighth-century B.C. Siloam Inscription,[452] which describes how the Hezekiah channel was dug simultaneously from either end (2 Chron. 32:30).[453] At the same time, elaborate excavations of the southern wall isolated for the first time a wall stretching across the mouth of the Tyropoeon, connecting the Southeastern and Southwestern hills.[454]

Perhaps it could be said that the third creative period began with the work of Raymond Weill. Although the area Weill excavated on the Southeastern hill was comparatively small, he first employed the stratigraphic excavation method at Jerusalem and provided penetrating new insights into Jerusalem's history before the time of David. His labors forever dispelled all doubt that the Southeastern hill exercised historical supremacy in earliest times. Following World War I, various teams explored north of the city,[455] discovering sections of the "third [northern] wall" of Josephus, begun by Herod Agrippa I and completed by the Zealots just prior to the siege of Jerusalem in A.D. 70. Subsequent excavations through the 1950s unearthed a cemetery, walls, and towers from the pre-Christian era, and the citadel at the Jaffa Gate was further explored.[456]

The fourth creative period was initiated with the protracted archaeological expedition under the capable leadership of Kathleen Kenyon. Between 1961 and 1967, this British School of Archaeology project explored several regions of Jerusalem, focusing principally upon the Southeastern hill near the Gihon, the mouth of the Tyropoeon, the territory immediately south of the Temple area, and the Armenian Gardens just inside the west section of the 16th-century walls. Since 1968, the Hebrew University has intermittently undertaken archaeological research in and near the city, especially on the east side. During those same years, Israel's Department of Antiquities has engaged in excavations of what was known prior to the 1948 war as the Jewish Quarter. As part of this latter work, the discovery of the so-called "broad wall" proved beyond cavil that the period of "first temple" Jerusalem had spread west of the Tyropoeon valley.

The fifth creative period is represented by a mélange of more recent noteworthy efforts at a variety of locations within Jerusalem's landscape. Included in these ventures is work among tombs, at the Church of the Holy Sepulchre, on the so-called "Warren's shaft," on the tunnel northwest of the Temple mount, on the towers and wall enclosing the Gihon spring, and perhaps above all on the area in and around the Siloam pool and in the Hinnom.[457]

HISTORY

Ancient flint implements found in the plain of the Rephaim, just west of Jerusalem, constitute the earliest evidence of existence of humankind in the area of Jerusalem. Near the beginning of the fourth millennium B.C., a sedentary group apparently first occupied the Southeastern hill, based on artifactual remains recovered from graves built on bedrock.[458] By 1800 B.C., the crest of the Southeastern hill was walled in rudimentary form, massive towers were erected around the Gihon complex, and the Siloam Channel apparently conveyed water from the Gihon spring southward into the Siloam pool.

In the 15th century B.C. or thereabouts, extensive building activities were initiated and measurably improved fortification methods were introduced at Jerusalem. Beginning some 160 feet down the eastern slope of the Southeastern hill, the city's occupants undertook to construct platform terraces, engineered to be filled up to the level of the top of the hill and reinforced by a series of ribs designed to hold and retain the immense fill that would have been required. The residents also erected a strong masonry rampart near the bottom of the slope, below a spot where some natural sinkholes existed that perhaps provided internal access to the waters of the Gihon. This enterprise procured an enlarged land area on the summit, a much stronger and more permanent city wall, and perhaps even some sort of water access during times of siege. Apparently the northern perimeter of this fortress extended to just south of the modern (16th-century) south wall.

Jerusalem could not be taken and held by the Israelites at the point of their first entry into the land (Josh. 15:63; Judg. 1:21); it didn't fall into Israelite hands until David's band wrested the city from Jebusite control (2 Sam. 5:6–9; 1 Chron. 11:4–8). How the capture was effected logistically has been debated in recent times. It had earlier been believed that Joab surreptitiously climbed through some sort of shaft from the Gihon and took the Jebusites by surprise, based on the biblical reference to the "water shaft" (*ṣinnôr*, 2 Sam. 5:8). Yet subsequent research has rendered this view untenable.[459] Whether David's men fought their way up the slopes by the use of scaling hooks (another possible meaning of *ṣinnôr*)[460] or in other ways, the incorporation of Jerusalem into David's kingdom and its transformation into some sort of a royal city

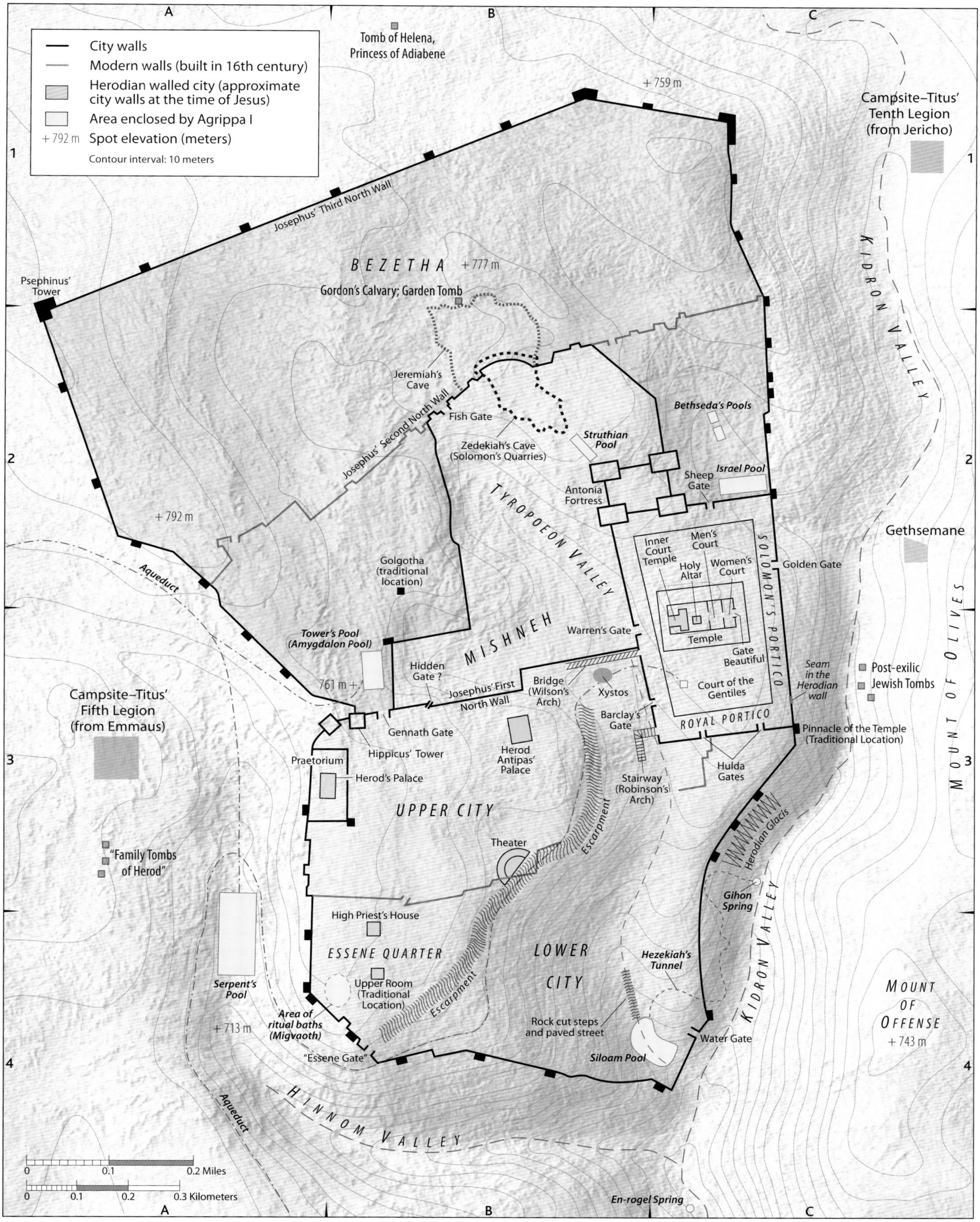
City walls
Modern walls (built in 16th century)
Herodian walled city (approximate city walls at the time of Jesus)
Area enclosed by Agrippa I
+ 792 m Spot elevation (meters)
Contour interval: 10 meters
A
B
C
1
2
3
4
Tomb of Helena, Princess of Adiabene
+ 759 m
Campsite–Titus' Tenth Legion (from Jericho)
Josephus' Third North Wall
BEZETHA
+ 777 m
Gordon's Calvary; Garden Tomb
Psephinus' Tower
KIDRON VALLEY
Jeremiah's Cave
Josephus' Second North Wall
Fish Gate
Bethseda's Pools
Struthian Pool
Zedekiah's Cave (Solomon's Quarries)
Israel Pool
Sheep Gate
Antonia Fortress
TYROPOEON VALLEY
+ 792 m
Gethsemane
Inner Court Temple
Men's Court
Holy Altar
Women's Court
Temple
SOLOMON'S PORTICO
Golden Gate
Aqueduct
Golgotha (traditional location)
MOUNT OF OLIVES
Warren's Gate
Tower's Pool (Amygdalon Pool)
MISHNEH
Gate Beautiful
Seam in the Herodian wall
Post-exilic Jewish Tombs
Hidden Gate ?
761 m +
Josephus' First North Wall
Bridge (Wilson's Arch)
Xystos
Court of the Gentiles
Campsite–Titus' Fifth Legion (from Emmaus)
Barclay's Gate
ROYAL PORTICO
Pinnacle of the Temple (Traditional Location)
Gennath Gate
Hippicus' Tower
Herod Antipas' Palace
Praetorium
Herod's Palace
Stairway (Robinson's Arch)
Hulda Gates
UPPER CITY
Escarpment
Herodian Glacis
Theater
"Family Tombs of Herod"
Gihon Spring
High Priest's House
ESSENE QUARTER
LOWER CITY
Hezekiah's Tunnel
KIDRON VALLEY
Serpent's Pool
Upper Room (Traditional Location)
Escarpment
MOUNT OF OFFENSE
+ 743 m
+ 713 m
Area of ritual baths (Migvaoth)
Rock cut steps and paved street
Water Gate
"Essene Gate"
Siloam Pool
HINNOM VALLEY
Aqueduct
0
0.1
0.2 Miles
0
0.1
0.2
0.3 Kilometers
En-rogel Spring

would have required substantial construction. The king is said to have fortified the city walls and to have prepared an extension of the city (2 Sam. 5:9; 1 Chron. 11:8).

David is said also to have constructed a royal residence in Jerusalem (2 Sam. 5:11). A text from Nehemiah (12:37) suggests that this edifice may have lain near the east side of the Southeastern hill. It was apparently from a window of this house that Michal peered out and saw her husband behaving in what she perceived as an undignified manner (2 Sam. 6:16). It was also from the roof of this palace that David gazed out upon Bathsheba as she bathed (2 Sam. 11:2–5), and later that his son Absalom publicly engaged in sexual intercourse with his father's concubines (2 Sam. 16:21–22).

By bringing the ark of the covenant into Jerusalem (2 Sam. 6:12–19; 1 Chron. 15:25–29), implying that Yahweh would also be residing there, David displayed perhaps his most profound leadership. In this perceptive act, he merged for the first time in Israel's history its political and religious centers. Henceforth, Jerusalem would take on the character of a "royal city" as well as a "holy city," and would be known as the "city of David" (2 Sam. 5:9) as well as the "city of God" (Ps. 46:4). From then on, adult healthy male Jews would be making their pilgrimages *to Jerusalem* to participate in festival seasons. It remained only for David to make permanent this arrangement, to enshrine Yahweh in Jerusalem forever by building him a temple (2 Sam. 7:1–17), but the execution of his dream was reserved for one of David's sons (2 Sam. 7:12–13; 1 Chron. 28:3).

Solomon inherited a kingdom from his father that was extensive and basically secure. Nevertheless, new and additional military measures had to be introduced into Jerusalem and the surrounding terrain. He is said to have fortified certain key cities, including Jerusalem,[461] and to have transformed some of them into military bases where a standing army was deployed (1 Kings 9:15–23). [**See map 64.**] And although his reign was not entirely peaceful, history records no significant military campaigns that he was obliged to undertake. All of Israel, from Dan to Beersheba, was said to have enjoyed peace and prosperity during Solomon's tenure (1 Kings 4:25), and he is remembered more for wisdom and architecture than for war.

Solomon was the great Old Testament builder of Jerusalem. His most significant building enterprise was undoubtedly the first Temple. Erected on the summit of the Temple hill, the edifice required some seven years to construct. With a suggested tripartite floor plan, the Temple faced east, the direction of the rising sun, and was a magnificent building (1 Kings 6:1–38; 7:13–51). Following the completion of the Temple, Solomon had the furniture of the Tabernacle, including the ark, moved from Zion (2 Chron. 5). The event was crowned by a manifestation of God's presence (1 Kings 8:10).

At the center of the Muslim sacred enclosure, known today as the Haram esh-Sherif ("the noble sanctuary"), stands the Dome of the Rock. [**See map 97.**] Embedded under this shrine is a large rock long venerated as the spot over which stood the courtyard of the Solomonic Temple. Though such a tradition may be based on fact, nothing definitively dating from that era has yet been exhumed from the sacred precinct.

Solomon also built Jerusalem's city walls (1 Kings 3:1; 9:15). This probably means that he extended the Canaanite walls to enclose the enlarged area of his own city. Though it is unlikely that Solomon expanded his city to the south or east, to encompass the Temple required constructing an extension wall to the north.[462] The position of the city walls depicted on **map 93** is largely speculative, based on a modicum of archaeological discovery.

Jerusalem and Judea were repeatedly assaulted throughout the period of the divided monarchy [**map 68**], but it was only with the onslaught of Nebuchadnezzar's Babylonian forces that the city capitulated and fell. [**See map 80.**] In 539 B.C., in the immediate aftermath of the fall of Babylon to the Persians [**map 86**], king Cyrus issued his now-famous proclamation allowing dispossessed peoples to be repatriated (2 Chron. 36:22–23; Ezra 1:1–4). Thereupon, a humble company returned to Jerusalem under the direction of Sheshbazzar. Referred to as the "prince" of Judah (Ezra 1:8), the term is commonly assumed to mark Sheshbazzar as a person of Davidic descent. Apparently not long thereafter a group of some 50,000 returnees arrived in Jerusalem under the able leadership of Zerubbabel, also of Davidic descent and designated as "governor" of Judah (Ezra 3:8–13; 5:16). Later, in the days of Artaxerxes I, Ezra the priest led a smaller company back to Jerusalem (Ezra 7:1–26).

Although these returnees had been permitted to rebuild, adorn, and enrich the Temple, the city itself remained almost empty (Neh. 11:1). Its walls and gates remained broken and dilapidated (Neh. 1:3). Moved by reports of these miserable conditions, Nehemiah decided to leave his esteemed post as cupbearer to king Artaxerxes I and travel to Jerusalem (Neh. 1:1—2:8). Earlier returnees had focused on the Temple itself; Nehemiah's concern was the city walls. His is the most comprehensive description of Jerusalem's post-exilic city walls and topography (Neh. 2:11–16). And spurred on by his energetic enthusiasm, various groups of people in and around Jerusalem undertook the rebuilding task. Their work may have included incorporating into Jerusalem the Tower of Hananel (Jer. 31:38; Neh. 3:1; 12:39; Zech. 14:10), which became known during the Hasmonean period as the Baris.

In 332 B.C., Jerusalem and the remainder of Judea peacefully submitted to the army of Alexander the Great. [**See map 88.**] But peace was soon thoroughly shattered as the Ptolemy and Seleucid dynasties sparred for control of the region [**map 87**], and as the latter dynasty in particular sought to legislate Hellenism in Jerusalem. [**See maps 91 and 92.**] A call for national autonomy that had fanned the flames

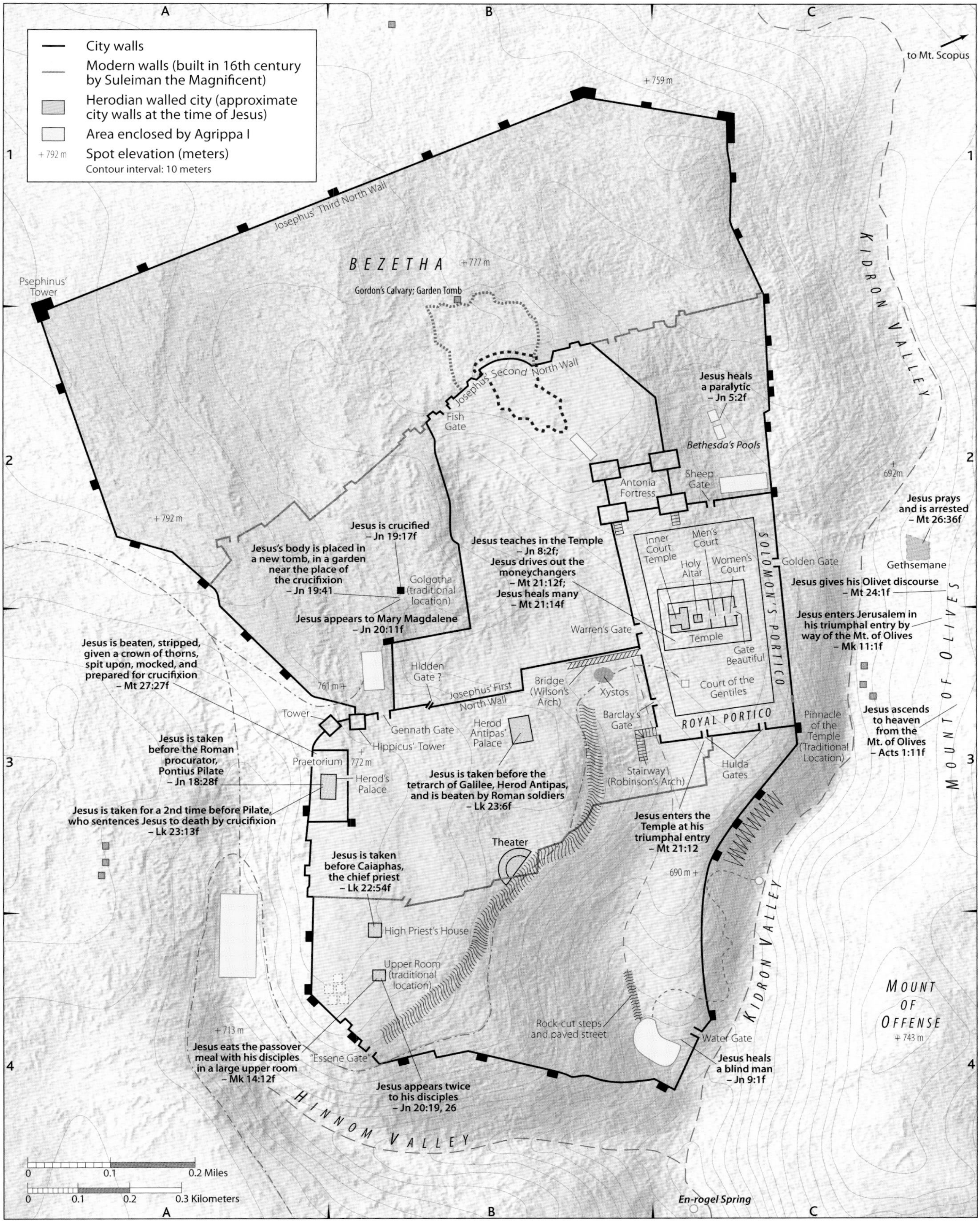
City walls
Modern walls (built in 16th century by Suleiman the Magnificent)
Herodian walled city (approximate city walls at the time of Jesus)
Area enclosed by Agrippa I
+ 792 m Spot elevation (meters)
Contour interval: 10 meters
Josephus' Third North Wall
BEZETHA
Gordon's Calvary; Garden Tomb
Psephinus' Tower
Josephus' Second North Wall
Fish Gate
Jesus heals a paralytic – Jn 5:2f
Bethesda's Pools
Antonia Fortress
Sheep Gate
KIDRON VALLEY
Jesus prays and is arrested – Mt 26:36f
Gethsemane
Jesus is crucified – Jn 19:17f
Jesus's body is placed in a new tomb, in a garden near the place of the crucifixion – Jn 19:41
Golgotha (traditional location)
Jesus appears to Mary Magdalene – Jn 20:11f
Jesus teaches in the Temple – Jn 8:2f; Jesus drives out the moneychangers – Mt 21:12f; Jesus heals many – Mt 21:14f
Inner Court Temple
Men's Court
Holy Altar
Women's Court
Temple
Gate Beautiful
SOLOMON'S PORTICO
Golden Gate
Jesus gives his Olivet discourse – Mt 24:1f
Jesus enters Jerusalem in his triumphal entry by way of the Mt. of Olives – Mk 11:1f
Warren's Gate
Jesus is beaten, stripped, given a crown of thorns, spit upon, mocked, and prepared for crucifixion – Mt 27:27f
Hidden Gate ?
Josephus' First North Wall
Bridge (Wilson's Arch)
Xystos
Court of the Gentiles
Barclay's Gate
ROYAL PORTICO
Pinnacle of the Temple (Traditional Location)
Jesus ascends to heaven from the Mt. of Olives – Acts 1:11f
MOUNT OF OLIVES
Tower
Gennath Gate
Hippicus' Tower
Herod Antipas' Palace
Jesus is taken before the Roman procurator, Pontius Pilate – Jn 18:28f
Praetorium
Herod's Palace
Jesus is taken before the tetrarch of Galilee, Herod Antipas, and is beaten by Roman soldiers – Lk 23:6f
Stairway (Robinson's Arch)
Hulda Gates
Jesus is taken for a 2nd time before Pilate, who sentences Jesus to death by crucifixion – Lk 23:13f
Jesus enters the Temple at his triumphal entry – Mt 21:12
Theater
Jesus is taken before Caiaphas, the chief priest – Lk 22:54f
High Priest's House
Upper Room (traditional location)
KIDRON VALLEY
MOUNT OF OFFENSE
Rock-cut steps and paved street
Water Gate
Jesus eats the passover meal with his disciples in a large upper room – Mk 14:12f
"Essene Gate"
Jesus heals a blind man – Jn 9:1f
Jesus appears twice to his disciples – Jn 20:19, 26
HINNOM VALLEY
En-rogel Spring
to Mt. Scopus
+ 759 m
+ 777 m
+ 792 m
761 m +
772 m
690 m +
+ 692m
+ 713 m
+ 743 m
0 0.1 0.2 Miles
0 0.1 0.2 0.3 Kilometers

of a Maccabean revolt eventually gave way to pleas for "law and order" upon the death of Alexander Janneus in 76 B.C. and the temporary ascension of his wife Salome Alexandra. Many grudgingly accepted her assumption of his political duties, but considered it unthinkable that she should also assume his role as high priest. So at her death, sectarian strife ensued concerning who should become the bona fide high priest. The Pharisees backed Salome's son John Hyrcanus II. The Sadducees supported Aristobulus II.

The civil war that resulted profited only the Romans. When citizens from both groups appealed to Rome, Pompey decided in favor of Hyrcanus. In response, the partisans of Aristobulus isolated themselves inside the Temple and defied his order, so Pompey laid siege to Jerusalem. In 63 B.C., the wall was breached and the Romans broke into the Temple. Pompey simply dissolved the Hasmonean syncretism and added Jerusalem to the Roman province of Syria.[463] But the rivalry between the two groups continued after the death of Pompey and even after the assassination of Julius Caesar, eventually resulting in the Roman Senate's appointment of Herod as "king of the Jews."[464] [**See further discussion at map 99**; cf. Matt. 2:1–4; Luke 1:5.]

During his 33-year reign in Jerusalem (37–4 B.C.), Herod dramatically transformed the external aspect of the city. He transferred the seat of government to the Southwestern hill and, according to Josephus, either erected or refurbished many architectural monuments, including a lavish palace, a hippodrome, a xystos (arena for athletic contests), a theater and an amphitheater, and a vast aqueduct network.[465] He transformed the Maccabean fortress (Baris) into a much larger structure and renamed it Antonia, in honor of the triumvir Mark Antony.[466]

The church of the Holy Sepulchre, Jerusalem, traditionally believed to cover the site of the crucifixion.

In the Temple area proper, he enlarged the esplanade on the north and especially on the south side, giving it a rectangular shape.[467] The Temple's construction began in 20 B.C., but was not completed until around A.D. 64, just six years prior to its complete demolition by Titus (cf. John 2:20).[468]

The New Testament gospels contain much information about Jesus and Jerusalem, particularly during his passion week. An examination of **map 95** shows that, in the days leading up to his crucifixion, Jesus came into contact with all five of Jerusalem's hills, as well as some surrounding areas.

The location of Jesus' crucifixion, in particular, has generated a fair amount of discussion and interest. What are the specifications of the New Testament in this regard? First, Jesus was crucified outside the city walls but near the city and in the vicinity of a city gate (John 19:17–20; Matt 27:32; Heb. 13:12–13). [**See map 95.**] Second, Jesus was crucified near a busy, well-traveled street—not on a "hill far away" (Matt. 27:39; implied in Mark 15:21; Luke 23:26). Roman writer Quintilian stated: "Whenever we crucify the guilty, the most crowded roads are chosen, where the most people can see and be moved by this fear."[469] Thousands of prisoners were crucified along the Appian Way, between Rome and Capua. It is pertinent to recall, in this regard, that all four gospels mention an inscription containing the charge against Jesus that was affixed to his gallows or hung around his neck (Matt. 27:37; Mark 15:26; Luke 23:38; John 19:19–20). One can only surmise that such an inscription, written in three different languages, was designed *to be read* by all (John 19:20a). And third, the crucifixion site was near a garden that contained at least one recently hewn but unused tomb (John 19:41; Matt. 27:60).

Christians today commonly identify one of two locations for Christ's crucifixion: either the site of the Church of the Holy Sepulchre, or the site of the so-called "Gordon's Calvary." Knowledgeable authorities have demonstrated that the site of Gordon's Calvary is problematic for a number of reasons: (1) the site can only trace back its roots as far as the second half of the 19th century and no further;[470] (2) a site to the

finally fell into pieces, but from the fragments great modern states, such as England, France, and Italy, have grown, and its civilization in a modified form has passed into modern life."[482]

This recent appraisal of the *pax Romana* is very similar to one expressed centuries ago by Eusebius, the eminent church historian, bishop of Caesarea, and metropolitan of Jerusalem during the era of Constantine. But his perspective was one of divine providence:

"The power of the Romans came to its zenith at precisely the moment of Jesus's unexpected sojourn among men, at the time when Augustus [Caesar] first acquired absolute power over all nations, defeating Cleopatra and putting an end to the succession of the Ptolemies . . . [and from] that day to this the Jewish nation has been subject to the Romans as likewise the Cappadocians and Macedonians, Bithynians and Greeks; in a word all the nations who now fall under Roman rule. And no one could deny that the synchronizing of this with the beginning of the teaching about the Savior is of God's arrangement, if he considered the difficulty of the disciples taking their journey to foreign lands, had the nations been at war with one another, or their diversities of government preventing relations between them. But when all these were abolished, they could accomplish their mission quite fearlessly and safely, since the Supreme God had smoothed the way before them."[483]

map 98

The expansion of the Roman Empire was a gradual and sometimes involuntary movement. It began as early as 260 B.C., when Sicily, Sardinia, and Corsica were annexed to a unified Italy. By the end of the Punic Wars, around 146 B.C., Macedonia, Tripolitania, and Achaia had been engulfed, and then over the next century Rome succeeded in adding Asia, Bithynia and Pontus, Cilicia, Syria, Cyrenaica, Gaul, Belgica, and parts of Hispania. The days of Augustus Caesar (27 B.C.–A.D. 14) saw the provinces of Egypt, Judea, Galatia, Cappadocia, Armenia, Illyricum, and the rest of Hispania added to the empire. Claudius (A.D. 41–54) vanquished Mauretania, Britannia, and Dacia; Trajan (A.D. 98–117) annexed Nabatea. The mountainous territory between the Black and Caspian seas and the expansive region of Mesopotamia were later acquired, but held only temporarily by Rome.[484]

Unreconstructed remains of a Roman amphitheater at the Sicilian city of Syracuse.

THE RISE OF HEROD THE GREAT

Herod the Great was one of the few non-Roman personalities during the Roman era who achieved extraordinary political status and power that lasted for a period of decades. Born into an aristocratic Idumean family[485] that had converted to Judaism during the time of John Hyrcanus I [**map 92**], Herod consistently allied himself with Rome throughout his lifetime.

In 40 B.C. the Parthians invaded Syria, endangering Herod's life because of his opposition to the Hasmoneans and Parthians. He fled Judea for Rome where, as a loyal client of Mark Antony, he was unanimously elected "king of Judea" by the Roman Senate (Luke 1:5; Matt. 2:1–4).[486] Armed with this newfound authority and Roman military support, Herod sailed early the following year from Rome to the port at Ptolemais, where he commenced a fierce two-year campaign culminating in the Roman recapture of Jerusalem in the early spring of 37 B.C.[487] Herod ruled there as king for the next 33 years, until his death in 4 B.C.[488]

Herodium, a fortress in the Judean Wilderness east of Bethlehem, was erected by Herod the Great by moving the ground from one hill to the top of another and then surmounting the structure with a heavily fortified emplacement. Herod was buried at Herodium.

Herod's transforming embellishments of Jerusalem have already been discussed [**map 94**], but he was no less active outside his capital city. Having received from Augustus Caesar the hamlet of Strato's Tower, Herod ambitiously undertook to create a worthy seat of Roman provincial rule in Judea. He named the new city Caesarea in honor of his new patron. Caesarea was endowed with most of the architectural accoutrements found in any major Roman city (temple of Augustus, theater, amphitheater, hippodrome, aqueducts, forum, basilica, and baths).[489] Its vast harbor represented the earliest known use of hydraulic cement in underwater construction east of Italy. [**See map 110.**] Herod also enlarged and strongly fortified the city of Samaria, in the heartland of his domain, in appreciation for its support in his struggles to win Judea. He renamed it Sebaste ("Augustus" in Latin)[490] and repopulated it with colonists loyal to his throne. Finally, Herod raised an immense shrine at Hebron over the place memorialized as the burial spot of the Hebrew patriarchs.

Herod also constructed or enlarged other cities throughout his kingdom, including Panias, Kedesh, Bathyra, Bethsaida, Sepphoris, Tiberias, Agrippina, Antipatris, Qiryat Bene-Hassan, Phaselis, Docus, Jericho, Anthedon, Ashkelon,

The Rise of Herod the Great

map 99

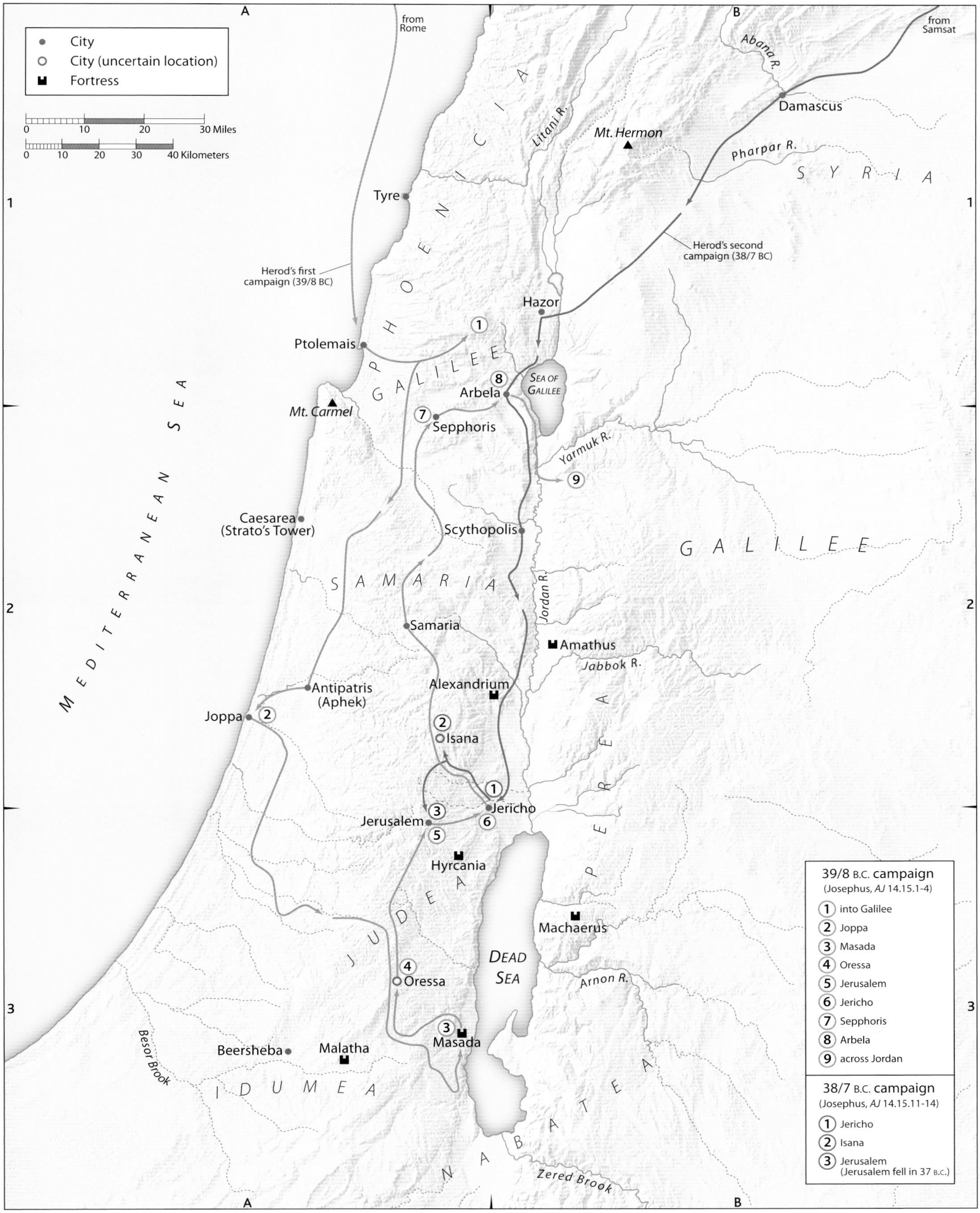

Remains of part of the long aqueduct built by Herod the Great to convey water from Mt. Carmel to the metropolis of Caesarea. Part of the structure lies inundated by sand dunes today.

Livias, and Callirrhoe. [**See map 100.**] And he enriched cities beyond his kingdom (e.g., Sidon, Tyre, Damascus, Byblos, Beirut, but also Syrian Antioch, Rhodes, Chios, Athens, and Sparta).

Yet despite this somewhat grandiose and very expensive construction, Herod never felt at ease in his relationship with the Jews. Therefore, he also engaged in erecting military fortresses within his kingdom, creating a chain of defensive positions he could use if he should have to flee Judea a second time.[491] In the eastern sector of his kingdom he erected Alexandrium, Cyprus, Hyrcania, and Herodium (where eventually he would be buried). In the south he constructed the fortresses of Malatha and Masada. And across the Jordan River, Herod built Amathus, Esbus (Heshbon), and Machaerus (where in due course Herod Antipas would have John the Baptist beheaded; cf. Matt. 14:3–12). Altogether, Herod engaged in building projects at more than 25 locations throughout his kingdom alone.[492]

At Herod's death and in accordance with his will, Augustus Caesar divided the Idumean's kingdom into three parts, each to be ruled by one of Herod's sons.[493] Archelaus, the eldest, was appointed ethnarch[494] over Samaria, Judea, and Idumea (Matt. 2:22); his second son, Herod Antipas, was nominated tetrarch and given the territories of Galilee and Perea (Matt. 14:1; Luke 3:1); his third son, Herod Philip, was also appointed tetrarch and assigned Iturea, Gaulanitis, Batanea, Trachonitis, and Auranitis (Luke 3:1; Matt. 14:3).[495]

In an apparent attempt to justify their appointments, each of Herod's sons sought to mimic their father's pattern of greatness by building cities. Archelaus enlarged the royal palace at Jericho in splendid fashion and created a new city in a northern suburb that he named after himself. Herod Antipas erected the Galilean city of Tiberias (named for Tiberius Caesar; cf. John 6:23). [**See map 102.**] And Herod Philip greatly expanded the site of Panias, renaming his construction Caesarea Philippi (cf. Matt 16:13).[496]

The area that became known as the "Decapolis" was largely comprised of a series of post-Alexandrian Hellenized colonial cities founded in the east. They had been occupied by Greek-speaking immigrants who were strongly opposed to either Jewish or Nabatean rule as early as Alexander Janneus. Liberated and converted into "free cities" during the time of Pompey,[497] they were loosely attached to the province of Syria. However, Augustus Caesar ceded nominal control over part of this area to Herod the Great, despite repeated local protests to Rome.[498] Upon Herod's death, this region was officially separated from Herod's kingdom and was not given to any of his sons. Rather, it was reattached to the province of Syria.[499]

Herod's 33-year reign represented a period of much peace and stability for the subjects of his realm. Still, his death became an occasion for a resurgence of strong anti-Roman sentiment and even hostility that may be seen on the pages of the New Testament (e.g., Matt. 22:16–22) and perhaps climaxed in the year A.D. 66. [**See map 115.**] Contributing to these feelings were his sometimes brutal enforcement of law, his personal paranoia, his open disregard for certain Jewish traditions (such as the implications of sponsoring Roman games), his control over other Jewish institutions (the Sanhedrin), and perhaps above all his burdensome, oppressive taxation system.

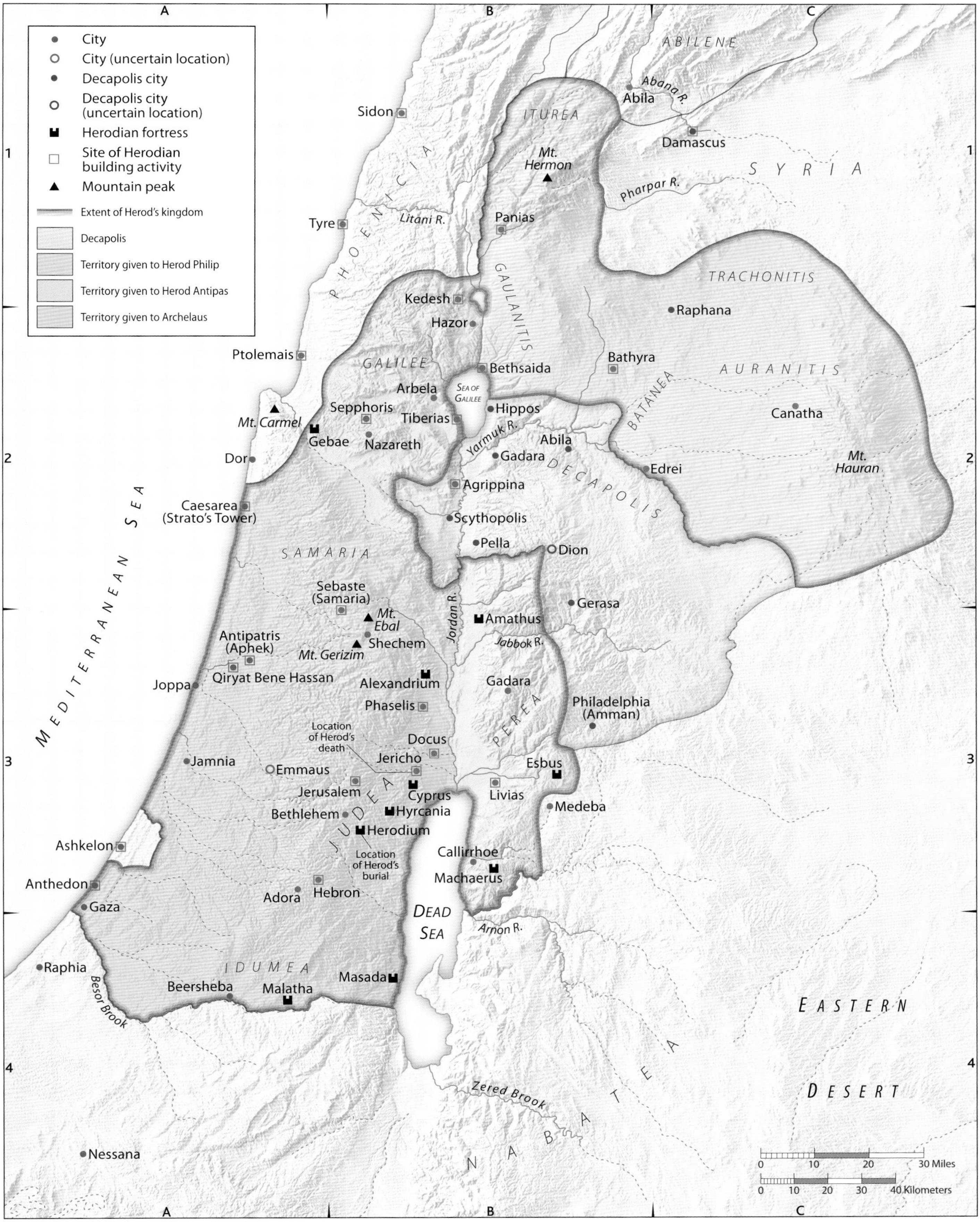
City
City (uncertain location)
Decapolis city
Decapolis city (uncertain location)
Herodian fortress
Site of Herodian building activity
Mountain peak
Extent of Herod's kingdom
Decapolis
Territory given to Herod Philip
Territory given to Herod Antipas
Territory given to Archelaus
A
B
C
1
2
3
4
ABILENE
Abana R.
Abila
Damascus
SYRIA
Pharpar R.
Sidon
ITUREA
Mt. Hermon
PHOENICIA
Litani R.
Tyre
Panias
GAULANITIS
TRACHONITIS
Raphana
Kedesh
Hazor
Ptolemais
GALILEE
Bethsaida
Bathyra
AURANITIS
BATANEA
Arbela
Sea of Galilee
Sepphoris
Hippos
Canatha
Mt. Carmel
Tiberias
Yarmuk R.
Gebae
Nazareth
Abila
Gadara
Dor
Edrei
Mt. Hauran
DECAPOLIS
Agrippina
MEDITERRANEAN SEA
Caesarea (Strato's Tower)
Scythopolis
Pella
Dion
SAMARIA
Sebaste (Samaria)
Mt. Ebal
Jordan R.
Gerasa
Amathus
Shechem
Jabbok R.
Antipatris (Aphek)
Mt. Gerizim
Qiryat Bene Hassan
Joppa
Alexandrium
Gadara
Phaselis
PEREA
Philadelphia (Amman)
Location of Herod's death
Docus
Jericho
Esbus
Jamnia
Emmaus
Jerusalem
Cyprus
Livias
Medeba
Bethlehem
Hyrcania
JUDEA
Herodium
Ashkelon
Location of Herod's burial
Callirrhoe
Machaerus
Anthedon
Adora
Hebron
Gaza
DEAD SEA
Arnon R.
IDUMEA
Raphia
Masada
Besor Brook
Beersheba
Malatha
EASTERN
DESERT
NABATEA
Zered Brook
Nessana
0 10 20 30 Miles
0 10 20 30 40 Kilometers

JESUS' EARLY YEARS

"Surely even the wrath of men shall praise the Lord." (cf. Ps. 76:10a)

This appears to be an apt characterization of the circumstances surrounding the birth of Jesus Christ. Augustus Caesar (earlier known as Octavian) issued a decree for a census to be taken across the whole Roman world. The census would require Joseph, then residing in Nazareth of Galilee, to journey approximately 70 miles south to the Judean hamlet of Bethlehem to be enrolled there, because he was from David's lineage. And while Joseph was in Bethlehem with his betrothed wife, Mary, the time of her delivery arrived (Luke 2:1–7) [**1**]. God had used the decree of a Roman Caesar to make possible a scenario in which Jesus would be born in Bethlehem of Judea, precisely as had been declared by the prophet Micah many years before (Mic. 5:2).

The gospel of Luke (2:7) declares that, at his birth, Jesus was laid in a "manger" (*phatnē*) because there was no room for his family in the "inn" (*kataluma*). To gain a historical conception of this context and to free oneself of some unhelpful stereotypes, it is useful to see how both of these words were utilized elsewhere by the gospel writer Luke.

In classical literature, *kataluma* can mean either a private house or a traveler's inn,[500] yet the gospel of Luke otherwise employed this word to describe only a "guest room" in a private house (Luke 22:11; cf. Mark 14:14). It is no less significant that Luke was also aware of a separate term (*pandoxeion*) to designate an overnight lodging place for travelers (Luke 10:34).[501] Most lower- and middle-class first-century Palestinian family houses were simple: one large, sometimes partitioned, room divided into an upper and lower section and/or built over a natural or man-made cave. Animals might take shelter at night in part of the lower section. In such houses, the *phatnē* ("feeding trough")[502] would have been either a carved limestone box or a notched outcropping of rock. It is most reasonable to assume that Joseph would have sought refuge for Mary and himself in the house of a family member in Bethlehem (Luke 1:39–40). However, because the "guest room" was apparently already taken—perhaps by another extended family member also there as a result of the census—it was necessary for Joseph and Mary to stay in the lower part of the family house, where there would also have been an animal's feeding trough.

From as early as A.D. 150, Christian literature repeatedly described Christ's birthplace as a cave.[503] Even earlier, the oral tradition of a cave in Bethlehem associated with Christ's birthplace was deeply established. The emperor Hadrian (A.D. 117–138) apparently converted the cave into a sanctuary to Adonis (Tammuz) in an unsuccessful attempt to eliminate the veneration of the site by Jewish Christians.[504] In the time of Jerome—a resident of Bethlehem who lived for years in a cave adjacent to the one identified as the site of Christ's birthplace—Christians and non-Christians alike were said to have been shown the cave where Christ was born and the

The Church of the Nativity dominates Manger Square, Bethlehem.

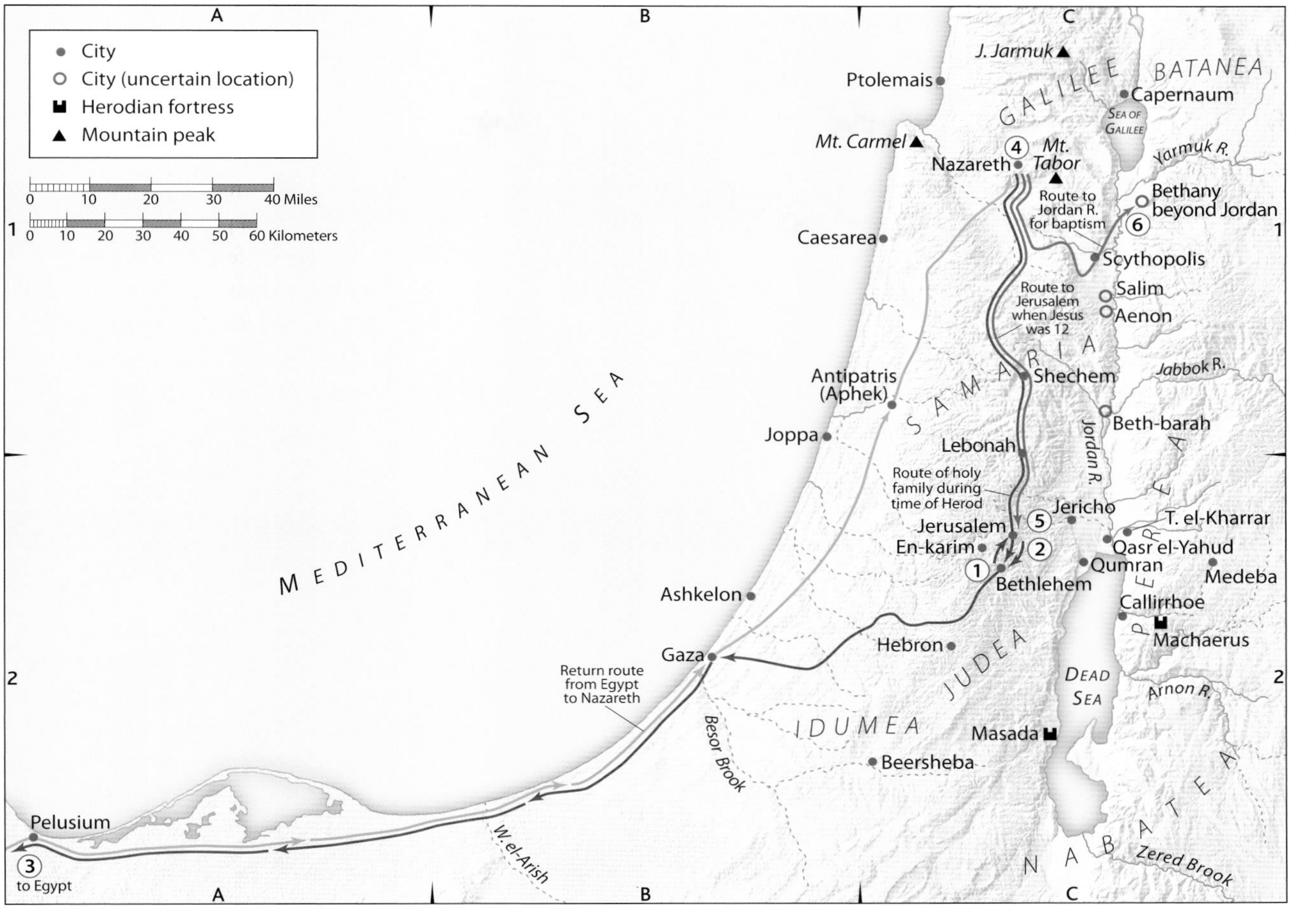

manger where he was placed. Origen further declared that the cave was famous in those parts even among people alien to the faith.[505] He went on to aver that the manger [*phatnē*] of Luke 2:7 was still known in Bethlehem in his day, that it was a rock groove with plain clay walls in a side cave approximately three meters by three meters in size.[506] Today the Church of the Nativity, begun by Constantine and completed by Justinian, stands over a series of caves, including the cave of the nativity.

Acting according to Mosaic prescription (Lev. 12:2–8), Jesus' parents piously brought him to Jerusalem about 40 days after his birth and presented him to be consecrated to the Lord (Luke 2:22–24), after which they returned to Bethlehem [**2**]. When magi from the East later came to Herod at Jerusalem with their troubling inquiry concerning the whereabouts of a newborn "king of the Jews," they were dispatched to Bethlehem where they found and worshiped the child (Matt. 2:1–11).

Warned in a dream of impending treachery by Herod the Great, Joseph took Mary and Jesus and fled under the cover of darkness from Bethlehem to Egypt (Matt. 2:13–14) [**3**]. Later, upon learning of Herod's death, Joseph brought his family out of Egypt, presumably intending to return to the environs of Bethlehem. But he discovered that Herod's son Archelaus had ascended to his father's throne in Judea. So Joseph, directed by God to withdraw into the district of Galilee, took Mary and the young boy to Nazareth (Matt. 2:19–23) [**4**].

It was in the tiny, sleepy, and geographically remote Galilean village of Nazareth that Jesus grew into manhood. At the age of twelve, Jesus' parents again took him to Jerusalem, this time to celebrate the Passover [**5**]. At the conclusion of the feast, Jesus' parents traveled northward a day's journey, possibly to the vicinity of Lebonah, supposing he was in the caravan returning to Galilee. When they discovered him missing, they returned to Jerusalem and found Jesus in the Temple, sitting among learned teachers who were astonished at his wisdom (Luke 2:41–47). He returned with his parents to Nazareth, where he remained for the balance of the so-called "silent years."

Jesus was about 30 years old when he began his public ministry (Luke 3:23).

It appears that the ministry of Christ and that of John the Baptist commenced in the 15th year of Tiberias Caesar—A.D. 27–28 (Luke 3:1). Although John was born of priestly lineage (Luke 1:5–7) and hailed according to tradition from the Judean town of En-karim, immediately southwest of Jerusalem,[507] his preaching and baptizing efforts were concentrated in the Jordan River valley. John's baptism of Jesus in the Jordan is recorded in all three synoptic gospels

Herod the Great sought relief from his acute medical ailments in the hot springs and mineral pools of Callirrhoe, known today as Zarqa Ma'in.

(Matt. 3:13–17; Mark 1:9–11; Luke 3:21–22), but unfortunately the location of the baptismal site is unspecified.

The fourth gospel records that John was baptizing at Bethany beyond Jordan (John 1:28; cf. 3:26), at Aenon[508] near Salim (3:23), but those texts do not explicitly identify Jesus as one being baptized. Already in the third century Origen knew of a baptismal site of Jesus opposite Jericho,[509] and offered the stunning, even brash, proposal that "we ought not to read 'Bethania,' but 'Bethabara' [in John 1:28]."[510] Today the modern state of Israel locates a baptismal site at Qasr el-Yahud (about where Bethabara is situated on the Medeba map),[511] while Jordanian authorities look to the site of T. el-Kharrar,[512] about five miles north of the Dead Sea on the east side of the river.

It seems that the question of the location of Jesus' baptismal site ultimately depends upon whether one is supposed to interpret this portion of the gospel of John chronologically. Perhaps favoring a chronological interpretation are John's additional distinctive references to the three annual Passovers (2:13; 6:4–5; 11:55–56) and his unique mention of other chronological facts in the life of Christ (1:39; 4:6; 19:14). Here in context, Jesus first began to gather disciples at John's baptismal site at Bethany beyond Jordan (1:35–42; cf. 1:28); the "next day" he decided to travel to Galilee (1:43–51); and the "third day" he attended a marriage in Cana of Galilee (2:1–11). It appears, then, that Jesus traveled from John's baptismal site to Cana in Galilee in two days' time, by inclusive reckoning.[513] Accordingly, Bethany and Cana could not have been separated by a distance greater than a group of men could walk without difficulty in two days. Travel between Jerusalem and Galilee via Samaria in New Testament times took three whole days, and medieval travel between Jerusalem and Tiberias, via the Jordan River route, consumed four days.[514] In the case of John 1 and 2, one must consider lost time as a result of Philip having to locate Nathaniel and then bring him to Jesus—who then conversed with him—combined with additional time consumed in having to cross the river itself. Such evidence allows for confidently asserting that a journey from the vicinity of Jericho to Cana in Galilee in two days' time is most highly improbable.

As a counterpoint, Bethany beyond Jordan (*Bēthania peran toû 'Iordanou*) in John 1:28 could instead be referencing Batanea (Old Testament Bashan).[515] Bashan was a territory often described as being "beyond the Jordan" (e.g., Num. 32:32; Deut. 3:8; 4:47; Josh. 9:10).[516] In such a scenario, one would be justified in looking farther north along the Jordan (Matt. 4:15), perhaps not far from the Jordan-Yarmuk confluence, where the region of Bashan/Batanea was contiguous to the Jordan.[517] [**See map 5.**] From this vicinity, it would of course be possible to travel to Cana in two days' time [**6**].

John's fervent denunciation of royal wickedness would earn him imprisonment and eventual decapitation (Matt. 14:1–12; Mark 6:14–29; Luke 3:18–20) at the hands of Herod Antipas, probably at the Herodian fortress at Machaerus.[518] His corpse was taken by his disciples and buried in a tomb (Mark 6:29), located according to an early Christian tradition in the town of Sebaste/Samaria.[519]

JESUS' MOVE TO CAPERNAUM

Not long after Jesus emerged from the wilderness, having successfully withstood a period of temptation (Matt. 4:1–11), he established the headquarters of his ministry at the town of Capernaum ("village of Nahum," cf. Matt. 4:12–13; Luke 4:16–32). Located along the northwestern shore of the Sea of Galilee, the Capernaum of Jesus' day was a prosperous fishing village, though unwalled and small of size. [**See map 14.**] The town was situated near the border between the domains of Herod Antipas, who ruled over Galilee, and Herod Philip, who ruled over Transjordanian vistas to the north and east. [**See map 100.**] Therefore, it would have had a customs station (Matt. 17:24; cf. Matt. 9:10–11). Perhaps it was from customs duties near Capernaum that Jesus called Matthew to follow him (Mark 2:13–14), just as he had called Andrew and Peter from their fishing profession in the same vicinity to become "fishers of men" (Matt. 4:18–20).

Roman archaeological remains exhumed from Capernaum have been impressive indeed. They include a two-story, pillared limestone synagogue measuring 67 feet in length and 60 feet in width. Apparently dating to the fourth century A.D., this structure featured a gable roof and galleries on three sides, benches for the synagogue hierarchy, and a fountain for ceremonial washings. The surrounding galleries and colonnades exhibit a wide array of Corinthian capitals and carved stone cornices decorated with such images as the menorah, the shofar, the hexagram star, and the ark of the covenant, in addition to various geometric patterns. This limestone basilica was constructed over an earlier basaltic foundation, thought to be the vestige of a synagogue that dates back into the New Testament era.[520] Immediately to the south of the synagogue stand the remains of a large octagonal Christian church dating to the fifth century, erected over the remains of a modest first-century house where graffiti on the plastered walls mentions "Peter"— suggesting that the house may have belonged to the apostle Peter[521] (Matt 8:14; Mark 1:29; Luke 4:38).

Scholars often express puzzlement over Jesus' choice of Capernaum in Galilee, since this clearly ran counter to the dominant expectation within Judaism that Jerusalem would be the center and focus of the Messiah and the Messianic age.[522] Did Jesus base his ministry in Capernaum because it was not a thoroughly Jewish city? Or did he settle there because that was where his message was readily welcomed? There is undoubtedly a measure of truth in both ideas, and both rather sharply differentiated Capernaum from Nazareth, although Christ seems not to have ministered much to the Gentiles of Galilee. But his reason(s) for choosing Capernaum may also have included geography. The city was very near to the Great Trunk Road, the international artery of trade and transportation that arched across the Fertile Crescent and ultimately linked Egypt and Mesopotamia. [**See map 27.**] Unlike the small, sleepy, and isolated village of Nazareth, Capernaum was situated near a critical junction, a conduit through which coursed a steady stream of humanity traveling from many diverse sectors and countries of the Near East. Jesus perceptively carried his message into Capernaum's synagogue, houses, alleys, and surrounding fields, which pulsated with the activities and congestion of internationalism.

Part of the reconstructed fourth century A.D. synagogue at Capernaum.

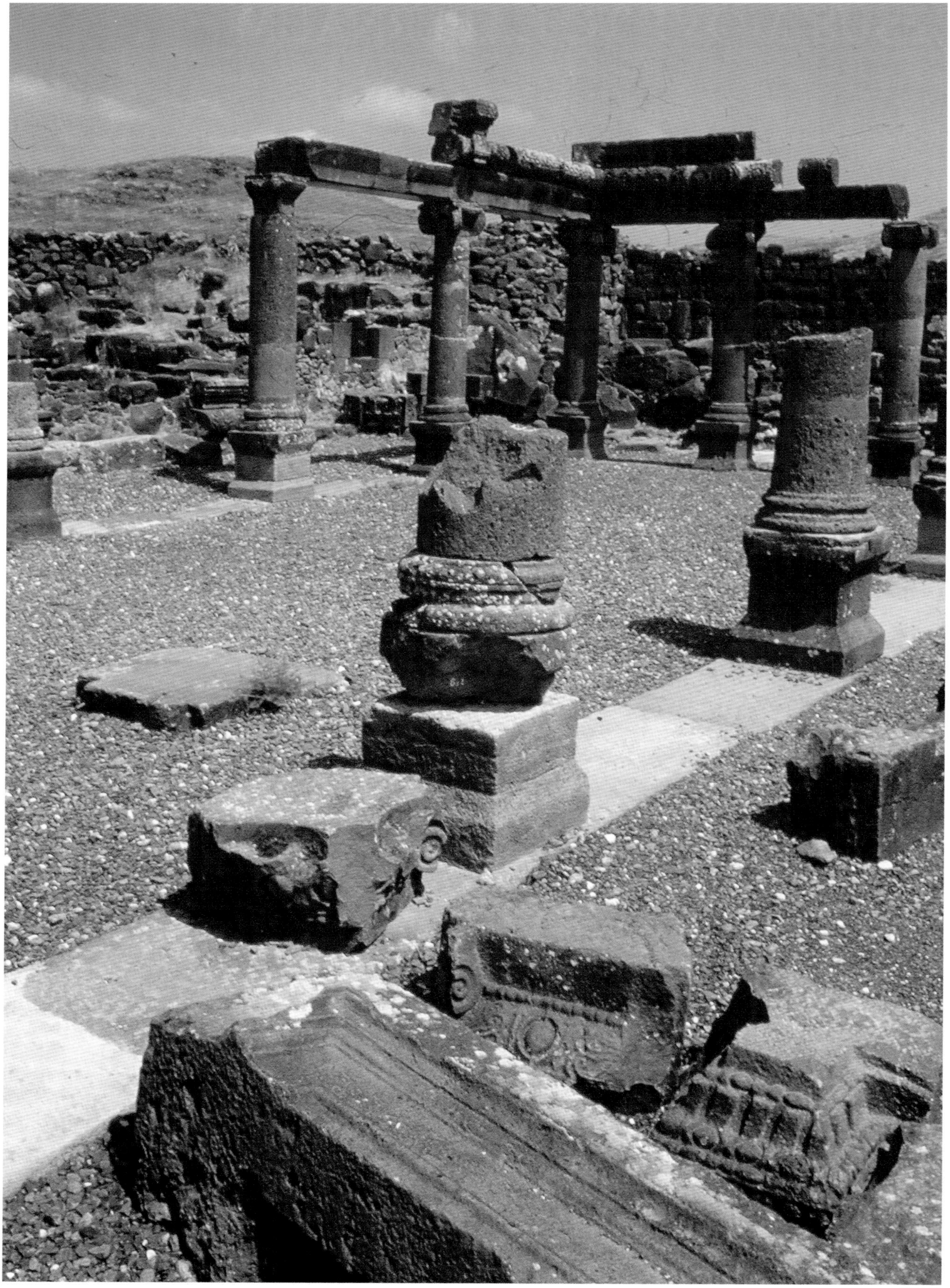

Jesus' Ministry in Galilee

map 102

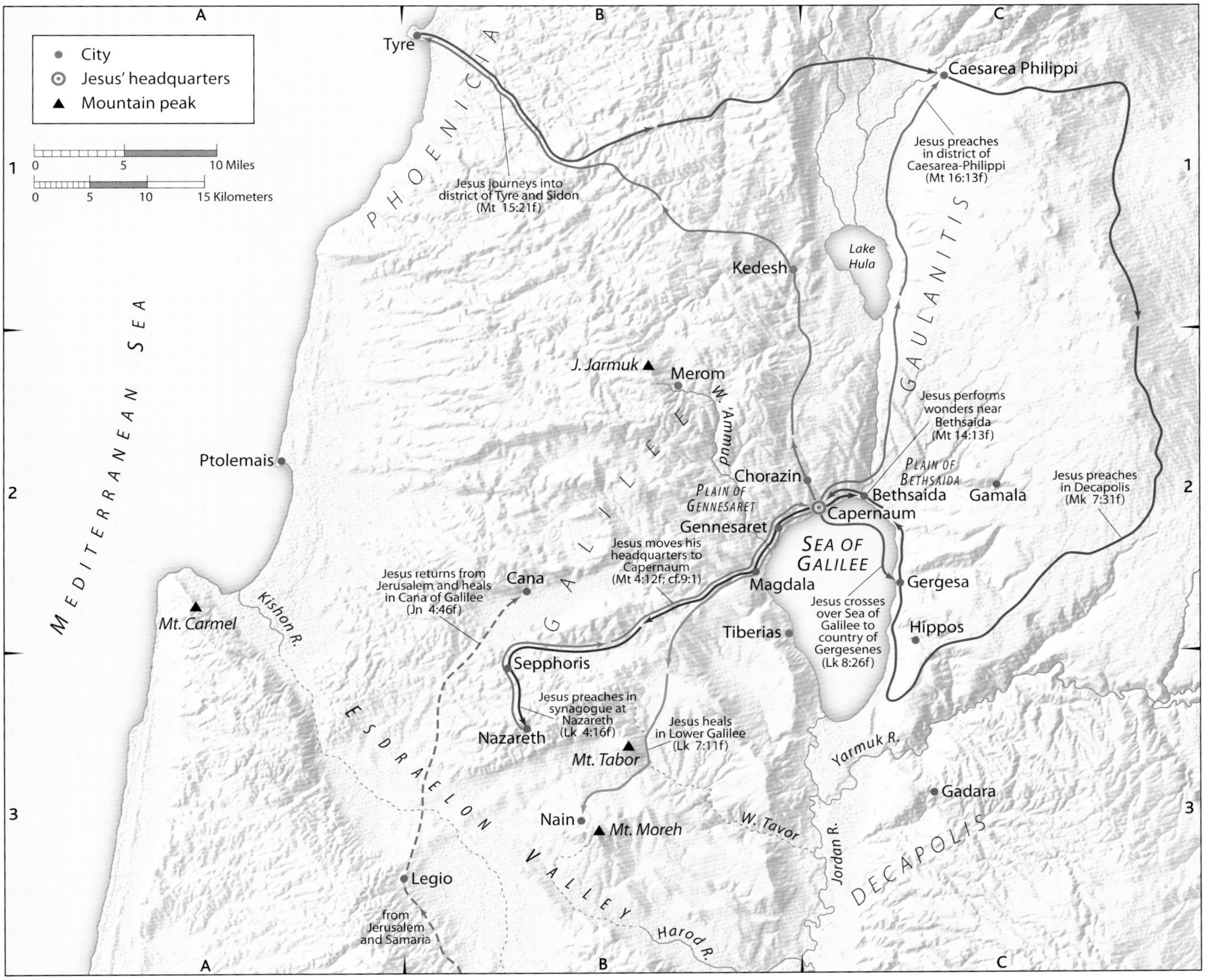

One may ponder when considering that the early apostolic movement apparently swept in a northern and northwestern direction from Jerusalem. Yet some of the earliest and most important Christian evidences—including the earliest archaeologically attested Christian church structure and the earliest New Testament manuscript found outside of Egypt, both found at Dura-Europos—are to be found in Mesopotamian territory *northeast* of Jerusalem. [**See map 116.**] Ponder, that is, until one realizes that such evidence is but one of the happy consequences of Jesus' astute move to Capernaum.[523]

Many modern Christians are familiar with a poem entitled "One Solitary Life." This lovely literary piece expounds upon the many things that Jesus never did and the many places Jesus never went. Yet understand that by anchoring his ministry at Capernaum, it became relatively unnecessary for Jesus to travel great distances. Many of those who heard and believed his words in Capernaum would become instant and far-flung ambassadors of the Christian gospel—men and women whose vocational travels would carry the message of Christ from the northern shores of the Sea of Galilee to the ends of the Roman world.

Partially restored synagogue at Chorazin.

Jesus' Ministry in Palestine

map 103

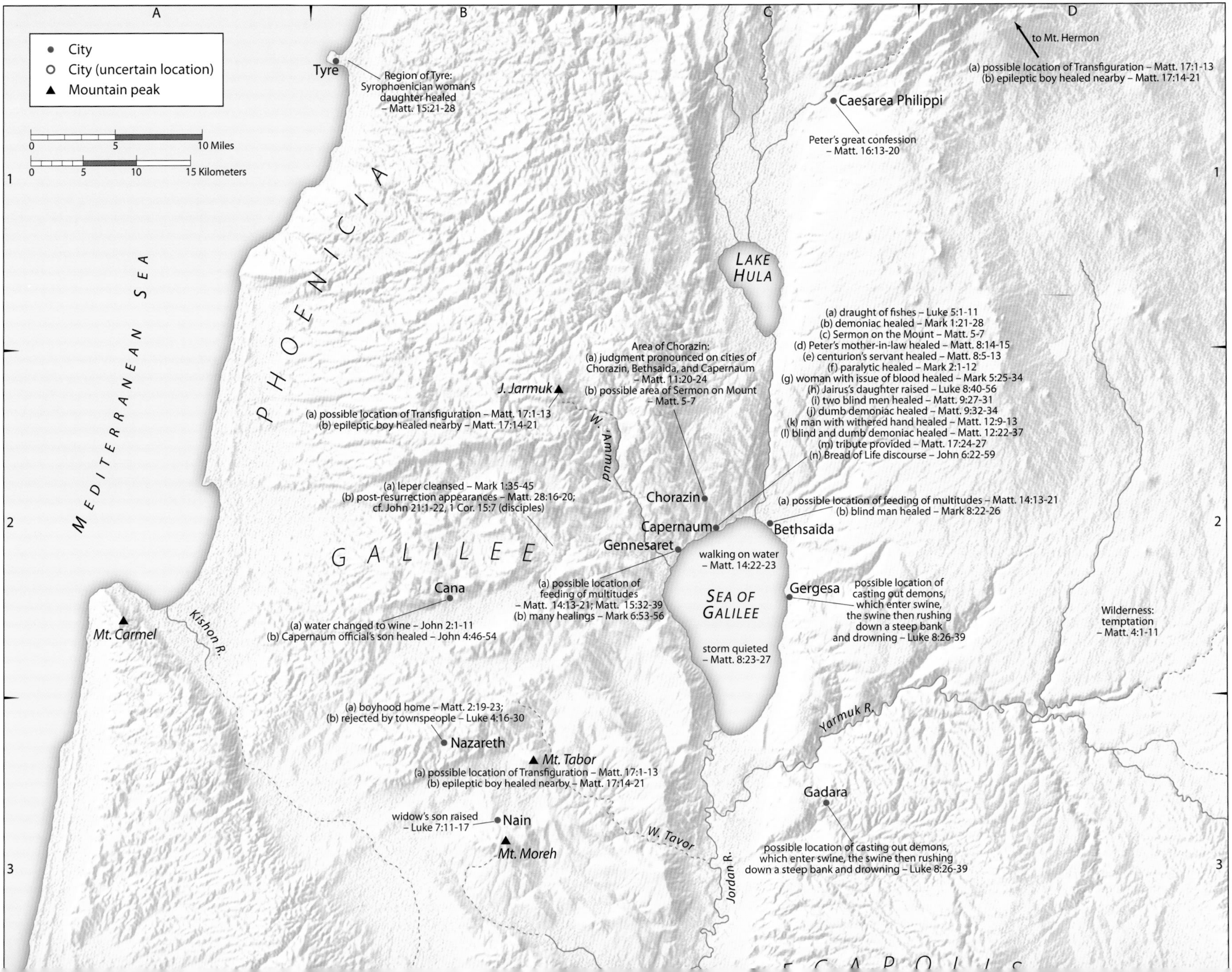

City
City (uncertain location)
Mountain peak
0 5 10 Miles
0 5 10 15 Kilometers
A
B
C
D
1
2
3
MEDITERRANEAN SEA
PHOENICIA
GALILEE
Tyre
Region of Tyre: Syrophoenician woman's daughter healed – Matt. 15:21-28
Caesarea Philippi
Peter's great confession – Matt. 16:13-20
to Mt. Hermon
(a) possible location of Transfiguration – Matt. 17:1-13
(b) epileptic boy healed nearby – Matt. 17:14-21
LAKE HULA
J. Jarmuk
(a) possible location of Transfiguration – Matt. 17:1-13
(b) epileptic boy healed nearby – Matt. 17:14-21
W. 'Ammud
Area of Chorazin:
(a) judgment pronounced on cities of Chorazin, Bethsaida, and Capernaum – Matt. 11:20-24
(b) possible area of Sermon on Mount – Matt. 5-7
(a) draught of fishes – Luke 5:1-11
(b) demoniac healed – Mark 1:21-28
(c) Sermon on the Mount – Matt. 5-7
(d) Peter's mother-in-law healed – Matt. 8:14-15
(e) centurion's servant healed – Matt. 8:5-13
(f) paralytic healed – Mark 2:1-12
(g) woman with issue of blood healed – Mark 5:25-34
(h) Jairus's daughter raised – Luke 8:40-56
(i) two blind men healed – Matt. 9:27-31
(j) dumb demoniac healed – Matt. 9:32-34
(k) man with withered hand healed – Matt. 12:9-13
(l) blind and dumb demoniac healed – Matt. 12:22-37
(m) tribute provided – Matt. 17:24-27
(n) Bread of Life discourse – John 6:22-59
(a) leper cleansed – Mark 1:35-45
(b) post-resurrection appearances – Matt. 28:16-20; cf. John 21:1-22, 1 Cor. 15:7 (disciples)
Chorazin
Capernaum
Gennesaret
(a) possible location of feeding of multitudes – Matt. 14:13-21
(b) blind man healed – Mark 8:22-26
Bethsaida
walking on water – Matt. 14:22-23
SEA OF GALILEE
storm quieted – Matt. 8:23-27
Gergesa
possible location of casting out demons, which enter swine, the swine then rushing down a steep bank and drowning – Luke 8:26-39
(a) possible location of feeding of multitudes – Matt. 14:13-21; Matt. 15:32-39
(b) many healings – Mark 6:53-56
Cana
(a) water changed to wine – John 2:1-11
(b) Capernaum official's son healed – John 4:46-54
Mt. Carmel
Kishon R.
Wilderness: temptation – Matt. 4:1-11
(a) boyhood home – Matt. 2:19-23;
(b) rejected by townspeople – Luke 4:16-30
Nazareth
Mt. Tabor
(a) possible location of Transfiguration – Matt. 17:1-13
(b) epileptic boy healed nearby – Matt. 17:14-21
Yarmuk R.
Gadara
possible location of casting out demons, which enter swine, the swine then rushing down a steep bank and drowning – Luke 8:26-39
widow's son raised – Luke 7:11-17
Nain
Mt. Moreh
W. Tavor
Jordan R.

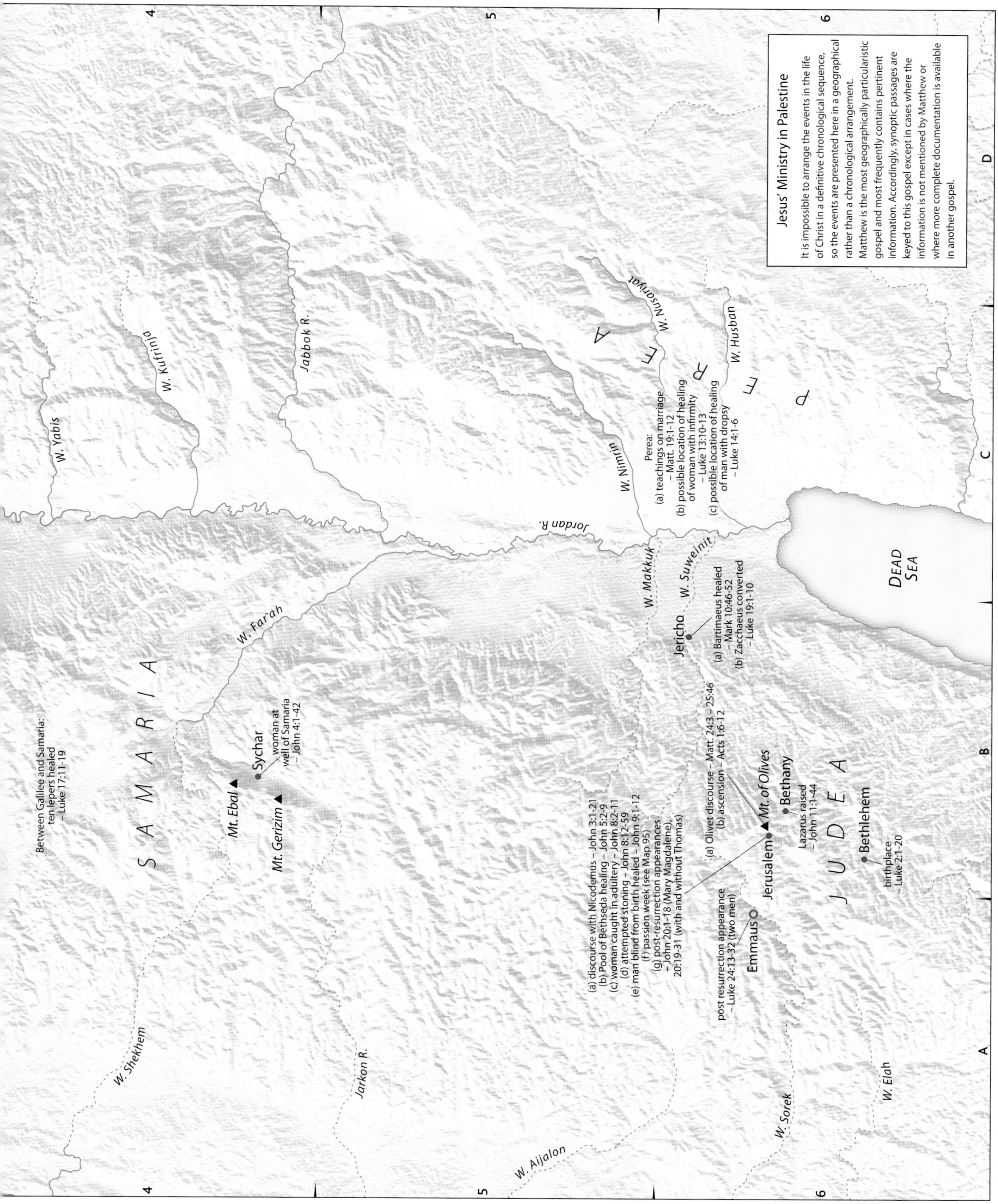
Jesus' Ministry in Palestine
It is impossible to arrange the events in the life of Christ in a definitive chronological sequence, so the events are presented here in a geographical rather than a chronological arrangement. Matthew is the most geographically particularistic gospel and most frequently contains pertinent information. Accordingly, synoptic passages are keyed to this gospel except in cases where the information is not mentioned by Matthew or where more complete documentation is available in another gospel.
Between Galilee and Samaria: ten lepers healed – Luke 17:11-19
SAMARIA
Mt. Ebal
Mt. Gerizim
Sychar
woman at well of Samaria – John 4:1-42
W. Farah
W. Shekhem
Jarkon R.
W. Aijalon
W. Sorek
W. Elah
W. Yabis
W. Kufrinja
Jabbok R.
Jordan R.
W. Nimrin
W. Nusriyat
W. Husban
PEREA
Perea: (a) teachings on marriage – Matt. 19:1-12 (b) possible location of healing of woman with infirmity – Luke 13:10-13 (c) possible location of healing of man with dropsy – Luke 14:1-6
W. Makkuk
W. Suweinit
DEAD SEA
Jericho
(a) Bartimaeus healed – Mark 10:46-52 (b) Zacchaeus converted – Luke 19:1-10
(a) discourse with Nicodemus – John 3:1-21 (b) Pool of Bethseda healing – John 5:2-9 (c) woman caught in adultery – John 8:2-11 (d) attempted stoning – John 8:12-59 (e) man blind from birth healed – John 9:1-12 (f) passion week (see Map 95) (g) post-resurrection appearances – John 20:1-18 (Mary Magdalene), 20:19-31 (with and without Thomas)
Jerusalem
Mt. of Olives
(a) Olivet discourse – Matt. 24:3 – 25:46 (b) ascension – Acts 1:6-12
Bethany
Lazarus raised – John 11:1-44
Emmaus
post resurrection appearance – Luke 24:13-32 (two men)
JUDEA
Bethlehem
birthplace – Luke 2:1-20

JESUS' JOURNEYS TO JERUSALEM

Jesus made numerous trips to Jerusalem during his lifetime, though we cannot be certain exactly how many. The answer may ultimately depend on the length of Christ's public ministry. We are informed that Jesus was approximately thirty years of age when he inaugurated his ministry (Luke 3:23), but information concerning the duration of his mission is nowhere disclosed in the gospels. We can compare Luke 3:1 with Matthew 27:2–26 and determine that his entire ministry occurred while Pontius Pilate was governor of Judea (A.D. 26–36). Historically, estimates have ranged from one year (based on Luke 4:18–19)[524] to twenty years (based on John 8:57),[525] though the latter view appears to be obviated by the Pontius Pilate linkages. Many New Testament scholars today argue for either two years[526] or three years.[527]

Nor is our quest helped by the fact that the gospel of John apparently records Jesus' attendance in Jerusalem at three Passovers (2:13; 6:4–5; 11:55–56). The New Testament documents Jesus' attendance at only one Passover before age thirty (Luke 2:41–42), yet the same text categorically declares that Joseph and Mary fastidiously attended the Passover every year. Surely by cultural prescription and personal inclination, Jesus would have accompanied his parents on most of those occasions (John 4:16). John also tells us that he could not record *everything* that Jesus did and said (20:30). And then, of course, healthy adult male Jews were required to make pilgrimages to Jerusalem three times annually—Passover/*Pesah*, Pentecost/*Shabu`ot*, and Tabernacles/*Succot* (cf. Lev. 23; Deut. 16). Accordingly, it seems prudent to leave open the question of how many trips Jesus may have made to Jerusalem throughout his lifetime.

The historian Josephus records, "It was the custom of the Galileans [in the time of Jesus] when they came to the holy city at the festivals, to take their journeys through the country of the Samaritans; at this time there lay, in the road they took, a village that was called Ginae, which was situated in the limits of Samaria and the great plain."[528] The name Ginae is reflected in the modern city name of Jenin, located near where the Jezreel valley gives way in the south to the mountains of Samaria. So Jewish pilgrims from Galilee would have utilized the direct route to Jerusalem, passing the cities of Sebaste, Sychar, Lebonah, and Bethel along the way.[529] It is reasonable to conclude, therefore, that Jesus also used this direct route going to and from the holy city. He certainly returned northward along this route on one occasion, for it was at the well of Sychar where Jesus met the woman of Samaria and discussed with her the nature of true religion (John 4:3–6).

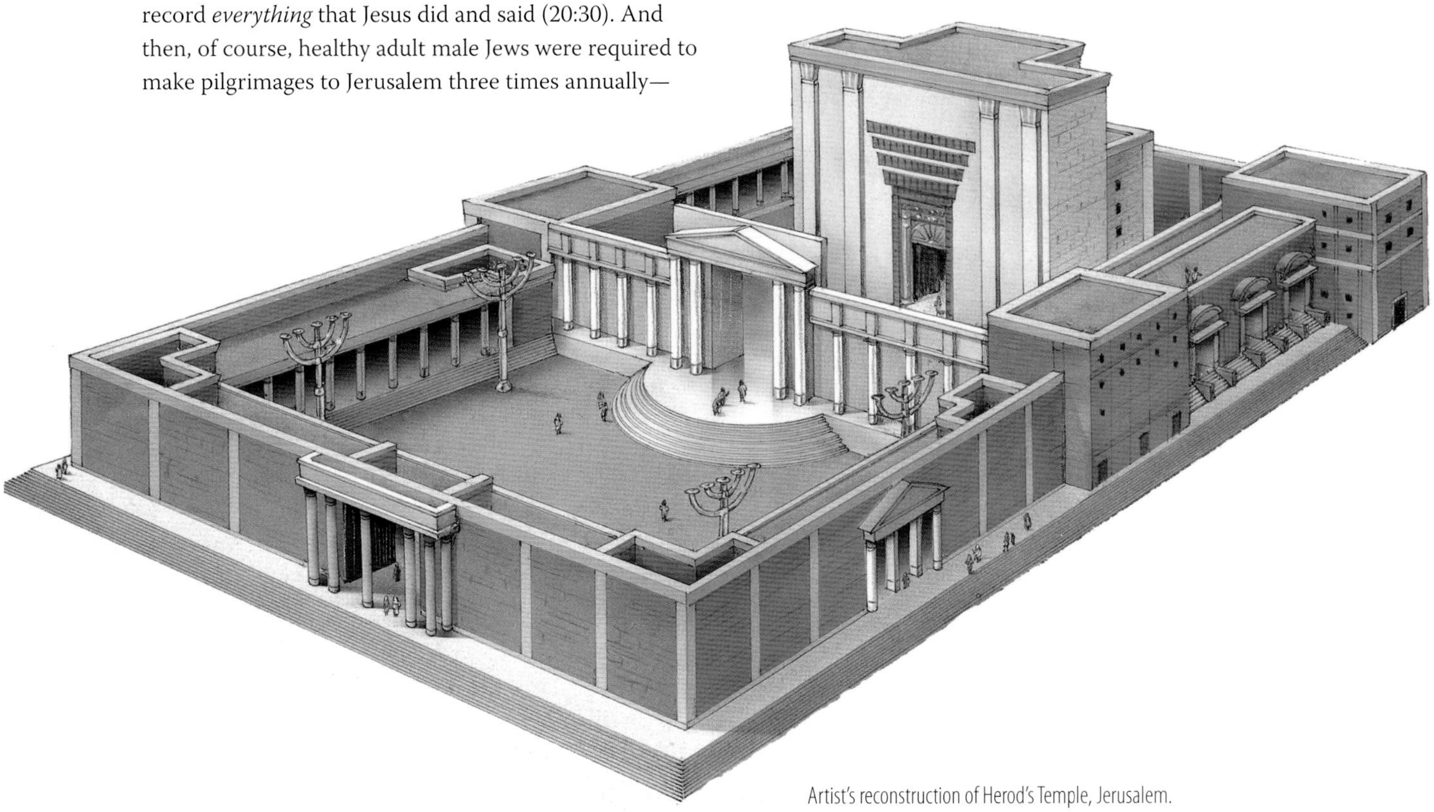

Artist's reconstruction of Herod's Temple, Jerusalem.

Jesus' Journeys to Jerusalem

map 104

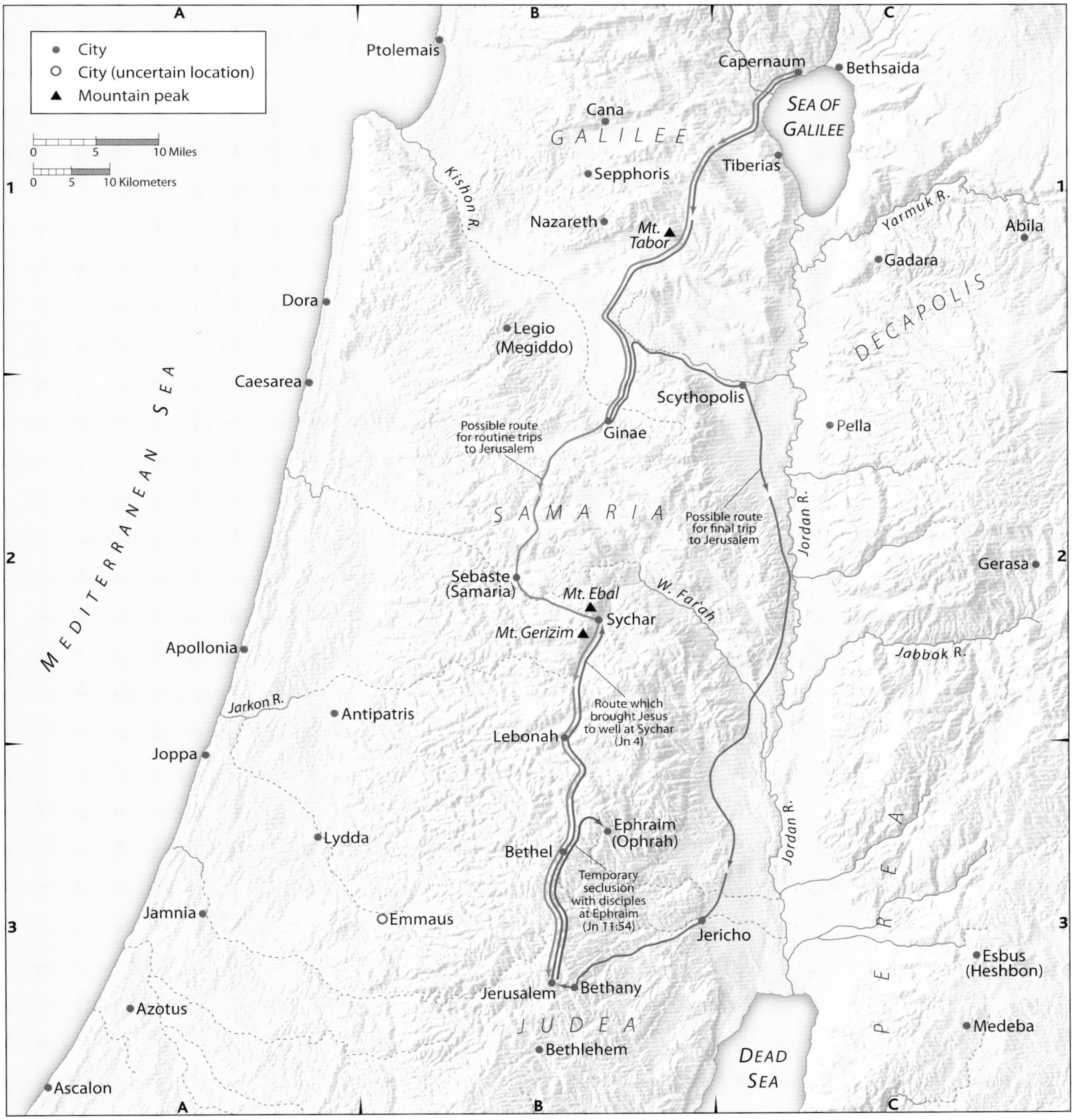

On what would be his final trip from Galilee to Jerusalem, it appears that Jesus again intended to take the direct route through Samaria. But he and his disciples were refused passage at a certain (unnamed) Samaritan village (Luke 9:51–56).[530] They were obliged to backtrack and to take another road that skirted Samaritan territory on their trip to Jerusalem. This route eventually brought them past the cities of Jericho (Matt. 19:1; 20:29; Mark 10:1, 46) and Bethany (John 11:1), so they evidently rerouted themselves east and likely chose the well-established roadway that ran along the western edge of the Jordan River valley from Scythopolis/Beth-shan, past Phaselis and Archelais, to Jericho. [**See map 27.**][531]

When Jesus arrived at Bethany, his friend Lazarus, who had been dead for four days, was raised back to life (John 11:17–44). When the religious establishment was informed of this and other "signs," their opposition and plotting against Christ reached an unprecedented level of intensity. Jesus went into temporary seclusion with some of his disciples at the town of Ephraim/Ophrah (John 11:45–54), north of Jerusalem, until his time had fully come.

JESUS' POST-RESURRECTION APPEARANCES

The doctrine of the resurrection of Christ has been an essential element of the teaching of the New Testament church since its very inception. It was unambiguously affirmed in early apostolic sermons (Acts 2:22–32; 3:15; 4:33; cf. Matt. 20:19; John 10:18), epistolary affirmations (Rom. 1:4; 4:24; 8:34; 1 Cor. 15:3–6; 1 Pet. 1:3; 3:21), and creedal formulae.[532] Serious differences in opinion had been debated with respect to the person or nature of Christ, yet the doctrine of the resurrection appears not to have been divisive among the mainstream Fathers of the early church. Christian believers from a host of ecclesiastical traditions, in every generation and on every continent, have fervently embraced this proclamation, despite the fact that the notion of rising from the dead has generally been rejected by ancient and modern people alike (Acts 17:32).

Perhaps the genius of such a tenet was best articulated by the apostle Paul who argued that without the keystone reality of Christ's resurrection, the edifice of Christian faith would collapse under its own weight and be shown to be ill-founded, if not fraudulent (1 Cor. 15:12–34). But quite to the contrary, he said, it was precisely Jesus' resurrection that formed the undergirding for Jesus' parousia (1 Thess. 1:10; Phil. 3:20–21; cf. 2 Cor. 4:14–15; 1 Thess. 4:14–18). It was the resurrection that validated Paul's sober claims about Jesus' unique status with God and his preeminent role on earth in what would be a new age (Eph. 1:20–23; Rom. 6:9–11; Phil. 3:10).

It seems that when the early apostles sought to substantiate Christ's resurrection, it was insufficient for them merely to point to an empty tomb in Jerusalem, especially since tomb robbing had long been a common practice throughout the Middle East (Matt. 28:11–15). In fact, it had been raised to a capital offense by the emperor in the New Testament era.[533] So the apostles anchored their claim on historical occasions when a resurrected Christ had appeared to them and others, had communicated with them, had eaten with them, had been touched by them, or had ascended before their eyes.

Based on the witness of the gospels, it is admittedly conjectural to comment on the exact number or the sequential order of the recorded post-resurrection appearances of Christ (John 21:14). Accordingly, in an endeavor to prevent overstatement, the map provides the data geographically. One can fairly clearly discern some thirteen different occasions when Christ is said to have made a post-resurrection appearance:

1. Jesus appeared (*ὁράω*) to Peter/Cephas in Jerusalem (Luke 24:34b; 1 Cor. 15:5a).
2. Jesus appeared (*φαίνομαι*) to Mary Magdalene beside the open tomb (Mark 16:9–11; Luke 24:1–11; John 20:11–18). Matthew 28:1–10 identifies Mary Magdalene, the other Mary (the mother of James and Joseph [Matt. 27:56]), and the wife of Cleopas (John 19:25). Mary Magdalene apparently touched him.
3. Jesus appeared (*ἵστημι*) to ten disciples in Jerusalem when Thomas was absent (Luke 24:36–43; John 20:19–23). They saw flesh and bones, and he ate with them.
4. Jesus appeared (*φανερόω*) to the disciples in Jerusalem, when Thomas was present (Mark 16:14–18; John 20:26–29). Thomas beheld his pierced hands and touched him.
5. Jesus appeared (*ὁράω*) to all the apostles at an undisclosed location, but presumably near Jerusalem (1 Cor. 15:7b).
6. Jesus appeared (*εἶδον, θεωρέω*) to Stephen in Jerusalem (Acts 7:55–56).
7. Jesus appeared (*ὁράω*) to James at an undisclosed location, but presumably near Jerusalem (1 Cor. 15:7a).
8. Jesus appeared (*φανερόω, ἐγγίζω . . . ἐπιγινώσκω*) to two disciples in the countryside on the road to Emmaus (Imwas?) (Mark 16:12–13; Luke 24:13–31).
9. Jesus appeared (*ὁράω*) to more than 500 believers at one time at an undisclosed location, but presumably near Jerusalem (1 Cor. 15:6). Most were still alive when Paul wrote his epistle.
10. Jesus appeared (*εἶδον*) to 11 disciples somewhere in Galilee (Matt. 28:16–20).
11. Jesus appeared (*φανερόω*) to seven disciples beside the Sea of Galilee (John 21:1–23).
12. Jesus appeared (*παρίστημι*) to his disciples atop the Mount of Olives (Acts 1:3–11; cf. Mark 16:19; 1 Cor. 15:5b).
13. Jesus appeared (*ὁράω*) to Saul/Paul on the road to Damascus (1 Cor. 15:8; cf. Acts 9:3–9).

Two remaining observations are noteworthy. First, biblical narrators sometimes chide the early disciples because they did not immediately recognize Jesus when he appeared (appearances #2, #3, and #8), were not expecting to meet him (#11 and #13), or did not believe the testimony of other eyewitnesses concerning his appearance(s) (#1, #2, #4, and #8). Such comments do not characterize individuals somehow involved in a pious fraud. Nor should a manufactured story have included the eyewitness testimony of either a solitary individual or a woman.[534] Second, Jesus appeared to persons who had been tutored to one degree or another in Judaism, who were likely familiar with the anthropological formula of much of early Judaism: *bāśār* ("body") + *rûaḥ* ("breath/spirit/inner self") = *nepheš* ("living being"). Therefore, it is doubtful that the notion of a non-corporeal resurrection could have arisen in such circles.[535]

EXTENSIVE TRAVELS OF THE APOSTLE PAUL

The distances traveled by the apostle Paul are nothing short of staggering. The New Testament registers the equivalent of about 13,450 miles that the great apostle journeyed. This estimation is only a calculation of approximate air miles, so when one takes into account the winding, circuitous roadways and tracks he necessarily had to employ, the total distance would exceed that figure by a sizeable margin.[541]

Moreover, it appears that the New Testament does not document *all* of Paul's missionary excursions. For example, there seem to have been unchronicled visits to Corinth (2 Cor. 12:14; 13:1) and Illyricum (Rom. 15:19). Paul also refers to shipwrecks of which we have no record (2 Cor. 11:25), and he expressed a desire to visit Spain (Rom. 15:24, 28; cf. 1:10–15). New Testament scholarship continues to debate whether Paul ever fulfilled this latter goal.[542]

Considering the means of transportation available in the Roman world, the average distance one could travel in a day, the primitive paths, and rugged, sometimes mountainous terrain over which one had to venture, it becomes almost unfathomable to imagine the sheer expenditure of the apostle's physical energy. Many of those miles carried Paul through unsafe and hostile environs controlled largely by bandits who eagerly awaited a victim (2 Cor. 11:26–27; cf. Luke 10:30). [**See Chapter One**]. Accordingly, the apostle's sterling commitment to the gospel of Christ entailed a spiritual vitality that was inextricably fused to superlative levels of physical stamina and courage.

The following is a list of Paul's documented journeys, with approximate air mileage for each:

1. Acts 9:1–30. Jerusalem—Damascus—(Arabia)—Jerusalem—Tarsus (690 miles, excluding his trip into the Arabian desert, the distance of which cannot be calculated, cf. Gal. 1:17–19; **see map 108**);
2. Acts 11:25–26. Tarsus—Antioch (90 miles; **see map 108**);
3. Acts 11:27–30; 12:25. Antioch—Jerusalem—Antioch (560 miles, cf. Gal. 2:1–10; **see map 108**);
4. Acts 13:4—14:28. First missionary journey (1,400 miles; **see map 110**);
5. Acts 15:3–30. Antioch—Jerusalem—Antioch (560 miles; **see map 108**);
6. Acts 15:39—18:22. Second missionary journey (2,800 miles; **see map 111**);
7. Acts 18:23—21:17. Third missionary journey (2,700 miles; **see map 112**);
8. Acts 23:31–33. Transported as a prisoner from Jerusalem to Caesarea (43 miles);
9. Acts 27:1—28:16. Transported as a prisoner to Rome (2,250 miles; **see map 113**);
10. Between a two-year imprisonment (Acts 28:30) and a second imprisonment in Rome (2 Tim. 1:16–17; 4:6–8, 16–18), the apostle apparently visited many places throughout the Roman Empire, including Crete (Titus 1:5), Miletus (2 Tim. 4:20), Ephesus (1 Tim. 1:20; 3:14; cf. 2 Tim. 2:17; 4:14), Colossae (Philem. 22), Troas (2 Tim. 4:13), Macedonia (1 Tim. 1:3), Nicopolis (Titus 3:12), and Corinth (2 Tim. 4:20)— at least 2,350 miles by constructing the shortest possible itinerary without regard to historical sequence. The actual total may have been closer to 2,750 miles.[543]

That portion of Antioch built on the slopes of Mt. Silpius is where the heart of the early Christian movement is thought to have been situated.

PAUL'S MISSIONARY JOURNEYS

It initially sounds rather far-fetched to suggest that the story of the early church as told in the book of Acts owes much of its shape to a pagan Macedonian monarch who lived centuries earlier. Closer inspection of certain details, however, reveals that this may very well have been the case. Seleucus I Nicator was one of the foremost generals of Alexander the Great, and he came to rule over most of the Asiatic provinces that had been part of Alexander's vast domain. [**See map 87.**] During the inauguration of the Seleucid era, Seleucus founded a number of metropolitan areas, including the preeminent city of Antioch itself, an enormous expanse of some 5,200 acres, all richly nourished by a copious supply of fresh water found in the adjacent plateau of Daphne to the south [**map 109**] and by its agriculturally productive basin to the northeast. [**See map 3.**]

Antioch in Syria was strategically situated in the narrow valley corridor of the Orontes River, which divided the northernmost outliers of the rugged Lebanon Mountains (Mt. Staurin, Mt. Silpius, Mt. Cassius) from the southernmost topography of the Amanus mountain range (Mt. Atallur). [**See map 109.**] It provided the easiest and most direct inland access from the northern sectors of the Mediterranean Sea into Cappadocia, Armenia, Mesopotamia, the Arabian Desert, and the whole of the East. (Chinese porcelains and silks have been found among Antioch's early archaeological remains.) Anyone traveling overland in antiquity from one side of the Taurus mountains to the other, whether between Asia Minor and Palestine or Egypt, or between Asia Minor and Mesopotamia, would almost automatically have been funneled geographically through this critical intersection.[544] For the Romans, Antioch became the single most strategic city in all of Asia and, behind Alexandria and Rome itself, the most important and largest city of the Roman Empire.[545]

After a large Jewish contingent assisted Seleucus in his pivotal victory over Antigonus at the battle of Ipsus in Phrygia, he bequeathed to the Jewish community certain sections inside the city of Antioch and sizeable tracts of land in the vicinity. Perhaps even more importantly, he offered citizenship to Jewish individuals at Antioch, and he granted them other political privileges equal to those afforded Macedonians and Greeks.[546] Later, when other Antiochian and Alexandrian citizens implored the Roman generals Vespasian and Titus to revoke citizenship for Jews, their pleadings went unheeded and Jews continued to retain their favored status in Antioch.[547] So even while Vespasian and Titus were vigorously engaged in crushing Jewish insurrection in Jerusalem and Palestine [**map 115**], they were simultaneously proclaiming free citizenship for Jews residing in and around Antioch, roughly 300 miles away.

Not astonishing, therefore, there developed a large and well-established Jewish population at Antioch in Syria by the middle of the first Christian century, and the city contained many Greek-speaking synagogues.[548] Because it was the Seleucid and Roman administrative and political center, Antioch also enjoyed a sizeable non-Jewish population, with an estimated total population of 500,000. The city maintained a cosmopolitan and eclectic interest in philosophical and religious enquiry, as well as a high level of public order and police protection. These factors combined to create a pervasive atmosphere in Antioch in which the Christian message could be safely propagated and spontaneously received.

As early believers faced increasing and recurring persecution following the death of Stephen, many scattered from Jerusalem to other regions where they found safe refuge, including Phoenicia, Cyprus, and Antioch. Some of the unnamed missionaries proclaimed the Good News in the city of Antioch, and great numbers believed and turned to the Lord (Acts 11:19–21).

When rumors of widespread conversions reached the church in Jerusalem, the elders sent Barnabas to Antioch to investigate and report back. Barnabas quickly saw that the work flourished. He went to Tarsus (the capital of Cilicia), located Saul (later to be known as Paul the apostle), and brought him to the Syrian metropolis to assist in instructing the new converts. So strong did the emerging movement become that disciples of Jesus were first called "Christians" at Antioch (Acts 11:22–26).[549] Later, when famine had spread across parts of western Asia, it was the fellowship at Antioch that sent assistance to the believers suffering in Jerusalem (Acts 11:27–30). Consequently, it comes as no surprise that it was this preeminent Christian base that commissioned and was the starting point for all three missionary journeys of the apostle Paul.

PAUL'S FIRST MISSIONARY JOURNEY

The initial mission from Antioch involved Paul and Barnabas, supported by John Mark, a cousin of Barnabas (Col. 4:10). From Antioch's port city on the Mediterranean, Seleucia Pieria [**map 109**], they took a boat to Cyprus, the birthplace of Barnabas (Acts 4:36), and arrived at the port city of Salamis. Though partially destroyed in an earthquake in 15 B.C., Salamis in the first Christian century featured a temple of Zeus, a gymnasium (open-air sports ground where teenagers received physical education and academic training), and a theater that sat 20,000 persons. Its large Jewish community required several synagogues (Acts 13:3–5). In what would become a personal ministerial pattern in other cities, Paul preached on the Sabbath in a synagogue.

The missionary party departed Salamis, crossed the entire island, and came to the city of [New] Paphos (Acts 13:6a).[550] Several unverifiable traditions suggest the route(s) Paul may have used to cross Cyprus and the places he may have stopped en route to Paphos.[551] Had he followed the existing Roman road along the southern coast, his group would have passed the intermediate towns of Kition, Amathus, and Kourion before arriving at New Paphos.

Paphos served as the seat of the island's government in the New Testament era, and the city was known for its temple and cult of the goddess Aphrodite, who allegedly emerged from the foam of the sea very near the city. Upon their arrival, the missionaries were summoned to appear before the Roman proconsul,[552] who desired to hear their message personally. Here Paul faced his first opposition and also had the first conversion to his message. A Jewish prophet named Bar-Jesus (*Elymas* is a Greek word meaning "sorcerer"), almost certainly a member of the proconsul's staff, sought to confound the apostle's message and to dissuade the proconsul. But Paul withstood him, and Bar-Jesus was struck with blindness (Acts 13:6b–12). Seeing what had occurred and becoming enamored of the gospel, the proconsul—Sergius Paulus—believed and became a disciple of Christ.[553] As a result of this event, western Cyprus became the first Christian-ruled district within the Roman Empire. And following this encounter with Sergius Paulus in the narrative, and

The Early Travels of the Apostle Paul

map 108

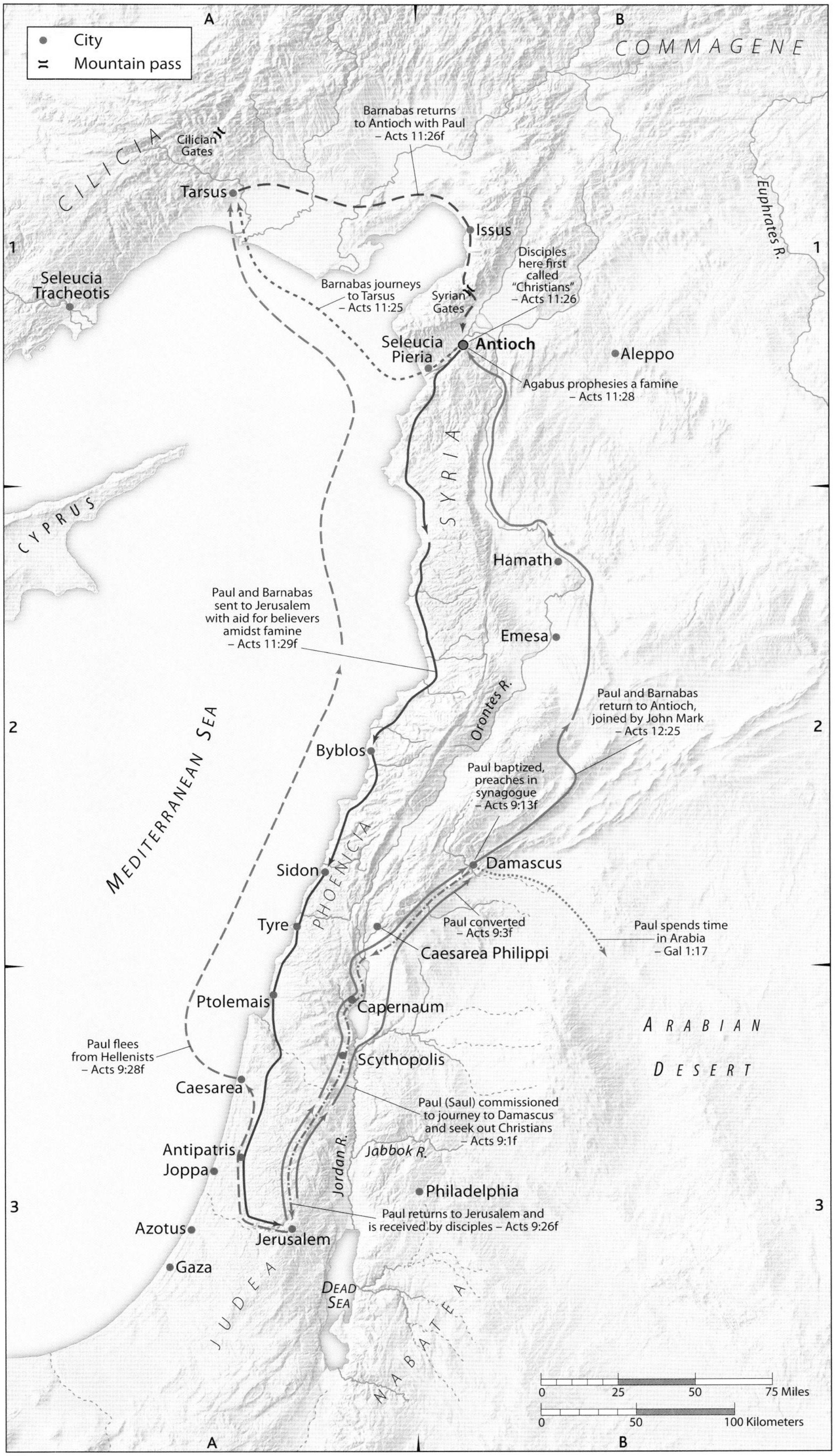

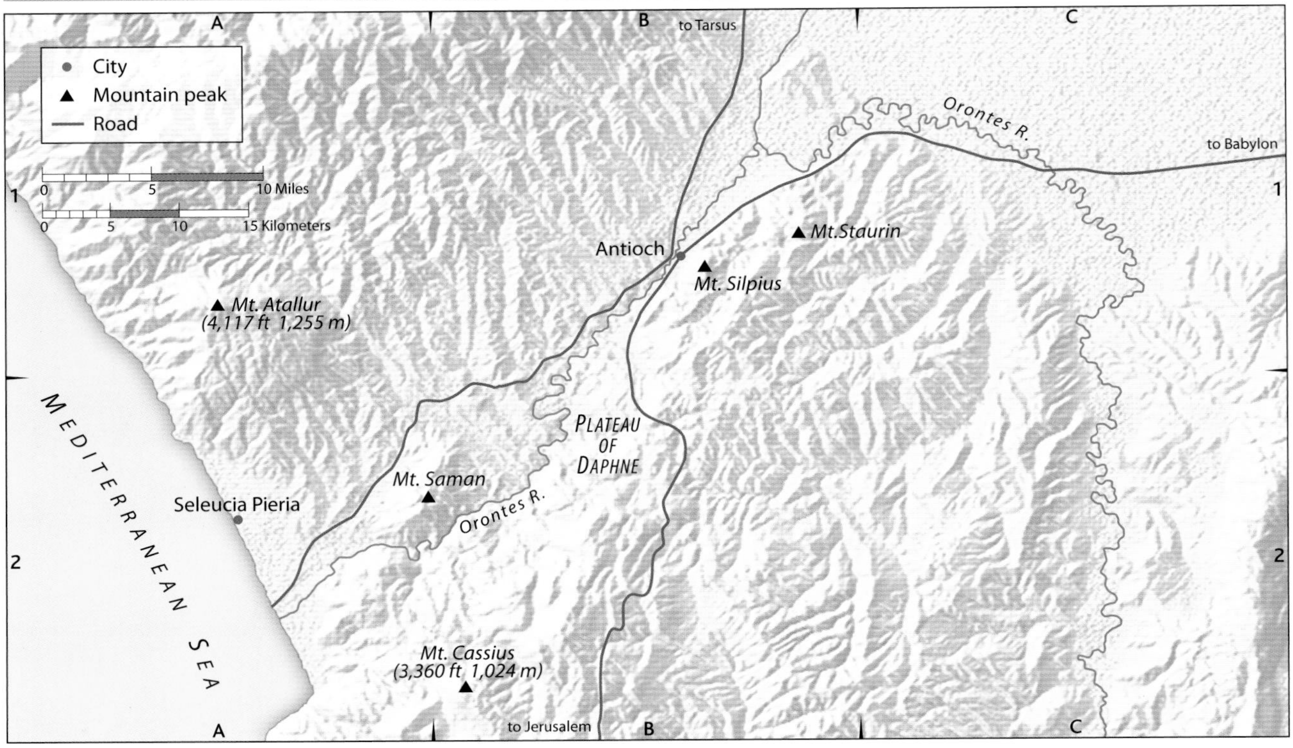

consistently throughout the epistles, the apostle is henceforth referenced by his Roman name (Paul) and no longer by his Jewish name (Saul).

Paul and his entourage left Cyprus and sailed to the mainland of Asia Minor at Perga.[554] The only event Luke associated with Perga was the departure of John Mark, who left the missionary party and returned to Jerusalem (Acts 13:13). Why Mark left the other missionaries at this point is unknown and widely debated in the literature. Did he depart because of lingering uncertainty about a Gentile mission, which perhaps was still thought to have been blasphemous (cf. Gal. 2:13)? Was he jealous that Paul had assumed leadership over his own kinsman? Did he fear the dangers they had to face? Was he ill or homesick? Or were the extremely rugged Taurus mountains too demanding for him? All of these possibilities have been suggested.

Regardless of John Mark's reasoning, Paul and Barnabas proceeded without him from Perga to Antioch in Pisidia (Acts 13:14). This stretch of their itinerary would have taken them through the Taurus mountain range near the Cestrus River, by way of the cities of Termessos, Comana, Lysinia, and Apollonia on a Roman military road—Via Sebaste—that had been constructed by Augustus as early as 6 B.C.[555] The dense forestation of the Taurus, coupled with its high altitude, would have made passage to its north side nearly impossible any other way.[556]

Again on the Sabbath, Paul preached in the synagogue in Antioch. This time his message so stirred the imagination of his audience that he was invited to speak again the following Sabbath. On that occasion, however, he was reviled by Jewish leaders and redirected his efforts toward the Gentiles in the region. Many believed Paul's message, a fact that further inflamed Jewish hostilities. As a result, the orthodox Jewish leaders insidiously created a disaffection within Antioch, and the two missionaries were driven from the territory (Acts 13:14b–52). A Christian church is being excavated in Antioch of Pisidia today, constructed over a first-century synagogue, which may or may not prove to be related to the place of Paul's preaching.

Entering the district of Lycaonia, Paul and Barnabas commenced their ministry there in the city of Iconium. The eastern sector of the Via Sebaste extended southeast from Antioch in Pisidia into the province of Lycaonia, past the towns of Neapolis and Tiberiopolis, and on to Iconium.[557] Paul and Barnabas remained in Iconium for a long time (Acts 14:1–6), and many were captivated by their message. But after they learned of a plot to stone them, they fled to the nearby town of Lystra, an important center of commerce in the eastern Roman world. While there, Paul healed a man who had been crippled from birth. The people of Lystra were astonished and thought they were being visited by the gods. They identified Paul as Hermes/Mercury because he was the speaker, and Barnabas as Zeus/Jupiter, perhaps because of his seniority and more imposing appearance. When the people tried to offer sacrifices to them (Acts 14:6b–18), Paul and Barnabas strongly insisted that they were mere mortals.[558]

Afterward, Jews from Antioch in Pisidia and Iconium succeeded in tracing the missionaries to Lystra, where they persuaded some individuals to stone Paul. The apostle was dragged out of the city and left for dead (Acts 14:19). The effectiveness of this delegation from abroad supports the notion that there was a Jewish population and perhaps even a synagogue in Lystra, though neither is explicitly mentioned in the text. Paul's mission to Lystra must ultimately be judged a success, however, if only because of the conversion of the family of Timothy (2 Tim. 1:5; Acts 16:1–3).

The final city visited on this first journey was Derbe, now known to be located at Kerti Hüyük, thanks to a mid-second-century limestone inscription and a fourth- or fifth-century inscribed stone slab found there.[559] Derbe was the only place in Asia on this journey where the apostles were not persecuted. (Note the omission of Derbe in Paul's later assessment of his persecutions [2 Tim. 3:11].) The fact that many disciples were made while Paul and Barnabas remained in Derbe allows for the inference that they may have stayed there for a considerable time (Acts 14:20–21a). One such disciple, Gaius, is later referenced by name (Acts 20:4).

At Derbe, Paul would have been less than 100 miles from his hometown of Tarsus, and only about 200 miles away from Antioch in Syria, the final destination of his first journey. Nevertheless, instead of taking a direct route east, passing through the Cilician Gates, and arriving in Antioch in about ten days, Paul's concern for the fledgling churches compelled him to retrace his steps and travel nearly 700 miles before concluding his journey. His choice of itinerary would have taken him back through towns where only a short time earlier he had received harsh treatment and rejection, which would have required a healthy dose of fearlessness on his part. But Paul had important business to conduct along his selected route: he "strengthened the disciples," "encouraged believers to remain strong amidst many tribulations," and "appointed elders in every church" (Acts 14:22–23). Following a brief preaching mission in Perga, Paul went down to the Mediterranean port of Attalia, the chief port of Pamphylia at the time.[560] The missionaries embarked on a ship headed home to Antioch, where they spent "no little time" with the believers there (Acts 14:24–28).

Paul's First Missionary Journey **map 110**

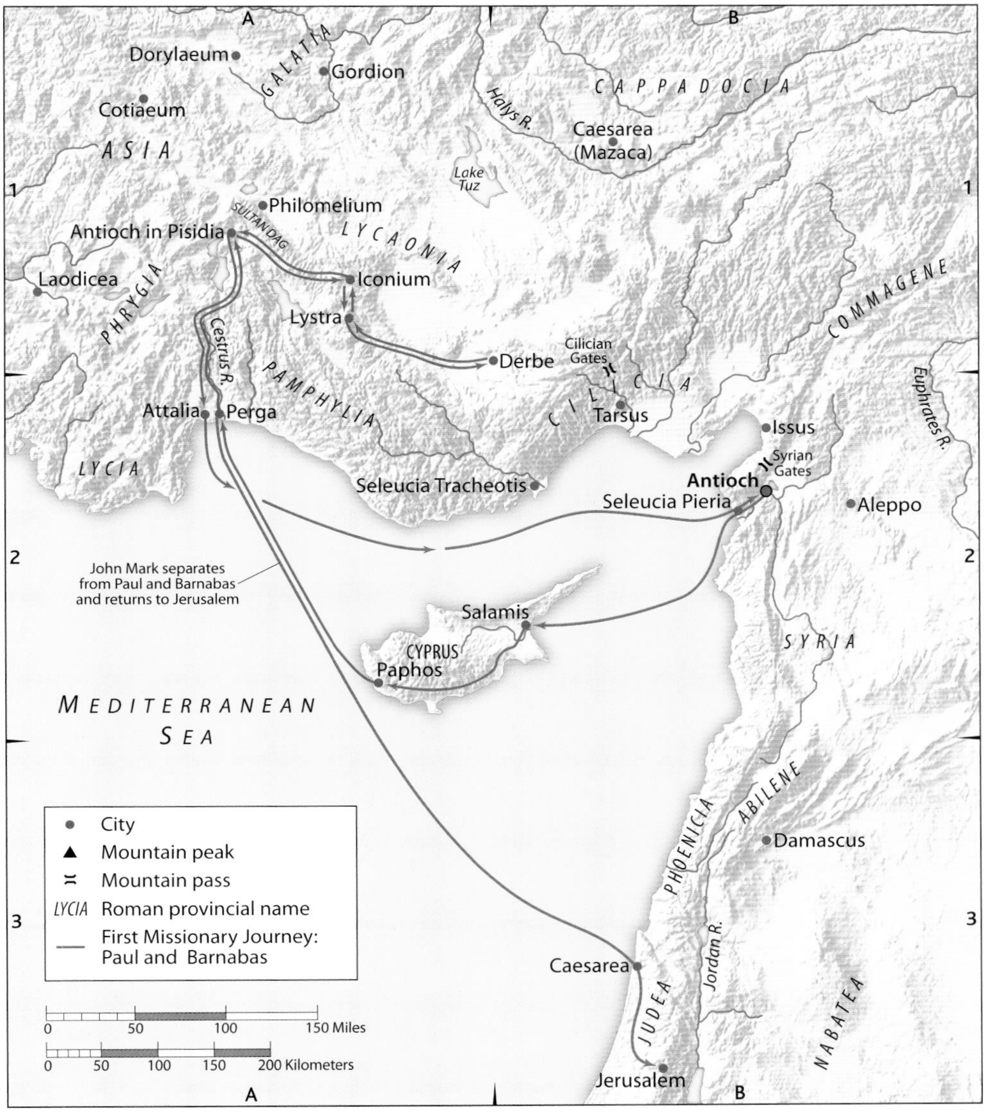

PAUL'S SECOND MISSIONARY JOURNEY

After spending time in Antioch and Jerusalem (Acts 15:1–35), Paul suggested to Barnabas that they revisit their Christian brothers and sisters in the towns of their first journey. While they were still in the planning stages, however, a sharp disagreement arose between them. Barnabas urged that John Mark accompany them, but Paul wanted nothing to do with the idea of taking along someone who earlier had withdrawn from their mission. Therefore they went their separate ways. Barnabas took Mark and sailed toward Cyprus, his homeland (Acts 15:36–39). Relieved of the Cyprian ministry, Paul recruited Silas, a Jew with Roman citizenship who was an important member of the church in Jerusalem (Acts 15:22–32; 16:40). (Paul and John Mark were later reconciled [Col. 4:10; 2 Tim. 4:11]. Similarly, the later text of 1 Corinthians 9:6 seems to reflect Paul's sympathetic awareness of the ministry of Barnabas.)

Paul and Silas proceeded north from Antioch, through the Syrian Gates and later through the Cilician Gates,[561] into the provinces of Cilicia and Galatia (Acts 15:41). They came to Derbe and passed on to Lystra, strengthening believers along the way. In the latter town, they met a young man named Timothy. Timothy's mother and/or grandmother may have been among Paul's earliest converts at Lystra (2 Tim. 1:5). Timothy himself may have become a disciple under Paul's tutelage (1 Cor. 4:17; 1 Tim. 1:2). His reputation among the believers in the Lycaonian region and his Jewish heritage (Acts 16:1) made Timothy a desirable and eventually an effective missionary companion of the apostle. So Timothy joined Paul and Silas, and they set out on the Roman road westward, probably intending to follow it as far west as Ephesus (precisely the route Paul employed on his third journey).[562]

However, when they approached the province of Asia, they were "forbidden by the Holy Spirit from entering" (Acts 16:6b). That would have left them obliged to leave a paved road, veer northward toward Bithynia and Pontus, and begin a trek across what at that time would have been a narrow, unpaved dirt trackway.[563] Their most likely route would have them follow the trackway between Antioch in Pisidia and its neighboring mountain in the north (Sultan Dag) in a northwest direction, across central Phrygia as far as the city of Cotiaeum (Kütahya). At Cotiaeum the trackway took a sharp turn to the northeast and proceeded as far as the prominent Roman city of Dorylaeum (Eskişehir). From Dorylaeum, the main trackway north ran to the northwest in the direction of Nicaea (Iznik) and Prusa (Bursa), staying north of the heights of the Mysian Olympus (Ulu Dag). It was along this stretch of roadway, probably not far from Nicaea, that Paul's party was again barred from entering their province of choice, Bithynia (Acts 16:7). Instead, they went west on a Roman trackway that passed through the province of Mysia and arrived at Alexandrian Troas (Acts 16:8), a port on the Aegean coast near the fabled city of Troy.[564] Founded by Alexander the Great and converted into a Roman colony by Augustus Caesar, Troas was a regular port of call for vessels traveling between Asia and Macedonia (Acts 20:5).

While staying at Troas with Silas and Timothy, Paul received his "Macedonian call," and the stage was set for the gospel to spread into Europe (Acts 16:9; cf. 2 Cor. 2:12–13). Some have speculated that the "man of Macedonia" was none other than Luke himself, author of the book of Acts.[565] A plausible basis of support for this premise can be found in the three so-called "we" passages of the book of Acts (16:10–17; 20:5—21:18; and 27:1—28:16).[566] Unlike the remainder of Acts, these three narratives are written in the first person and seem to reflect an actual eyewitness account. Yet despite the clear indications of Luke's authorship, speculation concerning the identity of the "man of Macedonia" is just that—speculation. Very few New Testament scholars today ardently embrace that possibility.

From Troas, Paul immediately set sail for Europe, now with Silas, Timothy, and Luke. Trade winds must have been favorable because the journey between Troas and Neapolis (Kavala) took only two days, while the inbound leg between Neapolis and Troas on Paul's third journey took five days (Acts 20:6). Their night en route was spent on Samothrace, a mountainous island that served as the seat of the mystery cult in Roman religion. From Neapolis, Paul and his compatriots made their way directly to Philippi. Between Neapolis and Thessalonica, Paul and his party were able to travel on the Egnatian Way, a nearly 500-mile paved arterial roadway stretching between Byzantium/Istanbul on the Marmara Sea and Dyrrhacium on the Adriatic Sea.[567] It was, in effect, a continuation of the Appian Way that spanned the Italian territory from Rome to Brundisium on the Adriatic, thus joining the eastern provinces with Italy. [**See map 26.**]

Philippi, named for the father of Alexander, was the largest and most important site in all of northern Greece at that time. About 100 years before Paul's visit, in 42 B.C., the plains of Philippi served as the site of a crushing defeat inflicted on Brutus and Cassius by the forces of Mark Antony and Octavian (later Augustus Caesar). Caesar converted Philippi into a Roman colony, and the city served as home for many of the military veterans of this and later conflicts. It was the only Roman colony to be so designated in the book of Acts (16:12). As a colony, its municipal authority was placed in the hands of two "magistrates" (Acts 16:20), known in Latin as "praetors" (Phil. 1:13; Matt. 27:27; Acts 23:35).

Following his earlier pattern, Paul sought opportunity at Philippi to preach on the Sabbath. In this case, however, he spoke at "a place of prayer outside the gate beside the river" (Acts 16:13, 16), probably a feeder stream of the Gangites River that was near the southwestern part of the city. Given Luke's unusual and even opaque terminology here, this suggests that Philippi had a very small Jewish population and may not have had a synagogue.[568] Paul's initial preaching efforts at Philippi were rewarded when Lydia believed and was baptized, together with her entire household. She was from the city of Thyatira in the province of Asia, and was in Philippi as a "seller of purple." (An inscription found at Philippi makes mention of "purple dyers" from "Thyatira" and suggests they may have worked there as a guild.)[569] Ironically, Paul's first recorded convert in Europe hailed from the very Asian province from which he had been prohibited to enter and evangelize (Acts 16:6b).

But later the apostle exorcised a spirit from a slave girl, and her owners realized they could no longer profit from exploiting her strange gift. Paul and Silas were dragged into the Roman agora (marketplace) before the tribunal, publicly beaten, and imprisoned (Acts 16:18–24; cf. 1 Thess. 2:2).[570] Around midnight, as Paul and Silas were praying and singing hymns deep inside the prison, an earthquake opened the prison doors and loosened the prisoners' fetters. The jailer, supposing that his prisoners had escaped and that he would have to pay the

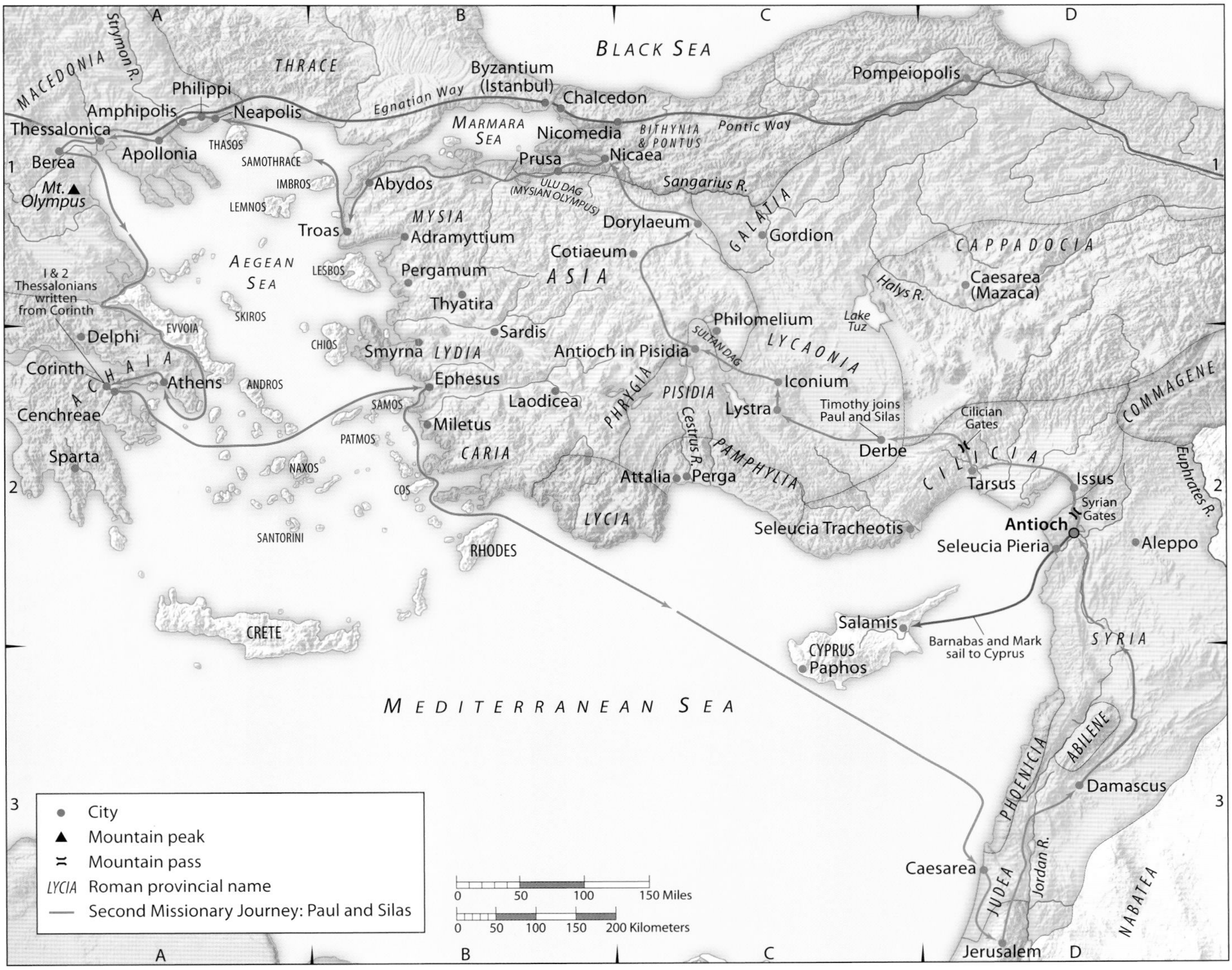

price of their lives with his own, prepared to commit suicide. But Paul assured him that not one prisoner had escaped. Terrified and probably confounded, the jailer entered Paul's jail cell, where he was captivated by the message of Christ and was converted. Whereupon, he took Paul and Silas to his house, cared for their physical needs, and was baptized, along with all his family. In the morning the magistrates discovered they had beaten Roman citizens and offered their apologies. Still, they requested that Paul leave Philippi, probably fearing reprisal if news of the beating were noised abroad (Acts 16:25–40).

Paul and his company, presumably without Luke, journeyed along the Egnatian Way, past Amphipolis[571] and Apollonia, as far as Thessalonica (Acts 17:1). Thessalonica was a harbor city at a strategic juncture along the Egnatian Way, near an intersection with another major roadway that linked the Aegean Sea northward to the Danube River.[572] Perhaps it was due to this distinctive geographical setting that Paul later wrote that the faith of the Thessalonian church had "gone throughout the world" (1 Thess. 1:8). Paul's party apparently found lodging in Thessalonica with a man named Jason. And for three successive Sabbaths, Paul expounded mightily from the Scriptures concerning Christ. Many believed, but again the ire of local Jewish leaders was aroused and they incited a mob to storm Jason's house. Unable to find Paul or Silas inside, Jason was taken and beaten for harboring seditionists (Acts 17:2–9).

Paul and his companions left Thessalonica under cover of darkness and journeyed the short distance to Berea. Their ministry in the synagogue there met with a receptive audience, and it appears that many individuals believed and a sizeable church was founded. But when news of this Berean ministry reached the ears of some Jews in Thessalonica, they went to Berea and sought to harm Paul. Silas and Timothy remained behind as Paul was quickly ushered out of Berea and taken down to the Aegean Sea (probably to Dium, site of a Roman colony near the northern base of Mt. Olympus), where he embarked on a ship headed to Athens (Acts 17:10–15).

From his ship, Paul could have viewed Mt. Olympus, the mythic home of Zeus, chief god in the Greek pantheon, but it was the myriad of gods that comprised the pantheon that confronted him in Athens.[573] Distraught at the bewildering array of deities worshiped in this city, Paul lost no time engaging in debate both in the Jewish synagogue and in the agora. Even though much of its former greatness was by then diminished, Athens was still the intellectual center of the ancient world in Paul's day. When word spread that a new teacher of religion from the East had arrived, Paul was invited to speak before the Areopagus, a court said to have been founded by Athena herself and which in earlier days had been the seat for the high council of Athens.

Since he was addressing people with no Jewish background at all, Paul did not follow his normal procedure of going to a synagogue and demonstrating how the promises of the Old Testament were realized through the death and resurrection of Christ. Instead, he began an eloquent address with the Greek view of God as creator, who was everywhere present within the universe. He supported his argument with a reference to a nearby altar "to an unknown god" (Acts 17:22–27a) and quoted from Greek poets—Aratus ("we are indeed his offspring" [17:28b]) and presumably Epimenedes ("in him we live and move and have our being" [17:28a]). But as soon as Paul came to the doctrine of the resurrection of Christ, his philosophical audience was immediately and strongly divided. Some mocked him (Acts 17:32); others referred to him as a "seed-picker" (*spermologos* [Acts 17:18])—an uncomplimentary term for someone who hung around the Areopagus and picked up scraps of information here and there;[574] still others believed. Among this latter group were Dionysius, a member of the Areopagus, and a woman named Damaris (Acts 17:34).[575] In the end, Paul left Athens having made a few converts, but apparently without having founded a church there. From Athens, he headed west to Corinth.

Corinth was a sprawling seaport city situated on a three-and-a-half-mile isthmus of land separating the Aegean and Adriatic seas, with a harbor on both.[576] By crossing this isthmus to get from one sea to the other, travelers and merchants could avoid making the time-consuming and extremely treacherous voyage around the entire Peloponnesus. Nero unsuccessfully attempted to construct a canal across, but in Paul's day a stone track across the isthmus permitted land transport of vessels directly from one sea to the other. Corinth possessed a rich supply of fresh water, and the city played host to the Isthmian Games,[577] a pan-Hellenic festival held every two years in honor of Poseidon/Neptune, god of the sea. These Games attracted many delegates, athletes, visitors, and merchants, generating much new revenue for local residents. Paul may have personally benefited from the Games, as great numbers of tents would have been needed to shelter visitors (1 Cor. 9:24–27).

As a strategically located cosmopolitan center with much international commerce and trade, Corinth enjoyed lavish prosperity, which appealed to many unsavory people. Such an atmosphere meant the city had become a notoriously immoral place. The Greek word *korinthiazō* meant "to practice fornication" (1 Cor. 5:1–11; 6:15–20; 7:1–2), and more than 1,000 female sacred prostitutes were attached to the temple of Aphrodite in Corinth.[578] The city also had other great temples as well as many other accoutrements of a major Roman city.

New Testament scholars believe they are able to date Paul's 18-month stay in Corinth fairly precisely (Acts 18:11). When he arrived, Paul found Priscilla and Aquila, Jews who had just arrived from Rome (Acts 18:2b), having been banished from that city as part of Claudius's purge in the ninth year of his reign (A.D. 49).[579] Toward the end of Paul's stay in Corinth, he was brought before Gallio, the proconsul of Achaia (Acts 18:12), who happened to be a stepbrother of the Roman poet and playwright Seneca. An inscription from Claudius, discovered at Delphi, mentions a Junius Gallio as proconsul of Achaia. It is dated to the year A.D. 52 and enables one to determine that Gallio was proconsul of Achaia between the dates of July 1, 51 and July 1, 52.[580] So it appears Paul arrived at Corinth in the winter (perhaps January) of A.D. 50, shortly after the arrival of Priscilla and Aquila in late A.D. 49, and he departed in the late summer of A.D. 51.[581]

On the road near the Roman theater in Corinth is carved a limestone inscription of a man named Erastus describing how a section of the road near the theater was laid at his expense in return for his "aedileship." An *aedile* was a prominent elected colony official responsible for the upkeep and welfare of city property, including streets, public buildings, the agora, and the like.[582] Based on results of its excavation, this pavement is believed to have been laid around A.D. 50,[583] the time when Paul was in Corinth. And although the personal name Erastus was relatively rare in first-century writings, Paul made reference to a Christian fellow worker from Corinth named Erastus (Rom. 16:23, written from Corinth), whom he described as the city "treasurer." This word approximates the work of a Corinthian aedile, and it is fairly commonly believed that Paul's Christian associate and the individual mentioned in the pavement inscription may have been one and the same person.[584]

As fellow tentmakers or leather workers, it was quite natural that Paul should become the associate, friend, and even houseguest of Priscilla and Aquila (Acts 18:3; cf. 1 Cor. 4:12). Some time during that period, the couple embraced the Good News and later traveled with Paul as far as Ephesus. Still later, Priscilla and Aquila were said even to have risked death for the sake of Paul and the gospel (Rom. 16:3–4). Many others

The Seven Churches of Asia

map 114

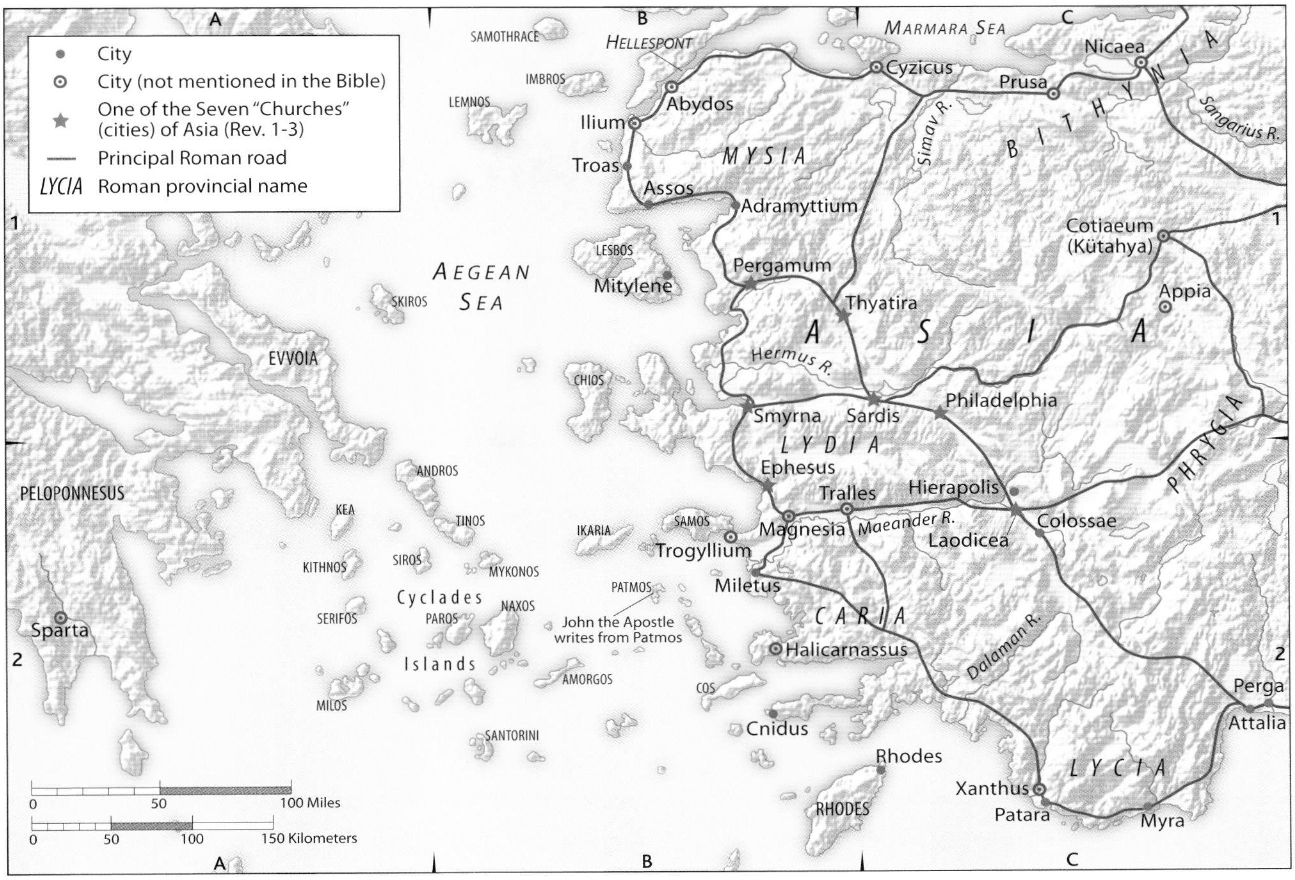

The seven cities, without exception, were situated on principal Roman routes used by, among others, postal carriers.[628] A carrier from Patmos could have landed at the port of Ephesus (Rev. 2:1–7) and traveled north through Smyrna (Rev. 2:8–11) to Pergamum (Rev. 2:12–17). From there he could have circled southeastward and proceeded directly along the Roman artery past Thyatira (Rev. 2:18–29), Sardis (Rev. 3:1–6), Philadelphia (Rev. 3:7–13), and on to Laodicea (Rev. 3:14–22).[629]

Were that the case, it follows that John's exhortations were not in the form of seven discreet letters addressed to and read by seven individual churches. Most likely they formed a common circulating letter (cf. Galatians), the whole of which was to be read in sequence by each successive church addressed when the letter arrived.

The Library of Celsus, Ephesus.

THE FIRST JEWISH REVOLT

Throughout much of the first Christian century a combination of Hellenistic secularism, Roman politics, and Jewish ideology created a strange alchemy in Palestinian culture and society. The Roman procurators were sometimes cruel and defiant, sometimes corrupt or contemptuous of Jewish religious practices, and always eager to impose an excessive tax burden. Jewish sectarianism, in response, had long been a breeding ground for voices of insurrection and resistance movements. Even among those who had attempted to avoid confrontation with Rome, increasingly bold and bitterly resentful sounds could be heard concerning Rome's tyrannical imperialism.[630] Then there was the Jewish nationalist sect known as the Zealots that was fervently and absolutely committed to the creation of an independent Jewish state at any cost. (Josephus referred to this as a "fourth philosophy," in contrast to the three longstanding philosophical groups of Pharisees, Sadducees, and Essenes.)[631] Suspicions fanned mutual animosities, and covert intrigue often gave way to open hostility. An atmosphere had been created in Judea in which revolution was imminent.

The lofty and isolated mesa of Masada is crowned with architecture from the time of Herod the Great. A 300-foot elevated siege ramp built by the Romans is visible on its west side (right side of the picture), in order to employ siege machines and battering rams to capture the city, thus ending the First Jewish Revolt.

A series of altercations occurred in rapid succession during the spring and early summer of A.D. 66 that ignited the explosion of revolt. Jewish anger was violently inflamed at Caesarea when an unscrupulous individual offered a "pagan" sacrifice at the entrance of a Jewish synagogue, desecrating the house of worship. When Jewish authorities attempted to halt the offense, a cry of violence arose from the general population of Caesarea, and the Jews were obliged to steal away rather quickly with their Torah scroll to a nearby town.[632]

Swift Jewish retaliation for the Caesarean affront came in the form of a theological edict: all sacrifices by foreigners, including those brought for the Caesar himself, would henceforth be refused in Jerusalem. Only Jewish countrymen would be permitted to enter the sacred precincts of the Temple. Soon thereafter, the Roman procurator Gessius Florus (A.D. 64–66) appeared in Jerusalem and, probably as an act of reprisal, demanded an exorbitant payment from the Temple treasury. When the Jews endeavored to rebuke the procurator for his outrageous demand, Florus ordered his troops to murder and plunder at will. Jewish citizens were subjected to rape, public whipping, looting, and crucifixion. Altogether there were about 3,600 Jewish casualties, including some children.[633]

Jerusalem immediately erupted into revolt. Jewish insurgents swarmed through the streets, first overpowering the Roman soldiers and driving them from the Upper City, and then setting fire to the Herodian palace of Agrippa II and the house of the high priest (who was perceived as having been solicitous of Rome). [**See map 94.**] They torched the official archives, destroying all records of debts and debtors, and they assaulted and burned the Roman Antonia fortress. Meanwhile, other rebels occupied the fortresses of Masada, Machaerus, and Cyprus, eventually returning to Jerusalem with a cache of armaments for their allies there.[634]

After word of the outbreak reached the governor Cestius Gallus, he immediately set out from Antioch in Syria toward Jerusalem with his 12th Imperial Legion and some additional troops, a total force said to number more than 30,000 men. He passed Ptolemais and Caesarea, and he set Lydda ablaze. But while attempting to ascend through the pass at Beth-horon,[635] Gallus's veteran forces were ambushed by the guerilla tactics at which the freedom fighters had become quite adept. Although the legionnaires finally arrived at

The First Jewish Revolt *map 115*

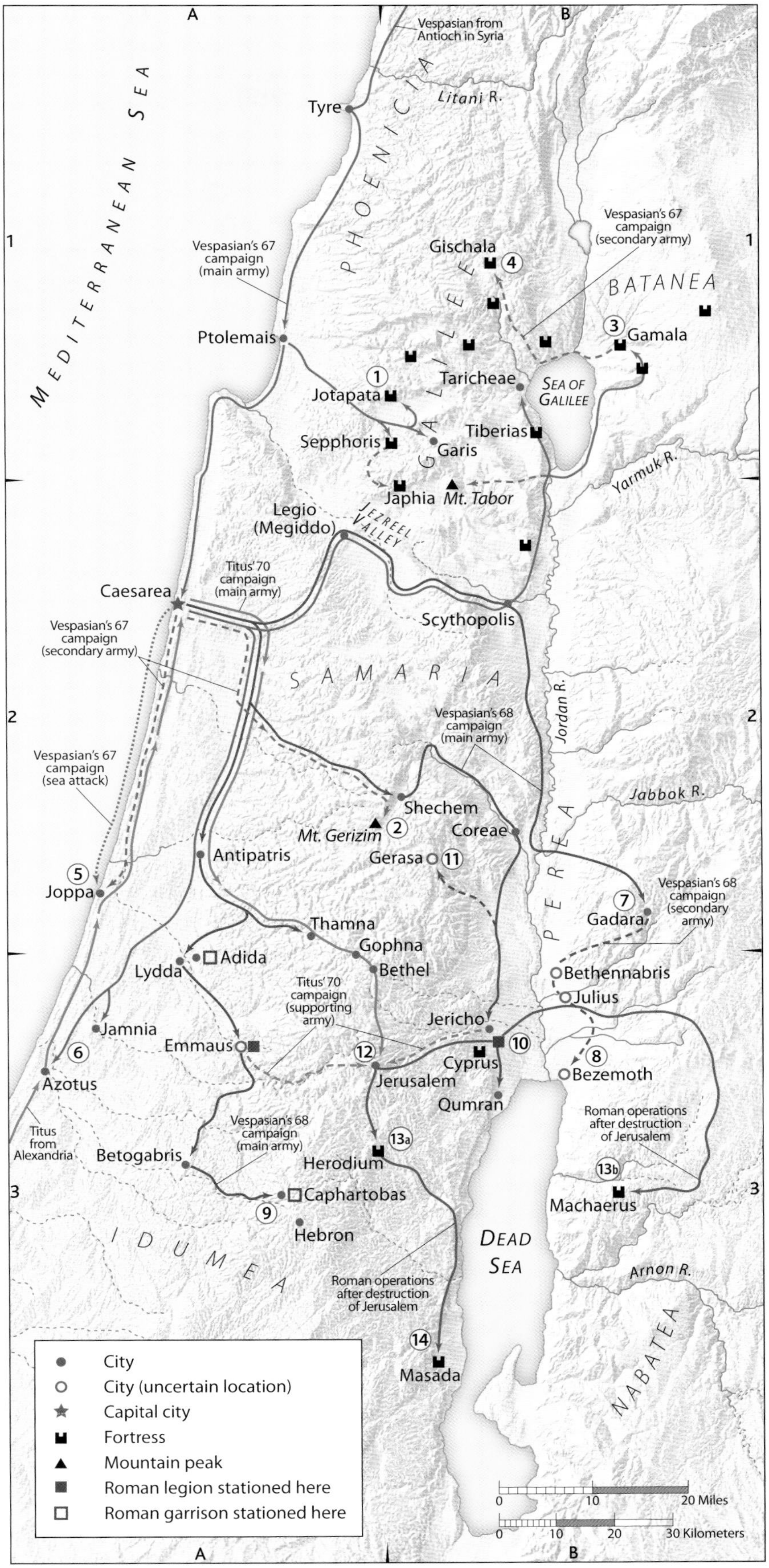

Jerusalem and even managed to breach the "third wall," they were unsuccessful in penetrating the inner city. In due course they were forced to disengage. Rome lost an imperial eagle, some siege equipment, and the better part of a rear guard as the Jews gained temporary national autonomy and prepared for a full-scale Roman counteroffensive. Command of the Galilean district—one of seven Jewish military divisions—was given to a priest named Joseph, known today as the historian Josephus Flavius.[636]

Rome did not disappoint. The emperor Nero ordered Vespasian to the battlefield. Vespasian was a general who had earlier distinguished himself in Germania and had masterfully added Britannia to the empire.[637] He mobilized three legions (the 5th, 10th, and 15th—an estimated force of between 55,500 and 57,500 men)[638] to suppress the Jewish menace once and for all. Upon his arrival at Ptolemais from Antioch in Syria in the spring of A.D. 67, Vespasian mapped out a skillful and deliberate strategy to gain an ever-tightening grip on the center of the revolt—Jerusalem. He began his systematic dismembering of the Jewish rebellion by attacking Galilee, one of Jerusalem's strongest philosophical allies. His forces swept into the fortress of Sepphoris without resistance. Josephus's troops had retreated to Jotapata, where they were forced to surrender some 47 days later [**1**]. Vespasian dispatched a secondary force to quell an uprising atop Mt. Gerizim [**2**] as he led his main army from Caesarea across the Jezreel valley[639] to Taricheae, the Galilean center of the revolt. A decisive battle ensued at the nearby cliffs of Arbel and then at the town itself, followed by a one-sided, extremely gruesome, bloody naval battle on the Sea of Galilee.[640]

The Romans quickly moved across the Jordan and subdued the imposing fortress at Gamala [**3**]. Vespasian dispatched his son Titus with the command to vanquish the revolutionaries at Gischala [**4**], succeeding both in silencing the rebellion in Galilee and in severing its lifeline to Babylonia. Before the onset of winter, Joppa fell before a land and sea attack [**5**], the cities of Jamnia and Azotus were brought under Roman control [**6**], and the transportation/communication corridor to Egypt was secured.[641]

After wintering his legionnaires at Caesarea and Scythopolis, Vespasian's A.D. 68 campaign was no less skillfully contrived. Tightening his grip on Jerusalem, Vespasian moved with alacrity to subjugate Perea and Idumea. When his forces had seized Gadara [**7**], he returned to Caesarea with his main army while a secondary force swept southward as far as Bezemoth [**8**], effectively neutralizing all major Transjordanian resistance apart from Machaerus. Vespasian at that point embarked on a southward mission from Caesarea into Idumea. He subdued Antipatris, Thamna, Lydda, and Emmaus, where he positioned the 5th Legion of soldiers. Continuing their southward advance, his troops captured Betogabris and Caphartobas, where a garrison of soldiers was deployed to further harass the Idumeans and to gain nominal control of Jerusalem's southern egress [**9**]. But his main army backtracked from Caphartobas toward Samaria, stationing an additional garrison at Adida along the way.[642] Vespasian himself marched eastward beyond Shechem, proceeded past Coreae, and captured New Testament Jericho, where he stationed the 10th Legion [**10**]. At the same time, a contingent of troops was sent north from Jericho to seize the town of Gerasa [**11**].[643] Roman legions now had complete control of the only highway from Jerusalem into the Transjordanian interior and beyond, the two major highways from the holy city to the Mediterranean Sea, and the city's southern outlet toward Hebron, Beersheba, and Egypt.

Vespasian returned to Caesarea in June, A.D. 68. He was preparing for an all-out offensive against Jerusalem itself, when he learned of the suicide of Nero.[644] During the next year, the imperium saw a rapid succession of occupants: Galba, Otho, and Vitellius. But a Flavian dynasty had arisen by late A.D. 69 and Vespasian himself ascended to the imperial throne in Rome. So it was his son Titus who was destined to subdue the remaining strongholds of Jewish resistance. In the spring of A.D. 70, Titus marched from Alexandria to Caesarea, approached Jerusalem from the north, and laid siege to the holy city directly [**12**]. Overpowered by the force of four determined Roman legions, Jerusalem fell to the forces of Titus in late August of that year. [**See map 96.**]

Following the capture of Jerusalem, three fortresses were all that remained of the revolt. Herodium [**13a**] and Machaerus [**13b**] fell with little difficulty, and only Masada remained. In A.D. 73, a new and ambitious provincial governor—Flavius Silva—turned his undivided attention toward the one remaining stronghold. After completely surrounding the site with a massive siege wall made of stones, Silva constructed an elevated ramp more than 300 feet high against the rock face of the fortress on the west side. Siege machines and battering rams from the top of the ramp would eventually do their damage and Masada would fall,[645] finally fulfilling (posthumously) Nero's dream of destroying the Jewish menace [**14**].

THE SPREAD OF CHRISTIANITY IN THE ROMAN WORLD

"One of the most amazing and significant facts of history is that within five centuries of its birth Christianity won the professed allegiance of the overwhelming majority of the population of the Roman Empire and even the support of the Roman state. Beginning as a seemingly obscure sect of Judaism, one of scores, even hundreds of religions and religious groups which were competing within that realm, revering as its central figure one who had been put to death by the machinery of Rome, and in spite of having been long proscribed by that government and eventually having the full weight of the state thrown against it, Christianity proved so far the victor that the Empire sought alliance with it and to be a Roman citizen became almost identical with being a Christian."[646]

Jesus' admonition to go into all the world and preach the Good News (Matt. 28:19) had been taken seriously indeed. Far from least among the factors that played a vital role in the spread of Christianity was a zealous apostolic response to the Great Commission. Environmental factors emanating from the Roman Empire also contributed to the rapid growth of the gospel. Lands within the empire were bequeathed an era of peace. Commerce flourished and travel became more accessible, and a great deal safer, than ever before. Highways built for commerce or Roman legions also served the messengers of the cross. Important too was the Greek language, used widely across the empire by Jews and Gentiles alike. This meant that Christianity could articulate its thought and doctrines in readily understandable forms.

But ironically, persecution also became a significant factor in the outward spread of Christianity—a testimony to the effectiveness of early missionary activities and apologetic writings. The most infamous of the early persecutions took place in and around Rome in A.D. 64 under Nero. According to Tacitus,[647] after Nero was accused of giving the order to set fire to Rome, which laid waste two-thirds of the city, the emperor sought to shift blame to Christians, who had spoken

Massive fortification walls from the Byzantine period surround the town of Nicaea (modern Iznik), east of Constantinople/Istanbul in northern Turkey, where the early church held its first ecumenical Council in the year A.D. 325.

The Spread of Christianity in the Roman World

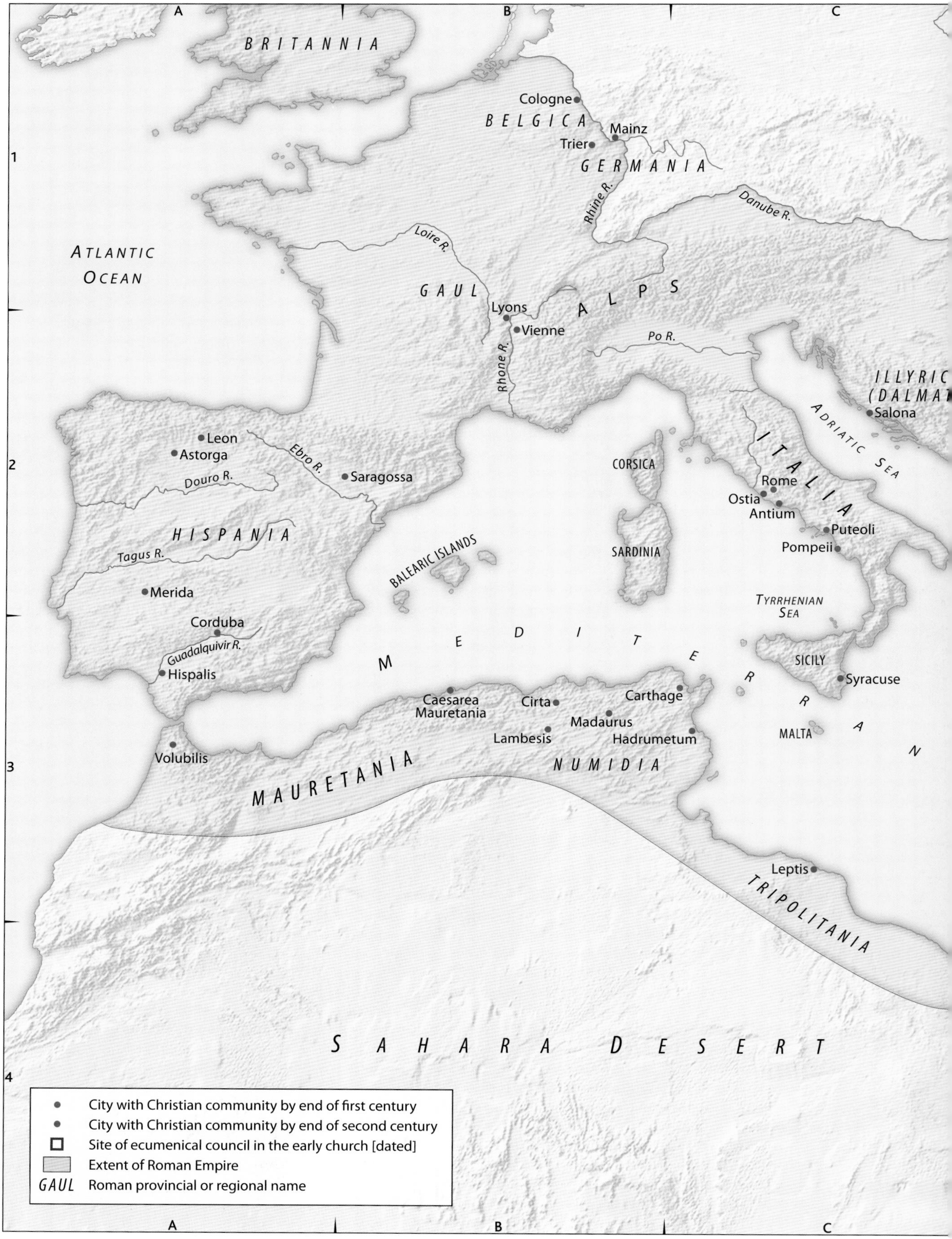

BRITANNIA
BELGICA
Cologne
Mainz
Trier
GERMANIA
Rhine R.
Danube R.
Loire R.
ATLANTIC OCEAN
GAUL
Lyons
Vienne
ALPS
Po R.
Rhone R.
ILLYRIC (DALMAT
Salona
ADRIATIC SEA
ITALIA
Leon
Astorga
Ebro R.
Douro R.
Saragossa
CORSICA
Rome
Ostia
Antium
Puteoli
Pompeii
HISPANIA
Tagus R.
SARDINIA
BALEARIC ISLANDS
Merida
TYRRHENIAN SEA
Corduba
Guadalquivir R.
Hispalis
MEDITERRAN
SICILY
Syracuse
Caesarea Mauretania
Cirta
Carthage
Madaurus
Lambesis
Hadrumetum
MALTA
Volubilis
NUMIDIA
MAURETANIA
Leptis
TRIPOLITANIA
SAHARA DESERT
City with Christian community by end of first century
City with Christian community by end of second century
Site of ecumenical council in the early church [dated]
Extent of Roman Empire
GAUL Roman provincial or regional name

SARMATIA
Dniester R.
Dnieper R.
Volga R.
DACIA
BOSPORUS
Danube R.
MOESIA
Anchialos
BLACK SEA
CAUCASUS MTS.
CASPIAN SEA
Debeltum
THRACE
Chalcedon
[451]
Amastris
Ionopolis
Sinope
Amisus
Constantinople
(Byzantium) [381]
BITHYNIA AND PONTUS
Philippi
Nicomedia
Apollonia
Parion
Nicaea [325]
Ancyra
Halys R.
Cyrus R.
AEGEAN SEA
Troas
MYSIA
PHRYGIA
CAPPADOCIA
ARMENIA
Araxes R.
Pergamum
Thyatira
Antioch in
Pisidia
GALATIA
Sardis
Hierapolis
Lake Tuz
Malatya
Lake Van
Athens
Ephesus
[431]
Laodicea
Iconium
Caesarea
Mazaca
Samsat
Beit Zabde
Corinth
Tralles
Colossae
Lystra
Lake Urmia
Sparta
Miletus
Derbe
CILICIA
Edessa
Nisibis
Attalia
Perga
Tarsus
Alexandreia
RHODES
Myra
Antioch
MESOPOTAMIA
Laodicea
Apamea
PARTHIA
CRETE
Cnossus
Gortyna
CYPRUS
Salamis
SYRIA
Tripolis
Paphos
Dura-
Europos
Tigris R.
Sidon
Damascus
Euphrates R.
SEA
See map 117,
page 275
Tyre
Apollonia
Jerusalem
Alexandria
Gaza
Naucratis
NABATEA
Memphis
Babylon
PERSIAN GULF
EGYPT
Antinoe
Nile R.
RED SEA
ARABIAN
DESERT
0 100 200 300 400 500 Miles
0 100 200 300 400 500 600 700 800 Kilometers

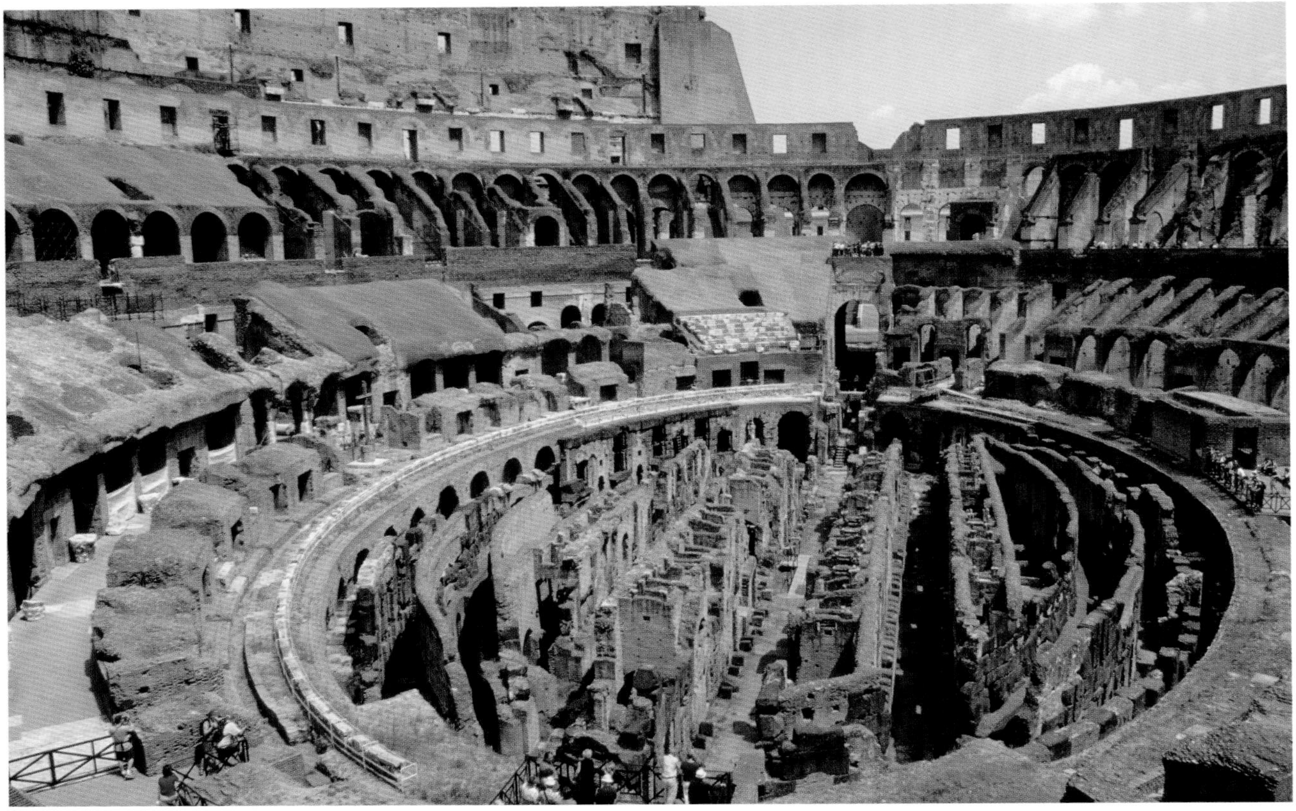

Remains of the Roman amphitheater at Rome known as the Colosseum, which was inaugurated by the emperor Vespasian and formally dedicated by his son Titus, the man who destroyed Jerusalem.

of a fiery end of the world. To deflect suspicion away from his own pyromaniacal deed, Nero afflicted Christians with relentless passion and ingenious brutality. Some believers were wrapped in the hides of wild beasts, to be torn to pieces by hungry dogs. Others, fastened to crosses, were set on fire to light Nero's gardens by night.[648] Such abuse and the subsequent round of persecutions under Domitian (A.D. 95), combined with greatly intensified hostility in Jerusalem from Jewish authorities, triggered a widespread movement of Christians to safer environs.

By the conclusion of the first century, Christianity stretched from Rome essentially as far east as the upper Mesopotamian valley, incorporating much of the Levant [**map 117**] and parts of Asia Minor, North Africa, and the Greek peninsula.[649] And by the end of the second century, the new movement had spread almost as far as the bounds of the empire itself, from Mesopotamia and Armenia (and perhaps even India) as far west as Belgica and Hispania, and possibly even into Britannia.[650]

Emerging dominant Christian centers included the cities of Antioch in Syria (where Paul's missionary enterprises originated, and where Ignatius exerted his considerable influence upon several early Christian doctrines) and Pella (where many Christians fled for safety in the wake of the first Jewish revolt, A.D. 66–73). [**See map 117.**] Mesopotamia had two major centers: one at Edessa (where at a very early date Christianity was made the official religion)[651] and the other at Dura-Europos (where the earliest known Christian house-church has been discovered by archaeologists).[652] North Africa also produced two important centers of Christian theology and scholarship—Alexandria and Carthage. Alexandria was the home of Origen, who wrote the first systematic treatise of Christian theology and who gave the church the Hexapla—six parallel translations of the Bible. It was also the base of Athanasius, an early bishop who ably defended the Trinitarian doctrine and the doctrine of the person of Christ. Carthage was where the influential Christian apologist Tertullian preached and engaged in his enormous writing output, and where Cyprian served as an early bishop to sow many doctrinal and ecclesiastical seeds that grew into fruition during the time of Augustine.

Not surprisingly, the preeminent Christian center in Europe was Rome itself. By the time of Eusebius (late third to early fourth century), the church of Rome was said to have had one bishop, 46 presbyters, seven deacons, 42 acolytes, 50 readers, exorcists, and doorkeepers, plus some 1,500 widows and poor persons under its care.[653] Ascendancy was also conferred upon Lyons during the days of Irenaeus's celebrated bishopric there.

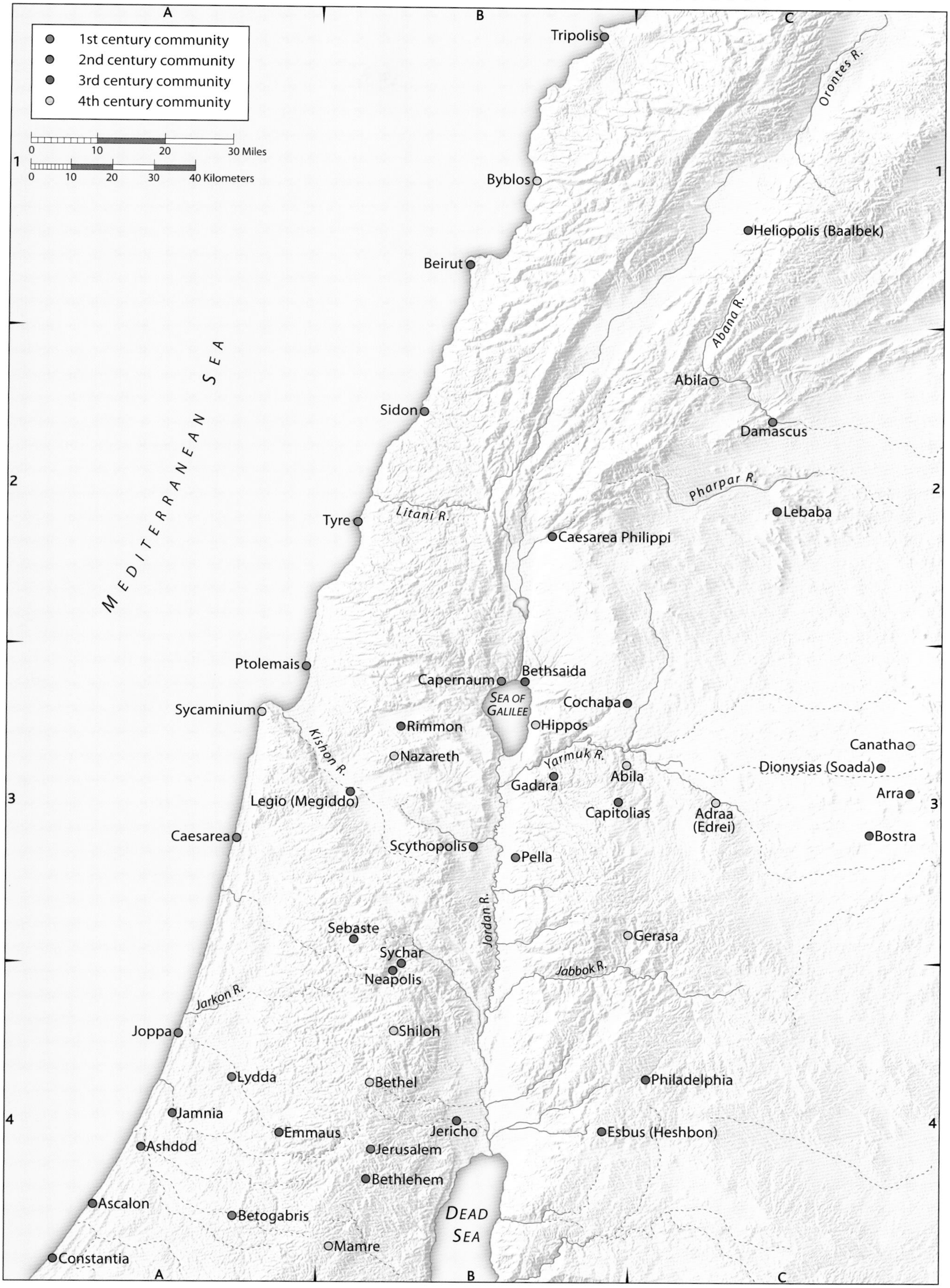

A
B
C
1st century community
2nd century community
3rd century community
4th century community
0 10 20 30 Miles
0 10 20 30 40 Kilometers
1
2
3
4
Tripolis
Orontes R.
Byblos
Heliopolis (Baalbek)
Beirut
Abana R.
Abila
Sidon
Damascus
MEDITERRANEAN SEA
Pharpar R.
Lebaba
Tyre
Litani R.
Caesarea Philippi
Ptolemais
Capernaum
Bethsaida
Sea of Galilee
Cochaba
Sycaminium
Rimmon
Hippos
Kishon R.
Nazareth
Canatha
Yarmuk R.
Abila
Dionysias (Soada)
Gadara
Legio (Megiddo)
Arra
Capitolias
Adraa (Edrei)
Caesarea
Bostra
Scythopolis
Pella
Jordan R.
Sebaste
Gerasa
Sychar
Neapolis
Jabbok R.
Jarkon R.
Joppa
Shiloh
Lydda
Bethel
Philadelphia
Jamnia
Jericho
Emmaus
Esbus (Heshbon)
Ashdod
Jerusalem
Bethlehem
Ascalon
Dead Sea
Betogabris
Mamre
Constantia

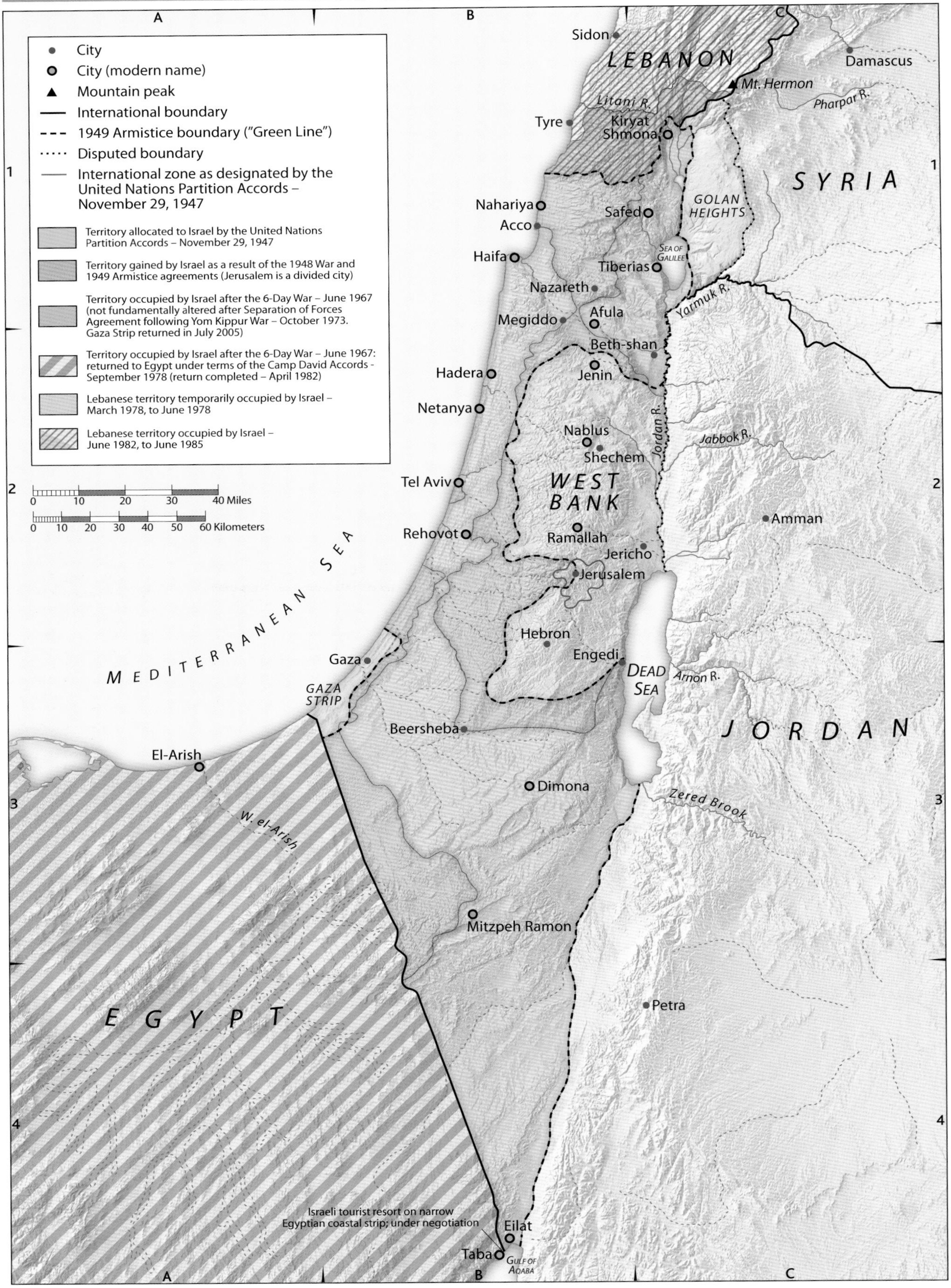
City
City (modern name)
Mountain peak
International boundary
1949 Armistice boundary ("Green Line")
Disputed boundary
International zone as designated by the United Nations Partition Accords – November 29, 1947
Territory allocated to Israel by the United Nations Partition Accords – November 29, 1947
Territory gained by Israel as a result of the 1948 War and 1949 Armistice agreements (Jerusalem is a divided city)
Territory occupied by Israel after the 6-Day War – June 1967 (not fundamentally altered after Separation of Forces Agreement following Yom Kippur War – October 1973. Gaza Strip returned in July 2005)
Territory occupied by Israel after the 6-Day War – June 1967: returned to Egypt under terms of the Camp David Accords - September 1978 (return completed – April 1982)
Lebanese territory temporarily occupied by Israel – March 1978, to June 1978
Lebanese territory occupied by Israel – June 1982, to June 1985
0 10 20 30 40 Miles
0 10 20 30 40 50 60 Kilometers
Sidon
LEBANON
Damascus
Mt. Hermon
Pharpar R.
Litani R.
Tyre
Kiryat Shmona
SYRIA
Nahariya
Safed
GOLAN HEIGHTS
Acco
Haifa
SEA OF GALILEE
Tiberias
Nazareth
Yarmuk R.
Afula
Megiddo
Beth-shan
Hadera
Jenin
Netanya
Jordan R.
Nablus
Jabbok R.
Shechem
Tel Aviv
WEST BANK
Amman
Rehovot
Ramallah
MEDITERRANEAN SEA
Jericho
Jerusalem
Hebron
Gaza
Engedi
DEAD SEA
Arnon R.
GAZA STRIP
Beersheba
JORDAN
El-Arish
Dimona
Zered Brook
W. el-Arish
Mitzpeh Ramon
Petra
EGYPT
Israeli tourist resort on narrow Egyptian coastal strip; under negotiation
Eilat
Taba
GULF OF AQABA

CHAPTER 1 NOTES

1 The expression "Middle East" seems to have originated in and around the British India Office during the 1880s (so C. R. Koppes, "Captain Mahan, General Gordon, and the Origins of the Term 'Middle East,'" *Middle Eastern Studies* 12/1, [1976], 95–98), at a time when the expansionist tendency of Great Britain and Russia was creating a struggle for influence in central Asia between Arabia and India, focusing on the Persian Gulf. It is likely that the expression originally designated Persia and adjacent territories, differentiated from the "Near East" (i.e., the eastern Mediterranean world) and the "Far East" (i.e., the western Pacific world); *contra* G. S. P. Freeman-Grenville, *Historical Atlas of the Middle East*, (New York: Simon & Schuster, 1993), preface. Despite what Kipling had penned concerning East and West never meeting, the twain *did* meet, and in modern times the two met initially in the Middle East. In any event, "Middle East" has become a common expression in political, socioeconomic, and military parlance since the 1900s, particularly in the English-speaking world. It is also employed today in conjunction with certain academic studies and in the names of book titles, documentaries and professional journals. (See also T. Scheffler, "'Fertile Crescent,' 'Orient,' 'Middle East': The Changing Mental Maps of Southwest Asia," *European Review of History* 10/2, [2003], 253–272.)

2 J. Michelet, *Histoire de France*, (Paris: A. Lacroix, 1833), 1.2, author's translation.

3 On December 26, 2004, virtually the whole world witnessed the catastrophic results of seismic activity, when an earthquake near the Aceh province of northwestern Indonesia displaced a segment of the ocean floor, creating a tsunami that killed an estimated 240,000 people. The greatest loss of human life as the result of an earthquake occurred in the Shaanxi province of central China on January 23, 1556, when perhaps as many as 830,000 died.

4 The bibliography here is extensive; see A. Kaloyeropoulou, ed., *Acta of the 1st International Scientific Congress on the Volcano of Thera*, (Athens: Archaeological Services of Greece, 1971) for many details; refer also to S.W. Manning, "The Bronze Age Eruption of Thera: Absolute Dating, Aegean Chronology and Mediterranean Cultural Interrelations," *Journal of Mediterranean Archaeology* 1/1, (1988), 17–82; P. M. Warren, "The Date of the Thera Eruption in Relation to Aegean-Egyptian Interconnections and the Egyptian Historical Chronology," in E. Czerny, I. Hein, H. Hunger, D. Melman, and A. Schwab, eds., *Timelines: Studies in Honour of Manfred Bietak*, (Leuven: Peeters, 2006), 305–321.

5 K. O. Emery and D. Neev, "Mediterranean Beaches of Israel," *Bulletin of the Geological Survey of Israel* 26, (1960), 9–10; D. J. Stanley and H. Sheng, "Volcanic shards from Santorini (Upper Minoan ash) in the Nile Delta, Egypt," *Nature* 320/6064, (1986), 733–735.

6 e.g., N. C. Flemming, *Archaeological Evidence for Eustatic Change of Sea Level and Earth Movements in the Western Mediterranean during the Last 2000 Years*, (Boulder, Colo.: Geological Society of America, 1969); R. Chapman, "Climatic Changes and Evolution of Landforms in the Eastern Province of Saudi Arabia," *Geological Society of America Bulletin* 82, (1971), 2713–2728; Van Zeist 1985; Shehadeh 1985; H. J. Bruins, "Comparative chronology of climate and human history in the Southern Levant from the Late Chalcolithic to the Early Arab Period," in O. Bar-Yosef and R. Kra, eds., *Late Quaternary Chronology and Paleoclimates of the Eastern Mediterranean*, (Tucson: Radiocarbon, 1994), 301–314; A. M. Rosen and S. A. Rosen, "Determinist or Not Determinist?: Climate, Environment, and Archaeological Explanation in the Levant," in S. R. Wolff, ed., *Studies in the Archaeology of Israel and Neighboring Lands*, (Chicago: University of Chicago Press, 2001), 535–549; M. Staubwasser and H. Weiss, "Holocene climate and cultural evolution in late prehistoric—early historic West Asia," *Quaternary Research* 66/3, (2006), 372–387; E. Linden, *The Winds of Change: Climate, Weather, and the Destruction of Civilizations*, (New York: Simon and Schuster, 2006), 9–178.

7 Captain John Smith is alleged to have stated in 1624: "Geography without History seemeth a carkasse without motion; so History without Geography wandreth as a Vagrant without a certaine habitation." (See G. M. Grosvenor, "New Atlas Unfurls Nation's History," *National Geographic* 174/3, [1988], 430.)

8 The actual statement is, "Civilization exists by geological consent, subject to change without notice." It is ascribed to Durant's *The Story of Philosophy* (e.g., *Cole's Quotables* #4607; *Rand Lindsly's Quotations* #21280; FamousQuotes.com; QuoteAddiction.com), though its presence in these sources cannot be cited by page number and is disputable. For an example of the undocumented usage of the quotation in scientific literature, see W. I. Rose, J. J. Bommer, and C. A. Sandoval, "Natural hazards and risk mitigation in El Salvador: An Introduction," *Geological Society of America, Special Paper* 3, (2004), 2.

9 Portions of this section draw upon the foreword in B. J. Beitzel, chief consultant, *Biblica, The Bible Atlas: A Social and Historical Journey Through the Lands of the Bible*, (London: Penguin Books Ltd., 2006).

10 So W. Bruggemann, *The Land*, (Philadelphia: Fortress Press, 1977); see also W. D. Davies, *The Gospel and the Land: Early Christianity and Jewish Territorial Doctrine*, (Berkeley: University of California Press, 1974), 15–48.

11 The expression "the holy land" (*admat haqqōdeš*) explicitly designating a territory inside ancient Canaan is found in biblical writings as early as Zechariah 2:12 (cf. Ps. 78:54 [*gᵉbûl qōdšô*], "[the border of] his holy land"). The same expression is found in apocryphal and pseudepigraphical writings (e.g., Wisd. of Sol. 12:3; 2 Macc. 1:7; 2 Bar. 63:10; 84:8; cf. W. D. Davies, *The Gospel and the Land: Early Christianity and Jewish Territorial Doctrine*, [Berkeley: University of California Press, 1974], 49–74). This terrain is otherwise identified as the "holy border" (4 Ezra 13:48), the "glorious land" (Dan. 11:16, 41), or, most commonly, "the land" (*hā'āreṣ*, e.g., Gen. 12:1, 6–7; Deut. 17:14; Josh. 19:49; Isa. 6:3b). Other writers as early as the first century a. d. (e.g., Pseudo-Philo, *Liber Antiquitatum Biblicarum*, 19:10) identified the land of Israel as "the holy land" (*terra sancta*), though Virgil (*Aeneid*, 3.73) had earlier employed similar phraseology to denote the island of Delos, which in Greek mythology was the birthplace of both Apollo and Diana. The expression "the promised land" does not occur in the Old Testament or other early writings; rather, this appears to be a Christian designation of the land given to Abraham and his seed (Heb. 11:9, *gēn tēs 'epaggelias*; and see Wilken 1988:233 for the later use of "holy land" to designate the area around Jerusalem as a *Christian* territory). Finally, as early as the time of Christ, the expression "the holy land" was employed metaphorically to refer to heaven (e.g., TestJob 33:5).

12 Josephus, *Antiquities of the Jews*, 17.299–303.

13 Josephus, *Antiquities of the Jews*, 17.339–340.

14 Portions of this section draw upon B. J. Beitzel, "Geography of the Levant," in S. Richard, ed., *Near Eastern Archaeology: A Reader*, (Winona Lake, Ind.: Eisenbrauns, 2003), 3–9 and the bibliography cited there.

15 J. H. Breasted, *Ancient Times: A History of the Early World*, (Boston: Ginn and Company, 1916), 100–101.

16 See Polybius (e.g., 5.48.16), Strabo (e.g., 2.1.26; 16.1.21–27), and Josephus (e.g., *War*, 4.531; *Antiquities of the Jews*, 1.244, 278, 285).

17 J. M. Wagstaff, *The Evolution of Middle Eastern Landscapes: An Outline to A.D. 1840*, (Totowa, N. J.: Barnes & Noble Books, 1985), 96–97; see also T. Jacobsen and R. M. Adams, "Salt and Silt in Ancient Mesopotamian Agriculture," *Science* 128/3334, (1958), 1251–1258.

18 T. B. Jones, *Ancient Civilization*, (Chicago: Rand McNally College Publishing Company, 1960), 46–49.

19 J. B. Pritchard, ed., *Ancient Near Eastern Texts Relating to the Old Testament*, (Princeton: Princeton University Press, 1969), 280; see also D. D. Luckenbill, *Ancient Records of Assyria and Babylonia*, (Chicago: University of Chicago Press, 1926–1927), 1.243 (§672); 1.294 (§821).

20 e.g., D. D. Luckenbill, *Ancient Records of Assyria and Babylonia*, (Chicago: University of Chicago Press, 1926–1927), 2.314 (§818).

21 e.g., Y. Aharoni and M. Avi-Yonah, *The Macmillan Bible Atlas*, (New York: Macmillan Publishing Company, 1993), 209 [with the fourth edition, this is now known as *The Carta Bible Atlas*]; J. Simons, *The Geographical and Topographical Texts of the Old Testament*, (Leiden: Brill, 1959), 102.

22 Lebo-hamath refers to a specific site and not to the more generic "entrance of Hamath" (cf. what would otherwise be a double preposition in 1 Kings 8:65; 2 Chron. 7:8; Amos 6:14, *millᵉbô' ḥᵉmāt*; see also *`ad lᵉbô' ḥᵉmāt* in 1 Chron. 13:5); note this as a translational change between the *RSV* and *NRSV*.

23 Egyptian (e.g., W. W. Hallo and K. L. Younger, Jr., eds., *The Context of Scripture*, [Leiden: Brill, 1997–2002], 2.21a; cf. Y. Aharoni, *The Land of the Bible: A Historical Geography*, [Philadelphia: Westminster Press, 1979], 72–73); Assyrian (A. M. Bagg, *Die Orts- und Gewässernamen der neuassyrischen Zeit*, Répertoire Géographique des Textes Cunéiformes 7/1, [Wiesbaden: Reichert, 2007], 151); classical (e.g., R. J. A. Talbert, ed., *Barrington Atlas of the Greek and Roman World*, [Princeton: Princeton University Press, 2000], 68 [B5]).

24 For the importance of this depression to Egypt, see A. F. Rainey and R. S. Notley, *The Sacred Bridge: Carta's Atlas of the Biblical World*, (Jerusalem: Carta, 2006), 80–82; as related to the aftermath of the Battle of Kadesh, see Rainey and Notley, 96–98; as related to the boundary of Amurru, see G. Kestemont, "La Nahr el-Kebir et le pays d'Amurru," *Berytus* 20, (1971), 47–55; Astour 1981:9–10; W. L. Moran, *The Amarna Letters*, (Baltimore: Johns Hopkins University Press, 1992), 388 (and note also Josh. 13:4b–5, where Israel's land yet to be possessed extended beyond Byblos, to Lebo-hamath, and as far as *the border of the Amorites*); as related to the boundary of Phoenicia, see Pliny, *Natural History*, 5.18.79; Strabo 16.2.12; 16.2.15.

25 cf. J. Simons, *The Geographical and Topographical Texts of the Old Testament*, (Leiden: Brill, 1959), 102; Y. Aharoni, *The Land of the Bible: A Historical Geography*, (Philadelphia: Westminster Press, 1979), 80 n. 40.

26 e.g., A. L. Oppenheim, *et al.*, eds., *The Assyrian Dictionary of the Oriental Institute of the University of Chicago*, (Chicago: The Oriental Institute, 1956), 4.8.

27 See this same kind of fluidity in Daniel 10:4, where the identical expression explicitly denotes the Tigris River.

28 Consider, for example, the following hymns: *Guide Me, O Thou Great Jehovah* ("When I tread the verge of Jordan, bid my anxious fears subside; bear me through the swelling current, land me safe on Canaan's side"); *On Jordan's Stormy Banks* ("On Jordan's stormy banks I stand, and cast a wishful eye to Canaan's fair and happy land, where my possessions lie"); *He Leadeth Me* ("And when my task on earth is done, when by Thy grace the victory's won; even death's cold wave I will not flee, since God through Jordan leadeth me"); and *I Won't Have to Cross Jordan Alone* ("When I come to the river at ending of day, when the last winds of sorrow have blown; there'll be somebody waiting to show me the way; I won't have to cross Jordan alone").

29 On this territorial gap, see Na`aman 1986b:39–73.

30 R. de Vaux, *The Early History of Israel*, (Philadelphia: Westminster Press, 1978), 555–556, and literature cited there.

31 The Genesis 15:18 text does utilize the expression *nᵉhar miṣ rayim*, but we have already observed that this verse seems to be describing idealized territorial terminal points rather than giving actual border delineations. Accordingly, and in the absence of text-critical support, I see little reason to propose with J. Simons (*The Geographical and Topographical Texts of the Old Testament*, [Leiden: Brill, 1959], 96) a textual emendation in Genesis (*nāhār* to *nahal*) that would bring it into geographical conformity with the Numbers, Joshua, and Ezekiel border texts.

32 A. L. Oppenheim, et al., eds., *The Assyrian Dictionary of the Oriental Institute of the University of Chicago*, (Chicago: The Oriental Institute, 1956), 11/1.125; cf. S. Parpola, *Neo-Assyrian Toponyms*, Alter Orient und Altes Testament 6, (Neukirchen-Vluyn: Butzon and Bercker Kevelaer, 1970), 256; see also J. B. Pritchard, ed., *Ancient Near Eastern Texts Relating to the Old Testament*, (Princeton: Princeton University Press, 1969), 286, 290, 292.

33 R. J. A. Talbert, ed., *Barrington Atlas of the Greek and Roman World*, (Princeton: Princeton University Press, 2000), map 70 (D3).

34 e.g., E. Orni and E. Efrat, *Geography of Israel*, (Jerusalem: Israel Universities Press, 1980), 125–126, 365.

35 N. Na`aman ("The Brook of Egypt and Assyrian Policy on the Border of Egypt," *Tel Aviv* 6, [1979], 68–90; "The Shihor of Egypt and Shur That Is before Egypt," *Tel Aviv* 7, [1980], 95–109) has proposed that the brook/wadi of Egypt should be identified, not with W. el-Arish, but with the Brook Besor, a stream that deposits its water into the Mediterranean about five miles south of Gaza, at T. el-`Ajjul. [**See map 4.**] According to him, the "brook/wadi of Egypt" only became associated with W. el-Arish in the intertestamental period. (See also H. Verreth, "The Egyptian Eastern Border Region in Assyrian Sources," *Journal of the American Oriental Society* 119/2, [1999], 235 n.15; cf. P. K. Hooker, "The Location of the Brook of Egypt," in M. P. Graham, W. P. Brown, and J. K. Kuan, eds., *History and Interpretation: Essays in Honour of John H. Hayes*, [Sheffield, England: JSOT Press, 1993], 203–214, who agrees that a name transfer did in fact occur, but that this took place in the late-Assyrian period). For a cogent rebuttal of Na`aman, see A.F. Rainey ("Toponymic Problems," *Tel Aviv* 9/2, [1982], 131–132; A. F. Rainey and R. S. Notley, *The Sacred Bridge: Carta's Atlas of the Biblical World*, [Jerusalem: Carta, 2006], 34–35, 283; cf. G. A. Buttrick, ed., *The Interpreter's Dictionary of the Bible*, [New York: Abingdon Press, 1962], 2.66–67; J. Simons, *The Geographical and Topographical Texts of the Old Testament*, [Leiden: Brill, 1959], 27).

36 e.g., M. H. Woudstra, *The Book of Joshua*, The New International Commentary on the Old Testament, (Grand Rapids: Eerdmans, 1981), 235; R. S. Hess, *Joshua: An Introduction and Commentary*, Tyndale Old Testament Commentaries, (Leicester, England: Inter-Varsity Press, 1996), 242, though see J. A. Soggin, *Joshua: A Commentary*, Old Testament Library, (Philadelphia: Westminster Press, 1972), 172.

37 I. Singer, "The Hittites and the Bible Revisited," in A. M. Maeir and P. de Miroschedji, eds., *"I Will Speak the Riddle of Ancient Times": Archaeological and Historical Studies in Honor of Amihai Mazar on the Occasion of His Sixtieth Birthday*, (Winona Lake, Ind.: Eisenbrauns, 2006), 725–727.

38 References to "Canaan" begin with an 18th-century B.C. text from Mari (B. Groneberg, *Die Orts- und Gewässernamen der altbabylonischen Zeit*, Répertoire Géographique des Textes Cunéiformes 3, [Wiesbaden: Reichert, 1980], 139; Archives royales de Mari: transcriptions et traductions 16/1.19). The term also appears as a territorial entity at Alalakh (D. J. Wiseman, *The Alalakh Tablets*, [London: British Institute of Archaeology in Ankara, 1953], 155), Ugarit (C. H. Gordon, *Ugaritic Textbook*, Analecta Orientalia 38, [Rome: Pontifical Biblical Institute, 1965], 421; G. del Olmo Lete and J. Sanmartín, eds., *A Dictionary of the Ugaritic Language in the Alphabetic Tradition*, Handbuch der Orientalistik 67, [Leiden: Brill, 2003], 1.449), Boghazkoy (G. F. del Monte and J. Tischler, *Die Orts- und Gewässernamen der hethitischen Texte*, Répertoire Géographique des Textes Cunéiformes 6/1, [Wiesbaden: Reichert, 1978], 208), Amarna (A. F. Rainey, "Who is a Canaanite? A Review of the Textual Evidence," *Bulletin of the American Schools of Oriental Research* 304, [1996], 6–10; K. Nashef, *Die Orts- und Gewässernamen der mittelbabylonischen und mittelassyrischen Zeit*, Répertoire Géographique des Textes Cunéiformes 5, [Wiesbaden: Reichert, 1982], 167; W. L. Moran, *The Amarna Letters*, [Baltimore: Johns Hopkins University Press, 1992], 389), and elsewhere in Egypt (M. Görg, "Der Name 'Kanaan' in ägyptischer Wiedergabe," *Biblische Notizen* 18, [1982], 26–27).

39 *Papyrus Anastasi* I; cf. J. B. Pritchard, ed., *Ancient Near Eastern Texts Relating to the Old Testament*, (Princeton: Princeton University Press, 1969), 557b; the town of Ammiya was situated in Canaan, but a number of sites not too far north were not; *Papyrus Anastasi* III and a number of campaign texts also connect Canaan with the fortress of Sile/T. Hebua, located near the lower reaches of the eastern Delta. [**See map 33.**]

40 M. C. Astour, "The Origin of the terms 'Canaan,' 'Phoenician,' and 'Purple,'" *Journal of Near Eastern Studies* 24, (1965), 346–350.

41 The phoeneme /`/ in Hebrew often appears in Akkadian as /H/ (A. F. Rainey, "The Toponymics of Eretz-Israel," *Bulletin of the American Schools of Oriental Research* 231, [1978], 9; cf. L. Koehler and W. Baumgartner, eds., *The Hebrew and Aramaic Lexicon of the Old Testament*, [Leiden: Brill, 2001], 1.485), and the final consonant of place names is often doubled in Akkadian (e.g., Amurru, Mitanni, Eshnunna, Si'annu, Ḫadatta, Kazallu, Kisurra, Ḫilakku, Izalla, etc.). See also A.L. Oppenheim, et al., eds., *The Assyrian Dictionary of the Oriental Institute of the University of Chicago*, (Chicago: The Oriental Institute, 1956), 8.379.

42 *Anchor Bible Dictionary*, 5.557–560; see also I. I. Ziderman "First Identification of Authentic *Tĕkēlet*," *Bulletin of the American Schools of Oriental Research* 265, (1987), 25–33; "Seashells and Ancient Purple Dyeing," *Biblical Archaeologist* 53/2, (1990), 98–101.

43 E. Stern, "The Persistence of Phoenician Culture," *Biblical Archaeology Review* 19/3, (1993), 47–49; cf. R. R. Stieglitz, "The Minoan Origin of Tyrian Purple," *Biblical Archaeologist* 57/1, (1994), 46–54.

44 See Job 41:6 (with the parallel word *ḥabbār* ["partner in trade"]); Isaiah 23:8 (with parallel word *saḥar* ["trading profit"]); Hosea 12:7 (where the word is related to "false balances of a scale"); Zephaniah 1:11 (where the word is related to "weighing silver"); cf. Proverbs 31:24; Zechariah 11:7, 11 (LXX); 14:21.

45 *Anchor Bible Dictionary*, 5.1059–1061, and literature cited there. For additional reading on the Sea Peoples, refer to M. C. Astour, "New Evidence on the Last Days of Ugarit," *American Journal of Archaeology* 69, (1965), 253–258; I. Singer, "The Origin of the Sea Peoples and Their Settlement on the Coast of Canaan," in M. Heltzer and E. Lipiński, eds., *Society and Economy In the Eastern Mediterranean (c. 1500—1000 B.C.)*, (Louvain: Peeters, 1988); D. B. Redford, *Egypt, Canaan, and Israel in Ancient Times*, (Princeton: Princeton University Press, 1992), 241–256; T. Dothan and M. Dothan, *People of the Sea: The Search for the Philistines*, (New York: Macmillan Publishing Company, 1992); L. E. Stager, "Biblical Philistines: A Hellenistic Literary Creation?," in A. M. Maeir and P. de Miroschedji, eds., *"I Will Speak the Riddle of Ancient Times": Archaeological and Historical Studies in Honor of Amihai Mazar*, (Winona Lake, Ind.: Eisenbrauns, 2006).

46 See most recently, I. Shai, "The Political Organization of the Philistines," in A. M. Maeir and P. de Miroschedji, eds., *"I Will Speak the Riddle of Ancient Times": Archaeological and Historical Studies in Honor of Amihai Mazar on the Occasion of His Sixtieth Birthday*, (Winona Lake, Ind.: Eisenbrauns, 2006), 347 n. 1, and literature cited there.

47 This view is heard both in some Jewish (e.g., L. H. Feldman, "Some Observations on the Name of Palestine," *Hebrew Union College Annual* 61, [1990], 1–23) as well as Christian (e.g., T. S. McCall, "Palestine vs. Israel as the Name of the Holy Land," Zola Levitt Letter, December, 1997 [see also www.levitt.com/essays/palestine.html]) circles, perhaps of a more Zionist inclination, as well as in more casual writing (e.g., *Biblical Archaeology Review* 32/5, [2006], 6c). I do not wish to denigrate Drs. Feldman or McCall in any way. To the contrary, I have chosen to use their names and cite their bibliographies because in my opinion they may represent the best expression of their respective schools of thought.

48 If it is argued that "Palestine" should not be used in contemporary writings and graphics because the name does not occur in the Bible, and, in that sense, it is not biblical, I should respond by enumerating the names of other geographical entities invariably utilized in contemporary discussions (including in many cases by those who decry the use of Palestine) that are likewise "unbiblical" in that sense: e.g., Mediterranean Sea, Dead Sea, Persian Gulf, Tigris river, Nile river, Egypt, Mesopotamia, Sumeria, Greece, and Turkey, to name a few.

49 The Assyrian version of Palestine was normally written either as *Pilištu* or *Palaštu* (cf. Hebrew *P'lešet*). For other early usage of the word, see A. M. Bagg, *Die Orts- und Gewässernamen der neuassyrischen Zeit*, Répertoire Géographique des Textes Cunéiformes 7/1, (Wiesbaden: Reichert, 2007), 189–191; S. Parpola, *Neo-Assyrian Toponyms*, Alter Orient und Altes Testament 6, (Neukirchen-Vluyn: Butzon and Bercker Kevelaer, 1970), 272.

50 W. W. Hallo and K. L. Younger, Jr., eds., *The Context of Scripture*, (Leiden: Brill, 1997–2002), 2.276; J. B. Pritchard, ed., *Ancient Near Eastern Texts Relating to the Old Testament*, (Princeton: Princeton University Press, 1969), 281.

51 Steindorff 1939:30–33; J. B. Pritchard, ed., *Ancient Near Eastern Texts Relating to the Old Testament*, (Princeton: Princeton University Press, 1969), 264.

52 Consult I. Shai, "The Political Organization of the Philistines," in A. M. Maeir and P. de Miroschedji, eds., *"I Will Speak the Riddle of Ancient Times": Archaeological and Historical Studies in Honor of Amihai Mazar on the Occasion of His Sixtieth Birthday*, (Winona Lake, Ind.: Eisenbrauns, 2006), 1.355–356; see also O. Margalith, "Where Did the Philistines Come From?," *Zeitschrift für die alttestamentliche Wissenschaft* 107/1, (1995), 102–103.

53 Admittedly, well over half of the citations occur in Josephus, where the historian is usually, but not always, rehearsing the storyline of the biblical Philistines, so they cannot be employed to bolster my contention. I would point out in passing, however, that Josephus utilizes the same word *Palaistinē* to cite both the Philistines and the country of the Philistines (e.g., Josephus, *Antiquities of the Jews*, 2.322–323, where this is explicit), and at one point near the conclusion of his *Antiquities* (20.259) Josephus does appear to use *Palaistinē* as a reference to the whole of Israel. (He speaks of his literary work containing the events that befell the Jews in Egypt, Syria and Palestine; cf. 1.145.) Many of the remaining citations generated are either ambiguous or insufficiently precise to be incorporated into my argument, and another handful are irrelevant because they refer either to a geographical entity in northern Mesopotamia near the Euphrates River (e.g., Pliny, *Natural History*, 6.31.132; Ovid, *Fasti*, 2.464) or to a Roman seaport on the Adriatic Sea (Julius Caesar, *Civil Wars*, 3.6.3; Lucan, *Civil War*, 5.460).

54 Because of space limitations, I can cite only some of the specimens here. There are additional citations, but these should be sufficient to make the point:

(1) Herodotus (fifth century B.C.; 2.104) speaks of Phoenicians and Syrians from Palestine who claim they learned the custom of circumcision from the Egyptians. Josephus (*Antiquities of the Jews*, 8.262; *Apion*, 1.168–171) explicitly rehearses this statement of Herodotus, but then adds his own interpretation: "Herodotus thus says that the Palestinian Syrians were circumcised; but the Jews are the only inhabitants of Palestine who adopt this practice. He must therefore have known this, and his allusion is to the Jewish nation" (cf. note also the repeated references in the Bible to the "uncircumcised" Philistines [Judg. 14:3; 15:18; 1 Sam. 14:6; 17:26, 36]);

(2) Aristotle (fourth century B.C.; *Meteorologica*, 2.359a.17–18), when describing how water becomes more dense when mixed with salt, talks about a lake in Palestine (Dead Sea) where you can bind man or beast and throw them into the lake, yet they will float and not sink; he adds that the lake is so bitter and salty that it contains no fish (and note that Vespasian is said to have tested this theory by ordering that certain persons who could not swim should have their hands bound behind their backs and thrown into the water of the Dead Sea [cf. Josephus, *War*, 4.476–477]);

(3) In the second century B.C., Agatharchides [5.89a, 89b, 89c] speaks several times of exploring the Red Sea and coming to Seal Island (Tiran), from where, he adds, there is a promontory stretching to the rock of the Arabs (Petra) and the country of Palestine (cf. similar declaration in Strabo 16.4.18);

(4) Philo (first century B.C.; *Abraham*, 133) at one point speaks of the land of the Sodomites, a part of Canaan afterwards called Palestinian Syria; his understanding of Palestinian Syria here is further clarified by the next example;

(5) Philo in another passage (*Every Good Man*, 75) asserts that Palestinian Syria has not failed to produce high moral excellence. In this country, he continues, live many of the very populous nation of the Jews, more than 4000 of whom are called Essenes;

(6) In one Strabo text (first century B.C.; *Geog Headings*, 1.16), the geographer lists cities and provinces found between Syria, the Arabian coast, and India, embedded in which is a reference to Palestine, seemingly incorporating the entire area between Phoenicia and Arabia; the passage reads "Adiabene and Mesopotamia, all of Syria, Phoenicia, Palestine, all of Arabia . . ." (cf. Pliny, *Natural History*, 5.69);

(7) Ovid (43 B.C.–A.D. 17; *Love*, 1.416) speaks of the seventh-day feast that the Syrians of Palestine observe (and note even L.H. Feldman ["Some Observations on the Name of Palestine," *Hebrew Union College Annual* 61, (1990), 14] concedes that this mention of the Sabbath thus makes a clear reference to the Jews);

(8) Statius (A.D. 45–96; *Silvae*, 5.1.213) in one text, where he is describing funeral gifts, juxtaposes Palestinian shrines and Hebrew essences;

(9) Statius in another passage (*Silvae*, 3.2.105) refers to an individual who had been given the standards of the East and the cohorts of Palestine (commonly understood to denote a military command on the Eastern front);

(10) Silius Italicus (A.D. 26–101; *Punica*, 3.606), in describing the various military feats of Vespasian, adds that his son (Titus) will take up his father's work and while still a youth will put an end to the war with the fierce people of Palestine (which focused on Galilee and Judea and culminated in Jerusalem in the year A.D. 70) **[see map 115]**; and

(11) The Sophist Dio Chrysostom (A.D. 40–112; *Testimony* 5) praises the Essenes in one text—a community, he adds, that is situated beside the Dead Sea, in the interior of Palestine near Sodom.

55 *Treatise of Shem* 1:11; 11:11; J. H. Charlesworth, ed., *The Old Testament Pseudepigrapha*, (Garden City, N.Y.: Doubleday, 1983), 1.474.

56 The Talmud normally refers to the land of Israel as "the Land" or "the West," and in a few cases as "Zion" or "this Country." Some of the more helpful citations of "Palestine" are found in *Qiddushin* 50a, 69b; *`Erubin* 19a; *Pesahim* 51a; *Bezak* 9a; *Rosh Hashanah* 9b; *Ta`anith* 2a, 9b, 10ab, 27a; *Mo`ed Qatan* 8a, 27a, and *Nedarim* 22a. For references to Palestine in Rabbinic literature, see G. Reeg, *Die Ortsnamen Israels nach der rabbinischen Literatur*, (Wiesbaden: Reichert, 1989), 514–516.

57 Refer also to D. M. Jacobson ("Palestine and Israel," *Bulletin of the American Schools of Oriental Research* 313, [1999], 65–74; "When Palestine Meant Israel," *Biblical Archaeology Review* 27/3, [2001], 42–47, 57), though I remain unconvinced that the word Palestine (*Palaistinē*) developed as the consequence of a Hellenistic pun on the word for "wrestler" (*palaistēs*).

58 The northern kingdom of Israel, according to A. M. Bagg, *Die Orts- und Gewässernamen der neuassyrischen Zeit*, Répertoire Géographique des Textes Cunéiformes 7/1, (Wiesbaden: Reichert, 2007), 221.

59 For the translation, see W. W. Hallo and K. L. Younger, Jr., eds., *The Context of Scripture*, (Leiden: Brill, 1997–2002), 2.137–138; J. B. Pritchard, ed., *Ancient Near Eastern Texts Relating to the Old Testament*, (Princeton: Princeton University Press, 1969), 320–321.

60 A. Lemaire, "'House of David' Restored in Moabite inscription," *Biblical Archaeology Review* 20/3, (1994), 37; cf. E. Lipiński, *On the Skirts of Canaan in the Iron Age*, Orientalia Lovaniensia Analecta 153, (Leuven: Peeters, 2006), 350.

61 Some of the biblical words and locations used in the Mesha Inscription include: *hesed* ("covenant loyalty," l. 17), *bāmâ* ("high place," l. 3), *ophel* ("mound," l. 22), Gad (l. 10), Yahweh (l. 18 [the earliest extra-biblical reference to the God of Israel]), and *bêt David* ("house/dynasty of David," l. 31). Several Moabite towns associated with the occupation of Moab by Transjordanian tribes are mentioned in the Mesha stone: e.g., Medeba (ll. 8, 30; cf. Josh. 13:9), Baal-meon (ll. 9, 30; cf. Num. 32:38), Kiriathaim (l. 10; cf. Num. 32:37), Sharon (l. 13; cf. 1 Chron. 5:16), Ataroth (ll. 10, 11; cf. Num. 32:34), Nebo (l. 14; cf. Num. 32:38), Aroer (l. 26; cf. Num. 32:34), Jahaz (ll. 19, 20; Josh. 13:18), Bezer (l. 27; cf. Josh. 20:8), Dibon (ll. 2, 21, 28; cf. Num. 32:34), and possibly Diblathaim (l. 30; cf. Num. 33:46).

62 Josephus, *War*, 3.35; cf. Pliny, *Natural History*, 5.75.

63 so Josephus, *War*, 2.573; 3.35; cf. 1.22; Judith 1:8.

64 *War*, 3.48.

65 *Mercator's World* 3/5, (1998), 13.

66 G. A. Smith, *The Historical Geography of the Holy Land*, (New York: Harper & Row, 1966), 206–215.

67 Note the location of Edrei **on map 5**. For a recent tabulation of Transjordanian place-names, see J. R. Bartlett, *Mapping Jordan Through Two Millennia*, Palestine Exploration Fund Annual 10, (Leeds, U. K.: Maney, 2008), 135–146.

68 Josephus, *Antiquities of the Jews*, 17.189, 319; *War*, 2.95; cf. *War*, 1.398–400; Strabo 16.2.20; see also R. S. Notley and Z. Safrai, *Eusebius, Onomasticon*, (Leiden: Brill, 2005), 107, 155: Gaulanitis, Trachonitis, Auranitis (Hauran), Batanea (Bashan), and Iturea.

69 *Anchor Bible Dictionary*, 1.573–574; L. Koehler and W. Baumgartner, eds., *The Hebrew and Aramaic Lexicon of the Old Testament*, (Leiden: Brill, 2001), 2.1055b; cf. Pliny, *Natural History*, 12.98; Diodorus 2.49.1; Strabo 16.2.41.

70 Eusebius (R. S. Notley and Z. Safrai, *Eusebius, Onomasticon*, [Leiden: Brill, 2005], 79); Josephus, *War*, 3.446; Pliny, *Natural History*, 5.74; Ptolemy, *Geog*, 5.14.18.

71 While I am following the list presented by Pliny (*Natural History*, 5.74), a definitive list of the ten cities—or even proof that there were only ten—is difficult to establish. Even as he delineates his own choice of cities, Pliny acknowledges that not all writers agree on this. **[See map 100.]** The second-century A.D. list from Ptolemy (*Geog*, 5.15–22–23) adds Edrei, Abila, Lysanias, Saana, Gadora, Capitolias, Heliopolis, and Bosra.

72 A Greek synonym for Abarim ("the region across," cf. Num. 27:12; 33:47–48; Deut. 32:49; Jer. 22:20); see also Eusebius (R. S. Notley and Z. Safrai, *Eusebius, Onomasticon*, [Leiden: Brill, 2005], 18).

73 Josephus, *Antiquities of the Jews*, 18.116–119; *War*, 3.44–47; 4:413–418.

74 For early documentation on the Nabateans, consult Diodorus 2.48.1–6; 19.94.1–97.6; Strabo 16.4.18.

75 For evidence of offshore, inundated habitational ruins near the Mediterranean coast, refer to E. Galili, D. Kaufman, and M. Weinstein-Evron, "8,000 Years Under the Sea," *Arch* 41/1, (1988); E. Galili et al., "Atlit-Yam: A Prehistoric Site on the Sea Floor off the Israeli Coast," *Journal of Field Archaeology* 20/2, (1993); A. Ronen, "Late Quaternary Sea Levels Inferred from Coastal Stratigraphy and Archaeology in Israel," in P. M. Masters and N. C. Flemming, eds., *Quaternary Coastlines and Marine Archaeology*, (London: Academic Press, Inc., 1983), 126–130; A. Raban, "Submerged Prehistoric Sites Off the Mediterranean Coast of Israel," in P. M. Masters and N. C. Flemming, eds., *Quaternary Coastlines and Marine Archaeology*, (New York: Academic Press, Inc., 1983), 215–232; A. Raban and E. Galili, "Recent Maritime Archaeological Research in Israel—A Preliminary Report," *International Journal of Nautical Archaeology* 14/4, (1985), 321–356.

76 cf. Judith 1:8; 3:9; 4:6; 7:3; 1 Maccabees 5:52; 12:49.

77 The apocalyptic language of Revelation 16:16 that mentions "Armageddon" has been interpreted in a bewildering number of ways. Although its exact meaning remains in doubt, it seems clear that the word itself was used symbolically to refer to a final decisive battle. In such a context, the name may be a pun on the place-name Megiddo, which would have conjured in the minds of first-century A.D. individuals familiar with Megiddo's military profile an image as profound and nuanced as words like "Gettysburg," "the Alamo," or "Pearl Harbor" would for someone today.

78 See, most recently, the lively and detailed overview of E. H. Cline, *The Battles of Armageddon*, (Ann Arbor: University of Michigan Press, 2002).

79 References to Mt. Carmel are found in: the Melqart votive inscription (W. Beyerlin, ed., *Near Eastern Religious Texts Relating to the Old Testament*, Old Testament Library, [Philadelphia: Westminster, 1978], 232–234); several temple lists from Egypt (Simons 1937:111, 157, 165); and the Black Obelisk (J. B. Pritchard, ed., *Ancient Near Eastern Texts Relating to the Old Testament*, [Princeton: Princeton University Press, 1969], 280; A. M. Bagg, *Die Orts- und Gewässernamen der neuassyrischen Zeit*, Répertoire Géographique des Textes Cunéiformes 7/1, [Wiesbaden: Reichert, 2007], 40–41; S. Parpola, *Neo-Assyrian Toponyms*, Alter Orient und Altes Testament 6, [Neukirchen-Vluyn: Butzon and Bercker Kevelaer, 1970], 57); cf. Tell el-Amarna tablets 288–289; W. L. Moran, *The Amarna Letters*, (Baltimore: Johns Hopkins University Press, 1992), 330–333.

80 C. K. Nyamweru, "The African Rift System," in W. M. Adams, A. S. Goudie, and A. R. Orme, eds., *The Physical Geography of Africa*, (New York: Oxford University Press, 1996), 18–33.

81 The bibliography here is extensive; consult e.g., C. K. Nyamweru, "The African Rift System," in W. M. Adams, A. S. Goudie, and A. R. Orme, eds., *The Physical Geography of Africa*, (New York: Oxford University Press, 1996), 18–33; I. G. Main and P.W. Burton, "Information Theory and the Earthquake Frequency-Magnitude Distribution," *Bulletin of the Seismological Society of America* 74/4, (1984), 1409–1426; *Atlas of Israel* 1970: 9–12, folio 9; 1985: map 9; N.C. Flemming, "Predictions of Relative Coastal Sea-Level Change in the Mediterranean Based on Archaeological, Historical and Tide-Gauge Data," in L. Jeftić, J. D. Milliman, and G. Sestini, eds., *Climatic Change and the Mediterranean*, (London: Edward Arnold, 1992), 268–271; Niemi, Ben-Avraham, and Gat 2000; Z. Ben-Avraham, T. M. Niemi, C. Heim, J. F. W. Negendank and A. Nur, "Holocene stratigraphy of the Dead Sea: Correlation of high-resolution Seismic reflection profiles to sediment cores," *Journal of Geophysical Research* 104/B8, (1999), 17, 617–17, 626; refer also to www.icdp—online.de/news/PDF_Files.

82 See A. Ben-Menahem and E. Aboodi, "Micro- and macroseismicity of the Dead-Sea Rift and off-coast Eastern Mediterranean," *Tectonophysics* 80, (1981), 199–233. For a study of historic earthquakes, including dates, epicenters, and approximate magnitudes, refer to R. Ken-Tor, A. Agnon, Y. Enzel, M. Stein, S. Marco, and J. Negendank, "High-resolution geological record of historic earthquakes in the Dead Sea basin," *Journal of Geophysical Research* 106/B2, (2001), 2228–2229; A. Shapira, "On the seismicity of the Dead Sea basin," in T. M. Niemi, Z. Ben- Avraham, and J. R. Gat, eds., *The Dead Sea: The Lake and Its Setting*, Oxford Monographs on Geology and Geophysics 36, (New York: Oxford University Press, 1997), 82; D. H. K. Amiran, E. Arieh, and T. Turcotte, "Earthquakes in Israel and Adjacent Areas: Macroseismic Observations since 100 B.C.E.," *Israel Exploration Journal* 44/3–4, (1994), 265–291; A. Ben-Menahem, "Four Thousand Years of Seismicity Along the Dead Sea Rift," *Journal of Geophysical Research* 96/B12, (1991), 20, 205–206; cf. N. Ambraseys, "Studies in historical seismicity and tectonics," in W.C. Brice, ed., *The Environmental History of the Near and Middle East since the Last Ice Age*, (New York: Academic Press, 1978), 185–210.; R. Ken-Tor, M. Stein, Y. Enzel, A. Agnon, S. Marco, and J. Negendank, "Precision of calibrated radiocarbon ages of historic earthquakes in the Dead Sea basin," *Radiocarbon* 43/3, (2001), 1371–1382; C. Migowski, R. Bookman, J. F. W. Negendank, and M. Stein, "Recurrence Pattern of Holocene Earthquakes along the Dead Sea Transform Revealed by Varve-Counting and Radiocarbon Dating of Lacustrine Sediments," *Earth and Planetary Science Letters* 222, (2004), 301–314; see also Josephus, *Antiquities of the Jews*, 15.121–122.

83 Watson 1895; cf. R. de Vaux, *The Early History of Israel*, (Philadelphia: Westminster Press, 1978), 386, 607.

84 *Atlas of Israel*, 1970, 3.4.

85 J. Garstang, *Joshua-Judges*, (London: Constable and Company, 1931), 136–139, pl. 25; cf. J. Garstang and J. B. E. Garstang, *The Story of Jericho*, (London: Marshall, Morgan & Scott, 1948), 139–140; See the earlier pessimism of de Vaux (*The Early History of Israel*, [Philadelphia: Westminster Press, 1978], 607 n.45); cf. D. H. K. Amiran, E. Arieh, and T. Turcotte, "Earthquakes in Israel and Adjacent Areas: Macroseismic Observations since 100 B.C.E.," *Israel Exploration Journal* 44/3–4, (1994), 282. More recently, serious scientific doubts have been cast upon Garstang's second-hand account, though there are really two separate issues here: (1) the location of the quake's epicenter, and (2) the extent of damage at Damiya; consult A. Shapira, R. Avni, and A. Nur, "A new estimate for the epicenter of the Jericho earthquake of 11 July 1927," *Israel Journal of Earth Sciences* 42/2, (1993), 93–96; R. Avni, D. Bowman, A. Shapira, and A. Nur, "Erroneous interpretation of historical documents related to the epicenter of the 1927 Jericho earthquake in the Holy Land," *Journal of Seismology* 6, (2002), 469–476. Nevertheless, similar catastrophic consequences at Damiya did take place in 1267, 1546, apparently in 1906 (R. St. John, *Roll Jordan Roll: The Life Story of a River and Its People*, [Garden City, N.Y.: Doubleday & Company, 1965], 121), and possibly on December 10, 1033, and on May 23, 1834.

86 Z. Gal, "Khirbet Roš Zayit—Biblical Cabul," *Biblical Archaeologist* 53/2, (1990), 88–97.

87 "Studies in Palestinian Geography," *The Biblical World* 4/6 (1894): 421–431.

88 M. Nun, *The Sea of Galilee and Its Fishermen in the New Testament*, (Ein Gev, Israel: Kinnereth Sailing Company, 1989).

89 W. F. Lynch, *Narrative of the United States Expedition to the River Jordan and the Dead Sea*, (Philadelphia: Lea and Blanchard, 1849), 217–265

90 Vogel 1982:1120.

91 M. Har-el, "The Pride of the Jordan: The Jungle of the Jordan," *Biblical Archaeologist* 41/2, (1978), 64–75.

92 H. Donner, *The Mosaic Map of Madaba*, (Kampen: Kok Pharos Publishing House, 1992), map.

93 Written either as *nekra thalassa* (Strabo, *Geog Headings*, 1.16) or as *nekron hudōr* (Dio Chrysostom, *Testimony*, 5).

94 K. Nebenzahl, *Maps of the Holy Land: Images of* Terra Sancta *through Two Millennia*, (New York: Abbeville Press, 1986), 19.

95 T. M. Niemi, The Life of the Dead Sea," *Biblical Archaeology Review* 34/1, (2008), 37–46.

96 A. Frumkin, G. Kadan, Y. Enzel, and Y. Eyal, "Radiocarbon chronology of the Holocene Dead Sea: attempting a regional correlation," *Radiocarbon* 43/3, (2001), 1179–1180; Y. Enzel et al., "Late Holocene climates of the Near East deduced from Dead Sea level variations and modern regional winter rainfall," *Quaternary Research* 60/3, (2003), 265–266.

97 G. Shapland, *Rivers of Discord: International Water Disputes in the Middle East*, (New York: St. Martin's Press, 1997), 5–56; A.

Soffer, *Rivers of Fire: The Conflict over Water in the Middle East*, (Lanham, Md.: Rowman & Littlefield Publishers, 1999), 119–203; J. A. Allan, *The Middle East Water Question*, (London: I. B. Tauris Publishers, 2002).

98 A. Oren, "Microbiological studies in the Dead Sea: 1892–1992," in T. M. Niemi, Z. Ben-Avraham, and J. R. Gat, eds., *The Dead Sea: The Lake and Its Setting*, Oxford Monographs on Geology and Geophysics 36, (New York: Oxford University Press, 1997), 205.

99 R. Carter, "Boat remains and maritime trade in the Persian Gulf during the sixth and fifth millennia B.C.," *Antiquity* 80/307, (2006), 57.

100 J. A. Harrell and M. D. Lewan, "Sources of mummy bitumen in ancient Egypt and Palestine," *Archaeometry* 44/2, (2002), 285–293; J. Rullkötter and A. Nissenbaum, "Dead Sea asphalt in Egyptian mummies: Molecular evidence," *Naturwissenschaften* 75/4, (1988), 618–621; note that the Egyptian word *mummiya* originally meant "bitumen."

101 Diodorus 2.48; Strabo 16.2.41.

102 A. Nissenbaum, "Shipping Lanes of the Dead Sea," *Rehovot* 11/1, (1991), 21.

103 See most recently T. M. Niemi, The Life of the Dead Sea," *Biblical Archaeology Review* 34/1, (2008), 45–49.

104 See S. M. Head, "Introduction," in A. J. Edwards and S. M. Head, eds., *Red Sea*, (Oxford: Pergamon Press, 1987), 2–4 for cross-sectional topographical profiles of the depths of the Red Sea.

105 Consult B. MacDonald, *"East of the Jordan": Territories and Sites of the Hebrew Scriptures*, (Boston: American Schools of Oriental Research, 2000), 21–43 for a useful overview.

106 Consult *Atlas of Israel*, 1970, 3/4.

107 There is no Hebrew or Greek word used in the Bible for "petroleum." The word "oil" occurs with great frequency in the Old Testament, of course, but that word without exception refers to olive oil, not petroleum (*šemen*; cf. Arab.—*samn*; Akk.—*šamnu*; Phoen. and Ug.—*šmn*). The word is sometimes explicitly juxtaposed to the word for "olive" (Ex. 27:20; 30:24) and is also used (1) in connection with trees ("wood of oil" was the natural way to refer to olive wood [1 Kings 6:23, 31–33; Isa. 41:19]); (2) as part of a dietary paradigm ("grain, wine, and oil" [Deut. 8:8; Ezek. 16:19]); (3) in medicine (Isa. 1:6; Luke 10:34; James 5:14); (4) as a reference to perfume (Ruth 3:3; 2 Sam. 12:20; Prov. 27:9; Song of Sol. 1:3; 5:1; Amos 6:6); and (5) as a softener of leather (2 Sam. 1:21). The word "fresh oil" (*yiṣhar*) is frequently paired with new wine (*tîrôš*) and refers to freshly crushed olive oil produce (Deut. 7:13; 11:14; Jer. 31:12; Hag. 1:11), not petroleum.

108 Marduk also played a magical function in Babylonian society.

109 W. E. Rast, *Through the Ages in Palestinian Archaeology*, (Philadelphia: Trinity Press International, 1992), 23–24; see A. Zertal, "The Water Factor during the Israelite Settlement Process in Canaan," in M. Heltzer and E. Lipiński, eds., *Society and Economy in the Eastern Mediterranean (c. 1500–1000 B.C.)*, (Louvain: Peeters, 1988), 341–352 for the water factor during the settlement process.

110 For similar claims in ancient secular texts, see J. B. Pritchard, ed., *Ancient Near Eastern Texts Relating to the Old Testament*, (Princeton: Princeton University Press, 1969), 257, 471.

111 J. Kay, "Human Dominion over Nature in the Hebrew Bible," *AAAG* 79/2, (1989), 216–217.

112 By the same token, the presence of dew became a signal of benevolence and blessing (Gen. 27:28; Deut. 33:28; Judg. 6:38; Job 29:19; Isa. 18:4; Hos. 14:5; Mic. 5:7; Zech. 8:12).

113 D. Baly, *The Geography of the Bible*, (New York: Harper & Row, 1974), 44–47, 221; E. Orni and E. Efrat, *Geography of Israel*, (Jerusalem: Israel Universities Press, 1980), 44, 147, 155; *Atlas of Israel* 1970: 4/1, maps R–T; *Anchor Bible Dictionary*, 5.124–125.

114 J. J. Bimson and J. P. Kane, eds., *New Bible Atlas*, (Leicester, England: Inter-Varsity Press, 1985), 15.

115 See also E. Levine, "The Land of Milk and Honey," *Journal for the Study of the Old Testament* 87, (2000), 43–57.

116 e.g., J. B. Pritchard, ed., *Ancient Near Eastern Texts Relating to the Old Testament*, (Princeton: Princeton University Press, 1969), 19b, 239b; W. W. Hallo and K. L. Younger, Jr., eds., *The Context of Scripture*, (Leiden: Brill, 1997–2002), 3.32a; cf. N. Na`aman, "Economic Aspects of the Egyptian Occupation of Canaan," *Israel Exploration Journal* 31/3–4, (1981), 181; E. D. Oren, "The Establishment of Egyptian Imperial Administration on the 'Ways of Horus': An Archaeological Perspective from North Sinai," in E. Czerny, et al., eds., *Timelines: Studies in Honour of Manfred Bietak*, Orientalia Lovaniensia Analecta 149, (Leuven: Peeters, 2006), 289.

117 *Anchor Bible Dictionary*, 6.1150; J. M. Wagstaff, *The Evolution of Middle Eastern Landscapes: An Outline to A.D. 1840*, (Totowa, N.J.: Barnes & Noble Books, 1985), 86.

118 cf. www.rehov.org/bee.htm; A. Mazar and N. Panitz-Cohen, "To What God? Altars and a House Shrine from Tel Rehov Puzzle Archaeologists," *Biblical Archaeology Review* 34/4, (2008), 42–44; A. Mazar, D. Namdar, N. Panitz-Cohen, R. Neumann, and S. Weiner 2008.

119 The expression, "a land flowing with milk and honey," is sometimes understood either as theological exaggeration (Y. Ben-Arieh, "Perceptions and Images of the Holy Land," in R. Kark, ed., *The Land That Became Israel: Studies in Historical Geography*, [New Haven: Yale University Press, 1990], 42) or environmental degradation (S. D. Waterhouse, "A Land Flowing with Milk and Honey," *Andrews University Seminary Studies* 1, [1963], 154). But the concept of environmental degradation is scientifically unsubstantiated, and theological exaggeration is unnecessary.

120 See R. J. A. Talbert, ed., *Barrington Atlas of the Greek and Roman World*, (Princeton: Princeton University Press, 2000), for the inclusion of aqueducts on classical maps; for the earlier Assyrian aqueduct of Sennacherib between Jerwan and Nineveh, see T. Jacobsen and S. Lloyd, *Sennacherib's Aqueduct at Jerwan*, Oriental Institute Publications 24, (Chicago: University of Chicago Press, 1935); E. G. Garrison, *A History of Engineering and Technology*, (Boca Raton: CRC Press, 1998), 32–36, 66–72.

121 D. Sperber, *The City in Roman Palestine*, (New York: Oxford University Press, 1998), 128–148.

122 D. P. Crouch, *Water Management in Ancient Greek Cities*, (New York: Oxford University Press, 1993), 338.

123 Y. Goldreich, "Temporal changes in the spatial distribution of rainfall in the Central Coastal Plain of Israel," in S. Gregory, ed., *Recent Climatic Change: A Regional Approach*, (London: Belhaven Press, 1988), 116–124.

124 W. A. Dando, "Biblical Famines, 1850 B.C.—A.D. 46: Insights for Modern Mankind," *Ecology of Food and Nutrition* 13/2, [1983], 231–249; "Famine," in A. S. Goudie, ed., *Encyclopedia of Global Change, Environmental Change and Human Society* (New York: Oxford University Press, 2002), 425–430.

125 See D. P. Crouch, *Water Management in Ancient Greek Cities*, (New York: Oxford University Press, 1993), 35–36 for some difficulties in absorbing early rains that are heavy.

126 See J. Katsnelson, "The Frequency of Hail in Israel," *Israel Journal of Earth-Sciences* 16, (1967), 1–4 for the extreme seasonality of hail.

127 See Y. Enzel et al., "Late Holocene climates of the Near East deduced from Dead Sea level variations and modern regional winter rainfall," *Quaternary Research* 60/3, (2003), 270.

128 See A. Horowitz, "Recent pollen sedimentation in Lake Kinneret, Israel," *Pollen et Spores* 11/2, (1969), 353–384; "Preliminary Palynological Indications as to the climate of Israel during the last 6000 years," *Paléorient* 2/2, (1974), 407–414; "Human Settlement Pattern in Israel: A Discussion of the Impact of Environment," *Expedition* 20/4, (1978), 55–58; *Palynology of arid lands*, (Amsterdam: Elsevier, 1992); J. Guiot, "Methodology of the last climatic cycle reconstruction from pollen data," *Palaeogeography, Palaeoclimatology, Palaeoecology* 80, (1990), 49–69); M. Fontugne et al., "Paleoenvironment, sapropel chronology and Nile River discharge during the last 20,000 years as indicated by deep-sea sediment records in the Eastern Mediterranean," in O. Bar-Yosef and R. Kra, eds., *Late Quaternary Chronology and Paleoclimates of the Eastern Mediterranean*, (Tucson: Radiocarbon, 1994), 75–77; N. Liphschitz, *Timber in Ancient Israel: Dendroarchaeology and Dendrochronology*, (Tel Aviv: Tel Aviv University, 2007); Van Zeist and Bottema 1982; Van Zeist 1985.

129 Refer to T. A. Wertime, "The Furnace versus the Goat: The Pyrotechnologic Industries and Mediterranean Deforestation in Antiquity," *Journal of Field Archaeology* 10/4, (1983), 446; cf. J. D. Hughes, "How the Ancients Viewed Deforestation," *Journal of Field Archaeology* 10/4, (1983), 439–443; E. Galili et al., "Atlit-Yam: A Prehistoric Site on the Sea Floor off the Israeli Coast," *Journal of Field Archaeology* 20/2, (1993), 152. Wertime (p. 450) reminds us that 1,000 donkey loads of juniper wood were required for a single limekiln to engage in one burn in the highlands of Greece. Households apparently also used dung for heating purposes. Dung is still used for fuel in homes across the contemporary Middle East.

130 J. B. Pritchard, ed., *The Harper Atlas of the Bible*, (New York: Harper & Row Publishers, 1987), 58; B. Golomb and Y. Kedar, "Ancient Agriculture in the Galilee Mountains," *Israel Exploration Journal* 21, (1971), 136–140; cf. Job 28:1–11.

131 S. Ahituv, "Economic Factors in the Egyptian Conquest of Canaan," *Israel Exploration Journal* 28/1–2, (1978), 100–101.

132 e.g., N. C. Flemming, *Archaeological Evidence for Eustatic Change of Sea Level and Earth Movements in the Western Mediterranean during the Last 2000 Years*, (Boulder, Colo.: Geological Society of America, 1969); W.C. Brice, ed., *The Environmental History of the Near and Middle East Since the Last Ice Age*, (London: Academic Press, 1978); T. M. Wigley, M. J. Ingram, and G. Farmer, eds., *Climate and History: Studies in past climates and their impact on Man*, (Cambridge: Cambridge University Press, 1981); S. Bottema and W. Van Zeist, "Palynological Evidence for the Climatic History of the Near East, 50,000–6,000 BP," in J. Cauvin and P. Sanlaville, eds., *Préhistoire du Levant: chronologie et organisation de l'espace depuis les origines jusqu'au VIe millénaire*, (Paris: Centre national de la recherche scientifique, 1981); A. F. Harding, ed., *Climatic Change in Later Prehistory*, (Edinburgh: Edinburgh University Press, 1982); J. L. Bintliff and W. Van Zeist, eds., *Palaeoclimates, Palaeoenvironments and Human Communities in the Eastern Mediterranean Region in Later Prehistory*, BAR International Series I, (Oxford: British Archaeological Reports, 1982), I 33 (i, ii); Shehadeh 1985; H. E. Wright et al., *Global Climates since the Last Glacial Maximum*, (Minneapolis: University of Minnesota Press, 1993); H. J. Bruins, "Comparative chronology of climate and human history in the Southern Levant from the Late Chalcolithic to the Early Arab Period," in O. Bar-Yosef and R. Kra, eds., *Late Quaternary Chronology and Paleoclimates of the Eastern Mediterranean*, (Tucson: Radiocarbon, 1994), 301–314; A. S. Issar, *Climate Changes during the Holocene and their Impact on Hydrological Services*, (Cambridge: Cambridge University Press, 2003); M. Staubwasser and H. Weiss, "Holocene climate and cultural evolution in late prehistoric—early historic West Asia," *Quaternary Research* 66/3, (2006), 372–387.

133 e.g., boat found beside the great pyramid of Cheops; cf. Old Kingdom texts (e.g., J. B. Pritchard, ed., *Ancient Near Eastern Texts Relating to the Old Testament*, [Princeton: Princeton University Press, 1969], 227, 416); cf. A. Ben-Tor, "The Relations between Egypt and the Land of Canaan during the Third Millennium B.C.," in G. Vermes and J. Neusner, eds., *Essays in Honour of Yigael Yadin*, (Totowa, N.J.: Allanheld, Osmun & Company, 1983), 12. Lebanese princes cutting timber as tribute appear in the upper register of the northeast exterior corner wall of the hypostyle hall at Karnak.

134 R. L. Hohlfelder, "Herod the Great's City on the Sea: Caesarea Maritima," *National Geographic* 171/2, (1987), 265.

135 N. Shepherd, *The Zealous Intruders: The Western Rediscovery of Palestine*, (San Francisco: Harper & Row Publishers, 1987), 202–205.

136 See Herodotus 1.28–33, 50–52, 94; 5.101; 6.125; Strabo 13.4.5; 14.5.28; Diodorus 9.10.6.

137 C. J. Hemer, *The Letters to the Seven Churches of Asia in Their Local Setting*, (Sheffield: JSOT Press, 1986), 131.

138 G. W. Treumann, *The Role of Wood in the Rise and Decline of the Phoenician Settlements on the Iberian Peninsula*, (Unpublished Ph.D. dissertation, University of Chicago, 1997), 102–175, has helpfully shown how the location of many port cities in the Mediterranean world, in effect, illustrates the guiding principle of regional topography. The same could be said of various cities situated at certain places along rivers (Ur on the Euphrates; Kanish on the Halys; Hamath on the Orontes; T. el-Amarna on the Nile, etc.) or at fords (Malatya on the Euphrates; Carchemish on the Euphrates; Aswan on the Nile; and possibly Aenon on the Lower Jordan).

139 For example, Jerusalem repeatedly resisted attack. **[See map 68.]** Samaria thwarted a prolonged siege during the time of Elisha (6:25), withstood the mighty Assyrian military machine for three years, and held off the assaults of John Hyrcanus for one year. And Masada succeeded in withstanding siege and all-out attack of the Roman 10th Legion with numerous auxiliary forces for seven months. (See S. E. Iakovidis, "The Impact of Trade Disruption on the Mycenaean Economy in the 13th—12th Centuries B.C.E.," in A. Biran and J. Aviram, eds., *Biblical Archaeology Today, 1990*, [Jerusalem: Israel Exploration Society, 1993], 314–315 for the placement of Mycenae in accordance with local topography.)

140 B. J. Beitzel, "Did Zimri–Lim Play a Role in Developing the Use of Tin-Bronze in Palestine?," in G. D. Young, M. W. Chavalas, and R. E. Averbeck, eds., *Crossing Boundaries and Linking Horizons*, (Bethesda, Md.: CDL Press, 1997), 135–139.

141 Stratification is nicely illustrated in J. N. Tubb and R. L. Chapman, *Archaeology and The Bible*, (London: Trustees of the British Museum, 1990), 26–29.

142 See A. F. Rainey, "Historical Geography," in J. F. Drinkard, Jr., G. L. Mattingly, and J. M. Miller, eds., *Benchmarks in Time and Culture: Essays in honor of Joseph A. Callaway*, (Atlanta: Scholars Press, 1988), 362.

143 F. Brown, S. R. Driver, and C. A. Briggs, eds., *A Hebrew and English Lexicon of the Old Testament*, (Oxford: Clarendon Press, 1966), 67; L. Koehler and W. Baumgartner, eds., *The Hebrew and Aramaic Lexicon of the Old Testament*, (Leiden: Brill, 2001), 1.80.

144 W. Helck (*Die Beziehungen Ägyptens zu Vorderasien im 3. und 2. Jahrtausend v. Chr.* ÄA 5, [Wiesbaden: Harrassowitz, 1971], 52, 121, 160) mentions as many as five Apheks in Egyptian sources (cf. *Anchor Bible Dictionary*, 1.275–277).

145 L. Koehler and W. Baumgartner, eds., *The Hebrew and Aramaic Lexicon of the Old Testament*, (Leiden: Brill, 2001), 2.1312.

146 This phenomenon also occurs outside the Bible. For example, classical literature cites at least 18 cities named Antioch, 14 named Alexandria, 14 called Seleucia, and 11 referred to as Ptolemais.

147 See also A. F. Rainey, "Historical Geography," in J. F. Drinkard, Jr., G. L. Mattingly, and J. M. Miller, eds., *Benchmarks in Time and Culture: Essays in honor of Joseph A. Callaway*, (Atlanta: Scholars Press, 1988), 359–362; B. MacDonald, *"East of the Jordan": Territories and Sites of the Hebrew Scriptures*, (Boston: American Schools of Oriental Research, 2000), 13–19; *IDBSupp* 825–827; cf. note some requisite cautions expressed by H. J. Franken, "The Problem of Identification in Biblical Archaeology," *Palestine Exploration Quarterly* 108, (1976), 3–11; and refer also to J. M. Miller, "Site Identification: A Problem Area in Contemporary Biblical Scholarship," *Zeitschrift des deutschen Palästina-Vereins* 99, (1983), 119–129; "Biblical Maps: How Reliable Are They?," *Bible Review* 3/4, (1987), 32–41.

148 See the site identifications of E. Robinson and E. Smith (*Biblical Researches in Palestine, and in the Adjacent Regions*, [Boston: Crocker and Brewster, 1868]; *Later Biblical Researches in Palestine, and in the Adjacent Regions*, [Boston: Crocker and Brewster, 1871]), who often embrace this line of reasoning.

149 See A. M. Bagg, *Die Orts- und Gewässernamen der neuassyrischen Zeit*, Répertoire Géographique des Textes Cunéiformes 7/1, [Wiesbaden: Reichert, 2007], 10–11; 1 Maccabees (e.g., 10:89), and Josephus (e.g., *Antiquities of the Jews*, 5.87; 6.30). Eusebius also confirms the site (R. S. Notley and Z. Safrai, *Eusebius, Onomasticon*, [Leiden: Brill, 2005], 22–23).

150 S. Gitin, "Philistia in Transition: The Tenth Century BCE and Beyond," in S. Gitin, A. Mazar, and E. Stern, eds., *Mediterranean Peoples in Transition: Thirteenth to Early Tenth Centuries BCE*, (Jerusalem: Israel Exploration Society, 1998), 173–174, 178; S. Gitin, "Excavating Ekron: Major Philistine City Survived by Absorbing Other Cultures," *Biblical Archaeology Review* 31/6, (2005), 51–53.

151 Portions of this section draw upon B. J. Beitzel, 1992a and 1992b.

152 G. D. Mumford and S. Parcak, "Pharaonic Ventures into South Sinai: El-Markha Plain Site 346," *Journal of Egyptian Archaeology* 89, (2003), 112; cf. D. French, "The Roman Road-system of Asia Minor," in H. Temporini and W. Haase, eds., *Aufstieg und Niedergang der Römischen Welt*, (Berlin: Walter de Gruyter, 1980), 729.

153 A. T. Olmstead, *History of Assyria*, (Chicago: University of Chicago Press, 1964), 271, 334, 555–556

154 cf. B. Isaac and I. Roll, "A Milestone of A.D. 69 from Judaea: the Elder Trajan and Vespasian," *Journal of Roman Studies* 66, (1976), 15–19; B. Isaac and I. Roll, *Roman Roads in Judaea: the Legio-Scythopolis Road*, BAR International Series 141, (Oxford: Archaeopress, 1982); I. Roll, "The Roman Road System in Judaea," *The Jerusalem Cathedra* 3, (1983); cf. D. French, *Roman Roads and Milestones of Asia Minor*, BAR International Series 329 (i, ii), (London: British Institute of Archaeology at Ankara, 1988).

155 cf. M. C. Astour, "841 B.C.: The First Assyrian Invasion of Israel," *Journal of the American Oriental Society* 91, (1971).

156 One extraordinary text from Mari refers to a caravan of 3,000 donkeys (A. Finet, "Adalšenni, roi Burundum," *Revue d'assyriologie et d'archéologie orientale* 60, [1966], 24–28; refer also to G. Wilhelm, "When a Mittani Princess Joined Pharaoh's Harem," *Archaeology Odyssey* 4/3, [2001], 28).

157 Herodotus 8.98.

158 W. Durant, *Caesar and Christ*, The Story of Civilization 3, (New York: Simon and Schuster, 1944), 323

159 R. J. Forbes, *Studies in Ancient Technology* 2, (Leiden: Brill, 1965), 138.

160 Numerous archival texts, itineraries, and military annals are available from all parts of the ancient Near Eastern world: Egypt, Babylonia, Assyria, Persia, and Asia Minor. Some of this considerable evidence comes from the second millennium B.C., and other portions derive from the first millennium B.C.

161 The Arabah road or a road through the center of the Sinai; G. I. Davies, "The Significance of Deuteronomy 1.2 for the Location of Mount Horeb," *Palestine Exploration Quarterly* 111/2, (1979), 99–101; *Anchor Bible Dictionary*, 5.1071–1073.

162 cf. Josephus, *Antiquities of the Jews*, 3.318; 11.135.

163 cf. N. P. Milner, ed., *Vegetius: Epitome of Military Science*, (Liverpool: Liverpool University Press, 1996), 10

164 Josephus, *Life*, 52; J. Wilkinson, *Jerusalem Pilgrimage 1099—1185*, (London: Hakluyt Society, 1988), 154

165 For why the title "Via Maris" is inappropriately applied to this transportation artery, see B.J. Beitzel, "The *Via Maris* in Literary and Cartographic Sources," *Biblical Archaeologist* 54/2, (1991), 64–75.

166 This branch may have seen limited usage throughout the rainy seasons of the Old Testament period and underwent a slightly circuitous modification in the Roman period. It is not pictured on the Peutinger map, the sole surviving specimen of a roadmap from the Roman era.

167 cf. A. L. Oppenheim, et al., eds., *The Assyrian Dictionary of the Oriental Institute of the University of Chicago*, (Chicago: The Oriental Institute, 1956), 6.108, 232; 17/2.101, where the same expression is employed to designate several Mesopotamian roadways.

168 D. F. Graf, "les routes romaines d'Arabie Pétrée," *Le Monde de la Bible* 59/2, (1989), 54–56.

169 See B. J. Beitzel, "The Old Assyrian Caravan Road in the Mari Royal Archives," in G. D. Young, ed., *Mari in Retrospect: Fifty Years of Mari and Mari Studies*, (Winona Lake, Ind.: Eisenbrauns, 1992), 35–57; G. J. Barjamovic, *The Historical Geography of Anatolia in the Assyrian Colony Period*, (Unpublished Ph.D. dissertation, University of Copenhagen, 2005); Wilkinson and Tucker 1995:53–57, 147–153.

CHAPTER 2 NOTES

1 Whether the verb of Nehemiah 9:25 (*ʿdn*) is a cognate of Eden or is merely a homonym remains an open question (e.g., F. Brown, S. R. Driver, and C. A. Briggs, eds., *A Hebrew and English Lexicon of the Old Testament*, [Oxford: Clarendon Press, 1966], 726b; L. Koehler and W. Baumgartner, eds., *The Hebrew and Aramaic Lexicon of the Old Testament*, [Leiden: Brill, 2001], 1.792b). The word in Ecclesiastes 4:3 (*ʿdn*) should be rendered adverbially ("not yet") and is not etymologically related to Eden. It would be tempting to identify the biblical reference to Beth-eden (Amos 1:5) in NW Mesopotamia (Bit-Adini, **map 79**) with the location of the garden, but such speculation is not sustainable on present evidence. A correlation of "precious/delightful things" with Eden probably explains why the LXX renders Eden as "paradise" and why the Vulgate further describes Eden as a "voluptuous" place. A Syriac cognate occurs (*ʿdn*, e.g., R. Payne Smith, ed., *A Compendious Syriac Dictionary*, [Winona Lake, Ind.: Eisenbrauns], 401), but this data is too late to be helpful. An Arabic root (*ǵadan*, e.g., H. Wehr, ed., *A Dictionary of Modern Written Arabic*, [Ithaca, N.Y.: Cornell University Press, 1966], 666b: "limpness, lethargy") appears to be unrelated to our word.

2 For the neo-Assyrian territory of Bit-Adini in NW Mesopotamia, cf. S. Parpola and M. Porter, *The Helsinki Atlas of the Near East in the Neo-Assyrian Period*, (Helsinki: Vammalan Kirjapaino Oy, 2001), 7.

3 e.g., A. L. Oppenheim, et al., eds. *The Assyrian Dictionary of the Oriental Institute of the University of Chicago*, (Chicago: The Oriental Institute, 1956), 4.33a; cf. M. Bonechi, *I nomi geografici dei testi di Ebla*, Répertoire Géographique des Textes Cunéiformes 12/1, (Wiesbaden: Reichert, 1993), 135.

4 e.g., C. H. Gordon, *Ugaritic Textbook*, Analecta Orientalia 38, (Rome: Pontifical Biblical Institute, 1965), 3.454a; G. del Olmo Lete and J. Sanmartín, eds., *A Dictionary of the Ugaritic Language in the Alphabetic Tradition*, Handbuch der Orientalistik 67, (Leiden: Brill, 2003), 1.150; L. Koehler and W. Baumgartner, eds., *The Hebrew and Aramaic Lexicon of the Old Testament*, (Leiden: Brill, 2001), 2.1944; see also R.S. Hess, "Eden—a Well-watered Place," *Bible Review*, 7/6 (1991), 30–32.

5 W. von Soden, ed., *Akkadisches Handwörterbuch*, (Wiesbaden: Harrassowitz, 1959–1975), 3.1378–79; cf. A. L. Oppenheim, et al., eds. *The Assyrian Dictionary of the Oriental Institute of the University of Chicago*, (Chicago: The Oriental Institute, 1956), 19.42–44.

6 The names Euphrates and Tigris are of Greek extraction. The Hebrew names translated Euphrates (*p*^{e}*rāt*) and Tigris (*hiddeqel*) are also found regularly in Akkadian texts designating the same rivers (*purattu*, e.g., R. Zadok, *Geographical Names According to New- and Late-Babylonian Texts*, Répertoire Géographique des Textes Cunéiformes 8, [Wiesbaden: Reichert, 1985], 396–398; *idiglat*, e.g., Zadok 1985, 361). As may be clear to the reader, this discussion having to do with the location of the garden of Eden is essentially adopting a Calvinist, not a Lutheran, view of ante-diluvian geography. Luther ("Lectures on Genesis Chapters 1—5," in J. Pelikan, ed., *Luther's Works*, [St. Louis: Concordia Publishing House, 1958], 1.87–91, 98–99) argued that even to ask where the garden was located in a contemporary world was an idle and imponderable question about something that had been completely obliterated.
For Luther, paradise had been lost not only in the Miltonian sense, but also because the deluge of Noah had laid waste to the surface of the earth and had fundamentally altered the geographical landscape of the world. On the other hand, Calvin (*Commentaries on the First Book of Moses Called Genesis*, [Grand Rapids: Eerdmans, 1948], 1.118–120), following a majority opinion at the time, insisted that ante-diluvian geography had not been materially disarranged or substantially disturbed as a result of the flood.

7 A. Scafi, *Mapping Paradise: A History of Heaven and Earth*, (Chicago: University of Chicago Press, 2006), 37–39.

8 Ben Sirach (Ecclesiastes) 24:25, 27; Jubilees 8:15; Jeremiah 2:18 (LXX); Qumran (*Genesis Apocryphon* from Qumran cave 1, col. 21.15, 18–19), and a possible citation in Pseudo-Philo (D. J. Harrington, "Biblical Geography in Pseudo-Philo's *Liber Antiquitatum Biblicarum*," in E. F. Campbell and R. G. Boling, eds., *Essays in Honor of George Ernest Wright*, [Missoula, Mont.: Scholars Press, 1976], 68b).

9 Josephus's etymologizing (*Antiquities of the Jews*, 1.38–39) is fanciful and unconvincing in this regard (Pishon = "multitude"; Gihon = "what wells up from the opposite world").

10 A. Scafi, *Mapping Paradise: A History of Heaven and Earth*, (Chicago: University of Chicago Press, 2006), 13, 35–40; T. Suárez, *Early Mapping of Southeast Asia*, (Singapore: Periplus Editions, 1999), 69, 105.

11 U. Cassuto, *A Commentary on the Book of Genesis: From Adam to Noah*, (Jerusalem: Magnes Press, 1961), 119–120; L. Koehler and W. Baumgartner, eds., *The Hebrew and Aramaic Lexicon of the Old Testament*, (Leiden: Brill, 2001), 1.110b.

12 e.g., C. F. Keil and F. Delitzsch, *Biblical Commentary on the Old Testament: Pentateuch*, (Grand Rapids: Eerdmans, 1969), 81–83; P. D. Huet, *Traité de la situation du paradis terrestre*, (Paris: Jean Anisson, 1691), pl. 3; D. Rohl, *Legend: The Genesis of Civilisation*, (London: Century, 1998), 46–68; M. Chahin, *The Kingdom of Armenia: A History*, (Richmond, Surrey: Curzon, 2001), 54.

13 E. A. Speiser, "The Rivers of Paradise," in J. J. Finkelstein and M. Greenberg, eds., *Oriental and Biblical Studies: Collected Writings of E.A. Speiser*, (Philadelphia: University of Pennsylvania Press, 1967a), 23–34; W. L. Holladay, ed., *A Concise Hebrew and Aramaic Lexicon of the Old Testament*, (Grand Rapids: Eerdmans, 1974), 361b; but see L. Koehler and W. Baumgartner, eds., *The Hebrew and Aramaic Lexicon of the Old Testament*, (Leiden: Brill, 2001), 2.1424b.

14 A recension (critical revision) of the Samaritan Pentateuch renders Gihon in verse 13 as "Askoph," which is the ancient name of the Kerkha River (cf. Herodotus 5.52—Choaspes).

15 cf. W. von Soden, ed., *Akkadisches Handwörterbuch*, (Wiesbaden: Harrassowitz, 1959–1975), 3.1426–1427; J.A. Brinkman, *A Political History of Post-Kassite Babylonia*, Analecta Orientalia 43, (Rome: Pontifical Biblical Institute, 1968), 269; S. Parpola, *Neo-Assyrian Toponyms*, Alter Orient und Altes Testament 6, (Neukirchen-Vluyn: Butzon and Bercker Kevelaer, 1970), 406; S. Parpola and M. Porter, *The Helsinki Atlas of the Near East in the Neo-Assyrian Period*, (Helsinki: Vammalan Kirjapaino Oy, 2001), 18; cf. F. Vallat, *Les noms géographiques des sources suso-élamites*, Répertoire Géographique des Textes Cunéiformes 11, (Wiesbaden: Reichert, 1993), 337–338; A. Fuchs, *Die Inschriften Sargons II. aus Khorsabad*, (Göttingen: Cuvillier, 1994), 466–467; K. L. Younger, Jr., "The Repopulation of Samaria (2 Kings 17:24, 27–31) in Light of Recent Study," in J. K. Hoffmeier and A. Millard, eds., *The Future of Biblical Archaeology: Reassessing Methodologies and Assumptions*, (Grand Rapids: Eerdmans, 2004), 264.

16 See most recently D. J. Hamblin, "Has the Garden of Eden Been Located at Last?" *Smithsonian* 18/2 (1987), 127–135; J. Sauer, "A New Climatic and Archaeological View of the Early Biblical Traditions," in M. D. Coogan, J. C. Exum, and L. E. Stager, eds., *Scripture and Other Artifacts: Essays on the Bible and Archaeology in Honor of Philip J. King*, (Louisville: Westminster/John Knox Press, 1994), 381–388; J. Sauer, "A Lost River of Eden: Rediscovering the Pishon," in M. D. Meinhardt, ed., *Mysteries of the Bible: From the Garden of Eden to the Shroud of Turin*, (Washington, D.C.: Biblical Archaeology Society, 2004), 3–11; but refer also to the 1575 Beroaldus map in A. Scafi, *Mapping Paradise: A History of Heaven and Earth*, (Chicago: University of Chicago Press, 2006), 296; consult M. Dietrich, "Das biblische Paradies und der babylonische Tempelgarten," in B. Janowski and B. Ego, eds., *Das biblische Weltbild und seine altorientalischen Kontexte*, Forschungen zum Alten Testament 32, (Tübingen: Mohr Siebeck, 2001), 311–320; K. A. Kitchen, *On the Reliability of the Old Testament*, (Grand Rapids: Eerdmans, 2003), 428–430.

17 A. N. S. Lane, *John Calvin: Student of the Church Fathers*, (Grand Rapids: Eerdmans, 1999), 6–7, 212, 240.

18 A. Scafi, *Mapping Paradise: A History of Heaven and Earth*, (Chicago: University of Chicago Press, 2006), 271–275.

19 J. Calvin, *Commentaries on the First Book of Moses Called Genesis*, (Grand Rapids: Eerdmans, 1948), 1.119–124. To reinforce what was obviously a novel interpretation, Calvin published a map depicting the flow of the rivers of Eden, which as far as I know was the first time a map was incorporated into a printed biblical commentary. (See A. Scafi, *Mapping Paradise: A History of Heaven and Earth*, [Chicago: University of Chicago Press, 2006], 272, for a copy of the map in Calvin's 1553 edition.)
In presenting his map, Calvin stated that he would "submit a plan to view, that the readers may understand where I think Paradise was placed by Moses" (Calvin 1948:1.120). Calvin's map was based ultimately on the cartographic theory of Claudius Ptolemy (K. Nebenzahl, *Maps of the Holy Land: Images of* Terra Sancta *through Two Millennia*, [New York: Abbeville Press, 1986], 16–17), the famous second-century mapmaker from Alexandria who is credited with creating a grid system of parallels and meridians that made possible the projection of a spherical world onto a flat surface. What Calvin labeled on his map as the lower Euphrates he identified in his text as the Gihon, and what he depicted as the lower Tigris he identified as the Pishon.

20 e.g., P. Lawrence, *The IVP Atlas of Bible History*, (Downers Grove, Ill.: InterVarsity Press, 2006), 15–17, most recently.

21 e.g., J. O. Thomson, *History of Ancient Geography*, (New York: Biblo and Tannen, 1965), 15.

22 e.g., Pliny, *Natural History*, 6.124–126.

23 J. A. Gifford, "Sea Levels and Ancient Seafaring," *American Institute of Nautical Archaeology Newsletter*, 3/2, (1976), 1–3; P. M. Masters and N. C. Flemming, eds., *Quaternary Coastlines and Marine Archaeology*, (New York: Academic Press, 1982); K. Lambeck and J. Chappell, "Sea level change through the last glacial cycle," *Science*, 292/5517 (2001), 679–686; V. Yanko-Hombach et al., eds., *The Black Sea Flood Question: Changes in Coastline, Climate and Human Settlement*, (Dordrecht, Netherlands: Springer, 2007), 230, 258–272, 798.

24 G. M. Lees and N. L. Falcon, "The Geographical History of the Mesopotamian Plains," *Geographical Journal*, 118/1 (1952), 24–39; C. E. Larsen, *Life and Land Use on the Bahrain Islands: The Geoarcheology of an Ancient Society*, (Chicago: University of Chicago Press, 1983), 1–5, 120–125.

25 The depiction in G. Barraclough (*The Times Atlas of World History*, [Maplewood, N.J.: Hammond, 1984], 37) is helpful in this regard, even if it dates to another period; see also J. M. Wagstaff, *The Evolution of Middle Eastern Landscapes: An Outline to* A.D. *1840*, (Totowa, N.J.: Barnes & Noble Books, 1985), 93–97. Traces of similar inundated habitational ruins from that general period are known along the shoreline of modern Israel (E. Galili, D. Kaufman, and M. Weinstein-Evron, "8,000 Years Under the Sea," *Archaeology*, 41/1, [1988], 66–67; E. Galili et al., "Atlit-Yam: A Prehistoric Site on the sea floor off the Israeli Coast," *Journal of Field Archaeology*, 20/2, [1993], 133–157; A. Ronen, "Late Quaternary sea levels inferred from coastal stratigraphy and archaeology in Israel," in P. M. Masters and N. C. Flemming, eds., *Quaternary Coastlines and Marine Archaeology*, [London: Academic Press, Inc., 1983], 126–130; A. Raban, "Submerged Prehistoric Sites Off the Mediterranean Coast of Israel," in P. M. Masters and N. C. Flemming, eds., *Quaternary Coastlines and Marine Archaeology*, [New York: Academic Press, Inc., 1983], 215–230; A. Raban and E. Galili, "Recent maritime archaeological research in Israel—A preliminary report," *International Journal of Nautical Archaeology*, 14/4, [1985], 321–356) and elsewhere in the Mediterranean (C. Davaras, *Guide to Cretan Antiquities*, [Park Ridge, N.J.: Noyes Press, 1976], 113).

26 Aside from its obsolete science, the ancient shoreline theory seems to be applied rather inconsistently by its adherents to the Persian Gulf, but not also to the Mediterranean Sea, the Nile delta, the Black Sea, or even the Dead Sea, where we know of substantial fluctuations in water levels over time.

27 cf. P. S. Alexander, "Notes on the 'Imago Mundi' of the Book of Jubilees," in G. Vermes and J. Neusner, eds., *Essays in Honour of Yigael Yadin*, (Totowa, N.J.: Allanheld, Osmun & Company, 1982), 202–203.

28 See also B. J. Beitzel, "Exegesis, Dogmatics and Cartography: A Strange Alchemy in Earlier Church Traditions," *Archaeology in the Biblical World*, 2/2, (1994), 8–21; J. O. Thomson, *History of Ancient Geography*, (New York: Biblo and Tannen, 1965), 27–33.

29 J. B. Pritchard, ed., *Ancient Near Eastern Texts Relating to the Old Testament*, (Princeton, N.J.: Princeton University Press, 1969), 303a; 451a.

30 Herodotus 1.15–16, 4.11–13.

31 For the Old Persian text, consult Kent 1953:117–123, 209; for the Akkadian text, see E. N. von Voigtlander, *The Bisitun Inscription of Darius the Great, Babylonian Version*, Corpus Inscriptionum Iranicarum 1/2, (London: Lund Humphries, 1978), 54–57; and for the Elamite text, refer to G. G. Cameron, "The Elamite Version of the Bisitun Inscriptions," *Journal of Cuneiform Studies*, 14, (1960), 59–68.

32 Medieval mapmakers, as they depicted the biblical world, often included the domain of Gog at a point north or northeast of Israel. The area of Gog may be surrounded by a distinct and sturdy-looking wall, presumably designed to restrain Gog's diabolical forces (B. J. Beitzel, "Exegesis, Dogmatics and Cartography: A Strange Alchemy in Earlier Church Traditions," *Archaeology in the Biblical World*, 2/2, [1994], 13–15; e.g., the "Psalter map," attached to a 1250 Latin manuscript of the book of Psalms).

33 K. Farrokh, *Shadows in the Desert: Ancient Persia at War*, (Oxford: Osprey Publishing, 2007), 24–36.

34 e.g., F. Vallat, *Les noms géographiques des sources suso-élamites*, Répertoire Géographique des Textes Cunéiformes 11, (Wiesbaden: Reichert, 1993), 109–110; R. Zadok, *Geographical Names According to New- and Late-Babylonian Texts*, Répertoire Géographique des Textes Cunéiformes 8, (Wiesbaden: Reichert, 1985), 186–188

35 Herodotus 3.94. It seems strange that Josephus (*Antiquities of the Jews*, 1.124) should identify Tubal with the Iberian peninsula.

36 S. Parpola, *Neo-Assyrian Toponyms*, Alter Orient und Altes Testament 6, (Neukirchen-Vluyn: Butzon and Bercker Kevelaer, 1970), 252–253; K. Nashef, *Die Orts- und Gewässernamen der mittelbabylonischen und mittelassyrischen Zeit*, Répertoire Géographique des Textes Cunéiformes 5, (Wiesbaden: Reichert, 1982), 199; M. Robbins, *Collapse of the Bronze Age: The Story of Greece, Troy, Israel, Egypt, and the Peoples of the Sea*, (New York: Authors Choice Press, 2001), 172–176.

37 J. H. Breasted, *Ancient Records of Egypt*, (New York: Russell & Russell, 1962), 3.240–252; K. A. Kitchen, *Ramesside Inscriptions, Historical and Biographical*, (Oxford: Blackwell, 1969), 4.2–12, 39–41.

38 F. Vallat, *Les noms géographiques des sources suso-élamites*, Répertoire Géographique des Textes Cunéiformes 11, (Wiesbaden: Reichert, 1993), 167; R. Zadok, *Geographical Names According to New- and Late-Babylonian Texts*, Répertoire Géographique des Textes Cunéiformes 8, (Wiesbaden: Reichert, 1985), 219–220; D. D. Luckenbill, *Ancient Records of Assyria and Babylonia*, (Chicago: University of Chicago Press, 1926–1927), 2.207, 2.213; cf. S. Parpola, *Neo-Assyrian Toponyms*, Alter Orient und Altes Testament 6, (Neukirchen-Vluyn: Butzon and Bercker Kevelaer, 1970), 178, 236–237.

39 Riphath is written "Diphath" in 1 Chronicles 1:6. Manuscript evidence and the Versions strongly support the reading "Riphath." The shape of the Hebrew letters [*d*] and [*r*] is graphically similar, and thus they can be easily confused.

40 *Antiquities of the Jews*, 1.126.

41 Hittite texts from Boghazköy make frequent mention of a site Takarama/Tagarama (L. L. Orlin, *Assyrian Colonies in Cappadocia*, [Paris: Mouton, 1970], 86; G. F. del Monte and J. Tischler, *Die Orts- und Gewässernamen der hethitischen Texte*, Répertoire Géographique des Textes Cunéiformes 6/1, [Wiesbaden: Reichert, 1978], 383–384), located in the vicinity of the Upper Euphrates near the site of modern Gürün, north of modern Malatya. [**See map 23**.] This same entity is apparently known as Til-garimmu (D. D. Luckenbill, *Ancient Records of Assyria and Babylonia*, [Chicago: University of Chicago Press, 1926–1927], 2.138, 2.148; S. Parpola, *Neo-Assyrian Toponyms*, Alter Orient und Altes Testament 6, [Neukirchen-Vluyn: Butzon and Bercker Kevelaer, 1970], 353–354) in later Akkadian texts, where the place must again be located near the Upper Euphrates River, probably near its western shore. (See H. Cazelles, "Zephaniah, Jeremiah, and Scythians in Palestine," in L. G. Perdue and B. W. Kovacs, eds., *A Prophet to the Nations*, [Winona Lake, Ind.: Eisenbrauns, 1984], 136.)

42 Y. L. Holmes, "The Location of Alashiya," *Journal of the American Oriental Society* 61, (1971), 426–429; J. D. Muhly, *Copper and Tin*, (New Haven: Connecticut Academy of Arts and Sciences, 1973), 176; M. C. Astour, "Ugarit and the Aegean," in H. A. Hoffner, Jr., ed., *Orient and Occident: Essays Presented to Cyrus H. Gordon on the Occasion of His Sixty-fifth Birthday*, 17–27, Alter Orient und Altes Testament 22, (Neukirchen-Vluyn: Butzon and Bercker Kevelaer, 1973), 18.

43 G. F. del Monte and J. Tischler, *Die Orts- und Gewässernamen der hethitischen Texte*, Répertoire Géographique des Textes Cunéiformes 6/1, (Wiesbaden: Reichert, 1978), 6; B. Groneberg, *Die Orts- und Gewässernamen der altbabylonischen Zeit*, Répertoire Géographique des Textes Cunéiformes 3, (Wiesbaden: Reichert, 1980), 10; D. J. Wiseman, *The Alalakh Tablets*, (London: British Institute of Archaeology in Ankara, 1953), 154; W. L. Moran, *The Amarna Letters*, (Baltimore: Johns Hopkins University Press, 1992), 104–113, 189; C. H. Gordon, *Ugaritic Textbook*, Analecta Orientalia 38, (Rome: Pontifical Biblical Institute, 1965), 3.360; G. del Olmo Lete and J. Sanmartín, eds., *A Dictionary of the Ugaritic Language in the Alphabetic Tradition*, Handbuch der Orientalistik 67, (Leiden: Brill, 2003), 1.67–68; J. B. Pritchard, ed., *Ancient Near Eastern Texts Relating to the Old Testament*, (Princeton: Princeton University Press, 1969), 29 n. 43.

241 M. Liverani, "The collapse of the Near Eastern regional system at the end of the Bronze Age: the case of Syria," in M. Rowlands, M. Larsen, and K. Kristiansen, eds., *Centre and Periphery in the Ancient World*, New Directions in Archaeology 1, (Cambridge: Cambridge University Press, 1987), 69–73.

242 D. L. Davis, "Sailing the Open Seas," *Archaeology Odyssey* 6/1, (2003), 61–62.

243 cf. A. J. Parker, *"Ancient Shipwrecks of the Mediterranean and the Roman Provinces,"* BAR International Series 580, (Oxford: Tempus Reparatum, 1992); J. S. Illsley, *"An indexed bibliography of underwater archaeology and related topics,"* (Oswestry, Shropshire: Anthony Nelson, 1996); M. Jurišić, *"Ancient Shipwrecks of the Adriatic: Maritime Transport during the First and Second Centuries A.D.,"* BAR International Series 828, (Oxford: Archaeopress, 2000). After **map 63** had been created, announcement was made of the accidental discovery of a hieroglyphically inscribed anchor and other artifacts dated to approximately 1000 B.C., found off the shore of Kyrenia on the northern coast of Cyprus. This find may prove to be another shipwreck site (*Turkish Daily News*, April 11, 2008).

244 For example, the western presence of certain technological innovations ascribed to Phoenician craftsmanship, such as cupellation (a tenth-century process in Spain where lead was heated so that the metal is converted into an oxide, leaving pure silver in its solid state) or novel artistic motifs of an oriental kind (e.g., warrior stelae) may very well suggest a Phoenician presence at this or that western location. However, this evidence is not decisive, in my opinion, unless it is found in a stratified context or controlled by some other objective criteria. J. N. Coldstream ("The First Exchanges between Euboeans and Phoenicians: Who Took the Initiative?," in S. Gitin, A. Mazar, and E. Stern, eds., *Mediterranean Peoples in Transition*, [Jerusalem: Israel Exploration Society, 1998], 353–355) and G. E. Markoe (*Phoenicians*, [Berkeley: University of California Press, 2000], 139) have shown clear evidence of direct contact between Tyre and Lefkandi (on the west coast of the Greek island of Euboea) in the form of tenth-century B.C. datable tombs containing distinctive Phoenician bowls and pitchers, and a 13th-century B.C. bronze statue of the Phoenician god Melqart has been discovered accidentally off the southern coast of Sicily. But how any of those objects got there or who was responsible is not yet clear. Even employing distinctive Phoenician pottery found in an unstratified context may be problematic in this regard. I wish therefore to confine my remarks to a fairly narrow slice of what I regard as more precise and unambiguous evidence.

245 so B. Peckham, "The Phoenician Foundation of Cities and Towns in Sardinia," in R. H. Tykot and T. K. Andrews, eds., *Sardinia in the Mediterranean: A Footprint in the Sea*, (Sheffield: Sheffield Academic Press, 1992), 412; G. E. Markoe, *Phoenicians*, (Berkeley: University of California Press, 2000), 170; *Anchor Bible Dictionary*, 5.352a; J. M. Sasson, ed., *Civilizations of the Ancient Near East*, (New York: Charles Scribner's Sons, 1995), 1324; A. Raban, "Near Eastern Harbors: Thirteenth—Seventh Centuries B.C.E.," in S. Gitin, A. Mazar, and E. Stern, eds., *Mediterranean Peoples in Transition*, (Jerusalem: Israel Exploration Society, 1998), 430.

246 J. D. Muhly, "Homer and the Phoenicians," *Berytus* 19, (1970), 45–46.

247 A bronze bowl/cup containing a Phoenician inscription was found in situ in an unplundered tomb (J) at Tekke, a northern necropolis of Knossus. On paleographic grounds, F. M. Cross ("Newly Found Inscriptions in Old Canaanite and Early Phoenician Scripts," *Bulletin of the American Schools of Oriental Research* 238, [1980], 17; see now *Leaves from an Epigrapher's Notebook: Collected Papers in Hebrew and West Semitic Palaeography and Epigraphy*, [Winona Lake, Ind.: Eisenbrauns, 2003], 227–230) dated this inscription to the late 11th century B.C. (so J. Naveh, *Early History of the Alphabet: An Introduction to West Semitic Epigraphy and Palaeography*, [Leiden: Brill, 1982], 40–41; E. Puech, "Présence phénicienne dans les îles à la fin du IIe millénaire," *Revue Biblique* 90/3, [1983], 385–391; O. Negbi, "Early Phoenician Presence in the Western Mediterranean," in M. S. Balmuth, ed., *Nuragic Sardinia and the Mycenaean World*, BAR International Series 387, [Oxford: BAR, 1987], 248; E. Lipiński, "Notes d'épigraphie phénicienne et punique," *Orientalia Lovaniensia Periodica* 14, [1983], 130–133 dates the bowl to c. 1000 B.C.). Such a date appears to be corroborated by the fact that the tomb also contained some "early Greek protogeometric" pottery as well as a Late Minoan IIIc seal (1200–1000 B.C.). Moreover, across the island on Crete's southern coast numerous fragments of distinctive 10th-century Phoenician pottery have been found in stratified contexts at Temple A (925–800 B.C.) at Kommos (J. Boardman, "Aspects of 'Colonization'," *Bulletin of the American Schools of Oriental Research* 322, [2001], 36), which points to some sort of ongoing Phoenician initiative there.

248 These texts include the Nora stela (Corpus Inscriptionum Semiticarum 1.145), dated by Cross ("The Oldest Phoenician Inscription from Sardinia: The Fragmentary Stele from Nora," in D. M. Golomb, ed., *"Working With No Data": Semitic and Egyptian Studies Presented to Thomas O. Lambdin*, [Winona Lake, Ind.: Eisenbrauns, 1987], 65–72) on the basis of a detailed paleographic analysis to the 11th century B.C., a date accepted by a host of scholars, including J. Naveh (*Early History of the Alphabet: An Introduction to West Semitic Epigraphy and Palaeography*, [Leiden: Brill, 1982], 40–41, 59); E. Puech ("Présence phénicienne dans les îles à la fin du IIe millénaire," *Revue Biblique* 90/3, [1983], 385–391); O. Negbi ("Early Phoenician Presence in the Western Mediterranean," in M. S. Balmuth, ed., *Nuragic Sardinia and the Mycenaean World*, BAR International Series 387, [Oxford: BAR, 1987], 248); M. Balmuth ("Phoenician Chronology in Sardinia: Prospecting, Trade and Settlement before 900 B.C.," in T. Hackens and G. Moucharte, eds., *Studia Phoenicia IX: Travaux du Groupe de contact interuniversitaire d'études phéniciennes et puniques sous les auspices du Fonds National de la Recherche Scientifique*, [Louvain: Université Catholique de Louvain, 1992], 218); and G. S. Webster and M. Teglund ("Toward the Study of Colonial-Native Relations in Sardinia from c. 1000 B.C.—A.D. 456," in R. H. Tykot and T. K. Andrews, eds., *Sardinia in the Mediterranean: A Footprint in the Sea*, [Sheffield: Sheffield Academic Press, 1992], 448). E. Lipiński (*Itineraria Phoenicia*, Orientalia Lovaniensia Analecta 127, [Leuven: Peeters, 2004]) down dates the fragment to the ninth or early eighth centuries B.C. In addition, a small stone fragment found at Bosa (Corpus Inscriptionum Semiticarum 1.162), in northwest Sardinia about 100 miles from Nora, consisting of a few letters but part of a monumental inscription, is dated paleographically by F. M. Cross to the ninth century B.C. ("Phoenicians in the West: The Early Epigraphic Evidence," *Studies in Sardinian Archaeology* 2, [1986], 120). Moreover, leading Sardinian scholars (F. Barreca, "Phoenicians in Sardinia: The Bronze Figurines," *Studies in Sardinian Archaeology* 2, [1986], 131–133; M. Balmuth, 218–222) have long argued that Phoenicians were present on both the northern and southern coasts of Sardinia by 1000 B.C., basing their claim on Phoenician bronze figurines found at numerous Sardinian sites but dated only on stylistic grounds. More recently, however, F. R. Serra Ridgway ("Commentary: some remarks on A. M. Bisi's paper Near Eastern Bronzes in Sardinia; imports and influences," in M. S. Balmuth, ed., *Nuragic Sardinia and the Mycenaean World*, BAR International Series 387, [Oxford: BAR, 1987], 251–252) has reported the tantalizing discovery of a portion of one such figurine found in a sealed locus that cannot be dated later than the 10th century B.C. (cf. C. Burgess, "The East and the West: Mediterranean Influence in the Atlantic World in the Later Bronze Age, c. 1500–700 B.C.," in C. Chevillot and A. Coffyn, *L'Age du Bronze atlantique*, [Dordogne, France: Association des Musées du Sarladais, 1991], 36).

249 F. González de Canales, P. L. Serrano, and G. J. Llompart (*El emporio fenicio precolonial de Huelva (ca. 900–770 a.C.)*, [Madrid: Biblioteca Nueva, 2004]; and "The Pre-colonial Phoenician Emporium of Huelva ca 900–770 B.C.," *Bulletin Antieke Beschaving* 81, [2006], 13–29).

250 González de Canales et al., "The Pre-colonial Phoenician Emporium of Huelva ca 900–770 B.C.," *Bulletin Antieke Beschaving* 81, (2006), 13.

251 In regard to these samples, taken from the Phoenician stratum, the quality of the determinations was assessed as excellent, having yielded a mean calibrated age of 930–830 B.C., with a low error analysis (± 25 years) and a high degree of probability (94 percent) (A. J. Nijboer and J. van der Plicht, "An interpretation of the radiocarbon determinations of the oldest indigenous-Phoenician stratum thus far, excavated at Huelva, Tartessos [south-west Spain]," *Bulletin Antieke Beschaving* 81, [2006], 31).

252 González de Canales et al., "The Pre-colonial Phoenician Emporium of Huelva ca 900–770 B.C.," *Bulletin Antieke Beschaving* 81, (2006), 27.

253 A. R. Rodríguez, "The Iron Age Iberian Peoples of the Upper Guadalquivir Valley," in M. Díaz-Andreu and S. Keay, eds., *The Archaeology of Iberia*, (London: Routledge, 1997), 175–191; Lipiński 1992:166.

254 e.g., K. Kilian, "Mycenaean Colonization: Norm and Variety," in J.-P. Descœudres, ed., *Greek Colonists and Native Populations*, (Oxford: Clarendon Press, 1990), 465; e.g., S. Pomeroy et al., *Ancient Greece: A Political, Social, and Cultural History*, (New York: Oxford University Press, 1999), 90–95.

255 C. Burgess, "The East and the West: Mediterranean Influence in the Atlantic World in the Later Bronze Age, c. 1500–700 B.C.," in C. Chevillot and A. Coffyn, *L'Age du Bronze atlantique*, [Dordogne, France: Association des Musées du Sarladais, 1991], 33 speculates that Hiram permitted Solomon a share in his already existing Tarshish trade as a quid pro quo for access to the new trade on the Red Sea and Ophir. J. M. Miller and J. H. Hayes (*A History of Ancient Israel and Judah*, [Louisville: Westminster/John Knox Press, 2006], 208) argue more soberly that the Red Sea venture was really "a Phoenician undertaking in which Solomon was allowed to participate" because he controlled access to the Gulf of Aqaba. I submit that their inferential argument might just as well be applied to the evidentiary record that exists for Phoenicians on the Mediterranean, as it is not clear to me how a joint nautical venture to a foreign port on the Mediterranean is inherently any more hyperbolic or exaggerated than a similar claim for the Red Sea, where no distinctive Iron Age evidence of Phoenician nauticalism of any kind has yet been discovered.

256 A. F. Rainey and R. S. Notley, *The Sacred Bridge: Carta's Atlas of the Biblical World*, (Jerusalem: Carta, 2006), 177; A. F. Rainey, "Aspects of Life in Ancient Israel," in R. E. Averbeck, M. W. Chavalas, and D. B. Weisberg, eds., *Life and Culture in the Ancient Near East*, (Bethesda, Md.: CDL Press, 2003), 264.

257 W. W. Hallo, "Sumer and the Bible: A Matter of Proportion," in J. K. Hoffmeier and A. Millard, eds., *The Future of Biblical Archaeology*, (Grand Rapids: Eerdmans, 2004), 174–175; J. Bright, *A History of Israel*, (Philadelphia: Westminster Press, 1981), 221–223; cf. J. Gray, *I and II Kings, A Commentary*, Old Testament Library, (London: SCM Press Ltd., 1970), 135–136.

258 I. Beit-Arieh, "Edomites Advance into Judah," *Biblical Archaeology Review* 22/6, (1996), 28–36; E. Lipiński, *On the Skirts of Canaan in the Iron Age*, Orientalia Lovaniensia Analecta 153, (Leuven: Peeters, 2006), 370–418.

259 so S. Japhet, *I & II Chronicles: A Commentary*, Old Testament Library, (Louisville: Westminster/John Knox Press, 1993), 666; L. C. Allen, *The First and Second Books of Chronicles*, The New Interpreter's Bible, (Nashville: Abingdon Press, 1999), 3.521.

260 *contra* T. R. Hobbs, "The 'Fortresses of Rehoboam': Another Look," in L. M. Hopfe, ed., *Uncovering Ancient Stones: Essays in Memory of H. Neil Richardson*, (Winona Lake, Ind.: Eisenbrauns, 1994), 41–61.

261 Unless specified to the contrary, regnal dates for the kings of Israel and Judah are adopted from E. R. Thiele (*The Mysterious Numbers of the Hebrew Kings*, [Exeter, Devon: The Paternoster Press, 1965]; cf. M. Cogan, "Chronology," in D. N. Freedman, ed., *The Anchor Bible Dictionary*, [New York: Doubleday, 1992], 1.1010; A. F. Rainey, "Down-to-Earth Biblical History," *Journal of the American Oriental Society* 122/3, [2002], 545; B. J. Beitzel, chief consultant, *Biblica, The Bible Atlas: A Social and Historical Journey Through the Lands of the Bible*, [London: Penguin Books Ltd., 2006], 498). Beyond the Assyriological data, dates near the beginning of the divided monarchy may also be helpfully addressed by means of the chronologically discreet but contemporary Tyrian king list, on which consult *Anchor Bible Dictionary*, 5.356; W. H. Barnes, *Studies in the Chronology of the Divided Monarchy of Israel*, Harvard Semitic Monographs 48, (Atlanta: Scholars Press, 1991), 29–55; F. M. Cross, "Newly Discovered Inscribed Arrowheads of the 11th Century B.C.E.," in A. Biran and J. Aviram, eds., *Biblical Archaeology Today, 1990*, (Jerusalem: Israel Exploration Society, 1993), 540 n.3; F. M. Cross, *Leaves from an Epigrapher's Notebook: Collected Papers in Hebrew and West Semitic Palaeography and Epigraphy*, (Winona Lake, Ind.: Eisenbrauns, 2003), 207 n.3; Liverani 2006:166–174.

262 see most recently, E. Blyth, *Karnak: Evolution of a temple*, (London: Routledge, 2006).

263 The triumphant battle reliefs at Karnak include those of Thutmose III (1479–1425 B.C.; six reliefs), probably the greatest military strategist in Egyptian history, who undertook at least 21 military campaigns into Asia and boasted that he had even "crossed the Euphrates" to rout the enemy. This grand tradition was continued by Amenhotep II (1427–1400 B.C.; two reliefs), Amenhotep III (1390–1352 B.C.; one relief), Horemheb (1323–1295 B.C.; one relief), Seti I (1294–1279 B.C.; two reliefs), Ramses II (1279–1213 B.C.; two reliefs), Merneptah (1213–1203 B.C.; one relief), Shishak (945–924 B.C.; one relief), and Taharqa (690–664 B.C.; one relief). One pauses to note here a rather unbroken succession between Thutmose III and Merneptah, then a 260-year hiatus until Shishak, followed by another 245-year interval until Taharqa.

264 The inscription records the date of the quarrying of Shishak's slabs as, "21st year, second month of the third season" (stela 100; K. A. Kitchen, *The Third Intermediate Period in Egypt (1100–650 B.C.)*, [Warminster, England: Aris & Phillips Ltd., 1973], 73 n.358). It was normal procedure for pharaohs to commence erecting their triumphal battle reliefs immediately upon returning from their victorious battles. In this case we know that Shishak's reign ended near the end of his 21st year (which probably explains why his relief panels were never finished), so there is every reason to conclude that he also acted in this manner. This all means that Shishak's Asiatic campaign was concluded not too long before the date on his quarry inscription. Shishak began his reign in the year 945 B.C. (so E. Blyth, *Karnak: Evolution of a temple*, [London: Routledge, 2006], xxiv; W. W. Hallo and W. K. Simpson, *The Ancient Near East: A History*, [New York: Harcourt Brace College Publishers, 1998], 299; K. A. Kitchen, "Egypt, History of (Chronology)," in D. N. Freedman, ed., *The Anchor Bible Dictionary*, [New York: Doubleday, 1992], 2.329; W. J. Murnane, *The Penguin Guide to Ancient Egypt*, [Harrisonburg, Va.: R. R. Donnelley & Sons Company. 1983], 354) or 946 B.C. (so E.F. Wente, Review of K. A. Kitchen, *The Third Intermediate Period of Egypt*, *Journal of Near Eastern Studies* 35/4, [1976], 278), and therefore his 21st year would be either 926/925 B.C. (Wente) or 925/924 B.C. (Hallo and Simpson; Kitchen; Murnane), depending on whether it was an autumn or spring campaign.

265 e.g., A. Mazar, *Archaeology of the Land of the Bible 10,000–586 B.C.E.*, (New York: Doubleday, 1990), 398; e.g., Y. Aharoni, *The Land of the Bible: A Historical Geography*, (Philadelphia: Westminster Press, 1979), 323–330; R. Cohen, "Iron Age Fortresses in the Central Negev," *Bulletin of the American Schools of Oriental Research* 236, (1980), 61–79; G. Barkay, "The Iron Age II-III," in A. Ben-Tor, ed., *The Archaeology of Ancient Israel*, (New Haven: Yale University Press, 1992), 323–327; M. Haiman, "Negev," in S. Richard, ed., *Near Eastern Archaeology: A Reader*, (Winona Lake, Ind.: Eisenbrauns, 2003), 282; A. Faust, "The Negev 'Fortresses' in Context: Reexamining the 'Fortress' Phenomenon in Light of General Settlement Processes of the Eleventh—Tenth Centuries B.C.E.," *Journal of the American Oriental Society* 126/2, (2006), 153–154. **[See map 44.]**

266 Some critics attack the authenticity of the relief itself. Since there is no other record in Egyptian documentation of a campaign by Shishak into Asia, they argue that Shishak sought to make himself great at home by simply manufacturing in stone what some of his predecessors had actually accomplished in Asia (e.g., J. Wellhausen, *Israelitische und Jüdische Geschichte*, [Berlin: Georg Reimer, 1914], 68 n.1). They contend that no one had written of such things for more than 250 years at Karnak. However, the Egyptian orthography of Shishak's relief differs markedly from earlier reliefs (A. F. Rainey and R. S. Notley, *The Sacred Bridge: Carta's Atlas of the Biblical World*, [Jerusalem: Carta, 2006], 185), and of the 150 or so place names that appear on the panels of his relief, about 50 names are unique to Shishak and are not found on earlier reliefs, including such places as Gibeon [#23], Beth-horon [#24], Aijalon [#26], Tappuah [#39], Penuel [#53], Adam [#56], Mahanaim [#22], Succoth [#55], and the Jordan River [#150]. This almost certainly means that Shishak's invasion route differed from any of his Egyptian predecessors and took him inland into the hill country of Judah and Samaria, even apparently crossing the Jordan River. **[See map 44.]** Anyone wishing to follow the easiest route from the Great Trunk Road to Jerusalem would quite naturally have passed the sites of Aijalon, Beth-horon, and Gibeon. **[See map 27.]** Such novel elements can do nothing but help authenticate both the relief and the events it described.

267 D. Rohl, *Pharaohs and Kings: A Biblical Quest*, (New York: Crown Publishers, Inc., 1995), 163.

268 Redford (*Anchor Bible Dictionary*, 5.1221b) has shown that Shishak and the entire 22nd dynasty that he founded was of Libyan descent. (His army is said to have included elements from Libya [2 Chron. 12:3b].) In addition, Shishak's name derives from a perfectly transparent Libyan root, recorded also in Akkadian and in Greek.

269 Some wish to ascribe the Rehoboam account to Josiah (e.g., E. Junge, *Der Wiederaufbau des Heerwesens des Reiches Juda unter Josia*, [Stuttgart: W. Kohlhammer, 1937], 73–80; V. Fritz, "The 'List of Rehoboam's Fortresses' in 2 Chr. 11:5–12—A Document from the Time of Josiah," *Eretz-Israel* 15, [1981], 50*), because the "motif of building" in Chronicles should be taken to indicate a king who enjoys the blessings of God as the result of obedience, which is at variance with the Chronicler's verdict about Rehoboam (2 Chron. 12:1–8, 14). Others ascribe the account to Hezekiah (e.g., N. Na`aman, "Hezekiah's Fortified Cities and the *LMLK* Stamps," *Bulletin of the American Schools of Oriental Research* 261, [1986], 5–21; S. L. McKenzie, *1–2 Chronicles*, Abingdon Old Testament Commentaries, [Nashville: Abingdon Press, 2004], 265–266; S. S. Tuell, *First and Second Chronicles*, Interpretation, [Louisville: John Knox Press, 2001], 159; P. R. Ackroyd, *I & II Chronicles, Ezra, Nehemiah*, [London: SCM Press, 1973], 131), either on text critical grounds (the similarity of wording in 1 Kings 14:25 and 2 Kings 18:13, where Sennacherib invades Judah and Jerusalem) or on archaeological grounds (distribution throughout Judah of wine jars, with handles bearing a royal *l^emelek* ["belonging to/for the king"] stamp, associated with Hezekiah and his preparations for the Assyrian war). The textual argument here may be coincidental in nature and is mitigated by the fact that a similar stylistic formula is also found in other texts as well where a list of fortified cities is clearly not in view (e.g., 2 Kings 15:29; 16:5; 18:9; 25:1). There is also the fact, as pointed out by S. Japhet (*I & II Chronicles: A Commentary*, Old Testament Library, [Louisville: Westminster/John Knox Press, 1993], 678), that cities were said to have been "saved" during the days of Hezekiah (2 Chron. 32:21–23), meaning that an Assyrian threat was ultimately averted in his time.

270 cf. H. G. M. Williamson, *1 and 2 Chronicles*, New Century Bible Commentary, (Grand Rapids: Eerdmans Publishing Company, 1982), 240–241; J. Myers, *I Chronicles*, Anchor Bible, (Garden City, N.Y.: Doubleday & Company, 1965), 69; C. Mangan, *1–2 Chronicles, Ezra, Nehemiah*, (Wilmington, Del.: Michael Glazier, Inc., 1982), 96; cf. J. Miller, "Rehoboam's Cities of Defense and the Levitical City List," in L. G. Perdue, et al., eds., *Archaeology and Biblical Interpretation: Essays in Memory of D. Glenn Rose*, (Atlanta: John Knox Press, 1987), 278–282.

271 e.g., F. Clancy, "Shishak/Shoshenq's Travels," *Journal for the Study of the Old Testament* 86, (1999), 20.

272 E. Blyth, *Karnak: Evolution of a temple*, (London: Routledge, 2006), xviii, 187–212.

273 According to D. Edelman ("Forward," in L. K. Handy, ed., *The Age of Solomon: Scholarship at the Turn of the Millennium*, [Leiden: Brill, 1997], xviii), this may only be a legibility question.

274 Some of the "lists" included in the history of David and Solomon must have been prepared by such scribes as part of their administrative record-keeping. For example: a list of David's "mighty men" (2 Sam. 23:8–39); a list of David's wives and children (2 Sam. 3:2–5; 1 Chron. 3:1–9); a list of David's military victories (2 Sam. 8:1–14; 21:15–22); a list of David's census (2 Sam. 24:1–9); a list of David's cabinet officials (2 Sam. 8:15–18; 20:23–26); a list of Solomon's cabinet officials (1 Kings 4:2–6); a list of Solomon's 12 administrative districts (1 Kings 4:7–19); and a list of numerous military and civil officials (1 Chron. 27).

275 For example: "the scroll of the Acts of Solomon" (1 Kings 11:41), "the history of Nathan the prophet" (2 Chron. 9:29), "the scroll of the chronicles of the kings of Judah" (1 Kings 14:29), "the chronicles of Shemaiah the prophet and Iddo the Seer" (2 Chron. 12:15), and "the scroll of the chronicles of the kings of Israel" (1 Kings 14:19).

276 cf. K. van der Toorn, *Scribal Culture and the Making of the Hebrew Bible*, (Cambridge: Harvard University Press, 2007), 23, 82.

277 J. Taylor, "The Third Intermediate Period (1069–664 B.C.)," in I. Shaw, ed., *The Oxford History of Ancient Egypt*, (Oxford: Oxford University Press, 2002), 335–336.

278 cf. J. A. Brinkman, *A Political History of Post-Kassite Babylonia*, Analecta Orientalia 43, (Rome: Pontifical Biblical Institute, 1968), 240 n.1544(b).

279 J. B. Pritchard, ed., *Ancient Near Eastern Texts Relating to the Old Testament*, (Princeton: Princeton University Press, 1969), 283a; W. W. Hallo and K. L. Younger, Jr., eds., *The Context of Scripture*, (Leiden: Brill, 1997–2002), 2.285, 287.

280 J. B. Pritchard, ed., *Ancient Near Eastern Texts Relating to the Old Testament*, (Princeton: Princeton University Press, 1969), 282–283; W. W. Hallo and K. L. Younger, Jr., eds., *The Context of Scripture*, (Leiden: Brill, 1997–2002), 2.290, 291.

281 Archaeological remains from Gezer amply attest to its destruction at this time (E. Stern, ed., *The New Encyclopedia of Archaeological Excavations in the Holy Land*, [Jerusalem: Israel Exploration Society and Carta, 1993], 2.505b), and Tiglath-pileser's own artists created a palace relief on a wall at Nimrud that commemorated the victory (J. B. Pritchard, ed., *The Ancient Near East in Pictures Relating to the Old Testament*, [Princeton: Princeton University Press, 1954], 129 [#369]).

282 cf. J. B. Pritchard, ed., *Ancient Near Eastern Texts Relating to the Old Testament*, (Princeton: Princeton University Press, 1969), 284a; W. W. Hallo and K. L. Younger, Jr., eds., *The Context of Scripture*, (Leiden: Brill, 1997–2002), 2.222, 291, 292.

283 See also J. B. Pritchard, ed., *The Ancient Near East in Pictures Relating to the Old Testament*, (Princeton: Princeton University Press, 1954), 129–132 (#371–374) for battle scenes of Sennacherib at Lachish, found in his palace at Nineveh.

284 J. B. Pritchard, ed., *Ancient Near Eastern Texts Relating to the Old Testament*, (Princeton: Princeton University Press, 1969), 288a; W. W. Hallo and K. L. Younger, Jr., eds., *The Context of Scripture*, (Leiden: Brill, 1997–2002), 2.303; for the same expression, see also Hallo and Younger, 2.286; A. L. Oppenheim, et al., eds., *The Assyrian Dictionary of the Oriental Institute of the University of Chicago*, (Chicago: The Oriental Institute, 1956), 7:212; Tell el-Amarna tablets 105.8–9; (cf. 2 Kings 18:14—19:37; 2 Chron. 32:2–22; Isa. 36:2—37:38).

285 The circumstances of Sennacherib's murder are recorded in the Bible (2 Kings 19:37; Isa. 37:38) and in extrabiblical literature. Like the Old Testament, the Babylonian Chronicle (A. K. Grayson, *Assyrian and Babylonian Chronicles*, [Winona Lake, Ind.: Eisenbrauns, 2000], 81) and a later Nabonidus text (J. B. Pritchard, ed., *Ancient Near Eastern Texts Relating to the Old Testament*, (Princeton: Princeton University Press, 1969), 309a) ascribe his death to the treachery of one of his sons (and in the latter text, as in the Old Testament, a theological explanation of Sennacherib's death is offered). Also like the Old Testament, an Esarhaddon prism (J. B. Pritchard, ed., *Ancient Near Eastern Texts Relating to the Old Testament*, [Princeton: Princeton University Press, 1969], 289) indicates that the perpetrator(s) escaped to another land (T. C. Mitchell, *The Bible in the British Museum: Interpreting the Evidence*, [New York: Paulist Press, 2004], 73–74). S. Parpola ("The Murderer of Sennacherib," in B. Alster, ed., *Death in Mesopotamia*, [Copenhagen: Akademisk Forlag, 1980], 171–182) has now shown that the name of Sennacherib's murderer was his eldest surviving son—Arad-Mulissi—which he understands to be the same person as the Adrammelech of 2 Kings 19:37 (so W. W. Hallo and K. L. Younger, Jr., eds., *The Context of Scripture*, [Leiden: Brill, 1997–2002], 3.244). Whatever the case, the reporting of this later event, occurring in faraway Assyria, represents a quite unusual piece of Judahite historiography written decades after Sennacherib's campaign to Jerusalem.

286 Minor kings in this battle were from Byblos, Arvad, Arabia, Ammon, Egypt, and a few additional cities. Significantly, the entry in Shalmaneser's monolith includes "Gindibu' the Arabian." This is apparently the first time someone called an "Arab" is mentioned by name in extrabiblical literature (I. Eph`al, *The Ancient Arabs: Nomads on the Borders of the Fertile Crescent 9th–5th Centuries B.C.*, [Jerusalem: The Magnes Press, 1982], 21, 75–76). R. Byrne ("Early Assyrian Contacts with Arabs and the Impact on Levantine Vassal Tribute," *Bulletin of the American Schools of Oriental Research* 331, [2003], 12–17) argues that Assyrian attestations of "Arab(s)" beginning in the ninth century B.C. and thereafter, as well as their possible depiction in eighth-century B.C. Assyrian reliefs, is not a reflection of the appearance of a new immigrant group but is rather a function of geography as Assyrians moved deeper into the Levant and into the Eastern Desert (Arab homeland). Similarly, it is in a ninth century B.C. context that the Bible first uses the word "Arab" or "Arabian" to denote an inhabitant of Arabia (2 Chron. 17:11; 21:16; 22:1; cf. 1 Kings 10:15). Earlier biblical texts seem to designate that area as "the land of the east" (Gen. 25:6) and its residents as "the people of the east" (Judg. 6:3, 33; 7:12; 8:10; 1 Kings 4:30; cf. L. Koehler and W. Baumgartner, eds., *The Hebrew and Aramaic Lexicon of the Old Testament*, [Leiden: Brill, 2001], 2.1070).

287 so E. Ebeling and B. Meissner, eds., *Reallexikon der Assyriologie* 10/1–2, (Berlin: Walter de Gruyter, 1928), 131–132; S. Mittman and G. Schmitt, eds., *Tübinger Bibelatlas*, (Stuttgart: Deutsche Bibelgesellschaft, 2001), B/IV/14; A. F. Rainey and R. S. Notley, *The Sacred Bridge: Carta's Atlas of the Biblical World*, (Jerusalem: Carta, 2006), 200; Y. Ikeda, "Royal Cities and Fortified Cities," *Iraq* 41/1, (1979), 79–84, 87; M. C. Astour, "The Partition of the Confederacy of Mukiš-Nuḫašše-Nii by Šuppiluliuma: A Study in Political Geography of the Amarna Age," *Orientalia [New Series]* 38/3, (1969), 412.

288 see W. W. Hallo and K. L. Younger, Jr., eds., *The Context of Scripture*, (Leiden: Brill, 1997–2002), 2.261–264; T. C. Mitchell, *The Bible in the British Museum: Interpreting the Evidence*, (New York: Paulist Press, 2004), 49–50; consult J. B. Pritchard, ed., *The Ancient Near East in Pictures Relating to the Old Testament*, (Princeton: Princeton University Press, 1954), 153 (#443).

289 cf. D. D. Luckenbill, *Ancient Records of Assyria and Babylonia*, (Chicago: University of Chicago Press, 1926–1927), 1.239 (§652), 240 (§§654, 659).

290 While various chronological schemes show deviation at some other points, this datum is taken as established verity by a wide array of chronological authorities, e.g., J. Finegan, *Handbook of Biblical Chronology*, (Princeton: Princeton University Press, 1964), 196 (§303); E. R. Thiele, *The Mysterious Numbers of the Hebrew Kings*, (Exeter, Devon: The Paternoster Press, 1965), 11, 66, 205; J. H. Hayes and P. K. Hooker, *A New Chronology for the Kings of Israel and Judah*, (Atlanta: John Knox Press, 1988), 29, 35; W. H. Barnes, *Studies in the Chronology of the Divided Monarchy of Israel*, Harvard Semitic Monographs 48, (Atlanta: Scholars Press, 1991), 153; G. Galil, *The Chronology of the Kings of Israel and Judah*, (Leiden: Brill, 1996), 32, 44; A. F. Rainey, "Stones for Bread: Archaeology versus History," *Near Eastern Archaeology* 64/3, (2001), 146.

291 cf. Mesha Inscription; for its translation, see most recently W. W. Hallo and K. L. Younger, Jr., eds., *The Context of Scripture*, (Leiden: Brill, 1997–2002), 2.137–138; A. Lemaire, "Notes d'épigraphie nord-ouest sémitique," *Syria* 64/3, (1987), 205–217; A.F. Rainey, "The Chronicler and his Sources—Historical and Geographical," in M. P. Graham, K. G. Hoglund, and S. L. McKenzie, eds., *The Chronicler as Historian*, (Sheffield: Sheffield Academic Press, 1997), 305–307; E. Lipiński, *On the Skirts of Canaan in the Iron Age*, Orientalia Lovaniensia Analecta 153, (Leuven: Peeters, 2006), 335–337.

292 The four dated inscriptions include (1) two large Bull-Colossi found at Nimrud/Calah (see W. W. Hallo and K. L. Younger, Jr., eds., *The Context of Scripture*, [Leiden: Brill, 1997–2002], 2.266–267; E. Ebeling and B. Meissner, eds., *Reallexikon der Assyriologie*, [Berlin: Walter de Gruyter, 1928], 3.42–48); (2) a Marble Slab found at Assur (Hallo and Younger, 2.267–268; Ebeling and Meissner 3.50–56); (3) the so-called "Kurba'il Statue" found at Nimrud/Calah (Hallo and Younger, 2.268–269; Ebeling and Meissner 3.58–61); and (4) the now-famous "Black Obelisk" found at Nimrud/Calah. (For the text, consult Hallo and Younger, 2.269–270; Ebeling and Meissner 3.62–71, 149–150; for a depiction of the sculpture, see J. B. Pritchard, ed., *The Ancient Near East in Pictures Relating to the Old Testament*, [Princeton: Princeton University Press, 1954], 120–125 [#351–361, especially #355]; T. C. Mitchell, *The Bible in the British Museum: Interpreting the Evidence*, [New York: Paulist Press, 2004], 51–54). While these texts vary slightly in some peripheral details, on the following central claims of military achievement they all concur: Shalmaneser III boasted that, in his 18th year, he crossed the Euphrates River for the 16th time and marched to Mt. Senir (Mt. Hermon?). From there he first launched an attack into Mt. Hauran, following which he stated that he received tribute from the people of Tyre, Sidon, and from "Jehu, man of Bit-Humri."

293 so J. Finegan, *Handbook of Biblical Chronology*, (Princeton: Princeton University Press, 1964), 196 (§304); E. R. Thiele, *The Mysterious Numbers of the Hebrew Kings*, (Exeter, Devon: The Paternoster Press, 1965), 66, 76, 205; J. H. Hayes and P. K. Hooker, *A New Chronology for the Kings of Israel and Judah*, (Atlanta: John Knox Press, 1988), 42–43; W. H. Barnes, *Studies in the Chronology of the Divided Monarchy of Israel*, Harvard Semitic Monographs 48, (Atlanta: Scholars Press, 1991), 156; G. Galil, *The Chronology of the Kings of Israel and Judah*, (Leiden: Brill, 1996), 33, 45; A.F. Rainey, "Stones for Bread: Archaeology versus History," *Near Eastern Archaeology* 64/3, (2001), 146; E. Lipiński, *On the Skirts of Canaan in the Iron Age*, Orientalia Lovaniensia Analecta 153, (Leuven: Peeters, 2006), 170.

294 On the Jehoram/Joram and Jehoash/Joash orthography of kings' names, I have followed W. H. Barnes (*Studies in the Chronology of the Divided Monarchy of Israel*, Harvard Semitic Monographs 48, [Atlanta: Scholars Press, 1991], 152–153) and K. L. Younger, Jr. ("'Hazael, Son of a Nobody': Some Reflections in Light of Recent Study," in P. Bienkowski, C. Mee, and E. Slater, eds., *Writing and Ancient Near Eastern Society: Papers in Honour of Alan R. Millard*, [London: T. & T. Clark, 2005], 250–252) in an attempt to reflect consistently a presumed northern and southern dialect. Thus, in this volume, "Jehoram" and "Jehoash" are named as kings of Judah, while "Joram" and "Joash" are kings of Israel.

295 E. R. Thiele, *The Mysterious Numbers of the Hebrew Kings*, (Exeter, Devon: The Paternoster Press, 1965), 16–38; Thiele has been followed explicitly, e.g., by M. C. Astour, "841 B.C.: The First Assyrian Invasion of Israel," *Journal of the American Oriental Society* 91, (1971), 383–384; A. F. Rainey, "Stones for Bread: Archaeology versus History," *Near Eastern Archaeology* 64/3, (2001), 146; K. A. Kitchen, "How We Know When Solomon Ruled," *Biblical Archaeology Review* 27/5, (2001), 34 [front jacket of the fascicle is mislabeled as 27/4]; and implicitly by a host of scholars.

296 Were that the case, it follows that the accession of Jehu would also have to be brought forward by three or four years, to about 838/837 B.C., which would be impossible if, according to the Bull-Colossi, Marble Slab, Kurba'il Statue, and Black Obelisk he paid tribute as king to Shalmaneser in the latter's 18th year (841 B.C.). Alternatively, were one to argue that Jehu might not have paid tribute in the first year of his reign, presuming Jehu's accession to have occurred around 846/845 B.C., then Ahab's death necessarily would also have taken place some 12 years earlier, or about 858/857 B.C., which again would not be possible if king Ahab was still alive in 853 to fight Shalmaneser at Qarqar.

297 The exact geographical circumstances of Ahaziah's death remain unclear. According to 2 Kings 9:27–28, he was wounded at Ibleam and fled to Megiddo where he died. But 2 Chronicles 22:9 reports that Ahaziah was captured while hiding in Samaria and taken to Jehu at an unspecified location, presumably the capital city (so S. Japhet, *I & II Chronicles: A Commentary*, Old Testament Library, [Louisville: Westminster/John Knox Press, 1993], 823), where he was put to death. Technically speaking, the city of Megiddo was located in the region of Samaria, but all other citations of Samaria in Chronicles clearly refer to the *city* of Samaria, not the *region* of Samaria. Other attempts at harmonization are briefly discussed by R. B. Dillard (*2 Chronicles*, Word Bible Commentary, [Waco: Word Books, 1987], 172–173).

298 N. Postgate, "Ancient Assyria—A Multi-Racial State," *ARAM* 1/1, (1989), 3.

299 *Anchor Bible Dictionary*, 4.737.

300 tablet 16; cf. tablet 15.

301 See J. B. Pritchard, ed., *Ancient Near Eastern Texts Relating to the Old Testament*, (Princeton: Princeton University Press, 1969), 295; E. Blyth, *Karnak: Evolution of a temple*, (London: Routledge, 2006), 87, 208.

302 J. Oates and D. Oates, *Nimrud: An Assyrian Imperial City Revealed*, (London: British School of Archaeology in Iraq, 2001), 36–42.

303 Consult B. J. Beitzel, chief consultant, *Biblica, The Bible Atlas: A Social and Historical Journey Through the Lands of the Bible*, (London: Penguin Books Ltd., 2006), 499; L. J. Mykytiuk, *Identifying Biblical Persons in Northwest Semitic Inscriptions of 1200–539 B.C.E.*, (Atlanta: Society of Biblical Literature, 2004); M. Cogan, *The Raging Torrent: Historical Inscriptions from Assyria and Babylonia Relating to Ancient Israel*, (Jerusalem: Carta, 2008).

304 Tiglath-pileser III: 744–727 (2 Kings 15:29); Shalmaneser V: 727–722 (2 Kings 17:3); Sargon II: 722–705 (Isa. 20:1); Sennacherib: 705–681 (2 Kings 18:13); Esarhaddon: 681–669 (2 Kings 19:37); and Ashurbanipal (Osnappar): 669–627 (Ezra 4:10). (Osnappar is generally regarded as a reference to Ashurbanipal, e.g., H. G. M Williamson, *Ezra, Nehemiah*, Word Bible Commentary, [Waco: Word Books, 1985], 55; *Anchor Bible Dictionary*, 5.50.)

305 Mt. Carmel was known by Shalmaneser as "Baal-rosh," cf. role of Baal in the Elijah narratives.

306 S. Yamada, *The Construction of the Assyrian Empire: A Historical Study of the Inscriptions of Shalmaneser III (859–824 B.C.) Relating to His Campaigns to the West*, (Leiden: Brill, 2000), 185–195.

307 E. Ebeling and B. Meissner, eds., *Reallexikon der Assyriologie*, (Berlin: Walter de Gruyter, 1928), 3.211; W. W. Hallo and K. L. Younger, Jr., eds., *The Context of Scripture*, (Leiden: Brill, 1997–2002), 2.276n. 4; D. D. Luckenbill, *Ancient Records of Assyria and Babylonia*, (Chicago: University of Chicago Press, 1926–1927), 1.262 (§739); not mentioned in the Old Testament.

308 W. W. Hallo and K. L. Younger, Jr., eds., *The Context of Scripture*, (Leiden: Brill, 1997–2002), 2.276—Adad-nirari III otherwise identified Samaria as "the land of Humri" (Omri).

309 cf. W. W. Hallo and K. L. Younger, Jr., eds., *The Context of Scripture*, (Leiden: Brill, 1997–2002), 2.290, 292?

310 A. Millard, *The Eponyms of the Assyrian Empire 910–612 B.C.*, (Helsinki: Helsinki University Press, 1994), 45.

311 See also W. W. Hallo and K. L. Younger, Jr., eds., *The Context of Scripture*, (Leiden: Brill, 1997–2002), 2.286, 291, probably including such towns as Yiron, Merom, and Daberath. [**See map 40.**]

312 H.Tadmor, "The Southern Border of Aram," *Israel Exploration Journal* 12/2, (1962), 118–119.

313 A. Millard, *The Eponyms of the Assyrian Empire 910–612 B.C.*, (Helsinki: Helsinki University Press, 1994), 45.

314 J. B. Pritchard, ed., *The Ancient Near East in Pictures Relating to the Old Testament*, (Princeton: Princeton University Press, 1954), #366; *Anchor Bible Dictionary*, 1.491.

315 See W. W. Hallo and K. L. Younger, Jr., eds., *The Context of Scripture*, (Leiden: Brill, 1997–2002), 2.292, where Tiglath-pileser indicated that he spared Samaria.

316 See also A. F. Rainey and R. S. Notley, *The Sacred Bridge: Carta's Atlas of the Biblical World*, (Jerusalem: Carta, 2006). During the three-year siege, the city of Shechem fell to the Assyrians, as clearly attested by the discovery of an Assyrian seal among the debris of a house. (See E. Stern, ed., *The New Encyclopedia of Archaeological Excavations in the Holy Land*, [Jerusalem: Israel Exploration Society and Carta, 1993], 4.1353–1354; cf. M. Cogan and H. Tadmor, *II Kings*, Anchor Bible, [Garden City, N.Y.: Doubleday & Company, 1988], 228, illustration 11[a]).

317 W. W. Hallo and W. K. Simpson, *The Ancient Near East: A History*, (New York: Harcourt Brace College Publishers, 1998), 133.

318 A. K. Grayson, *Assyrian and Babylonian Chronicles*, (Winona Lake, Ind.: Eisenbrauns, 2000), 73.

319 e.g., W. W. Hallo and K. L. Younger, Jr., eds., *The Context of Scripture*, (Leiden: Brill, 1997–2002), 2.293–294, 295 (twice), 296–297, 297, 298 (twice); cf. K. L. Younger, Jr., "Recent Study on Sargon II, King of Assyria: Implications for Biblical Studies," in M. W. Chavalas and K. L. Younger, Jr., eds., *Mesopotamia and the Bible*, (Grand Rapids: Baker, 2002), 291.

320 His fifth regnal year, in the month Tebet, month 10 (December); cf. W. W. Hallo and K. L. Younger, Jr., eds., *The Context of Scripture*, (Leiden: Brill, 1997–2002), 1.467.

321 See K. L. Younger, Jr., "The Deportations of the Israelites," *Journal of Biblical Literature* 117/2, (1998), 215–227.

322 J. B. Pritchard, ed., *Ancient Near Eastern Texts Relating to the Old Testament*, (Princeton: Princeton University Press, 1969), 286–287.

323 W. W. Hallo and K. L. Younger, Jr., eds., *The Context of Scripture*, (Leiden: Brill, 1997–2002), 2.294, 296–297, 297, 299–300. An additional tablet that may be related to this event speaks of the Assyrian seizure of the city of Azekah. The text indicates that it had previously been captured and fortified by "[ ]iah of the land of Judah" (Hallo and Younger, 2.304–305). It had earlier been thought that this partially legible king of Judah was "[Uzz]iah," and thus the text would date to the reign of Tiglath-pileser III. But it has more recently been argued that the king in view was "[Hezek]iah" (2 Kings 18:8), and thus the text should be related either to Sennacherib or more likely to Sargon. If the latter, it most likely pertains to his purge of Philistia in the year

712 B.C. (e.g., H. Tadmor, "The Campaigns of Sargon II of Assur: A Chronological-Historical Study," *Journal of Cuneiform Studies* 12, [1958], 22–40, 77–100; G. Galil, "A New Look at the 'Azekah Inscription'," *Revue Biblique* 102, [1995], 321–329). Map 77 reflects this quite plausible view of recent scholarship, though admittedly additional evidence of corroboration is still required.

324 W. R. Gallagher, *Sennacherib's Campaign to Judah*, (Leiden: Brill, 1999).

325 Rassam Cylinder, §§49–51, §§42–43.

326 J. B. Pritchard, ed., *The Ancient Near East in Pictures Relating to the Old Testament*, (Princeton: Princeton University Press, 1954), 129–132 (#371–374).

327 e.g., W. W. Hallo and W. K. Simpson, *The Ancient Near East: A History*, (New York: Harcourt Brace College Publishers, 1998), 134.

328 J. Ur, "Sennacherib's Northern Assyrian Canals: New Insights from Satellite Imagery and Aerial Photography," *Iraq* 67/1, (2005), 320–321, 335–343.

329 Included among the library's remains are pieces such as the *Descent of Ishtar into Hades*, *Enuma Elish* (the Babylonian account of creation), *Ludlul bēl nēmeqi* (a so-called "Babylonian Job"), and the *Gilgamesh Epic*, (a so-called Babylonian account of the flood). But rather than being a flood story per se, this work is believed today to address the question of how a human being might attain immortality (e.g., W. G. Lambert, *Babylonian Wisdom Literature*, [Winona Lake, Ind.: Eisenbrauns, 1996], 11–12).

330 A. K. Grayson, *Assyrian and Babylonian Chronicles*, (Winona Lake, Ind.: Eisenbrauns, 2000), 87–90; D. J. Wiseman, *Chronicles of Chaldean Kings*, (London: British Museum, 1961), 5–11.

331 A. K. Grayson, *Assyrian and Babylonian Chronicles*, (Winona Lake, Ind.: Eisenbrauns, 2000), 94–95; D. J. Wiseman, *Chronicles of Chaldean Kings*, (London: British Museum, 1961), 13–15.

332 A. K. Grayson, *Assyrian and Babylonian Chronicles*, (Winona Lake, Ind.: Eisenbrauns, 2000), 92–93; D. J. Wiseman, *Chronicles of Chaldean Kings*, (London: British Museum, 1961), 15–17.

333 A. K. Grayson, *Assyrian and Babylonian Chronicles*, (Winona Lake, Ind.: Eisenbrauns, 2000), 95–96; D. J. Wiseman, *Chronicles of Chaldean Kings*, (London: British Museum, 1961), 18–20.

334 See B. J. Beitzel, chief consultant, *Biblica, The Bible Atlas: A Social and Historical Journey Through the Lands of the Bible*, (London: Penguin Books Ltd., 2006), 328–329 for evidence of Josiah's expansionist tendencies north and west.

335 A. K. Grayson, *Assyrian and Babylonian Chronicles*, (Winona Lake, Ind.: Eisenbrauns, 2000), 97–100; D. J. Wiseman, *Chronicles of Chaldean Kings*, (London: British Museum, 1961), 23–28; cf. Jeremiah 46:1–2.

336 cf. Pliny, *Natural History*, 5.13.66–67.

337 Josephus, *Antiquities of the Jews*, 20.17–91.

338 e.g., Josephus, *Wars*, 2.520; 5.474; 6.567.

339 Compare the Babylonian king list (W. W. Hallo and K. L. Younger, Jr., eds., *The Context of Scripture*, [Leiden: Brill, 1997–2002], 1.462) with the Babylonian Chronicle (A. K. Grayson, *Assyrian and Babylonian Chronicles*, [Winona Lake, Ind.: Eisenbrauns, 2000], 73–77).

340 *Anchor Bible Dictionary*, 4.744–745.

341 e.g., M. Dietrich, *The Babylonian Correspondence of Sargon and Sennacherib*, State Archives of Assyria 17, (Helsinki: Helsinki University Press, 2003), 25, 119; J.A. Brinkman, "Merodach-Baladan II," in R. D. Biggs and J. A. Brinkman, eds., *Studies Presented to A. Leo Oppenheim*, (Chicago: Oriental Institute of the University of Chicago Press, 1964), 12–18.

342 D. J. Wiseman, *Chronicles of Chaldean Kings*, (London: British Museum, 1961) 1961:69.

343 ibid:69.

344 A. K. Grayson, *Assyrian and Babylonian Chronicles*, (Winona Lake, Ind.: Eisenbrauns, 2000), 100.

345 Ibid.: 100.

346 A. K. Grayson, *Assyrian and Babylonian Chronicles*, (Winona Lake, Ind.: Eisenbrauns, 2000), 102; D. J. Wiseman, *Chronicles of Chaldean Kings*, (London: British Museum, 1961) 1961:72–73.

347 Several cuneiform tablets exhumed from Babylon, and dating to the reign of Nebuchadnezzar (J. B. Pritchard, ed., *Ancient Near Eastern Texts Relating to the Old Testament*, [Princeton: Princeton University Press, 1969], 308b; D. W. Thomas, ed., *Documents from Old Testament Times*, [New York: Harper & Row Publishers, 1958], 86) detail various and somewhat generous food allotments to a "Ya'u-kinu [Jehoiachin] king of the land of Judah." Jehoiachin was released from Babylonian prison in the 37th year of his captivity (560 B.C) (2 Kings 25:27–30; Jer. 52:31–34).

348 Y. Aharoni, "Arad: Its Inscriptions and Temple," *Biblical Archaeologist* 31/1, (1968), 17–18.

349 This source is ostracon 4, found in the gate complex of Lachish (W. W. Hallo and K. L. Younger, Jr., eds., *The Context of Scripture*, [Leiden: Brill, 1997–2002], 3.80).

350 E. Stern, ed., *The New Encyclopedia of Archaeological Excavations in the Holy Land*, (Jerusalem: Israel Exploration Society and Carta, 1993), 3.907–909; *Anchor Bible Dictionary*, 4.121–123, though dated there to the Assyrian conquest.

351 cf. Ezekiel 24:1–2; Jeremiah 33:4; see also Josephus, *Antiquities of the Jews*, 10.116.

352 B. J. Beitzel, chief consultant, *Biblica, The Bible Atlas: A Social and Historical Journey Through the Lands of the Bible*, (London: Penguin Books Ltd., 2006), 336–337.

353 2 Kings 25:1–3; Jeremiah 39:1–2; 52:4–6, i.e., from the tenth month of Zedekiah's ninth year until the fourth month of his eleventh year; cf. Josephus, *Antiquities of the Jews*, 10.116.

354 B. Oded, *Mass Deportations and Deportees in the Neo-Assyrian Empire*, (Wiesbaden: Reichert, 1979), 18–22.

355 Cuneiform literature augments the biblical data for the northern kingdom at several places, including a record of a given numbers of deportees. From an Assyrian perspective, approximately 40,000 people of Israel were deported (about one-tenth of the estimated population). These deportations took place in conjunction with Tiglath-pileser III's campaign in 733 B.C., after which he declared that he deported around 13,500 people from various cities in Galilee (W. W. Hallo and K. L. Younger, Jr., eds., *The Context of Scripture*, [Leiden: Brill, 1997–2002], 2.286), and the victory of Sargon II who boasted in several different texts that he deported from Samaria either 27,280 people (Hallo and Younger, 2.295) or 27,290 people (Hallo and Younger, 2.296). On the other hand, Sennacherib declared, rather hyperbolically, that he carried off more than 200,000 people from Judah (Hallo and Younger, 2.303).

356 S. Parpola and M. Porter, *The Helsinki Atlas of the Near East in the Neo-Assyrian Period*, (Helsinki: Vammalan Kirjapaino Oy, 2001), map 4.

357 Cuneiform tablets from several sites in central Palestine (Samaria, Gezer, T. Hadid [near modern Lod]) presumably relate to individuals from various Mesopotamian locales who were forcibly relocated *to* Samaria by Sargon II. See N. Na`aman and R. Zadok, "Assyrian Deportations to the Province of Samerina in the Light of Two Cuneiform Tablets from Tel Hadid," *Tel Aviv* 27, (2000), 159–188; cf. Sargon's similar claims of deporting Arabs to Samaria (R. Byrne, "Early Assyrian Contacts with Arabs and the Impact on Levantine Vassal Tribute," *Bulletin of the American Schools of Oriental Research* 331, [2003], 12).

358 For proposed locations of these sites, see R. Zadok, "Geographical and Onomastic Notes," *Journal of the Ancient Near Eastern Society* 8, (1976), 113–126; R. Zadok, *Geographical Names According to New- and Late-Babylonian Texts*, Répertoire Géographique des Textes Cunéiformes 8, (Wiesbaden: Reichert, 1985), 36, 12, 267; N. Na`aman and R. Zadok, "Sargon II's Deportations to Israel and Philistia (716–708 B.C.)," *Journal of Cuneiform Studies* 40/1, (1988), 44; S. Parpola and M. Porter, *The Helsinki Atlas of the Near East in the Neo-Assyrian Period*, (Helsinki: Vammalan Kirjapaino Oy, 2001).

359 P. Sanlaville, "L'espace géographique de Mari," *Mari, Annales de Recherches Interdisciplinaires* 4, (1985), 21; A. Bossuyt, L. Bronze, and V. Ginsburgh, "On Invisible Trade Relations between Mesopotamian Cities during the Third Millennium B.C.," *Professional Geographer* 53/3, (2001), 375.

360 P. Briant, *From Cyrus to Alexander: A History of the Persian Empire*, (Winona Lake, Ind.: Eisenbrauns, 2002), 22–24.

361 Herodotus 1.74–75.

362 A. K. Grayson, *Assyrian and Babylonian Chronicles*, (Winona Lake, Ind.: Eisenbrauns, 2000), 109–110.

363 W. W. Hallo and K. L. Younger, Jr., eds., *The Context of Scripture*, (Leiden: Brill, 1997–2002), 2.198.

364 *Anchor Bible Dictionary*, 2.445–455, and the extensive bibliography cited there; cf. W. W. Hallo and K. L. Younger, Jr., eds., *The Context of Scripture*, (Leiden: Brill, 1997–2002), 3.116–134, 141–198.

365 A. K. Grayson, *Assyrian and Babylonian Chronicles*, (Winona Lake, Ind.: Eisenbrauns, 2000), 109–110.

366 In Cyrus's own words, as contained in the so-called "Cyrus Cylinder" (adapted from W. W. Hallo and K. L. Younger, Jr., eds., *The Context of Scripture*, [Leiden: Brill, 1997–2002], 2.315; cf. 1 Esdras 2:1–7; Josephus, *Antiquities of the Jews*, 11.1–18).

367 For Mesopotamian references to Persis, see R. Zadok, *Geographical Names According to New- and Late-Babylonian Texts*, Répertoire Géographique des Textes Cunéiformes 8, (Wiesbaden: Reichert, 1985), 247–248; F. Vallat, *Les noms géographiques des sources suso-élamites*, Répertoire Géographique des Textes Cunéiformes 11, (Wiesbaden: Reichert, 1993), 207–211; S. Parpola, *Neo-Assyrian Toponyms*, Alter Orient und Altes Testament 6, (Neukirchen-Vluyn: Butzon and Bercker Kevelaer, 1970), 274–275.

368 The evolution of the Persian (Achaemenid) Empire is far more complex than the rather simple overview presented here. For more complete information, consult E. M. Yamauchi, *Persia and the Bible*, (Grand Rapids: Baker Book House, 1990); P. Briant, *From Cyrus to Alexander: A History of the Persian Empire*, (Winona Lake, Ind.: Eisenbrauns, 2002); J. Curtis and N. Tallis, *Forgotten Empire: The World of Ancient Persia*, (London: British Museum Press, 2005); K. Farrokh, *Shadows in the Desert: Ancient Persia at War*, (Oxford: Osprey Publishing, 2007).

369 cf. the Cyrus Cylinder; W. W. Hallo and K. L. Younger, Jr., eds., *The Context of Scripture*, (Leiden: Brill, 1997–2002), 2.315; Babylonian Chronicle, A. K. Grayson, *Assyrian and Babylonian Chronicles*, (Winona Lake, Ind.: Eisenbrauns, 2000), 109–110.

370 P. Briant, *From Cyrus to Alexander: A History of the Persian Empire*, (Winona Lake, Ind.: Eisenbrauns, 2002), 44–49; K. Farrokh, *Shadows in the Desert: Ancient Persia at War*, (Oxford: Osprey Publishing, 2007), 44.

371 Herodotus 5.52–53; Many parts of this roadway had been in existence long before Darius came to the throne. It is but one of several "royal" roads within the Persian's domain (Diodorus 19.19.2; Pseudo-Aristotle, *Oeconomia*, 2.2.14b; P. Briant, *From Cyrus to Alexander: A History of the Persian Empire*, [Winona Lake, Ind.: Eisenbrauns, 2002], 357). For the expression "royal road" in Akkadian (*girri šarri*) consult A.L. Oppenheim, et al., eds., *The Assyrian Dictionary of the Oriental Institute of the University of Chicago*, (Chicago: The Oriental Institute, 1956), 5.90; for the same expression in Hebrew (*derek hammelek*), see L. Koehler and W. Baumgartner, eds., *The Hebrew and Aramaic Lexicon of the Old Testament*, (Leiden: Brill, 2001), 1.232.

372 Herodotus 5.54; so P. Briant, *From Cyrus to Alexander: A History of the Persian Empire*, (Winona Lake, Ind.: Eisenbrauns, 2002), 357–364.

373 This segment of Greek history is far more complex and detailed than can be presented here. For more complete information, the reader is advised to consult W.G. Sinnegen and C. A. Robinson, *Ancient History*, (New York: Macmillan Publishing Company, 1981); S. Pomeroy et al., *Ancient Greece: A Political, Social, and Cultural History*, (New York: Oxford University Press, 1999); P. Briant, *From Cyrus to Alexander: A History of the Persian Empire*, (Winona Lake, Ind.: Eisenbrauns, 2002). The data derives ultimately from various classical writers: e.g., Plutarch, Diodorus of Sicily, Arrian, and Quintus Curtius.

374 Arrian, *Anabasis*, 1.2.3; Plutarch 15.1–2.

375 Diodorus 17.23.2.

376 Diodorus 17.23.4ff; Plutarch 17.1ff; Josephus, *Antiquities of the Jews*, 11.313ff.

377 Plutarch 18.2.

378 Diodorus 17.39.1.

379 Diodorus 17.40.5; Quintus Curtius 4.2.1.

380 Plutarch 25.4f; Diodorus 17.48.7.

381 Josephus, *Antiquities of the Jews*, 11.329–339; cf. Pseudo-Callisthenes, *Romance of Alexander*, 2.24; see also A. F. Rainey and R. S. Notley, *The Sacred Bridge: Carta's Atlas of the Biblical World*, (Jerusalem: Carta, 2006), 298–299 for relevant rabbinic literature; C. Ritter, *The Comparative Geography of Palestine and the Sinaitic Peninsula*, (New York: Greenwood Press, 1968), 2.24 for a brief critical discussion of the visit to Jerusalem.

382 Josephus, *Antiquities of the Jews*, 11.337; cf. Daniel 8:21; 11:3; Enoch 90:1–5.

383 Josephus, *Antiquities of the Jews*, 11.340–344.

384 e.g., Quintus Curtius 4.8.9–10; cf. Arrian, *Anabasis*, 2.25.4; Josephus, *Apion*, 2.42–43, but see C. T. R. Hayward, *The Jewish Temple: A non-biblical sourcebook*, (New York: Routledge, 1996), 18–25.

385 Diodorus 17.52; Quintus Curtius 4.8.1ff.

386 W. G. Sinnegen and A. Robinson, Jr., *Ancient History*, (New York: Macmillan Publishing Company, 1981), 262.

387 The size of Darius's army at Gaugamela ranges from 500,000 (Justin 2.12.5) to 1,000,000 (Diodorus 17.53.3; Plutarch 31.1; Arrian 3.8.6).

388 Diodorus 17.53.4.

389 Diodorus 17.55.6ff; Plutarch 33.3ff; Arrian, *Anabasis*, 3.14.1ff.

390 Diodorus 17.64.3; 65.4; 70.1.

391 Diodorus 17.74.3–5.

392 Diodorus 17.73.2.

393 As a former student of Aristotle, Alexander had been taught about the sphericity of the earth and that the entire inhabited world, from Gibraltar to India, was relatively small and probably surrounded on all sides by an ocean. In that regard, Alexander took with him surveyors entrusted with keeping daily ledgers of his campaign, recording distances between stops, and describing features of soil and landscape along the way. It is quite clear that Alexander's expedition became a primary source of new cartographic data in the classical world.

394 Diodorus 17.86.5.

395 Diodorus 17.94.5.

396 Diodorus 17.104.3.

397 Diodorus 17.108.6.

398 Diodorus 17.117.5ff.

399 so Pliny, *Natural History*, 5.91; Strabo 12.2.7–9; Xenophon, *Anabasis*, 1.2.21; Arrian, *Anabasis* 2.4.3.

400 so Strabo 14.5.18; Arrian, *Anabasis*, 2.7.1.

401 so Arrian, *Anabasis*, 2.5.1; Diodorus 14.20.3–5; 17.32.2.

402 J. D. Montagu, *Battles of the Greek and Roman Worlds*, (London: Greenhill Books, 2000), 102–103.

403 Plutarch, *Alexander*, 19.1–3.

404 Quintus Curtius 3.2.1–9; other estimates include 400,000 (Diodorus 17.31.2; Justin 11.9.1) or even 600,000 personnel (Arrian, *Anabasis*, 2.8.8).

405 Quintus Curtius 3.8.17 .

406 M. Bennett, "Alexander at Issus (Turkey, 333 B.C.)," in M. Stephenson, ed., *Battlegrounds: Geography and the History of Warfare*, (Washington D.C.: National Geographic, 2003), 14–20.

407 Diodorus 17.34.7–9; Plutarch, *Alexander*, 20.10; Quintus Curtius 3.11.27.

408 Ecclesiasticus discusses a loss of faith that permeated this new environment; Jubilees represents a polemic against religious laxity resulting from exposure to this new culture; cf. Greek Additions to the book of Esther.

409 E. Schürer, *The History of the Jewish People in the Age of Jesus Christ*, (Edinburgh: T. & T. Clark, 1979), 2.381–414, 550–590; A. J. Levine, "Visions of Kingdoms: From Pompey to the First Jewish Revolt," in M. D. Coogan, ed., *The Oxford History of the Biblical World*, (New York: Oxford University Press, 2001), 364–379; J. C. VanderKam, *From Joshua to Caiaphas: High Priests After the Exile*, (Minneapolis: Fortress Press, 2004).

410 J. M. Wagstaff, *The Evolution of Middle Eastern Landscapes: An Outline to A.D. 1840*, (Totowa, N.J.: Barnes & Noble Books, 1985), 144–145.

411 *Encyclopaedia Judaica* 16.991–992; cf. Josephus, *Antiquities of the Jews*, 12.160ff.

412 S. Schwartz, "A New View on the Social Type and Political Ideology of the Hasmonean Family," *Journal of Biblical Literature* 112/2, (1993), 306.

413 D. Sperber, "Objects of Trade between Palestine and Egypt in Roman Times," *Journal of the Economic and Social History of the Orient* 19/2, (1976), 113–115.

414 L. I. A. Levine, "The Age of Hellenism: Alexander the Great and the Rise and Fall of the Hasmonean Kingdom," in H. Shanks, ed., *Ancient Israel*, (Washington D.C.: Biblical Archaeology Society, 1988), 179.

415 R. J. H. Shutt, "Letter of Aristeas," in J. H. Charlesworth, ed., *The Old Testament Pseudepigrapha* 2, (Garden City, N.Y.: Doubleday & Company, 1985), 12–34.

416 R. Harrison, "Hellenization in Syria-Palestine: The Case of Judea in the Third Century B.C.E.," *Biblical Archaeologist* 57/2, (1994), 98–107.

417 1 Maccabees 1:10–15; 2 Maccabees 4:7–12; Josephus, *Antiquities of the Jews*, 12.237ff.

418 Josephus, *Antiquities of the Jews*, 12.251–252.

419 1 Maccabees 1:21–23, 54–64; 2 Maccabees 5:15–16; 6:1–12; Josephus, *Antiquities of the Jews*, 12.248ff; cf. Daniel 11:30–31.

420 1 Maccabees 2:1ff; cf. Josephus, *War*, 1.45.

421 Josephus, *Antiquities of the Jews*, 12.265; *War*, 1.36.

422 1 Maccabees. 3:10–12.

423 1 Maccabees 3:13–26.

424 cf. Josephus, *Antiquities of the Jews*, 12.292.

425 1 Maccabees 3:38–4:25; 2 Maccabees 8:8–29.

426 1 Maccabees 4:26–35; 2 Maccabees 11:1–14; Josephus, *War*, 1.41ff.

427 1 Maccabees 4:36–61; cf. John 10:22.

428 The events bringing a Hasmonean state into existence are recalled in detail in Josephus, *Antiquities of the Jews*, 13; *War*, 1; books of Maccabees.

429 A paraphrase of T. Szulc ("Abraham: Journey of Faith," *National Geographic* 200/6, [2001], 126).

430 See most recently A. F. Rainey and R. S. Notley, *The Sacred Bridge: Carta's Atlas of the Biblical World*, (Jerusalem: Carta, 2006), 72–75, 93, 186–188.

431 Whether the name Jerusalem originally appeared in the poorly preserved panels of Egyptian king Shishak must remain an open question (D. Edelman, "Foreword," in L. K. Handy, ed., *The Age of Solomon: Scholarship at the Turn of the Millennium*, [Leiden: Brill, 1997], xviii). The view of G. A. Smith (*Jerusalem: the Topography, Economics and History from the Earliest Times to A.D. 70*, [New York: A. C. Armstrong and Son, 1908], 1.268), that Jerusalem occurs in the Shishak registers under the title Rabbat ("capital city"), is a case of special pleading and is untenable on several grounds. Likewise, Rohl's assertion (*Pharaohs and Kings: A Biblical Quest*, [New York: Crown Publishers, Inc., 1995], 149–150) that Shalem (Jerusalem) is found atop the north pylon of the Ramesseum is not commonly accepted by scholarship, though in his eighth year, Ramses II did undertake a campaign into the southern Levant, including into Canaan.

432 A. K. Grayson, *Assyrian and Babylonian Chronicles*, (Winona Lake, Ind.: Eisenbrauns, 2000), 99–100.

433 Found in the Egyptian Execration Texts now housed in Berlin (K. Sethe, *Die Ächtung feindlicher Fürsten, Völker und Dinge auf altägyptischen Tongefässscherben des mittleren Reiches*, [Berlin: Akademie der Wissenschaften, 1926], 53 [group f18]; but see N. Na`aman, "Canaanite Jerusalem and its Central Hill Country Neighbours in the Second Millennium B.C.E.," *Ugarit-Forschungen* 24, [1992], 278–279) and Brussels (G. Posener, *Princes et pays d'Asie et de Nubie: Textes hiératiques sur des figurines d'envoûtement du Moyen Empire*, [Brussels: Fondation Éyptologique Reine Élisabeth, 1940], 39–45, 86 [E45]; cf. A. Ben-Tor, "Do the Execration Texts Reflect an Accurate Picture of the Contemporary Settlement Map of Palestine?," in Y. Amit et al., eds., *Essays on Ancient Israel in Its Near Eastern Context*, [Winona Lake, Ind.: Eisenbrauns, 2006], 66–70).

434 L. Koehler and W. Baumgartner, eds., *The Hebrew and Aramaic Lexicon of the Old Testament*, (Leiden: Brill, 2001), 1.437; A. F. Rainey and R. S. Notley, *The Sacred Bridge: Carta's Atlas of the Biblical World*, (Jerusalem: Carta, 2006), 58; *Anchor Bible Dictionary*, 3.751.

435 From the Abdi-Hepa correspondence found at T. el-Amarna; W. L. Moran, *The Amarna Letters*, (Baltimore: Johns Hopkins University Press, 1992), 328–334; W. W. Hallo and K. L. Younger, Jr., eds., *The Context of Scripture*, (Leiden: Brill, 1997–2002), 3.237–239.

436 i.e., the so-called "bull inscription"; see D. D Luckenbill, (*The Annals of Sennacherib*, Oriental Institute Publications 2, [Chicago: University of Chicago Press, 1924], 70; cf. G. Smith, *History of Sennacherib*, [Edinburgh: Williams and Norgate, 1878], 60–63) and the so-called "Oriental Institute prism" (Luckenbill, 31–33; cf. W. W. Hallo and K. L. Younger, Jr., eds., *The Context of Scripture*, [Leiden: Brill, 1997–2002], 2.302–303; S. Parpola, *Neo-Assyrian Toponyms*, Alter Orient und Altes Testament 6, [Neukirchen-Vluyn: Butzon and Bercker Kevelaer, 1970], 375).

437 G. del Olmo Lete and J. Sanmartín, eds., *A Dictionary of the Ugaritic Language in the Alphabetic Tradition*, Handbuch der Orientalistik 67, (Leiden: Brill, 2003), 820; C. H. Gordon, *Ugaritic Textbook*, Analecta Orientalia 38, (Rome: Pontifical Biblical Institute, 1965), 3.490; *Anchor Bible Dictionary*, 5.1152–1153; cf. Genesis 14:18.

438 Consult L. Koehler and W. Baumgartner, eds., *The Hebrew and Aramaic Lexicon of the Old Testament*, (Leiden: Brill, 2001), 1.25; F. Brown, S. R. Driver, and C. A. Briggs, eds., *A Hebrew and English Lexicon of the Old Testament*, (Oxford: Clarendon Press, 1966), 436.

439 See also D. M. Jacobson, "Palestine and Israel," *Bulletin of the American Schools of Oriental Research* 313, (1999), 67; cf. Josephus, *Antiquities of the Jews*, 7.67; *War*, 6.438.

440 cf. Eusebius, *Onomasticon*, #618.

441 e.g., H. W. Hertzberg, *I & II Samuel: A Commentary*, Old Testament Library, (Philadelphia: Westminster Press, 1964), 414.

442 e.g., V. P. Hamilton, *The Book of Genesis: Chapters 18—50*, The New International Commentary on the Old Testament, (Grand Rapids: Eerdmans, 1995), 102–103; R. B. Dillard, *2 Chronicles*, Word Bible Commentary, (Waco: Word Books, 1987), 27.

443 e.g., *War*, 1.39; *Antiquities of the Jews*, 14.477.

444 e.g., the 1475 map of Brandis de Schass; see E. Laor, *Maps of the Holy Land: Cartobibliography of Printed Maps, 1475–1900*, (New York: Alan R. Liss, Inc., 1986), 18.

445 Y. Tsafrir, L. Di Segni, and J. Green, *Tabula Imperii Romani: Iudaea, Palaestina*, (Jerusalem: Israel Academy of Sciences and Humanities, 1994), maps.

446 Y. Shiloh, "Underground Water Systems in Eretz-Israel in the Iron Age," in L.G. Perdue, L. E. Toombs, and G. L. Johnson, eds., *Archaeology and Biblical Interpretation: Essays in Memory of D. Glenn Rose*, (Atlanta: John Knox Press, 1987), 215–222.

447 A. Mazar, "The Aqueducts of Jerusalem," in Y. Yadin, ed., *Jerusalem Revealed: Archaeology in the Holy City 1968–1974*, (New Haven: Yale University Press and the Israel Exploration Society, 1976), 79–84; cf. Josephus, *Antiquities of the Jews*, 18.60; *War*, 2.175.

448 For more complete information, consult D. Bahat, *The Illustrated Atlas of Jerusalem*, (New York: Simon & Schuster, 1990), 16–19; E. Stern, ed., *The New Encyclopedia of Archaeological Excavations in the Holy Land*, (Jerusalem: Israel Exploration Society and Carta, 1993), 2.801–804; G. J. Wightman, *The Walls of Jerusalem: From the Canaanites to the Mamluks*, (Sydney: University of Sydney, 1993); cf. F. J. Bliss, *The Development of the Palestine Exploration Fund*, (New York: Charles Scribner's Sons, 1906).

449 Other notable early work in and around Jerusalem was conducted by individuals such as Niebuhr, Pococke, Bonomi, Catherwood, Arundale, and Clark. (See F. J. Bliss, *The Development of the Palestine Exploration Fund*, [New York: Charles Scribner's Sons, 1906], 137–183).

450 E. Robinson and E. Smith, *Biblical Researches in Palestine, and in the Adjacent Regions*, (Boston: Crocker and Brewster, 1868); *Later Biblical Researches in Palestine, and in the Adjacent Regions*, (Boston: Crocker and Brewster, 1871).

451 See F. J. Bliss, *The Development of the Palestine Exploration Fund*, (New York: Charles Scribner's Sons, 1906), 184–223.

452 The recent assertion that the Siloam tunnel and the inscription date to the Hasmonean period in the second century B.C. (J. Rogerson and P. R. Davies, "Was the Siloam Tunnel Built by Hezekiah?," *Biblical Archaeologist* 59/3, [1996], 138–149) has been effectively rebutted: paleographically, orthographically, philologically (R. S. Hendel, "The Date of the Siloam Inscription: A Rejoinder to Rogerson and Davies," *Biblical Archaeologist* 59/4, [1996], 233–237; J. Hackett et al., "Defusing Pseudo-Scholarship: The Siloam Inscription Ain't Hasmonean," *Biblical Archaeology Review* 23/2, [1997], 41–50, 68), geologically (D. Gill, "The Geology of the City of David and Its Ancient Subterranean Waterworks," in D. T. Ariel and A. DeGroot, eds., *Various Reports*, [Jerusalem: Hebrew University, 1996], 22), and radiometrically (A. Frumkin, A. Shimron, and J. Rosenbaum, "Radiometric dating of the Siloam Tunnel, Jerusalem," *Nature* 425/6954, [2003], 169–171). An in-depth analysis of the text itself may be found in K. L. Younger, Jr., "The Siloam Tunnel Inscription: an Integrated Reading," *Ugarit-Forschungen* 26 (1994), 543–556.

453 The logistics of cutting out this tunnel are discussed by S. Rosenberg ("The Siloam Tunnel Revisited," *Tel Aviv* 25/1, [1998], 116–130), though it continues to be debated whether the tunnelers were following a natural karstic crack in the rock, were being guided by acoustical communications from the surface, or were pursuing some other process.

454 The work of F. J. Bliss (*The Development of the Palestine Exploration Fund*, [New York: Charles Scribner's Sons, 1906]).

455 The Southeastern hill was again the subject of a campaign by Weill, of a team under the supervision of Macalister and Duncan, and of an expedition led by Crowfoot and Fitzgerald. From 1925 to 1927, Sukenik, Mayer, and Fisher discovered sections of the northern wall of Josephus.

456 Iliffe unearthed a cemetery, and Johns excavated the citadel at the Jaffa gate. John's unstinting efforts were rewarded with the discovery of walls and towers from the pre–Christian era. Just prior to World War II, Hamilton carried on work outside the northeastern wall near St. Stephen's gate; from 1949 to 1953, Testa conducted excavations at Bethphage.

457 These discoveries and other work has been conducted by Barkay, Broshi, Gill, Bahat, Mazar (e.g., E. Mazar, "The Solomonic Wall in Jerusalem," in A. M. Maeir and P. de Miroschedji, eds., *"I Will Speak the Riddles of Ancient Times": Archaeological and Historical Studies in Honor of Amihai Mazar*, [Winona Lake, Ind.: Eisenbrauns, 2006], 775–786; cf. J. Cahill, "Jerusalem in David and Solomon's Time," *Biblical Archaeology Review* 30/6, [2004], 20–31, 62–63), and Reich, Shukron, and the Israel Antiquities Authority (e.g., R. Reich and E. Shukron, "The History of the Gihon Spring in Jerusalem," *Levant* 36, [2004], 211–223; H. Shanks, "Everything You Ever Knew About Jerusalem Is Wrong (Well, Almost)," *Biblical Archaeology Review* 25/6, [1999], 20–35; cf. D. Ussishkin, "The Original Length of the Siloam Tunnel in Jerusalem," *Levant*, [1976], 82–95).

458 G. Auld and M. Steiner, *Jerusalem I: From the Bronze Age to the Maccabees*, (Cambridge: The Lutterworth Press, 1996), 22–33.

459 R. Reich and E. Shukron, "Light at the End of the Tunnel," *Biblical Archaeology Review* 25/1, (1999), 22–33, 72; H. Shanks, "Everything You Ever Knew About Jerusalem Is Wrong (Well, Almost)," *Biblical Archaeology Review* 25/6, [1999], 20–35.

460 L. Koehler and W. Baumgartner, eds., *The Hebrew and Aramaic Lexicon of the Old Testament*, (Leiden: Brill, 2001), 2.1038.

461 See A. Lemaire, "The United Monarchy: Saul, David and Solomon," in H. Shanks, ed., *Ancient Israel: A Short History from Abraham to the Roman Destruction of the Temple*, (Washington D.C.: Biblical Archaeology Society, 1988), 106–108; E. Mazar, "The Solomonic Wall in Jerusalem," in A. M. Maeir and P. de Miroschedji, eds., *"I Will Speak the Riddles of Ancient Times": Archaeological and Historical Studies in Honor of Amihai Mazar*, (Winona Lake, Ind.: Eisenbrauns, 2006), 775–786.

462 Remains of an early occupation of the northern section of the Southwestern hill (the so-called "broad wall") have been attributed by some writers to a Solomonic expansion to the west, though I consider this rather implausible and am more inclined to associate this wall with the westward expansion of Jerusalem in the time of Hezekiah (e.g., 2 Kings 22:14; 2 Chron. 32:5; 34:22). (See also N. Na`aman, "When and How Did Jerusalem Become a Great City? The Rise of Jerusalem as Judah's Premier City in the Eighth-Seventh Centuries B.C.E.," *Bulletin of the American Schools of Oriental Research* 347, [2007], 21–56.)

463 R. Seager, *Pompey the Great*, (Oxford: Blackwell Publishing, 2002), 58–59; D. Saddington, "The administration and the army in Judaea in the early Roman period (From Pompey to Vespasian, 63 B.C.—A.D. 79)," in M. Sharon, ed., *Pillars of Smoke and Fire: The Holy Land in History and Thought*, (Johannesburg: Southern Book Publishers Ltd., 1988), 33–35; S. J. D. Cohen, "Roman Domination: The Jewish Revolt and the Destruction of the Second Temple," in H. Shanks, ed., *Ancient Israel*, (Washington D.C.: Biblical Archaeology Society, 1988), 205–235.

464 Though Pompey had left Hyrcanus in charge of Jerusalem, three times in the next decade Aristobulus or his compatriots attempted to gain control. Throughout these assaults, Hyrcanus was supported by his Roman patron and a wily Idumean (Edomite) named Antipater. At the death of Pompey, Hyrcanus and Antipater aligned themselves with Rome and Julius Caesar, whereas a son of Aristobulus, Mattathias Antigonus, found a welcome embrace with the Parthians. When Caesar was assassinated in 44 B.C., Mark Antony established Antipater's two sons—Phasael and Herod—as tetrarchs of Judah (Josephus, *Antiquities of the Jews*, 14.324–326). But Roman preoccupation with political affairs outside Palestine provided Antigonus an opportunity. With the aid of the Parthians in 40 B.C., Antigonus attacked Jerusalem, forcing Phasael, Herod, and Antipater into a defensive posture. In an effort to negotiate a truce, Phasael and Hyrcanus journeyed to Galilee to meet the Parthian king. But they walked into a trap, and both were taken prisoner (Josephus, 14.337–348). When Herod discovered the treachery, he moved quickly into the fortress at Masada, on to Petra, and finally to Egypt (Josephus, 14.352–376). From there, Herod set sail for Rome where, through the patronage of Mark Antony, the Senate unanimously appointed him to the post of "king of the Jews."

465 Josephus, *Antiquities of the Jews*, 15.268; 15.317–322; 17.255; *War*, 2.44; 6.377.

466 *War*, 1.402.

467 D. M. Jacobson, "Herod's Roman Temple," *Biblical Archaeology Review* 28/2, (2002), 18–27, 60–61; E. Stern, ed., *The New Encyclopedia of Archaeological Excavations in the Holy Land*, (Jerusalem: Israel Exploration Society and Carta, 1993), 2.736–740; cf. Josephus, *Antiquities of the Jews*, 1.401ff.

468 The dimensions of Herod's temple were approximately 2,500 feet by 1,000 feet, with two concentric courts giving added dimension to the structure. The outer court (the "Court of the Gentiles") was the only area where non-Jews could enter. Archaeology has yielded up several Greek inscriptions warning Gentiles not to go beyond this court and transgress the inner court. [**See picture at map 112.**] The inner court had three subdivisions: one for women, one for men, and one for priests and Levites. Surrounding the Temple hill, a massive supporting wall was constructed, portions of which still stand today. A small section of the western perimeter of this wall is known today as the "western [wailing] wall." [For Herod's extensive architectural contributions throughout Judea, **see map 100.**]

469 *Declamationes minores* 274.

470 C. G. Gordon, "Eden and Golgotha," *Palestine Exploration Fund Quarterly Statement*, (1885), 78–81; reprinted in R. P. Gordon, *Holy Land, Holy City: Sacred Geography and the Interpretation of the Bible*, (Carlisle, U.K.: Paternoster, 2004), 127–133.

471 cf. G. Barkay and A. Kloner, "Jerusalem Tombs From the Days of the First Temple," *Biblical Archaeology Review* 12/2, (1986), 22–39.

472 J. Wilkinson, *Egeria's Travels to the Holy Land*, (Jerusalem: Ariel Publishing House, 1981), 36–46; Eusebius, *Onomasticon* § 365; cf. W. E. Rast, *Through the Ages in Palestinian Archaeology*, (Philadelphia: Trinity Press International, 1992), 170–172.

473 Hadrian's visit to Jerusalem is known both from classical writers (Epiphanius, *Weights and Measures*, 14.54c; Dio Cassius, *Roman History*, 69.12.1; cf. J. L. Sheler, *Is the Bible True? How Modern Debates and Discoveries Affirm the Essence of the Scriptures*, [New York: Harper SanFrancisco, 1999], 114–117; *Anchor Bible Dictionary*, 3.761–762) and from archaeological remains. His name appears on a block of stone that was apparently the base of a statue; it has been reused and placed upside down in the exterior southern wall of the Temple (D. Bahat, *The Illustrated Atlas of Jerusalem*, [New York: Simon & Schuster, 1990], 67). See **map 96** for other architecture commonly ascribed to Hadrian; see also E. Mazar, "Hadrian's Legion Encamped on the Temple Mount," *Biblical Archaeology Review* 32/6, (2006), 52–58, 82–83. This was the occasion when Hadrian renamed the city Aelia Capitolina, in honor of the Capitoline Jupiter. Roman coins minted just after that time sometimes bear the official Roman name of the city and depict an image of Jupiter on the reverse side (G. Vermes and F. Millar, *The History of the Jewish People in the Age of Jesus Christ (175 B.C.—A.D. 135)*, [Edinburgh: T. & T. Clark, 1973], 1.553–555). Dio Cassius also stated that while Hadrian was there, he erected on the former site of the Temple a new temple to Jupiter (Zeus) that, the writer added, led in due course to the second Jewish Revolt (A.D. 132–135); (cf. Jerome, *Commentary on Isaiah*, 1.2.9 [Corpus Christianorum Series Latina 73.33]).

474 so Eusebius, *Life of Constantine*, 3.26.

475 *Letter to Paulinus*, 58.3 (The Fathers of the Church 6.120).

476 Eusebius, *Life of Constantine*, 3.30–32; cf. W. H. C. Frend, *The Archaeology of Early Christianity*, (Minneapolis: Fortress Press, 1996), 2–5; J. Wilkinson, *Egeria's Travels to the Holy Land*, (Jerusalem: Ariel Publishing House, 1981), 164–165; J. Finegan, *The Archeology of the New Testament: The Life of Jesus and the Beginning of the Early Church*, (Princeton: Princeton University Press, 1969), 120–121, 163–165.

477 Eusebius, *Ecclesiastical History*, 4.5; cf. his tabular enumeration at index A.

478 Vespasian had stationed two legions at strategic points to keep Jerusalem isolated inside Judea (the 5th Legion Macedonica at Emmaus and the 10th Legion Fretensis at Jericho). Titus also mustered the 12th Legion Fulminata and the 15th Legion Apollinaris, and he had the support of a considerable body of Syrian auxiliaries, 2,000 handpicked troops from Alexandria, 3,000 from the Euphrates, plus a cadre of lancers, cavalry, mercenaries, siege engines, and a supply train.

479 Every major act of Titus in the year A.D. 70 is described in ample detail by Josephus, (*War*, 5.1; 5.39–46; 5.47–50; 7.17–20).

480 H. Geva, "Searching for Roman Jerusalem," *Biblical Archaeology Review* 23/6, (1997), 34–45, 72–73.

481 *War*, 7.17–20; E. Mazar, "Hadrian's Legion Encamped on the Temple Mount," *Biblical Archaeology Review* 32/6, (2006), 52–58, 82–83.

482 W. G. Sinnegen and C. A. Robinson, *Ancient History*, (New York: Macmillan Publishing Company, 1981), 373.

483 Eusebius, *Demonstratio Evangelica*, 3.7.139–140.

484 For a more detailed description of the development of the Roman Empire, consult G. Picard, *The Ancient Civilization of Rome*, (New York: Cowles Book Company, 1969); W. G. Sinnegen and C. A. Robinson, *Ancient History*, (New York: Macmillan Publishing Company, 1981); T. Cornell and J. Matthews, *Atlas of the Roman World*, (New York: Checkmark Books, 1982); J. Boardman, J. Griffin, and O. Murray, *The Oxford History of the Classical World*, (New York: Oxford University Press, 1986); M. Grant, *Atlas of Classical History*, (New York: Oxford University Press, 1994); N. Constable, *Historical Atlas of Ancient Rome*, (New York: Checkmark Books, 2003); and M. T. Boatwright, D. J. Gargola, and R. J. A. Talbert, *The Romans: From Village to Empire*, (New York: Oxford University Press, 2004).

485 It is sometimes alleged that Herod the Great was born at Ascalon/Ashkelon. Eusebius (*Ecclesiastical History*, 1.6.2–3) cites Julius Africanus to the effect that Herod's father, Antipas, had spent his childhood as a servant in the temple of Apollo in Ascalon. When Antipas was given reign over all of Idumea, he established very close trade relations between the Nabateans and the city of Ascalon (Josephus, *Antiquities of the Jews*, 14.10). Josephus (*War*, 1.422) also reports on baths, fountains, and colonnades Herod erected in Ascalon for the population there and that, upon his death, Herod bequeathed a palace in Ascalon to Augustus Caesar.

486 Josephus, *Antiquities of the Jews*, 14.385; *War*, 1.282–286.

487 Josephus, *Antiquities of the Jews*, 14.394–467.

488 During Herod's rule he successfully transferred his subservient loyalties from Mark Antony to Octavian, the nephew of Julius Caesar. (Octavian was later named "Augustus Caesar" by the Senate.) Antony had committed suicide in the immediate aftermath of the battle of Actium (cf. Josephus, *Antiquities of the Jews*, 15.161–164; 17.246; *War*, 1.386–397) when the Second Triumvirate was officially dissolved. At that point Octavian was acknowledged as the uncontested master of the whole Roman Empire, and Herod came to be known as his "friend and ally."

489 cf. Josephus, *Antiquities of the Jews*, 15.331–341; 16.136–141.

490 Josephus, *War*, 1.403.

491 Josephus, *Antiquities of the Jews*, 15.292–295.

492 V. H. Matthews, *Manners and Customs in the Bible*, (Peabody, Mass.: Hendrickson, 1988), 206–213; J. McRay, *Archaeology and the New Testament*, (Grand Rapids: Baker Book House, 1991), 91–149.

493 Josephus, *Antiquities of the Jews*, 17.317–320; *War*, 2.93–100.

494 Ethnarch ("governor") was a title of intermediate rank, lower than king and higher than tetrarch. The literal meaning of "tetrarch" was "ruler of a fourth part," but the term had come to mean "minor ruler" in a more general sense.

495 In this case, Herod's domain was divided into four parts: Archelaus was given half and each of his brothers was given a fourth (Josephus, *Antiquities of the Jews*, 17.318–319; *War*, 2.94–95). Matthew 2:22 and Josephus (*Antiquities of the Jews*, 18.93) loosely refer to Archelaus as "king"; Mark 6:14 and 6:26 offer the same description of Herod Antipas. It should also be noted that the cities of Azotus, Jamnia, and Phaselis inside Archelaus's domain were given to Herod's sister, Salome, under Archelaus's supervision (Josephus, *Antiquities of the Jews*, 17.321–323; *War*, 2.98). After Archelaus was removed by Augustus Caesar in A.D. 6 and banished to Gaul, Gaza and its suburbs were transferred to the proconsul of Syria.

496 Josephus, *Antiquities of the Jews*, 17.339–341; 18.36–38; *War*, 2.168.

497 Josephus, *Antiquities of the Jews*, 14.75–76; *War*, 1.155–157.

498 Josephus, *Antiquities of the Jews*, 15.351–360.

499 Josephus, *Antiquities of the Jews*, 17.320.

500 J. H. Moulton and G. Milligan, *The Vocabulary of the Greek Testament Illustrated from the Papyri and other Non-Literary Sources*, (Grand Rapids: Eerdmans, 1930), 329; H. Liddell, R. Scott, and H. S. Jones, *A Greek-English Lexicon*, (Oxford: Clarendon Press, 1968), 899; G. W. H. Lampe, *A Patristic Greek Lexicon*, (Oxford: Clarendon Press, 1961), 711.

501 cf. W. Bauer, W. F. Arndt, F. W. Gingrich, and F. W. Danker, *A Greek-English Lexicon of the New Testament*, (Chicago: University of Chicago Press, 1979), 612; H. Liddell, R. Scott, and H. S. Jones, *A Greek-English Lexicon*, (Oxford: Clarendon Press, 1968), 1296–1297; J. H. Moulton and G. Milligan, *The Vocabulary of the Greek Testament Illustrated from the Papyri and other Non-Literary Sources*, (Grand Rapids: Eerdmans, 1930), 476; G. W. H. Lampe, *A Patristic Greek Lexicon*, (Oxford: Clarendon Press, 1961), 1002; and notice the presence of an innkeeper (*pandoxeus*) who could supply food and care; cf. Josephus, *Antiquities of the Jews*, 8.41; and see LXX use in Job 6:5; 39:9; Isaiah 1:3.

502 W. Bauer, W.F. Arndt, F. W. Gingrich, and F. W. Danker, *A Greek-English Lexicon of the New Testament*, (Chicago: University of Chicago Press, 1979), 1050; J. H. Moulton and G. Milligan, *The Vocabulary of the Greek Testament Illustrated from the Papyri and other Non-Literary Sources*, (Grand Rapids: Eerdmans, 1930), 665; R. E. Brown, *The Birth of the Messiah: A Commentary on the infancy narratives in Matthew and Luke*, (Garden City, N.Y.: Image Books, 1979), 399; see G. A. Buttrick, ed., *The Interpreter's Dictionary of the Bible*, (New York: Abingdon Press, 1962), 3.257 for a picture of such a manger; at Lachish, a small cave beneath a private house contained a small masonry manger.

503 so *Protevangelium of James*, 18.1**;** see also Justin Martyr (*Dialogue with Trypho*, 78.5; cf. 70.1); Origen (*contra Celsum*, 1.51; *Commentary on the Gospel of Matthew*, 10:17); Jerome (*Ep. 108.12, ad Eustochium Virginem; Homily 88, On the Nativity of the Lord*).

504 so Jerome (*Ep. 58.3, ad Paulinum*); D. Baldi, *Enchiridion Locorum Sanctorum. Documenta S. Evangelii Loca Respicientia*, (Jerusalem: Franciscan Printing Press, 1982), 83–91; E. Stern, ed., *The New Encyclopedia of Archaeological Excavations in the Holy Land*, (Jerusalem: Israel Exploration Society and Carta, 1993), 1.204–205; P. W. L. Walker, *Holy City, Holy Places? Christian Attitudes to Jerusalem and the Holy Land in the Fourth Century*, (Oxford: Clarendon Press, 1990), 181–184; cf. Hadrian's similar actions at Jerusalem.

505 *contra Celsum* 1.51.

506 cf. D. Baldi, *Enchiridion Locorum Sanctorum. Documenta S. Evangelii Loca Respicientia*, (Jerusalem: Franciscan Printing Press, 1982), 91.

507 See J. Wilkinson, *Jerusalem Pilgrimage 1099—1185*, (London: Hakluyt Society, 1988), 72–73.

508 According to the early travels of Egeria (J. Wilkinson, *Egeria's Travels to the Holy Land*, [Jerusalem: Ariel Publishing House, 1981], 110–111, but see 161) and the Medeba map (H. Donner, *The Mosaic Map of Madaba*, [Kampen: Kok Pharos Publishing House, 1992], map and 37), Aenon was situated about eight miles south of Scythopolis (opposite the outflow of the W. Yabis), where some lush springs of ed-Der rise near T. Sheikh Salim (so D. Baldi, *Enchiridion Locorum Sanctorum. Documenta S. Evangelii Loca Respicientia*, [Jerusalem: Franciscan Printing Press, 1982], 215–217). Moreover, the copper scroll of Qumran (3Q15.12.6) describes an Essene group that practiced baptism, which settled near this place (cf. Discoveries in the Judaean Desert, 4.262; B. Pixner, "Unravelling the Copper Scroll Code: a Study on the Topography of 3Q15," *Revue de Qumran* 11/3, [1983], 335–338, 357–361).

509 *Anchor Bible Dictionary*, 1.703–705.

510 In his *Commentary on the Gospel of John* (The Fathers of the Church 80.6.204–206; cf. 89.13.455), Origen even offered an etymological defense for his point of view. (Origen's assertion influenced the translations of the *KJV* and the *NKJV*.)

511 A site known as Bethabara is known from the sixth-century Medeba mosaic map (H. Donner, *The Mosaic Map of Madaba*, [Kampen: Kok Pharos Publishing House, 1992], map and 38); that site was located contiguous to the western bank of the Jordan, not far from the Dead Sea.

512 R. G. Khouri, "Where John Baptized: Bethany beyond the Jordan," *Biblical Archaeology Review* 31/1, (2005), 34–43.

513 This is the view espoused by D. A. Carson, *The Gospel According to John*, (Grand Rapids: Eerdmans, 2000), 167–168; R. W. Yarbrough, *John*, Everyman's Bible Commentary, (Chicago: Moody Press, 1991), 29; E. Haenchen, *A Commentary on the Gospel of John, Chapters 1–6*, Hermeneia, (Philadelphia: Fortress, 1980), 172; C. K. Barrett, *The Gospel According to St. John*, (Philadelphia: Westminster Press, 1978), 189–190; L. Morris, *The Gospel According to John*, The New International Commentary on the New Testament, (Grand Rapids: Eerdmans Publishing Company, 1971), 177; R. E. Brown, *The Gospel According to John (i–xii)*, Anchor Bible, (Garden City, N.Y.: Doubleday & Company, 1966), 97; E. F. Harrison, *John: The Gospel of Faith*, (Chicago: Moody Press, 1962), 21; W. Hendrickson, *Exposition of the Gospel According to John*, (Grand Rapids: Baker Book House, 1953), 113.

514 Josephus, *Life*, 52; see J. Wilkinson, *Jerusalem Pilgrimage 1099—1185*, (London: Hakluyt Society, 1988), 154.

515 Batanea is the Hellenized transliteration of the Aramaic spelling of the Hebrew name Bashan; so W. H. Brownlee, "Whence the Gospel According to John?," in J. H. Charlesworth, ed., *John and Qumran*, (London: Geoffrey Chapman, 1972), 169; cf. *Anchor Bible Dictionary*, 1.704; L. Koehler and W. Baumgartner, eds., *The Hebrew and Aramaic Lexicon of the Old Testament*, (Leiden: Brill, 2001), 1.165. The proto–Semitic phoneme /θ/ appears in Hebrew as a /š/ but in Aramaic as a /t/ (so A. F. Rainey, "The Toponymics of Eretz-Israel," *Bulletin of the American Schools of Oriental Research* 231, [1978], 9).

516 LXX: *peran toû Iordanou*; cf. Josephus, *Antiquities of the Jews*, 8.37; In the Old Testament, the expression "beyond the Jordan" may denote territory east of the Jordan River (e.g., Num. 34:15; Deut. 4:49; 32:32; Josh. 1:14; 2:10; 9:10; 13:8; 18:7) or west of the Jordan (e.g., Gen. 50:10–11; Num. 32:19; Deut. 3:20; Josh. 5:1; 9:1; 12:7; 22:7; Isa. 9:1), often but not always depending on the perspective of the narrator; see also M. H. Woudstra, *The Book of Joshua*, The New International Commentary on the Old Testament, (Grand Rapids: Eerdmans, 1981), 153–154.

517 For a similar viewpoint, refer to W. R. Wilson, *Travels in The Holy Land, Egypt*, (London: Longman, Brown, Green, and Longmans, 1847), 2.31–32; C. Kopp, *The Holy Places of the Gospels*, (New York: Herder and Herder, 1963), 129–137; W. H. Brownlee, "Whence the Gospel According to John?," in J. H. Charlesworth, ed., *John and Qumran*, (London: Geoffrey Chapman, 1972), 168–173; R. Riesner, "Bethany beyond the Jordan (John 1:28)," *Tyndale Bulletin* 38, (1987), 29–63; P. Lawrence, *The IVP Atlas of Bible History*, (Downers Grove, Ill.: InterVarsity Press, 2006), 139; *Anchor Bible Dictionary*, 1.703–705.

518 so Josephus, *Antiquities of the Jews*, 18.119; cf. C. Ritter, *The Comparative Geography of Palestine and the Sinaitic Peninsula*, (New York: Greenwood Press, 1968), 3.70–71; 4.322.

519 See J. Wilkinson, *Egeria's Travels to the Holy Land*, (Jerusalem: Ariel Publishing House, 1981), 201.

520 *Anchor Bible Dictionary*, 1.868; J. McRay, *Archaeology and the New Testament*, (Grand Rapids: Baker Book House, 1991), 70–72 (cf. Mark 1:21; Luke 7:2–5).

521 V. Corbo, *The House of Saint Peter at Capharnaum*, Publications of the Studium Biblicum Franciscanum 5, (Jerusalem: Franciscan Printing Press, 1969), 53–69**;** *Anchor Bible Dictionary*, 1.867–868; E. Stern, ed., *The New Encyclopedia of Archaeological Excavations in the Holy Land*, (Jerusalem: Israel Exploration Society and Carta, 1993), 1.295; J. Wilkinson, *Egeria's Travels to the Holy Land*, (Jerusalem: Ariel Publishing House, 1981), 194–196.

522 W. D. Davies, *The Gospel and the Land: Early Christianity and Jewish Territorial Doctrine*, (Berkeley: University of California Press, 1974), 235–236; although refer to Jerome *Commentary on Isaiah* 9:1 (Patrologia Latina 24.125 §130) for an early Christian tradition that the Messiah would appear in Galilee.

523 E. M. Meyers and L. M. White, "Jews and Christians in a Roman World," *Archaeology* 42/2, (1989), 32–33**;** *Anchor Bible Dictionary*, 2.242–243; H. T. Frank, *Bible, Archaeology and Faith*, (New York: Abingdon Press, 1971), 306–307; W. H. C. Frend, *The Archaeology of Early Christianity*, (Minneapolis: Fortress Press, 1996), 198–199; Tatian's *Diatessaron*; J. McRay, *Archaeology and the New Testament*, (Grand Rapids: Baker Book House, 1991), 354.

524 The view of Clement of Alexandria (*Stromata*, 1.21) and Origen (*De principiis*, 4.5; cf. *contra Celsum*, 2.12; cf. *Homilies on Luke*, 32.5).

525 The view of Irenaeus (*Adversus haereses*, 2.22.5–6).

526 e.g., D. A. Carson and D. J. Moo, *An Introduction to the New Testament*, (Grand Rapids: Zondervan, 2005), 125–126.

527 e.g., H. Hoehner, *Chronological Aspects of the Life of Christ*, (Grand Rapids: Zondervan, 1977), 55–63.

528 Josephus, *Antiquities of the Jews*, 20.118.

529 Consult also Josephus, *Life*, 52, and see the same road used by various medieval pilgrims, so J. Wilkinson, *Jerusalem Pilgrimage 1099—1185*, (London: Hakluyt Society, 1988), 110–111, 230, 238.

530 Only a few years later, a bloody and protracted incident took place at Ginae between Samaritans and Jewish pilgrims intending to go to Jerusalem (Josephus, *Antiquities of the Jews*, 20.118–136). The incident is indicative of the hostilities that sometimes existed between Samaritans and Jewish pilgrims, and it illustrates why pilgrims normally traveled in caravan style (Luke 2:44).

531 It has sometimes been suggested that such an alternative route would have allowed Jesus and his disciples to pass completely beyond Samaritan territory and cross the Jordan River for passage through the safer environs of Jewish Perea to Jerusalem (e.g., G. C. Morgan, *The Gospel According to John*, [London: Fleming H. Revell Company, 1933], 71). This view, however, is based on an extremely broad and general interpretation of John 4:9, tellingly belied in the text by Jesus' own involvement with the woman from Sychar (cf. Luke 17:11–19). In any event, the Rift Valley roadway lay beyond the Samaritan highlands and was effectively out of Samaria. Moreover, this route would have avoided the strenuous and perilous task of crossing the Jordan River twice on a one-way journey. Finally, the Rift Valley road is clearly documented and was well known throughout the Roman period. (See I. Roll, "The Roman Road System in Judaea," *The Jerusalem Cathedra* 3, [1983], 136–161; Y. Tsafrir, L. Di Segni, and J. Green, *Tabula Imperii Romani: Iudaea, Palaestina*, [Jerusalem: Israel Academy of Sciences and Humanities, 1994], maps.) No corresponding road existed along the entire eastern stretches of the Jordan valley as far south as the vicinity of Jericho.

532 e.g., Ignatius, *Tralles*, 9.2; Polycarp, *Philippians*, 2.2; Irenaeus, *Adversus haereses*, 1.10.1; 3.4.2; Aristides, *Apology*; Tertullian, *De praescriptione haereticorum*, 13.4; *Adversus Praxean* 2.1; *De virginibus velandis* 1.3; Origen, *De principiis*, 1.4; cf. early church councils beginning with Nicaea in A.D. 325; see J. Pelikan and V. Hotchkiss, *Creeds & Confessions of Faith in the Christian Tradition*, (New Haven: Yale University Press, 2003), 1.37–154.

533 A. Millard, *Discoveries from the Time of Jesus*, (Oxford: Lion Publishing, 1990), 134–135.

534 Josephus, *Antiquities of the Jews*, 4.219.

535 According to Josephus (*War*, 2.150–166; *Antiquities of the Jews*, 18.12–22), Pharisees subscribed to the doctrine of the bodily resurrection of the righteous, unlike either the Sadducees, who maintained that both soul and body perish at death, or the Essenes who held, in effect, to the immortality of the soul, following Greek thought (Mark 12:18–27; Acts 23:6–8).

536 Recognition of selectivity in the Pentecost account has led numerous New Testament scholars to relate Luke's list to an ancient astrological treatise of Paulus Alexandrinus having to do with the twelve signs of the zodiac, thus suggesting a worldwide outlook at Pentecost. For a description and critique of this viewpoint, see B. M. Metzger, "Ancient Astrological Geography and Acts 2:9–11," in W. W. Gasque and R. P. Martin, eds., *Apostolic History and the Gospel*, (Grand Rapids: Eerdmans, 1970), 123–133.

537 The strongest manuscript evidence at Acts 8:5 supports the reading, "*the* city of Samaria" (see F. F. Bruce, *The Book of Acts*, The New International Commentary on the New Testament, [Grand Rapids: Eerdmans, 1988], 163 n.17; B. M. Metzger, *A Textual Commentary on the Greek New Testament*, [New York: United Bible Societies, 1975], 355–356), not just any city in the region of Samaria. According to Justin Martyr (*First Apologia*, 26) Simon Magus hailed from the Samarian town of Gitta (T. Gatt?), about 11 miles northwest of Sebaste, and hence for him this event transpired there, not at Sebaste.

538 I. Roll, "The Roman Road System in Judaea," *The Jerusalem Cathedra* 3, (1983), 139–141; Y. Tsafrir, L. Di Segni, and J. Green, *Tabula Imperii Romani: Iudaea, Palaestina*, (Jerusalem: Israel Academy of Sciences and Humanities, 1994), 118–119, maps; cf. Peutinger map depicts a road running southwest from Jerusalem, past Betogabris, and on to the coastal plain.

539 Y. Rapuano, "Did Philip Baptize the Eunuch at Ein Yael?," *Biblical Archaeology Review* 16/6, (1990), 44–49.

540 E. Robinson and E. Smith (*Biblical Researches in Palestine, and in the Adjacent Regions*, [Boston: Crocker and Brewster, 1868], 2.46–48; *Later Biblical Researches in Palestine, and in the Adjacent Regions*, [Boston: Crocker and Brewster, 1871], 3.278) and F. F. Bruce (*The Book of Acts*, The New International Commentary on the New Testament, [Grand Rapids: Eerdmans, 1988], 177, but he wrongly located the springs at a point northeast of Gaza.) A very rich Christian tradition also exists that locates the baptismal site at Beth-zur, about five miles north of Hebron (so Eusebius, *Onomasticon* 52.1; Bordeaux Pilgrim [J. Wilkinson, *Egeria's Travels to the Holy Land*, (Jerusalem: Ariel Publishing House, 1981), 162]; Peter the Deacon [Wilkinson, 188]; Medeba map [H. Donner, *The Mosaic Map of Madaba*, (Kampen: Kok Pharos Publishing House, 1992), 26, map]). While plausible, this location is geographically improbable because of difficult routing implications inherent in a road from Jerusalem, past Beth-zur, to Gaza. It would require the eunuch to take either a circuitous roundabout from Hebron back up to Marisa or, worse yet, to follow the road south from Hebron to Beersheba, and then go northwest as far as Gaza. It would seem that, in either event, someone traveling by carriage on the central ridge road as far south as Hebron, en route to Egypt, would most likely have continued an essentially southward course past Beersheba and beyond, via the Way to Shur, directly into Egypt. **[See map 34.]**

541 For estimated miles based on roadway configuration, see E. M. Yamauchi, "On the Road with Paul," *Christian History* 14/3, (1995), 18 [17,285 miles]; E. Schnabel, *Early Christian Mission*, (Leicester, England: Apollos, 2004), 1288 [15,500 miles]; refer also to R. Jewett, *A Chronology of Paul's Life*, (Philadelphia: Fortress Press, 1979), 59–61 [the outbound leg of Paul's second journey as far as Corinth totals approximately 1820 miles, taking him an estimated 68 actual travel days]; J. Murphy-O'Connor, "On the Road and on the Sea with St. Paul," *Bible Review* 1/1, (1985), 41.

542 Early indications that Paul actually traveled to Spain include 1 Clement 5:1–7 ("Paul reached the farthest bounds of the west"); the *Muratorian Canon* ("Luke tells 'the excellent Theophilus' that the various incidents took place in his presence, and indeed he makes this quite clear by omitting the passion of Peter, as well as Paul's journey when he set out from Rome to Spain"); and the *Acts of Peter* (see E. Hennecke and W. Schneemelcher, eds., *New Testament Apocrypha*, [Philadelphia: Westminster Press, 1964], 2.279–287; cf. F. F. Bruce, *Paul: Apostle of the Heart Set Free*, [Grand Rapids: Eerdmans, 1977], 446–450). Paul's journey to Spain was later taken as historical fact by both John Chrysostom, an early bishop of Constantinople (*Homilies on Matthew 75.2; Homilies on 1 Corinthians* 13.6; *Homilies on 2 Timothy* [2 Tim. 4:20]; *Homilies on Hebrews*, Argument 2), and by Jerome (*De uiris illustribus*, 5; O. F. A. Meinardus, *St. Paul's Last Journey*, [New Rochelle, N.Y.: Caratzas Brothers, 1979], 126; F. F. Bruce, *Paul: Apostle of the Heart Set Free*, [Grand Rapids: Eerdmans, 1977], 449). If Paul did make it to Spain, what he would have met is nicely described in J. S. Richardson, *The Romans in Spain*, (Cambridge, Mass.: Blackwell Publishers, 1996).

543 If one were to follow the historically more probable post-imprisonment itineraries of Paul proposed by G. D. Fee (*1 and 2 Timothy, Titus*, New International Biblical Commentary, [Peabody, Mass.: Hendrickson Publishers, 1988], 3–5) or F. F. Bruce (*Paul: Apostle of the Heart Set Free*, [Grand Rapids: Eerdmans, 1977], 446–448), an approximate total of 2,750 airline miles would have been traveled.

544 e.g., Hattušili I, Muršili I, Sea Peoples, Ashurbanipal, Cyrus the Younger, Alexander the Great, various Seleucid kings, Vespasian in A.D. 67, Trajan, many Christian pilgrims (Egeria, Pilgrim of Bordeaux), Abu Bakr, many Crusaders, Suleiman the Magnificent.

545 R. R. Hann, "Judaism and Jewish Christianity in Antioch: Charisma and Conflict in the First Century," *Journal of Religious History* 14/4, (1987), 341–343; J. M. Wagstaff, *The Evolution of Middle Eastern Landscapes: An Outline to A.D. 1840*, (Totowa, N.J.: Barnes & Noble Books, 1985), 134; cf. note the prominent place accorded Antioch on the Peutinger map, from the Roman period (K. Nebenzahl, *Maps of the Holy Land: Images of* Terra Sancta *through Two Millennia*, [New York: Abbeville Press, 1986], 20–21); Antioch's port—Seleucia Pieria—some 25 miles downstream and also constructed by Seleucus—came to acquire its own political, commercial, and military significance.

546 W. A. Meeks and R. L. Wilken, *Jews and Christians in Antioch in the First Four Centuries of the Common Era*, (Ann Arbor, Mich.: Scholars Press, 1978), 1–52; cf. Josephus, *War*, 7.44–45.

547 Josephus, *Antiquities of the Jews*, 12.119–124; *War*, 12.100–115.

548 cf. Acts 6:5; Josephus, *War*, 7.43–46.

549 This is the sort of detail unlikely to have been invented by Luke (so W. A. Meeks and R. L. Wilken, *Jews and Christians in Antioch in the First Four Centuries of the Common Era*, [Ann Arbor, Mich.: Scholars Press, 1978], 15–16). Initially, "Christian(s)" appears to have been a term applied to believers by non-believers (Acts 11:26; 26:28). Tacitus [*Annals*, 15.44] relates how Nero, in an attempt to deflect attention away from his own pyromaniacal act, blamed "Christians" for starting the fire that ravaged Rome. Euodius, the first bishop of Antioch, was apparently the first believer to use "Christian(s)" as a designation for the new entity, beyond Jews and Gentiles (refer to A.S. von Stauffenberg, *Die Römische Kaisergeschichte bei Malalas*, [Stuttgart: W. Kohlhammer, 1931], 25 [§247.2]; cf. E. Jeffreys, M. Jeffreys, and R. Scott, *The Chronicle of John Malalas: A Translation*, [Melbourne: University of Sydney, 1986], 131). Ignatius, the second bishop of Antioch, seems to be the first person to have used the word "Christianity" (*christianismos*; see *Romans*, 3.3; *Magnesians*, 10.1.3 [twice]; *Philadelphia*, 6.1; cf. *Ante-Nicene Fathers*, 1.182–183, 210–211). Ignatius also employed the word "Christian" (*christianos*) both as a noun (e.g., *Romans*, 3.2; *Magnesians*, 4.1; *Polycarp*, 7.3) and as an adjective (e.g., *Tralles*, 6.1; cf. *Didache*, 12.4; Theophilus [an early bishop of Antioch] *Ad Autolycum*, 1.1, 12). Another designation of early believers, employed both as a self-designation and by outsiders, was "the Way" or "followers of the Way" (Acts 9:2; 19:9, 23; 22:4; 24:14, 22). In early Islam, the expression "people of the Book" was often used to denote Christians.

550 cf. Pliny, *Natural History*, 5.130, as over against the nearby Phoenician port of Old Paphos (Strabo 14.6.3).

551 It is not even certain Paul took a single route, as Cyprus contained at least 15 towns at the time (Pliny, *Natural History*, 5.130).

552 In peaceable districts, called "senatorial provinces," no Roman troops were deployed and rule was maintained by a "proconsul,"

who was responsible to the Senate. In more troublesome districts, called "imperial provinces," troops were deployed and rule was maintained by a legate ("governor"), who was responsible directly to the Emperor.

553 For a possible identification of Sergius Paulus of Acts with a Lucius Sergius Paulus found on several early Latin inscriptions, refer most recently to R. Riesner, *Paul's Early Period: Chronology, Mission Strategy, Theology*, (Grand Rapids: Eerdmans, 1998), 137–146; E. J. Schnabel, *Early Christian Mission*, (Leicester, England: Apollos, 2004), 1084–1089.

554 Strabo (14.4.2) located the harbor at Perga about seven miles inland, up the Cestrus River, where there was an Artemis temple perhaps as significant as the one at Ephesus. Nearby was a stadium almost 800 feet long and a large theater to accommodate some 14,000 people. The *Acts of Barnabas* (Ante-Nicene Fathers, 8.493b) indicates that Paul had a two-month stay in Perga.

555 See D. French, *Roman Roads and Milestones of Asia Minor*, BAR International Series 329 (i, ii), (London: British Institute of Archaeology at Ankara, 1988), maps 5, 8; R. J. A. Talbert, ed., *Barrington Atlas of the Greek and Roman World*, (Princeton: Princeton University Press, 2000), maps 62, 65; W. M. Calder and G. E. Bean, *A Classical Map of Asia Minor*, (London: British Institute of Archaeology at Ankara, 1957), map; D. French, "Acts and the Roman Roads of Asia Minor," in D. W. J. Gill and C. Gempf, eds., *The Book of Acts in Its Graeco-Roman Setting*, (Grand Rapids: Eerdmans, 1994), 50–52; S. Mitchell and M. Waelkens, *Pisidian Antioch: The Site and its Monuments*, (London: Gerald Duckworth & Company, 1998), 2–4.

556 Technically speaking, this Antioch was not in the province of Pisidia (contra Ptolemy, *Geography*, 5.5.4 and see Asia map 1; Pliny, *Natural History*, 5.24.94) but was rather in Phrygia Galatica near Pisidia (cf. Strabo 12.6.4; 12.8.14). However, since there was already another Antioch in Phrygia (Antiochia ad Maeandrum, see R. J. A. Talbert, ed., *Barrington Atlas of the Greek and Roman World*, [Princeton: Princeton University Press, 2000], map 65 [A2]), this city became known as "Antioch in/of/by/toward Pisidia." Eighteen different "Antiochs" were founded in the Seleucid era, of which nine were situated in Asia Minor (cf. I. H. Marshall, *The Acts of the Apostles*, Tyndale New Testament Commentaries, [Grand Rapids: Eerdmans, 1980], 222).

557 At Iconium the Via Sebaste split: one branch ran almost due east and came to the Via Taurus and the Cilician Gates [**map 89**], and the other branch veered south from Iconium and came to the site of Lystra, where it bent southeast and passed several sites, including Laranda and Derbe (Kerti Hüyük, not Devrişehir), before it converged with the more northerly leg that stretched from Iconium directly toward the Cilician Gates (D. French, *Roman Roads and Milestones of Asia Minor*, BAR International Series 329 [i, ii], [London: British Institute of Archaeology at Ankara, 1988], maps 2, 5, 8; R. J. A. Talbert, ed., *Barrington Atlas of the Greek and Roman World*, [Princeton: Princeton University Press, 2000], maps 65, 66; W. M. Calder and G. E. Bean, *A Classical Map of Asia Minor*, [London: British Institute of Archaeology at Ankara, 1957], map; S. Mitchell and M. Waelkens, *Pisidian Antioch: The Site and its Monuments*, [London: Gerald Duckworth & Company, 1998], 2–4).

558 Ovid (*Metamorphoses*, 8.620–719) relates an early first-century story in which Zeus and Hermes (son of Zeus and grandson of Atlas) disguised themselves as mortals, went to the province of Phrygia, and took up residence with an elderly couple who were very poor but who nevertheless generously lavished upon their guests several courses of rich food and drink. But when an empty bowl on their table miraculously kept refilling itself with wine and the couple's interest was piqued, the two gods revealed their true identity and explained why they had really come to visit (cf. J. L. Kelso, *An Archaeologist Follows the Apostle Paul*, [Waco: Word Books, 1970], 48; see also C. J. Hemer, *The Book of Acts in the Setting of Hellenistic History*, Wissenschaftliche Untersuchungen zum Neuen Testament 49, [Tübingen: J. C. B. Mohr, 1989], 111, n. 24).

559 The earlier inscription was discovered on the site, making reference to the "people of Derbe" (M. Ballance, "The Site of Derbe; A New Inscription," *Anatolian Studies* 7, [1957], 147–151). The latter reads "Michael, bishop of Derbe," and was found on Kerti Hüyük by local residents who carried it to another site about two and a half miles away (B. van Elderen, "Some Archaeological Observations on Paul's Second Missionary Journey," in W. W. Gasque and R. P. Martin, eds., *Apostolic History and the Gospel*, [Grand Rapids: Eerdmans, 1970], 156–161; cf. *The International Standard Bible Encyclopedia* 1.924–925).

560 For evidence of a Roman road connecting Perga and Attalia, see R. J. A. Talbert, ed., *Barrington Atlas of the Greek and Roman World*, (Princeton: Princeton University Press, 2000), map 65; D. French, "Acts and the Roman Roads of Asia Minor," in D. W. J. Gill and C. Gempf, eds., *The Book of Acts in Its Graeco-Roman Setting*, (Grand Rapids: Eerdmans, 1994), map 5.

561 Diodorus 17.32.2; Arrian 2.5.1; Pliny, *Natural History*, 5.91; Strabo 12.2.9.

562 For the road system across Asia Minor, see D. French, "The Roman Road-system of Asia Minor," in H. Temporini and W. Haase, eds., *Aufstieg und Niedergang der Römischen Welt*, (Berlin: Walter de Gruyter, 1980), 698–729; R. J. A. Talbert, ed., *Barrington Atlas of the Greek and Roman World*, (Princeton: Princeton University Press, 2000), maps 56, 61–62, 65. About 100 years prior to Paul, Cicero had marched a Roman army across essentially this same terrain, but in the opposite direction, from Ephesus to Tarsus. Cicero's trip took an estimated total of five months, and the orator described his journey as "difficult" and passing over "hot and dusty roads" (*Epistulae ad Atticum*, 107–120 [5.14–6.7]; *Epistulae ad familiares*, 103, 105 [15.2–3]).

563 adopting the terminology of D. French, "The Roman Road-system of Asia Minor," in H. Temporini and W. Haase, eds., *Aufstieg und Niedergang der Römischen Welt*, (Berlin: Walter de Gruyter, 1980), 703.

564 D. French, *Roman Roads and Milestones of Asia Minor*, BAR International Series 329 (i, ii), (London: British Institute of Archaeology at Ankara, 1988), maps 7–8, 10; R.J.A. Talbert, ed. *Barrington Atlas of the Greek and Roman World*, (Princeton: Princeton University Press, 2000), maps 52, 62; W. M. Calder and G. E. Bean, *A Classical Map of Asia Minor*, (London: British Institute of Archaeology at Ankara, 1957), map; D. French, "Acts and the Roman Roads of Asia Minor," in D. W. J. Gill and C. Gempf, eds., *The Book of Acts in Its Graeco-Roman Setting*, (Grand Rapids: Eerdmans, 1994), 53–54; S. Mitchell, *Anatolia: Land, Men, and Gods in Asia Minor*, (Oxford: Clarendon Press, 1993), maps 2–4, 6–8.

565 W. M. Ramsay, *St. Paul the Traveller and the Roman Citizen*, (London: Hodder and Stoughton, 1897), 200–205. According to this theory, Luke had been practicing medicine (Col. 4:14) in Philippi and, either hearing of the apostle's arrival at Troas or by prior arrangement, he met Paul and pleaded with him to bring the gospel to Europe. F. F. Bruce (*The Book of Acts*, The New International Commentary on the New Testament, [Grand Rapids: Eerdmans, 1988], 308; *Commentary on the Book of Acts*, The New International Commentary on the New Testament, [Grand Rapids: Eerdmans, 1971], 328) argues that Luke was practicing medicine in Troas.

566 On the second missionary journey, Luke joined Paul at Troas and stayed behind when Paul left Philippi (Acts 16:10–17). On the third missionary journey, Luke joined Paul upon his return to Philippi and traveled as far as Assos; at Assos Luke traveled by ship whereas Paul traveled overland to Troas, where they were reunited and traveled by ship to Caesarea and then overland to Jerusalem (20:5—21:18). And on Paul's journey from Caesarea to Rome, Luke accompanied him the whole way (Acts 27:1—28:16).

567 R. J. A. Talbert, ed., *Barrington Atlas of the Greek and Roman World*, (Princeton: Princeton University Press, 2000), maps 49–52.

568 But see E. J. Schnabel, *Early Christian Mission*, (Leicester, England: Apollos, 2004), 1153.

569 F. F. Bruce, *The Book of Acts*, The New International Commentary on the New Testament, (Grand Rapids: Eerdmans, 1988), 311; C. J. Hemer, *The Book of Acts in the Setting of Hellenistic History*, Wissenschaftliche Untersuchungen zum Neuen Testament 49, (Tübingen: J. C. B. Mohr, 1989), 114–115.

570 The Roman marketplace at Philippi and the foundations of the judgment seat (*bēma*) can still be seen today.

571 Amphipolis figured prominently in the fifth- to fourth-century B.C. Peloponnesian Wars. A fifth-century B.C. wooden bridge still spans the Strymon River. Alexander the Great erected a large stone lion monument at Amphipolis to mark the grave of more than 250 of his men who had died nearby at the battle of Chaeronea (E. M. Sanford, *The Mediterranean World in Ancient Times*, [New York: Ronald Press Company, 1951], 220–223, 277–281).

572 M. Grant, *The Ancient Mediterranean*, (London: Weidenfeld and Nicolson, 1969), 305–306; cf. R. J. A. Talbert, ed., *Barrington Atlas of the Greek and Roman World*, (Princeton: Princeton University Press, 2000), map 50.

573 It appears that Silas and Timothy temporarily rejoined Paul in Athens (1 Thess. 3:1), from where Timothy was dispatched back to Thessalonica (1 Thess. 3:2) and Silas was sent elsewhere in Macedonia (Acts 18:5), perhaps to Philippi. Paul apparently stayed alone in Athens (1 Thess. 3:1) and later traveled to Corinth, where both Silas and Timothy eventually rejoined the apostle (Acts 18:5; 1 Thess. 3:6).

574 W. Bauer, W. F. Arndt, F. W. Gingrich, and F. W. Danker, *A Greek-English Lexicon of the New Testament*, (Chicago: University of Chicago Press, 1979), 937; J. H. Moulton and G. Milligan, *The Vocabulary of the Greek Testament Illustrated from the Papyri and other Non-Literary Sources*, (Grand Rapids: Eerdmans, 1930), 583; cf. G. W. H. Lampe, *A Patristic Greek Lexicon*, (Oxford: Clarendon Press, 1961), 1249.

575 Eusebius (*Ecclesiastical History*, 4.23) recorded that Dionysius became the first bishop of Athens, and O. F. A. Meinardus (*St. Paul in Greece*, [New Rochelle, N.Y.: Caratzas Brothers, 1979], 57) indicated that he suffered martyrdom during the Domitian persecutions toward the end of the first century.

576 Strabo 8.6.20: Cenchreae on the Aegean (cf. Acts 18:18; Rom. 16:1, written from Corinth), Lechaion on the Adriatic (cf. Strabo 8.6.22; Diodorus 22.8.6).

577 Strabo 8.6.20.

578 H. Liddell, R. Scott, and H. S. Jones, *A Greek-English Lexicon*, (Oxford: Clarendon Press, 1968), 981; Strabo 8.6.20.

579 Suetonius, *Life of Claudius*, 25.4; cf. J. Finegan, *Handbook of Biblical Chronology*, (Princeton: Princeton University Press, 1964), 319; C. J. Hemer, *The Book of Acts in the Setting of Hellenistic History*, Wissenschaftliche Untersuchungen zum Neuen Testament 49, (Tübingen: J. C. B. Mohr, 1989), 167–168.

580 E. J. Schnabel, *Early Christian Mission*, (Leicester, England: Apollos, 2004), 46; R. Riesner, *Paul's Early Period: Chronology, Mission Strategy, Theology*, (Grand Rapids: Eerdmans, 1998), 193–211; F. F. Bruce, *The Book of Acts*, The New International Commentary on the New Testament, (Grand Rapids: Eerdmans, 1988), 352n. 38; F. F. Bruce, *New Testament History*, (Garden City, N.Y.: Doubleday & Company, 1980), 297–299; R. Jewett, *A Chronology of Paul's Life*, (Philadelphia: Fortress Press, 1979), 38–40.

581 D. A. Carson and D. J. Moo, *An Introduction to the New Testament*, (Grand Rapids: Zondervan, 2005), 367.

582 R. Laurence, *The Roads of Roman Italy*, (London and New York: Routledge, 1999), 41, 52–54.

583 so J. McRay, *Archaeology and the New Testament*, (Grand Rapids: Baker Book House, 1991), 331.

584 Refer to the detailed discussion of G.Theissen, *The Social Setting of Pauline Christianity*, (Philadelphia: Fortress Press, 1982), 75–83; cf. D. J. Moo, *The Epistle to the Romans*, The New International Commentary on the New Testament, (Grand Rapids: Eerdmans, 1996), 936; but see D. W. J. Gill, "Acts and the Urban Élites," in D. W. J. Gill and C. Gempf, eds., *The Book of Acts in Its Graeco-Roman Setting*, (Grand Rapids: Eerdmans, 1994), 112.

585 *anōterikos*; W. Bauer, W. F. Arndt, F. W. Gingrich, and F. W. Danker, *A Greek-English Lexicon of the New Testament*, (Chicago: University of Chicago Press, 1979), 92; H. Liddell, R. Scott, and H. S. Jones, *A Greek-English Lexicon*, (Oxford: Clarendon Press, 1968), 170; cf. G. W. H. Lampe, *A Patristic Greek Lexicon*, (Oxford: Clarendon Press, 1961), 166.

586 See R. J. A. Talbert, ed., *Barrington Atlas of the Greek and Roman World*, (Princeton: Princeton University Press, 2000), maps 61–62, 65; S. Mitchell, *Anatolia: Land, Men, and Gods in Asia Minor*, (Oxford: Clarendon Press, 1993), map 7; D. French, *Roman Roads and Milestones of Asia Minor*, BAR International Series 329 (i, ii), (London: British Institute of Archaeology at Ankara, 1988), maps 5–6, 8.

587 It may be that Paul penned his letters to the Colossians and to Philemon (perhaps the "letter to Laodicea" of Colossians 4:16?) while he was a prisoner at Ephesus, or still later while he was imprisoned in Rome. In either event, those churches in the Lycus River valley would not have owed their genesis to the apostle Paul, though he did express a desire to visit the churches in that vicinity (Philem. 22).

588 For example: Paul's three months on Malta (Acts 28:1–10); *any* place where he stayed only a day or two; and cities inherent in a given itinerary but with no record of his evangelistic efforts (e.g., Smyrna and Pergamum).

589 Strabo 12.8.15.

590 See most recently J. Romer and E. Romer, *The Seven Wonders of the World*, (London: Seven Dials, 2005), 129–164.

591 A large section of extravagant first-century Roman private residences has been excavated at Ephesus and is currently in process of restoration. What is currently being uncovered is likely to be directly related to Paul and his mission. A number of these somewhat lavish houses contain art representing the *ixthus* symbol.

592 so I. H. Marshall, *The Acts of the Apostles*, Tyndale New Testament Commentaries, (Grand Rapids: Eerdmans, 1980), 325.

593 One Greek text tradition adds "after remaining at Trogyllium" in Acts 20:15, thus creating the sequence Mitylene, Chios, Samos, Trogyllium, Miletus. The town of Trogyllium was situated on the end of the Turkish peninsula, opposite Samos. [**See map 114**; Strabo 14.1.12–14]. And see Strabo 14.1.6–7 for a description of four harbors at Miletus and a discussion of the city's notable sons.

594 A fourth-century B.C. ship found wrecked just offshore from Kyrenia, on the northern coast of Cyprus, apparently had taken a similar itinerary as Paul's vessel. Among its cargo were jars of wine from Samos, millstones from Cos, and expensive wines from Rhodes. According to O. F. A. Meinardus (*St. Paul in Greece*, [New Rochelle, N.Y.: Caratzas Brothers, 1979], 101), there is a local Christian tradition that, while at Rhodes, Paul appointed Prochorus (Acts 6:5) as bishop of this island.

595 See B. M. Rapske, "Acts, Travel and Shipwreck," in D. W. J. Gill and C. Gempf, eds., *The Book of Acts in Its Graeco-Roman Setting*, (Grand Rapids: Eerdmans, 1994), 11–14.

596 H. Dessau, ed., *Inscriptiones latinae selectae*, (Chicago: Ares Publishers, 1979), 1.531–532 (#2683).

597 E. Dąbrowa, "The commanders of Syrian legions, 1st-3rd c. A.D.," in D. L. Kennedy, ed., *The Roman Army in the East*, Journal of Roman Archaeology, Supplementary Series 18, (Ann Arbor, Mich.: Cushing-Malloy Inc., 1996), 277–296.

598 C. J. Hemer, *The Book of Acts in the Setting of Hellenistic History*, Wissenschaftliche Untersuchungen zum Neuen Testament 49, (Tübingen: J. C. B. Mohr, 1989), 362–364.

599 Strabo 13.1.51; Pliny, *Natural History*, 13.2.5.

600 According to one Greek text tradition at Acts 27:5, the trip from Caesarea to Myra took 15 days (cf. *The Jerusalem Bible* "fortnight"). Given what is known about average daily distances made on this sector of the Mediterranean during the Roman period, this tradition corresponds rather closely to the historical reality.

601 P. Garnsey, "Grain for Rome," in P. Garnsey, K. Hopkins, and C. R. Whittaker, eds., *Trade in the Ancient Economy*, (Berkeley: University of California Press, 1983), 118–119; cf. P. Temin, "A Market Economy in the Early Roman Empire," *Journal of Roman Studies* 91, (2001), 176–179.

602 H. Dessau, ed., *Inscriptiones latinae selectae*, (Chicago: Ares Publishers, 1979), 2/1.450–451 (#5908); The vestiges of numerous large, long granary storerooms for warehousing imperial grain can still be seen at Myra. The city also possessed other accoutrements of a prominent Roman city, including much imperial statuary, some of the finest known examples of rock-cut Lycian tombs, and a well-preserved theater that could seat some 11,000 spectators. While we have no such record in the biblical text, a book in the New Testament Apocrypha, *Acts of Paul and Thecla*, indicates that Paul preached the Good News while at Myra. (See W. Schneelmecher, ed., *New Testament Apocrypha*, [Louisville: Westminster/John Knox, 2003], 2.222–223.)

603 Within ten years of Paul's journey, Josephus [*Life* 3] also made a nautical voyage from Palestine to Rome, and he also suffered shipwreck. There were said to have been some 600 passengers aboard the ship of Josephus, of which only 80 survived. Late Roman scholars calculate that, from high antiquity down to the advent of the Muslim period, perhaps as many as 30,000 ships were lost in the Mediterranean, owing to either foul weather or warfare. (See also M. Jurišić, "*Ancient Shipwrecks of the Adriatic: Maritime Transport during the First and Second Centuries* A.D.," BAR International Series 828, (Oxford: Archaeopress, 2000); J. S. Illsley, "*An indexed bibliography of underwater archaeology and related topics*," [Oswestry, Shropshire: Anthony Nelson, 1996]; A. J. Parker, "*Ancient Shipwrecks of the Mediterranean and the Roman Provinces*," BAR International Series 580, [Oxford: Tempus Reparatum, 1992].)

604 B. M. Rapske, "Acts, Travel and Shipwreck," in D. W. J. Gill and C. Gempf, eds., *The Book of Acts in Its Graeco-Roman Setting*, (Grand Rapids: Eerdmans, 1994), 29–36.

605 so I. H. Marshall, *The Acts of the Apostles*, Tyndale New Testament Commentaries, (Grand Rapids: Eerdmans, 1980), 406; F. F. Bruce, *Commentary on the Book of Acts*, The New International Commentary on the New Testament, (Grand Rapids: Eerdmans, 1971), 506.

606 For classical references to this port and town, consult Strabo 10.4.3; Ptolemy, *Geography*, 3.15.3; and see Europe map 10.

607 *Epitoma Rei Militaris*; see also the assessment of Livy (*History*, 31.47.1), Pliny (*Natural History*, 2.47.122–125), and Hesiod (*Opera et Die*, 663).

608 Historical data from antiquity show, on the one hand, that mariners on the Gulf of Lion or much of the Tyrrhenian Sea, even in the middle of summer, tended to face weather so adverse as to render sailing an extremely dangerous enterprise. On the other hand, these data demonstrate that the eastern Mediterranean was good even for winter travel (J.H. Pryor, *Geography, technology, and war: Studies in the maritime history of the Mediterranean*, [Cambridge: Cambridge University Press, 1992], 1–3, 87–88); according to vessel ledgers from Elephantine, Rhodes and Egypt experienced virtually year-round open seas and trade (B. Porten and A. Yardeni, "Social, Economic, and Onomastic Issues in the Aramaic Ostraca of the Fourth Century B.C.E.," in O. Lipschits and M. Oeming, eds., *Judah and Judeans in the Persian Period*, [Winona Lake, Ind.: Eisenbrauns, 2006], 462–463, 468–470, 476–479) and ships from the east brought olive oil to Carthage even in mid-winter (J. Beresford, "A Reassessment of the Sailing Season in Late Antiquity"; Paper presented before the Fourth Biennial Conference of the Society for Late Antiquity, San Francisco State University [March 8–11, 2001]). In earlier times, Wenamun's round-trip from Egypt to

Phoenicia commenced in January and ended in May of the same year (W. W. Hallo and K. L. Younger, Jr., eds., *The Context of Scripture*, [Leiden: Brill, 1997–2002], 1.89–93).

609 Suetonius (*Life of Claudius*, 18; cf. B. M. Rapske, "Acts, Travel and Shipwreck," in D. W. J. Gill and C. Gempf, eds., *The Book of Acts in Its Graeco-Roman Setting*, [Grand Rapids: Eerdmans, 1994], 26); Pliny (*Natural History*, 2.125) asserted in one text that not even the fury of raging winter storms could close the sea, and Tacitus (*Annals*, 12.43) lamented that the life of the whole Roman nation had been staked on cargo-ships and accidents at sea.

610 For Mediterranean geography and climatology, consult M. Grant and R. Kitzinger, eds., *Civilization of the Ancient Mediterranean*, (New York: Scribner's, 1988), 1.101–113; 2.765–769; P. Guibout, *Atlas hydrologique de la Méditerranée*, (Paris: IFREMER, 1987); and M. and R. Beckinsale, *Southern Europe: a Systematic Geographical Study*, (New York: Holmes & Meier Publishers, 1975), 2–36.

611 G. E. Markoe, *Phoenicians*, (Berkeley: University of California Press, 2000), 181; M. E. Aubet, *The Phoenicians and the West*, (Cambridge: Cambridge University Press, 2001), 159–160; J. H. Pryor, *Geography, technology, and war: Studies in the maritime history of the Mediterranean*, (Cambridge: Cambridge University Press, 1992), 22–23; the Syrtis was described by Lucan (refer to O. A. W. Dilke, "Graeco-Roman Perception of the Mediterranean," in M. Galley and L. L. Sebaï, eds., *L'Homme Méditerranéen et la Mer: Actès du Troisième Congrès International d'études des Cultures de la Méditerranée Occidentale*, [Tunis: Salammbô, 1985], 55, and Dio Chrysostum, [*Libyan Myth* 7–9, The Loeb Classical Library, 1.238–239]) as a sort of nautical "black hole".

612 P. Throckmorton, *The Sea Remembers: Shipwrecks and Archaeology*, (New York: Weidenfeld & Nicolson, 1987), 8–10, 78–80.

613 Larger Roman ships routinely carried as many as 12 to 15 lead or stone anchors, sometimes weighing as much as two tons each (G. Kapitän, "Ancient Anchors—technology and classification," *International Journal of Nautical Archaeology* 13/1, [1984], 38). One recovered early Mediterranean shipwreck apparently included 24 anchors.

614 The phrase interpreted "reef" is *topon dithalasson*—"a place with sea on both sides" (so W. Bauer, W. F. Arndt, F. W. Gingrich, and F. W. Danker, *A Greek-English Lexicon of the New Testament*, [Chicago: University of Chicago Press, 1979], 245b; H. Liddell, R. Scott, and H. S. Jones, *A Greek-English Lexicon*, [Oxford: Clarendon Press, 1968], 427b).

615 See Ptolemy, *Tetrabiblios*, 1.9; Strabo 1.3.2.

616 Thucydides 6.2–5; Strabo 6.2.4.

617 D. P. Crouch, *Water Management in Ancient Greek Cities*, (New York: Oxford University Press, 1993), 132–149.

618 e.g., St. Gennaro; cf. Cicero, *Verres*, 2.4.115–119 for the city's resplendence.

619 Thucydides 4.24.4; Strabo 6.1.6.

620 For a description of this port during the New Testament era, consult N. C. Flemming, *Archaeological Evidence for eustatic change of sea level and earth movements in the Western Mediterranean during the last 2000 years*, (Boulder, Colo.: Geological Society of America, 1969), 40.

621 T. Suárez, *Early Mapping of Southeast Asia*, (Singapore: Periplus Editions, 1999), 61–62.

622 See A. Raban, "Coastal Processes and Ancient Harbour Engineering," in A. Raban, ed., *Archaeology of Coastal Changes*, BAR International Series 404, (Oxford: B.A.R., 1988), 187–189; cf. A. Raban, "The Heritage of Ancient Harbour Engineering in Cyprus and the Levant," in V. Karageorghis and D. Michaelides, eds., *Proceedings of the Inter-National Symposium: Cyprus and the Sea*, (Nicosia: University of Cyprus, 1995), 176; K. G. Holum et al., *King Herod's Dream: Caesarea on the Sea*, New York: W. W. Norton & Company, 1988), 101.

623 *War*, 2.7.1; Josephus, *Antiquities of the Jews*, 17.12.1.

624 R. J. A. Talbert, ed., *Barrington Atlas of the Greek and Roman World*, (Princeton: Princeton University Press, 2000), map 44.

625 According to one Greek text tradition at Acts 28:16, Julius handed Paul over to a *stratopedarch*—possibly the prefect of the praetorium guard in Rome (I. H. Marshall, *The Acts of the Apostles*, Tyndale New Testament Commentaries, [Grand Rapids: Eerdmans, 1980], 420); cf. N. Constable, *Historical Atlas of Ancient Rome*, (New York: Checkmark Books, 2003), 88–89.

626 C. J. Hemer, *The Letters to the Seven Churches of Asia in Their Local Setting*, (Sheffield: JSOT Press, 1986), 2–12.

627 R. J. A. Talbert, ed., *Barrington Atlas of the Greek and Roman World*, (Princeton: Princeton University Press, 2000), maps 56, 61–62, 65; D. French, *Roman Roads and Milestones of Asia Minor*, BAR International Series 329 (i, ii), (London: British Institute of Archaeology at Ankara, 1988), maps 5–6, 8, 11.

628 C. J. Hemer, "Seven Cities of Asia Minor," in R. K. Harrison, ed., *Major Cities of the Biblical World*, (Nashville: Thomas Nelson Publishers, 1985), 235–236.

629 Refer to the classic discussion in C. J. Hemer, *The Letters to the Seven Churches of Asia in Their Local Setting*, (Sheffield: JSOT Press, 1986); see also J. Freely, *The Aegean Coast of Turkey*, (Istanbul: Redhouse Press, 1996); O. F. A. Meinardus, *St. John of Patmos and the Seven Churches of the Apocalypse*, (Athens, Greece: Lycabettus Press, 1998).

630 A. J. Levine, "Visions of Kingdoms: From Pompey to the First Jewish Revolt," in M. D. Coogan, ed., *The Oxford History of the Biblical World*, (New York: Oxford University Press, 2001), 360–369; W. D. Davies, *The Gospel and the Land: Early Christianity and Jewish Territorial Doctrine*, (Berkeley: University of California Press, 1974), 95–97.

631 Josephus, *Antiquities of the Jews*, 13.171–173; 18.11–25; *War*, 4.121–161; 7.268–274; cf. Pliny, *Natural History*, 5.15.73.

632 Josephus, *War*, 2.289–292, cf. A. J. Levine, "Visions of Kingdoms: From Pompey to the First Jewish Revolt," in M. D. Coogan, ed., *The Oxford History of the Biblical World*, (New York: Oxford University Press, 2001), 380–386.

633 Josephus, *War*, 2.284–410.

634 Josephus, *War*, 2.425–432, 484–486; E. Schürer, *The History of the Jewish People in the Age of Jesus Christ*, (Edinburgh: T. & T. Clark, 1979), 1.336–355, 2.381–414, 550–590.

635 See Y. Tsafrir, L. Di Segni, and J. Green, *Tabula Imperii Romani: Iudaea, Palaestina*, (Jerusalem: Israel Academy of Sciences and Humanities, 1994), maps.

636 Josephus, *War*, 2.513–555, 562–568.

637 Josephus, *War*, 3.3–8; Tacitus, *Agricola*, 7–9, 13, 17.

638 Josephus, *War*, 3.65–69.

639 See B. Isaac and I. Roll, *Roman Roads in Judaea: the Legio-Scythopolis Road*, BAR International Series 141, (Oxford: Archaeopress, 1982).

640 Josephus, *War*, 3.462–542.

641 Josephus, *War*, 4.1–134.

642 See S. Mittman and G. Schmitt, eds., *Tübinger Bibelatlas*, (Stuttgart: Deutsche Bibelgesellschaft, 2001), B/V/17; Y. Tsafrir, L. Di Segni, and J. Green, *Tabula Imperii Romani: Iudaea, Palaestina*, (Jerusalem: Israel Academy of Sciences and Humanities, 1994), map; B. Isaac and I. Roll, *Roman Roads in Judaea: the Legio-Scythopolis Road*, BAR International Series 141, (Oxford: Archaepress, 1982), fig 3, for a Roman road from Jerusalem west past Adida and Lydda, where it joined the Great Trunk Road.

643 Josephus, *War*, 4.412–490.

644 Josephus, *War*, 4.491–496.

645 Josephus, *War*, 7.275–419.

646 K. S. Latourette, *A History of Christianity*, (New York: Harper & Row Publishers, 1959), 3.65.

647 Tacitus, *Annals*, 15.38–44.

648 See the correspondence of Pliny the Younger, *Letters*, 10.96–97; Suetonius, *Nero*, 16.3; Eusebius, *Ecclesiastical History*, 143–183.

649 Y. Tsafrir, "Ancient Churches in the Holy Land," *Biblical Archaeology Review* 19/5, (1993), 26–39; T. Dowley, ed., *The Baker Atlas of Christian History*, (Grand Rapids: Baker Book House, 1997), 74.

650 See S. Mittman and G. Schmitt, eds., *Tübinger Bibelatlas*, (Stuttgart: Deutsche Bibelgesellschaft, 2001), B/VI/2; H. Chadwick and G. R. Evans, eds., *Atlas of the Christian Church*, (Oxford: Equinox, 1987), 21–25; J. B. Pritchard, ed., *The Harper Atlas of the Bible*, (New York: Harper & Row Publishers, 1987), 183; A. Harnack, *The Mission and Expansion of Christianity in the First Three Centuries*, (New York: Williams and Norgate, 1908), 2.272–274.

651 See J. B. Segal, *Edessa: "The Blessed City,"* (Oxford: Clarendon Press, 1970).

652 See B. Goldman, ed., *The Discovery of Dura-Europos*, (New Haven: Yale University Press, 1979), 89–117; cf. J. L. Kugel and R. A. Greer, *Early Biblical Interpretation*, (Philadelphia: Westminster Press, 1986), 200–201.

653 Eusebius, *Ecclesiastical History*. book 6, chapter 43, ("Of Novatus, his manners and habits, and his heresy"), (Grand Rapids: Baker, 1971), 265.

MAP CITATION INDEX

In scope, the Map Citation Index is intended to contain all geographical data appearing on the maps, alphabetically arranged according to map number, not page number. Brackets are employed to qualify or further define homonyms (*e.g.* Abila [Decapolis]). Alternate names of a geographical entity either from a different period of time or from a different language are referenced within parentheses containing the word "*See*" immediately following an entry name. Map location of a given entity is indicated by a set of parenthesis containing an alpha-numeric grid coordinate: data found in bold print (*e.g.* **B3**) refer to placement on the four-map Palestinian city map (map #22, pp. 68-71); other parenthesized data provide the locational coordinates of an entity the first time it appears on a map in the volume. Entries preceded by the symbol + are judged to be of uncertain location.

GENERAL INDEX

GENERAL READING

In addition to this general bibliography of reference materials and selected monographs, useful information having to do with geography, history, archaeology, and biblical interpretation may be gleaned from the Notes contained in the *Atlas*.

Adams, W. M., A. S. Goudie, and A. R. Orne, eds., *The Physical Geography of Africa*, (London: Oxford University Press, 1996).

Allan, J. A., *The Middle East Water Question: Hydropolitics and the Global Economy*, (London: I. B. Tauris, 2001).

Bahat, D., *The Illustrated Atlas of Jerusalem*, (New York: Simon & Schuster, 1990).

Bartlett, J. R., *Mapping Jordan Through Two Millennia*, Palestine Exploration Fund Annual 10, (Leeds, UK: 2008).

Beitzel, B. J., chief consultant, *Biblica, the Bible Atlas: A Social and Historical Journey Through the Lands of the Bible*, (Camberwell, Australia: Penguin Books, Ltd., 2006).

Boatright, M. T., D. J. Gargola, and R. J. A. Talbert, *The Romans: From Village to Empire* (Oxford: Oxford University Press, 2004).

Carson, D. A., and D. J. Moo, *An Introduction to the New Testament*, 2nd ed., (Grand Rapids, MI: Zondervan, 2005).

Coogan, M. D., ed., *The Oxford History of the Biblical World*, (New York: Oxford University Press, 1998).

Crouch, D. P., *Water Management in Ancient Greek Cities*, (Oxford: Oxford University Press, 1993).

Dorsey, D. A., *The Roads and Highways of Ancient Israel*, (Baltimore: Johns Hopkins Press, 1991).

Freedman, D. N., gen. ed., *The Anchor Bible Dictionary*, 6 vols., (New York: Doubleday, 1992).

French, D., *Roman Roads and Milestones of Asia Minor*, 2 vols., BAR International Series 392, (Oxford: BAR, 1988).

Grayson, A. K., *Assyrian and Babylonian Chronicles*, (Winona Lake, IN: Eisenbrauns, 2000).

Hallo, W. W., and K. L. Younger, Jr., eds., *The Context of Scripture*, 3 vols., (Leiden: Brill, 1997-2002).

Harrison, R. K., ed., *Major Cities of the Biblical World*, (Nashville, TN: Thomas Nelson Publishers, 1985).

Hemer, C. J., *The Letters to the Seven Churches of Asia in Their Local Setting*, Journal for the Study of the New Testament, Supplement Series 11, (Sheffield, UK: JSOT Press, 1986).

Hoffmeier, J. K., *Ancient Israel in Sinai*, (New York: Oxford University Press, 2005).

Hunt, N. B., *Historical Atlas of Ancient Mesopotamia*, (New York: Checkmark Books, 2004).

Isbouts, J.-P., *The Biblical World: An Illustrated Atlas*, (Washington D.C.: National Geographic, 2007).

Kitchen, K. A., *On the Reliability of the Old Testament*, (Grand Rapids, MI: Eerdmans Publishing Company, 2003).

Lawrence, P., *The IVP Atlas of Bible History*, (Downers Grove, IL: InterVarsity Press, 2006).

Mehler, C., project ed., *Atlas of the Middle East*, (Washington D.C.: National Geographic, 2003).

Meyers, E. M., ed., *The Oxford Encyclopedia of Archaeology in the Near East*, 5 vols., (New York: Oxford University Press, 1997).

Montagu, J. D., *Battles of the Greek and Roman Worlds*, (London: Greenhill Books, 2000).

Parpola, S., and M. Porter, *The Helsinki Atlas of the Near East in the Neo-Assyrian Period*, (Helsinki: Vammalan Kirjapaino Oy, 2001).

Pritchard, J. B., ed., *Ancient Near Eastern Texts Relating to the Old Testament*, 3rd ed., (Princeton, NJ: Princeton University Press, 1969).

Rainey, A. F., and R. S. Notley, *The Sacred Bridge: Carta's Atlas of the Biblical World*, (Jerusalem: Carta, 2006).

Riesner, R., *Paul's Early Period: Chronology, Mission Strategy, Theology*, (Grand Rapids, MI: Eerdmans Publishing Company, 1998).

Sasson, J. M., ed., *Civilizations of the Ancient Near East*, 4 vols., (New York: Charles Scribner's Sons, 1995).

Schnabel, E. J., *Early Christian Mission*, 2 vols., (Leicester, UK: Apollos, 2004).

Shaw, I., ed., *The Oxford History of Ancient Egypt*, (Oxford: Oxford University Press, 2000).

Staccioli, R. A., *The Roads of the Romans*, (Los Angeles: J. Paul Getty Museum, 2003).

Stern, E., A. Gilboa, and J. Aviram, eds., *The New Encyclopedia of Archaeological Excavations in the Holy Land*, 4 vols., (New York: Simon & Schuster, 1993).

Thiele, E. R., *The Mysterious Numbers of the Hebrew Kings*, (Grand Rapids, MI: Eerdmans Publishing Company, 1965).

Tsafrir, Y., L. Di Segni, and J. Green, *Tabula Imperii Romani Iudaea-Palestina: Eretz Israel in the Hellenistic, Roman and Byzantine Periods*, 2 vols., (Jerusalem: Israel Academy of Sciences and Humanities, 1994).

Wilken, R. L., *The Land Called Holy: Palestine in Christian History and Thought*, (New Haven, CT: Yale University Press, 1992).

Wilkinson, J., *Jerusalem Pilgrimage 1099-1185*, (London: Hakluyt Society, 1988).

Wiseman, D. J., *Chronicles of Chaldean Kings (626-556 B.C.) in the British Museum*, (London: Trustees of the British Museum, 1961).

Yamauchi, E., *Persia and the Bible*, (Grand Rapids, MI: Baker Book House, 1990).